Front Plate 3 Elevation data for Honolulu, Hawaii displayed using a quadmesh to define control points for a Bezier surface. (Courtesy of Brian Wylie, University of New Mexico and Sandia National Laboratories.)

Front Plate 4 Wire frame of the quadmesh showing lower resolution in flat areas. (Courtesy of Brian Wylie, University of New Mexico and Sandia National Laboratories.)

INTERACTIVE COMPUTER GRAPHICS
A Top-Down Approach with OpenGL™

THIRD EDITION

EDWARD ANGEL

Addison
Wesley

Boston San Francisco New York
London Toronto Sydney Tokyo Singapore Madrid
Mexico City Munich Paris Cape Town Hong Kong Montreal

Senior Acquisitions Editor	Maite Suarez-Rivas
Executive Editor	Susan Hartman Sullivan
Assistant Editor	Lisa Hogue
Executive Marketing Manager	Michael Hirsh
Production Supervisor	Kim Ellwood
Project Management	P. M. Gordon Associates, Inc.
Compositor	Windfall Software, using ZzTEX
Cover Design/Design Manager	Gina Hagen Kolenda
Prepress and Manufacturing	Caroline Fell

Access the latest information about Addison-Wesley titles from our World Wide Web site:
www.awlonline.com

Many of the designations used by manufacturers and sellers to distinguish their products are claimed as trademarks. Where those designations appear in this book, and Addison-Wesley was aware of a trademark claim, the designations have been printed in initial caps or all caps.

The programs and applications presented in this book have been included for their instructional value. They have been tested with care but are not guaranteed for any purpose. The publisher does not offer any warranties or representations, nor does it accept any liabilities with respect to the programs or applications.

Library of Congress Cataloging-in-Publication Data

Angel, Edward
    Interactive computer graphics : a top-down approach with OpenGL / Edward Angel—
3rd ed.
      p. cm.
    Includes bibliographical references and index.
    ISBN 0-201-77343-0
    1. Computer graphics. 2. OpenGL. 3. Interactive computer systems. I. Title.
T385 A514 2003
006.6′6—dc21   2002074555

2 3 4 5 6 7 8 9 10—CRW—05 04 03

To Rose Mary

Contents

Preface

This book is an introduction to computer graphics, with an emphasis on applications programming. In the first edition, which was published in 1997, I noted that in the seven years since my previous graphics text, the field had experienced enormous growth—a rate of growth that exceeded most people's expectations, including my own. In the five years since, we have seen even more changes. Feature-length computer-animated movies have become commercial and artistic successes. The use of computer effects in movies is standard and it is often almost impossible to distinguish live action from computer-generated effects. Recent hardware has blurred the distinction between computers and game boxes. The explosion of interest in graphical applications over the Internet has continued.

Not only have graphics capabilities increased but costs have been reduced for both high- and low-end workstations. Within the last few years the cost of a graphics system that can generate over ten million three-dimensional polygons per second with lighting and texture mapping has dropped from over $100,000 to a few thousand dollars. Even computers that cost less than $1000 can support basic three-dimensional graphics applications. The availability of special-purpose graphics boards for personal computers has been especially significant. These boards provide workstation performance starting at about $100. On the software side, OpenGL remains the standard programmer's interface both for writing application programs and for developing high-level products in the scientific community.

A Top-Down Approach

These recent advances and the success of the first two editions of this text have reinforced my belief in a top-down, programming-oriented approach to introductory computer graphics. Although many computer science and engineering departments now support more than one course in the subject, most students will take only a single course. Such a course is placed in the curriculum after students have already studied programming, data structures, algorithms, software engineering, and basic mathematics. A class in computer graphics allows the instructor to build on these topics in a way that can be both informative and fun. I want these students to be programming three-dimensional applications as soon as possible. Low-level algorithms, such as those that draw lines or fill polygons, can be dealt with later, after students are creating graphics.

John Kemeny, a pioneer in computer education, used a familiar automobile analogy: You don't have to know what's under the hood to be literate, but unless you know how to program, you'll be sitting in the back seat instead of driving. That same analogy applies to the way we teach computer graphics. One approach—the algorithmic approach—is to teach everything about what makes a car function: the engine, the transmission, the combustion process. A second approach—the survey approach—is to hire a chauffeur, to sit back, and to see the world as a spectator. A third approach—the programming approach that I have adopted here—is to teach you how to drive and how to take yourself wherever you want to go. As the old auto-rental commercial used to say, "Let us put *you* in the driver's seat."

Programming with OpenGL and C

When I began teaching computer graphics 20 years ago, the greatest impediment to implementing a programming-oriented course, and to writing a textbook for that course, was the lack of a widely accepted graphics library or application programmer's interface (API). Difficulties included high cost, limited availability, lack of generality, and high complexity. The development of OpenGL resolved most of the difficulties many of us had experienced with other APIs (such as GKS and PHIGS), and with the alternative of using home-brewed software. OpenGL today is supported by most workstation suppliers and is available for most platforms through third-party vendors. It is bundled with all recent versions of Microsoft Windows and with the Apple Macintosh operating system. There is also an OpenGL API called Mesa that can be compiled for most systems and is included with most Linux distributions.

A graphics class teaches far more than the use of a particular API, but a good API makes it easier to teach key graphics topics, such as three-dimensional graphics, shading, client–server graphics, modeling, and implementation algorithms. OpenGL's extensive capabilities and well-defined architecture lead to a stronger foundation for teaching both theoretical and practical aspects of the field, and for teaching important new capabilities, such as texture mapping and compositing, that, until recently, were not supported in any API.

I switched my classes to OpenGL about 8 years ago, and the results astounded me. By the middle of the semester, *every* student was able to write a moderately complex three-dimensional program that required understanding of three-dimensional viewing and event-driven input. In 15 years of teaching computer graphics, I had never come even close to this result. That class led me to rewrite my previous book from scratch.

This is a textbook on computer graphics; it is not an OpenGL manual. Consequently, I do not cover all aspects of the OpenGL API, but rather explain only what is necessary for mastering this book's contents. I present OpenGL at a level that should permit users of other APIs to have little difficulty with the material. For students who want more detail on OpenGL, my recent book, *OpenGL: A Primer* (Addison-Wesley, 2002), should be a valuable supplement.

In this edition, I use both C and C++, with C as the dominant language. There are two reasons for this decision. First, OpenGL is not object-oriented, so using C++ or Java would not add significantly to the basic presentation, unless I were to insert an object-oriented geometric library between OpenGL and the user. I have not taken this step, despite its appealing features, because it would detract from the graphics and would make the book less accessible to students who are good programmers, but who are unfamiliar with object-oriented languages. Second, my experience has been that object-oriented approaches shield the user from what is going on inside (as they should), whereas, in an introduction to computer graphics, I want readers to be aware of what is happening at the lowest levels. Although the use of computer graphics is a wonderful way to introduce students to object-oriented programming, in my view, an object-oriented approach is not the most effective way to teach graphics to computer science and engineering students. The exception to this view is when I introduce scene graphs that are object oriented and benefit from the use of C++. My undergraduate students use C++ in their beginning courses, but have no difficulty in using the code in this book with either C or C++.

Within the computer graphics community, there has been much discussion of the future of OpenGL and whether it will be replaced by DirectX. Among computer graphics educators, however, there is little doubt that OpenGL will continue to be the API of choice for their classes. Although DirectX is the standard for game development, in the opinion of many of us, it is not well suited for teaching computer graphics or for users who want to develop their own applications. In addition to being specific to Windows platforms, DirectX requires far more code for basic portable applications. At the higher levels, OpenGL and DirectX support similar functionality in similar ways. Hence, users of this book should be able to move to DirectX with little difficulty when required.

Intended Audience

This book is suitable for advanced undergraduates and first-year graduate students in computer science and engineering and for students in other disciplines who have good programming skills. The book also will be useful to many professionals. I have taught approximately 100 short courses for professionals; my experiences with those students have had a great influence on what I have chosen to include in the book.

Prerequisites for using this text are good programming skills in C or C++, an understanding of basic data structures (linked list, trees), and a rudimentary knowledge of linear algebra and trigonometry. I have found that the mathematical backgrounds of computer science students, whether of undergraduates or of graduates, vary considerably. Hence, I have integrated much of the linear algebra and geometry that is required for fundamental computer graphics into the text. I have also summarized this material in two appendices.

Organization of the Book

The book is organized as follows. Chapter 1 overviews the field and introduces image formation by optical devices; thus, we start with three-dimensional concepts immediately. Chapter 2 introduces programming using OpenGL. Although the example program that we develop—each chapter has one or more complete programming examples—is two-dimensional, it is embedded in a three-dimensional setting. Chapter 3 discusses interactive graphics in a modern client–server setting and develops event-driven graphics programs. Chapters 4 and 5 concentrate on three-dimensional concepts; Chapter 4 is concerned with defining and manipulating three-dimensional objects, whereas Chapter 5 is concerned with viewing them. Chapter 6 introduces light–material interactions and shading. These chapters should be covered in order, and can be done in about 10 weeks of a 15-week semester.

The next seven chapters can be read in almost any order. All seven are somewhat open ended, and can be covered at a survey level, or individual topics can be pursued in depth. Chapter 7 introduces many of the new discrete capabilities that are now supported in graphics hardware and by OpenGL. All these techniques involve working with various buffers. It concludes with a short discussion of aliasing problems in computer graphics. Chapter 8 surveys implementation. It gives one or two major algorithms for each of the basic steps in the viewing pipeline. Chapter 9 contains a number of topics that fit loosely under the heading of hierarchical and object-oriented graphics. The topics range from building models that encapsulate the relationships between the parts of a model to high-level approaches to graphics over the Internet. It includes a simple scene graph API.

Curves and surfaces are discussed in Chapter 10. Chapter 11 introduces procedural methods as a way to escape the limits of building geometric models with polygons. It includes material on language-based models, fractals, and particle systems. Chapter 12 provides an introduction to scientific visualization. Not only is this area one of great current interest, it gives us a chance to demonstrate almost all the techniques developed in previous chapters. Chapter 13 is new and surveys alternate approaches to rendering. It includes expanded discussions of ray tracing and radiosity and an introduction to image-based rendering and parallel rendering.

Programs, primarily from the first part of the book, are included in Appendix A. They are also available electronically (see the Supplements section).

Changes from the Second Edition

The reaction of readers of the first and second editions of this book was overwhelmingly positive, especially to the use of OpenGL and the top-down approach. But there are always improvements to be made and recent advances to be added. This third edition addresses these issues.

I have made three types of changes from the second edition. First, I have enhanced the discussion of the more mathematical topics. Second, I have added material of current interest, such as scene graphs and alternate rendering methods. Third, I have included more OpenGL examples. These changes led to a reorganization of the second half of the book. These changes should have only minor effects on the teaching of a one semester introductory course, but should make it easier for instructors to use the book for a two-semester class.

Chapters 1 and 2 contain minor updates. In Chapter 3, I added material on the use of the exclusive-or writing mode so that readers would be able to develop applications that used rubberbanding. I also added a section on picking using selection mode.

Some of Chapter 4 has been rewritten to make the mathematical topics clearer. I also added a section on quaternions at the end of the chapter that fits well with the expanded treatment of smooth rotations in this edition.

Chapter 5 is largely unchanged.

Chapter 6 now focuses on pipeline rendering and the material on global rendering has been moved to Chapter 13.

The information in Chapter 7 has been moved forward (from Chapter 9) to reflect the growing importance of mapping and the use of discrete buffers. There is more detail on using OpenGL's texture mapping functions and many additional code examples.

Chapter 8, formerly Chapter 7, is largely unchanged.

The new Chapter 9, formerly Chapter 8, contains an extensive treatment of scene graphs and uses a scene graph developed by one of my students, Ye Cong, as a class project. I debated about using a "standard" scene graph, such as those in VRML or Java3D, but came to the conclusion that there is no standard and it is unclear whether or not these candidates will survive as long as the third edition. However, I do believe the concepts are important and thus decided to go with a simple scene graph that students could work with using code I could place on the Web.

Chapter 10 now contains an introduction to subdivision curves and surfaces. Chapters 11 and 12 are largely unchanged from the second edition.

Chapter 13 is new. It contains expanded introductions to ray tracing and radiosity, including a discussion of the rendering equation, which was covered in

Chapter 6 in the previous two editions. I have added an introduction to image-based rendering, an area of great recent interest that encompasses a multitude of approaches. I have added a section on parallel rendering that is related to my own interests and also should gain importance as clusters of PCs with commodity graphics cards replace supercomputers built with specialized hardware.

Appendix A contains added examples. Appendix B now contains a short section on eigenvalues and eigenvectors to support topics such as smooth rotation.

Supplements

The CD that accompanies the book includes software tools (recent distributions of GLUT and MESA), source code and Windows binaries for the examples in the text (and some additional examples), OpenGL man pages (in html and ps formats), my OpenGL tutorial (in pdf format) from SIGGRAPH 2001, and Nate Robins' OpenGL tutorials.

The following support material is available to all readers of this book.

- Program code
- Solutions to selected exercises

Please visit http://www.aw.com/cssupport for more information on obtaining these supplements.

Additional support materials are only available to instructors adopting this textbook for classroom use. Please contact your school's Addison-Wesley representative for information on obtaining access to this material, including

- Solutions to all exercises
- Figure files in three formats so that you can create your own lecture notes
- Tutorial lecture notes on OpenGL.

All of this information and more is available on my Web site

http://www.cs.unm.edu/~angel

Programs from the book, as well as additional sample programs, are available over the Internet via anonymous ftp at:

ftp.cs.unm.edu   under pub/angel/BOOK

I welcome suggestions regarding other supplements that readers would find useful, as well as comments on the book itself:

angel@cs.unm.edu

Acknowledgments

I have been fortunate over the past few years to have worked with wonderful students at the University of New Mexico. They were the first to get me interested in OpenGL, and I have learned much from them. They include Hue

Bumgarner-Kirby (Walker), Ye Cong, Pat Crossno, Tommie Daniel, Lisa Desjarlais, Kim Edlund, Lee Ann Fisk, Maria Gallegos, Brian Jones, Christopher Jordan, Max Hazelrigg, Sheryl Hurley, Thomas Keller, Ge Li, Pat McCormick, Al McPherson, Martin Muller, David Munich, Jim Pinkerton, Jim Prewett, Dave Rogers, Hal Smyer, Dave Vick, and Brian Wylie. Many of the examples in the Color Plates section were created by these students.

The first edition of this book was written during my sabbatical; various parts were written in five different countries. The experience speaks well for the versatility of portable computers and the universality of the Internet. Nevertheless, the task would not have been accomplished without the help of a number of people and institutions that made their facilities available to me. I am greatly indebted to Jonas Montilva and Chris Birkbeck of the Universidad de los Andes (Venezuela), to Rodrigo Gallegos and Aristides Novoa of the Universidad Tecnologica Equinoccial (Ecuador), to Long Wen Chang of the National Tsing Hua University (Taiwan), and to Kin Hong Wong and Pheng Ann Heng of the Chinese University of Hong Kong. Ramiro Jordan of ISTEC and the University of New Mexico made possible many of these visits. John Brayer and Jason Stewart at the University of New Mexico and Helen Goldstein at Addison-Wesley somehow managed to get a variety of items to me wherever I happened to be. My Web site contains a description of my adventures writing the first edition.

The second and third editions was written in New Mexico and benefited greatly from the feedback of hundreds of instructors and students who used these editions and sent me their comments. Many of the changes from earlier editions are responses to their requests and comments.

Silicon Graphics and Apple Computer were generous in making equipment available to me. Conix Enterprises, Portable Graphics, Template Graphics, and Metrowerks were kind enough to provide software so that I could test sample programs on a variety of platforms. David Kirk and Mark Kilgard at NVidia were kind enough to provide cards for testing many of the recent algorithms.

A number of other people provided significant help. I thank Ben Bederson, Gonzalo Cartagenova, Tom Caudell, Kathi Collins, Kathleen Danielson, Roger Ehrich, Robert Geist, Chuck Hansen, Mark Henne, Bernard Moret, Dick Nordhaus, Helena Saona, Dave Shreiner, Vicki Shreiner, Gwen Sylvan, and Mason Woo. Mark Kilgard, Brian Paul, and Nate Robins are owed a great debt by the OpenGL community for creating software that enables OpenGL code to be developed over a variety of platforms.

At the University of New Mexico, the High Performance Computing Center and IBM provided support for many of my visualization projects. The Computer Science Department, the National Science Foundation, Sandia National Laboratories, and Los Alamos National Laboratory have supported many of my students and research projects that led to parts of this book. David Beining and the Lodestar Planetarium have provided tremendous support for the Full Dome Project (Sheryl Hurley, Christopher Jordan, Laurel Ladwig, Hue (Bumgarner-Kirby) Walker) that provided the cover images and some of the images in the Color Plate section.

Reviewers of my manuscript drafts provided a variety of viewpoints on what I should include and what level of presentation I should use. These reviewers included Hamid Arabnia (University of Georgia), Wayne Carlson (Ohio State University), Jim X. Chen (George Mason University), Norman Chin (Silicon Graphics), Andrew Duchowski (Clemson University), Matthew Evett (Eastern Michigan University), Michael Garland (University of Illinois), Scott Grissom (University of Illinois, Springfield), Ardeshir Goshtasby (Wright State University), John C. Kelly, Jr. (North Carolina A&T State University), Kwan-Liu Ma (University of California, Davis), David McAllister (North Carolina State University), Tom McReynolds (Silicon Graphics), Jim Miller (University of Kansas), Dick Phillips (formerly Los Alamos National Laboratories), Yang Wang (Southwest Missouri State University), Jane Wilhelms (University of California, Santa Cruz), Edward Wong (Brooklyn Polytechnic Institute), and Mike Wozny (Rensselaer Polytechnic Institute). Although the final decisions may not reflect their views—which often differed considerably from one another—each reviewer forced me to reflect on every page of the manuscript.

I acknowledge the entire production team at Addison-Wesley; these people, in addition to doing their usual great job, took on the additional burden of working with someone who was never in one place for long. My editors, Peter Gordon and Maite Suarez-Rivas, have been a pleasure to work with through three editions of this book and the Open Primer. Through three books, Paul Anagnostopoulos at Windfall Software has always been more than helpful in assisting me with TeX problems. I am especially grateful to Lyn Dupré. I am not a natural writer. If the readers could see the original draft of this book, they would understand the wonders that Lyn does with a manuscript.

My wife, Rose Mary Molnar, created the figures for my first graphics book, many of which form the basis for the figures in this book. Wisely choosing not to fight over use of our only notebook computer, she was able to preserve our relationship and to contribute in a thousand other ways.

Graphics Systems
and Models

Of all the characteristics we associate with the new millennium, it is clear that computer and communication technologies have become dominant forces in our lives. Activities as wide-ranging as filmmaking, publishing, banking, and education continue to undergo revolutionary changes as these technologies alter the ways in which we conduct our daily activities. The combination of computers, networks, and the complex human visual system, through computer graphics, has led to new ways of displaying information, seeing virtual worlds, and communicating with both other people and machines.

Computer graphics is concerned with all aspects of producing pictures or images using a computer. The field began humbly more than 40 years ago, with the display of a few lines on a **cathode-ray tube (CRT)**; now, we can generate images that are nearly indistinguishable from photographs. We routinely train pilots with simulated airplanes, generating graphical displays of a virtual environment in real time. Feature-length movies made entirely by computer have been successful both critically and financially.

In this chapter, we start our journey with a short discussion of applications of computer graphics. Then, we overview graphics systems and imaging. Throughout this book, our approach stresses the relationships between computer graphics and image formation by familiar methods, such as drawing by hand and photography. We shall see that these relationships can help us to design application programs, graphics libraries, and architectures for graphics systems.

In this book, we introduce a particular graphics software system, **OpenGL**, which has become a widely accepted standard for developing graphics applications. Fortunately, OpenGL is easy to learn, and it possesses most of the characteristics of other popular graphics systems. Our approach is top-down. We want you to start writing, as quickly as possible, application programs that will generate graphical output. After you begin writing simple programs, we shall discuss how the underlying graphics library and the hardware are implemented. This chapter should give you a sufficient overview for you to proceed to writing programs.

1.1 Applications of Computer Graphics

The development of computer graphics has been driven both by the needs of the user community and by advances in hardware and software. The applications of computer graphics are many and varied; we can, however, divide them into four major areas:

1. Display of information
2. Design
3. Simulation and animation
4. User interfaces

Although many applications span two or more of these areas, the development of the field was based on separate work in each.

1.1.1 Display of Information

Classical graphics techniques arose as a medium to convey information among people. Although spoken and written languages serve a similar purpose, the human visual system is unrivaled both as a processor of data and as a pattern recognizer. More than 4000 years ago, the Babylonians displayed floor plans of buildings on stones. More than 2000 years ago, the Greeks were able to convey their architectural ideas graphically, even though the related mathematics was not developed until the Renaissance. Today, the same type of information is generated by architects, mechanical designers, and draftspeople using computer-based drafting systems.

For centuries, cartographers have developed maps to display celestial and geographical information. Such maps were crucial to navigators as these people explored the ends of the earth; maps are no less important today in fields such as geographic information systems. Now, maps can be developed and manipulated in real time over the Internet.

Over the past 100 years, workers in the field of statistics have explored techniques for generating plots that aid the viewer in determining the information in a set of data. Now, we have computer plotting packages that provide a variety of plotting techniques and color tools, and that can handle multiple large data sets. Nevertheless, it is still the human's ability to recognize visual patterns that ultimately allows us to interpret the information contained in the data.

Medicine poses interesting and important data-analysis problems. New imaging technologies—such as computed tomography (CT), magnetic resonance imaging (MRI), ultrasound, and positron-emission tomography (PET)—generate three-dimensional data that must be subjected to algorithmic manipulation to provide useful information. Color Plate 20 shows an image of a person's head in which the skin is displayed as transparent and the muscles are displayed as opaque. Although the data were collected by a medical imaging system, computer graphics produced the image that shows the structures.

Supercomputers now allow researchers in many areas to solve previously intractable problems. The field of scientific visualization provides graphical tools that help these researchers to interpret the vast quantity of data that they generate. In fields such as fluid flow, molecular biology, and mathematics, images generated by conversion of data to geometric entities that can be displayed have yielded new insights into complex processes. For example, Color Plate 19 shows fluid dynamics in the mantle of the earth. The system used a mathematical model to generate the data; various visualization techniques that we discuss in Chapters 8, 9, and 12 produced the visualization.

1.1.2 Design

Professions such as engineering and architecture are concerned with design. Starting with a set of specifications, engineers and architects seek a cost-effective and esthetic solution that satisfies the specifications. Design is an iterative process. Rarely in the real world is a problem specified such that there is a unique optimal solution. Design problems are either *overdetermined*, such that they possess no optimal solution, or *underdetermined*, such that they have multiple solutions. Thus, the designer works in an iterative manner. She generates a possible design, tests it, and then uses the results as the basis for exploring other solutions.

The power of the paradigm of humans interacting with images on the screen of a CRT was recognized by Ivan Sutherland over 40 years ago. Today, the use of interactive graphical tools in computer-aided design (CAD) pervades fields such as architecture and the design of mechanical parts and of very-large-scale integrated (VLSI) circuits. In many such applications, the graphics is used in a number of distinct ways. For example, in a VLSI design, the graphics provides an interactive interface between the user and the design package, usually by means of such tools as menus and icons. In addition, after the user evolves a possible design, other tools analyze the design and display the analysis graphically. Color Plates 9 and 10 show two views of the same architectural design. Both images were generated with the same CAD system. They demonstrate the importance of having the tools available to generate different images of the same objects at different stages of the design process.

1.1.3 Simulation and Animation

Once graphics systems evolved to be capable of generating sophisticated images in real time, engineers and researchers began to use them as simulators. One of the most important uses has been in the training of pilots. Graphical flight simulators have proved both to increase safety and to reduce training expenses. The use of special VLSI chips has led to a generation of arcade games as sophisticated as flight simulators. Games and educational software for home computers are almost as impressive. Color Plate 16 shows a physical robot and the corresponding graphical simulation. The simulator can be used for designing the robot, for planning its path, and for simulating its behavior in complex environments.

The success of flight simulators led to the use of computer graphics for animation in the television, motion-picture, and advertising industries. Entire animated movies can now be made by computer at a cost less than that of movies made with traditional hand-animation techniques. The use of computer graphics with hand animation allows the creation of technical and artistic effects that are not possible with either alone. While computer animations have a distinct look, we can also generate photorealistic images by computer. Often, images that we see on television, in movies, and in magazines are so realistic that we cannot distinguish computer-generated or computer-altered images from photographs. In Chapters 6 and 7, we discuss many of the lighting effects used to produce computer animations. Color Plates 11–13 are three scenes from a computer-generated video. The artists and engineers who created these scenes used commercially available software. The plates demonstrate our ability to generate realistic environments, such as the factory in Plate 11; to simulate robots, as shown in Plate 12; and to create special effects, such as the sparks in Plate 13. The images in Color Plate 31 show another example of the use of computer graphics to generate an effect that, although it looks realistic, could not have been created otherwise. The images in Color Plates 23 and 24 also are realistic renderings.

The field of virtual reality (VR) has opened up many new horizons. A human viewer can be equipped with a display headset that allows her to see separate images with her right eye and her left eye so that she has the effect of stereoscopic vision. In addition, her body location and position, possibly including her head and finger positions, are tracked by the computer. She may have other interactive devices available, including force-sensing gloves and sound. She can then act as part of a computer-generated scene, limited only by the image-generation ability of the computer. For example, a surgical intern might be trained to do an operation in this way, or an astronaut might be trained to work in a weightless environment. Color Plate 22 shows one frame of a VR simulation of a simulated patient used for remote training of medical personnel.

1.1.4 User Interfaces

Our interaction with computers has become dominated by a visual paradigm that includes windows, icons, menus, and a pointing device, such as a mouse. From a user's perspective, windowing systems such as the X Window system, Microsoft Windows, and the Macintosh operating system differ only in details. More recently, millions of people have become users of the Internet. Their access is through graphical network browsers, such as Netscape and Internet Explorer, that use these same interface tools. We have become so accustomed to this style of interface that we often forget that what we are doing is working with computer graphics.

Although we are familiar with the style of graphical user interface used on most workstations, advances in computer graphics have made possible other forms of interfaces. Color Plate 14 shows the interface used with a high-level modeling package. It demonstrates the variety both of the tools available in such packages and of the interactive devices the user can employ in modeling geometric objects.

1.2 A Graphics System

A computer graphics system is a computer system; as such it must have all the components of a general-purpose computer system. Let us start with the block diagram in Figure 1.1. There are five major elements in our system:

1. Processor
2. Memory
3. Frame buffer
4. Output devices
5. Input devices

This model is general enough to include workstations, personal computers, graphics terminals attached to a central time-shared computer, and sophisticated image-generation systems. Although all the components, with the exception of the frame buffer, are present in a standard computer, it is the way each element is specialized for computer graphics that characterizes this diagram as a portrait of a graphics system.

1.2.1 Pixels and the Frame Buffer

At present, almost all graphics systems are raster based. A picture is produced as an array—the **raster**—of picture elements, or **pixels**, within the graphics system.

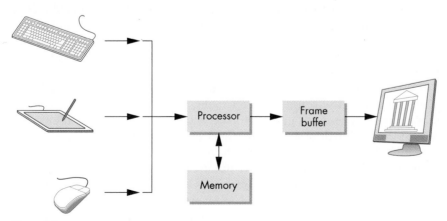

Figure 1.1 A graphics system.

figure 1.2 Pixels. (a) Image of Yeti the cat. (b) Detail of area around one eye showing individual pixels.

As we can see from Figure 1.2, each pixel corresponds to a location, or small area, in the image. Collectively, the pixels are stored in a part of memory called the **frame buffer**. In high-end systems, the frame buffer is implemented with special types of memory chips—video random-access memory (VRAM) or dynamic random-access memory (DRAM)—that enable fast redisplay of the contents of the frame buffer. The **depth** of the frame buffer, defined as the number of bits that are used for each pixel, determines properties such as how many colors can be represented on a given system. For example, a 1-bit-deep frame buffer allows only two colors, whereas an 8-bit-deep frame buffer allows 2^8 (=256) colors. In **full-color** systems, there are 24 (or more) bits per pixel. Such systems can display sufficient colors to represent most images realistically. They are also called **true-color** systems, or **RGB-color** systems, because individual groups of bits in each pixel are assigned to each of the three primary colors—red, green, and blue—used in most displays. In simpler systems, the frame buffer is part of standard memory. The frame buffer can be viewed as the core element of a graphics system. Its **resolution**—the number of pixels in the frame buffer—determines the detail that you can see in the image.

In a very simple system, the frame buffer holds only the colored pixels that are displayed on the screen. In most systems, the frame buffer holds far more information, such as depth information needed for creating images from three-dimensional data. In these systems, the frame buffer can be looked at as consisting of multiple buffers, one or more of which are **color buffers** that hold the colored pixels that are displayed. For now, we can use the terms *frame buffer* and *color buffer* synonymously without confusion.

In a simple system, there may be only one **processor**, which must do both the normal processing and the graphical processing. The main graphical function of the processor is to take specifications of graphical primitives (such as lines, circles, and polygons) generated by application programs, and to assign values to the pixels in the frame buffer that best represent these entities. The converting of geometric entities to pixel assignments in the frame buffer is known as **rasterization**, or **scan conversion**. Sophisticated graphics systems are characterized by various special-purpose processors, each custom-tailored to specific graphics functions.

1.2.2 Output Devices

The dominant type of display, and the one that we assume is used on our system, is the **cathode-ray tube** (**CRT**). A simplified picture of a CRT is shown in Figure 1.3. When electrons strike the phosphor coating on the tube, light is emitted. The direction of the beam is controlled by two pairs of deflection plates. The output of the computer is converted, by digital-to-analog converters, to voltages across the x and y deflection plates. Light appears on the surface of the CRT when a sufficiently intense beam of electrons is directed at the phosphor.

If the voltages steering the beam change at a constant rate, the beam will trace a straight line, visible to a viewer. Such a device is known as the **random-scan** or **calligraphic** CRT, because the beam can be moved directly from any position to any other position. If intensity of the beam is turned off, the beam can be moved to a new position without changing any visible display. This configuration was the basis of early graphics systems that predated the present raster technology.

A typical CRT will emit light for only a short time—usually, a few milliseconds—after the phosphor is excited by the electron beam. For a human to see a steady image on most CRT displays, the same path must be retraced, or **refreshed**, by the beam at least 50 times per second.

In a raster system, the graphics system takes pixels from the frame buffer and displays them as points on the surface of the display. The entire contents of the frame buffer are displayed on the CRT at a rate high enough to avoid flicker. This rate is called the **refresh rate**. There are two fundamental ways

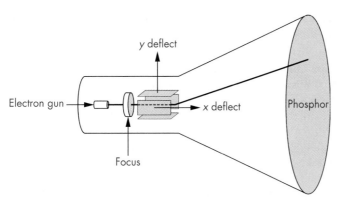

Figure 1.3 The cathode-ray tube (CRT).

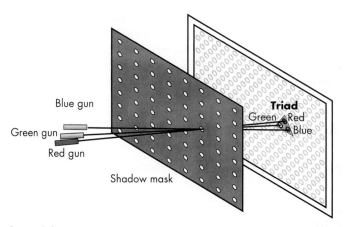

Figure 1.4 Shadow-mask CRT.

that pixels are displayed on a CRT. In a **noninterlaced** system, the pixels are displayed row by row, or scan line by scan line, at the refresh rate, which is usually 50 to 85 times per second, or 50 to 85 Hertz (Hz). In an **interlaced** display, odd rows and even rows are refreshed alternately. Interlaced displays are used in commercial television. In an interlaced display operating at 60 Hz, the screen is redrawn in its entirety only 30 times per second, although the visual system is tricked into thinking the refresh rate is 60 Hz rather than 30 Hz. Viewers located near the screen, however, can tell the difference between the interlaced and noninterlaced displays. Noninterlaced displays are becoming more widespread, even though these displays process pixels at twice the rate of the interlaced display.

Color CRTs have three different colored phosphors (red, green, and blue), arranged in small groups. One common style arranges the phosphors in triangular groups called **triads**, each triad consisting of three phosphors, one of each primary. Most color CRTs have three electron beams, corresponding to the three types of phosphors. In the shadow-mask CRT (Figure 1.4), a metal screen with small holes—the **shadow mask**—ensures that an electron beam excites only phosphors of the proper color.

Although CRTs are still the most common display device, they are not the only type. However, most other output technologies are also raster. The liquid-crystal displays (LCDs) used in portable computers are raster displays which, depending on the particular technology, may or may not have to be refreshed. Other devices such as plasma panels and digital projection systems are also raster devices. Most hard-copy devices, such as printers and plotters, are also raster based but cannot be refreshed.

1.2.3 Input Devices

Most graphics systems provide a keyboard and at least one other input device. The most common input devices are the mouse, the joystick, and the data tablet. Each provides positional information to the system, and each usually is equipped with one or more buttons to provide signals to the processor. Often called **pointing devices**, these devices allow a user to indicate a particular location on the display. We study these devices in Chapter 3.

1.3 Images: Physical and Synthetic

The usual pedagogical approach to teaching computer graphics is to start with a discussion of how to construct raster images of simple two-dimensional geometric entities (for example, points, line segments, and polygons) in the frame buffer. Next, most textbooks discuss how to define mathematical objects in the computer based on the set of two-dimensional geometric entities. This approach works well for creating simple images of simple objects. In modern systems, however, we want to exploit the capabilities of the software and hardware to create realistic images of computer-generated three-dimensional objects—a task that involves many aspects of image formation, such as lighting, shading, and properties of materials. Because such functionality is supported by most present computer graphics systems, we prefer to set the stage for creating these images here, rather than to expand a limited model later.

Computer-generated images are synthetic or artificial, in the sense that the objects being imaged do not exist physically. In this chapter, we argue that the preferred method to form computer-generated images is similar to traditional imaging methods. Hence, before we discuss the mechanics of writing programs to generate images, we discuss the way images are formed by optical systems, such as cameras and the human visual system. We construct a model of the image-formation process that we can then use to understand and develop computer-generated imaging systems.

In this chapter, we make minimal use of mathematics. We want to establish a paradigm for creating images and to present a computer architecture for implementing that paradigm. Details are presented in subsequent chapters, where we discuss implementation. There, we generate the relevant equations.

1.3.1 Objects and Viewers

We live in a world of three-dimensional objects. We usually refer to the location of a point on an object in terms of some convenient reference system. We can measure the distance between points in space, and thus between various objects. The development of many branches of mathematics, including geometry and trigonometry, was in response to the desire to systematize conceptually simple ideas, such as the measurement of size and distance. Often, we seek to represent our understanding of such spatial relationships with pictures or images, such as maps, paintings, and photographs. Likewise, the development of many physical devices—including cameras, microscopes, and telescopes—was tied to the desire to visualize spatial relationships among objects. Hence, there is a fundamental link between the physics and the mathematics of image formation—one that we exploit in our development of computer image formation.

Two basic entities must be part of any image-formation process, be it mathematical or physical: *object* and *viewer*. The object exists in space independent of any image-formation process and of any viewer. In computer graphics, where we deal with synthetic objects, we form objects by specifying the positions in space of various geometric primitives, such as points, lines, and polygons. In most graphics systems, a set of locations in space, or of **vertices**, is sufficient to define, or approximate, most objects. For example, a line can be defined by two vertices, a polygon can be defined by an ordered list of vertices, and a sphere can be specified by two vertices that specify its center and any point on its circumference. One of the main functions of a CAD system is to provide an interface that makes it easy for a user to build a synthetic model of the world. In Chapter 2, we show how OpenGL allows us to build simple objects; in Chapter 9, we learn to define objects in a manner that incorporates relationships among objects.

Every imaging system must provide a means of forming images from objects. To form an image, we must have someone, or something, that is viewing our objects, be it a human, a camera, or a digitizer. It is the **viewer** that forms the image of our objects. In the human visual system, the image is formed on the back of the eye, on the retina. In a camera, the image is formed in the film plane. It is easy to confuse images and objects. We usually see an object from our single perspective and forget that other viewers, located in other places, will see the same object differently. Figure 1.5(a) shows an image as seen by viewer A. In the scene are two other observers, B and C; they appear as objects to viewer A. Figures 1.5(b) and (c) show the images seen by B and C, respectively.

Figure 1.6 shows a camera system viewing a building. Here, we can observe that both the object and the viewer exist in a three-dimensional world. However,

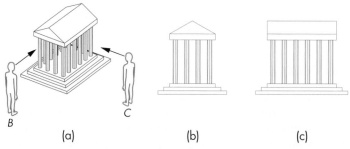

(a)   (b)   (c)

Figure 1.5 Image seen by three different viewers. (a) A's view. (b) B's view. (c) C's view.

Figure 1.6 Camera system.

the image that they define—what we find on the film plane—is two-dimensional. The process by which the specification of the object is combined with the specification of the viewer to produce a two-dimensional image is the essence of image formation, and we shall study it in detail.

1.3.2 Light and Images

Much information is missing from the preceding description of image formation. For example, we have yet to mention light. If there were no light sources, the objects would be dark, and there would be nothing visible in our image. We have not indicated how color enters the picture, or what are the effects of different kinds of surfaces on the objects.

Taking a more physical approach, we can start with the arrangement in Figure 1.7, which shows a simple physical imaging system. Again, we see a physical object and a viewer (the camera); now, however, there is a light source in the scene. Light from the source strikes various surfaces of the object, and a portion of the reflected light enters the camera through the lens. The details of the interaction between light and the surfaces of the object determine how much light enters the camera.

Light is a form of electromagnetic radiation. Electromagnetic energy travels as waves that can be characterized by either their wavelengths or their frequencies.[1] The electromagnetic spectrum (Figure 1.8) includes radio waves, infrared (heat), and a portion that causes a response in our visual systems. This **visible spectrum**, which has wavelengths in the range of 350 to 780 nanometers (nm), is called **light**. A given light source has a color determined by the energy that it emits at various wavelengths. Wavelengths in the middle of the range, around 520 nm,

---

1. The relationship between frequency f and wavelength λ is $f\lambda = c$, where c is the speed of light.

Figure 1.7 A camera system with a light source.

are seen as green; those near 450 nm are seen as blue; and those near 650 nm are seen as red. Just as with a rainbow, light at wavelengths between red and green we see as yellow, and wavelengths shorter than blue generate violet light.

Light sources can emit light either as a set of discrete wavelengths or continuously. A laser, for example, emits light at a single wavelength, whereas an incandescent lamp emits energy over a range of wavelengths. Fortunately, in computer graphics, except for recognizing that distinct frequencies are visible as distinct colors, we rarely need to deal with the wave nature of light.

Instead, we can follow a more traditional path that is correct when we are operating with sufficiently high light levels, and at a scale where the wave nature of light is not a significant factor. **Geometric optics** models light sources as emitters of light energy that have a fixed rate or intensity. Light travels in straight lines, from the sources to those objects with which it interacts. An ideal **point source** emits energy from a single location at one or more frequencies equally in all directions. More complex sources, such as a light bulb, can be

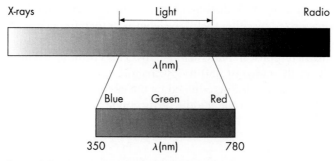

Figure 1.8 The electromagnetic spectrum.

characterized as emitting light over an area and by emitting more light in one direction than another. A particular source is characterized by the intensity of light that it emits at each frequency, and by that light's directionality. We consider only point sources for now. More complex sources often can be modeled by a number of carefully placed point sources. Modeling of light sources is discussed in Chapter 6.

Another simplification that we will make, for now, is to consider purely **monochromatic** lighting—a source of a single frequency. Because we can add together the contributions of light at various frequencies, this assumption does not restrict us, but it will make our development clearer. This assumption is equivalent to discussing only the brightness of a light, rather than the light's particular color or hue—an approach that is analogous to discussing black-and-white television before examining color television.

1.3.3 Ray Tracing

We can start building an imaging model by following light from a source. Consider the scene in Figure 1.9; it is illuminated by a single point source. We include the viewer in the figure because we are interested in the light that reaches her eye. The viewer can also be a camera, as shown in Figure 1.10. A **ray** is a semi-infinite line that emanates from a point and travels to infinity in a particular direction. Because light travels in straight lines, we can think in terms of rays of light emanating in all directions from our point source. A portion of these infinite rays contributes to the image on the film plane of our camera. For example, if the source is visible from the camera, some of the rays go directly from the source through the lens of the camera, and strike the film plane. Most rays go off to infinity, neither entering the camera directly nor striking any of the objects. These rays contribute nothing to the image, although they may be seen by some other viewer. The remaining rays strike and illuminate objects. These rays can interact

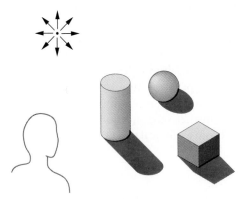

Figure 1.9 Scene with a single point source.

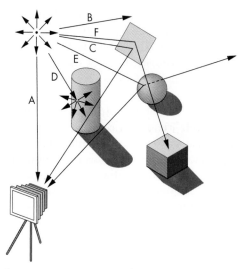

Figure 1.10 Ray tracing. Ray A goes directly through the lens, whereas ray B misses everything and travels to infinity. Ray C bounces off a mirror and enters the camera. Ray D hits a diffuse surface and generates (infinite) new rays that, in principle, can contribute to the image. Ray E hits a surface that is partially transparent, and generates a transmitted ray and a reflected ray. Ray F is reflected from a surface, but strikes another surface that absorbs it.

with the objects' surfaces in a variety of ways. For example, if the surface is a mirror, a reflected ray might—depending on the orientation of the surface— enter the lens of the camera and contribute to the image. Other surfaces, known as **diffuse surfaces**, scatter light in all directions. If the surface is transparent, the light ray from the source can pass through it, perhaps being bent or **refracted**, and may interact with other objects, enter the camera, or travel to infinity without striking another surface. Figure 1.10 shows six of the possibilities.

Ray tracing is an image-formation technique that is based on these ideas and that can form the basis for producing computer-generated images. We can use the ray-tracing model to simulate physical effects as complex as we wish, as long as we are willing to carry out the requisite computing.[2] Although the ray-tracing model is a close approximation to the physical world, it is not well suited for fast computation. We can, however, make one further simplification that will lead us to a more viable computational method. From a physical perspective, if an object

---

2. In Chapter 13, we shall examine ray tracing as method for creating computer-generated images.

emits light, we cannot tell whether we are looking at an object that is reflecting light, or whether the object is emitting light from internal energy sources. For example, a mirror that reflects light from a source toward the viewer looks like a light source. If we can see an object, it is illuminated by a source, or it is an emitter of light, or it is both. We cannot tell by looking at the object which combination we are seeing.

Let's assume that all our objects are uniformly bright—a scenario that might be difficult to accomplish in practice, but often is a reasonable goal when we place lights in an environment. From the perspective of the viewer, a red triangle appears to have the same shade of red at every point, and is indistinguishable from a uniformly red emitter of light. Given this assumption, we can dispense with sources, and can use simple trigonometric methods to calculate the image. In Chapter 6, we relax this assumption, adding light sources and more complex material properties, still without getting into the full complexity of the ray tracer.

We now introduce two imaging systems: the human visual system and the pinhole camera. The human visual system is extremely complex, but still obeys the physical principles of all imaging systems. We introduce it not only as an example of an imaging system, but also because understanding its properties will help us to exploit the capabilities of computer-graphics systems. The pinhole camera is a simple example of an imaging system that will enable us to understand the functioning of cameras and of other optical imagers. We emulate it to build a model of image formation.

1.4 The Human Visual System

Our extremely complex visual system has all the components of a physical imaging system, such as a camera or a microscope. The major components of the visual system are shown in Figure 1.11. Light enters the eye through the lens and cornea, a transparent structure that protects the eye. The iris opens and closes to adjust the amount of light entering the eye. The lens forms an image on a two-dimensional structure called the retina at the back of the eye. The rods and cones (so named because of their appearance when magnified) are light sensors and are located on the retina. They are excited by electromagnetic energy in the range of 350 to 780 nm.

The rods are low-level-light sensors that account for our night vision; the cones are responsible for our day vision. The sizes of the rods and cones, coupled with the optical properties of the lens and cornea, determine the **resolution** of our visual systems, or our **visual acuity**. Resolution is a measure of what size objects we can see. More technically, it is a measure of how close we can place two points and still recognize that there are two distinct points.

The sensors in the human eye do not react uniformly to light energy at different wavelengths. There are three types of cones and a single type of rod. Whereas intensity is a physical measure of light energy, **brightness** is a measure of how intense we perceive the light emitted from an object to be. The human

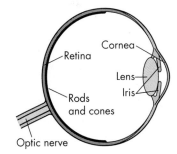

Figure 1.11 The human visual system.

Figure 1.12 CIE standard
observer curve.

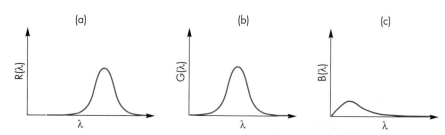

Figure 1.13 Cone sensitivity curves.

visual system does not have the same response to a monochromatic (single-frequency) red light as to a monochromatic green light. If these two lights were to emit energy with the same intensity, they would appear to us to have different brightness, because of the unequal response of the cones to red and green light. Relative brightness response at different frequencies is shown in Figure 1.12. This curve, which gives the relative sensitivity of the human visual system at visible-light frequencies, is known as the Commision Internationale de L'Eclairage **(CIE) standard observer curve**. It shows that we are most sensitive to green light, and least to red and blue. This curve also closely matches the sensitivity of the monochromatic sensors used in black-and-white film and in black-and-white video cameras.

Brightness is an overall measure of how we react to the intensity of light. Human color-vision capabilities are due to the different sensitivities of the three types of cones. Each type has its own sensitivity curve, as shown by Figure 1.13. Of the three curves, one is centered in the blue range, one in the green, and the third in the yellow.[3] The major consequence of having three types of cones is that most image-production systems, such as film and video, can work with three basic or **primary** colors. We can use standard primaries to approximate any color that we can perceive. We discuss color in Chapter 2.

The initial processing of light in the human visual system is based on the same principles as are used by most optical systems. However, the human visual system has a back end much more complex than that of a camera or telescope. The optic nerves are connected to the rods and cones in an extremely complex arrangement that has many of the characteristics of a sophisticated signal processor. The final processing is done in a part of the brain called the visual cortex, where high-level functions, such as object recognition, are carried out. We shall omit any discussion of high-level processing; instead we can simply think in terms of an image that is conveyed from the rods and cones to the brain.

---

3. The curve centered in the yellow is often referred to as the *red curve* to be compatible with other three-color systems used in film and video. The key point is that there are three types of sensors, rather than that the individual response curves are centered at particular frequencies.

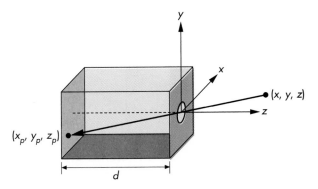

Figure 1.14 Pinhole camera.

1.5 The Pinhole Camera

The pinhole camera in Figure 1.14 provides an example of image formation that we can understand with a simple geometric model. A **pinhole camera** is a box with a small hole in the center of one side of the box; the film is placed inside the box on the side opposite the pinhole. Suppose that we orient our camera along the z-axis, with the pinhole at the origin of our coordinate system. We assume that the hole is so small that only a single ray of light, emanating from a point, can enter it. The film plane is located a distance d from the pinhole. A side view (Figure 1.15) allows us to calculate where the image of the point (x, y, z) is on the film plane $z = -d$. Using the fact that the two triangles in Figure 1.15 are similar, we find that the y coordinate of the image is at y_p, where

$$y_p = -\frac{y}{z/d}.$$

A similar calculation, using a top view, yields

$$x_p = -\frac{x}{z/d}.$$

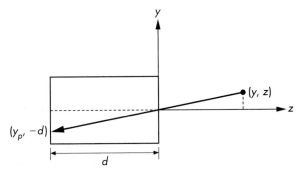

Figure 1.15 Side view of pinhole camera.

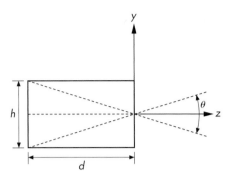

Figure 1.16 Angle of view.

The point $(x_p, y_p, -d)$ is called the **projection** of the point (x, y, z). In our idealized model, the color on the film plane at this point will be the color of the point (x, y, z). The **field** or **angle of view** of our camera is the angle made by the largest object that our camera can image on its film plane. We can calculate the field of view with the aid of Figure 1.16.[4] If h is the height of the camera, the angle of view θ is

$$\theta = 2 \tan^{-1} \frac{h}{2d}.$$

The ideal pinhole camera has an infinite **depth of field**: Every point within its field of view is in focus. The image of a point is a point. The pinhole camera has two disadvantages. First, because the pinhole is so small—it admits only a single ray from a point source—almost no light enters the camera. Second, the camera cannot be adjusted to have a different angle of view.

The jump to more sophisticated cameras and to other imaging systems that have lenses is a small one. By replacing the pinhole with a lens, we solve the two problems of the pinhole camera. First, the lens gathers more light than can pass through the pinhole. The larger the aperture of the lens, the more light that lens can collect. Second, by picking a lens with the proper focal length—a selection equivalent to choosing d for the pinhole camera—we can achieve any desired angle of view (up to 180 degrees). Lenses, however, do not have an infinite depth of field: Not all distances from the lens are in focus.

For our purposes, in this chapter, we can work with a pinhole camera whose focal length is the distance d from the front of the camera to the film plane. Like the pinhole camera, computer graphics produces images in which all objects are in focus.

---

4. If we consider the problem in three, rather than two, dimensions, then the diagonal length of the film will substitute for h. See Exercise 1.1.

Figure 1.17 Imaging system.

1.6 The Synthetic-Camera Model

Our models of optical imaging systems lead directly to the conceptual foundation for modern three-dimensional computer graphics. We look at creating a computer-generated image as being similar to forming an image using an optical system. This paradigm has become known as the **synthetic-camera model**. Consider the imaging system shown in Figure 1.17. We again see objects and a viewer. In this case, the viewer is a bellows camera.[5] The image is formed on the film plane at the back of the camera. So that we can emulate this process to create artificial images, we need to identify a few basic principles.

First, the specification of the objects is independent of the specification of the viewer. Hence, we should expect that, within a graphics library, there will be separate functions for specifying the objects and the viewer.

Second, we can compute the image using simple trigonometric calculations. We can derive these calculations in a straightforward manner. Consider the side view of the camera and a simple object in Figure 1.18. The view on the left is similar to that of the pinhole camera. We obtain the view on the right by noting the similarity of the two triangles: We move the image plane in front of the lens, and, in three dimensions, work with the arrangement of Figure 1.19. We find the image of a point on the object by drawing a line, called a **projector**, from the point to the center of the lens, or the **center of projection**. Note that all projectors are rays emanating from the center of projection. In our synthetic camera, the film plane that we have moved in front of the lens is called the **projection plane**. The image of the point is located where the projector passes

---

5. In a bellows camera, the front plane of the camera, where the lens is located, and the back of the camera, the film plane, are connected by flexible sides. Thus, we can move the back of the camera independently of the front of the camera, introducing additional flexibility in the image-formation process. We use this flexibility in Chapter 5.

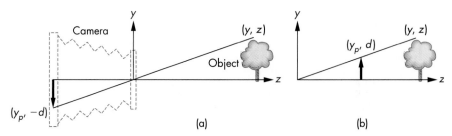

Figure 1.18 Equivalent views of image formation (a) with the image formed on the back of the camera, and (b) with the image plane moved in front of the camera.

through the projection plane. In Chapter 5, we discuss this process in detail and derive the relevant mathematical formulas.

We must also consider the limited size of the image. As we saw, not all objects can be imaged onto the pinhole camera's film plane. The angle of view expresses this limitation. In the synthetic camera, we can move this limitation to the front by placing a **clipping rectangle**, or **clipping window**, in the projection plane (Figure 1.20). This rectangle acts as a window through which a viewer, located at the center of projection, sees the world. Given the location of the center of projection, the location and orientation of the projection plane, and the size of the clipping rectangle, we can determine which objects will appear in the image.

Figure 1.19 Imaging with the synthetic camera.

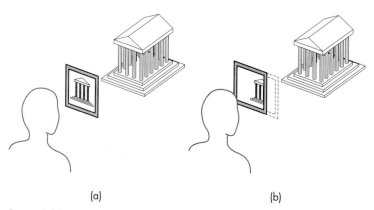

         (a)   (b)

Figure 1.20 Clipping (a) with window in initial position, and (b) with window shifted.

1.7 The Programmer's Interface

There are numerous ways that a user can interact with a graphics system. With completely self-contained packages, such as are used in the CAD community, a user develops images through interactions with the display, using input devices, such as a mouse and a keyboard. In a typical application, such as the painting program in Figure 1.21, she sees menus and icons that represent possible actions. By clicking on these items, the user guides the software and produces images without having to write programs.

Of course, someone has to develop the code for these applications, and many of us, despite the sophistication of commercial products, still have to write our own graphics application programs (and even enjoy doing so).

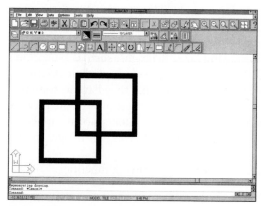

Figure 1.21 Interface for a painting program.

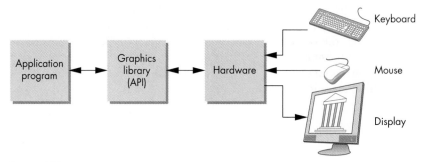

Figure 1.22   Application programmer's model of graphics system.

1.7.1 Application Programmer's Interfaces

The interface between an application program and a graphics system can be specified through a set of functions that resides in a graphics library. These specifications are called the **application programmer's interface (API)**. The application programmer's model of the system is shown in Figure 1.22. The application programmer sees only the API, and is thus shielded from the details of both the hardware and the software implementation of the graphics library. From the perspective of the writer of an application program, the functions available through the API should match the conceptual model that the user wishes to employ to specify images.

1.7.2 The Pen-Plotter Model

Historically, most early graphics systems were two-dimensional systems. The conceptual model that they used is now referred to as the *pen-plotter model*, referencing the output device that was available on these systems. A **pen plotter** (Figure 1.23) produces images by moving a pen held by a gantry, a structure that can move the pen in two orthogonal directions around the paper. The plotter can raise and lower the pen as required to create the desired image. Pen plotters are still in use; they are well suited for drawing large diagrams, such as blueprints. Various APIs—such as LOGO, GKS, and PostScript—all have their origins in this model. Although they differ from one another, what they have in common is that they view the process of creating an image as being similar to the process of drawing on a pad of paper. The user works on a two-dimensional surface of some size. She moves a pen around on this surface, leaving an image on the paper.

Figure 1.23   Pen plotter.

We can describe such a graphics system with two drawing functions:

```
moveto(x,y);
lineto(x,y);
```

Execution of the `moveto` function moves the pen to the location (x, y) on the paper without leaving a mark. The `lineto` function moves the pen to (x, y) and draws a line from the old to the new location of the pen. Once we add a few initialization and termination procedures, as well as the ability to change pens to alter the drawing color or line thickness, we have a simple—but complete—graphics system. Here is a fragment of a simple program in such a system:

```
moveto(0, 0);
lineto(1, 0);
lineto(1, 1);
lineto(0, 1);
lineto(0,0);
```

This fragment would generate the output in Figure 1.24(a). If we added the code

```
moveto(0, 1);
lineto(0.5, 1.866);
lineto(1.5, 1.866);
lineto(1.5, 0.866);
lineto(1, 0);
moveto(1, 1);
lineto(1,5,1.866);
```

we would have the image of a cube formed by an oblique projection, as is shown in Figure 1.24(b).

For certain applications, such as page layout in the printing industry, systems built on this model work well. For example, the PostScript page-description language, a sophisticated extension of these ideas, is a standard for controlling printers and typesetters.

We are much more interested, however, in the three-dimensional world. The pen-plotter model does not extend well to three-dimensional graphics systems. For example, if we wish to use the pen-plotter model to produce the image of a three-dimensional object on our two-dimensional pad, either by hand or by computer, then we have to figure out where on the page to place two-dimensional points corresponding to points on our three-dimensional object. These two-dimensional points are, as we saw in Section 1.5, the projections of points in three-dimensional space. The mathematical process of determining projections is an application of trigonometry. We develop the mathematics of projection in Chapter 5; understanding projection is crucial to understanding three-dimensional graphics. We prefer, however, to use an API that allows users to work directly in the domain of their problems and to use computers to carry out the details of the projection process automatically, without the users having to make any trigonometric calculations within the application program. That approach should be a boon to users who have difficulty learning to draw various projections on a drafting board or sketching objects in perspective.

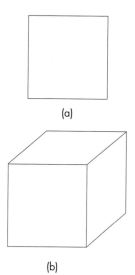

(a)

(b)

Figure 1.24 Output of pen-plotter program for (a) a square, and (b) a projection of a cube.

More important, users can rely on hardware and software implementations of projections within the implementation of the API that are far more efficient than would be any possible implementation of projections within their programs.

1.7.3 Three-Dimensional APIs

The synthetic-camera model is the basis for a number of popular APIs, including OpenGL, PHIGS, Direct3D, VRML, and JAVA-3D.

If we are to follow the synthetic-camera model, we need functions in the API to specify

- Objects
- Viewer
- Light sources
- Material properties

Objects are usually defined by sets of vertices. For simple geometric objects—such as line segments, rectangles, and polygons—there is a simple relationship between a list of vertices and the object. For more complex objects, there may be multiple ways of defining the object from a set of vertices. A circle, for example, can be defined by three points on its circumference, or by its center and one point on the circumference.

Most APIs provide similar sets of primitive objects for the user. These primitives are usually those that can be displayed rapidly on the hardware. The usual sets include points, line segments, polygons, and, sometimes, text. OpenGL defines primitives through lists of vertices. The following code fragment defines a triangular polygon in OpenGL through five function calls:

```
glBegin(GL_POLYGON);
    glVertex3f(0.0, 0.0, 0.0);
    glVertex3f(0.0, 1.0, 0.0);
    glVertex3f(0.0, 0.0, 1.0);
glEnd( );
```

Note that, by adding additional vertices, we can define an arbitrary polygon. If we change the type parameter, GL_POLYGON, we can use the same vertices to define a different geometric primitive. For example, the type GL_LINE_STRIP uses the vertices to define two connected line segments, whereas the type GL_POINTS uses the same vertices to define three points.

Some APIs let the user work directly in the frame buffer by providing functions that read and write pixels. Some APIs provide curves and surfaces as primitives; often, however, these types are approximated by a series of simpler primitives within the application program. OpenGL provides access to the frame buffer, curves, and surfaces.

We can define a viewer or camera in a variety of ways. Available APIs differ both in how much flexibility they provide in camera selection and in how many different methods they allow. If we look at the camera in Figure 1.25, we can identify four types of necessary specifications:

1. **Position**   The camera location usually is given by the position of the center of the lens (the center of projection).
2. **Orientation**   Once we have positioned the camera, we can place a camera coordinate system with its origin at the center of projection. We can then rotate the camera independently around the three axes of this system.
3. **Focal length**   The focal length of the lens determines the size of the image on the film plane or, equivalently, the portion of the world the camera sees.
4. **Film plane**   The back of the camera has a height and a width. On the bellows camera, and in some APIs, the orientation of the back of the camera can be adjusted independently of the orientation of the lens.

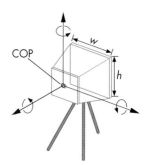

Figure 1.25 Camera specification.

These specifications can be satisfied in various ways. One way to develop the specifications for the camera location and orientation uses a series of coordinate-system transformations. These transformations convert object positions represented in the coordinate system that specifies object vertices to object positions in a coordinate system centered at the center of projection. This approach is useful, both for doing implementation and for getting the full set of views that a flexible camera can provide. We use this approach extensively, starting in Chapter 5.

Having many parameters to adjust, however, can also make it difficult to get a desired image. Part of the problem lies with the synthetic-camera model. Classical viewing techniques, such as are used in architecture, stress the *relationship* between the object and the viewer, rather than the *independence* that the synthetic-camera model emphasizes. Thus, the classical two-point perspective of a cube in Figure 1.26 is a *two-point* perspective because of a particular relationship between the viewer and the planes of the cube (see Exercise 1.6). Although the OpenGL API allows us to set transformations with complete freedom, it also provides helpful extra functions. For example, consider the two function calls

```
gluLookAt(cop_x, cop_y, cop_z, at_x, at_y, at_z, ...);
glPerspective(field_of_view, ...);
```

The first function call points the camera from a center of projection toward a desired point; the second selects a lens for a perspective view. However, none

Figure 1.26 Two-point perspective of a cube.

of the APIs built on the synthetic-camera model—OpenGL, PHIGS, VRML—provide functions for specifying desired relationships between the camera and an object.

Light sources can be defined by their location, strength, color, and directionality. APIs provide a set of functions to specify these parameters for each source. Material properties are characteristics, or attributes, of the objects, and such properties are usually specified through a series of function calls at the time that each object is defined. Both light sources and material properties depend on the models of light–material interactions supported by the API. We discuss such models in Chapter 6.

1.7.4 A Sequence of Images

In Chapter 2, we begin our detailed discussion of the OpenGL API that we will use throughout this book. OpenGL will allow you to write graphical application programs. The images defined by your programs will be formed automatically by the hardware and software implementation of the image-formation process.

Here, we look at a sequence of images that shows what we can create using the OpenGL API. We present these images as an increasingly more complex series of renderings of the same objects. The sequence not only loosely follows the order in which we present related topics, but also reflects how graphics systems have developed over the past 30 years.

Color Plate 1 shows one of the planet objects as on the front and back covers of this book. Color Plate 2 shows the object rendered using only line segments. Although the object consists of many parts, and although the programmer may have used sophisticated data structures to model each part and the relationships among the parts, the rendered object shows only the outlines of the parts. This type of image is known as a **wireframe** image, because we can see only the edges of surfaces: Such an image would be produced if the objects were constructed with stiff wires that formed a frame with no solid material between the edges. Before raster-graphics systems became available, wireframe images were the only type of computer-generated images that we could produce.

In Color Plate 3, the same object has been rendered with flat polygons. Certain surfaces are not visible because there is a solid surface between them and the viewer; these surfaces have been removed by a hidden-surface-removal (HSR) algorithm. Most raster systems can fill the interior of polygons with a solid color in the same time that they can render a wireframe image. Although the objects are three dimensional, each surface is displayed in a single color, and the image fails to show the three-dimensional shapes of the objects. Early raster systems could produce images of this form.

In Chapters 2 and 3, we show you how to generate images composed of simple geometric objects—points, line segments, and polygons. In Chapters 4 and 5, you will learn how to transform objects in three dimensions, and how to obtain a desired three-dimensional view of a model, with hidden surfaces removed.

Color Plate 4 introduces a light source and a smooth shading of the object; it shows that the object is three dimensional and gives the appearance of a smooth surface. We develop shading models that are supported by OpenGL in Chapter 6. These shading models are also supported in the hardware of high-end graphics workstations; generating the shaded image on one of these systems takes the same amount of time as does generating a wireframe image.

Color Plate 5 shows a more sophisticated wireframe model that was con-structed using NURBS surfaces that we introduce in Chapter 10. Such surfaces give the application programmer great flexibility in the design process but are ultimately rendered using line segments and polygons.

In Color Plates 6 and 7, we add surface texture to our object; texture is one of the effects that we discuss in Chapter 7. The most sophisticated workstations now support texture mapping in hardware, so rendering of a texture-mapped image requires no additional time. In Color Plate 6, we use a technique called bump mapping that gives the appearance of a rough surface even though we render flat polygons. Color Plate 7 shows an environmental map applied to the surface of the object, which gives the surface the appearance of a mirror.

Color Plate 8 shows a small area of the rendering of the object using an environmental map. The image on the left shows the jagged artifacts known as aliasing errors that are due to the discrete nature of the frame buffer. The image on the right has been rendered using a smoothing or antialiasing method that we shall study in Chapters 7 and 8.

Not only do these images show what is possible with available hardware and a good API, but they are also simple to generate, as we shall see in subsequent chap-ters. In addition, just as the images show incremental changes in the renderings, the programs are incrementally different from one another.

1.7.5 The Modeling–Rendering Paradigm

Another approach to image formation can also be pursued: In many situations—especially in CAD applications and in development of realistic images, such as for movies—we can separate the modeling of the scene from the production of the image—the **rendering** of the scene. Hence, we can look at image formation as the two-step process shown in Figure 1.27. Although the tasks are the same as those that we have been discussing, this block diagram suggests that we might implement the modeler and the renderer with different software and hardware. For example, consider the production of a single frame in an animation. We

Figure 1.27 The modeling–rendering pipeline.

first want to design and position our objects. This step is highly interactive, and we do not need to work with detailed images of the objects. Consequently, we prefer to carry out this step on a graphical workstation. Once we have designed the scene, we want to render it, adding light sources, material properties, and a variety of other detailed effects, to form a production-quality image. This step requires a tremendous amount of computation, so we prefer to use a number-cruncher machine. Not only is the optimal hardware different in the modeling and rendering steps, but also the software that we use may be different.

The interface between the modeler and renderer can be as simple as a file produced by the modeler that describes the objects and that contains additional information important only to the renderer, such as light sources, viewer location, and material properties. Pixar's RenderMan Interface follows this approach and uses a file format that allows modelers to pass models to the renderer in text format. One of the other advantages of this approach is that it allows us to develop modelers that, although they use the same renderer, are custom-tailored to particular applications. Likewise, different renderers can take as input the same interface file. It is even possible, at least in principle, to dispense with the modeler completely, and to use a standard text editor to generate an interface file. For any but the simplest scenes, however, users cannot edit lists of information for a renderer. Rather, they use interactive modeling software. Because we must have at least a simple image of our objects to interact with a modeler, most modelers use the synthetic-camera model to produce these images in real time.

This paradigm has become popular as a method for generating computer games and images over the World Wide Web. Models, including the geometric objects, lights, cameras, and material properties, are placed in a data structure called a **scene graph** that is passed to a renderer or game engine. We shall examine scene graphs in Chapter 9.

1.8 Graphics Architectures

On one side of the API is the application program. On the other is some combination of hardware and software that implements the functionality of the API. Researchers have taken various approaches to developing architectures to support graphics APIs.

Early graphics systems used general-purpose computers with the standard von Neumann architecture. Such computers are characterized by a single processing unit that processes a single instruction at a time. A simple model of these early graphics systems is shown in Figure 1.28. The display in these systems was based on a CRT display that included the necessary circuitry to generate a line segment connecting two points. The job of the host computer was to run the application program and to compute the endpoints of the line segments in the image (in units of the display). This information had to be sent to the display at a rate high

Figure 1.28   Early graphics system.

enough to avoid flicker on the display. In the early days of computer graphics, computers were so slow that refreshing even simple images, containing a few hundred line segments, would burden an expensive computer.

1.8.1 Display Processors

The earliest attempts to build special-purpose graphics systems were concerned primarily with relieving the general-purpose computer from the task of refreshing the display continuously. These **display processors** had conventional architectures (Figure 1.29), but included instructions to display primitives on the CRT. The main advantage of the display processor was that the instructions to generate the image could be assembled once in the host and sent to the display processor, where they were stored in the display processor's own memory as a **display list** or **display file**. The display processor would then execute repetitively the program in the display list, at a rate sufficient to avoid flicker, independently of the host, thus freeing the host for other tasks. This architecture has become closely associated with the client–server architectures that we discuss in Chapter 3.

1.8.2 Pipeline Architectures

The major advances in graphics architectures parallel closely the advances in workstations. In both cases, the ability to create special-purpose VLSI circuits was the key enabling technology development. In addition, the availability of cheap solid-state memory led to the universality of raster displays.

Figure 1.29   Display-processor architecture.

Figure 1.30 Arithmetic pipeline.

For computer graphics applications, the most important use of custom VLSI circuits has been in creating **pipeline** architectures. The concept of pipelining is illustrated in Figure 1.30 for a simple arithmetic calculation.

In our pipeline, there is an adder and a multiplier. If we use this configuration to compute $a + (b * c)$, the calculation takes one multiplication and one addition—the same amount of work required if we use a single processor to carry out both operations. However, suppose that we have to carry out the same computation with many values of a, b, and c. Now, the multiplier can pass on the results of its calculation to the adder, and can start its next multiplication while the adder carries out the second step of the calculation on the first set of data. Hence, whereas it takes the same amount of time to calculate the results for any one set of data, when we are working on two sets of data at one time, our total time for calculation is shortened markedly. Here, the rate at which data flows through the system, the **throughput** of the system, has been doubled.

We can construct pipelines for more complex arithmetic calculations that will afford even greater increases in throughput. Of course, there is no point in building a pipeline unless we will do the same operation on many data sets. But that is just what we do in computer graphics, where large sets of vertices must be processed in the same manner.

Suppose that we have a set of vertices that defines a set of primitives. Because our representation is given in terms of locations in space, we can refer to the set of primitive types and vertices as the **geometry** of the data. In a complex scene, there may be thousands—even millions—of vertices that define the objects. We must process all these vertices in a similar manner to form an image in the frame buffer. If we think in terms of processing the geometry of our objects to obtain an image, we can employ the block diagram in Figure 1.31, which shows the four major steps in the imaging process:

1. Transformation
2. Clipping
3. Projection
4. Rasterization

In subsequent chapters, we discuss the details of these steps. Here, we are content to show that these operations can be pipelined.

Figure 1.31 Geometric pipeline.

1.8.3 Transformations

Many of the steps in the imaging process can be viewed as transformations between representations of objects in different coordinate systems. For example, in our discussion of the synthetic camera, we observed that a major part of viewing is to convert to a representation of objects from the system in which they were defined to a representation in terms of the coordinate system of the camera. A further example of a transformation arises when we finally put our images onto a CRT display or other output device. The internal representation of objects—whether in the camera coordinate system or perhaps in a system used by the graphics software—eventually must be represented in terms of the coordinate system of the display. We can represent each change of coordinate systems by a matrix. We can represent successive changes in coordinate systems by multiplying, or **concatenating**, the individual matrices into a single matrix. In Chapter 4, we examine these operations in detail. Because multiplying one matrix by another matrix yields a third matrix, a sequence of transformations is an obvious candidate for a pipeline architecture. In addition, because the matrices that we use in computer graphics will always be small (4×4), we have the opportunity to use parallelism within the transformation blocks in the pipeline.

1.8.4 Clipping

The second fundamental operation in the implementation of computer graphics is **clipping**. We do clipping because of the limitation that no imaging system can see the whole world at once. The human retina has a limited size corresponding to an approximately 90-degree field of view. Cameras have film of limited size, and we can adjust their fields of view by selecting different lenses. We obtain the equivalent property in the synthetic camera by placing a **clipping rectangle** of limited size in the projection plane, as we saw in Figure 1.20. Objects whose projections are within the window appear in the image. Those that are outside do not, and are said to be clipped out. Objects whose projections straddle the edges of the window are partly visible in the image.

Clipping can occur at various stages in the imaging process. For simple geometric objects, we can determine from its vertices whether or not an object is clipped out. Because clippers work with vertices, clippers can be inserted with transformers into the pipeline. Clipping can even be subdivided further into a sequence of pipelined clippers (see Exercises 1.4 and 1.5). Efficient clipping algorithms are developed in Chapter 8.

1.8.5 Projection

In general, three-dimensional objects are kept in three dimensions as long as possible, as they pass through the pipeline. Eventually, after multiple stages of transformation and clipping, the geometry of the remaining primitives (those that have not been clipped out and will appear in the image) must be projected into two-dimensional objects. There are various projections that we can implement; we shall see in Chapter 5 that we can implement this step using 4×4 matrices, and, thus, also fit it in the pipeline.

1.8.6 Rasterization

Finally, our projected objects must be represented as pixels in the frame buffer. We discuss this scan-conversion or rasterization process in Chapters 7 and 8 for the standard primitives, such as line segments and polygons. Because the refreshing of the display is carried out automatically by the hardware, the details are of minor concern to the applications programmer. Thus, we can think of the rasterizer as being the end of the pipeline.

1.8.7 Performance Characteristics

There are two fundamentally different types of processing in our architecture. At the front end, there is geometric processing, based on processing vertices through the various clippers and transformers. This processing is ideally suited for pipelining, and it usually involves floating-point calculations. The geometry engine developed by Silicon Graphics was a VLSI implementation for many of these operations in a special-purpose chip that became the basis for a series of fast graphics workstations. Later, floating-point accelerator chips, such as the Intel i860, put 4×4 matrix-transformation units on the chip, reducing a matrix multiplication to a single instruction. Graphics workstations and add-on graphics boards use Application-Specific Integrated Circuits (ASICs) that perform many of the graphics operations at the chip level.

Pipeline architectures are the dominant type of high-performance system. As we add more boxes to the pipeline, however, it takes more time for a single datum to pass through the system. This time is called the **latency** of the system; we must balance it against increased throughput in evaluating the performance of a pipeline.

Beginning with rasterization and including many features that we discuss later, processing involves a direct manipulation of bits in the frame buffer. This back-end processing is fundamentally different from front-end processing, and we implement it most effectively using architectures that have the ability to move blocks of bits quickly. The overall performance of a system is characterized by how fast we can move geometric entities through the pipeline and by how many pixels per second we can alter in the frame buffer. Consequently, the fastest graphics workstations are characterized by pipelines at the front ends and parallel bit processors at the back ends.

Pipeline architectures dominate the graphics field, especially where real-time performance is of importance. Our presentation has made a case for using such an architecture to implement the hardware in a system. However, we can also make as strong a case for pipelining being the basis of a complete software implementation of an API. The power of the synthetic-camera paradigm is that the latter works well in both cases. However, where realism is important, other types of renderers will perform better at the expense of requiring more computation time. In Chapter 13, we shall introduce two of the most important rendering alternatives: ray tracing and radiosity.

1.9 Summary and Notes

In this chapter, we have set the stage for our top-down development of computer graphics. We presented the overall picture so that you can proceed to writing graphics applications programs in the next chapter without feeling that you are working in a vacuum.

We have stressed that computer graphics is a method of image formation that should be related to classical methods of image formation—in particular, to image formation in optical systems, such as in cameras. In addition to explaining the pinhole camera, we have introduced the human visual system; both are examples of imaging systems. In Chapter 2, when we discuss color graphics, we shall see that understanding the perceptual aspects of the human visual system will help us to produce images that meet our expectations.

We described three distinct image-formation paradigms, each of which has applicability in computer graphics. The synthetic-camera model has two important consequences for computer graphics. First, it stresses the independence of the objects and the viewer—a distinction that leads to a good way of organizing the functions that will be in a graphics library. Second, it leads to the notion of a pipeline architecture, in which each of the various stages in the pipeline performs distinct operations on geometric entities, then passes on the transformed objects to the next stage.

We also introduced the idea of tracing rays of light to obtain an image. This paradigm is especially useful in understanding the interaction between light and materials that is essential to physical image formation. Ray tracing provides an alternative way to develop a computer-graphics system. Were we to attempt such development, however, we would have to alter the paradigm, because, of all the rays leaving a source, only a small fraction enter the imaging system, and the time spent tracing most rays is wasted. In Chapter 13, we shall see a practical method that is based on casting rays from the center of projection. All such rays must contribute to the image.

The modeling–rendering paradigm is becoming increasingly important. A good graphics workstation can generate millions of line segments or polygons per second at the resolution of up to 1280×1024 pixels. Such a workstation can shade the polygons using a simple shading model, and can display only visible surfaces at this rate. However, realistic images may require a resolution of up to 4000×6000 pixels to match the capabilities of film, and may use light and material effects that cannot be implemented in real time. Even as the power of available hardware and software continues to grow, modeling and rendering have such different goals that we can expect the distinction between a modeling system and a rendering system to survive.

Our next step will be to explore the application side of graphics programming. We use the OpenGL API, which is powerful, is supported on most platforms, and has a distinct architecture that will allow us to use it to understand how computer graphics works, from an application program to a final image on a display.

1.10 Suggested Readings

There are many excellent graphics textbooks. The book by Newman and Sproull [New73] was the first to take the modern point of view of using the synthetic-camera model. The various versions of Foley et al. [Fol90, Fol94] have been the standard references for the past decade. Other good texts include Hearn and Baker [Hea94] and Hill [Hil01]. Foley, as well as Hearn and Baker, use PHIGS, whereas Angel [Ang90] uses GKS.

Good general references include *Computer Graphics*, the quarterly journal of SIGGRAPH (the Association for Computing Machinery's Special Interest Group on Graphics), *IEEE Computer Graphics and Applications*, and *Visual Computer*. The summer issue of *Computer Graphics* contains the proceedings of the annual SIGGRAPH conference and includes the latest techniques. Of particular interest to newcomers to the field are the state-of-the-art videotapes available from SIGGRAPH, and the notes from tutorial courses taught at that conference. The latter are available on CD-ROM.

Sutherland's doctoral dissertation, "Project Sketchpad," published as *Sketchpad: A Man–Machine Graphical Communication System* [Sut63] was probably the seminal paper in the development of interactive computer graphics. Sutherland was the first person to realize the power of the new paradigm in which humans interacted with images on a CRT display. Videotape copies of film of his original work are still available.

Tufte's books [Tuf83, Tuf90, Tuf97] show the importance of good visual design, and contain considerable historical information on the development of graphics. The article by Carlbom and Paciorek [Car78] gives a good discussion of some of the relationships between classical viewing, as used in fields such as architecture, and viewing by computer.

Many books describe the human visual system. Pratt [Pra78] gives a good short discussion for working with raster displays. Also see Glassner [Gla95], Wyszecki and Stiles [Wys82], and Hall [Hal89].

Exercises

1.1 The *focal length* of a camera lens is the distance from the center of the lens to the point at which parallel rays of light will all be focused. For a pinhole camera, the focal length is the distance from the pinhole to the film plane. The dimensions of a frame of 35-mm film are about 24 mm × 36 mm. Assuming that the human visual system has an angle of view of 90 degrees, what focal length should we use with 35-mm film to achieve a natural view?

1.2 In computer graphics, objects such as spheres are usually approximated by simpler objects constructed from flat polygons (polyhedra). Start with a regular tetrahedron, which is constructed from four triangles. Find its vertices, assuming that it is centered at the origin and has one vertex on the y-axis. Derive an algorithm for obtaining increasingly closer approximations to a unit sphere, based on subdividing the faces of the tetrahedron.

1.3 Consider the clipping of a line segment defined by the latter's two endpoints. Show that you require only the endpoints to determine whether the line segment is not clipped, is partially visible, or is clipped out completely.

1.4 For a line segment, show that clipping against the top of the clipping rectangle can be done independently of the clipping against the other sides. Use this result to show that a clipper can be implemented as a pipeline of four simpler clippers.

1.5 Extend Exercises 1.3 and 1.4 to clipping against a three-dimensional right parallelepiped.

1.6 Consider the perspective views of the cube shown in Figure 1.32. The one on the left is called a *one-point perspective* because parallel lines in one direction of the cube—along the sides of the top—converge to a *vanishing point* in the image. In contrast, the image on the right is a *two-point perspective*. Characterize the particular relationship between the viewer, or a simple camera, and the cube that determines why one is a two-point perspective and the other a one-point perspective.

Figure 1.32 Perspectives of a cube.

1.7   The memory in a frame buffer must be fast enough to allow the display to be refreshed at a rate sufficiently high to avoid flicker. A typical workstation display can have a resolution of 1280×1024 pixels. If it is refreshed 72 times per second, how fast must the memory be? That is, how much time can we take to read one pixel from memory? What is this number for a 480×640 display that operates at 60 Hz but is interlaced?

1.8   Movies are generally produced on 35-mm film that has a resolution of approximately 2000×3000 pixels. What implication does this resolution have for producing animated images for television as compared with film?

1.9   Consider the design of a two-dimensional graphical API for a specific application, such as for VLSI design. List all the primitives and attributes that you would include in your system.

1.10   It is possible to design a color CRT that uses a single electron gun and does not have a shadow mask. The single beam is turned on and off at the appropriate times to excite the desired phosphors. Why might such a CRT be more difficult to design, as compared to the shadow-mask CRT?

1.11   In a typical shadow-mask CRT, if we want to have a smooth display, the width of a pixel must be about three times the width of a triad. Assume that a monitor displays 1280×1024 pixels, has a CRT diameter of 50 cm, and has a CRT depth of 25 cm. Estimate the spacing between holes in the shadow mask.

2

Graphics Programming

Our approach to computer graphics is programming oriented. Consequently, we want you to get started programming graphics as soon as possible. To this end, we introduce a minimal application programmer's interface (API). This API is sufficient to allow you to program many interesting two- and three-dimensional problems, and to familiarize you with the basic graphics concepts.

We regard two-dimensional graphics as a special case of three-dimensional graphics. This perspective allows us to get started, even though we touch on three-dimensional concepts lightly in this chapter. Our two-dimensional code will execute without modification on a three-dimensional system.

Our development uses a simple but informative problem: the Sierpinski gasket. It shows how we can generate an interesting and, to many people, unexpectedly sophisticated graphics plot using only a handful of graphics functions. We use OpenGL as our API, but our discussion of the underlying concepts is broad enough to encompass most modern systems, including the Programmer's Hierarchical Graphics System (PHIGS), the Graphical Kernel System (GKS), JAVA-3D, and DirectX. The functionality that we introduce in this chapter is sufficient to allow you to write sophisticated two-dimensional programs that do not require user interaction. We conclude the chapter with an example of a three-dimensional application.

2.1 The Sierpinski Gasket

We use as a sample problem the drawing of the Sierpinski gasket—an interesting shape that has a long history and that is of interest in areas such as fractal geometry. The Sierpinski gasket is an object that can be defined recursively and randomly; in the limit, however, it has properties that are not at all random.

Suppose that we start with three vertices in the plane. Assume that their locations, as specified in some convenient coordinate system,[1] are (x_1, y_1), (x_2, y_2), and (x_3, y_3). The construction proceeds as follows:

1. Pick an initial point at random inside the triangle.
2. Select one of the three vertices at random.
3. Find the point halfway between the initial point and the randomly selected vertex.
4. Display this new point by putting some sort of marker, such as a small circle, at its location.
5. Replace the initial point with this new point.
6. Return to step 2.

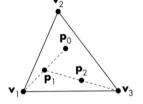

Figure 2.1 Generation of the Sierpinski gasket.

Thus, each time that we generate a point, we display it on the output device. This process is illustrated in Figure 2.1, where $\mathbf{p}_0$ is the initial point, and $\mathbf{p}_1$ and $\mathbf{p}_2$ are the first two points generated by our algorithm.

Before we develop the program, you might try to figure out what the resulting image will be. Try to construct it on paper; you might be surprised by your results.

A possible form for our graphics program might be this:

```
main( )
{
    initialize_the_system();

    for(some_number_of_points)
    {
        pt = generate_a_point();
        display_the_point(pt);
    }

    cleanup();
}
```

Although our final OpenGL program will have a slightly different organization, it will be almost that simple. We develop the program in stages. First, we concentrate on the core: generating and displaying points. There are two questions that we must answer: How do we represent points in space? and Should we use a two-dimensional, three-dimensional, or other representation?

---

1. In Chapter 4, we expand the concept of a coordinate system to the more general formulation of a *frame*.

2.2 Programming Two-Dimensional Applications

For two-dimensional applications, such as the Sierpinski gasket, although we could use a pen-plotter API, such an approach would limit us. Instead, we choose to start with a three-dimensional world; we regard two-dimensional systems, such as our pad, as special cases. Mathematically, we view the two-dimensional plane, or a simple two-dimensional curved surface, as a subspace of a three-dimensional space. Hence, statements—both practical and abstract—about the bigger three-dimensional world will hold for the simpler two-dimensional one.

Suppose that we assume that our pad has infinite area (we limit its size later) and corresponds to the plane $z = 0$. We can represent a point in the plane as $\mathbf{p} = (x, y, 0)$ in the three-dimensional world, or as $\mathbf{p} = (x, y)$ in the two-dimensional subspace corresponding to our pad. OpenGL, like most three-dimensional graphics systems, allows us to use either representation, with the underlying internal representation being the same, regardless of which form the user chooses. We can implement representations of points in a number of ways, but the simplest is to think of a three-dimensional point as being represented by a triplet:

$$\mathbf{p} = \begin{bmatrix} x \\ y \\ z \end{bmatrix}.$$

For now, we ignore the question of what coordinate system $\mathbf{p}$ is represented in.

We often use the term *vertex*, rather than *point*. A **vertex** is a location in space; we use two-, three-, and four-dimensional spaces in computer graphics. We use vertices to define the atomic geometric objects that are recognized by our graphics system. The simplest geometric object is a point in space, which is specified by a single vertex. Two vertices define a line segment, a second geometric object; three vertices can determine either a triangle or a circle; four determine a quadrilateral, and so on.

OpenGL has multiple forms for many functions. The variety of forms allows the user to select the one best suited for her problem. For the vertex function, we can write the general form

```
glVertex*
```

where the * can be interpreted as either two or three characters of the form nt or ntv, where n signifies the number of dimensions (2, 3, or 4); t denotes the data type, such as integer (i), float (f), or double (d); and v, if present, indicates that the variables are specified through a pointer to an array, rather than through an argument list. We shall use whatever form is best suited for our discussion, leaving the details of the various other forms to the *OpenGL Reference Manual* [Ope01b]. Regardless of which form a user chooses, the underlying representation is the same, just as our pad can be looked at as either a two-dimensional space or the subspace of three-dimensional space corresponding to the plane $z = 0$. In Chapter 4, we shall see that the underlying representation is four-dimensional; however, we do not need to worry about that fact yet.

In OpenGL, we often use basic OpenGL types, such as GLfloat and GLint, rather than the C types, such as float and int. These types are defined in the header files and usually in the obvious way—for example,

```
#define GLfloat float
```

However, use of the OpenGL types allows additional flexibility for implementations where, for example, we might want to change floats to doubles without altering existing application programs.

Returning to the vertex function, if the user wants to work in two dimensions with integers, then the form

```
glVertex2i(GLint xi, GLint yi)
```

is appropriate, and

```
glVertex3f(GLfloat x, GLfloat y, GLfloat z)
```

specifies a position in three-dimensional space using floating-point numbers. Finally, if we use an array to store the information for a three-dimensional vertex,

```
GLfloat vertex[3]
```

then we can use

```
glVertex3fv(vertex)
```

Vertices can define a variety of geometric objects; different numbers of vertices are required depending on the object. We can group as many vertices as we wish, using the functions glBegin and glEnd. The argument of glBegin specifies the geometric type that we want our vertices to define. Hence, a line segment can be specified by

```
glBegin(GL_LINES);
  glVertex2f(x1,y1);
  glVertex2f(x2,y2);
glEnd();
```

We can use the same data to define a pair of points, by using the form

```
glBegin(GL_POINTS);
  glVertex2f(x1,y1);
  glVertex2f(x2,y2);
glEnd();
```

We can now look at the heart of our Sierpinski gasket program. Suppose that we choose to generate all our points within a 500×500 square whose lower-left-hand corner is at $(0, 0)$—a convenient, but easily altered, choice.

First, we must consider how we wish to represent geometric data in our program. We could employ the most basic representation of separate x, y, and z variables (in three dimensions). Many programmers prefer a more object-oriented approach, such as using a data type point3 for a three-dimensional vertex and point2 for a two-dimensional point. In an object-oriented language, we could then have statements such as

```
new_point = old_point + random_number
```

Unfortunately, neither C nor OpenGL is oriented this way (at least at present). As a compromise between a truly low-level view and a high-level abstraction, we use a two-element array for two-dimensional points:

```
typedef GLfloat point2[2];
```

We create a function, called display, that generates 5000 points each time that it is called. We assume that an array of triangle vertices vertices[3] is defined in display as an array of type point2:

```
void display(void)
{
    point2 vertices[3] = {{0.0, 0.0}, {250.0, 500.0},
                                      {500.0, 0.0}};
            /* an arbitrary triangle */
    static point2 p = {75.0 ,50.0};
             /* or set to any desired initial point */
    int j, k;
    int rand(); /* standard random-number generator */

    for(k=0;k<5000;k++)
    {
      /* pick a random vertex from 0,1,2 */

      j=rand()%3;

      /* compute new point */

      p[0] = (p[0] + vertices[j][0])/2;
      p[1] = (p[1] + vertices[j][1])/2;

      /* display new point */

      glBegin(GL_POINTS);
        glVertex2fv(p);
```

```
        glEnd();
    }
    glFlush();
}
```

The function rand is a standard random-number generator that produces a new random integer each time that it is called. We use the modulus operator to reduce these random integers to the three integers 0, 1, and 2. For a small number of iterations, the particular characteristics of the random-number generator are not crucial, and any other random-number generator should work at least as well as rand.

The call to glFlush ensures that points are rendered to the screen as soon as possible. If you leave it out, the program should work correctly, but you may notice a delay in a busy or networked environment. We still do not have a complete program; Figure 2.2 shows the output we expect to see.

We have now written the core of the program. But we still have to worry about such issues as the following:

1. In what colors are we drawing?
2. Where on the screen does our image appear?
3. How large will the image be?
4. How do we create an area of the screen—a window—for our image?
5. How much of our infinite pad will appear on the screen?
6. How long will the image remain on the screen?

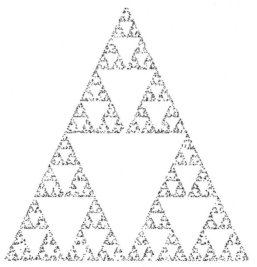

Figure 2.2 The Sierpinski gasket as generated with 5000 random points.

The answers to all these questions are important, even though, at first, they may appear to be peripheral to our major concerns. As we shall see, the basic code that we develop to answer these questions and to control the placement and appearance of our renderings will not change substantially across programs. Hence, the effort that we expend now will be repaid later.

2.2.1 Coordinate Systems

At this point, you may be puzzled about how to interpret the values of x, y, and z in our specification of vertices. In what units are they? Are they in feet, meters, microns? Where is the origin? In each case, the simple answer is that it is up to you.

Originally, graphics systems required the user to specify all information, such as vertex locations, directly in units of the display device. If that were true for high-level application programs, we would have to talk about points in terms of screen locations in pixels or centimeters from a corner of the display. There are obvious problems with this method, not the least of which is the absurdity of using distances on the computer screen to describe phenomena where the natural unit might be light years (such as in displaying astronomical data) or microns (for integrated-circuit design). One of the major advances in graphics software systems occurred when the graphics systems allowed users to work in any coordinate system that those users desired. The advent of **device-independent graphics** freed application programmers from worrying about the details of input and output devices. The user's coordinate system became known as the **world coordinate system** or the **application or problem coordinate system**. Within the slight limitations of floating-point arithmetic on our computers, we can use any numbers that fit our application.

Units on the display were first called **physical-device coordinates** or just **device coordinates**. For raster devices, such as most CRT displays, we use the term **raster coordinates** or **screen coordinates**.[2] Screen coordinates are always expressed in some integer type, because the center of any pixel in the frame buffer must be located on a fixed grid, or, equivalently, because pixels are inherently discrete and we can address them using integers.

At some point, the values in world coordinates must be mapped into device coordinates, as shown in Figure 2.3. The graphics system, rather than the user, is responsible for this task, and the mapping is performed automatically as part of the rendering process. As we shall see in the next few sections, the user needs to specify only a few parameters—such as the area of the world that she would like to see and the size of the display—to define this mapping.

---

2. OpenGL makes a distinction between raster and screen coordinates, but this distinction will not be important until we work with how the OpenGL pipeline is implemented in Chapter 8.

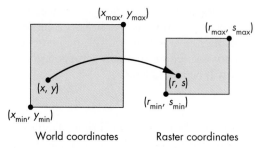

World coordinates   Raster coordinates

Figure 2.3 Mapping from world coordinates to raster coordinates.

2.3 The OpenGL API

We have the heart of a simple graphics program; now, we want to gain control over how our objects appear on the display. We also want to control the flow of the program, and we have to interact with the window system. Before completing our program, we describe the OpenGL API in more detail. Because vertices are represented in the same manner internally, whether they are specified as two- or three-dimensional entities, everything that we do here will be equally valid in three dimensions. Of course, we can do much more in three dimensions, but we are only getting started. In this chapter, we concentrate on how we specify primitives to be displayed; we leave interaction to Chapter 3.

OpenGL's structure is similar to that of most modern APIs, including Java3D and DirectX. Hence, any effort that you put into learning OpenGL will carry over to other software systems. Although OpenGL is easy to learn, compared with other APIs, it is nevertheless powerful. It supports the simple two- and three-dimensional programs that we develop in Chapters 2 through 6; it also supports the advanced rendering techniques that we study in Chapters 8 through 13.

Our prime goal is to study computer graphics; we are using an API to help us attain that goal. Consequently, we do not present all OpenGL functions, and we omit many details. However, our sample programs will be complete. More detailed information on OpenGL and on other APIs is given in the Suggested Readings section at the end of the chapter.

2.3.1 Graphics Functions

Our basic model of a graphics package is a **black box**, a term that engineers use to denote a system whose properties are described by only its inputs and outputs; nothing is known about its internal workings. We can think of the graphics system as a box whose inputs are function calls from a user program; measurements from input devices, such as the mouse and keyboard; and possibly other input, such as messages from the operating system. The outputs are primarily the graphics

Figure 2.4 Graphics system as a black box.

sent to our output devices. For now, we can take the simplified view of inputs as function calls and outputs as primitives displayed on our CRT screen, as shown in Figure 2.4. Although OpenGL is the particular system that we use, all graphics APIs have a similar structure.

We describe an API through the functions in its library. A good API may contain hundreds of functions, so it is helpful to divide the functions into seven groups by their functionality:

1. The **primitive functions** define the low-level objects or atomic entities that our system can display. Depending on the API, the primitives can include points, line segments, polygons, pixels, text, and various types of curves and surfaces.

2. If primitives are the *what* of an API—the objects that can be displayed— then attributes are the *how*. That is, the attributes govern the way that a primitive appears on the display. **Attribute functions** allow us to perform operations ranging from choosing the color with which we display a line segment, to picking a pattern with which to fill the inside of a polygon, to selecting a typeface for the titles on a graph.

3. Our synthetic camera must be described if we are to create an image. As we saw in Chapter 1, we must describe its position and orientation in our world, and must select the equivalent of a lens. This process not only will fix the view, but also will allow us to clip out objects that are too close or too far away. The **viewing functions** allow us to specify various views, although APIs differ in the degree of flexibility in choosing a view that they provide.

4. One of the characteristics of a good API is that it provides the user with a set of **transformation functions** that allows her to carry out transformations of objects, such as rotation, translation, and scaling. Our developments of viewing in Chapter 5 and of modeling in Chapter 9 will make heavy use of matrix transformations.

5. For interactive applications, an API must provide a set of **input functions** to allow us to deal with diverse forms of input that characterize modern graphics systems. We need functions to deal with devices such as keyboards, mice, and data tablets. In Chapter 3, we introduce functions for working with three different input modes and with a variety of input devices.

6. In any real application, we also have to worry about handling the complexities of working in a multiprocessing multiwindow environment—usually

an environment where we are connected to a network and there are other users. The **control functions** enable us to communicate with the window system, to initialize our programs, and to deal with any errors that take place during the execution of our programs.

7. If we are to write device-independent programs, we should expect the implementation of the API to take care of differences between devices, such as how many colors are supported or the size of the display. However, there are applications where we need to know some properties of the particular implementation. For example, we would probably chose to do things differently if we knew in advance that we were working with a display that could support only two colors rather than one with millions of colors. More generally, within our applications we can often use other information within the API, including camera parameters or values in the frame buffer. A good API will provide this information through a set of **inquiry** functions.

2.3.2 The Graphics Pipeline and State Machines

If we put together some of these perspectives toward graphics APIs, we can obtain another view, one closer to the way OpenGL, in particular, actually is organized and implemented. We can think of the entire graphics system as a **state machine**, a black box that contains a finite-state machine. This state machine has inputs that come from the application program and that may change the state of the machine or cause the machine to produce a visible output. From the perspective of the API, graphics functions are of two types: those that define primitives that flow through a pipeline inside the state machine and those that change the state inside the machine. In OpenGL, functions such as glVertex are of the first type, whereas almost all other functions are of the second type.

One important consequence of this view is that in OpenGL most parameters are persistent; their values remain unchanged until we explicitly change them through functions that alter the state. For example, once we set a color, that color remains the *present color* until it is changed through a color-altering function. One consequence of this view is that attributes which we may consider as bound to objects—a red line or a blue circle—are in fact part of the state and a line will be drawn in red only if the present color state calls for drawing in red. Although within our applications it is usually harmless, and often even preferable, to think of attributes as bound to primitives, there can be annoying consequences if we neglect to make state changes when needed or lose track of the present state.

2.3.3 The OpenGL Interface

OpenGL function names begin with the letters gl and are stored in a library usually referred to as GL (or OpenGL in Windows). There are a few related libraries that we also use. The first is the **graphics utility library (GLU)**. This library uses only GL functions, but contains code for creating common

Figure 2.5 Library organization.

objects, such as spheres, and other tasks that users prefer not to have to write repeatedly. This library is available in all OpenGL implementations. The second library addresses the problems of interfacing with the window system. We use a readily available library called the **GL Utility Toolkit (GLUT)**. It provides the minimum functionality that should be expected in any modern windowing system. We introduce a few of its functions in this chapter, and describe more of them in Chapter 3, where we consider input and interaction in detail. Figure 2.5 shows the organization of the libraries for an X Window system environment. The GLX library provides the minimum "glue" between OpenGL and the X Window system. GLX is used by GLUT, and thus this library and various others are called from the OpenGL libraries, but the application program does not need to refer to these libraries directly. A similar organization holds for other environments. For example, with Microsoft Windows a library called wgl replaces GLX; otherwise Figure 2.5 is unchanged.

OpenGL makes heavy use of macros to increase code readability and to avoid the use of magic numbers. Thus, strings such as GL_FILL and GL_POINTS are defined in header (.h) files. In most implementations, one of the "include" lines

```
#include <GL/glut.h>
```

or

```
#include <glut.h>
```

is sufficient to read in glut.h, gl.h, and glu.h.

2.4 Primitives and Attributes

Within the graphics community, there has been an ongoing debate about which primitives should be supported in an API. The debate is an old one and has never been fully resolved. On the minimalist side, the contention is that an

Figure 2.6 The OpenGL pipeline.

API should contain a small set of primitives that all hardware can be expected to support. In addition, the primitives should be orthogonal, each giving a capability unobtainable from the others. Minimal systems typically support lines, polygons, and some form of text (strings of characters), all of which can be generated efficiently in hardware. On the other end are systems that can also support a variety of primitives, such as circles, curves, surfaces, and solids. The argument here is that users need more complex primitives to build sophisticated applications easily. However, because few hardware systems can be expected to support the large set of primitives that is the union of all the desires of the user community, a program developed with such a system probably would not be portable, because few implementations could be expected to support the entire set of primitives.

OpenGL takes an intermediate position. The basic library has a small set of primitives. The GLU libary contains a richer set of objects derived from the basic library.

OpenGL supports two classes of primitives: **geometric primitives** and **raster primitives**. Geometric primitives are described within the problem domain and include points, line segments, polygons, curves, and surfaces. These primitives pass through a geometric pipeline, as shown in Figure 2.6, where they are subject to series of geometric operations that determine whether a primitive is visible, where on the screen it appears if it is visible, and the rasterization of the primitive into pixels in the frame buffer. Because geometric primitives can be described by their spatial properties, they can be manipulated by operations such as rotation and translation within the user domain. In addition, they can be used as building blocks for other geometric objects using these same operations. Raster primitives, such as arrays of pixels, lack geometric properties and cannot be manipulated in space in the same way as geometric primitives. They pass through a separate parallel pipeline on their way to the frame buffer. We shall defer our discussion of raster primitives until Chapter 7.

The basic OpenGL geometric primitives are specified via points in space or vertices. Thus, the programmer defines her objects with sequences of the form

```
glBegin(type);
    glVertex*(...);
    .
    .
    .
    glVertex*(...);
glEnd();
```

The value of type specifies how OpenGL interprets the vertices to define geometric objects. Other code and OpenGL function calls can occur between glBegin and glEnd. For example, we can change attributes or perform calculations for the next vertex between glBegin and glEnd, or between two invocations of glVertex. A major conceptual difference between the basic geometric types is whether or not they have interiors. All the basic types will be defined either in terms of vertices or by finite pieces of lines, called **line segments**—in contrast to lines that are infinite in extent. Of course, a single line segment is itself specified by a pair of vertices, but the line segment is of such importance that we can consider it to be a basic graphical entity. You can use line segments to define approximations to curves, or you can use a sequence of line segments to connect data values for a graph. You can also use line segments for the edges of closed objects, such as polygons, that have interiors.

If we wish to display points or line segments, we have a few choices in OpenGL (Figure 2.7). The primitives and their type specifications include the following:

Points (GL_POINTS) Each vertex is displayed at a size of at least one pixel.

Line segments (GL_LINES) The line-segment type causes successive pairs of vertices to be interpreted as the endpoints of individual segments. Note that, because the interpretation is done on a pairwise basis, successive segments usually are disconnected.

Polylines (GL_LINE_STRIP, GL_LINE_LOOP) If successive vertices (and line segments) are to be connected, we can use the line strip or **polyline** form. Many curves can be approximated via a suitable polyline. If we wish the polyline to be

Figure 2.7 Point and line-segment types.

Figure 2.8   Filled objects.

Figure 2.9   Methods of displaying a polygon.

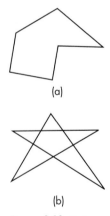

(a)

(b)

Figure 2.10   Polygons. (a) Simple. (b) Nonsimple.

Figure 2.11   Convexity.

closed, we can locate the final vertex in the same place as the first, or we can use the GL_LINE_LOOP type, which will draw a line segment from the final vertex to the first, thus creating a closed path.

2.4.1 Polygon Basics

Line segments and polylines can model the edges of objects, but closed objects also may have interiors (Figure 2.8). We usually reserve the name **polygon** to refer to an object that has a border that can be described by a line loop, but has an interior.[3] Polygons play a special role in computer graphics because we can display them rapidly and can use them to approximate curved surfaces. The performance of graphics systems is measured by the number of polygons per second that can be displayed. We can display a polygon in a variety of ways. We can display only its edges. We can fill its interior with a solid color or a pattern, and we can display or not display the edges, as shown in Figure 2.9. Although the outer edges of a polygon are defined easily by an ordered list of vertices, if the interior is not well defined, then the polygon may be rendered incorrectly. Three properties will ensure that a polygon will be displayed correctly: It must be simple, convex, and flat.

In two dimensions, as long as no pair of edges of a polygon cross each other, we have a **simple** polygon. As we can see from Figure 2.10, simple two-dimensional polygons have well-defined interiors. Although the locations of the vertices determine whether or not a polygon is simple, the cost of testing is sufficiently high (see Exercise 2.14) that most graphics systems require that the application program do any necessary testing. We can ask what a graphics system will do if it is given a nonsimple polygon to display and whether there is a way to define an interior for a nonsimple polygon. We shall examine these questions in Chapter 8.

From the perspective of implementing a practical algorithm to fill the interior of a polygon, simplicity alone is often less than desired. Some APIs guarantee a consistent fill from implementation to implementation only if the polygon is convex. An object is **convex** if all points on the line segment between any two points inside the object, or on its boundary, are inside the object (Figure 2.11). Although, so far, we have been dealing with only two-dimensional objects, this definition makes reference neither to the type of object nor to the number of dimensions. Convex objects include triangles, tetrahedra, rectangles, circles, spheres, and parallelepipeds (Figure 2.12). There are various tests for convexity; see Exercise 2.20. However, like simplicity testing, convexity testing is expensive and usually is left to the application program.

In three dimensions, polygons present a few more difficulties, because, unlike all two-dimensional objects, they are not necessarily flat. One property that most graphics systems exploit, and that we shall use, is that any three vertices that are

---

3. The term *fill area* is sometimes used instead of *polygon*.

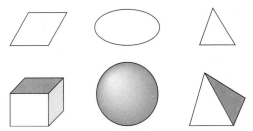

Figure 2.12   Convex objects.

not collinear determine both a triangle and the plane in which that triangle lies. Hence, if we always use triangles, we are safe—we can be sure that these objects will be rendered correctly. Often, we are almost forced to use triangles because typical rendering algorithms are guaranteed to be correct only if the vertices form a flat convex polygon. In addition, hardware and software often support a triangle type that is rendered much faster than is a polygon with three vertices.

2.4.2 Polygon Types in OpenGL

Let us return to the OpenGL types. For objects with interiors, we can specify the following types (Figure 2.13):

Polygons (GL_POLYGON) The edges are the same as they would be if we used line loops. Successive vertices define line segments, and a line segment connects the final vertex to the first. The interior is filled according to the state of the relevant attributes. Note that a mathematical polygon has an inside and an outside that are separated by the edge. The edge itself has no width. Consequently, most graphics systems allow you to fill the polygon with a color or pattern or to draw lines around the edges, but not to do both. In OpenGL, we can use the function glPolygonMode to select edges instead of fill (the default). However, if we want to draw a polygon that is filled and to display its edges, then we have to draw it twice, once in each mode, or to draw a polygon and a line loop with the same vertices.

Figure 2.13   Polygon types.

Figure 2.14 Triangle strip, quadrilateral strip, and triangle fan.

Triangles and Quadrilaterals (GL_TRIANGLES, GL_QUADS) These objects are special cases of polygons. Successive groups of three and four vertices are interpreted as triangles and quadrilaterals, respectively. Using these types may lead to a rendering more efficient than that obtained with polygons.

Strips and Fans (GL_TRIANGLE_STRIP, GL_QUAD_STRIP, GL_TRIANGLE_FAN) These objects are based on groups of triangles or quadrilaterals that share vertices and edges. In the triangle strip, for example, each additional vertex is combined with the previous two vertices to define a new triangle (Figure 2.14). For the quadstrip, we combine two new vertices with the previous two vertices to define a new quadrilateral. A triangle fan is based on one fixed point. The next two points determine the first triangle, and subsequent triangles are formed from one new point, the previous point, and the first (fixed) point.

2.4.3 Drawing a Sphere

Fans and strips also allow us to approximate many curved surfaces simply. For example, one way to construct an approximation to a sphere is to use a set of polygons defined by lines of longitude and latitude as in Figure 2.15. We can do so very efficiently using either quad strips or triangle strips. Consider a unit sphere. We can describe it by the three equations

$$x(\theta, \phi) = \sin \theta \cos \phi,$$
$$y(\theta, \phi) = \cos \theta \cos \phi,$$
$$z(\theta, \phi) = \sin \phi.$$

If we fix θ and draw curves as we change ϕ, we get circles of constant longitude. Likewise, if we fix ϕ and vary θ, we obtain circles of constant latitude. By generating points at fixed increments of θ and ϕ, we can define quadrilaterals as in Figure 2.15. The code for the quadrilaterals corresponding to increments of 20 degrees in θ, and 20 degrees in ϕ is

Figure 2.15 Sphere approximation with quadrilaterals.

```
c=M_PI/180.0; //degrees to radians, M_PI = 3.14159...
for(phi=-80.0; phi<=80.0; phi+=20.0)
{
    glBegin(GL_QUAD_STRIP);
    for(theta=-180.0; theta<=180.0;theta+=20.0)
```

```
    {
        x=sin(c*theta)*cos(c*phi);
        y=cos(c*theta)*cos(c*phi);
        z=sin(c*phi);
        glVertex3d(x,y,z);
        x=sin(c*theta)*cos(c*(phi+20.0));
        y=cos(c*theta)*cos(c*(phi+20.0));
        z=sin(c*(phi+20.0));
        glVertex3d(x,y,z);
    }
    glEnd();
}
```

However, we have a problem at the poles where we can no longer use strips because all lines of latitude converge there. We can, however, use two triangle fans, one at each pole as follows:

```
glBegin(GL_TRIANGLE_FAN);
glVertex3d(x,y,z);
c=M_PI/180.0;
z=sin(c*80.0);
for(thet=-180.0; theta<=180.0;theta+=20.0)
{
    x=sin(c*theta)*cos(c*80.0);
    y=cos(c*theta)*cos(c*80.0);
    glVertex3d(x,y,z);
}
glEnd();
x=y=0;
z=-1;
glBegin(GL_TRIANGLE_FAN);
glVertex3d(x,y,z);
z=-sin(c*80.0);
for(theta=-180.0;theta<=180.0;theta+=20.0)
{
    x=sin(c*theta)*cos(c*80.0);
    y=cos(c*theta)*cos(c*80.0);
    glVertex3d(x,y,z);
}
glEnd();
```

2.4.4 Text

Graphical output in applications such as data analysis and display requires annotation, such as labels on graphs. Although, in nongraphical programs, textual output is the norm, text in computer graphics is problematic. In nongraphical applications, we are usually content with a simple set of characters, always displayed in the same manner. In computer graphics, however, we often wish to display text in a multitude of fashions by controlling type styles, sizes, colors, and other parameters. We also want to have available a choice of fonts. **Fonts** are families of type faces of a particular style, such as Times, Computer Modern, or Helvetica.

There are two forms of text: stroke and raster. **Stroke text** (Figure 2.16) is constructed as are other graphic primitives. We use vertices to define line segments or curves that outline each character. If the characters are defined by closed boundaries, we can fill them. The advantage of stroke text is that it can be defined to have all the detail of any other object, and, because it is defined in the same way as are other graphical objects, it can be manipulated by our standard transformations and viewed like any other graphical primitive. An obvious advantage to stroke text is that, as we make a stroke character bigger or rotate it, it retains its detail and appearance. Consequently, we need to define a character only once, and can use transformations to generate it at the desired size and orientation.

Defining a full 128- or 256-character stroke font, however, can be complex, and the font can take up significant memory and processing time. The standard PostScript fonts are defined by polynomial curves, and they illustrate all the advantages and disadvantages of stroke text. The various PostScript fonts can be used for both high- and low-resolution applications. Often, developers mitigate the problems of slow rendering of such stroke characters by putting considerable processing power in the printer. This strategy is related to the client–server concepts that we discuss in Chapter 3.

Raster text (Figure 2.17) is simple and fast. Characters are defined as rectangles of bits called **bit blocks**. Each block defines a single character by the pattern of 0 and 1 bits in the block. A raster character can be placed in the frame buffer rapidly by a **bit-block-transfer (bitblt)** operation, which moves the block of bits using a single instruction. We discuss bitblt in Chapter 7; OpenGL allows the application program to use functions that allow direct manipulation of the contents of the frame buffer.

Computer Graphics

Figure 2.16 Stroke text (PostScript font).

Figure 2.17 Raster text.

Figure 2.18 Raster-character replication.

You can increase the size of raster characters only by **replicating** or duplicating pixels, a process that gives larger characters a blocky appearance (Figure 2.18). Other transformations of raster characters, such as rotation, may not make sense, because the transformation may move the bits defining the character to locations that do not correspond to the location of pixels in the frame buffer. In addition, because raster characters often are stored in read-only memory (ROM) in the hardware, a particular font might be of limited portability.

Because stroke and bitmap characters can be created from other primitives, OpenGL does not have a text primitive. However, GLUT provides a few bitmap and stroke character sets that are defined in software and are portable. For example, we can put out a bitmap character that is 8 × 8 pixels by

```
glutBitmapCharacter(GLUT_BITMAP_8_BY_13, c)
```

where c is the number of the ASCII characters that we wish to be placed on the display. The character is placed at the present **raster position** on the display, a location that is part of the graphics state, is measured in pixels, and can be altered by the various forms of the function glRasterPos*. We return to text in Chapter 3. There, we shall see that both stroke and raster text can be implemented most efficiently through display lists.

2.4.5 Curved Objects

The primitives in our basic set have all been defined through vertices. With the exception of the point type, all either consist of line segments or use line segments to define the boundary of a region that can be filled with a solid color or a pattern. We can take two approaches to creating a richer set of objects.

First, we can use the primitives that we have to approximate curves and surfaces. For example, if we want a circle, we can use a regular polygon of n sides. Likewise, we can approximate a sphere with a regular polyhedron. More generally, we approximate a curved surface by a mesh of convex polygons—a **tessellation**—which can occur either at the rendering stage or within the user program.

The other approach, which we explore in Chapter 10, is to start with the mathematical definitions of curved objects, and then to build graphics functions to implement those objects. Objects such as quadric surfaces and parametric polynomial curves and surfaces are well understood mathematically, and we can specify them through sets of vertices. For example, we can define a sphere by its center and a point on its surface, or we can define a cubic polynomial curve by four points.

Most graphics systems give us aspects of both approaches. In OpenGL, we can use the utility library (GLU) for a collection of approximations to common curved surfaces, and we can write functions to define more of our own. We can also use the advanced features of OpenGL to work with parametric polynomial curves and surfaces.

2.4.6 Attributes

In a modern graphics system, there is a distinction between what the type of a primitive is and how that primitive is displayed. A red solid line and a green dashed line are the same geometric type, but each is displayed differently. An **attribute** is any property that determines how a geometric primitive is to be rendered. Color is an obvious attribute, as are the thickness of a line and the pattern used to fill a polygon. Several of these attributes are shown in Figure 2.19 for lines and polygons.

Attributes may be associated with, or **bound** to, primitives at various points in the modeling and rendering pipeline. Bindings may not be permanent. At this point, we are concerned with immediate-mode graphics. In **immediate mode**, primitives are not stored in the system, but rather are passed through the system for possible display as soon as they are defined. The present values of attributes are part of the state of the graphics system. When a primitive is defined, the present attributes for that type are used, and it is displayed immediately. There is no memory of the primitive in the system. Only the primitive's image appears on the display; once erased from the display, it is lost. In Chapter 3, we introduce

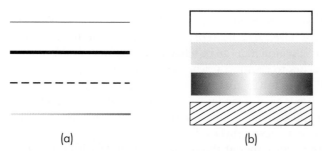

(a)   (b)

Figure 2.19 Attributes for (a) lines and (b) polygons.

Figure 2.20 Stroke-text attributes.

display lists, which will enable us to keep objects in memory, so that these objects can be redisplayed.[4]

Each geometric type has a set of attributes. For example, a point has a color attribute and a size attribute. Line segments can have color, thickness, and type (solid, dashed, or dotted). Filled primitives, such as polygons, have more attributes, because we must specify enough parameters to specify how the fill should be done. We can fill with a solid color or a pattern. We can decide not to fill the polygon and to display only its edges. If we fill the polygon, we might also display the edges in a color different from that of the interior.

In systems that support stroke text as a primitive, there is a variety of attributes. Some of these attributes are demonstrated in Figure 2.20; they include the direction of the text string, the path followed by successive characters in the string, the height and width of the characters, the font, and the style (bold, italic, underlined).

2.5 Color

Color is one of the most interesting aspects of both human perception and computer graphics. Full exploitation of the capabilities of the human visual system with computer graphics requires a far deeper understanding of the anatomy,

---

4. OpenGL's emphasis on immediate-mode graphics and a pipeline architecture works well for interactive applications, but that emphasis is a fundamental difference between OpenGL and systems such as PHIGS that use a database paradigm, in which geometric entities reside in a central data store and can thus be recalled as desired.

physiology, and psychophysics of the human than we can present here. We can, however, expand the model of the human visual system from Chapter 1 to obtain a useful color model.

Light is the part of the electromagnetic spectrum that occupies wavelengths from about 350 to 780 nm. The shorter wavelengths in the visible spectrum we see as blues; the longer wavelengths we see as reds; we see the middle ones as greens. Other than those colors generated by means of pure spectral sources, such as lasers, or by passed light through extremely narrow filters, colors are combinations of wavelengths. A color can be characterized by a function $C(\lambda)$, as shown in Figure 2.21, whose value for a given wavelength λ in the visible spectrum gives the strength of that wavelength in the color.

Although this characterization is accurate in terms of a physical color whose properties we can measure, it does not take into account how we *perceive* color. To understand this distinction, we consider one of the key tasks in using color in computer graphics: color matching. Suppose that we have a color characterized by a distribution $C(\lambda)$ that we would like to match on the screen of our CRT. Do we have to match C for every λ? A monitor that could do such matching for all visible colors is beyond our ability to construct. Fortunately, we do not need such a monitor, because our visual systems are consistent with a three-primary-color model.

Color in computer graphics is based on what has become known as the **three-color theory**.[5] Using the **additive color model**, we think of a color as being formed from three primary colors that are mixed to form the desired color. A good analogy is to consider three colored spotlights (Figure 2.22) whose intensities can be varied. All three are focused on the same spot on a dark screen. Each of the three spotlights adds to the screen light that is reflected back to our eyes; we see a single color.

We can attempt to match a given color by adjusting the intensities of the individual spotlights. Although we might not be able to match all colors in this way with a particular set of primaries, if we use standard red, green, and blue spotlights, we can come close. We can represent this matching process abstractly as follows. We let $\mathbf{C}$ represent the color that we are trying to match, and $\mathbf{R}$, $\mathbf{G}$, and $\mathbf{B}$ represent the three spotlights. A color match is specified by the equation

$$\mathbf{C} = T_1\mathbf{R} + T_2\mathbf{G} + T_3\mathbf{B},$$

where T_1, T_2, and T_3 are the strengths, or intensities, of the three spotlights. These intensities are called the **tristimulus values**. We can characterize the target color, relative to the particular set of primaries—our spotlights—by the triplet (T_1, T_2, T_3).

Figure 2.21 A color distribution.

---

5. The major exception is in the printing industry, which uses a four-color process for reasons that have more to do with the practical aspects of printing than with fundamental conceptual differences with three-color theory.

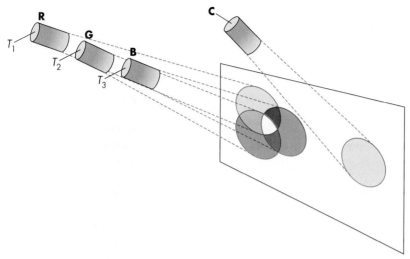

Figure 2.22 Additive color matching.

Obviously, most of the information about the distribution of $C(\lambda)$ cannot be in (T_1, T_2, T_3); we have reduced a continuous function to three numbers. That, however, is exactly what our visual systems do. The color receptors in our eyes—the cones—are of three different types. Type i, $i \in \{1, 2, 3\}$, has a sensitivity curve $S_i(\lambda)$, so, when it is exposed to a color distribution $C(\lambda)$, it measures and sends back to the brain a number

$$A_i = \int S_i(\lambda) C(\lambda) d\lambda,$$

where the integration is over the visible wavelengths. Thus, the brain perceives the color through a triplet (A_1, A_2, A_3), rather than as a continuous distribution $C(\lambda)$.

Putting it all together, we get the **basic tenet of three-color theory**: *If two colors produce the same tristimulus values, then they are visually indistinguishable*. Two colors that match visually are known as **metameric pairs**; they have the same tristimulus values, although their distributions as a function of λ may be different. For a visual match, we need to match only a color's tristimulus values.

There are many matters that we are not exploring fully here. Most concern the differences among various sets of primaries, or the limitations conferred by the physical constraints of real devices. The primaries that characterize the receptors in the eye neither are the same as the CRT primaries, nor are the same as the primaries for film, or for a printer. In addition, the tristimulus values that we use to match a color on our CRT screen must be positive, because we are adding light to the screen. We are also limited by the maximum intensity that we can produce with a device or perceive with our visual systems. Hence, although we can relate mathematically the tristimulus values in one set of primaries to the

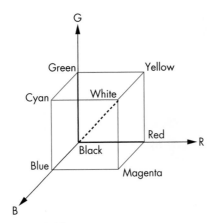

Figure 2.23   Color solid.

values in another, we may not always be able to produce the same color in both systems. The range of colors that we can produce on a given system with a given set of primaries is called that system's **color gamut**.

We have used an additive color model that is appropriate for CRT displays, transparencies, and slide (positive) film. In such systems, the primaries are usually red, green, and blue. We can view a color as a point in a **color solid**, as shown in Figure 2.23 and in Color Plate 21. We draw the solid using a coordinate system corresponding to the three primaries. The distance along a coordinate axis represents the amount of the corresponding primary in the color. If we normalize the maximum value of each primary to be 1, then we can represent any color that we can produce with this set of primaries as a point in a unit cube. The vertices of the cube correspond to black (no primaries on); red, green, and blue (one primary fully on); the pairs of primaries, cyan (green and blue fully on), magenta (red and blue fully on), and yellow (red and green fully on); and white (all primaries fully on). The principal diagonal of the cube connects the origin (black) with white. All colors along this line have equal tristimulus values and appear as shades of gray. We can answer questions such as whether the color gamuts for two sets of primaries match by viewing them in terms of how the color cube for one set of primaries maps to the color space of another set.

With additive color, primaries add light to an initially black display, yielding the desired color. For processes such as commercial printing and painting, a **subtractive color model** is more appropriate. Here, we start with a white surface, such as a sheet of paper. Colored pigments remove color components from light that is striking the surface. If we assume that white light hits the surface, a particular point will be red if all components of the incoming light are absorbed by the surface except for wavelengths in the red part of the spectrum, which are reflected. In subtractive systems, the primaries are usually the **complementary** colors: cyan, magenta, and yellow (CMY; Figure 2.24). We shall not explore

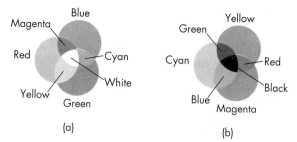

Figure 2.24 Color formation. (a) Additive color. (b) Subtractive color.

subtractive color here. You need to know only that an RGB additive system has a dual with a CMY subtractive system (see Exercise 2.8).

2.5.1 RGB Color

Now we can look at how color is handled in a graphics system from the programmer's perspective—that is, through the API. There are two different approaches. We shall stress the **RGB-color model**, because an understanding of it will be crucial for our later discussion of lighting and shading. Compared to the **indexed color model** (Section 2.5.2), it is a more difficult model to support in hardware, because of higher memory requirements, but modern systems support it more easily now that memory is cheaper. It is also possible for a system to support true color in software through the API, and to have the hardware use approximate techniques to implement a display visually close to an RGB-color display.

In a three-primary-color, additive-color RGB system, there are conceptually separate buffers for red, green, and blue images. Each pixel has separate red, green, and blue components that correspond to locations in memory (Figure 2.25). In a typical system, there might be a 1280×1024 array of pixels, and each pixel might consist of 24 bits (3 bytes): 1 byte for each of red, green, and blue. Such a frame buffer would have over 3 megabytes (MB) of memory that would have to be redisplayed at video rates. Until recently, this amount of memory was prohibitively expensive in all but the best systems.

As programmers, we would like to be able to specify any color that can be stored in the frame buffer. For our 24-bit example, there are 2^{24} possible colors, sometimes referred to as 16 M colors. where M denotes 1024^2. Other systems may have as many as 12 (or more) bits per color, or as few as 4 bits per color. Because our API should be independent of the particulars of the hardware, we would like to specify a color independently of the number of bits in the frame buffer, and to let the drivers and hardware match our specification as closely as possible to the available display. A natural technique is to use the color cube, and to specify color components as numbers between 0.0 and 1.0, where 1.0 denotes the maximum value of the corresponding primary, and 0.0 denotes a zero value

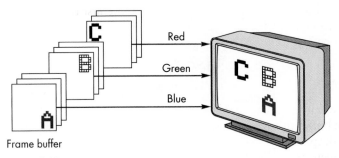

Frame buffer

Figure 2.25 RGB color.

of that primary. In OpenGL, we use the color cube as follows. To draw in red, we issue the function call

```
glColor3f(1.0, 0.0, 0.0);
```

The execution of this function will set the present drawing color to red. Because the color is part of the state, we continue to draw in red until the color is changed. The "3f" is used in a manner similar to the glVertex function: It conveys that we are using a three-color (RGB) model and that the values of the components are given as floats in C. If we use an integer or byte type to specify a color value, the maximum value of the chosen type corresponds to the primary fully on, and the minimum value corresponds to the primary fully off.

Later, we shall be interested in a four-color (RGBA) system. The fourth color (A) uses what is called the **alpha channel**, but is stored in the frame buffer, as are the RGB values; it can be set with four-dimensional versions of the color functions. In Chapter 7, we shall see various uses of the alpha channel, such as for creating fog effects or for combining images. Here, we need the alpha value to aid in the initialization of an OpenGL program. The alpha value will be treated by OpenGL as an **opacity** or **transparency** value. Transparency and opacity are complements of each other. An opaque object passes no light through it; a transparent object passes all light. An object can range from fully transparent to fully opaque.

One of the first tasks that we must do in a program is to clear an area of the screen—a drawing window—in which to display our output. We also must clear this window whenever we want to draw a new frame. By using the four-dimensional (RGBA) color system, we can create effects where the drawing window interacts with other windows that may be beneath it, by manipulating the opacity assigned to the window when it is cleared. The function call

```
glClearColor(1.0, 1.0, 1.0, 1.0);
```

defines a four-color clearing color that is white, because the first three components are set to 1.0, and is opaque, because the alpha component is 1.0. We can then use the function glClear to make the window on the screen solid and white.

2.5.2 Indexed Color

Many systems have frame buffers that are limited in depth. For example, we might have a frame buffer that has a spatial resolution of 1280×1024, but each pixel is only 8 bits deep. We could divide these 8 bits into smaller groups of bits to assign to red, green, and blue. Although this technique is adequate in a few applications, it usually does not give us enough flexibility in color assignment, and breaking apart individual bytes into small groups of bits can affect performance.

Rather, we can follow an analogy with an artist who paints in oils. The oil painter can produce an almost infinite number of colors by mixing together a limited number of pigments from tubes. We say that the painter has a potentially large color **palette**. At any one time, however, perhaps due to a limited number of brushes, the painter uses only a few colors. In this fashion, our painter can create an image that, although it contains a small number of colors, expresses the painter's desires because she can choose the few colors from a large palette.

Returning to the computer model, we can argue that, if we can choose, for each application, a limited number of colors from a large selection (our palette), we should be able to create good-quality images most of the time.

We can select colors by interpreting our limited-depth pixels as **indices**, rather than as color values. These indices correspond to lines or entries in a table. Suppose that our frame buffer has k bits per pixel. Each pixel value or index is an integer between 0 and $2^k - 1$. Suppose that we can display colors with an accuracy of m bits; that is, we can choose from 2^m reds, 2^m greens, and 2^m blues. Hence, we can produce any of 2^{3m} colors on the display, but the frame buffer can specify only 2^k of them. We handle the specification through a user-defined **color-lookup table** that is of size $2^k \times 3m$ (Figure 2.26). The user program fills the 2^k entries (rows) of the table with the desired colors, using m bits for each of red, green, and blue. Once the user has constructed the table, she can specify a color by its index, which points to the appropriate entry in the color-lookup table (Figure 2.27). For $k = m = 8$, a common configuration, she can choose 256 out of 16 M colors. The 256 entries in the table constitute the user's color palette.

If we are in color-index mode, the present color is selected by a function such as

```
glIndexi(element);
```

that selects a particular color out of the table. Setting and changing the entries in the color-lookup table involves interacting with the window system, a topic discussed in Chapter 3. One difficulty is that, if the window system and underlying hardware support only a limited number of colors, the window system may have

Input	Red	Green	Blue
0	0	0	0
1	$2^m - 1$	0	0
.	0	$2^m - 1$	0
.	.	.	.
.	.	.	.
$2^k - 1$	.	.	.

|← m bits →|← m bits →|← m bits →|

Figure 2.26 Color-lookup table.

only a single color table that must be used for all its windows, or it might have to juggle multiple tables, one for each window on the screen. GLUT allows us to set the entries in a color table for each window through the function

```
glutSetColor(int color, GLfloat red, GLfloat blue, GLfloat green)
```

Historically, color-index mode was important because it required less memory for the frame buffer and fewer other hardware components. However, the cost issue is less important now, and color-index mode presents a few problems. For a standard 8-bit (256-color) frame buffer, we can usually find a limited set of colors to represent a single image adequately. However, when we are working with dynamic images that must be shaded, we usually need more colors. Thus, for the most part, we shall assume that we are using RGB color.

2.5.3 Setting of Color Attributes

For our simple example program, we use RGB color. We have three attributes to set. The first is the clear color, which is set to white by the function call

```
glClearColor(1.0, 1.0, 1.0, 1.0);
```

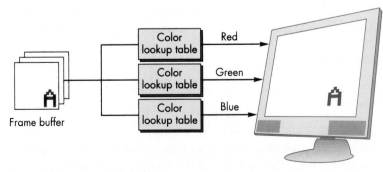

Figure 2.27 Indexed color.

We can select the rendering color for our points by setting the color state variable to red through the function call

```
glColor3f(1.0, 0.0, 0.0);
```

We can set the size of our rendered points to be 2 pixels wide, by using

```
glPointSize(2.0);
```

Note that attributes, such as the point size and line width, are specified in terms of the pixel size. Hence, if two displays have different-sized pixels (due to their particular screen dimensions and resolutions), the rendered images may appear slightly different. Certain graphics APIs, in an attempt to ensure that identical displays will be produced on all systems with the same user program, specify all attributes in a device-independent manner. Unfortunately, ensuring that two systems produce the same display has proved to be a difficult implementation problem. OpenGL has chosen a more practical balance between desired behavior and realistic constraints.

2.6 Viewing

We can now put a variety of graphical information into our two-dimensional world, and we can describe how we would like these objects to appear, but we do not yet have a method for specifying exactly which of these objects should appear on the screen. Just as what we record in a photograph depends on where we point the camera and what lens we use, we have to make similar viewing decisions in our program.

A fundamental concept that emerges from the synthetic-camera model that we introduced in Chapter 1 is that the specification of the objects in our scene is completely independent of our specification of the camera. Once we have specified both the scene and the camera, we can compose an image. The camera forms an image by exposing the film, whereas the computer system forms an image by carrying out a sequence of operations in its viewing pipeline. The application program needs to worry only about specification of the parameters for the objects and the camera, just as the casual photographer does not have to worry about how the shutter works or the details of the photochemical interaction of film with light.

There are default viewing conditions in computer image formation that are similar to the settings on a basic camera with a fixed lens. However, a camera that has a fixed lens and that sits in a fixed location forces us to distort our world to take a picture. We can create pictures of elephants only if we place the animals sufficiently far from the camera, or of ants if we put the insects relatively close to the lens. We prefer to have the flexibility to change the lens to make it easier to form an image of a collection of objects. The same is true when we use our graphics system.

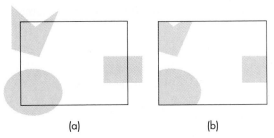

(a)   (b)

Figure 2.28 Two-dimensional viewing. (a) Objects
before clipping. (b) Image after clipping.

2.6.1 Two-Dimensional Viewing

Two-dimensional viewing is based on taking a rectangular area of our two-dimensional world and transferring its contents to the display, as shown in Figure 2.28. The area of the world that we image is known as the **viewing rectangle** or **clipping rectangle**. Objects inside the rectangle are in the image; objects outside are **clipped out** and are not displayed. Objects that straddle the edges of the rectangle are partially visible in the image. The size of the window on the display, and where this window is placed on the display, are independent decisions that we examine in Section 2.7.

Remember that, in our view, two-dimensional graphics is a special case of three-dimensional graphics. Our viewing rectangle is in the plane $z = 0$ within a three-dimensional **viewing volume**, as shown in Figure 2.29. If we do not specify a viewing volume, OpenGL uses its default, a $2 \times 2 \times 2$ cube, with the origin in the center. In terms of our two-dimensional plane, the bottom-left corner is at $(-1.0, -1.0)$, and the upper-right corner is at $(1.0, 1.0)$.

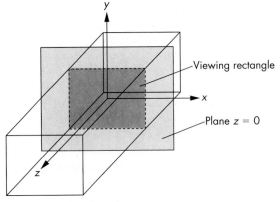

Figure 2.29 Viewing volume.

2.6.2 The Orthographic View

The two-dimensional view that we have described is a special case of the **orthographic projection** that we discuss in Chapter 5. This simple orthographic projection takes a point (x, y, z) and projects it into the point $(x, y, 0)$, as shown in Figure 2.30. Because our two-dimensional world consists of only the plane $z = 0$, the projection has no effect; however, we can employ the machinery of a three-dimensional graphics system to produce our image. In OpenGL, an orthographic projection with a right-parallelepiped viewing volume is specified via

```
void glOrtho(GLdouble left, GLdouble right, GLdouble bottom,
    GLdouble top, GLdouble near, GLdouble far)
```

Note that the near and far distances are measured from the camera. In OpenGL, the camera starts off at the origin pointing in the negative z direction as in Figure 2.31. The orthographic projection "sees" only those objects in the volume specified by viewing volume. Unlike a real camera, the orthographic projection can include objects behind the camera. Thus, as long as the plane $z = 0$ is located between near and far, the two-dimensional plane will intersect the viewing volume. If using a three-dimensional volume seems strange in a two-dimensional application, the function

```
void gluOrtho2D(GLdouble left, GLdouble right,
    GLdouble bottom, GLdouble top)
```

in the utility library may make your program more consistent with its two-dimensional structure. This function is equivalent to glOrtho, with near and

Figure 2.30 Orthographic projection.

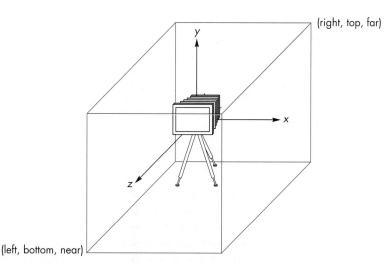

Figure 2.31 The default camera and an orthographic view volume.

far set to -1.0 and 1.0, respectively. In Chapters 4 and 5, we discuss moving the camera and creating more complex views.

2.6.3 Matrix Modes

Pipeline graphics systems have an architecture that depends on multiplying together, or concatenating, a number of transformation matrices to achieve the desired image of a primitive. Like most other OpenGL variables, the values of these matrices are part of the state of the system and remain in effect until changed. The two most important matrices are the **model-view** and **projection** matrices. At any time, the state includes values for both of these matrices, which start off set to identity matrices. In Chapter 4, we study a set of OpenGL functions to manipulate these matrices. The usual sequence is to modify the initial identity matrix by applying a sequence of transformations. There is only a single set of functions that can be applied to any type of matrix. We select the matrix to which the operations apply by first setting the **matrix mode**, a variable that is set to one type of matrix and is also part of the state. The default matrix mode is to have operations apply to the model-view matrix, so, to alter the projection matrix, we must first switch modes. The following sequence is common for setting a two-dimensional viewing rectangle:

```
glMatrixMode(GL_PROJECTION);
glLoadIdentity();
gluOrtho2D(0.0, 500.0, 0.0, 500.0);
glMatrixMode(GL_MODELVIEW);
```

This sequence defines a 500×500 viewing rectangle with the lower-left corner of the rectangle at the origin of the two-dimensional system. It then switches the matrix mode back to model-view mode. It is a good idea, in complex programs, always to return to a given matrix mode, in this case model-view mode, to avoid problems caused by your losing track of which matrix mode the program is in at a given time.

2.7 Control Functions

We are almost done with our first program, but we still must discuss the minimal interactions with the window and operating systems. If we look at the details for a specific environment, such as the X Window system on a UNIX platform or Windows on a PC, we see that the programmer's interface between the graphics system and the operating and window systems can be complex. Exploitation of the possibilities open to the application programmer requires knowledge specific to these systems. In addition, the details can be different for two different environments, and discussing these differences will do little to enhance our understanding of computer graphics.

Rather than deal with these issues in detail, we look at a minimal set of operations that must take place from the perspective of the graphics application program. The OpenGL Utility Toolkit (GLUT) is a library of functions that provides a simple interface between the systems. Details specific to the underlying windowing or operating system are inside the implementation, rather than being part of its API. Operationally, we add another library to our standard library search path. Both here and in Chapter 3, GLUT will help us to understand the interactions that characterize modern interactive graphics systems, including a wide range of APIs, operating systems, and window systems. The application programs that we produce using GLUT should run under multiple window systems.

2.7.1 Interaction with the Window System

The term *window* is used in a number of different ways in the graphics and workstation literature. We use **window** or **screen window** to denote a rectangular area of our display that, by default, is the screen of a CRT. We are concerned only with raster displays. A window has a height and width, and, because the window displays the contents of the frame buffer, positions in the window are measured in **window** or **screen coordinates**,[6] where the units are pixels.

In a modern environment, we can display many windows on the CRT screen. Each can have a different purpose, ranging from editing a file to monitoring our system. We use the term **window system** to refer to the multiwindow environment provided by systems such as the X Window system and Microsoft Windows. The window in which the graphics output appears is one of the windows managed by the window system. Hence, to the window system, the graphics window is a particular type of window—one in which graphics can be displayed or rendered. References to positions in this window are relative to one corner of the window. We have to be careful about which corner is the origin. Usually, the lower-left corner is the origin, and has window coordinates $(0,0)$. However, virtually all raster systems display their screens in the same way as commercial television systems do—from top to bottom, left to right. From this perspective, the top-left corner should be the origin. Our OpenGL commands assume that the origin is bottom left, whereas information returned from the windowing system, such as the mouse position, often has the origin at the top left and thus requires us to convert the position from one coordinate system to the other.

Note also that, although our screen may have a resolution of, say, 1280 × 1024 pixels, the window that we use can have any size, up to the full screen

---

6. In OpenGL, window coordinates are three-dimensional, whereas screen coordinates are two-dimensional. Both systems use units measured in pixels, but window coordinates retain depth information.

size. Thus, the frame buffer must have a resolution equal to the screen size. Conceptually, if we use a window of 300 × 400 pixels, we can think of it as corresponding to a 300 × 400 frame buffer, even though it uses only a part of the real frame buffer.

Before we can open a window, there must be interaction between the windowing system and OpenGL. In GLUT, this interaction is initiated by the function call

```
glutInit(int *argcp, char **argv)
```

The two arguments allow the user to pass command-line arguments, as in the standard C main function, and are usually the same as in main. We can now open an OpenGL window using the GLUT function:

```
glutCreateWindow(char *title)
```

where the title at top of the window is given by the string title.

The window that we create has a default size, a position on the screen, and characteristics such as use of RGB color. We can also use GLUT functions before window creation to specify these parameters. For example, the code

```
glutInitDisplayMode(GLUT_RGB | GLUT_DEPTH | GLUT_DOUBLE);
glutInitWindowSize(480, 640);
glutInitWindowPosition(0,0);
```

specifies a 480 × 640 window in the top-left corner of the display. We specify RGB rather than indexed (GLUT_INDEX) color; a depth buffer for hidden-surface removal; and double rather than single (GLUT_SINGLE) buffering. The defaults, which are all we need for now, are RGB color, no hidden-surface removal, and single buffering. Thus, we do not need to request these options explicitly, but specifying them makes the code clearer. Note that parameters are logically OR-ed together in the argument to glutInitDisplayMode.

2.7.2 Aspect Ratio and Viewports

The **aspect ratio** of a rectangle is the ratio of the rectangle's width to its height. The independence of the object, viewing, and workstation window specifications can cause undesirable side effects if the aspect ratio of the viewing rectangle, specified by glOrtho, is not the same as the aspect ratio of the window specified by glutInitWindowSize. If they differ, as depicted in Figure 2.32, objects are distorted on the screen. This distortion is a consequence of our default mode of operation, in which the entire clipping rectangle is mapped to the display window. The only way that we can map the entire contents of the clipping rectangle to the entire display window is to distort the contents of the former to fit inside the latter. We can avoid this distortion if we ensure that the clipping rectangle and

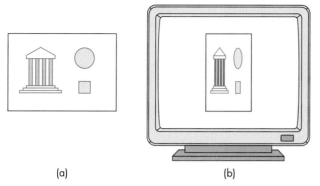

Figure 2.32 Aspect-ratio mismatch. (a) Viewing rectangle.
(b) Display window.

display window have the same aspect ratio. Another, more flexible method is to use the concept of a viewport. A **viewport** is a rectangular area of the display window. By default, it is the entire window, but it can be set to any smaller size in pixels via the function

```
void glViewport(GLint x, GLint y, GLsizei w, GLsizei h)
```

where (x,y) is the lower-left corner of the viewport (measured relative to the lower-left corner of the window), and w and h give the height and width, respectively. The types are all integers that allow us to specify positions and distances in pixels. Primitives are displayed in the viewport, as shown in Figure 2.33. For a given window, we can adjust the height and width of the viewport to match the aspect ratio of the clipping rectangle, thus preventing any object distortion in the image.

The viewport is part of the state. If we change the viewport between rendering objects or redisplay the same objects with the viewport changed, we achieve the

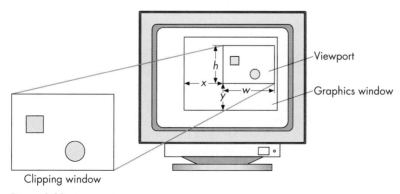

Figure 2.33 A mapping to the viewport.

effect of multiple viewports with different images in different parts of the window. We see further uses of the viewport in Chapter 3, where we consider interactive changes in the size and shape of the window.

2.7.3 The `main`, `display`, and `myinit` Functions

In principle, we should be able to combine the simple initialization code with our code from Section 2.1 to form a complete OpenGL program that generates the Sierpinski gasket. Unfortunately, life in a modern system is not that simple. There are two problems: One is generic to all graphics systems; the second has more to do with problems of interacting with the underlying windowing system.

In immediate-mode graphics, a primitive is rendered to the screen as soon as it is defined; the system uses the present state to determine the primitive's appearance. Subsequently, the program goes on to the next statement. In an interactive program, we would continue to generate more primitives. However, for an application such as our sample program, we draw a few primitives and are finished. As the application ends, the screen may clear before we have even had a chance to see our output. A simple solution for our simple program might be to insert a delay, such as via a standard function such as `sleep(enough_time)`. For any but the most trivial applications, however, we need a more sophisticated mechanism. In Chapter 3, we discuss event processing, which will give us greater interactive control in our programs. For now, we can use the GLUT function

```
void glutMainLoop();
```

whose execution will cause the program to begin an event-processing loop. If there are no events to process, the program will sit in a wait state, with our graphics on the screen, until we terminate the program through some external means, such as by hitting the "kill" key.

Graphics are sent to the screen through a function called the **display callback**. This function is specified through the GLUT function

```
void glutDisplayFunc(void (*func)(void))
```

Here, `func` is the name of the function that will be called whenever the windowing system determines that the OpenGL window needs to be redisplayed. One of these times is when the window is first opened; thus, if we put all our graphics into this function (for our noninteractive example), `func` will be executed once and our gasket will be drawn. Although it may appear that our use of the display function is merely a convenience for organizing our program, the display function is required by GLUT. Other examples of when a display callback occurs include when the window is moved from one location on the screen to another, and when a window in front of the OpenGL window is destroyed, making visible the whole OpenGL window.

Following is a main program that works for most noninteractive applications:

```
#include <GL/glut.h>

void main(int argc, char **argv)
{

    glutInit(&argc,argv);
    glutInitDisplayMode (GLUT_SINGLE | GLUT_RGB);
    glutInitWindowSize(500,500);
    glutInitWindowPosition(0,0);
    glutCreateWindow("simple  OpenGL example");
    glutDisplayFunc(display);
    myinit();
    glutMainLoop();
}
```

We use an initialization function myinit()[7] to set the OpenGL state variables dealing with viewing and attributes—parameters that we prefer to set once, independently of the display function. The standard "include" (.h) file for GLUT is loaded before the beginning of the function definitions. In most implementations, the compiler directive

```
#include <GL/glut.h>
```

will add in the header files for the GLUT library, the OpenGL library (gl.h), and the OpenGL utility library (glu.h). The macro definitions for our standard values, such as GL_LINES and GL_RGB, are in these files.

2.7.4 Program Structure

Every program we write will have the same structure as our gasket program. We shall always use the GLUT toolkit. The main function will then consist of calls to GLUT functions to set up our window(s) and to make sure that the local environment supports the required display properties. The main will also name the required callbacks and callback functions. Every program must have a display callback, and most will have other callbacks to set up interaction. The myinit function will set up user options, usually through OpenGL functions on the GL and GLU libraries. Although these options could be set in main, it is probably clearer to keep GLUT functions separate from OpenGL functions. In most programs, most of the graphics output will be generated in the display callback.

---

7. We hope to avoid confusion by using the same function names as those in the *OpenGL Programmer's Guide* [Ope01a] and in the GLUT documentation [Kil94a].

2.8 The Gasket Program

Using our main function, we can now write the myinit and display functions, and thus complete the program that will generate the Sierpinski gasket. We draw red points on a white background. We also set up a two-dimensional coordinate system, so that our points are defined within a 500×500 square with the origin in the lower-left corner.

Here are the two functions:

```
void myinit(void)
{
/* attributes */

    glClearColor(1.0, 1.0, 1.0, 1.0); /* white background */
    glColor3f(1.0, 0.0, 0.0); /* draw in red */

/* set up viewing */

    glMatrixMode(GL_PROJECTION);
    glLoadIdentity();
    gluOrtho2D(0.0, 500.0, 0.0, 500.0);
    glMatrixMode(GL_MODELVIEW);
}

void display( void )
{
    typedef GLfloat point2[2]; /* define a point data type */

    point2 vertices[3]={{0.0,0.0},{250.0,500.0},{500.0,0.0}};
        /*triangle */

    int i, j, k;
    int rand(); /* standard random--number generator */
    point2 p ={75.0,50.0}; /* arbitrary point
                                inside triangle*/

    glClear(GL_COLOR_BUFFER_BIT);  /*clear  the window */

/* compute and output 5000 new points */

    for( k=0; k<5000; k++)
    {
        j=rand()%3; /* pick a vertex at random */

/* Compute point halfway between vertex and old point */

        p[0] = (p[0]+vertices[j][0])/2.0;
        p[1] = (p[1]+vertices[j][1])/2.0;
```

```
    /* plot point */
    glBegin(GL_POINTS);
        glVertex2fv(p);
    glEnd();
  }

  glFlush();
}
```

Our display function has an arbitrary triangle (three vertices) defined in it, and an arbitrary initial point is defined within this triangle. It also has a loop that will generate a fixed number of (5000) points. A call to the OpenGL function glFlush has been included; it will force the system to plot the points on the display as soon as possible.

A complete listing of this program, and of the other example programs that we generate in subsequent chapters, is given in Appendix A.

2.9 Polygons and Recursion

The output from our gasket program (Figure 2.2) shows considerable structure. If we were to run the program with more iterations, then much of the randomness in the image would disappear. Examining this structure, we see that, regardless of how many points we generate, there are no points in the middle. If we draw line segments connecting the midpoints of the sides of the original triangle, then we divide the original triangle into four triangles, the middle one containing no points (Figure 2.34).

Looking at the other three triangles, we see that we can apply the same observation to each of them; that is, we can subdivide each of these triangles into four triangles by connecting the midpoints of the sides, and each middle triangle will contain no points.

This structure suggests a second method for generating the Sierpinski gasket— one that uses polygons instead of points, and does not require the use of a random-number generator. One advantage of using polygons is that we can fill solid areas on our display. Our strategy is to start with a single triangle, to subdivide it into four smaller triangles by bisecting the sides, and then to remove the middle triangle from further consideration. We repeat this procedure on the remaining triangles until the size of the triangles that we are removing is small enough—about the size of one pixel—that we can draw the remaining triangles.

We can implement the process that we just described through a recursive program. We start its development with a simple function that draws a single triangular polygon given three arbitrary vertices:

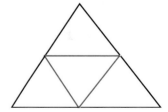

Figure 2.34 Bisecting of the sides of a triangle.

```
void triangle(point2 a, point2 b, point2 c)

{
```

```
        glBegin(GL_TRIANGLES);
            glVertex2fv(a);
            glVertex2fv(b);
            glVertex2fv(c);
        glEnd();
}
```

Suppose that the vertices of our original triangle are given by the array

```
point2 v[3];
```

then the midpoints of the sides are given by the array m[3], which can be computed using the code

```
for(j=0; j<2; j++) m[0][j]=(v[0][j]+v[1][j])/2.0;
for(j=0; j<2; j++) m[1][j]=(v[0][j]+v[2][j])/2.0;
for(j=0; j<2; j++) m[2][j]=(v[1][j]+v[2][j])/2.0;
```

With these six points, we can use triangle to draw the three triangles formed by (v[0], m[0], m[1]), (v[2], m[1], m[2]), and (v[1], m[2], m[0]). We do not really want simply to draw these triangles; we want to subdivide them. Hence, we make the process recursive. We define a recursive function divide_triangle(point2 a, point2 b, point2 c, int k) that will draw the triangles only if k is zero. Otherwise, it will subdivide the triangle specified by a, b, and c, and decrease k. Here is the code:

```
void divide_triangle(point2 a, point2 b, point2 c, int k)
{
    point2 ab, ac, bc;
    int j;
    if(k>0)
    {
/* compute midpoints of sides */

        for(j=0; j<2; j++) ab[j]=(a[j]+b[j])/2;
        for(j=0; j<2; j++) ac[j]=(a[j]+c[j])/2;
        for(j=0; j<2; j++) bc[j]=(b[j]+c[j])/2;

/* subdivide all but inner triangle */

        divide_triangle(a, ab, ac, k-1);
        divide_triangle(c, ac, bc, k-1);
        divide_triangle(b, bc, ab, k-1);
    }
    else triangle(a,b,c); /* draw triangle at
                              end of recursion */

}
```

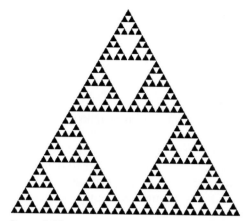

Figure 2.35 Triangles after five subdivisions.

The display function is now almost trivial. It uses a global[8] value of n determined by the main program to fix the number of subdivision steps we would like, and it calls `divide_triangle` once.

```
void display(void)
{
    glClear(GL_COLOR_BUFFER_BIT);
    divide_triangle(v[0], v[1], v[2], n);
    glFlush();
}
```

The rest of the program is the same as our previous gasket program, except that we read in the value of n. Output for five subdivision steps is shown in Figure 2.35.

The complete program is given in Appendix A.

2.10 The Three-Dimensional Gasket

We have argued that two-dimensional graphics is a special case of three-dimensional graphics, but we have not yet seen a true three-dimensional program. Next, we convert our two-dimensional Sierpinski gasket program to a program that will generate a three-dimensional gasket. We can follow either of

---

8. Note that often we have no convenient way to pass variables to OpenGL functions and callbacks other than through global parameters. Although we prefer not to pass values in such a manner, because the form of these functions is fixed, we have no good alternative.

the two approaches that we used for the two-dimensional gasket. Both extensions start in a similar manner, replacing the initial triangle with a tetrahedron
(Figure 2.36).

Figure 2.36 Tetra-
hedron.

2.10.1 Use of Three-Dimensional Points

Because every tetrahedron is convex, the midpoint of a line segment between a
vertex and any point inside a tetrahedron also is inside the tetrahedron. Hence,
we can follow the same procedure as before, but this time, instead of the three
vertices required to define a triangle, we need four initial vertices to define the
tetrahedron. Note that, as long no three vertices are collinear, we can choose
the four vertices of the tetrahedron at random without affecting the character of
the result.

The required changes are primarily in the function display. We define a three-
dimensional point data type

```
typedef GLfloat point3[3];
```

Then we initialize the vertices of the tetrahedron; for instance, we can use the
code

```
point3 vertices[4]={{0.0,0.0,0.0},{250.0,500.0,100.0},
                   {500.0,250.0,250.0},{250.0,100.0,250.0}};
                   /* vertices of an arbitrary tetrahedron */

point3 p ={250.0,100.0,250.0}; /* arbitrary initial point */
```

We now use the function glVertex3fv to define points. One problem for the
three-dimensional gasket that we did not have with the two-dimensional gasket
is that, because points are not restricted to a single plane, it may be difficult
to envision the three-dimensional structure from the two-dimensional image
displayed. To get around this problem, we have added a color function that makes
the color of each point depend on that point's location, so we can understand
the resulting image more easily. Here is the display function:

```
void display()
{
/* computes and plots a single new point */

  int rand();
  int i;
  j=rand()%4; /* pick a vertex at random */

/* Compute point halfway between vertex and old point */
```

```
  p[0] = (p[0]+vertices[j][0])/2.0;
  p[1] = (p[1]+vertices[j][1])/2.0;
  p[2] = (p[2]+vertices[j][2])/2.0;

/* plot point */

  glBegin(GL_POINTS);
   glColor3f(p[0]/250.0,p[1]/250.0,p[2]/250.0);
   glVertex3fv( p );
  glEnd();

/* replace old point by new */

  old.x=new.x;
  old.y=new.y;
  old.z=new.z;

  glFlush();

}
```

We are now working in three dimensions, so we define a three-dimensional clipping volume (in `main.c`) by

```
glOrtho(-500.0 , 500.0, -500.0, 500.0 ,-500.0, 500.0);
```

Figure 2.37 and Front Plate 1 show that if we generate enough points, the resulting figure will look like the initial tetrahedron with increasingly smaller tetrahedrons removed.

2.10.2 Use of Polygons in Three Dimensions

Following our second approach, we note that the faces of a tetrahedron are the four triangles determined by its four vertices. We can then apply our subdivision algorithm to each of the triangle faces. Thus, the code is almost the same as in two dimensions. Our triangle routine now uses points in three dimensions, rather than in two dimensions:

```
void triangle(point3 a, point3 b, point3 c)
{
    glBegin(GL_POLYGON);
        glVertex3fv(a);
        glVertex3fv(b);
        glVertex3fv(c);
    glEnd();
}
```

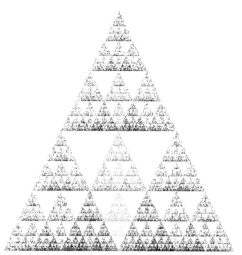

Figure 2.37 Three-dimensional Sierpinski gasket.

Our code for divide_triangle does the same:

```
void divide_triangle(point3 a, point3 b, point3 c, int k)
{
    point3 ab, ac, bc;
    int j;
    if(k>0)
    {
        for(j=0; j<3; j++) ab[j]=(a[j]+b[j])/2;
        for(j=0; j<3; j++) ac[j]=(a[j]+c[j])/2;
        for(j=0; j<3; j++) bc[j]=(b[j]+c[j])/2;
        divide_triangle(a, ab, ac, k-1);
        divide_triangle(c, ac, bc, k-1);
        divide_triangle(b, bc, ab, k-1);
    }
    else triangle(a,b,c); /* draw triangle
                             at end of recursion */
}
```

We can then generate our subdivided tetrahedron by applying triangle subdivision to each of the four original triangles that form the surface of the tetrahedron:

```
void tetrahedron( int n )
{
    glColor3f(1.0,0.0,0.0);
    divide_triangle(v[0], v[1], v[2], k);
    glColor3f(0.0,1.0,0.0);
```

```
      divide_triangle(v[3], v[2], v[1], k);
      glColor3f(0.0,0.0,1.0);
      divide_triangle(v[0], v[3], v[1], k);
      glColor3f(0.0,0.0,0.0);
      divide_triangle(v[0], v[2], v[3], k);
}
```

where n is the number of subdivision steps. We have also assigned a different color to each face to make the output clearer. There is just one more problem that we must address before we have a useful three-dimensional program.

2.10.3 Hidden-Surface Removal

If you execute the code in the previous section, you might be confused by the results. The program draws triangles in the order that they are specified in the program. This order is determined by the recursion in our program and not by the geometric relationship between the triangles. Each triangle is drawn (filled) in a solid color and is drawn over those triangles that have already been rendered to the display.

Contrast this order to the way that we would see the triangles if we were to construct the three-dimensional Sierpinski gasket out of small solid tetrahedra. We would see only those faces of tetrahedra that were in front of all other faces as seen by a viewer. Figure 2.38 shows a simplified version of this **hidden-surface** problem. From the viewer's position, she sees quadrilateral A clearly, but triangle B is blocked from her view, and triangle C is only partially visible. Without going into the details of any specific algorithm, you should be able to convince yourself that, if we have the position of the viewer and the triangles, then we should be able to draw the triangles such that the correct image is obtained. Algorithms for ordering objects so that they are drawn correctly are called **visible-surface algorithms** or **hidden-surface–removal algorithms**, depending on how we look at the problem. We discuss such algorithms in detail in Chapters 4 and 8.

For now, we can simply use a particular hidden-surface–removal algorithm, called the **z-buffer** algorithm, that is supported by OpenGL. This algorithm can be turned on (enabled) and off (disabled) easily. In our main program, we must request the auxiliary storage, a z or depth buffer, by modifying the initialization of the display mode to the following:

```
glutInitDisplayMode(GLUT_SINGLE | GLUT_RGB | GLUT_DEPTH);
```

Note that the z buffer is one of the buffers that make up the frame buffer. We enable the algorithm by the function call

```
glEnable(GL_DEPTH_TEST)
```

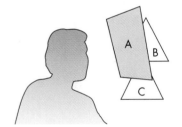

Figure 2.38 The hidden-surface problem.

Figure 2.39 Three-dimensional gasket after five
recursion steps.

either in main.c or in an initialization function such as myinit.c. Because the
algorithm stores information in the depth buffer, we must clear this buffer
whenever we wish to redraw the display; thus, we modify the clear procedure in
the display function:

```
glClear(GL_COLOR_BUFFER_BIT | GL_DEPTH_BUFFER_BIT);
```

The display callback is

```
void display()
{
  glClear(GL_COLOR_BUFFER_BIT | GL_DEPTH_BUFFER_BIT);
  tetrahedron(n);
  glFlush();
}
```

The results are shown in Figure 2.39 and Front Plate 2 for a recursion of five
steps. The complete program is given in Appendix A.

2.11 Summary and Notes

In this chapter, we introduced the OpenGL API and applied the basic concepts
that we learned in Chapter 1. Although the first application that we used to
develop our first program was two-dimensional, we took the path of looking
at two-dimensional graphics as a special case of three-dimensional graphics. We
then were able to extend the example to three dimensions with minimal work.

The Sierpinski gasket provides a nontrivial beginning application. A few extensions and mathematical issues are presented in the exercises at the end of this

chapter. We give a more detailed introduction to fractal geometry in Chapter 11, where we use these concepts to generate realistic-looking objects. The texts in the Suggested Readings section provide many other examples of interesting curves and surfaces that can be generated with simple programs.

The historical development of graphics APIs and graphical models illustrates the importance of starting in three dimensions. The pen-plotter model from Chapter 1 was used for many years and is the basis of many important APIs, such as Postscript. Work to define an international standard for graphics APIs began in the 1970s and culminated with the adoption of GKS by the International Standards Organization (ISO) in 1984. However, GKS had its basis in the pen-plotter model, and, being a two-dimensional API, was of limited utility in the CAD community. Although the standard was extended to three dimensions with GKS-3D, the limitations imposed by the original underlying model led to a standard that was lacking in many aspects. The PHIGS and PHIGS+ APIs, started in the CAD community, are inherently three-dimensional, and are based on the synthetic-camera model.

The modeling–rendering paradigm is illustrated by Pixar's RenderMan Interface. Although the specification is for an interface between the modeler and the renderer, the interface is based on a high-quality renderer (Reyes) that, among other applications, is used to create animated films. This interface makes use of the synthetic-camera model.

OpenGL is derived from the GL API, which is based on implementing the synthetic-camera model with a pipeline architecture. GL was developed for Silicon Graphics workstations that incorporated a pipeline architecture that originally was implemented with special-purpose VLSI chips. Hence, although PHIGS and GL have much in common, GL was designed specifically for high-speed real-time rendering. OpenGL was a result of application users realizing the advantages of GL programming and wanting to carry these advantages to other platforms. Because it removed input and windowing functions from GL and concentrated on the rendering aspects of the API, OpenGL emerged as a new API that is portable but that retains the features that make GL such a powerful API.

Recently, two other APIs have become popular. Java3D exploits many of the advantages of Java such as the machine independence of its byte code. It makes use of scene graphs (Chapter 9) and is usually implemented on top of OpenGL. That is, applications that are written for Java3D generate code that can be sent over the World Wide Web and interpreted locally using interpreters written in OpenGL.

Within the game community, the dominance of Windows makes it possible for game developers to write code for a single platform. DirectX only runs on Windows platforms and is optimized for speed on these systems. Although much DirectX code looks like OpenGL code, the coder can make use of device-dependent features that are available in commodity graphics cards. Consequently, applications written in DirectX do not have the portability and stability of OpenGL applications. Thus, we see DirectX dominate the game world, whereas scientific and engineering applications generally are written in OpenGL. For OpenGL programmers who want to use features specific to certain hardware, OpenGL has an extension mechanism for accessing these features at the cost of portability.

Our examples and programs have shown how we describe and display geometric objects in a simple manner. In terms of the modeling–rendering paradigm that we presented in Chapter 1, we have focused on the modeling. However, our models are completely unstructured. Representations of objects are lists of vertices and attributes. In Chapter 9, we shall learn to construct hierarchical models that can represent relationships among objects. Nevertheless, at this point, you should be able to write interesting programs. Complete the exercises at the end of the chapter, and extend a few of the two-dimensional problems to three dimensions.

2.12 Suggested Readings

The Sierpinski gasket provides a good introduction to the mysteries of fractal geometry; there are good discussions in several texts [Bar93, Hil90, Man82, Pru90].

The pen-plotter API is used by Postscript [Ado85] and LOGO [Pap81]. LOGO provides turtle graphics, an API that is both simple to learn and capable of describing several of the two-dimensional mathematical curves that we use in Chapter 10; see Exercise 2.4.

GKS [ANSI85], GKS-3D [ISO88], PHIGS [ANSI88], and PHIGS+ [PHIG89] are both U.S. and international standards. Their formal descriptions can be obtained from the American National Standards Institute (ANSI) and from ISO. Numerous textbooks use these APIs [Ang90, End84, Fol94, Hea94, Hop83, Hop91].

The X Window system [Sch88] has become the standard on UNIX workstations and has influenced the development of window systems on other platforms. Recent versions of the X Window system include the PHIGS extensions to X (PEX).

The Renderman interface is described in [Ups89].

The two standard references for OpenGL are the *OpenGL Programmer's Guide* [Ope01a] and the *OpenGL Reference Manual* [Ope01b]. There is also a formal specification of OpenGL [Seg92]. The second edition of the *Programmer's Guide* uses the GLUT library that was developed by Mark Kilgard [Kil94b]. The Programmer's Guide provides many more code examples using OpenGL. GLUT was developed for use with the X Window System [Kil96], but there are now versions available for Windows. The first edition of the *Programmer's Guide* used a simpler toolkit, aux, to interface to the X Window system. Conversion of programs written using aux to programs using GLUT is a trivial exercise. Much of this information and many of the example programs are available over the Internet. Representative sites are listed at the beginning of Appendix A.

The companion book to this book, *OpenGL: A Primer* [Ang02] contains details of the OpenGL functions used here and more examples.

The Java 3D API is described in [Swo00]. The graphics part of the DirectX PI was originally known as Direct3D. Version 8.0 of DirectX is used in [McC01].

Exercises

2.1   A slight variation on generating the Sierpinski gasket with triangular polygons yields the *fractal mountains* used in computer-generated animations. After you find the midpoint of each side of the triangle, perturb this location before subdivision. Generate these triangles without fill. Later, you can do this exercise in three dimensions and add shading. After a few subdivisions, you should have generated sufficient detail that your triangles look like a mountain.

2.2   The Sierpinski gasket, as generated in Exercise 2.1, demonstrates many of the geometric complexities that are studied in fractal geometry (Chapter 11). Suppose that you construct the gasket with mathematical lines that have length but no width. In the limit, what percentage of the area of the original triangle remains after the central triangle has been removed after each subdivision? Consider the perimeters of the triangles remaining after each central triangle is removed. In the limit, what happens to the total perimeter length of all remaining triangles?

2.3   At the lowest level of processing, we manipulate bits in the frame buffer. OpenGL has pixel-oriented commands that allow users to access the frame buffer directly. You can experiment with simple raster algorithms, such as drawing lines or circles, by using the OpenGL function glPoint, as the basis of a simple virtual-frame-buffer library. Write a library that will allow you to work in a frame buffer that you create in memory. The core functions should be WritePixel and ReadPixel. Your library should allow you to set up and display your frame buffer, and to run a user program that reads and writes pixels.

2.4   *Turtle graphics* is an alternative positioning system that is based on the concept of a turtle moving around the screen with a pen attached to the bottom of his shell. The turtle's position can be described by a triplet (x, y, θ), giving the location of the center and the orientation of the turtle. A typical API for such a system includes functions such as

```
init(x,y,theta); /* initialize position and orientation
                    of turtle */
forward(distance);
right(angle);
left(angle);
pen(up_down);
```

Implement a turtle-graphics library using OpenGL.

Figure 2.40 Generation of the Koch snowflake.

2.5   Use your turtle-graphics library from Exercise 2.4 to generate the Sierpinski gasket and fractal mountains of Exercises 2.1 and 2.2.

2.6   Space-filling curves have interested mathematicians for centuries. In the limit, these curves have infinite length, but they are confined to a finite rectangle and never cross themselves. Many of these curves can be generated iteratively. Consider the "rule" pictured in Figure 2.40 that replaces a single line segment with four shorter segments. Write a program that starts with a triangle and iteratively applies the replacement rule to all the line segments. The object that you generate is called the Koch snowflake. For other examples of space-filling curves, see [Hil01, Bar93].

2.7   You can generate a simple maze starting with a rectangular array of cells. Each cell has four sides. You remove sides (except from the perimeter of all the cells) until all the cells are connected. Then you create an entrance and an exit by removing two sides from the perimeter. A simple example is shown in Figure 2.41. Write a program using OpenGL that takes as input the two integers N and M, and then draws an $N \times M$ maze.

2.8   Describe how you would adapt the RGB color model in OpenGL to allow you to work with a subtractive color model.

Figure 2.41 Maze.

2.9   We saw that a fundamental operation in graphics systems is to map a point (x, y), which lies within a clipping rectangle, to a point (x_s, y_s), which lies in the viewport of a window on the screen. Assume that the two rectangles are defined by OpenGL function calls

```
glViewport(u, v, w , h);
gluOrtho2D(x_min, x_max, y_min, y_max);
```

Find the mathematical equations that map (x, y) into (x_s, y_s).

2.10   Many graphics APIs use relative positioning. In such a system, the API contains functions such as

```
move_rel(x,y);
line_rel(x,y);
```

for drawing lines and polygons. The move_rel function moves an internal position, or cursor, to a new position; the line_rel function moves the cursor and defines a line segment between the old cursor position and the new position. What are the advantages and disadvantages of relative positioning, as compared to the absolute positioning used in OpenGL? Describe how you would add relative positioning to OpenGL.

2.11   In Section 2.4, in determining whether or not a point is inside a polygon, we ignored potential problems that might arise if one or more sides of the polygon are parallel to a scan line. What are these problems? How would you handle them?

2.12   In practice, testing each point in a polygon to determine whether it is inside or outside the polygon is extremely inefficient. Describe the general strategies that you might pursue to avoid point-by-point testing.

2.13   In Section 2.4, we saw that OpenGL defines polygons using lists of vertices. How could you use OpenGL to define polygons by their edges?

2.14   Devise a test to determine whether a two-dimensional polygon is simple.

2.15   Figure 2.42 shows a set of polygons called a *mesh*; these polygons share some edges and vertices. Find one or more simple data structures that represent the mesh. A good data structure should include information on shared vertices and edges. Using OpenGL, find an efficient method for displaying a mesh represented by your data structure.

Figure 2.42   Polygonal mesh.

2.16   In OpenGL, we can associate a color with each vertex. If the endpoints of a line segment have different colors assigned to them, OpenGL will interpolate between the colors as it renders the line segment. It will do the same for polygons. Use this property to display the *Maxwell triangle*: an equilateral triangle whose vertices are red, green, and blue. What is the relationship between the Maxwell triangle and the color cube?

2.17   We can simulate many realistic effects using computer graphics by incorporating simple physics in the model. Simulate a bouncing ball in two dimensions, incorporating both gravity and elastic collisions with a surface. You can model the ball with a closed polygon that has a sufficient number of sides to look smooth.

2.18   An interesting, but difficult, extension of Exercise 2.17 is to simulate a game of pool or billiards. You will need to have multiple balls that can interact with the sides of the table and with one another. *Hint:* Start with two balls, and consider how to detect possible collisions.

2.19   A certain graphics system with a CRT display is advertised to display any four out of 64 colors. What does this statement tell you about the frame buffer, and about the quality of the CRT?

2.20   Devise a test for the convexity of a two-dimensional polygon.

2.21   One problem for beginning users of OpenGL is the number of forms of the basic functions such as glVertex. In a language such as C++, we can use a single name and let the compiler pick the correct version by the type of the arguments. In C++, write a library to sit between OpenGL and a user program that minimizes the number of functions that the application programmer needs.

Input and Interaction

We now turn to the development of interactive graphics programs. Interactive computer graphics opens up a myriad of applications, ranging from inter- active design of buildings, to control of large systems through graphical interfaces, to virtual-reality systems, to computer games.

Our discussion has three main parts. First, we introduce the variety of devices available for interaction. We consider input devices from two different perspec- tives: (1) the way that the physical devices can be described by their real-world properties, and (2) the way that these devices appear to the application program. We then consider client–server networks and client–server graphics. We use these ideas to develop event-driven input for our graphics programs. Finally, we de- velop a paint program that demonstrates the important features of interactive graphics programming.

3.1 Interaction

One of the most important advances in computer technology was enabling users to interact with computer displays. More than any other event, Ivan Sutherland's Project Sketchpad launched the present era of *interactive* computer graphics. The basic paradigm that he introduced is deceptively simple. The user sees an image on the display. She reacts to this image by means of an interactive device, such as a mouse. The image changes in response to her input. She reacts to this change, and so on. Whether we are writing programs using the tools available in a modern window system or using the human–computer interface in an interactive museum exhibit, we are making use of this paradigm.

In the 40 years since Sutherland's work, there have been many advances in both hardware and software, but the viewpoint and ideas that he introduced still dominate interactive computer graphics. These influences range from how we conceptualize the human–computer interface to how we can employ graphical data structures that allow for efficient implementations.

In this chapter, we take an approach slightly different from that in the rest of the book. Although rendering is the prime concern of most modern APIs, including of OpenGL, interactivity is an important component of many applica- tions. OpenGL, however, does not support interaction directly. The major reason for this omission is that the system architects who designed OpenGL wanted to increase its portability by allowing the system to work in a variety of environments. Consequently, windowing and input functions were left out of the API. Although this decision makes renderers portable, it makes more difficult discussions of interaction that do not include specifics of the windowing system. In addition, because any application program must have at least a minimal interface to the windowing environment, we cannot avoid such issues completely if we want to write complete, nontrivial programs. If interaction is omitted from the API, the application programmer is forced to worry about the often arcane details of her particular environment.

We can avoid such potential difficulties by using a simple library, or toolkit, as we did in Chapter 2. The toolkit can provide the minimal functionality that is expected on virtually all systems, such as opening of windows, use of the keyboard and mouse, and creation of pop-up menus through the toolkit's API. We adopt this approach, even though it may not provide all the features of any particular windowing system, and may produce code that neither makes use of the full capabilities of the window system, nor is as efficient as would be the code written in terms of the particular environment.

We use the term *windowing system*, as we did in Chapter 2, to include the total environment provided by systems such as the X Window system, Microsoft Windows, and the Macintosh operating system. Graphics programs that we develop will render into a window within one of these environments. The terminology used in the windowing-system literature may obscure the distinction between, for example, an X window and the OpenGL window into which our graphics are rendered. However, you will usually be safe if you regard the OpenGL window as a particular type of X window. Our use of the GLUT toolkit will enable us to avoid the complexities inherent in the interactions among the windowing system, the window manager, and the graphics system. Just as it did in Chapter 2, GLUT will allow our sample programs to be independent of any particular window system.

We start by describing several interactive devices and the variety of ways that we can interact with them. We then put these devices in the setting of a client–server network. Then, we introduce an API for minimal interaction. Finally, we shall generate sample programs.

3.2 Input Devices

We can think about input devices in two distinct ways. The obvious one is to look at them as physical devices, such as a keyboard or a mouse, and to discuss how they work. Certainly, we need to know something about the physical properties of our input devices, so such a discussion is necessary if we are to obtain a full understanding of input. However, from the perspective of an application programmer, we almost never want to use anything about the particular characteristics of a physical device in an application program. Rather, we prefer to treat input devices as *logical* devices whose properties are specified in terms of what they do from the perspective of the application program. A **logical device** is characterized by its high-level interface with the user program, rather than by its physical characteristics. Logical devices are familiar to all writers of high-level programs. For example, data input and output in C are done through functions such as printf, scanf, getchar, and putchar, whose arguments use the standard C data types, and through input (cin) and output (cout) streams in C++. When we output a string using printf, the physical device on which the output appears could be a printer, a terminal, or a disk file. This output could even be the input to another program. The details of the format required by the destination device are of minor concern to the writer of the application program.

In computer graphics, the use of logical devices is slightly more complex, because the forms that input can take are more varied than the strings of bits or characters to which we are usually restricted in nongraphical applications. For example, we can use the mouse—a physical device—either to select a location on the screen of our CRT, or to indicate which item in a menu we wish to select. In the first case, an x, y pair (in some coordinate system) is returned to the user program; in the second, the application program may receive an integer as the identifier of an entry in the menu. The separation of physical from logical devices allows us to use the same physical devices in two markedly different logical ways. It also allows the same program to work, without modification, if the mouse is replaced by another physical device, such as a data tablet or trackball.

3.2.1 Physical Input Devices

From the physical perspective, each device has properties that make it more suitable for certain tasks than for others. We take the view used in most of the workstation literature that there are two primary types of physical devices: pointing devices and keyboard devices. The **pointing device** allows the user to indicate a position on the screen, and almost always incorporates one or more buttons to allow the user to send signals or interrupts to the computer. The **keyboard device** is almost always a physical keyboard, but can be generalized to include any device that returns character codes[1] to a program.

The mouse (Figure 3.1) and trackball (Figure 3.2) are similar in use and, often, in construction. A typical mechanical mouse when turned over looks like a trackball. In both devices, the motion of the ball is converted to signals sent back to the computer by pairs of encoders inside the device that are turned by the motion of the ball. The encoders measure motion in two orthogonal directions.

There are many variants of these devices. Some use optical detectors, rather than mechanical detectors, to measure motion. Optical mice measure distance

Figure 3.1 Mouse.

Figure 3.2 Trackball.

---

1. We use the American Standard Code for Information Interchange (ASCII), although nothing we do restricts us to this particular choice, other than that ASCII is the prevailing code used.

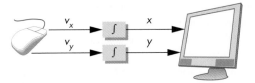

Figure 3.3 Cursor positioning.

traveled by counting lines on a special pad. Small trackballs are popular with portable computers because they can be incorporated directly into the keyboard. There are also various pressure-sensitive devices used in keyboards that perform similar functions to the mouse and trackball, but that do not move; their encoders measure the pressure exerted on a small knob that often is located between two keys in the middle of the keyboard.

We can view the output of the mouse or trackball as two independent values provided by the device. These values can be considered as positions and converted—either within the graphics system or by the user program—to a two-dimensional location in either screen or world coordinates. If it is configured in this manner, we can use the device to position a marker (cursor) automatically on the display; however, we rarely use these devices in this direct manner.

It is not necessary that the output of the mouse or trackball encoders be interpreted as a position. Instead, either the device driver or a user program can interpret the information from the encoder as two independent velocities (see Exercise 3.4). The computer can then integrate these values to obtain a two-dimensional position. Thus, as a mouse moves across a surface, the integrals of the velocities yield x, y values that can be converted to indicate the position for a cursor on the screen, as shown in Figure 3.3. By integrating the distance traveled by the ball as a velocity, we can use the device as a variable-sensitivity input device. Small deviations from rest cause slow or small changes; large deviations cause rapid large changes. With either device, if the ball does not rotate, then there is no change in the integrals, and a cursor tracking the position of the mouse will not move. In this mode, these devices are **relative-positioning** devices, because changes in the position of the ball yield a position in the user program; the absolute location of the ball (or of the mouse) is not used by the application program.

Relative positioning, as provided by a mouse or trackball, is not always desirable. In particular, these devices are not suitable for an operation such as tracing a diagram. If, while the user is attempting to follow a curve on the screen with a mouse, she lifts and moves the mouse, the absolute position on the curve being traced is lost. **Data tablets** provide absolute positioning. A typical data tablet (Figure 3.4) has rows and columns of wires embedded under its surface. The position of the stylus is determined through electromagnetic interactions between signals traveling through the wires and sensors in the stylus. Touch-sensitive transparent screens that can be placed over the face of a CRT have

Figure 3.4 Data tablet.

many of the same properties as the data tablet. Small, rectangular pressure-sensitive touchpads are embedded in the keyboards of many portable computers. These touchpads can be configured as either relative- or absolute-positioning devices.

The **lightpen** has a long history in computer graphics. It was the device used in Sutherland's original Sketchpad. The lightpen contains a light-sensing device, such as a photocell (Figure 3.5). If the lightpen is positioned on the face of the CRT at a location opposite where the electron beam strikes the phosphor, the light emitted exceeds a threshold in the photodetector, and a signal is sent to the computer. Because each redisplay of the frame buffer starts at a precise time, we can use the time at which this signal occurs to determine a position on the CRT screen (see Exercise 3.19). Hence, we have a direct-positioning device. The lightpen is not as popular as the mouse, data tablet, and trackball. One of its major deficiencies is that it has difficulty obtaining a position that corresponds to a dark area of the screen.

Figure 3.5 Lightpen.

One other device, the **joystick** (Figure 3.6), is worthy of mention. The motion of the stick in two orthogonal directions is encoded, interpreted as two velocities, and integrated to identify a screen location. The integration implies that, if the stick is left in its resting position, there is no change in the cursor position, and the farther the stick is moved from its resting position, the faster the screen location changes. Thus, the joystick is a variable-sensitivity device. The other advantage of the joystick is that the device can be constructed with mechanical elements, such as springs and dampers, that give resistance to a user who is pushing the stick. Such mechanical feel, which is not possible with the other devices, makes the joystick well suited for applications such as flight simulators and games.

Figure 3.6 Joystick.

For three-dimensional graphics, we might prefer to use three-dimensional input devices. Although various such devices are available, none have yet won the widespread acceptance of the popular two-dimensional input devices. A **spaceball** looks like a joystick with a ball on the end of the stick (Figure 3.7); however, the stick does not move. Rather, pressure sensors in the ball measure the forces applied by the user. The spaceball can measure not only the three direct forces (up–down, front–back, left–right), but also three independent twists. Thus, the device measures six independent values and has six **degrees of freedom**. Such an input device could be used, for example, both to position and to orient a camera.

Other three-dimensional devices, such as laser-based structured-lighting systems and laser-ranging systems, measure three-dimensional positions. Numerous tracking systems used in virtual-reality applications sense the position of the user. Virtual-reality and robotics applications often need more degrees of freedom than the two to six provided by the devices that we have described. Devices such as data gloves can sense motion of various parts of the human body, thus providing many additional input signals.

Figure 3.7 Spaceball.

We shall not use three-dimensional input in our code, although there is nothing in the API that restricts the input to two dimensions.

3.2.2 Logical Devices

We can now return to looking at input from inside the application program—that is, from the logical point of view. Two major characteristics describe the logical behavior of an input device: (1) the measurements that the device returns to the user program, and (2) the time when the device returns those measurements.

Some APIs, such as PHIGS and GKS, consider six classes of logical input devices. Because input in a modern window system cannot always be disassociated completely from the properties of the physical devices, OpenGL does not take this approach. Nevertheless, we describe the six classes briefly, because they show the variety of input forms that a developer of graphical applications may want, and they also show how OpenGL can provide similar functionality.

1. **String**   A string device is a logical device that provides ASCII strings to the user program. Usually, this logical device is implemented by means of a physical keyboard. In this case, the terminology is consistent with the terminology used in most window systems and OpenGL, which do not distinguish between the logical string device and the keyboard.
2. **Locator**   A locator device provides a position in world coordinates to the user program. It is usually implemented by means of a pointing device, such as a mouse or a trackball. In OpenGL, we usually use the pointing device in this manner, although we have to do the conversion from screen coordinates to world coordinates within our own programs.
3. **Pick**   A pick device returns the identifier of an object to the user program. It is usually implemented with the same physical device as a locator but has a separate software interface to the user program. In OpenGL, we can use a process called *selection* to accomplish picking.
4. **Choice**   Choice devices allow the user to select one of a discrete number of options. In OpenGL, we can use various widgets provided by the window system. A **widget** is a graphical interactive device, provided by either the window system or a toolkit. Typical widgets include menus, scrollbars, and graphical buttons. Most widgets are implemented as special types of windows. For example, a menu with n selections acts as choice device, allowing us to select one of n alternatives.
5. **Dial**   Dials (or valuators) provide analog input to the user program. Here again, widgets within various toolkits usually provide this facility through graphical devices, such as slidebars.
6. **Stroke**   A stroke device returns an array of locations. Although we can think of a stroke as similar to multiple uses of a locator, it is often implemented such that an action, such as pushing down a mouse button, starts the transfer of data into the specified array, and a second action, such as releasing the button, ends this transfer.

3.2.3 Measure and Trigger

The manner by which physical and logical input devices provide input to an application program can be described in terms of two entities: a measure process and a device trigger. The **measure** of a device is what the device returns to the user program. The **trigger** of a device is a physical input on the device with which the user can signal the computer. For example, the measure of a keyboard contains a string, and the trigger can be the "return" or "enter" key. For a locator, the measure includes the position, and the associated trigger can be a button on the pointing device.

In addition to its obvious parts, the measure can include other information, such as status. For example, a pick device will return in its measure the identifier of the object to which the user is pointing. If the physical device is a mouse, the trigger is a mouse button. When we develop an application program, we have to account for the user triggering the device while she is not pointing to an object. If the measure consists of only an object identifier, we face problems in constructing code that takes care of this situation correctly. We can resolve the problem more easily if part of the measure is a status variable that indicates that the user was not pointing to an object, or that the cursor was outside the window, when the trigger occurred.

3.2.4 Input Modes

In addition to the multiple types of logical input devices, we can obtain the measure of a device in three distinct modes. Each mode is defined by the relationship between the measure process and the trigger. Normally, the initialization of the input device starts a measure process. The initialization may require an explicit function call in some APIs, or it may occur automatically. In either case, once the measure process is started, the measure is taken and placed in a buffer, even though the contents of the buffer may not yet be available to the program. For example, the position of a mouse is tracked continuously by the underlying window system, regardless of whether the application program needs mouse input.

In **request mode**, the measure of the device is not returned to the program until the device is triggered. This input mode is standard in nongraphical applications, such as a typical C program that requires character input. When we use a function such as scanf, the program halts when it encounters this statement and waits while we type characters at our terminal. We can backspace to correct our typing, and we can take as long as we like. The data are placed in a keyboard buffer whose contents are returned to our program only after a particular key, such as the "enter" key (the trigger), is depressed. For a logical device, such as a locator, we can move our pointing device to the desired location, and then trigger the device with its button; the trigger will cause the location to be returned to the application program. The relationship between measure and trigger for request mode is as shown in Figure 3.8.

Figure 3.8 Request mode.

Sample-mode input is immediate. As soon as the function call in the user program is encountered, the measure is returned. Hence, no trigger is needed (Figure 3.9). In sample mode, the user must have positioned the pointing device or entered data using the keyboard before the function call, because the measure is extracted immediately from the buffer.

One characteristic of both request- and sample-mode input in APIs that support them is that the user must identify which device is to provide the input. We usually interface with the devices through functions such as

```
request_locator(device_id, &measure);
sample_locator(device_id, &measure);
```

which have as their parameters the identifier of the particular device and a location in the user program to place the measure of the device. Consequently, we ignore any other information that becomes available from any input device other than the one specified in the function call. Both request and sample modes are useful for situations where the program guides the user, but are not useful in applications where the user controls the flow of the program. For example, a flight simulator might have multiple input devices—such as a joystick, dials, buttons, and switches—most of which can be used at any time by the pilot. Writing programs to control the simulator with only sample- and request-mode input is nearly impossible, because we do not know what devices the pilot will use at any point in the simulation. More generally, sample- and request-mode input are not sufficient for handling the variety of possible human–computer interactions that arise in a modern computing environment.

Our third mode, **event mode**, can handle these other interactions. We introduce it in three steps. First, we show how event mode can be described as another mode within our measure–trigger paradigm. Second, we discuss the basics of client and servers where event mode is the preferred interaction mode. Third, we show an event-mode interface to OpenGL using GLUT, and we write demonstration programs using this interface.

Suppose that we are in an environment with multiple input devices, each with its own trigger and each running a measure process. Each time that a device

Figure 3.9 Sample mode.

Figure 3.10 Event–mode model.

is triggered, an **event** is generated. The device measure, with the identifier for the device, is placed in an **event queue**. This process of placing events in the event queue is completely independent of what the application program does with these events. One way that the application program can work with events is shown in Figure 3.10. The user program can examine the front event in the queue or, if the queue is empty, can wait for an event to occur. If there is an event in the queue, the program can look at the event's type and then decide what to do. This method is used in the APIs for GKS and PHIGS.

Another approach is to associate a function called a **callback** with a specific type of event. We take this approach, because it is the one currently used with the major windowing systems and because it has been proved to work well in client–server environments.

3.3 Clients and Servers

So far, our approach to input has been isolated from all other activities that might be happening in our computing environment. We have looked at our graphics system as a monolithic box that has limited connections to the outside world, other than through our carefully controlled input devices and a display. Networks and multiuser computing have changed this picture dramatically, and to such an extent that, even if we had a single-user isolated system, its software probably would be configured as a simple client–server network.

If computer graphics is to be useful for a variety of real applications, it must function well in a world of distributed computing and networks. In this world, our building blocks are entities called **servers** that can perform tasks for **clients**. Clients and servers can be distributed over a network (Figure 3.11) or contained entirely within a single computational unit. Familiar examples of servers include print servers, which can allow sharing of a high-speed printer among users; compute servers, such as remotely located supercomputers, accessible from user programs; file servers that allow users to share files and programs, regardless of into what machine they are logged; and terminal servers that handle dial-in access. Users and user programs that make use of these services are clients or client programs.

It is less obvious what we should call a workstation connected to the network: It can be both a client and a server, or, perhaps more to the point, a workstation may run client programs and server programs concurrently.

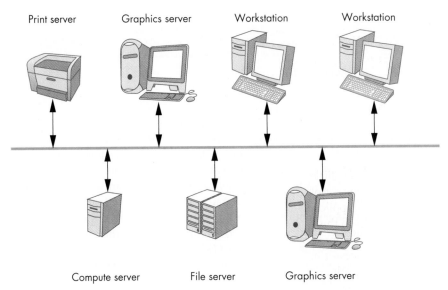

Figure 3.11 Network.

The model that we use here was popularized by the X Window system. We use much of that system's terminology, which is now common to most window systems and fits well with graphical applications.

A workstation with a raster display, a keyboard, and a pointing device, such as a mouse, is a **graphics server**. The server can provide output services on its display, and input services through the keyboard and pointing device. These services potentially are available to clients anywhere on the network.

Our OpenGL application programs are clients that use the graphics server. Within an isolated system, this distinction may not be apparent as we write, compile, and run the software on a single machine. However, we also can run the same application program using other graphics servers on the network.

3.4 Display Lists

Display lists illustrate how we can use clients and servers on a network to improve interactive graphics performance. Display lists have their origins in the early days of computer graphics. As we saw in Chapter 1, the original architecture of a graphics system was based on a general-purpose computer (or host) connected, through digital-to-analog converters, to a CRT (Figure 3.12). The computer would send out the necessary information to redraw the display at a rate sufficient

Figure 3.12 Simple graphics architecture.

to avoid noticeable flicker.[2] At that time (circa 1960), computers were slow and expensive, so the cost of keeping even a simple display refreshed was prohibitive for all but a few applications.

The solution to this problem was to build a special-purpose computer, called a **display processor**, with an organization like that illustrated in Figure 3.13. The display processor had a limited instruction set, most of which was oriented toward drawing primitives on the CRT. The user program was processed in the host computer, resulting in a compiled list of instructions that was then sent to the display processor, where the instructions were stored in a **display memory** as a **display file** or **display list**. For a simple noninteractive application, once the display list was sent to the display processor, the host was free for other tasks, and the display processor would execute its display list repeatedly at a rate sufficient to avoid flicker. In addition to resolving the bottleneck due to burdening the host, the display processor introduced the advantages of special-purpose rendering hardware.

Today, the display processor of old has become a graphics server, and the user program on the host computer has become a client. The major bottleneck is no longer the rate at which we have to refresh the display (although that is still a significant problem), but rather the amount of traffic that passes between the client and server. In addition, the use of special-purpose hardware now characterizes high-end systems.

We can send graphical entities to a display in one of two ways. We can send the complete description of our objects to the graphics server. For our typical geometric primitives, this transfer entails sending vertices, attributes, and primitive types, in addition to viewing information. In our fundamental mode of operation, **immediate mode**, as soon as the program executes a statement that defines a primitive, that primitive is sent to the server for display, and no memory of it is retained in the system.[3] To redisplay the primitive after a clearing of the screen, or in a new position after an interaction, the program must redefine the

---

2. This rate depends on the phosphors in the CRT, but we usually assume it to be in the range of 50 to 85 Hz, or one-half that rate if the display is interlaced.

3. The *image* of the primitive is retained in the frame buffer, but objects and images are not the same.

Figure 3.13 Display-processor architecture.

primitive and then must resend the primitive to the display. For complex objects in highly interactive applications, this process can cause a considerable quantity of data to pass from the client to the server.

Display lists offer an alternative to this method of operation. This second method is called **retained-mode** graphics. We define the object once, then put its description in a display list. The display list is stored in the server and redisplayed by a simple function call issued from the client to the server. In addition to conferring the obvious advantage of reduced network traffic, this model also allows the client to take advantage of any special-purpose graphics hardware that might be available in the graphics server. Thus, in many situations, the optimum configuration consists of a good numerical-processing computer that executes the client program and a special-purpose graphics computer for the server—an old idea used with great efficiency in modern systems.

There are, of course, a few disadvantages to the use of display lists. Display lists require memory on the server, and there is the overhead of creating a display list. Although this overhead often is offset by the efficiency of the execution of the display list, it might not be if the data are changing.

3.4.1 Definition and Execution of Display Lists

Display lists have much in common with ordinary files. There must be a mechanism to define (create) and manipulate (place information in) them. The definition of what contents of a display list are permissible should be flexible enough to allow considerable freedom to the user. OpenGL[4] has a small set of functions to manipulate display lists, and places only a few restrictions on display-list contents. We develop several simple examples to show the functions' use.

Display lists are defined similarly to geometric primitives. There is a `glNewList` at the beginning and a `glEndList` at the end, with the contents in between. Each

---

4. PHIGS contains *structures* and GKS contains *segments*, both of which provide many of the characteristics of OpenGL display lists.

display list must have a unique identifier—an integer that is usually macro-defined in the C program by means of a #define directive to an appropriate name for the object in the list. For example, the following code defines a red box. The code is similar to code from Chapter 2, but this time places the information in a display list:

```
#define BOX 1 /* or some other unused integer */

glNewList(BOX,  GL_COMPILE);
    glBegin(GL_POLYGON);
        glColor3f(1.0, 0.0, 0.0);
        glVertex2f(-1.0, -1.0);
        glVertex2f( 1.0, -1.0);
        glVertex2f( 1.0,  1.0);
        glVertex2f(-1.0,  1.0);
    glEnd();
glEndList();
```

The flag GL_COMPILE tells the system to send the list to the server but not to display its contents. If we want an immediate display of the contents, we can use the GL_COMPILE_AND_EXECUTE flag instead.

Each time that we wish to draw the box on the server, we execute the function

```
glCallList(BOX);
```

Just as it does with other OpenGL functions, the present state determines which transformations are applied to the primitives in the display list. Thus, if we change the model-view or projection matrices between executions of the display list, the box will appear in different places or even will no longer appear, as the following code fragment demonstrates:

```
glMatrixMode(GL_PROJECTION);
for(i= 1 ; i<5; i++)
{
    glLoadIdentity();
    gluOrtho2D(-2.0*i  , 2.0*i , -2.0*i , 2.0*i );
    glCallList(BOX);
}
```

Each time that glCallList is executed, the box is redrawn, albeit with a different clipping rectangle.

In succeeding chapters, we introduce various transformation matrices that will enable us to use display lists for modeling. Note that, because we can change state from within a display list, we have to be careful to avoid allowing these changes to have undesirable—and often unexpected—effects later. For example, our box display list changes the drawing color. Each time that the display list is executed, the drawing color is set to red; unless the color is set to some other value, primitives defined subsequently in the program also will be colored red. The easiest safeguard is to use the matrix and attribute stacks provided by OpenGL. A **stack** is a data structure in which the item placed most recently in the structure is the first removed. We can save the present values of attributes and matrices by placing, or **pushing**, them on the top of the appropriate stack; we can recover them later by removing, or **popping**, them from the stack. A standard—and safe—procedure is always to push both the attributes and matrices on their own stacks when we enter a display list, and to pop them when we exit. Thus, we usually see the function calls

```
glPushAttrib(GL_ALL_ATTRIB_BITS);
glPushMatrix();
```

at the beginning of a display list, and

```
glPopAttrib();
glPopMatrix();
```

at the end. We use matrix and attributes stacks extensively in Chapter 9 to build and display hierarchical models.

A few additional functions are available that make it easier to work with display lists. Often, we want to work with multiple display lists, as we demonstrate with the next example. We can create multiple lists with consecutive identifiers more easily if we use the function glGenLists(number), which returns the first integer (or base) of number consecutive integers that are unused labels. The function glCallLists allows us to execute multiple display lists with a single function call. Text generation is a good example of how we can make excellent use of the options available through display lists. Section 3.4.2 contains OpenGL details; you may want to skip it the first time that you read this chapter. It illustrates the flexibility that the API provides to the application programmer for dealing with troublesome problems that arise in working with text. We encounter many of these issues again in Chapter 9 when we discuss graphics and the World Wide Web.

3.4.2 Text and Display Lists

In Chapter 2, we introduced both stroke and raster text. Regardless of which type we choose to use, we need a reasonable amount of code to describe a set of characters. For example, suppose that we use a raster font in which each character is stored as a 12×10 pattern of bits. It takes 15 bytes to store each character. If we want to display a string by the most straightforward method, we can send each character to the server each time that we want it displayed. This transfer requires the movement of at least 15 bytes per character. If we define a stroke font using only line segments, each character can require a different number of lines. If we use filled polygons for characters, as in Figure 3.14, we see that an "I" is fairly simple to define, but we may need many line segments to get a sufficiently smooth "O." On the average, we need many more than 15 bytes per character to represent a stroke font. For applications that display large quantities of text, sending each character to the display every time that it is needed can place a significant burden on our graphics systems.

A more efficient strategy is to define the font once, using a display list for each character, and then to store the font on the server using these display lists. This solution is similar to what is done for bitmap fonts on standard alphanumeric display terminals. The patterns are stored in read-only memory (ROM) in the terminal, and each character is selected and displayed based on a single byte: its ASCII code. The difference here is one of both quantity and quality. We can define as many fonts as our display memory can hold, and we can treat stroke fonts like other graphical objects, allowing us to translate, scale, and rotate them as desired.

The basics of defining and displaying a character string (1 byte per character) using a stroke font and display lists provide a simple but important example of the use of display lists in OpenGL. The procedure is essentially the same for a raster font. We can define either the standard 96 printable ASCII characters or we can define patterns for a 256-character extended ASCII character set.

First, we define a function OurFont(char c), which will draw any ASCII character c that can appear in our string. The function might have a form like

```
void OurFont(char c)
    {
        switch(c)
        {
            case 'a':
                . . .
            break;
            case 'A':
                . . .
            break;
                . . .
        }
    }
```

Within each case, we have to be careful about the spacing; each character in the string must be displayed to the right of the previous character. We can use the translate function glTranslate to get the desired spacing. Suppose that we are defining the letter "O," and we wish it to fit in a unit square. The corresponding part of OurFont might be

```
case 'O':
    glTranslatef(0.5, 0.5, 0.0); /* move to center */
    glBegin{GL_QUAD_STRIP);
    for (i=0; i<=12; i++)  /* 12 vertices */
```

(a) Input Output

(b)

Figure 3.14 Stroke characters. (a) Filled strings. (b) Magnified outlines.

```
      {
            angle = 3.14159 /6.0 * i; /* 30 degrees in radians */
            glVertex2f(0.4*cos(angle); 0.4*sin(angle));
            glVertex2f(0.5*cos(angle), 0.5*sin(angle));
      }
      glEnd();
      glTranslatef(0.5, -0.5, 0.0); /* move to lower right */
      break;
```

This code approximates the circle with 12 quadrilaterals. Each will be filled according to the present state. Although we do not discuss the full power of transformations until Chapter 4, here we explain the use of the translation function in this code. We are working with two-dimensional characters. Hence, each character is defined in the plane $z = 0$, and we can use whatever coordinate system we wish to define our characters. We assume that each character fits inside a box.[5] The usual strategy is to start at the lower-left corner of the first character in the string, and to draw one character at a time, drawing each character such that we end at the lower-right corner of that character's box, which is the lower-left corner of the successor's box.

The first translation moves us to the center of the "O" character's box, which we set to be a unit square. We then define our vertices using two concentric circles centered at this point (Figure 3.15). One way to envision the translation function is to say that it shifts the origin for all the drawing commands that follow. After the 12 quadrilaterals in the strip are defined, we move to the lower-right corner of the box. The two translations accumulate; as a result of these translations, we are in the proper position to start the next character. Note that, in this example, we do not want to push and pop the matrices. Other characters can be defined in a similar manner.

Although our code is inelegant, its efficiency is of little consequence, because the characters are generated only once and then are sent to the graphics server as a compiled display list.

Suppose that we want to generate a 256-character set. The required code, using the OurFont function, is as follows:

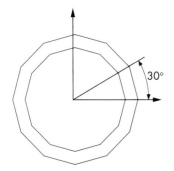

Figure 3.15 Drawing of the letter "O."

```
base = glGenLists(256); /* return index of first of 256
                           consecutive available ids */
for(i=0; i<256; i++)
{
      glNewList(base + i, GL_COMPILE);
      OurFont(i);
      glEndList();
}
```

---

5. Each character may have a different size and thus be in a box of unique dimensions, or, if we are defining a fixed-width monotype font (such as the one used to set code in this book), all characters will have boxes of the same size.

When we wish to use these display lists to draw individual characters, rather than offsetting the identifier of the display lists by base each time, we can set an offset with

```
glListBase(base);
```

Finally, our drawing of a string is accomplished in the server by the function call

```
char *text_string;
```

```
glCallLists( (GLint) strlen(text_string), GL_BYTE, text_string);
```

which makes use of the standard C library function strlen to find the length of input string text_string. The first argument in the function glCallLists is the number of lists to be executed. The third is a pointer to an array of a type given by the second argument. The identifier of the kth display list executed is the sum of the list base (established by glListBase) and the value of the kth character in the array of characters.

3.4.3 Fonts in GLUT

In general, we prefer to use an existing font, rather than to define our own. GLUT provides a few raster and stroke fonts.[6] They do not make use of display lists; in the final example in this chapter, however, we create display lists to contain one of these GLUT fonts. We can access a single character from a **monotype**, or evenly spaced, font by the function call

```
glutStrokeCharacter(GLUT_STROKE_MONO_ROMAN, int character)
```

GLUT_STROKE_ROMAN provides proportionally spaced characters. You should use these fonts with caution. Their size (approximately 120 units maximum) may have little to do with the units of the rest of your program; thus, they may have to be scaled. We usually control the position of a character by using a translation before the character function is called. In addition, each invocation of glutStrokeCharacter includes a translation to the bottom right of the character's box, to prepare for the next character. Scaling and translation affect the OpenGL state, so here we should be careful to use glPushMatrix and glPopMatrix as necessary, to prevent undesirable positioning of objects defined later in the program.

Raster or bitmap characters are produced in a similar manner. For example, a single 8×13 character is obtained using

```
glutBitmapCharacter(GLUT_BITMAP_8_BY_13, int character)
```

---

6. We can also access fonts that are provided by the windowing system at the expense of code portability.

Positioning of bitmap characters is considerably simpler than is that of stroke characters, because bitmap characters are drawn directly in the frame buffer and are not subject to geometric transformations, whereas stroke characters are. OpenGL keeps, within its state, a **raster position**. This position identifies where the next raster primitive will be placed; it can be set using the function `glRaster-Pos*()`. The user program typically moves the raster position one character to the right each time that `glutBitmapCharacter` is invoked. This change does not affect subsequent rendering of geometric primitives. If characters have different widths, we can use the function `glutBitmapWidth(font, char)` to return the width of a particular character. Thus, when we define a sequence of characters, we often see code such as

```
glRasterPos2i(rx, ry);
glutBitmapCharacter(GLUT_BITMAP_8_BY_13, k);
rx+=glutBitmapWidth(GLUT_BITMAP_8_BY_13, k);
```

We use bitmap characters in our example of a painting program later in this chapter, using display lists.

The case for always using display lists is strong, and we return to them when we discuss hierarchical modeling in Chapter 9. At this point, however, we are more interested in clarity and brevity than in efficiency. Hence, we do not use display lists in many of our examples. Most user code can be encapsulated between a `glNewList` and `glEndList`. Thus, you should be able to convert most code to use display lists with little effort.

3.5 Programming Event-Driven Input

In this section, we develop event-driven input through a number of simple examples that use the callback mechanism that we introduced in Section 3.2. We examine various events that are recognized by the window system and, for those of interest to our application, we write callback functions that govern how the application program responds to these events.

3.5.1 Using the Pointing Device

We start by altering the `main` function in the gasket program from Chapter 2. In the original version, we used functions in the GLUT library to put a window on the screen, and then entered the event loop by executing the function `glutMainLoop`. In that chapter, we entered the loop but did nothing. We could not even terminate the program, except through an external mechanism. Our first example will remedy this omission by using the pointing device to terminate a program. We accomplish this task by having the program execute a standard termination function called `exit` when a particular mouse button is depressed.

We discuss only those events recognized by GLUT. A window system such as the X Window system recognizes many more events. However, the GLUT library will recognize a set of events that is common to most window systems, and is sufficient for developing basic interactive graphics programs that can be used with multiple window systems. Two types of events are associated with the pointing device, which is conventionally assumed to be a mouse. A **move event** is generated when the mouse is moved with one of the buttons depressed. If the mouse is moved without a button being held down, this event is classified as a **passive move event**. After a move event, the position of the mouse—its measure—is made available to the application program. A **mouse event** occurs when one of the mouse buttons is either depressed or released. A button being held down does not generate an event until the button is released.[7] The information returned—the measure—includes the button that generated the event, the state of the button after the event (up or down), and the position of the cursor tracking the mouse in screen coordinates. We specify the mouse callback function, usually in the `main` function, by means of the GLUT function

```
glutMouseFunc(mouse)
```

The mouse callback must have the form

```
void mouse(int button, int state, int x, int y)
```

Within the callback function, we define the actions that we want to take place if the specified event occurs. There may be multiple actions defined in the mouse callback function corresponding to the many possible button and state combinations. For our simple example, we want the depression of the left mouse button to terminate the program. The required callback is the single-line function

```
void mouse(int button, int state,
   int x, int y)
{
    if(button == GLUT_LEFT_BUTTON && state == GLUT_DOWN)
            exit();
}
```

If any other mouse event—such as a depression of one of the other buttons—occurs, no response action will occur, because no callback corresponding to these events has been defined, or **registered**, with the window system.

Our next example illustrates the benefits of the program structure that we introduced in the previous chapter. We write a program to draw a small box at each location on the screen where the mouse cursor is located at the time that the left button is pushed. A push of the middle button terminates the program.

---

7. Certain systems count the pushing and the releasing of a button as only a single event.

First, we look at the main program, which is much the same as our previous examples.[8]

```
int main(int argc, char **argv)
{

    glutInit(&argc,argv);
    glutInitDisplayMode(GLUT_SINGLE | GLUT_RGB);
    glutCreateWindow("square");
    myinit();
    glutReshapeFunc(myReshape);
    glutMouseFunc(mouse);
    glutDisplayFunc(display);
    glutMainLoop();
}
```

The **reshape event** is generated whenever the window is resized, such as by a user interaction; we discuss it next. We do not use the required display callback in this example, because the only time that primitives will be generated is when a mouse event occurs. Because GLUT requires that every program have a display callback, we must include this callback, although it can have an empty body:

```
void display(){ }
```

The mouse callbacks are again in the function mouse.

```
void mouse(int btn, int state, int x, int y)
{
  if(btn==GLUT_LEFT_BUTTON && state==GLUT_DOWN) drawSquare(x,y);
  if(btn==GLUT_MIDDLE_BUTTON && state==GLUT_DOWN) exit();
}
```

Because only the primitives are generated in drawSquare, the desired attributes must have been set elsewhere, such as in our initialization function myinit.

We need three global variables. The size of the window may change dynamically, and its present size should be available, both to the reshape callback and to the drawing function drawSquare. If we want to change the size of the squares that we draw, we may find it beneficial also to make the square-size parameter global. Our initialization routine selects a clipping window that is the same size as the window created in main, and selects the viewport to correspond to the entire window. This window is cleared to black. Note that we could omit the setting of the window and viewport here, since we are merely setting them to

---

8. We use naming conventions for callbacks similar to those in the *OpenGL Programmer's Guide* [Ope01a].

the default values. However, it is illustrative to compare this code with what we do in the reshape callback in Section 3.5.2.

```
/* globals */

GLsizei wh = 500, ww = 500; /* initial window size */
GLfloat size = 3.0;   /*one-half of side length of square */

void myinit(void)
{
   /* set viewing conditions */

      glViewport(0,0,ww,wh);
      glMatrixMode(GL_PROJECTION);
      glLoadIdentity();
      gluOrtho2D(0.0, (GLdouble) ww , 0.0, (GLdouble) wh);
      glMatrixMode(GL_MODELVIEW);

      /* set clear color to black, and clear window */

      glClearColor (0.0, 0.0, 0.0, 1.0);
      glClear(GL_COLOR_BUFFER_BIT);
      glFlush();
}
```

Our square-drawing routine has to take into account that the position returned from the mouse event is in the window system's coordinate system, which has its origin at the top left of the window. Hence, we have to flip the y value returned, using the present height of the window (the global wh). We pick a random color using the standard random-number generator rand().

```
void drawSquare(int x, int y)
{

      y=wh-y;
      glColor3ub( (char) rand()%256, (char) rand()%256,
                              (char) rand()%256);
      glBegin(GL_POLYGON);
          glVertex2f(x+size, y+size);
          glVertex2f(x-size, y+size);
          glVertex2f(x-size, y-size);
          glVertex2f(x+size, y-size);
      glEnd();
      glFlush();
}
```

After we insert the necessary include statements, we have a program that works, as long as the window size remains unchanged.

3.5.2 Window Events

Most window systems allow a user to resize the window, usually by using the mouse to drag a corner of the window to a new location. This event is an example of a **window event**. If such an event occurs, the user program can decide what to do.[9] If the window size changes, we have to consider three questions:

1. Do we redraw all the objects that were in the window before it was resized?
2. What do we do if the aspect ratio of the new window is different from that of the old window?
3. Do we change the sizes or attributes of new primitives if the size of the new window is different from that of the old?

There is no single answer to any of these questions. If we are displaying the image of a real-world scene, our reshape function probably should make sure that no shape distortions occur. But this choice may mean that part of the resized window is unused, or that part of the scene cannot be displayed in the window. If we want to redraw the objects that were in the window before it was resized, we need a mechanism for storing and recalling them. Often, we do this recall by encapsulating all drawing in a single function, such as the `display` function used in Chapter 2, which was registered as the display callback function. In the present example, however, that is probably not the best choice, because we decide what we draw interactively.

In our square-drawing example, we ensure that squares of the same size are drawn, regardless of the size or shape of the window. We clear the screen each time that it is resized, and we use the entire new window as our drawing area. The reshape event returns in its measure the height and width of the new window. We use these values to create a new OpenGL clipping window using `gluOrtho2D`, as well as a new viewport with the same aspect ratio. We then clear the window to black. Thus, we have the callback

```
void myReshape(GLsizei w, GLsizei h)
{

    /* adjust clipping box */

    glMatrixMode(GL_PROJECTION);
    glLoadIdentity();
    gluOrtho2D(0.0, (GLdouble)w, 0.0, (GLdouble)h);
    glMatrixMode(GL_MODELVIEW);
    glLoadIdentity();
```

---

9. Unlike most other callbacks, there is a default reshape callback, although it might not do what the user desires.

```
/* adjust viewport and clear */

glViewport(0,0,w,h);
glClearColor (0.0, 0.0, 0.0, 1.0);
glClear(GL_COLOR_BUFFER_BIT);
glFlush();
}
```

The complete square-drawing program is given in Appendix A.

There are other possibilities here. We could change the size of the squares to match the increase or decrease of the window size. We have not considered other events, such as a window movement without resizing, an event that can be generated by a user who drags the window to a new location, and we have not specified what to do if the window is hidden behind another window and then is exposed (brought to the front). There are callbacks for these events, and we can write simple functions similar to myReshape for them, or we can rely on the default behavior of GLUT. Another simple change that we can make to our program is to have new squares generated as long as one of the mouse buttons is held down. The relevant callback is the motion callback, which we set through the function

```
glutMotionFunc(drawSquare);
```

Each time the system senses the motion, a new square is drawn—an action that allows us to draw pictures using a brush with a square tip.

3.5.3 Keyboard Events

We can also use the keyboard as an input device. Keyboard events are generated when the mouse is in the window and one of the keys is depressed. Although in many window systems the release of a key generates a second event, GLUT does not have a callback for this event. The ASCII code for the key pressed and the location of the mouse are returned. All the keyboard callbacks are registered in a single callback function, such as

```
glutKeyboardFunc(keyboard);
```

For example, if we wish to use the keyboard only to exit the program, we can use the callback function

```
void keyboard(unsigned char key, int x, int y)
{
    if(key=='q' || key == 'Q') exit( );
}
```

GLUT includes functions that allow the user to define actions using the meta keys, such as the control and alt keys. These special keys can be important when we are using one- or two-button mice as we can then define the same functionality as having left, right, and middle buttons as we have assumed in this chapter.

3.5.4 The Display and Idle Callbacks

Of the remaining callbacks, two merit special attention. We have already seen the display callback, which we used in Chapter 2. This function is specified in GLUT by the function

```
glutDisplayFunc(display);
```

It is invoked when GLUT determines that the window should be redisplayed. One such situation occurs when the window is opened initially. Because we know that a display event will be generated when the window is first opened, the display callback is a good place to put the code that generates most noninteractive output. GLUT requires every program to have a display callback.

The display callback can be used in other contexts, such as in animations, where various values defined in the program may change. We can also use GLUT to open multiple windows. The state includes the present window, and we can render different objects into different windows by changing the present window. We can also **iconify** a window by replacing it with a small symbol or picture. Consequently, interactive and animation programs will contain many calls for the reexecution of the display function. Rather than call it directly, we use the GLUT function

```
glutPostRedisplay()
```

Using this function, rather than invoking the display callback directly, avoids extra or unnecessary drawings of the screen by setting a flag inside GLUT's main loop indicating that the display needs to be redrawn. At the end of each execution of the main loop, GLUT uses this flag to determine whether the display function will be executed. Thus, using `glutPostRedisplay` ensures that the display will be drawn at most once each time the program goes through the main loop.

The **idle callback** is invoked when there are no other events. Its default is the null function. A typical use of the idle callback is to continue to generate graphical primitives through a display function while nothing else is happening (see Exercise 3.2). We illustrate both the display and the idle callbacks in the paint programs that we develop in Sections 3.8 and 3.9.

We can change most callback functions during program execution by specifying a new callback function. We can also disable a callback by setting its callback function to NULL.

3.5.5 Window Management

GLUT also supports both multiple windows and subwindows of a given window. We can open a second top-level window (with the label "second window") by

```
id=glutCreateWindow("second window");
```

The returned integer value allows us to select this window as the current window into which objects will be rendered by

```
glutSetWindow(id);
```

We can make this window have properties different from those of other windows by invoking the `glutInitDisplayMode` before `glutCreateWindow`. Furthermore, each window can have its own set of callback functions, because callback specifications refer to the present window.

3.6 Menus

We could use our graphics primitives and our mouse callbacks to construct various graphical input devices. For example, we could construct a slidebar as shown in Figure 3.16, using filled rectangles for the device, text for any labels, and the mouse to get the position. Much of the code would be tedious to develop, however, especially if we tried to create visually appealing and effective graphical devices (widgets). Most window systems provide a toolkit that contains a set of widgets, but, because our philosophy is not to restrict our discussion to any particular window system, we shall not discuss the specifics of such widgets sets. Fortunately, GLUT provides one additional feature, **pop-up menus**, that we can use with the mouse to create sophisticated interactive applications.

Figure 3.16 Slidebar.

Using menus involves taking a few simple steps. We must define the entries in the menu. We must link the menu to a particular mouse button. Finally, we must define a callback function corresponding to each menu entry. We can demonstrate simple menus with the example of a pop-up menu that has three entries. The first selection allows us to exit our program. The second and third change the size of the squares in our `drawSquare` function. We name the menu callback `demo_menu`. The function calls to set up the menu and to link it to the right mouse button should be placed in our `main` function. They are

```
glutCreateMenu(demo_menu);
glutAddMenuEntry("quit",1);
glutAddMenuEntry("increase square size", 2);
glutAddMenuEntry("decrease square size", 3);
glutAttachMenu(GLUT_RIGHT_BUTTON);
```

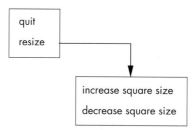

Figure 3.17 Structure of hierarchical menus.

The second argument in each entry's definition is the identifier passed to the callback when the entry is selected. Hence, our callback function is

```
void demo_menu(int id)
{
    if(id == 1) exit( );
    else if (id == 2) size = 2 * size;
    else if (size > 1) size = size/2;
    glutPostRedisplay( );
}
```

The call to glutPostRedisplay requests a redraw through the glutDisplayFunc callback, so that the screen is drawn again without the menu.

GLUT also supports hierarchical menus, as shown in Figure 3.17. For example, suppose that we want the main menu that we create to have only two entries. The first entry still causes the program to terminate, but now the second causes a submenu to pop up. The submenu contains the two entries for changing the size of the square in our square-drawing program. The following code for the menu (which is in main) should be clear:

```
sub_menu = glutCreateMenu(size_menu);
glutAddMenuEntry("Increase square size", 2);
glutAddMenuEntry("Decrease square size", 3);
glutCreateMenu(top_menu);
glutAddMenuEntry("Quit",1);
glutAddSubMenu("Resize", sub_menu);
glutAttachMenu(GLUT_RIGHT_BUTTON);
```

Writing the callback functions, size_menu and top_menu, should be a simple exercise for you (Exercise 3.5).

3.7 Picking

Picking is the logical input operation that allows the user to identify an object on the display. Although the action of picking uses the pointing device, the information that the user wants returned to the application program is not a position. A pick device is considerably more difficult to implement on a modern system than is a locator.

Such was not always the case. Old display processors could accomplish picking easily by means of a lightpen. Each redisplay of the screen would start at a precise time. The lightpen would generate an interrupt when the redisplay passed its sensor. By comparing the time of the interrupt with the time that the redisplay began, the processor could identify an exact place in the display list, and subsequently could determine which object was being displayed.

One reason for the difficulty of picking in modern systems is the forward nature of their rendering pipelines. Primitives are defined in an application program and move forward through a sequence of transformations and clippers until they are rasterized into the frame buffer. Although much of this process is reversible in a mathematical sense, the hardware is not reversible. Hence, converting from a location on the display to the corresponding primitive is not a direct calculation. There are also potential uniqueness problems; see Exercises 3.11 and 3.12.

There are at least three ways to deal with this difficulty. One process, known as **selection**, involves adjusting the clipping region and viewport such that we can keep track of which primitives in a small clipping region are rendered into a region near the cursor. These primitives go into a **hit list** that can be examined later by the user program. OpenGL supports this approach, and we shall discuss it after we discuss two simpler, but less general, strategies.

A simple approach is to use **bounding rectangles**, or **extents**, for objects of interest. The extent of an object is the smallest rectangle, aligned with the coordinates axes, that contains the object. It is relatively easy to determine which rectangles in world coordinates correspond to a particular point in screen coordinates. If the application program maintains a simple data structure to relate objects and bounding rectangles, approximate picking can be done within the application program. We demonstrate a simple example of this approach in Section 3.8.

Another simple approach involves using the back buffer and an extra rendering. Recall that the back buffer is not displayed and thus we can use it for purposes other than forming the image we will display when we swap the front and back buffers. Suppose that we render our objects into the back buffer, each in a distinct color. The application programmer is free to determine an object's contents by simply changing colors wherever a new object definition appears in the program.

We can perform picking in four steps that are initiated by a pick function in the application. First, we draw the objects into the back buffer with the pick colors. Second, we get the position of the mouse using the mouse callback. Third, we use the function glReadPixels() to find the color at the position in the frame buffer corresponding to the mouse position. Finally, we search a table of colors to find which object corresponds to the color read. We must follow this process by a normal rendering into the back buffer. There are some subtleties to the use of glReadPixels(), which we shall consider in Chapter 7.

3.7.1 Picking and Selection Mode

The difficult problem in implementing picking within the OpenGL pipeline is that we cannot go backward directly from the position of the mouse to primitives that were rendered close to that point on the screen. OpenGL provides a somewhat complex process using a rendering mode called **selection mode** to do picking at the cost of an extra rendering each time we that we do a pick. The basic idea of selection mode is that the objects in a scene can be rendered but not necessarily to the color buffer. As we render objects, OpenGL can keep track of which objects render to any chosen area by determining whether they are in a specified clipping volume, which does not have to be the same as the clipping volume used to render into the color buffer. There are a number of steps and functions that are required to do picking. We shall examine each step and then put them together in a simple program. The function glRenderMode lets us select one of three modes: normal rendering to the color buffer (GL_RENDER), selection mode (GL_SELECT), or feedback mode (GL_FEEDBACK). Feedback mode can be used to obtain a list of the primitives that were rendered. We will not discuss this mode. The return value from glRenderMode can be used to determine the number of hits in selection mode or primitives in feedback mode.

When we enter selection mode and render a scene, each primitive that renders within the clipping volume generates a message called a **hit** that is stored in a buffer called the **name stack**. We use the function glSelectBuffer to identify an array for the selection data. There are four functions for initializing the name stack, for pushing and popping information on it, and for manipulating the top entry on the stack. The information that we produce is called the **hit list** and can be examined after the rendering to obtain the information needed for picking. The function

```
void glSelectBuffer(GLsizei n, GLunint *buff)
```

specifies the array buff of size n in which to place selection data. The function

```
void glInitNames()
```

initializes the name stack. The function

```
void glPushName(GLuint name)
```

pushes name on the name stack. The function

```
void glPopName()
```

pops the top name from the name stack. Finally, the function

```
void glLoadName(GLuint name)
```

replaces the top of the name stack with `name`. In general, each object that we wish to identify is a set of primitives to which we assign the same integer name. Before we render the object, we load its name on the name stack. We cannot load a name onto an empty stack, so we usually enter an unused name onto the stack when we initialize it, for example, by

```
glInitNames();
glPushName(0);
```

We usually use the mouse callback to enter selection mode and leave selection mode before the end of the mouse callback. When we return to render mode, `glRenderMode` returns the number of hits that have been processed. We then examine the hit list. We also change the clipping volume within the mouse callback so that we obtain hits in the desired region, usually an area that is close to the location of the mouse. We can set the clipping volume in two ways. We could simply set a the view volume through `gluOrtho2D` (or use other viewing functions). We would probably first want to save the present clipping volume with a `glPushMatrix`. Then any primitive that fell within this new clipping volume would generate a hit regardless of where the mouse is located. This option works for selection, but when we pick we want only those objects that render near the cursor.

Suppose that we want all the objects that render into a small user-defined rectangle centered at the cursor. The size of the rectangle is a measure of how sensitive we want our picking to be. This rectangle is a small part of the viewport. Given the viewport, the location of the cursor, the size of the rectangle, and the clipping window, we can find a new clipping window such that all the objects in the new clipping window render into the full viewport. Mathematically, this is an exercise in proportions and involves the inverse of the projection matrix. We can let OpenGL do this calculation for us through the GLU function `gluPickMatrix`, which is applied before `glOrtho2D` when we are in selection mode. The function call has the form

```
gluPickMatrix( x,y,w,h,*vp);
```

and creates a projection matrix for picking that restricts drawing to a $w \times h$ area centered at (x,y) in window coordinates within the viewport vp. Figure 3.18 illustrates the process for a two-dimensional application. In Figure 3.18(a) we see the normal window and the image on the display. We also see the cursor with a small box around it indicating the area in which, if a primitive is rendered, we will count it as a hit. Figure 3.18(b) shows the window and display after the window has been changed by `gluPickMatrix`. Note that the world window has been changed so that only those objects that were in the pick rectangle are in the new window and these objects now occupy the whole viewport. It is for this reason that we do not want this image to appear on the screen.

Assuming that we have set up the viewing conditions for normal rendering during initialization or in the reshape callback, the mouse and display callbacks are of the form

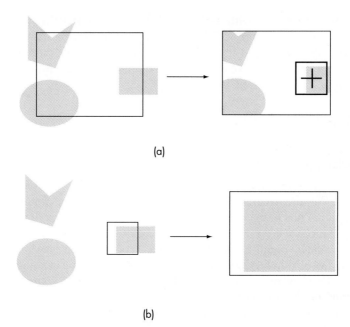

Figure 3.18 (a) Normal window and display. (b) Window and display after applying pick matrix.

```
void mouse(int button, int state, int x, int y )
{
    GLuint nameBuffer[SIZE]; /* define SIZE elsewhere */
    GLint hits;
    GLint viewport[4];
    If( button == GLUT_LEFT_BUTTON && state == GLUT_DOWN)
    {
        /* initialize the name stack */

        glInitNames( );
        glPushName( 0 );
        glSelectBuffer( SIZE, nameBuffer);

        /* set up viewing for selection mode */

        glGetIntegerv(GL_VIEWPORT, viewport);
        glMatrixMode(GL_PROJECTION);

        /* save original viewing matrix */

        glPushMatrix();
        glLoadIdentity( );

        /* N x N pick area around cursor */
```

```
        /* must invert mouse y to get in world coords */

        gluPickMatrix( (GLdouble) x, (GLdouble)
            ( viewport[3] - y), N, N, viewport);

        /* same clipping window as in reshape callback */

        gluOrtho2D (xmin, xmax, ymin, ymax);

        draw_objects(GL_SELECT);
        glMatrixMode(GL_PROJECTION);

        /* restore viewing matrix */

        glPopMatrix();
        glFlush();

        /* return to normal render mode */

        hits = glRendrerMode(GL_RENDER);

        /* process hits from selection mode rendering */

        processHits(hits, nameBuff);

        /* normal render */

        glutPostRedisplay();
    }
}

void display( )
{
    glClear( GL_COLOR_BUFFER_BIT);
    draw_objects(GL_RENDER);
    glFlush();
}
```

Note that we have to call the function that draws the objects directly rather than use glutPostRedisplay twice in the mouse callback because GLUT will only do one execution of the display callback each time through the event loop. Here is a simple function that draws two partially overlapping rectangles:

```
void drawObjects(GLenum mode)
{
    if(mode == GL_SELECT) glLoadName(1);
    glColor3f(1.0, 0.0, 0.0);
    glRectf(-0.5, -0.5, 1.0, 1.0);
```

```
if(mode == GL_SELECT) glLoadName(2);
glColor3f(0.0, 0.0, 1.0);
glRectf(-1.0, -1.0, 0.5, 0.5);
}
```

Note that we need to change only the top element on the name stack. If we had a hierarchical object, as we shall discuss in Chapter 9, we could use glPushName so that we could have multiple names on the stack for a given hit. For an object with multiple parts, all the parts that were close to the cursor would have their names placed in the same stack. The final piece we need to write is the function that examines the name stack. We will have it print out how many were placed in the stack for each left mouse click and the names of any objects that were picked. The hit buffer contains one record for each hit. Thus, every object that is rendered near the mouse cursor will generate a record. If there are no names on the hit list because no primitives were rendered near the mouse cursor, then there is a zero for the hit record. Otherwise, we find three types of information, all stored as integers. First there is the number of names on the name stack when there was a hit. For our example, this number can only be 1. It is followed by two integers which give scaled minimum and maximum depths for the hit primitive. As we are working in two dimensions, these values will not provide us useful information. For three-dimensional applications, we can use these values to determine the front object that was picked. These three integers are followed by entries in the name stack. For our example, we will find the identifier of either the red or the blue rectangle here (a 1 or a 2). The following function will print out this information.

```
void processHits (GLint hits, GLuint buffer[])
{
  unsigned int i, j;
  GLuint names, *ptr;

  printf ("hits = %d\n", hits);
  ptr = (GLuint *) buffer;

   /* Loop over number of hits */

  for (i = 0; i < hits; i++)
   {
      names = *ptr;

      /*skip over number of names and depths */

      ptr += 3;

      /* check each name in record */

     for (j = 0; j < names; j++)
```

```
      {
       if(*ptr==1) printf ("red rectangle\n");
       else printf ("blue rectangle\n");

      /* go to next hit record */

        ptr++;
      }
    }
}
```

Picking presents a number of other difficulties for the implementor. One is that, if an object is defined hierarchically, like those we discuss in Chapter 9, then it is a member of a set of objects. When the object is indicated by the pointing device, a list of all objects in the set of which it is a member should be returned to the user program.

Graphics APIs usually do not specify how close to an object we must point for the object to be identified. One reason for this omission is to allow multiple ways of picking. For example, if we use the bounding-rectangle strategy, we might not point to any point contained in the object. Another reason for this lack of preciseness is that humans are not accurate at positioning devices. Although the display at which we point might have a high resolution, we may find it difficult to indicate reliably with our pointing device the location on the screen corresponding to a given pixel.

3.8 A Simple Paint Program

We illustrate the use of callbacks, display lists, and interactive program design by developing a simple paint program. Paint programs have most of the features of sophisticated CAD programs. Any paint program should demonstrate most of the following features:

- It should have the ability to work with geometric objects, such as line segments and polygons. Given that geometric objects are defined through vertices, the program should allow us to enter vertices interactively.
- It should have the ability to manipulate pixels, and thus to draw directly into the frame buffer.
- It should provide control of attributes such as color, line type, and fill patterns.
- It should include menus for controlling the application.
- It should behave correctly when the window is moved or resized.

Our sample program demonstrates these principles, and incorporates many of the features that we introduced in the small examples that we have developed.

Figure 3.19 shows the initial display that a user sees. The five boxes are buttons that select from the five drawing modes: line segment, rectangle, triangle,

Figure 3.19 Initial display of paint program.

pixel, and text. The left mouse button selects the mode. If line-segment mode is selected, the next two clicks of the left mouse button while the cursor is outside the menu area give the locations of the endpoints. After the second endpoint is located, the line segment is drawn in the present color. Rectangle and triangle modes are similar: In rectangle mode, we select the diagonal corners; in triangle mode, we locate the three vertices. A new mode can be selected at any time. In pixel mode, successive mouse clicks give positions for randomly colored rectangles that can have a side length of two or more pixels. In text mode, the user types in a string of characters that appear on the display starting where the mouse was clicked most recently.

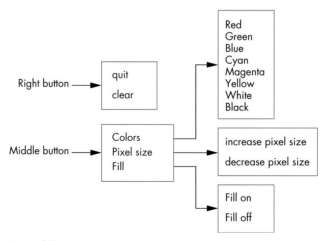

Figure 3.20 Menu structure of paint program.

The menus (Figure 3.20) are controlled by the middle and right mouse buttons. The right button allows us either to clear the screen or to terminate the program. The middle button allows us to change the drawing color, to select between fill and no fill for the triangles and rectangles, and to change the size of the pixel rectangles.

The most difficult part of the design process is deciding what functionality to place in each of the functions. The decisions reflected in our code are consistent with our previous examples. Many of the functions in our program are the same as those in our previous examples. We employ the following functions:

```
void mouse(int btn, int state , int x, int y); /* mouse callback */
void key( unsigned char c, int x, int y);      /* keyboard callback */
void display(void);                            /* display callback */
void drawSquare(int x, int y);                 /* random--color square
                                                  function*/

void myReshape(GLsizei, GLsizei);              /* reshape callback */
void myinit(void);                             /* initialization function */
void screen_box(int x, int y, int s);          /* box--drawing
                                                  function */


void right_menu(int id);                       /* menu callbacks */
void middle_menu(int id);
void color_menu(int id);
void pixel_menu(int id);
void fill_menu(int id);
int pick(int x, int y);                        /* mode--selection
                                                  function */
```

We have used most of these functions in our previous examples; thus, the main function is similar to the main function in our other examples:

```
int main(int argc, char **argv)
{
    int c_menu, p_menu, f_menu;

    glutInit(&argc,argv);
    glutInitDisplayMode (GLUT_SINGLE | GLUT_RGB);
    glutCreateWindow("Paint");
    glutDisplayFunc(display);
    c_menu = glutCreateMenu(color_menu);
    glutAddMenuEntry("Red",1);
    glutAddMenuEntry("Green",2);
    glutAddMenuEntry("Blue",3);
    glutAddMenuEntry("Cyan",4);
    glutAddMenuEntry("Magenta",5);
    glutAddMenuEntry("Yellow",6);
    glutAddMenuEntry("White",7);
    glutAddMenuEntry("Black",8);
```

```
p_menu = glutCreateMenu(pixel_menu);
glutAddMenuEntry("increase pixel size", 1);
glutAddMenuEntry("decrease pixel size", 2);
f_menu = glutCreateMenu(fill_menu);
glutAddMenuEntry("fill on", 1);
glutAddMenuEntry("fill off", 2);
glutCreateMenu(right_menu);
glutAddMenuEntry("quit",1);
glutAddMenuEntry("clear",2);
glutAttachMenu(GLUT_RIGHT_BUTTON);
glutCreateMenu(middle_menu);
glutAddSubMenu("Colors", c_menu);
glutAddSubMenu("Pixel size", p_menu);
glutAddSubMenu("Fill", f_menu);
glutAttachMenu(GLUT_MIDDLE_BUTTON);
myinit ();
glutReshapeFunc (myReshape);
glutMouseFunc (mouse);
glutKeyboardFunc(key);
glutMainLoop();

}
```

The function myinit clears the window, sets up global variables, and defines and compiles display lists for 128 characters.

```
void myinit(void)
{
/* set up a font in display list */
    int i;
    base = glGenLists(128);
    for(i=0;i<128;i++)
    {
            glNewList(base+i, GL_COMPILE);
            glutBitmapCharacter(GLUT_BITMAP_9_BY_15, i);
    /* change to a stroke font by substituting next line */
            /*glutStrokeCharacter(GLUT_STROKE_ROMAN,i); */
            glEndList();
    }
    glListBase(base);

    glViewport(0,0,ww,wh);

/* Pick 2D clipping window to match size of X window.
This choice avoids the need to scale object coordinates
each time that the window is resized */
```

```
        glMatrixMode(GL_PROJECTION);
        glLoadIdentity();
        glOrtho(0.0, (GLdouble) ww , 0.0, (GLdouble) wh ,
                                -1.0, 1.0);

/* set clear color to white and clear window */

        glClearColor (1.0, 1.0, 1.0, 1.0);
        glClear(GL_COLOR_BUFFER_BIT);
        glFlush();
}
```

The function display clears the window, sets the background to white, and then draws the buttons. The buttons are drawn as rectangles with sides that are 10% of the window height and width; they thus change size when the window is resized. Otherwise, the code here draws only simple primitives.

The function myReshape is the same reshape callback that we introduced in Section 3.5.

The function pick detects which object on the screen has been selected by the mouse and thus works in conjunction with the mouse callback function mouse. OpenGL supports a method for doing general object selection that is complex to implement. When we are interested in only rectangular areas of the screen, such as the drawing area and the buttons, it is simpler to implement our own pick method within the application program. Our procedure works as follows. Once a mouse event is detected, mouse uses pick to identify on which part of the screen the mouse is located. Because the buttons are rectangular boxes, we can detect directly whether the mouse is inside a button or in the drawing area; we return this information to mouse, which then does most of the work of drawing. Once an area has been identified by means of pick, the code chooses a proper mode, and determines whether it needs to output a primitive or to store the mouse location. For example, if the user indicated a triangle by first clicking on the appropriate button, the program must store two positions; then, when it receives the third position, it can draw the triangle. The appropriate code in mouse is

```
case (TRIANGLE):        /* pick detected click in triangle box */
    switch(count)       /* switch on number of vertices */
    {
      case(0):          /* store first vertex */
        count++;
        xp[0] = x;
        yp[0] = y;
        break;
      case(1):          /* store second vertex */
        count++;
        xp[1] = x;
        yp[1] = y;
        break;
```

```
case(2):          /* third vertex: draw triangle */
  if(fill) glBegin(GL_POLYGON);
  else glBegin(GL_LINE_LOOP);
      glVertex2i(xp[0],wh-yp[0]);
      glVertex2i(xp[1],wh-yp[1]);
      glVertex2i(x,wh-y);
  glEnd();
  draw_mode=0;  /* reset mode */
  count=0;
```

Note that the first mouse click selects triangle mode; subsequent clicks count and store vertices. However, if the mouse is clicked on another button before the third vertex is selected, a new object is selected and drawn.

The function key renders characters entered from the keyboard to characters on the display.

```
void key(unsigned char k, int xx, int yy)
{
   if(draw_mode!=TEXT) return; /* draw characters until
                                      mode changes */
   glRasterPos2i(rx,ry);
   glCallList(k);  /* Display list for character k */
   rx+=glutBitmapWidth(GLUT_BITMAP_9_BY_15,k);
}
```

A typical display from the middle of a drawing is shown in Figure 3.21. Although our paint program is simple and is limited in the facilities that it provides the user, we should be able to add more functionality easily. Straightforward

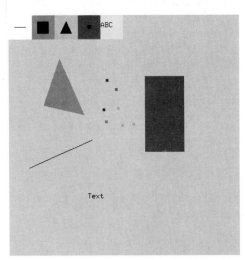

Figure 3.21 Output from painting program.

exercises are adding the ability to switch from raster to stroke text, allowing multiple fonts, adding line attributes (width and type), allowing selection of fill methods (solid or patterns), and adding more objects (arbitrary polygons, circle approximations, and curves). However, making the paint program function as smoothly as commercial products do is much more difficult (although possible), for reasons that we discuss in Section 3.9

The complete program is given in Appendix A.

3.9 Animating Interactive Programs

So far, our programs have been static; once a primitive was placed on the display, its image did not change until the screen was cleared. Suppose that we want to create a picture in which one or more objects are changing or moving, and thus their images must change. For example, we might want to have an animated character walk across the display, or we might want to move the viewer over time. We can gain insight into how we can handle these cases through a simple example in which we have a single rotating object.

3.9.1 The Rotating Square

Consider a two-dimensional point where

$$x = \cos \theta,$$
$$y = \sin \theta.$$

This point lies on a unit circle regardless of the value of θ. The three points $(-\sin \theta, \cos \theta)$, $(-\cos \theta, -\sin \theta)$, and $(\sin \theta, -\cos \theta)$ also lie on the unit circle, and the four points are equidistant apart along the circumference of the circle, as shown in Figure 3.22. Thus, if we connect the points to form a polygon, we will have a square centered at the origin whose sides are of length $\sqrt{2}$.

Assuming that the value of θ is a global variable, we can display this cube with the display function

```
void display()
{
  glClear(GL_COLOR_BUFFER_BIT);
  glBegin(GL_POLYGON);
    thetar = theta/((2*3.14159)/360.0); /* convert degrees
                                            to radians */
    glVertex2f(cos(thetar), sin(thetar));
    glVertex2f(-sin(thetar), cos(thetar));
    glVertex2f(-cos(thetar), -sin(thetar));
    glVertex2f(sin(thetar), -cos(thetar));
  glEnd();
}
```

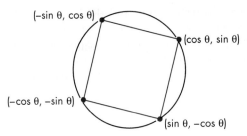

figure 3.22 Square constructed from four points on a circle.

Our display function will work for any value of θ, but suppose that we change θ as the program is running, thus rotating the square about the origin. We can display the rotated cube by simply reexecuting the display function through a call to glutPostRedisplay.

Now suppose that we want to increase θ by a fixed amount whenever nothing else is happening. We can use the idle callback for this operation. Thus, in our main program, we specify the idle callback

```
glutIdleFunc(idle);
```

and define the function as

```
void idle()
{
  theta+=2 /* or some other amount */
  if(theta >= 360.0 theta-=360.0;
  glutPostRedisplay();
}
```

This program will work, but we want to make one further change: We would like to be able to turn on and turn off the rotation feature. We can accomplish this change by using the mouse function to change the idle function. We identify the mouse callback as

```
glutMouseFunc(mouse)
```

Then, this function can be written as

```
void mouse(int button, int state, int x, int y)
{
  if(button==GLUT_LEFT_BUTTON&&state==GLUT_DOWN)
     glutIdleFunc(idle);
  if(button==GLUT_MIDDLE_BUTTON&&state=GLUT_DOWN)
     glutIdleFunc(NULL);
}
```

Thus, the left mouse button starts the cube rotating, and the middle mouse button stops the rotation. We call the full program `single_double.c`; it is given in Appendix A. If you run the program, the display probably will not look like a rotating cube. Rather, you will see parts of cubes changing over time. What went wrong? We consider this question next.

3.9.2 Double Buffering

When we redisplay our CRT, we want to do so at a rate sufficiently high that we cannot notice the clearing and redrawing of the screen. For most of us, a CRT display must be refreshed at a rate between 50 and 85 times per second, or we will notice the display flickering. In a graphics system, this requirement means that the contents of the frame buffer must be redrawn at this refresh rate. As long as the contents of the frame buffer are unchanged and we refresh at the 50- to 85-Hz rate, we should not notice the refresh taking place.[10] If we change the contents of the frame buffer during a refresh, we may see undesirable artifacts of how we generate the display.

One manifestation of this problem occurs if the display being drawn is complex and cannot be drawn in a single refresh cycle. In this case, we see different parts of objects on successive refreshes. If an object is moving, its image may be distorted on the display. Another example occurs with the repetitive clearing and redrawing of an area of the screen, as occurs in our rotating square program. Even though the square is a simple object and is rendered in a refresh cycle, in our program there is no coupling between when new cubes are drawn into the frame buffer and when the frame buffer is redisplayed by the hardware. Thus, depending on exactly when the frame buffer is displayed, only part of the square may be in this buffer.

Double buffering can provide a solution to these problems. Suppose that we have two color buffers at our disposal, conventionally called the front and back buffers. The **front buffer** always is the one displayed, whereas the **back buffer** is the one into which we draw. We can swap the front and back buffers at will from the application program. When we swap buffers, a display callback is invoked. Hence, if we put our rendering into the display callback, the effect will be to update the back buffer automatically. We can set up double buffering by using the option `GLUT_DOUBLE`, instead of `GLUT_SINGLE` in `glutInitDisplayMode`. The buffer-swap function using GLUT is

```
glutSwapBuffers();
```

---

10. If the display is interlaced, the odd and even lines in the frame buffer are displayed alternately, giving a true refresh rate of one-half of the specified rate. On such displays, you probably will notice the slight shifts of objects up and down on alternate refresh cycles.

If we have a complex display to generate, we can draw it into the back buffer, using multiple refresh cycles if needed, and swap buffers when done.

Double buffering is standard in animation, where the primitives, attributes, and viewing conditions may change continuously. We can generate a smooth display using double buffering by putting the drawing functions into a display callback. Within this callback, the first step is to clear the front buffer through `glClear`, and the final step is to invoke `glutSwapBuffers`.

For our rotating cube, we have to make two small changes to go from single to double buffering. First, we request a double buffered display in our `main` function by

```
glutInitDisplayMode(GLUT_RGB | GLUT_DOUBLE);
```

In our display function, we add the line

```
glutSwapBuffers();
```

after we have finished drawing our cube.

Double buffering does not solve all problems that we encounter with animated displays. If the display is complex, we still may need multiple frames to draw the image into the frame buffer. Double buffering does not speed up this process; it only ensures that we never see a partial display. However, we are often able to have visibly acceptable displays at rates as low as 10 to 20 frames per second if we use double buffering.

3.9.3 Other Buffering Problems

There are other problems that arise in interactive programming that cannot be solved with double buffering alone. Returning to our paint program, suppose that we want to add an elapsed-time clock in one corner of the screen to remind our users of how much time they have spent using our program (Figure 3.23).

In most systems, we can obtain the time of day from the system either as an ASCII string or as seconds elapsed since some initial time. By calling this function repeatedly, perhaps as part of the idle callback, we can compute elapsed time in seconds, which we can then convert to another form, such as *hours:minutes:seconds*. Finally, we can attempt to display these numbers as text.

Consider what happens if we add this elapsed-time facility to our original paint program, which used only single buffering because double buffering was not necessary. You will probably notice the elapsed-time clock flickering as the program clears the part of the screen under the clock and redisplays the new time. We can try to fix this problem by changing over to double buffering.

If we do so, the clock part of the display no longer will flicker, but we will have created a more serious problem: The objects we painted will flicker. A moment of thought should reveal the problem. Because we are using immediate-mode graphics, objects that we create by painting are drawn into the frame buffer only

Figure 3.23 Paint program with clock.

once. Each object will be in one of the two buffers, but it will not be in both. Thus, although we have stopped the clock from flickering, the objects that we paint may now flicker.

There are solutions to this problem. For our paint program, we could use display lists to store objects as they are painted. We could then clear the entire frame buffer after each swap and redraw into it all the now retained objects. However, we would have created a much more complex program with significant overhead, especially if we used a new display list for each character or even each pixel that we created. Of course, we could modify such a program so that we could edit and store the images we paint; in general, however, this approach is less than ideal.

What we really would like to do is to have each object that we create by painting appear in both the front buffer and the back buffer. OpenGL supports a variety of buffers that make up the frame buffer. The front and back buffers are color buffers that hold information that can be displayed on the screen. Normally, when we use double buffering, we would like OpenGL to draw into the back buffer, but we can control which color buffer is used for drawing through the function glDrawBuffer(). The default, when double buffering has been enabled, is equivalent to

```
glDrawBuffer(GL_BACK);
```

If we use

```
glDrawBuffer(GL_FRONT_AND_BACK);
```

primitives will be rendered into both the front and back buffers. Thus, by switching the drawing buffer in our program, we can draw the primitives that we specify interactively in both buffers but update the clock only in the back buffer, swapping buffers whenever the clock has been completely redrawn.

In Chapter 7, we shall discuss how some of these buffers can be used to create new effects.

3.10 Design of Interactive Programs

Defining what characterizes a good interactive program is difficult, but recognizing and appreciating a good interactive program is easy. Such programs include features such as these:

1. A smooth display, showing neither flicker nor any artifacts of the refresh process
2. A variety of interactive devices on the display
3. A variety of methods for entering and displaying information
4. An easy-to-use interface that does not require substantial effort to learn
5. Feedback to the user
6. Tolerance for user errors
7. A design that incorporates consideration of both the visual and motor properties of the human

The importance of these features and the difficulty of designing a good interactive program should never be underestimated. The field of human–computer interaction (HCI) is an active one, and we shall not shortchange you by condensing it into a few pages. Our concern in this book is computer graphics; within this topic, our primary interest is rendering. However, there are a few topics common to computer graphics and HCI that we can pursue to improve our interactive programs.

3.10.1 Toolkits, Widgets, and the Frame Buffer

In our paint program, we have used interactive tools, such as pop-up menus, that were provided by GLUT, and graphical buttons that we constructed in our programs. There are many more possibilities, such as slidebars, dials, hot areas of the screen, sound, and icons. Usually, these tools are supplied with various toolkits, although there is nothing to prevent us from writing our own. In general, these toolkits use callbacks to interface with application programs, and should be a simple extension of our development.

However, the simple model of rendering geometric objects into a color buffer is not sufficient to support many of these operations. Two examples illustrate the limitations of geometric rendering and show why, at times, we need to work directly in the frame buffer. First, consider our pop-up menus. When a menu callback is invoked, the menu appears over whatever was on the display. After we make our selection, the menu disappears, and the screen is restored to the state in which it was before the menu was displayed.

Our second example is **rubberbanding**, a technique used for displaying line segments (and other primitives) that change as they are manipulated interactively. In our painting program, we indicated the endpoints of our desired line segment by two successive mouse locations. We did not have a mechanism for ensuring that any particular relationship would hold between these two locations, and we were not able to interact with the display to help us place the points. Suppose that, after we locate the first point, then, as we move the mouse, a line segment is drawn automatically (and is updated on each refresh), from the first location to the present position of the mouse, as shown in Figure 3.24. This process is called **rubberbanding** because the line segment that we see on the display appears to be an elastic band, with one end fixed to the first location and the second end stretched to wherever the cursor moves. Note that, before each new line segment appears, the previous line segment must be erased. Usually, the rubberbanding begins when a mouse button is depressed, and continues until the button is released, at which time a final line segment is drawn.

We cannot implement this sequence of operations using only what we have presented so far. One way to implement these operations is to store the part of the display under the menu (or line) and to copy it back when the menu (or line) is no longer needed. Unfortunately, this description of what we want to do is in terms of what bits are on the display, or, equivalently, of what is contained in the frame buffer. One potential solution does not involve primitives in the application program; it involves only their scan-converted images. Consequently, a set of operations for implementing such operations should be described in terms of the contents of the frame buffer—that is, in terms of blocks of bits with what are called bit-block-transfer (bitblt) operations. We can take this approach once we have discussed bits and pixels in Chapter 7. There is another approach, supported by most OpenGL implementations that can provide many of these capabilities in a simple manner that we shall explore next.

Figure 3.24 Rubber-band line.

3.11 Logic Operations

When a program specifies a primitive that is visible, OpenGL renders it into a set of colored pixels that are written into the present drawing buffer. In the default mode of operation, these pixels simply replace the the corresponding pixels that are already in the frame buffer. Thus, if we start with a color buffer that has been cleared to black and draw a blue rectangle that is 10×10 pixels, then 100 blue pixels are copied into the color buffer, replacing 100 black pixels. In this mode, called **copy or replacement mode**, it does not matter what color the original pixels under the rectangle were before they were colored blue, because the blue pixels replace pixels of any color that were there. Although this mode of writing into a buffer may seem obvious, it is not the only way to do the write operation.

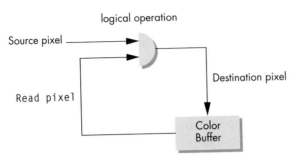

Figure 3.25 Pixel-writing model.

Consider the model in Figure 3.25, where we consider the writing of a single pixel into a color buffer. The pixel that we want to write is called the **source pixel**. The pixel in the drawing buffer that the source pixel will affect is called the **destination pixel**. In copy mode, the source pixel replaces the destination pixel. But suppose that the implementation can first look at the destination pixel and use its value in combination with the source pixel to determine the value to place in the color buffer.

Although we could pick the function that combines the source and destination pixels in an infinite number of ways, most hardware supports only bitwise operations between the pixels. There are 16 possible functions between two bits. Each defines a **writing mode**. We shall discuss these modes in more detail in Chapter 7. At this point, we are interested in two of these functions. The first is replacement mode in which each bit in the source pixel replaces the corresponding bit in the destination pixel.

The other mode is the **exclusive OR** or **XOR mode** in which corresponding bits in each pixel are combined using the exclusive or logical operation. If s and d are corresponding bits in the source and destination pixels, we can denote the new destination bit as d', and it is given by

$$d' = d \oplus s,$$

where $\oplus$ denotes the XOR operation. The most interesting property of the XOR operation is that if we apply it twice, we return to the original state. That is,

$$d = (d \oplus s) \oplus s,$$

Thus, if we draw something in XOR mode, we can erase it by simply drawing it a second time.

OpenGL supports all 16 logic modes. Copy mode (GL_COPY) is the default. If we wish to change modes, we must enable logic operations

```
glEnable(GL_COLOR_LOGIC_OP);
```

and change to XOR mode when desired by

```
glLogicOp(GL_XOR);
```

3.11.1 Drawing Erasable Lines

Using the XOR drawing mode, we can draw erasable lines in a variety of ways. Here is one simple method. Suppose that the OpenGL window is 500×500 pixels and the clipping window is a unit square with the origin at the lower-left corner. We use the mouse to get the first endpoint and store this point in world coordinates

```
xm = x/500.;
ym = (500-y)/500.;
```

We then can get the second point and draw a line segment in XOR mode

```
xmm = x/500.;
ymm = (500-y)/500.;
glLogicOp(GL_XOR);
glBegin(GL_LINES);
    glVertex2f(xm, ym);
    glVertex2f(xmm, ymm);
glEnd();
glLogicOp(GL_COPY);
glFlush();
```

We switch back to copy mode in case we want to draw other objects in the normal mode. If we enter another point with the mouse, we first draw the same line in XOR mode and then a second line using the first endpoint and the mouse input

```
glLogicOp(GL_XOR);
glBegin(GL_LINES);
    glVertex2f(xm, ym);
    glVertex2f(xmm, ymm);
glEnd();
glFlush();
xmm = x/500.0;
ymm = (500-y)/500.0;
glBegin(GL_LINES);
    glVertex2f(xm, ym);
    glVertex2f(xmm, ymm);
glLogicOp(GL_COPY);
glEnd();
glFlush();
```

We can sequence these operations by using the right mouse button to enter these data and the left mouse button to indicate that we accept the line segment and wish to draw it in its final form

```
glLogicOp(GL_COPY);
glBegin(GL_LINES);
    glVertex2f(xm, ym);
    glVertex2f(xmm, ymm);
glEnd();
glFlush();
glLogicOp(GL_XOR);
```

We can keep track of vertices by adding a counter, as in the paint program, to store which endpoint is expected next.

This example is not quite a rubber-band line, which is drawn continuously as the user moves the mouse. We can get rubber-band line by using the same operations in conjunction with a motion callback. Thus, when the user first depresses a designated mouse button, the first location is saved through the mouse callback. As the mouse moves with the key depressed, line segments are drawn from the first point to a second point determined through the motion callback, each time first redrawing the previous line segment to erase it. When the mouse button is released, a final line segment is drawn in copy mode from the mouse callback. Here is the code for a rubber-band rectangle

```
void mouse(int btn, int state, int x, int y)
{

    if(btn==GLUT_LEFT_BUTTON && state == GLUT_DOWN)
    {
        xm = x/500.;
        ym = (500-y)/500.;
        glColor3f(0.0, 0.0, 1.0);
        glLogicOp(GL_XOR);
        first = 0;
    }
    if(btn==GLUT_LEFT && state == GLUT_UP)
    {
        glRectf(xm, ym, xmm, ymm);
        glFlush();
        glColor3f(0.0, 1.0, 0.0);
        glLogicOp(GL_COPY);
        xmm = x/500.0;
        ymm = (500-y)/500.0;
        glLogicOp(GL_COPY);
        glRectf(xm, ym, xmm, ymm);
        glFlush();
    }
}
```

```
void move(int x, int y)
{
    if( first == 1)
    {
        glRectf(xm, ym, xmm, ymm);
        glFlush();
    }
    xmm = x/500.0;
    ymm = (500-y)/500.0;
    glRectf(xm, ym, xmm, ymm);
    glFlush();
    first = 1;
}
```

3.11.2 XOR and Color

If you run our previous example, you should notice some odd color combinations where the temporary lines are drawn over pixels that have already been colored. In the example, we used blue for the temporary color as we did the rubberbanding and green for the final color. Suppose that we are using a system that stores color components to eight bits, so that blue is stored as the 24-bit RGB values (00000000, 00000000, 11111111). Suppose that the screen is cleared to white or (11111111, 11111111, 11111111). Then when we draw the blue line using XOR mode, we will see a line in the RGB color (11111111, 11111111, 00000000) or yellow, rather than blue, because the XOR operation is applied bitwise. It the line crosses a red object, it will be colored magenta inside the object. These possibly annoying visual effects are a consequence of our use of the XOR write mode and should make it clear why a final drawing using copy mode is required.

Another common use of the XOR mode is for drawing a cursor on the display. Cursors can be small rectangles, small crosses, or other shapes. Often in CAD programs we use crosshairs, two perpendicular lines that can extend to rulers on the edge of the display. If these objects are drawn in XOR mode, then we can move them around the screen without distorting anything else on the display. However, if there are objects on the display the color of the objects under the cursor will be altered as the cursor moves across them.

3.11.3 Cursors and Overlay Planes

Rubberbanding and cursors can place a significant burden on graphics systems as they require the display to be updated constantly. Although the use of XOR mode appears to simplify the process, XOR requires the system to read the present destination pixels before computing the new destination pixels. These operations are slower than simply copying source pixels to the frame buffer.

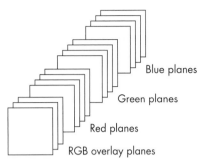

Figure 3.26 Color buffer with overlay planes.

An alternative is to provide hardware support for these types of interaction by providing extra bits in the color buffers by adding what are called **overlay planes**. Thus, a typical color buffer as in Figure 3.26 may have 8 bits for each of red, green, and blue and one red, one green, and one blue overlay plane.

The contents of the overlay planes are independent of what is in the color buffer. In addition, when the color buffer and overlay planes are displayed, the contents of the overlay planes act as if their values were copied into the color buffer. In other words, if there is a bit set in the red overlay plane and the corresponding bits in the blue and green overlay planes are not set, the corresponding point in the window will be red, regardless of what is in the matching 24 bits of the RGB-color buffer.

Overlay planes are a hardware feature and are not present in all systems. GLUT provides support for overlay planes in color index mode.

3.12 Summary and Notes

In this chapter, we have touched on a number of topics related to interactive computer graphics. These interactive aspects make the field of computer graphics exciting and fun. Although our API, OpenGL, is independent of any operating or window system, we recognize that any program must have at least minimal interaction with the rest of the computer system. We handled simple interactions by using a simple toolkit, GLUT, whose API provides the necessary additional functionality, without being dependent on a particular operating or window system.

We have been heavily influenced by the client–server perspective. Not only does it allow us to develop programs within a networked environment, but also it allows us to design programs that are portable yet can still take advantage of special features that might be available in the hardware. These concepts will be crucial in our discussion of object-oriented graphics and graphics for the World Wide Web in Chapter 9.

From the application programmer's perspective, various characteristics of interactive graphics are shared by most systems. We see the graphics part of the system as a server, consisting of a raster display, a keyboard, and a pointing device. In almost all workstations, we have to work within a multiprocessing windowed environment. Most likely, many processes are executing concurrently with the execution of your graphics program. However, the window system allows us to write programs for a specific window that act as though this window is the display device of a single-user system.

The overhead of setting up a program to run in this environment is small. Each application program contains a set of function calls that is virtually the same in every program. The use of logical devices within the application program frees the programmer from worrying about the details of particular hardware.

Within the environment that we have described, event-mode input is the norm. Although the other forms are available—request mode is the normal method used for keyboard input—event-mode input gives us far more flexibility in the design of interactive programs.

Interactive computer graphics is a powerful tool with unlimited applications. At this point, you should be able to write fairly sophisticated interactive programs. Probably the most helpful exercise that you can do now is to write one. The exercises at the end of the chapter provide suggestions.

3.13 Suggested Readings

Sutherland's Project Sketchpad is described in [Sut63].

Many of the conceptual foundations for the windows-icons-menus-pointing interfaces that we now consider routine were developed at the Xerox Palo Alto Research Center (PARC) during the 1970s; see [Sch87]. The mouse also was developed there [Eng68]. The familiar interfaces of today—such as the Macintosh Operating System, the X Window system, and Microsoft Windows—all have their basis in this work.

The volume by Foley and associates [Fol94] contains a thorough description of the development of user interfaces, with an emphasis on the graphical aspects. The books by Schneiderman [Sch97] and Nielson [Nie94] provide an introduction to HCI.

The X Window system [Sch88] was developed at the Massachusetts Institute of Technology and is the de facto standard in the UNIX workstation community. Recently, the development of the LINUX version for PCs has allowed the X Window system to run on these platforms too.

The input and interaction modes that we discussed grew out of the standards that led to GKS [ANSI85] and PHIGS [ANSI88]. These standards were developed for both calligraphic and raster displays; thus, they do not take advantage of the possibilities available on raster-only systems (see [Pik84, Gol83]).

Although we have used the GLUT toolkit [Kil94b] exclusively, we can also interface directly with the X Window system, with various X Window toolkits

[Kil94a, OSF89], and with Microsoft Windows. Also of interest is the use of scripting languages, such as tcl/tk [Ous94], to develop user interfaces that work with OpenGL. Additional details on GLUT are in the OpenGL Primer [Ang02]. There are also some other interface toolkits available for OpenGL. See the OpenGL website www.opengl.org.

Exercises

3.1   Explain problems that you face in defining a stroke font. Create a simple data structure that will allow you to define a set of stroke characters using only line segments.

3.2   Rewrite the Sierpinski-gasket program from Chapter 2 such that the left mouse button will start the generation of points on the screen, the right mouse button will halt the generation of new points, and the middle mouse button will terminate the program. Include a reshape callback.

3.3   Construct slidebars to allow users to define colors in the paint program. Your interface should let the user see a color before that color is used.

3.4   We can construct a virtual trackball from a mouse by mapping the mouse pad onto a ball. A major use of such a device is to allow the user to obtain velocities by using the mouse to "spin" the ball. Construct such a virtual device, and write a graphical application to demonstrate its use.

3.5   Alter the square-drawing program (Section 3.5) to incorporate menus like those described in Section 3.6.

3.6   Add an elapsed-time indicator in the paint program (Section 3.8) using a clock of your own design.

3.7   Creating simple games is a good way to become familiar with interactive graphics programming. Program the game of checkers. You can look at each square as an object that can be picked by the user. You can start with a program in which the user plays both sides.

3.8   Write a program that allows a user to play a simple version of solitaire. First, design a simple set of cards, using only our basic primitives. Your program can be written in terms of picking rectangular objects.

3.9   Simulating a pool or billiards game presents interesting problems. Here, as in Exercise 2.18, you must compute trajectories and detect collisions. The interactive aspects include initiating movement of the balls through a graphical cue stick, ensuring that the display is smooth, and creating a two-person game.

3.10   Rather than using buttons or menus to select options in an interactive program, we can make selections based on where in the window the mouse is located. Use this mechanism in the paint program (Section 3.8).

3.11 The mapping from a point in world coordinates to one in screen coordinates is well defined. It is not invertible because we go from three dimensions to two dimensions. Suppose, however, that we are working with a two-dimensional application. Is the mapping invertible? What problem can arise if you use a two-dimensional mapping to return a position in world coordinates by a locator device?

3.12 How do the results of Exercise 3.11 apply to picking?

3.13 In a typical application program, the programmer must decide whether or not to use display lists. Consider at least two applications. For each, list at least two factors in favor and at least two factors against the use of display lists. Using the fonts provided by GLUT, test whether what you wrote down is correct in practice.

3.14 Write an interactive program that will allow you to guide a graphical rat through the maze that you generated in Exercise 2.7. You can use the left and right buttons to turn the rat, and the middle button to move him forward.

3.15 Add rubber band lines and rectangles to the paint program.

3.16 Inexpensive joysticks, such as those used in toys and games, often lack encoders and contain only a pair of three-position switches. How might such devices function?

3.17 The orientation of an airplane is described by a coordinate system oriented as shown in Figure 3.27. The forward–backward motion of the joystick controls the up–down rotation with respect to the axis running along the length of the airplane, called the **pitch**. The right–left motion of the joystick controls the rotation about this axis, called the **roll**. Write a program that uses the mouse to control pitch and roll for the view seen by a pilot. You can do this exercise in two dimensions by considering a set of objects to be located far from the airplane, and then having the mouse control the two-dimensional viewing of these objects.

3.18 Consider a table with a two-dimensional sensing device located at the end of two linked arms, as shown in Figure 3.28. Suppose that the lengths of the two arms are fixed, and the arms are connected by simple (1-degree-of-freedom) pivot joints. Determine the relationship between the joint angles θ and ϕ and the position of the sensor.

3.19 Suppose that a CRT has a square face of 40×40 centimeters and is refreshed in a noninterlaced manner at a rate of 60 Hz. Ten percent of the time that the system takes to draw each scan line is used to return the CRT beam from the right edge to the left edge of the screen (the horizontal-retrace time), and 10 percent of the total drawing time is allocated for the beam to return from the lower-right corner of the screen to the upper-left corner after each refresh is complete (the vertical-retrace time). Assume that the resolution of the display is 1024×1024 pixels. Find a relationship between the time at which a lightpen detects the

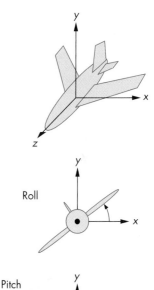

Figure 3.27 Airplane coordinate system.

Figure 3.28 Two-dimensional sensing arm.

beam and the lightpen's position. Give the result using both centimeters and screen coordinates for the location on the screen.

3.20 Circuit-layout programs are variants of paint programs. Consider the design of logical circuits using the Boolean AND, OR, and NOT functions. Each of these functions is provided by one of the three types of integrated circuits (gates), the symbols for which are shown in Figure 3.29. Write a program that allows the user to design a logical circuit by selecting gates from a menu and positioning them on the screen. Consider methods for connecting the outputs of one gate to the inputs of others.

3.21 Extend Exercise 3.20 to allow the user to specify a sequence of input signals. Have the program display the resulting values at selected points in the circuit.

3.22 Extend Exercise 3.20 to have the user enter a logical expression. Have the program generate a logical diagram from that expression.

3.23 Use the methods of Exercise 3.20 to form flowcharts for programs or images of graphs that you have studied in a data-structures class.

3.24 Plotting packages offer a variety of methods for displaying data. Write an interactive plotting application for two-dimensional curves. Your application should allow the user to choose the mode (polyline display of the data, bar chart, or pie chart), colors, and line styles.

3.25 The required refresh rate for CRT displays of 50 to 85 Hz is based on the use of short-persistence phosphors that emit light for extremely short intervals when excited. Long-persistence phosphors are available. Why are long-persistence phosphors not used in most workstation displays? In what types of applications might such phosphors be useful?

Figure 3.29 Symbols for logical circuits.

Geometric Objects and Transformations

We are now ready to concentrate on three-dimensional graphics. Much of this chapter is concerned with matters such as how to represent basic geometric types, how to convert between various representations, and what statements we can make about geometric objects, independent of a particular representation.

We begin with an examination of the mathematical underpinnings of computer graphics. This approach should avoid much of the confusion that arises from a lack of care in distinguishing among a geometric entity, its representation in a particular reference system, and a mathematical abstraction of it.

We use the notions of affine and Euclidean vector spaces to create the necessary mathematical foundation for later work. One of our goals is to establish a method for dealing with geometric problems that is independent of coordinate systems. The advantages of such an approach will be clear when we worry about how to represent the geometric objects with which we would like to work. The coordinate-free approach will prove to be far more robust than one based on representing the objects in a particular coordinate system or frame. This coordinate-free approach also leads to the use of homogeneous coordinates, a system that not only enables us to explain this approach, but also leads to efficient implementation techniques.

We use the terminology of abstract data types to reinforce the distinction between an object and its representation. Our development will show that the mathematics arise naturally from our desire to manipulate a few basic geometric data types. Much of what we present here is an application of vector spaces, geometry, and linear algebra. Appendices B and C cover the formalities of vector spaces and matrix algebra, respectively.

In a vein similar to the approach we took in Chapters 2 and 3, we develop a simple application program to illustrate the basic principles and to see how the concepts are realized within an API. In this chapter, our example is focused on the representation and transformations of a cube. We also consider how to specify transformations interactively and apply them smoothly.

4.1 Scalars, Points, and Vectors

In computer graphics, we work with sets of geometric objects, such as lines, polygons, and polyhedra. Such objects exist in a three-dimensional world and have properties that can be described by concepts such as length and angles. As we discovered working in two dimensions, we can define most geometric objects using a limited set of simple entities. These basic geometric objects and the relationships among them can be described using three fundamental types: scalars, points, and vectors.

Although each type can be looked at from a geometric perspective, each of these types also can be defined formally, as in Appendix B, as obeying a set of axioms. We can also take a purely programming-oriented view and look at how these entities are represented in code. Ultimately, we care about all three points of view, even though at first they may seem unrelated.

Although ultimately we will use a single instantiation of each type, we want to take great care in distinguishing between the abstract definition of each entity and any particular example, or implementation, of it. By taking care here, we can avoid many subtle pitfalls later. We start by examining each of the three approaches. Although we shall work in three-dimensional spaces, virtually all our results will hold in *n*-dimensional spaces.

4.1.1 The Geometric View

Our fundamental geometric object is a point. In a three-dimensional geometric system, a **point** is a location in the space. The only property that a point possesses is that point's location; a mathematical point has neither a size nor a shape.

Points are useful in specifying geometric objects but are not sufficient by themselves. We need real numbers to specify quantities such as the distance between two points. Real numbers—and complex numbers which we shall use occasionally—are examples of **scalars**. Scalars are objects that obey a set of rules that are abstractions of the operations of ordinary arithmetic. Thus, addition and multiplication are defined and obey the usual rules such as commutivity and associativity. Every scalar has multiplicative and additive inverses, which implicitly define subtraction and division.

We need one additional type—the **vector**—to allow us to work with directions. Physicists and mathematicians use the term *vector* for any quantity with direction and magnitude. Physical quantities, such as velocity and force, are vectors. A vector does not, however, have a fixed position in space.

In computer graphics, we often connect points with directed line segments, as shown in Figure 4.1. A line segment has both magnitude—its length—and direction—its orientation—and thus is a vector. Because vectors have no fixed position, the directed line segments shown in Figure 4.2 are identical because they have the same direction and magnitude. We shall often use the terms *vector* and *directed line segment* synonymously.

Figure 4.1 Directed line segment that connects points.

Figure 4.2 Identical vectors.

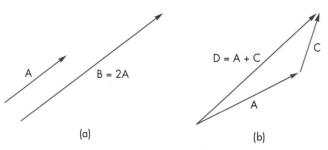

(a)

(b)

Figure 4.3 (a) Parallel line segments. (b) Addition of line segments.

Directed line segments can have their lengths changed by real numbers. Thus, in Figure 4.3(a), line segment A has the same direction as line segment B, but B has twice the length that A has, so we can write $B = 2A$. We can also combine directed line segments by the **head-to-tail rule**, as in Figure 4.3(b). Here, we connect the head of vector A to the tail of vector C to form a new vector D whose magnitude and direction are determined by the line segment from the tail of A to the head of C. We can call this new vector, D, the **sum** of A and C and write $D = A + C$. Because vectors have no fixed positions, we can move any two vectors as necessary to form their sum graphically. Note that we have described two operations: the addition of two vectors and the multiplication of a vector by a scalar.

If we consider the two directed line segments, A and E in Figure 4.4, with the same length but opposite directions, their sum, as defined by the head-to-tail addition, has no length. This sum forms a special vector called the **zero vector**, which we denote **0**, that has a magnitude of zero. Because it has no length, the orientation of this vector is undefined. Thus, we say that E is the **inverse** of A and we can write $E = -A$. By similar reasoning, scalar-vector expressions such as $A + 2B - 3C$ make sense.

Although we can multiply a vector by a scalar to change its length, there are no obvious sensible operations between two points or between a point and a scalar. There is, however, an operation between points and directed line segments (vectors), as is illustrated in Figure 4.5. We can use a directed line segment to move from a point to another. We call this operation **point-vector addition**, and it produces a new point. We can write this operation as $P = Q + v$. We see that the vector v displaces the point Q to the new location P.

Looking at things slightly differently, any two points define a line segment or vector between them. We call this operation **point-point subtraction**, and we can write it as $v = P - Q$. Because vectors can be multiplied by scalars, some expressions involving scalars, vectors, and points make sense, such as $P + 3v$, or $P - 2Q + 3v$, while others, such as $P + 3Q - v$, do not.

Figure 4.4 Inverse vectors

Figure 4.5 Point-vector addition.

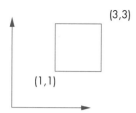

Figure 4.6 Object and coordinate system.

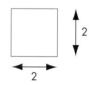

Figure 4.7 Object without coordinate system.

4.1.2 Coordinate-Free Geometry

Points exist in space regardless of any reference or coordinate system. Thus, we do not need a reference or coordinate system to define a point. This fact may seem counter to your experiences, but it is crucial to understanding geometry and how to build graphics systems. Consider the two-dimensional example in Figure 4.6. Here we see a coordinate system defined by two axes and a simple geometric object: a square. We can refer to the point at the lower-left corner of the square as having coordinates $(1,1)$ and note that the sides of the square are orthogonal to each other and that the point at $(3,1)$ is two units from the point at $(1,1)$. Now suppose that we remove the axes as in Figure 4.7. We can no longer specify where the points are. But those locations were relative to an arbitrary location and orientation of the original axes. What is more important is that the fundamental geometric relationships are preserved. The square is still a square; orthogonal lines are still orthogonal; distances between points remain the same.

Of course, we may find it inconvenient, at best, to refer to a specific point as "that point over there" or "the blue point to the right of the red one." Coordinate systems and frames (Section 4.3) solve this reference problem, but for now we want to see just how far we can get following a coordinate-free approach that does not require an arbitrary reference system.

4.1.3 The Mathematical View: Vector and Affine Spaces

We can regard scalars, points, and vectors as members of mathematical sets; then, we look at a variety of abstract spaces for representing and manipulating these sets of objects. Mathematicians have explored a variety of such spaces for applied problems, ranging from the solution of differential equations to the approximation of mathematical functions. The formal definitions of the spaces of interest to us—vector spaces, affine spaces, and Euclidean spaces—are given in Appendix B. We are concerned with only those examples in which the elements are geometric types.

We start with a set of scalars, any pair of which can be combined to form another scalar through two operations, called *addition* and *multiplication*. If these operations obey the closure, associativity, commutivity, and inverse properties described in Appendix B, the elements form a **scalar field**. Familiar examples of scalars include the real numbers, complex numbers, and rational functions.

Perhaps the most important mathematical space is the **(linear) vector space**. A vector space contains two distinct types of entities: vectors and scalars. In addition to the rules for combining scalars, within a vector space, we can combine scalars and vectors to form new vectors through **scalar–vector multiplication** and vectors with vectors through **vector–vector addition**. Examples of mathematical vector spaces include n-tuples of real numbers and the geometric operations on our directed line segments.

In a linear vector space, we do not necessarily have a way of measuring a scalar quantity. A **Euclidean space** is an extension of a vector space that adds a measure of size or distance and allows us to define such things as the length of a line segment.

An **affine space** is an extension of the vector space that includes an additional type of object: the point. Although there are no operations between two points or between a point and a scalar, there is an operation of *vector–point addition* that produces a new point. Alternately, we can say there is an operation called *point–point subtraction* that produces a vector from two points. Examples of affine spaces include the geometric operations on points and directed line segments that we introduced in Section 4.1.1.

In these abstract spaces, objects can be defined independently of any particular representation; they are simply members of various sets. One of the major vector-space concepts is that of representing a vector in terms of one or more sets of basis vectors. Representation provides the tie between abstract objects and their implementation. Conversion between representations leads us to geometric transformations.

4.1.4 The Computer-Science View

Although the mathematician may prefer to think of scalars, points, and vectors as members of sets that can be combined according to certain axioms, the computer scientist prefers to see them as **abstract data types** (**ADTs**). An ADT is a set of operations on data; the operations are defined independently of how the data are represented internally or of how the operations are implemented. The notion of *data abstraction* is fundamental to modern computer science. For example, the operation of adding an element to a list or of multiplying two polynomials can be defined independently of how the list is stored or of how real numbers are represented on a particular computer. People familiar with this concept should have no trouble distinguishing between objects (and operations on objects) and objects' representations (or implementations) in a particular system. From a computational point of view, we should be able to declare geometric objects through code such as

```
vector u,v;
point p,q;
scalar a,b;
```

regardless of the internal representation or implementation of the objects on a particular system. In languages, such as C++, we can use language features, such as classes and overloading of operators, so we can write lines of code, such as

```
q = p+a*v;
```

using our geometric data types. Of course, first we must define functions that perform the necessary operations; so that we can write them, we must look at the mathematical functions that we wish to implement. First, we shall define our objects. Then, we shall look to certain abstract mathematical spaces to help us with the operations among them.

4.1.5 Geometric ADTs

The three views of scalars, points, and vectors leave us with a mathematical and computational framework for working with our geometric entities. In summary, for computer graphics, our scalars are the real numbers using ordinary addition and multiplication. Our geometric points are locations in space, and our vectors are directed line segments. These objects obey the rules of an affine space. We can also create the corresponding ADTs in a program.

Our next step is to show how we can use our types to perform geometrical operations and to form geometric objects. We shall use the following notation: Greek letters $\alpha, \beta, \gamma, \ldots$ denote scalars; upper-case letters $P, Q, R, \ldots$ define points; and lower-case letters $u, v, w, \ldots$ denote vectors. We have not as yet introduced any reference system, such as a coordinate system; thus, for vectors and points, this notation refers to the abstract objects, rather than to these objects' representations in a particular reference system. We use boldface letters for the latter in Section 4.3. The **magnitude** of a vector v is a real number denoted by $|v|$. The operation of vector–scalar multiplication has the property that (see Appendix B)

$$|\alpha v| = |\alpha||v|,$$

and the direction of αv is the same as the direction of v if α is positive and the opposite direction if α is negative.

We have two equivalent operations that relate points and vectors. First, there is the subtraction of two points, P and Q—an operation that yields a vector v denoted by

$$v = P - Q.$$

A consequence of this operation is that, given any point Q and vector v, there is a unique point, P, that satisfies the preceding relationship. We can express this statement as follows: Given a point Q and a vector v, there is point a point P such that

$$P = v + Q.$$

Thus, P is formed by a point–vector addition operation. Figure 4.8 shows a visual interpretation of this operation. The head-to-tail rule gives us a convenient way of visualizing vector–vector addition. We obtain the sum $u + v$ as shown in Figure 4.9(a) by drawing the sum vector as connecting the tail of u to the head of v. However, we can also use this visualization, as demonstrated in Figure 4.9(b), to show that, for any three points P, Q, and R,

$$(P - Q) + (Q - R) = P - R.$$

Figure 4.8 Point–point subtraction.

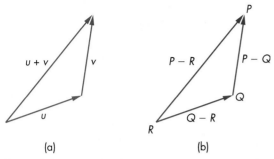

Figure 4.9 Use of the head-to-tail rule (a) for vectors, and (b) for points.

4.1.6 Lines

The sum of a point and a vector (or the subtraction of two points) leads to the notion of a line in an affine space. Consider all points of the form

$$P(\alpha) = P_0 + \alpha d,$$

where P_0 is an arbitrary point, d is an arbitrary vector, and α is a scalar that can vary over some range of values. Given the rules for combining points, vectors, and scalars in an affine space, for any value of α, the function $P(\alpha)$ yields a point. For geometric vectors (directed line segments), these points lie on a line, as shown in Figure 4.10. This form is known as the **parametric form** of the line, because we generate points on the line by varying the parameter α. For $\alpha = 0$, the line passes through the point P_0 and, as α is increased, all the points generated lie in the direction of the vector d. If we restrict α to nonnegative values, we get the **ray** emanating from P_0 and going in the direction of d. Thus, a line is infinitely long in both directions, a line segment is a finite piece of a line between two points, and a ray is infinitely long in one direction.

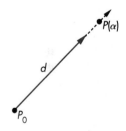

Figure 4.10 Line in an affine space.

4.1.7 Affine Sums

Whereas, in an affine space, the addition of two vectors, the multiplication of a vector by a scalar, and the addition of a vector and a point are defined, the addition of two arbitrary points and the multiplication of a point by a scalar are not. However, there is an operation called **affine addition** that has certain elements of these latter two operations. For any point Q, vector v, and positive scalar α,

$$P = Q + \alpha v$$

describes all points on the line from Q in the direction of v, as shown in Figure 4.11. However, we can always find a point R such that

$$v = R - Q;$$

Figure 4.11 Affine addition.

thus

$$P = Q + \alpha(R - Q) = \alpha R + (1 - \alpha)Q.$$

This operation looks like the addition of two points and leads to the equivalent form

$$P = \alpha_1 R + \alpha_2 Q,$$

where

$$\alpha_1 + \alpha_2 = 1.$$

4.1.8 Convexity

A **convex** object is one for which any point lying on the line segment connecting any two points in the object is also in the object. We saw the importance of convexity for polygons in Chapter 2. We can use affine sums to help us gain a deeper understanding of convexity. For $0 \le \alpha \le 1$, the affine sum defines the line segment connecting R and Q, as shown in Figure 4.12; thus, this line segment is a convex object. We can extend the affine sum to include objects defined by n points $P_1, P_2, \ldots, P_n$. Consider the form

$$P = \alpha_1 P_1 + \alpha_2 P_2 + \ldots + \alpha_n P_n.$$

We can show, by induction, that this sum is defined if and only if

$$\alpha_1 + \alpha_2 + \ldots + \alpha_n = 1.$$

The set of points formed by the affine sum of n points, under the additional restriction

$$\alpha_i \ge 0, \quad i = 1, 2, \ldots, n,$$

R

P(α)

Q

Figure 4.12 Line segment that connects two points.

Figure 4.13 Convex hull.

is called the **convex hull** of the set of points (Figure 4.13). It is easy to verify that the convex hull includes all line segments connecting pairs of points in $\{P_1, P_2, \ldots, P_n\}$. Geometrically, the convex hull is the set of points that we form by stretching a tight-fitting surface over the given set of points—**shrink wrapping** the points. It is the smallest convex object that includes the set of points. The notion of convexity is extremely important in the design of curves and surfaces; we return to it later, in Chapter 10.

4.1.9 Dot and Cross Products

Many of the geometric concepts relating the orientation between two vectors are in terms of the **dot** (**inner**) and **cross** (**outer**) **products** of two vectors. The dot product of u and v is written $u \cdot v$ (Appendix B) . If $u \cdot v = 0$, u and v are said to be **orthogonal**. In a Euclidean space, the magnitude of a vector is defined. The square of the magnitude of a vector is given by the dot product

$$|u|^2 = u \cdot u.$$

The angle between two vectors is given by

$$\cos \theta = \frac{u \cdot v}{|u||v|}.$$

In addition, $|u| \cos \theta = u \cdot v/|v|$ is the orthogonal projection of u onto v, as shown in Figure 4.14. Thus, the dot product expresses the geometric result that the shortest distance from a point (the end of the vector u) to the line segment v is obtained by drawing the vector orthogonal to v from the end of u. We can also see that the vector u is composed of the sum of the orthogonal projection on v and a vector orthogonal to v.

In vector space, vectors are **linearly independent** if we cannot write one in terms of the others using scalar-vector addition. A vector space has a **dimension**, which is the maximum number of linearly independent vectors that we can find. Given any three linearly independent vectors in a three-dimensional space, we can use the dot product to construct three vectors, each of which is orthogonal to the other two. This process is outlined in Appendix B. We can also use two nonparallel vectors, u and v, to determine a third vector n that is orthogonal to them (Figure 4.15). This vector is determined by the **cross product**

$$n = u \times v.$$

Note that we can use the cross product to derive three mutually orthogonal vectors in a three-dimensional space from any two nonparallel vectors. Starting again with u and v, we first compute n as before. Then, we can compute w by

$$w = u \times n,$$

and u, n, and w are mutually orthogonal.

The cross product is derived in Appendix C, using the representation of the vectors that gives a direct method for computing it. The magnitude of the cross product gives the sine of the angle θ between u and v

$$|\sin \theta| = \frac{|u \times v|}{|u||v|}.$$

Note that the vectors u, v, and n form a **right-handed coordinate system**; that is, if u points in the direction of the thumb of the right hand, and v points in the direction of the index finger, then n points in the direction of the middle finger.

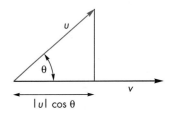

Figure 4.14 Dot product and projection.

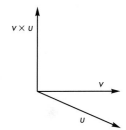

Figure 4.15 Cross product.

4.1.10 Planes

A **plane** in an affine space can be defined as a direct extension of the parametric line. From simple geometry, we know that three points, not on the same line, determine a unique plane. Suppose that P, Q, and R are three such points in an affine space. The line segment that joins P and Q is the set of points of the form

$$S(\alpha) = \alpha P + (1 - \alpha)Q, \qquad 0 \le \alpha \le 1.$$

Suppose that we take an arbitrary point on this line segment and form the line segment from this point to R, as shown in Figure 4.16. Using a second parameter β, we can describe points along this line segment as

$$T(\beta) = \beta S + (1 - \beta)R, \qquad 0 \le \beta \le 1.$$

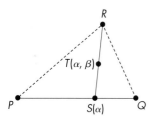

Figure 4.16 Formation of a plane.

Such points are determined by both α and β, and form the plane determined by P, Q, and R. Combining the preceding two equations, we obtain one form of the equation of a plane:

$$T(\alpha, \beta) = \beta[\alpha P + (1 - \alpha)Q] + (1 - \beta)R.$$

We can rearrange this equation in the form

$$T(\alpha, \beta) = P + \beta(1 - \alpha)(Q - P) + (1 - \beta)(R - P).$$

Noting that $Q - P$ and $R - P$ are arbitrary vectors, we have shown that a plane can also be expressed in terms of a point, P_0, and two nonparallel vectors, u, and v, as

$$T(\alpha, \beta) = P_0 + \alpha u + \beta v.$$

We can also observe that, for $0 \le \alpha, \beta \le 1$, all the points $T(\alpha, \beta)$ lie in the triangle formed by P, Q, and R. If a point P lies in the plane, then

$$P - P_0 = \alpha u + \beta v.$$

We can find a vector w that is orthogonal to both u and v, as shown in Figure 4.17. If we use the cross product

$$n = u \times v,$$

then the equation of the plane becomes

$$n \cdot (P - P_0) = 0.$$

Figure 4.17 Normal to a plane.

The vector n is perpendicular, or orthogonal, to the plane; it is called the **normal** to the plane. The forms $P(\alpha)$, for the line, and $T(\alpha, \beta)$, for the plane, are known as **parametric forms**, because they give the value of a point in space for each value of the parameters α and β.

4.2 Three-Dimensional Primitives

In a three-dimensional world, we can have a far greater variety of geometric objects than we could in two dimensions. When we worked in a two-dimensional plane in Chapter 2, we considered objects that were simple curves, such as line segments, and objects that had interiors, such as polygons. In three dimensions, we retain these objects, but they are no longer restricted to lie in the same plane.

Hence, curves become curves in space (Figure 4.18), and objects with interiors can become surfaces in space (Figure 4.19). In addition, we can have objects with volumes, such as parallelepipeds and ellipsoids (Figure 4.20).

We face two problems when we expand our graphics system to incorporate all these possibilities. First, the mathematical definitions of these objects can become complex. Second, we are interested in only those objects that lead to efficient implementations in graphics systems. The full range of three-dimensional objects cannot be supported on existing graphics systems, except by approximate methods.

Three features characterize three-dimensional objects that fit well with existing graphics hardware and software:

1. The objects are described by their surfaces and can be thought of as being hollow.
2. The objects can be specified through a set of vertices in three dimensions.
3. The objects either are composed of or can be approximated by flat convex polygons.

Figure 4.18 Curves in three dimensions.

Figure 4.19 Surfaces in three dimensions.

We can understand why we set these conditions if we consider what most modern graphics systems do best: They render triangular, or other flat, polygons. High-end systems can render more than 20 million small, flat polygons per second; boards in personal computers have rendering speeds greater than 5 million polygons per second.[1] The first condition implies that we need only two-dimensional primitives to model three-dimensional objects, because a surface is a two- rather than a three-dimensional entity. The second condition is an extension of our observations in Chapters 1 and 2. If an object is defined by vertices, we can use a pipeline architecture to process these vertices at high rates, and we can use the hardware to generate the images of the objects only during rasterization. The final condition is an extension from our discussion of two-dimensional polygons. Most graphics systems are optimized for the processing of points and polygons. In three dimensions, a polygon can be defined by an ordered list of vertices. However, if there are more than three vertices, they do not have to be in the same plane; if they are not, there is no simple way to define the interior of the object. Consequently, most graphics systems require that the user specify simple planar polygons, or the results of rasterizing the polygon are not guaranteed to be what the programmer might desire. Because triangular polygons are always flat, either the modeling system is designed always to produce triangles, or the graphics system provides a method to divide, or **tessellate**, an arbitrary polygon into triangular polygons. If we apply this same argument to a curved object, such as to a sphere, we realize that we should use an approximation to the sphere composed of small flat polygons. Hence, even if our modeling system

Figure 4.20 Volumetric objects.

---

1. Performance claims for graphics systems usually are quoted for three-dimensional triangles that can be generated by triangle strips. In addition, these triangles are shaded, lit, and texture mapped, as these functions can be implemented in hardware.

provides curved objects, we assume that a polygonal approximation is used for implementation.

The major exception to this approach is **constructive solid geometry** (**CSG**). In such systems, we build objects from a small set of volumetric objects through set operations such as union and intersection. We consider CSG models in Chapter 9. Although this approach is an excellent one for modeling, rendering CSG models is more difficult than is rendering surface-based polygonal models. Although this situation may not hold in the future, we discuss in detail only surface rendering.

All the primitives with which we work can be specified through a set of vertices. As we move away from abstract objects to real objects, we must consider how we represent points in space in a manner that can be used within our graphics systems.

4.3 Coordinate Systems and Frames

So far, we have considered vectors and points as abstract objects, without representing them in an underlying reference system. In a three-dimensional vector space, we can represent any vector w uniquely in terms of any three linearly independent vectors, v_1, v_2, and v_3 (see Appendix B), as

$$w = \alpha_1 v_1 + \alpha_2 v_2 + \alpha_3 v_3.$$

The scalars α_1, α_2, and α_3 are the **components** of w with respect to the **basis** v_1, v_2, and v_3. These relationships are shown in Figure 4.21. We can write the **representation** of w with respect to this basis as the column matrix

$$\mathbf{a} = \begin{bmatrix} \alpha_1 \\ \alpha_2 \\ \alpha_3 \end{bmatrix},$$

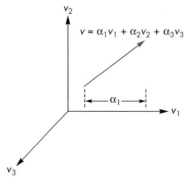

Figure 4.21   Vector derived from three basis vectors.

where boldface letters denote a representation in a particular basis, as opposed to the original abstract vector w. We can also write this relationship as

$$w = \mathbf{a}^T \begin{bmatrix} v_1 \\ v_2 \\ v_3 \end{bmatrix}.$$

We usually think of the basis vectors, v_1, v_2, v_3, as defining a **coordinate system**. However, for dealing with problems using points, vectors, and scalars, we need a more general method. Figure 4.22 shows one aspect of the problem. The three vectors form a coordinate system that is shown in Figure 4.22(a) as we would usually draw it, with the three vectors emerging from a single point. We could use these three basis vectors as a basis to represent any vector in three dimensions. Vectors, however, have direction and magnitude, but lack a position attribute. Hence, Figure 4.22(b) is equivalent, because we have moved the basis vectors, leaving their magnitudes and directions unchanged. Most people find this second figure confusing, even though mathematically it expresses the same the information as the first figure. We are still left with the problem of how to represent points—entities that have fixed positions.

Because an affine space contains points, in such a space, once we fix a particular reference point—the origin—we can represent all points unambiguously. The usual convention for drawing coordinate axes as emerging from the origin, as shown in Figure 4.22(a), makes sense in the affine space where both points and vectors have representations. However, this representation requires us to know *both* the reference point and the basis vectors. The origin and the basis vectors determine a **frame**. Loosely, this extension fixes the origin of the vector coordinate system at some point P_0. Within a given frame, every vector can be written uniquely as

$$w = \alpha_1 v_1 + \alpha_2 v_2 + \alpha_3 v_3,$$

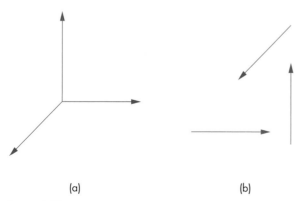

(a)   (b)

Figure 4.22 Coordinate system (a) with vectors emerging from a common point, and (b) with vectors moved.

just as in a vector space; in addition, every point can be written uniquely as

$$P = P_0 + \beta_1 v_1 + \beta_2 v_2 + \beta_3 v_3.$$

Thus, the representation of a particular vector in a frame requires three scalars; the representation of a point requires three scalars and the knowledge of where the origin is located. As we shall see in Section 4.3.4, by abandoning the more familiar notion of a coordinate system and a basis in that coordinate system in favor of the less familiar notion of a frame, we avoid the difficulties caused by vectors having magnitude and direction but no fixed position. In addition, we shall be able to represent points and vectors in a manner that will allow us to use matrix representations but that maintains a distinction between the two different geometric objects.

Points and vectors are two distinct geometric types. Graphical representations that equate a point with a directed line segment drawn from the origin to that point (Figure 4.23) should be regarded with suspicion. Thus, a correct interpretation of Figure 4.23 is that a given vector can be defined as going from a fixed reference point (the origin) to a particular point in space. Note that a vector, like a point, exists regardless of the reference system, but, as we shall see with both points and vectors, we eventually have to work with their representation in a particular reference system.

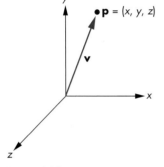

Figure 4.23 A dangerous representation of a vector.

4.3.1 Representations and N-tuples

Suppose that vectors e_1, e_2, and e_3 form a basis. The representation of any vector, v, is given by the components $(\alpha_1, \alpha_2, \alpha_3)$, where

$$v = \alpha_1 e_1 + \alpha_2 e_2 + \alpha_3 e_3.$$

The basis vectors[2] must themselves have representations that we can denote $\mathbf{e}_1$, $\mathbf{e}_2$, and $\mathbf{e}_3$ and are given by

$$\mathbf{e}_1 = (1, 0, 0)^T,$$
$$\mathbf{e}_2 = (0, 1, 0)^T,$$
$$\mathbf{e}_3 = (0, 0, 1)^T.$$

Consequently, in terms of representations, we can write the representation of any vector v as a column matrix $\mathbf{a}$ or as the 3-tuple $(\alpha_1, \alpha_2, \alpha_3)$ where

$$\mathbf{a} = \alpha_1 \mathbf{e}_1 + \alpha_2 \mathbf{e}_2 + \alpha_3 \mathbf{e}_3.$$

----

2. Many textbooks on vectors refer to these vectors as the unit basis $\mathbf{i}, \mathbf{j}, \mathbf{k}$ and write other vectors in the form $v = \alpha_1 \mathbf{i} + \alpha_2 \mathbf{j} + \alpha_2 \mathbf{k}$.

From this perspective, working with representations is equivalent to working with 3-tuples of scalars. These 3-tuples form a vector space known as the Euclidean $\mathbf{R}^3$ that is equivalent (or **homomorphic**) to the vector space of our original geometric vectors. From a practical perspective, it is almost always easier to work with 3-tuples than with other representations.

4.3.2 Changes of Coordinate Systems

Frequently, we are required to find how the representation of a vector changes when we change the basis vectors. For example, in OpenGL, we define our geometry using the coordinate system or frame that is natural for the application, which is known as the **world** or **user frame**. At some point, we want to know how these objects appear to the camera. It is natural at that point to convert from the user frame to the camera frame. This conversion is what is done by the model-view matrix.

Let us consider vectors first. Suppose that $\{v_1, v_2, v_3\}$ and $\{u_1, u_2, u_3\}$ are two bases. Each basis vector in the second set can be represented in terms of the first basis (and vice versa). Hence, there exist nine scalar components, $\{\gamma_{ij}\}$, such that

$$u_1 = \gamma_{11}v_1 + \gamma_{12}v_2 + \gamma_{13}v_3,$$
$$u_2 = \gamma_{21}v_1 + \gamma_{22}v_2 + \gamma_{23}v_3,$$
$$u_3 = \gamma_{31}v_1 + \gamma_{32}v_2 + \gamma_{33}v_3.$$

The 3×3 matrix

$$\mathbf{M} = \begin{bmatrix} \gamma_{11} & \gamma_{12} & \gamma_{13} \\ \gamma_{21} & \gamma_{22} & \gamma_{23} \\ \gamma_{31} & \gamma_{32} & \gamma_{33} \end{bmatrix}$$

is defined by these scalars, and

$$\begin{bmatrix} u_1 \\ u_2 \\ u_3 \end{bmatrix} = \mathbf{M} \begin{bmatrix} v_1 \\ v_2 \\ v_3 \end{bmatrix}.$$

The matrix $\mathbf{M}$ contains the information to go from a representation of a vector in one basis to its representation in the second basis. The inverse of $\mathbf{M}$ gives the matrix representation of the change from $\{u_1, u_2, u_3\}$ to $\{v_1, v_2, v_3\}$. Consider a vector w that has the representation $\{\alpha_1, \alpha_2, \alpha_3\}$ with respect to $\{v_1, v_2, v_3\}$; that is,

$$w = \alpha_1 v_1 + \alpha_2 v_2 + \alpha_3 v_3.$$

Equivalently,

$$w = \mathbf{a}^T \begin{bmatrix} v_1 \\ v_2 \\ v_3 \end{bmatrix},$$

where

$$\mathbf{a} = \begin{bmatrix} \alpha_1 \\ \alpha_2 \\ \alpha_3 \end{bmatrix}.$$

Assume that $\mathbf{b}$ is the representation of w with respect to $\{u_1, u_2, u_3\}$; that is,

$$w = \beta_1 u_1 + \beta_2 u_2 + \beta_3 u_3,$$

or

$$w = \mathbf{b}^T \begin{bmatrix} u_1 \\ u_2 \\ u_3 \end{bmatrix},$$

where

$$\mathbf{b} = \begin{bmatrix} \beta_1 \\ \beta_2 \\ \beta_3 \end{bmatrix}.$$

Then, using our representation of the second basis in terms of the first, we find that

$$w = \mathbf{b}^T \begin{bmatrix} u_1 \\ u_2 \\ u_3 \end{bmatrix} = \mathbf{b}^T \mathbf{M} \begin{bmatrix} v_1 \\ v_2 \\ v_3 \end{bmatrix} = \mathbf{a}^T \begin{bmatrix} v_1 \\ v_2 \\ v_3 \end{bmatrix}.$$

Thus,

$$\mathbf{a} = \mathbf{M}^T \mathbf{b}.$$

The matrix $(\mathbf{M}^T)^{-1}$ takes us from $\mathbf{a}$ to $\mathbf{b}$:

$$\mathbf{b} = (\mathbf{M}^T)^{-1} \mathbf{a}.$$

Thus, rather than working with our original vectors, typically directed line segments, we can work instead with their representations, which are 3-tuples or elements of $\mathbf{R}^3$. This result is important because it moves us from considering abstract vectors to working with column matrices of scalars—the vectors' representations. The important point to remember is that, whenever we work with columns of real numbers as "vectors," there is an underlying basis of which we must not lose track, lest we end up working in the wrong coordinate system.

These changes in basis leave the origin unchanged. We can use them to represent rotation and scaling of a set of basis vectors to derive another basis set, as shown in Figure 4.24. However, a simple translation of the origin, or change of frame, as shown in Figure 4.25, cannot be represented in this

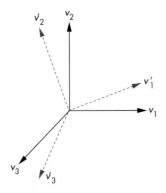

Figure 4.24 Rotation and scaling of a basis.

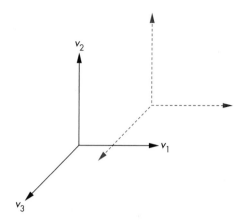

Figure 4.25 Translation of a basis.

way. After we complete a simple example, we introduce homogeneous coordinates, which allow us to change frames yet still use matrices to represent the change.

4.3.3 Example of Change of Representation

Suppose that we have a vector w whose representation in some basis is

$$\mathbf{a} = \begin{bmatrix} 1 \\ 2 \\ 3 \end{bmatrix}.$$

We can denote the three basis vectors as v_1, v_2, and v_3. Hence,

$$w = v_1 + 2v_2 + 3v_3.$$

Now suppose that we want to make a new basis from the three vectors v_1, v_2, and v_3:

$$u_1 = v_1,$$
$$u_2 = v_1 + v_2,$$
$$u_3 = v_1 + v_2 + v_3.$$

The matrix $\mathbf{M}$ is

$$\mathbf{M} = \begin{bmatrix} 1 & 0 & 0 \\ 1 & 1 & 0 \\ 1 & 1 & 1 \end{bmatrix}.$$

The matrix that converts a representation in v_1, v_2, and v_3 to one in which the basis vectors are u_1, u_2, and u_3 is

$$\mathbf{A} = (\mathbf{M}^T)^{-1}$$

$$= \begin{bmatrix} 1 & 1 & 1 \\ 0 & 1 & 1 \\ 0 & 0 & 1 \end{bmatrix}^{-1}$$

$$= \begin{bmatrix} 1 & -1 & 0 \\ 0 & 1 & -1 \\ 0 & 0 & 1 \end{bmatrix}.$$

In the new system, the representation of w is

$$\mathbf{b} = \mathbf{Aa} = \begin{bmatrix} -1 \\ -1 \\ 3 \end{bmatrix}.$$

That is,

$$w = -u_1 - u_2 + 3u_3.$$

If we are working in the space of 3-tuples ($\mathbf{R}^3$), rather than in an abstract setting, then we can associate v_1, v_2, and v_3 with the unit basis in $\mathbf{R}^3$:

$$\mathbf{e}_1 = \begin{bmatrix} 1 \\ 0 \\ 0 \end{bmatrix}, \qquad \mathbf{e}_2 = \begin{bmatrix} 0 \\ 1 \\ 0 \end{bmatrix}, \qquad \mathbf{e}_3 = \begin{bmatrix} 0 \\ 0 \\ 1 \end{bmatrix}.$$

We can make this example a little more concrete by considering the following variant. Suppose that we are working with the default (x, y, z) coordinate system, which happens to be orthogonal. We are given the three direction vectors whose representations are $(1, 0, 0)$, $(1, 1, 0)$, and $(1, 1, 1)$. Thus, the first vector points along the x-axis, the second points in a direction parallel to the plane $z = 0$, and the third points in a direction symmetric to the three basis directions. These three new vectors, although they are not mutually orthogonal, are linearly independent and thus define a new coordinate system that we can call the x', y', w' system. The original directions have representations in the x', w', z' given by the rows of the matrix $\mathbf{A}$.

4.3.4 Homogeneous Coordinates

Usually, our first inclination is to represent a point P located at (x, y, z) using a three-dimensional frame defined by P_0, v_1, v_2, and v_3, with the column matrix

$$\mathbf{p} = \begin{bmatrix} x \\ y \\ z \end{bmatrix},$$

where x, y, and z are the components of the basis vectors for this point, so that

$$P = P_0 + xv_1 + yv_2 + zv_3.$$

If we represent the point this way, then its representation is of the same form as the vector, that is,

$$w = \delta_1 v_1 + \delta_2 v_2 + \delta_3 v_3;$$

and the representation of w is the array or 3-tuple

$$\mathbf{w} = \begin{bmatrix} \delta_1 \\ \delta_2 \\ \delta_3 \end{bmatrix}.$$

Many references associate the point (x, y, z) with the vector defined by directed line segment from the origin to this point. This association can cause confusion. For example, the vector from the point $(1,1,1)$ to $(2,3,4)$ is the same as the vector from $(0,0,0)$ to $(1,2,3)$ because they have the same magnitude and direction, but we would not associate the first vector with point $(1,2,3)$ unless we fixed one end of it to $(0,0,0)$. We prefer to maintain points and vectors as distinct geometric types.

In addition, failure to distinguish between points and vectors can make implementation more difficult because a matrix multiplication in three dimensions cannot represent a change in frames. We take a different approach.

We use homogeneous coordinates to avoid these difficulties by using four-dimensional column matrices to represent both points and vectors in three dimensions. In the frame specified by (v_1, v_2, v_3, P_0), any point P can be written uniquely as

$$P = \alpha_1 v_1 + \alpha_2 v_2 + \alpha_3 v_3 + P_0.$$

If we agree to define the "multiplication" of a point by the scalars 0 and 1 as

$$0 \cdot P = \mathbf{0},$$
$$1 \cdot P = P,$$

then we can express this relation formally, using a matrix product, as

$$P = \begin{bmatrix} \alpha_1 & \alpha_2 & \alpha_3 & 1 \end{bmatrix} \begin{bmatrix} v_1 \\ v_2 \\ v_3 \\ P_0 \end{bmatrix}.$$

Strictly speaking, this expression is not a dot or inner product, because the elements of the matrices are dissimilar; nonetheless, the expression is computed as though it were an inner product by multiplying corresponding elements and summing the results. The four-dimensional row matrix on the right side of the equation is the **homogeneous-coordinate representation** of the point P in the frame determined by v_1, v_2, v_3, and P_0. Equivalently, we can say that P is represented by the column matrix

$$\mathbf{p} = \begin{bmatrix} \alpha_1 \\ \alpha_2 \\ \alpha_3 \\ 1 \end{bmatrix}.$$

In the same frame, any vector w can be written

$$w = \delta_1 v_1 + \delta_2 v_2 + \delta_3 v_3$$

$$= \begin{bmatrix} \delta_1 & \delta_2 & \delta_3 & 0 \end{bmatrix}^T \begin{bmatrix} v_1 \\ v_2 \\ v_3 \\ P_0 \end{bmatrix}.$$

Thus, w can be is represented by the column matrix

$$\mathbf{w} = \begin{bmatrix} \delta_1 \\ \delta_2 \\ \delta_3 \\ 0 \end{bmatrix}.$$

There are numerous ways to interpret this formulation geometrically. We simply note that we can carry out operations on points and vectors using their homogeneous-coordinate representations and ordinary matrix algebra. Consider, for example, a change of frames—a problem that caused difficulties when we used three-dimensional representations. If (v_1, v_2, v_3, P_0) and (u_1, u_2, u_3, Q_0) are two frames, then we can express the basis vectors and reference point of the second frame in terms of the first as

$$u_1 = \gamma_{11} v_1 + \gamma_{12} v_2 + \gamma_{13} v_3,$$
$$u_2 = \gamma_{21} v_1 + \gamma_{22} v_2 + \gamma_{23} v_3,$$
$$u_3 = \gamma_{31} v_1 + \gamma_{32} v_2 + \gamma_{33} v_3,$$
$$Q_0 = \gamma_{41} v_1 + \gamma_{42} v_2 + \gamma_{43} v_3 + P_0.$$

These equations can be written in the form

$$\begin{bmatrix} u_1 \\ u_2 \\ u_3 \\ Q_0 \end{bmatrix} = \mathbf{M} \begin{bmatrix} v_1 \\ v_2 \\ v_3 \\ P_0 \end{bmatrix},$$

where now $\mathbf{M}$ is the 4×4 matrix

$$\mathbf{M} = \begin{bmatrix} \gamma_{11} & \gamma_{12} & \gamma_{13} & 0 \\ \gamma_{21} & \gamma_{22} & \gamma_{23} & 0 \\ \gamma_{31} & \gamma_{32} & \gamma_{33} & 0 \\ \gamma_{41} & \gamma_{42} & \gamma_{43} & 1 \end{bmatrix}.$$

$\mathbf{M}$ is called the **matrix representation** of the change of frames.

We can also use $\mathbf{M}$ to compute the changes in the representations directly. Suppose that $\mathbf{a}$ and $\mathbf{b}$ are the homogeneous-coordinate representations either of two points or of two vectors in the two frames. Then,

$$\mathbf{b}^T \begin{bmatrix} u_1 \\ u_2 \\ u_3 \\ Q_0 \end{bmatrix} = \mathbf{b}^T \mathbf{M} \begin{bmatrix} v_1 \\ v_2 \\ v_3 \\ P_0 \end{bmatrix} = \mathbf{a}^T \begin{bmatrix} v_1 \\ v_2 \\ v_3 \\ P_0 \end{bmatrix}.$$

Hence,

$$\mathbf{a} = \mathbf{M}^T \mathbf{b}.$$

When we work with representations, as is usually the case, we are interested in $\mathbf{M}^T$, which is of the form

$$\mathbf{M}^T = \begin{bmatrix} \alpha_{11} & \alpha_{12} & \alpha_{13} & \alpha_{14} \\ \alpha_{21} & \alpha_{22} & \alpha_{23} & \alpha_{24} \\ \alpha_{31} & \alpha_{32} & \alpha_{33} & \alpha_{34} \\ 0 & 0 & 0 & 1 \end{bmatrix},$$

and is determined by 12 coefficients.

There are other advantages to using homogeneous coordinates that we explore extensively in later chapters. Perhaps the most important is that all affine (line-preserving) transformations can be represented as matrix multiplications in homogeneous coordinates. Although we have to work in four dimensions to solve three-dimensional problems when we use homogeneous-coordinate representations, less arithmetic work is involved. The uniform representation of all affine transformations makes carrying out successive transformations (concatenation) far easier than in three-dimensional space. In addition, modern hardware implements homogeneous-coordinate operations directly, using parallelism to achieve high-speed calculations.

4.3.5 Example of Change in Frames

Consider again the example of Section 4.3.3. If we again start with the basis vectors v_1, v_2, and v_3, and convert to a basis determined by the same u_1, u_2, and u_3, then the three equations are the same:

$$u_1 = v_1,$$
$$u_2 = v_1 + v_2,$$
$$u_3 = v_1 + v_2 + v_3.$$

The reference point does not change, so we add the equation

$$Q_0 = P_0.$$

Thus, the matrices in which we are interested are the matrix

$$\mathbf{M} = \begin{bmatrix} 1 & 0 & 0 & 0 \\ 1 & 1 & 0 & 0 \\ 1 & 1 & 1 & 0 \\ 0 & 0 & 0 & 1 \end{bmatrix},$$

its transpose, and their inverses.

Suppose that in addition to changing the basis vectors, we also want to move the reference point to the point that has the representation $(1, 2, 3, 1)$ in the original system. The displacement vector $v = v_1 + 2v_2 + 3v_3$ moves P_0 to Q_0. The fourth component identifies this entity as a point. Thus, we add to the three equations from the previous example the equation

$$Q_0 = P_0 + v_1 + 2v_2 + 3v_3,$$

and the matrix $\mathbf{M}^T$ becomes

$$\mathbf{M}^T = \begin{bmatrix} 1 & 1 & 1 & 1 \\ 0 & 1 & 1 & 2 \\ 0 & 0 & 1 & 3 \\ 0 & 0 & 0 & 1 \end{bmatrix}.$$

Its inverse is

$$\mathbf{A} = (\mathbf{M}^T)^{-1} = \begin{bmatrix} 1 & -1 & 0 & 1 \\ 0 & 1 & -1 & 1 \\ 0 & 0 & 1 & -3 \\ 0 & 0 & 0 & 1 \end{bmatrix}.$$

This pair of matrices allows us to move back and forth between representations in the two frames. Note that $\mathbf{A}$ takes the *point* $(1,2,3)$ in the original frame, whose representation is

$$\mathbf{p} = \begin{bmatrix} 1 \\ 2 \\ 3 \\ 1 \end{bmatrix},$$

to

$$\mathbf{p}' = \begin{bmatrix} 0 \\ 0 \\ 0 \\ 1 \end{bmatrix},$$

the origin in the new system. However, the *vector* $(1, 2, 3)$ which is represented as

$$\mathbf{a} = \begin{bmatrix} 1 \\ 2 \\ 3 \\ 0 \end{bmatrix}$$

in the original system is transformed to

$$\mathbf{b} = \begin{bmatrix} -1 \\ -1 \\ 3 \\ 0 \end{bmatrix},$$

a transformation that is consistent with the results from our example of change in coordinate systems, and that also demonstrates the importance of distinguishing between points and vectors.

4.3.6 Working with Representations

We usually work with representations rather than abstract points. Thus, when we specify a point, for example by glVertex3f(x,y,z), we are actually giving the representation of the point in some frame, usually the world frame used by the application. Changes of representation are thus given as in Section 4.3.2 by a relationship of the form

$$\mathbf{a} = \mathbf{C}\mathbf{b},$$

where $\mathbf{a}$ and $\mathbf{b}$ are the two representations of a point or vector in homogeneous coordinates. The problem is how to find $\mathbf{C}$ when we are working with representations. It turns out to be quite easy. Suppose that we are working in some frame and we specify another frame by its representation in this frame. Thus, if in the original system we specify a frame by the representations of three vectors, u, v, and n, and give the origin of the new frame as the point p, in homogeneous coordinates all four of these entities are 4-tuples or elements of $\mathbf{R}^4$.

Let's consider the inverse problem. The matrix

$$\mathbf{D} = \mathbf{C}^{-1}$$

converts from representations in the (u, v, n, p) frame to representations in the original frame. Thus, we must have

$$\mathbf{D} \begin{bmatrix} 1 \\ 0 \\ 0 \\ 0 \end{bmatrix} = \mathbf{u} = \begin{bmatrix} u_1 \\ u_2 \\ u_3 \\ 0 \end{bmatrix}.$$

Likewise,

$$
\mathbf{D}\begin{bmatrix} 0 \\ 1 \\ 0 \\ 0 \end{bmatrix} = \mathbf{v} = \begin{bmatrix} v_1 \\ v_2 \\ v_3 \\ 0 \end{bmatrix},
$$

$$
\mathbf{D}\begin{bmatrix} 0 \\ 0 \\ 1 \\ 0 \end{bmatrix} = \mathbf{n} = \begin{bmatrix} n_1 \\ n_2 \\ n_3 \\ 0 \end{bmatrix},
$$

$$
\mathbf{D}\begin{bmatrix} 0 \\ 0 \\ 0 \\ 1 \end{bmatrix} = \mathbf{p} = \begin{bmatrix} p_1 \\ p_2 \\ p_3 \\ 1 \end{bmatrix}.
$$

Putting these results together, we find

$$
\mathbf{DI} = \mathbf{D} = [\, u \quad v \quad n \quad p \,] = \begin{bmatrix} u_1 & v_1 & n_1 & p_1 \\ u_2 & v_2 & n_2 & p_2 \\ u_3 & v_3 & n_3 & p_3 \\ 0 & 0 & 0 & 1 \end{bmatrix},
$$

or

$$
\mathbf{C} = [\, u \quad v \quad n \quad p \,]^{-1} = \begin{bmatrix} u_1 & v_1 & n_1 & p_1 \\ u_2 & v_2 & n_2 & p_2 \\ u_3 & v_3 & n_3 & p_3 \\ 0 & 0 & 0 & 1 \end{bmatrix}^{-1}.
$$

Thus, the representation of a frame in terms of another frame gives us the inverse of the matrix we need to convert from representations in the first frame to representations in the second. Of course, we must compute this inverse, but computing the inverse of a 4×4 matrix should not present a problem.

4.3.7 Frames and ADTs

Thus far, our discussion has been mathematical. You may be wondering what all the mathematics has to do with programming. In this section, we address that question, starting with the notion of abstract data types to which we alluded earlier.

We have introduced a few geometric objects (for example, points, lines, and planes) that are important, either as primitives in a graphics system or as aids in defining other primitives. Thus, we would like to be able to write computer code such as

```
point3 p,q;
vector3 v,u;
```

and to expect to write programs in terms of these types. In a language like C++, which supports redefinition (overloading) of operators, statements such as

```
q=p+v;
u=p-q;
```

are valid, whereas statements such as

```
q=v;
u=p+q;
```

are detected as errors. The types could be implemented in a number of ways. In C++ and in other object-oriented languages, we could use features like constructors, destructors, and operator overloading to hide the details of the implementation from the applications programmer. C programmers might implement the point3 data type by using code such as

```
typedef float point3[4];
```

By using a four-dimensional array, we use homogeneous coordinate representations; by using

```
typedef float point2[4];
```

we are able to treat two-dimensional graphics as a special case of three-dimensional graphics. We could then implement functions to carry out our standard operations. This approach is taken in most graphics systems, including Java 3D, PHIGS, and OpenGL. However, it does not obviate certain difficulties. For example, consider the problem of initializing a point. In a standard C program, we might expect to see code fragments like

```
p={1.0,2.0,3.0};
```

There are two objections to this approach. First, we have mixed the implementation with the data type, and have subsequently created implementation-dependent code. Second, there is a question regarding what coordinate system or frame we are using.

We can solve the first problem by creating a set of functions that implements the abstract operations, rather than forcing a user to deal with implementation-dependent details. Hence, we would initialize a point through a function such as

```
p = new_point3(1.0, 2.0, 3.0);
```

and all operations would be done through functions, such as

```
point3 p,q;
vector3 v;
v = point_sub(p,q);
```

The second problem poses more difficulties in practice than in principle. As our discussion should have made clear, a representation of a point is with respect to a specific frame. Hence, one approach would be to have a type frame available as an additional graphical data type. The software would then allow the user to use a default frame or to change frames. The graphical functions could then either require the frame to be included explicitly in function calls, for example, as in the code

```
point3 p,q;
vector3 v;
frame f;
v = point_sub(p,q,f);
```

or all coordinates could be referenced to a present frame, as is done with attributes such as line type or color.

4.3.8 Frames in OpenGL

In OpenGL, we use two frames: the camera frame and the world frame. We can regard the camera frame as fixed. The model-view matrix positions the world frame relative to the camera frame. Thus, the model-view matrix converts the homogeneous-coordinate representations of points and vectors to their representations in the camera frame.[3] Because the model-view matrix is part of the state of the system, there is always a camera frame and a present world frame. OpenGL provides matrix stacks, so we can store model-view matrices or, equivalently, frames.

As we saw in Chapter 2, the camera is at the origin of its frame. The three basis vectors correspond to the up direction of the camera, the y direction; the direction the camera is pointing, the negative z direction; and a third orthogonal direction, x, that is placed so that the x, y, z directions form a right-handed coordinate system. We obtain other frames in which to place objects by performing homogeneous coordinate transformations that define new frames relative to the camera frame. We learn in Section 4.5 how to define these transformations; in Section 5.3 we use them to position the camera relative to our objects. Because changes of frame are represented by model-view matrices and we can store these matrices, we can save frames and move between frames by changing the present model-view matrix.

Before beginning a detailed discussion of what transformations are and how we use them in OpenGL, we present two examples. In the default settings (Figure 4.26[a]), the camera and world frames coincide with the camera pointing in the negative z direction. In many applications, it is natural to define objects

3. We could look at things the other way: We could regard the world frame as fixed. Which view we use is a matter of choice.

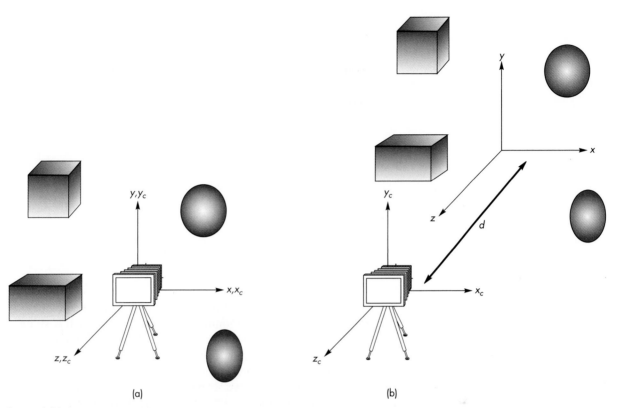

Figure 4.26 Camera and world frames (a) in default positions, and (b) after applying model-view matrix.

near the origin, such as a square centered at the origin or, perhaps, a group of objects whose center of mass is at the origin. It is also natural to set up our viewing conditions so that the camera sees only those objects that are in front of it. Consequently, to form images that contain all these objects, we must either move the camera away from the objects or move the objects away from the camera. Equivalently, we move the camera frame relative to the world frame. If we regard the camera frame as fixed and the model-view matrix as positioning the world frame relative to the camera frame, then the model-view matrix,

$$\mathbf{A} = \begin{bmatrix} 1 & 0 & 0 & 0 \\ 0 & 1 & 0 & 0 \\ 0 & 0 & 1 & -d \\ 0 & 0 & 0 & 1 \end{bmatrix},$$

moves a point (x, y, z) in the world frame to the point $(x, y, z - d)$ in the camera frame. Thus, by making d a suitably large positive number, we "move" the objects in front of the camera by moving the world frame relative to the camera frame (Figure 4.26[b]). Note that, as far as the user—who is working in world

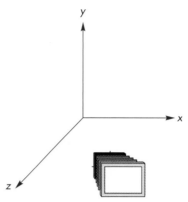

Figure 4.27 Camera at $(1,0,1)$ pointing toward the origin.

coordinates—is concerned, she is positioning objects as before. The model-view matrix takes care of the relative positioning of the frames. Using this strategy is almost always better than attempting to alter the positions of the object by changing their vertices to place them in front of the camera.

Let's look at another example working directly with representations. When we define our objects through vertices, we are working in the application frame (or world frame). The vertices specified by glVertex3f(x,y,z) are the representation of a point in that frame. Thus, we do not use the world frame directly but rather implicitly by representing points (and vectors) in it. Consider the situation in Figure 4.27.

Here we see the camera as positioned in the world frame. Using homogeneous coordinates, it is centered at a point $p = (1, 0, 1, 1)^T$ in world coordinates and points at the origin in the world frame. Thus the vector whose representation in the world frame is $\mathbf{n} = (-1, 0, -1, 0)^T$ is orthogonal to the back of the camera and points toward the origin. The camera is oriented so that its up direction is the same as the up direction in world coordinates and has the representation $\mathbf{v} = (0, 1, 0, 0)^T$. We can form an orthogonal coordinate system for the camera by using the cross product to determine a third orthogonal direction for the camera, which is $\mathbf{u} = (1, 0, -1, 0)^T$. We can now proceed as in Section 4.3.4 and derive the matrix $\mathbf{M}$ that converts the representation of points and vectors in the world frame to their representations in the camera frame. This matrix in homogenous coordinates is given by

$$
(\mathbf{M}^T)^{-1} = \begin{bmatrix} 1 & 0 & -1 & 1 \\ 0 & 1 & 0 & 0 \\ -1 & 0 & -1 & 1 \\ 0 & 0 & 0 & 1 \end{bmatrix}^{-1} = \begin{bmatrix} \frac{1}{2} & 0 & -\frac{1}{2} & 0 \\ 0 & 1 & 0 & 0 \\ -\frac{1}{2} & 0 & -\frac{1}{2} & 1 \\ 0 & 0 & 0 & 1 \end{bmatrix}.
$$

Note that the origin in the original frame is now one unit in the n direction from the origin in the camera frame or, equivalently at the point whose representation is $(0,0,1,1)$ in the camera frame.

In OpenGL, we can set a model-view matrix by sending an array of 16 elements to glLoadMatrix. For situations like the preceding, where we have the representation of one frame in terms of another through the specification of the basis vectors and the origin, it is a direct exercise to find the required coefficients. However, such is not usually the case. For most geometric problems, we usually go from one frame to another by a sequence of geometric transformations such as rotations, translations, and scales. We shall follow this approach in subsequent sections. But first, we shall look at a few simple approaches to building geometric objects.

4.4 Modeling a Colored Cube

We now have the tools we need to build three-dimensional graphical applications. Our tools are both conceptual and practical. We once again follow the pipeline approach that we pursued in our two-dimensional examples. Objects will again be defined in terms of sets of vertices. These vertices will pass through a number of transformations before the primitives that they define are rasterized in the frame buffer. The use of homogeneous coordinates not only will enable us to explain this process, but also will lead to efficient implementation techniques.

Consider the problem of drawing a rotating cube on the screen of our CRT. One frame of an animation is shown in Figure 4.28. We can identify a number of distinct tasks that we must perform to generate the image:

- Modeling
- Converting to the camera frame
- Clipping
- Projecting
- Removing hidden surfaces
- Rasterizing

We investigate each in turn. First, we shall see that three-dimensional objects can be represented, like two-dimensional objects, through a set of vertices. We shall also see that data structures will help us to incorporate the relationships among the vertices, edges, and faces of geometric objects. Such data structures are supported in OpenGL through a facility called *vertex arrays* that we introduce at the end of this section.

After we have modeled the cube, we can animate it using affine transformations. We introduce these transformations in Section 4.5. We use these transformations to alter OpenGL's model-view matrix. In Chapter 5, we use these transformations again as part of the viewing process. Our pipeline model will serve us well. Vertices will flow through a number of transformations in the pipeline, all of which will use our homogeneous-coordinate representation. At

Figure 4.28
One frame of cube animation.

the end of the pipeline awaits the rasterizer. At this point, we can assume it will do its job automatically, provided we perform the preliminary steps correctly.

4.4.1 Modeling of a Cube

The cube is as simple a three-dimensional object as we might expect to model and display. There are a number of ways, however, to model it. A CSG system would regard it as a single primitive. At the other extreme, the hardware processes the cube as an object consisting of eight vertices. Our decision to use surface-based models implies that we regard a cube either as the intersection of six planes, or as the six polygons that define its faces, called its **facets**. We start by assuming that the vertices of the cube are available through an array of vertices; for example, we could use

```
GLfloat vertices[8][3] = {{-1.0,-1.0,-1.0},{1.0,-1.0,-1.0},
   {1.0,1.0,-1.0}, {-1.0,1.0,-1.0}, {-1.0,-1.0,1.0},
   {1.0,-1.0,1.0}, {1.0,1.0,1.0}, {-1.0,1.0,1.0}};
```

We can adopt a more object-oriented form if we first define a three-dimensional point type

```
typedef GLfloat point3[3];
```

The vertices of the cube can then be defined as

```
point3 vertices[8] ={{-1.0,-1.0,-1.0},{1.0,-1.0,-1.0},
   {1.0,1.0,-1.0}, {-1.0,1.0,-1.0}, {-1.0,-1.0,1.0},
   {1.0,-1.0,1.0}, {1.0,1.0,1.0}, {-1.0,1.0,1.0}};
```

Our use of a `typedef` is a matter of convenience: OpenGL implements all vertices in four-dimensional homogeneous coordinates. Function calls using a three-dimensional type, such as `glVertex3fv`, have the values placed into four-dimensional form within the graphics system.

We can then use the list of points to define the faces of the cube. For example, one face is

```
glBegin(GL_POLYGON);
  glVertex3fv(vertices[0]);
  glVertex3fv(vertices[3]);
  glVertex3fv(vertices[2]);
  glVertex3fv(vertices[1]);
glEnd();
```

and we can define the other five faces in a similar manner. Note that we have defined three-dimensional polygons with exactly the same mechanism that we used to define two-dimensional polygons.

4.4.2 Inward- and Outward-Pointing Faces

We have to be careful about the order in which we specify our vertices when we are defining a three-dimensional polygon. We used the order 0, 3, 2, 1 for the first face. The order 1, 0, 3, 2 would be the same, because the final vertex in a polygon definition is always linked back to the first. However, the order 0, 1, 2, 3 is different. Although it describes the same boundary, the edges of the polygon are traversed in the reverse order—0, 3, 2, 1—as shown in Figure 4.29. In addition, each polygon has two sides. We can display either or both of them. First, however, we need a consistent way of identifying the faces.

We call a face **outward facing** if the vertices are traversed in a counterclockwise order when the face is viewed from the outside. This method is also known as the **right-hand rule** because, if you orient the fingers of your right hand in the direction the vertices are traversed, the thumb points outward.

In our example it was important to have defined the order as 0, 3, 2, 1, rather than as 0, 1, 2, 3, so that we could define the outer side of the back of the cube correctly.[4]

Figure 4.29 Traversal of the edges of a polygon.

4.4.3 Data Structures for Object Representation

We could now describe our cube through a set of vertex specifications. For example, we could use

`glBegin(GL_POLYGON)`

six times, each time followed by four vertices (via `glVertex`) and a `glEnd`, or we could use

`glBegin(GL_QUADS)`

followed by 24 vertices and a `glEnd`. Both of these methods work, but both fail to capture the essence of the cube's **topology**, as opposed to the cube's **geometry**. If we think of the cube as a polyhedron, we have an object—the cube—that is composed of six faces. The faces are each quadrilaterals that meet at vertices; each vertex is shared by three faces. In addition, pairs of vertices define edges of the quadrilaterals; each edge is shared by two faces. These statements describe the topology of a six-sided polyhedron. All are true, regardless of the location of the vertices—that is, regardless of the geometry of the object.[5]

---

4. *Back* here means as seen from the positive z direction. However, each face of an enclosed object, such as our cube, is an inside or outside face, regardless of from where we view it, as long as we view the face from outside the object.

5. We are ignoring special cases (singularities) that arise such as when three or more vertices lie along the same line, or when the vertices are moved so that we no longer have nonintersecting faces.

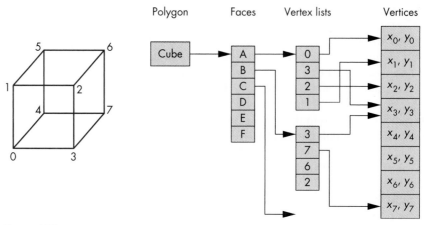

Figure 4.30 Vertex-list representation of a cube.

Throughout the rest of this book, we shall see that there are numerous advantages to building for our objects data structures that separate the topology from the geometry. In this example we use a structure, the vertex list, that is simple, is useful, and can be expanded later.

The data specifying the location of the vertices specify the geometry and can be stored as a simple list or array, such as in vertices[8]—the **vertex list**. The top-level entity is a cube; we regard it as being composed of six faces. Each face consists of four ordered vertices. Each vertex can be specified indirectly through its index. This data structure is shown in Figure 4.30. One of the advantages of this structure is that each geometric location appears only once, instead of being repeated each time it is used for a facet. If, in an interactive application, the location of a vertex is changed, the application needs to change that location only once, rather than searching for multiple occurrences of the vertex.

4.4.4 The Color Cube

We can use the vertex list to define a color cube. We assign the colors of the vertices of the color solid of Chapter 2 (black, white, red, green, blue, cyan, magenta, yellow) to the vertices. We define a function quad to draw quadrilateral polygons specified by pointers into the vertex list. Finally, the colorcube specifies the six faces, taking care to make them all outward-facing.

```
typedef GLfloat point3[3];

point3 vertices[8] ={{-1.0,-1.0,1.0},{-1.0,1.0,1.0},
    {1.0,1.0,1.0}, {1.0,-1.0,1.0}, {-1.0,-1.0,-1.0},
    {1.0,-1.0,-1.0}, {1.0,1.0,-1.0}, {-1.0,1.0,-1.0}};

GLfloat colors[8][3] = {{0.0,0.0,0.0},{1.0,0.0,0.0},
```

```
            {1.0,1.0,0.0}, {0.0,1.0,0.0}, {0.0,0.0,1.0},
            {1.0,0.0,1.0}, {1.0,1.0,1.0}, {0.0,1.0,1.0}};
    void quad(int a, int b, int c, int d)
    {
       glBegin(GL_QUADS);
          glColor3fv(colors[a]);
          glVertex3fv(vertices[a]);
          glColor3fv(colors[b]);
          glVertex3fv(vertices[b]);
          glColor3fv(colors[c]);
          glVertex3fv(vertices[c]);
          glColor3fv(colors[d]);
          glVertex3fv(vertices[d]);
       glEnd();
    }

    void colorcube()
    {
       quad(0,3,2,1);
       quad(2,3,7,6);
       quad(0,4,7,3);
       quad(1,2,6,5);
       quad(4,5,6,7);
       quad(0,1,5,4);
    }
```

4.4.5 Bilinear Interpolation

Although we have specified colors for the vertices of the cube, the graphics system must decide how to use this information to assign colors to points inside the polygon. There are many ways to use the colors of the vertices to fill in, or **interpolate**, colors across a polygon. Probably the most common method—one that we use in other contexts—is **bilinear interpolation**.

Consider the polygon in Figure 4.31. The colors C_0, C_1, C_2, and C_3 are the ones assigned to the vertices in the application program. We can use linear interpolation to interpolate colors[6] along the edges between vertices 0 and 1, and between 2 and 3, by using

$$C_{01}(\alpha) = (1 - \alpha)C_0 + \alpha C_1,$$
$$C_{23}(\alpha) = (1 - \alpha)C_2 + \alpha C_3.$$

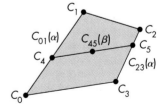

Figure 4.31 Bilinear interpolation.

---

6. Assume we are using RGB color and that the interpolation is applied individually to each primary color.

COP

Figure 4.32 Projection of polygon.

As α goes from 0 to 1, we generate colors, $C_{01}(\alpha)$ and $C_{23}(\alpha)$, along these two edges. For a given value of α, we obtain two colors, C_4 and C_5, on these edges. We can now interpolate colors along the line connecting the two points on the edges corresponding to C_4 and C_5:

$$C_{45}(\beta) = (1 - \beta)C_4 + \beta C_5.$$

For a flat quadrilateral, each color generated by this method corresponds to a point on the polygon. If the four vertices are not all in the same plane, then, although a color is generated, its location on a surface is not clearly defined.

A related algorithm, **scan-line interpolation**, avoids the flatness issue and can be made part of the scan-conversion process. A polygon is filled only when it is displayed. If we wait until rasterization, the polygon is first projected onto the two-dimensional plane (Figure 4.32). If we fill a quadrilateral scan line by scan line, as shown in Figure 4.33, then colors are assigned scan line by scan line on the basis of only two edges. OpenGL provides this method, not only for colors, but also, as we shall see in Chapter 6, for other values that can be assigned on a vertex-by-vertex basis.

We now have an object that we can display much as we did to the three-dimensional Sierpinski gasket in Section 2.9, using glOrtho to provide a basic orthographic projection. In Section 4.5 we introduce transformations, enabling us to animate the cube and also to construct more complex objects. First, however, we introduce an OpenGL 1.1 feature that not only reduces the overhead of generating our cube, but also gives us a higher-level method of working with the cube and with other polyhedral objects.

4.4.6 Vertex Arrays

Although we used vertex lists to model our cube, when we draw the cube we are making many calls to OpenGL functions. If we assign a color to each vertex, we make 50 OpenGL calls: six faces, each of which needs a glBegin, a glEnd, four

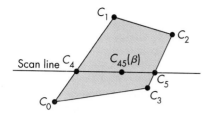

Figure 4.33 Scan-line interpolation.

calls to glColor, and four calls to glVertex. Each call involves overhead and data transfer. If, as we shall do in Chapter 6, we also specify a different normal vector at each vertex, we makes even more function calls to draw our cube. Hence, although we have used a data structure that helps us to conceptualize the cube as a three-dimensional geometric object, the code to draw it may not execute quickly.

Vertex arrays provide a method for encapsulating the information in our data structure such that we can draw polyhedral objects with only a few function calls. They allow us to define a data structure using vertices and pass this structure to the implementation. When the objects defined by these arrays need to be drawn, we can ask OpenGL to traverse the structure with just a few function calls.

There are three steps in using vertex arrays. First, we enable the functionality of vertex arrays. Second, we tell OpenGL where and in what format the arrays are. Third, we render the object. The first two steps can be part of the initialization; the third is typically part of the display callback. We illustrate for the cube.

OpenGL allows six different types of arrays (vertex, color, color index, normal, texture coordinate, and edge flag), corresponding to six items that can be set between a glBegin and a glEnd, although a given application usually requires only a subset of these types. For our rotating cube, we need only colors and vertices. We enable the corresponding arrays by

```
glEnableClientState(GL_COLOR_ARRAY);
glEnableClientState(GL_VERTEX_ARRAY);
```

The arrays are the same as before and can be set up as globals:

```
GLfloat vertices[] = {{-1.0,-1.0,-1.0},{1.0,-1.0,-1.0},
{1.0,1.0,-1.0}, {-1.0,1.0,-1.0}, {-1.0,-1.0,1.0},
{1.0,-1.0,1.0}, {1.0,1.0,1.0}, {-1.0,1.0,1.0}};

GLfloat colors[] = {{0.0,0.0,0.0},{1.0,0.0,0.0},
{1.0,1.0,0.0}, {0.0,1.0,0.0}, {0.0,0.0,1.0},
{1.0,0.0,1.0}, {1.0,1.0,1.0}, {0.0,1.0,1.0}};
```

We next identify where the arrays are by

```
glVertexPointer(3, GL_FLOAT, 0, vertices);
glColorPointer(3,GL_FLOAT, 0, colors);
```

The first three arguments state that the elements are three-dimensional colors and vertices stored as floats and that the elements are contiguous in the arrays. The fourth argument is a pointer to the actual array.

Now we have to provide the information in our data structure about the relationship between the vertices and the faces of the cube. We do so by specifying an array that holds the 24 ordered vertex indices for the six faces.

```
GLubyte cubeIndices[24]={0,3,2,1,2,3,7,6,0,4,7,
    3,1,2,6,5,4,5,6,7,0,1,5,4};
```

Thus, the first face is determined by the indices (0, 3, 2, 1), the second by (1, 2, 3, 7), and so on. Note that we have put the indices in an order that preserves outside-facing polygons. The index array can also be specified as a global.

Now we can render the cube through use of the arrays. When we draw elements of the arrays, all the enabled arrays (in this example, colors and vertices) are rendered. We have a few options regarding how to draw the arrays. We can use the function

```
glDrawElements(type, n, format, pointer)
```

Here type is the type of element, such as a line or polygon, that the arrays define; n is the number of elements that we wish to draw; format describes the form of the data in the index array, and pointer points to the first index to use.

For our cube, within the display callback we could make six calls to glDrawElements, one for each face:

```
for(i=0;i<6;i++)
    glDrawElements(GL_POLYGON, 4, GL_UNSIGNED_BYTE, &cubeIndex[4*i]);
```

Thus, once we have set up and initialized the arrays, each time that we draw the cube, we have only six function calls. We can rotate the cube as before; glDrawElements uses the present state when it draws the cube.

We can do even better though. Each face of the cube is a quadrilateral. Thus, if we use GL_QUADS, rather than GL_POLYGON, we can draw the cube with the single function call

```
glDrawElements(GL_QUADS, 24, GL_UNSIGNED_BYTE, cubeIndices);
```

because GL_QUADS starts a new quadrilateral after each four vertices.

4.5 Affine Transformations

A **transformation** is a function that takes a point (or vector) and maps that point (or vector) into another point (or vector). We can picture such a function by looking at Figure 4.34 or by writing down the functional form

$$Q = T(P)$$

for points, or

$$v = R(u)$$

for vectors. If we can use homogeneous coordinates, then we can represent both vectors and points as four-dimensional column matrices, and can define the transformation with a single function

$$\mathbf{q} = f(\mathbf{p}),$$

$$\mathbf{v} = f(\mathbf{u}),$$

Figure 4.34 Transformation.

that transforms the representations of both points and vectors in a given frame.

This formulation is too general to be useful, as it encompasses all single-valued mappings of points and vectors. In practice, even if we were to have a convenient description of the function $f()$, we would have to carry out the transformation on every point on a curve. For example, if we transform a line segment, a general transformation might require us to carry out the transformation for every point between the two endpoints.

Consider a restricted class of transformations. Let us assume that we are working in four-dimensional homogeneous coordinates. In this space, both points and vectors are represented as vertices—that is, as 4-tuples in a four-dimensional vector space.[7] We can obtain a useful class of transformations if we place restrictions on $f()$. The most important restriction is linearity. A function $f()$ is a **linear function** if and only if, for any scalars α and β, and any vertices p and q,

$$f(\alpha p + \beta q) = \alpha f(p) + \beta f(q).$$

The importance of such functions is that, if we know the transformations of vertices, we can obtain the transformations of linear combinations of vertices by linear combinations of transformations of the vertices. We do not have to recalculate the transformations for every linear combination.

In four-dimensional space, we work with the representations of points and vectors. A linear transformation then transforms the representation of a given point (or vector) into another representation of that point (or vector), and can

---

7. We consider only those functions that map vertices to other vertices and that obey the rules for manipulating points and vectors that we have developed in this chapter and in Appendix B.

always be written in terms of the two representations, $\mathbf{u}$ and $\mathbf{v}$, as a matrix multiplication:

$$\mathbf{v} = \mathbf{A}\mathbf{u},$$

where $\mathbf{A}$ is a square matrix. Comparing this expression with what we obtained in Section 4.3 for changes in frame, we can observe that, as long as $\mathbf{A}$ is nonsingular, each linear transformation corresponds to a change in frame. Hence, we can view a linear transformation in two equivalent ways: (1) as a change in the underlying representation, or frame, that yields a new representation of our vertices, or (2) as a transformation of the vertices within the same frame.

When we work with homogeneous coordinates, $\mathbf{A}$ is a 4×4 matrix that leaves unchanged the fourth (w) component of a representation. The matrix $\mathbf{A}$ is of the form

$$\mathbf{A} = \begin{bmatrix} \alpha_{11} & \alpha_{12} & \alpha_{13} & \alpha_{14} \\ \alpha_{21} & \alpha_{22} & \alpha_{23} & \alpha_{24} \\ \alpha_{31} & \alpha_{32} & \alpha_{33} & \alpha_{34} \\ 0 & 0 & 0 & 1 \end{bmatrix}.$$

The 12 values can be set arbitrarily, and we say this transformation has 12 *degrees of freedom*. However, points and vectors have slightly different representations in our affine space. Any vector is represented as

$$\mathbf{u} = \begin{bmatrix} \alpha_1 \\ \alpha_2 \\ \alpha_3 \\ 0 \end{bmatrix}.$$

Any point can be written as

$$\mathbf{p} = \begin{bmatrix} \beta_1 \\ \beta_2 \\ \beta_3 \\ 1 \end{bmatrix}.$$

If we apply an arbitrary $\mathbf{A}$ to a vector,

$$\mathbf{v} = \mathbf{A}\mathbf{u},$$

we see that only nine of the elements of $\mathbf{A}$ affect $\mathbf{u}$, and, thus, there are only 9 degrees of freedom in the transformation of vectors. Affine transformations of points have the full 12 degrees of freedom.

We can also show that affine transformations preserve lines. Suppose that we write a line in the form

$$P(\alpha) = P_0 + \alpha d,$$

where P_0 is a point and d is a vector. In any frame, the line can be expressed as

$$\mathbf{p}(\alpha) = \mathbf{p}_0 + \alpha \mathbf{d},$$

where $\mathbf{p}_0$ and $\mathbf{d}$ are the representations of P_0 and d in that frame. For any affine transformation matrix $\mathbf{A}$,

$$\mathbf{A}\mathbf{p}(\alpha) = \mathbf{A}\mathbf{p}_0 + \alpha\mathbf{A}\mathbf{d}.$$

Thus, we can construct the transformed line by first transforming $\mathbf{p}_0$ and $\mathbf{d}$, and using whatever line-generation algorithm we choose when the line segment must be displayed. If we use the two-point form of the line,

$$\mathbf{p}(\alpha) = \alpha\mathbf{p}_0 + (1 - \alpha)\mathbf{p}_1,$$

a similar result holds. We transform the representations of $\mathbf{p}_0$ and $\mathbf{p}_1$, and then construct the transformed line. Because there are only 12 elements in $\mathbf{M}$ that we can select arbitrarily, there are 12 degrees of freedom in the affine transformation of a line or line segment.

We have expressed these results in terms of abstract mathematical spaces. However, their importance in computer graphics is practical. We need only to transform the homogeneous-coordinate representation of the endpoints of a line segment to determine completely a transformed line. Thus, we can implement our graphics systems as a pipeline that passes endpoints through affine-transformation units, and we can finally generate the line at the rasterization stage.

Fortunately, most of the transformations that we need in computer graphics are affine. These transformations include rotation, translation, and scaling. With slight modifications, we can also use these results to describe the standard parallel and perspective projections.

4.6 Translation, Rotation, and Scaling

We have been going back and forth between looking at geometric objects as abstract entities and working with their representation in a given frame. When we work with application programs, we have to work with representations. In this section, first we show how we can describe the most important affine transformations independently of any representation. Then, we find matrices that describe these transformations by acting on the representations of our points and vectors. In Section 4.8, we shall see how these transformations are implemented in OpenGL.

We look at transformations as ways of moving to new positions a group of points that describes one or more geometric objects. Although there are many ways to transform one point to a new position, there will almost always be only a single way to move a collection of points to new positions with a single transformation, preserving the relationships among the vertices of the object. Hence, although we can find both a rotation matrix and a translation matrix that will move a point P_0 to the point Q_0, using these matrices on a set of points $\{P_0, P_1, P_2, \ldots\}$ will produce different results.

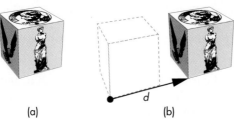

(a)   (b)

Figure 4.35 Translation. (a) Object in original
position. (b) Object translated.

4.6.1 Translation

Translation is an operation that displaces points by a fixed distance in a given
direction, as shown in Figure 4.35. To specify a translation, we need only to
specify a displacement vector d, because the transformed points are given by

$$P' = P + d$$

for all points P on the object. Note that this definition of translation makes no
reference to a frame or representation. Translation has 3 degrees of freedom, because we can specify the three components of the displacement vector arbitrarily.

4.6.2 Rotation

Rotation is more difficult to specify than translation, because more parameters
are involved. We start with the simple example of rotating a point about the
origin in a two-dimensional plane, as shown in Figure 4.36. Having specified a
particular point—the origin—we are in a particular frame. A two-dimensional
point at (x, y) in this frame is rotated about the origin by an angle θ to the
position (x', y'). We can obtain the standard equations describing this rotation
by representing (x, y) and (x', y') in polar form:

$$x = \rho \cos \phi,$$

$$y = \rho \sin \phi,$$

$$x' = \rho \cos(\theta + \phi),$$

$$y' = \rho \sin(\theta + \phi).$$

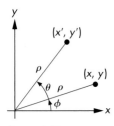

Figure 4.36 Two-
dimensional rotation.

Expanding these terms using the trigonometric identities for the sine and cosine
of the sum of two angles, we find

$$x' = \rho \cos \phi \cos \theta - \rho \sin \phi \sin \theta = x \cos \theta - y \sin \theta,$$

$$y' = \rho \cos \phi \sin \theta + \rho \sin \phi \cos \theta = x \sin \theta + y \cos \theta.$$

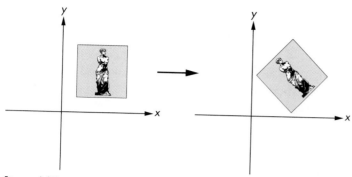

Figure 4.37 Rotation about a fixed point.

These equations can be written in matrix form as

$$\begin{bmatrix} x' \\ y' \end{bmatrix} = \begin{bmatrix} \cos\theta & -\sin\theta \\ \sin\theta & \cos\theta \end{bmatrix} \begin{bmatrix} x \\ y \end{bmatrix}.$$

We expand this form to three dimensions in Section 4.7.

Note three features of this transformation that extend to other rotations:

1. There is one point—the origin, in this case—that is unchanged by the rotation. We call this the **fixed point** of the transformation. Figure 4.37 shows a two-dimensional rotation about a different fixed point.
2. Knowing that the two-dimensional plane is part of three-dimensional space, we can reinterpret this rotation in three dimensions. In a right-handed system, when we draw the x- and y-axes in the standard way, the positive z-axis comes out of the page. Our definition of a positive direction of rotation is counterclockwise when we look down the positive z-axis toward the origin. We use this definition to define positive rotations about other axes.
3. Two-dimensional rotation in the plane is equivalent to three-dimensional rotation about the z-axis. Points in planes of constant z all rotate in a similar manner, leaving their z values unchanged.

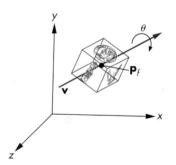

Figure 4.38 Three-dimensional rotation.

We can use these observations to define a general three-dimensional rotation that is independent of the frame. We must specify the three entities shown in Figure 4.38: a fixed point (P_f), a rotation angle (θ), and a line or vector about which to rotate. For a given fixed point, there are 3 degrees of freedom: the two angles necessary to specify the orientation of the vector, and the angle that specifies the amount of rotation about the vector.

Rotation and translation are known as **rigid-body transformations**. No combination of rotations and translations can alter the shape of an object; they can alter only the object's location and orientation. Consequently, rotation and translation alone cannot give us all possible affine transformations. The transformations in Figure 4.39 are affine, but they are not rigid-body transformations.

Figure 4.39 Non–rigid-body transformations.

Figure 4.40 Uniform and nonuniform scaling.

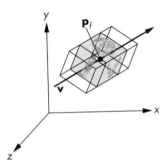

Figure 4.41 Effect of scale factor.

Figure 4.42 Reflection.

4.6.3 Scaling

Scaling is an affine non–rigid-body transformation. We can combine a properly chosen sequence of scalings, translations, and rotations to form any affine transformation. Scaling can make an object bigger or smaller, as shown in Figure 4.40, which illustrates both uniform scaling in all directions and scaling in a single direction. We need nonuniform scaling to build up the full set of affine transformations that we use in modeling and viewing.

Scaling transformations have a fixed point, as we can see from Figure 4.41. Hence, to specify a scaling, we can specify the fixed point, a direction in which we wish to scale, and a scale factor (α). For $\alpha > 1$, the object gets longer in the specified direction; for $0 \leq \alpha < 1$, the object gets smaller in that direction. Negative values of α give us **reflection** (Figure 4.42) about the fixed point, in the scaling direction.

4.7 Transformations in Homogeneous Coordinates

Most graphics APIs force us to work within some reference system. Although we can alter this reference system—usually a frame—we cannot work with high-level representations, such as the expression

$$Q = P + \alpha v.$$

Instead, we work with representations in homogeneous coordinates, and with expressions such as

$$\mathbf{q} = \mathbf{p} + \alpha \mathbf{v}.$$

Within a frame, each affine transformation is represented by a 4×4 matrix of the form

$$\mathbf{M} = \begin{bmatrix} \alpha_{11} & \alpha_{12} & \alpha_{13} & \alpha_{14} \\ \alpha_{21} & \alpha_{22} & \alpha_{23} & \alpha_{24} \\ \alpha_{31} & \alpha_{32} & \alpha_{33} & \alpha_{34} \\ 0 & 0 & 0 & 1 \end{bmatrix}.$$

4.7.1 Translation

Translation displaces points to new positions defined by a displacement vector. If we move the point $\mathbf{p}$ to $\mathbf{p}'$ by displacing by a distance $\mathbf{d}$, then

$$\mathbf{p}' = \mathbf{p} + \mathbf{d}.$$

Looking at their homogeneous-coordinate forms

$$\mathbf{p} = \begin{bmatrix} x \\ y \\ z \\ 1 \end{bmatrix}, \qquad \mathbf{p}' = \begin{bmatrix} x' \\ y' \\ z' \\ 1 \end{bmatrix}, \qquad \mathbf{d} = \begin{bmatrix} \alpha_x \\ \alpha_y \\ \alpha_z \\ 0 \end{bmatrix},$$

we see that these equations can be written component by component as

$$x' = x + \alpha_x,$$
$$y' = y + \alpha_y,$$
$$z' = z + \alpha_z.$$

This method of representing translation using the addition of column matrices does not combine well with our representations of other affine transformations. However, we can also get this result using the matrix multiplication:

$$\mathbf{p}' = \mathbf{T}\mathbf{p},$$

where

$$\mathbf{T} = \begin{bmatrix} 1 & 0 & 0 & \alpha_x \\ 0 & 1 & 0 & \alpha_y \\ 0 & 0 & 1 & \alpha_z \\ 0 & 0 & 0 & 1 \end{bmatrix}.$$

$\mathbf{T}$ is called the **translation matrix**. We sometimes write it as $\mathbf{T}(\alpha_x, \alpha_y, \alpha_z)$ to emphasize the three independent parameters.

It might appear that the fourth element of the column matrices is not necessary. However, it is not possible to get the same result using a three-dimensional version in the form $\mathbf{p}' = \mathbf{T}\mathbf{p}$. For this reason, the use of homogeneous coordinates is often seen as a clever trick that allows us to convert the addition of column matrices in three dimensions to matrix–matrix multiplication in four dimensions.

We can obtain the inverse of a translation matrix either by applying an inversion algorithm or by noting that, if we displace a point by the vector d, we can return to the original position by a displacement of $-d$. By either method, we find that

$$\mathbf{T}^{-1}(\alpha_x, \alpha_y, \alpha_z) = \mathbf{T}(-\alpha_x, -\alpha_y, -\alpha_z) = \begin{bmatrix} 1 & 0 & 0 & -\alpha_x \\ 0 & 1 & 0 & -\alpha_y \\ 0 & 0 & 1 & -\alpha_z \\ 0 & 0 & 0 & 1 \end{bmatrix}.$$

4.7.2 Scaling

For both scaling and rotation, there is a fixed point that is unchanged by the transformation. We let the fixed point be the origin, and we show how we can concatenate transformations to obtain the transformation for an arbitrary fixed point.

A scaling matrix with a fixed point of the origin allows for independent scaling along the coordinate axes. The three equations are

$$x' = \beta_x x,$$
$$y' = \beta_y y,$$
$$z' = \beta_z z.$$

These three equations can be combined in homogeneous form as

$$\mathbf{p}' = \mathbf{S}\mathbf{p},$$

where

$$\mathbf{S} = \mathbf{S}(\beta_x, \beta_y, \beta_z) = \begin{bmatrix} \beta_x & 0 & 0 & 0 \\ 0 & \beta_y & 0 & 0 \\ 0 & 0 & \beta_z & 0 \\ 0 & 0 & 0 & 1 \end{bmatrix}.$$

Note that, as is true of the translation matrix and, indeed, of all homogeneous coordinate transformations, the final row of the matrix does not depend on the particular transformation, but rather forces the fourth component of the transformed point to retain the value 1.

We obtain the inverse of a scaling matrix by applying the reciprocals of the scale factors:

$$\mathbf{S}^{-1}(\beta_x, \beta_y, \beta_z) = \mathbf{S}\left(\frac{1}{\beta_x}, \frac{1}{\beta_y}, \frac{1}{\beta_z}\right).$$

4.7.3 Rotation

We first look at rotation with a fixed point at the origin. There are 3 degrees of freedom corresponding to our ability to rotate independently about the three coordinate axes. We have to be careful, however, because matrix multiplication is not a commutative operation (Appendix C). Rotation about the x-axis by an angle θ followed by rotation about the y-axis by an angle ϕ does not give us the same result as the one that we obtain if we reverse the order of the rotations.

We can find the matrices for rotation about the individual axes directly from the results of the two-dimensional rotation that we developed in Section 4.6. We saw that the two-dimensional rotation was actually a rotation in three dimensions about the z-axis, and that the points remained in planes of constant z. Thus, in three dimensions, the equations for rotation about the z-axis by an angle θ are

$$x' = x \cos \theta - y \sin \theta,$$
$$y' = x \sin \theta + y \cos \theta,$$
$$z' = z;$$

or, in matrix form,

$$\mathbf{p}' = \mathbf{R}_z\mathbf{p},$$

where

$$\mathbf{R}_z = \mathbf{R}_z(\theta) = \begin{bmatrix} \cos\theta & -\sin\theta & 0 & 0 \\ \sin\theta & \cos\theta & 0 & 0 \\ 0 & 0 & 1 & 0 \\ 0 & 0 & 0 & 1 \end{bmatrix}.$$

We can derive the matrices for rotation about the x- and y-axes through an identical argument. If we rotate about the x-axis, the x values are unchanged, and we have a two-dimensional rotation in which points rotate in planes of constant x; for rotation about the y-axis, the y values are unchanged. The matrices are

$$\mathbf{R}_x = \mathbf{R}_x(\theta) = \begin{bmatrix} 1 & 0 & 0 & 0 \\ 0 & \cos\theta & -\sin\theta & 0 \\ 0 & \sin\theta & \cos\theta & 0 \\ 0 & 0 & 0 & 1 \end{bmatrix},$$

$$\mathbf{R}_y = \mathbf{R}_y(\theta) = \begin{bmatrix} \cos\theta & 0 & \sin\theta & 0 \\ 0 & 1 & 0 & 0 \\ -\sin\theta & 0 & \cos\theta & 0 \\ 0 & 0 & 0 & 1 \end{bmatrix}.$$

The signs of the sine terms are consistent with our definition of a positive rotation in a right-handed system.

Suppose that we let $\mathbf{R}$ denote any of our three rotation matrices. A rotation by θ can always be undone by a subsequent rotation by $-\theta$; hence,

$$\mathbf{R}^{-1}(\theta) = \mathbf{R}(-\theta).$$

In addition, noting that all the cosine terms are on the diagonal and the sine terms are off-diagonal, we can use the trigonometric identities $\cos(-\theta) = \cos\theta$ and $\sin(-\theta) = -\sin\theta$ to find

$$\mathbf{R}^{-1}(\theta) = \mathbf{R}^T(\theta).$$

In Section 4.8, we show how to construct any desired rotation matrix, with a fixed point at the origin, as a product of individual rotations about the three axes

$$\mathbf{R} = \mathbf{R}_z\mathbf{R}_y\mathbf{R}_x.$$

Using the fact that the transpose of a product is the product of the transposes in the reverse order, we see that, for any rotation matrix,

$$\mathbf{R}^{-1} = \mathbf{R}^T.$$

A matrix whose inverse is equal to its transpose is called an **orthogonal matrix**. Normalized orthogonal matrices correspond to rotations about the origin.

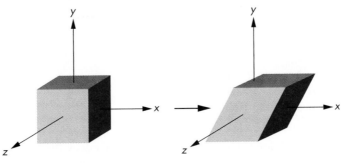

Figure 4.43 Shear.

4.7.4 Shear

Although we can construct any affine transformation from a sequence of rotations, translations, and scalings, there is one more affine transformation—the **shear** transformation—that is of such importance that we regard it as a basic type, rather than deriving it from the others. Consider a cube centered at the origin, aligned with the axes and viewed from the positive z-axis, as shown in Figure 4.43. If we pull the top to the right and the bottom to the left, we shear the object in the x direction. Note that neither the y nor the z values are changed by the shear, so we can call this operation x shear to distinguish it from shears of the cube in other possible directions. Using simple trigonometry on Figure 4.44, we see that each shear is characterized by a single angle θ; the equations for this shear are

$$x' = x + y \cot \theta,$$

$$y' = y,$$

$$z' = z,$$

Figure 4.44 Computation of the shear matrix.

leading to the shearing matrix

$$\mathbf{H}_x(\theta) = \begin{bmatrix} 1 & \cot \theta & 0 & 0 \\ 0 & 1 & 0 & 0 \\ 0 & 0 & 1 & 0 \\ 0 & 0 & 0 & 1 \end{bmatrix}.$$

We can obtain the inverse by noting that we need to shear in only the opposite direction; hence,

$$\mathbf{H}_x^{-1}(\theta) = \mathbf{H}_x(-\theta).$$

Figure 4.45 Application of transformations one at a time.

4.8 Concatenation of Transformations

In this section, we create examples of affine transformations by multiplying together, or **concatenating**, sequences of the basic transformations that we just introduced. Using this strategy is preferable to attempting to define an arbitrary transformation directly. The approach fits well with our pipeline architectures for implementing graphics systems.

Suppose that we carry out three successive transformations on a point **p**, creating a new point **q**. Because the matrix product is associative, we can write the sequence as

$$\mathbf{q} = \mathbf{CBAp},$$

without parentheses. However, the order in which we carry out the transformations does affect the efficiency of the calculation. In one view, we can carry out **A**, followed by **B**, followed by **C**—an order that corresponds to the grouping (Figure 4.45)

$$\mathbf{q} = (\mathbf{C}(\mathbf{B}(\mathbf{Ap}))).$$

If we are to transform a single point, this order is the most efficient, because each matrix multiplication involves multiplying a column matrix by a square matrix. If we have many points to transform, then we can proceed in two steps. First, we calculate

$$\mathbf{M} = \mathbf{CBA}.$$

Then, we use this matrix on each point

$$\mathbf{q} = \mathbf{Mp}.$$

This order corresponds to the pipeline in Figure 4.46, where we compute **M** first, then load it into a pipeline transformation unit. If we simply count operations,

Figure 4.46 Pipeline transformation.

we see that although we do a little more work in computing $\mathbf{M}$ initially, because $\mathbf{M}$ may be applied to tens of thousands of points, this extra work is insignificant compared with the savings we obtain by using a single matrix multiplication for each point. We now derive examples of computing $\mathbf{M}$.

4.8.1 Rotation About a Fixed Point

Our first example shows how we can alter the transformations that we defined with a fixed point at the origin (rotation, scaling, shear) to have an arbitrary fixed point. We demonstrate for rotation about the z-axis; the technique is the same for the other cases.

Consider a cube with its center at $\mathbf{p}_f$ and its sides aligned with the axes. We want to rotate the cube about the z-axis, but this time about its center $\mathbf{p}_f$, which becomes the fixed point of the transformation, as shown in Figure 4.47. If $\mathbf{p}_f$ were the origin, we would know how to solve the problem: We would simply use $\mathbf{R}_z(\theta)$. This observation suggests the strategy of first moving the cube to the origin. We can then apply $\mathbf{R}_z(\theta)$, and finally move the object back such that its center is again at $\mathbf{p}_f$. This sequence is shown in Figure 4.48. In terms of our basic affine transformations, the first is $\mathbf{T}(-\mathbf{p}_f)$, the second is $\mathbf{R}_z(\theta)$, and the final is $\mathbf{T}(\mathbf{p}_f)$. Concatenating them together, we obtain the single matrix

$$\mathbf{M} = \mathbf{T}(\mathbf{p}_f)\mathbf{R}_z(\theta)\mathbf{T}(-\mathbf{p}_f).$$

If we multiply out the matrices, we find that

$$\mathbf{M} = \begin{bmatrix} \cos\theta & -\sin\theta & 0 & x_f - x_f\cos\theta + y_f\sin\theta \\ \sin\theta & \cos\theta & 0 & y_f - x_f\sin\theta - y_f\cos\theta \\ 0 & 0 & 1 & 0 \\ 0 & 0 & 0 & 1 \end{bmatrix}.$$

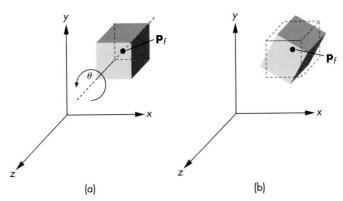

(a)   (b)

Figure 4.47 Rotation of a cube about its center.

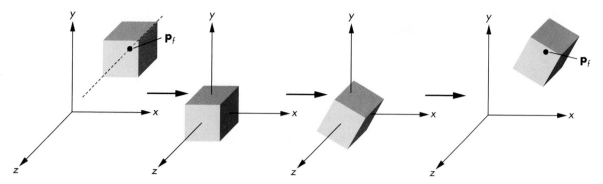

Figure 4.48 Sequence of transformations.

4.8.2 General Rotation

We now show that an arbitrary rotation about the origin can be composed of three successive rotations about the three axes. The order is not unique (see Exercise 4.10), although the resulting rotation matrix is. We form the desired matrix by first doing a rotation about the z-axis, then doing a rotation about the y-axis, and concluding with a rotation about the x-axis.

Consider the cube, again centered at the origin with its sides aligned with the axes, as shown in Figure 4.49(a). We can rotate it about the z-axis by an angle α to orient it as shown in Figure 4.49(b). We then rotate the cube by an angle β about the y-axis, as shown in a top view in Figure 4.50. Finally, we rotate the cube by an angle γ about the x-axis, as shown in a side view in Figure 4.51. Our final rotation matrix is

$$\mathbf{R} = \mathbf{R}_x \mathbf{R}_y \mathbf{R}_z.$$

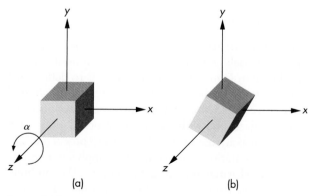

(a)   (b)

Figure 4.49 Rotation of a cube about the z-axis. The cube is shown (a) before rotation, and (b) after rotation.

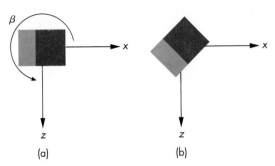

Figure 4.50 Rotation of a cube about the *y*-axis.

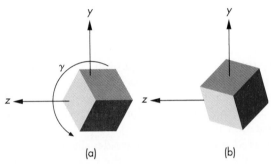

Figure 4.51 Rotation of a cube about the *x*-axis.

A little experimentation should convince you that we can achieve any desired orientation by proper choice of α, β, and γ, although, as we shall see in the example of Section 4.8.4, finding these angles can be tricky.

4.8.3 The Instance Transformation

Figure 4.52 Scene of simple objects.

Our example of a cube that can be rotated to any desired orientation suggests a generalization appropriate for modeling. Consider a scene composed of many simple objects, such as that shown in Figure 4.52. One option is to define each of these objects, through its vertices, in the desired location with the desired orientation and size. An alternative is to define each of the object types once at a convenient size, in a convenient place, and with a convenient orientation. Each occurrence of an object in the scene is an **instance** of that object's prototype, and we can obtain the desired size, orientation, and location by applying an affine transformation—the **instance transformation**—to the prototype. We can build a simple database to describe a scene from a list of object identifiers (such as 1 for a cube and 2 for a sphere) and of the instance transformation to be applied to each object.

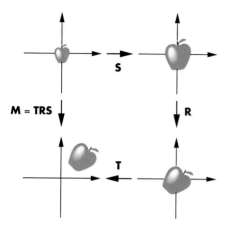

Figure 4.53 Instance transformation.

The instance transformation is applied in the order shown in Figure 4.53. Objects are usually defined in their own frames, with the origin at the center of mass and the sides aligned with the axes. First, we scale the object to the desired size. Then, we orient it with a rotation matrix. Finally, we translate it to the desired orientation. Hence, the instance transformation is of the form

$$\mathbf{M} = \mathbf{TRS}.$$

Modeling with the instance transformation works well not only with our pipeline architectures, but also with the display lists that we introduced in Chapter 3. A complex object that is used many times can be loaded into the server once as a display list. Displaying each instance of it requires only sending the appropriate instance transformation to the server.

4.8.4 Rotation About an Arbitrary Axis

Our final rotation example illustrates not only how we can achieve a rotation about an arbitrary point and line in space, but also how we can use direction angles to specify orientations. Consider rotating a cube, as shown in Figure 4.54. We need three entities to specify this rotation. There is a fixed point $\mathbf{p}_0$ that we assume is the center of the cube, a vector about which we rotate, and an angle of rotation. Note that none of these entities relies on a frame, and that we have just specified a rotation in a coordinate-free manner. Nonetheless, to find an affine matrix to represent this transformation, we have to assume that we are in some frame.

The vector about which we wish to rotate the cube can be specified in various ways. One way is to use two points, $\mathbf{p}_1$ and $\mathbf{p}_2$, defining the vector

$$\mathbf{u} = \mathbf{p}_2 - \mathbf{p}_1.$$

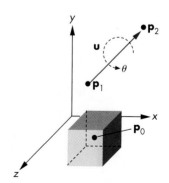

Figure 4.54 Rotation of a cube about an arbitrary axis.

Note that the order of the points determines the positive direction of rotation for θ, and that, although we draw $\mathbf{u}$ as passing through $\mathbf{p}_0$, only the orientation of $\mathbf{u}$ matters. Replacing $\mathbf{u}$ with a unit-length vector

$$\mathbf{v} = \frac{\mathbf{u}}{|\mathbf{u}|} = \begin{bmatrix} \alpha_x \\ \alpha_y \\ \alpha_z \end{bmatrix}$$

in the same direction simplifies the subsequent steps. We have already seen that moving the fixed point to the origin is a helpful technique. Thus, our first transformation is the translation $\mathbf{T}(-\mathbf{p}_0)$, and the final one is $\mathbf{T}(\mathbf{p}_0)$. After the initial translation, the required rotation problem is as shown in Figure 4.55. Our previous example (Section 4.8.2) showed that we could get an arbitrary rotation from three rotations about the individual axes. This problem is more difficult, because we do not know what angles to use for the individual rotations. Our strategy is to carry out two rotations to align the axis of rotation, $\mathbf{v}$, with the z-axis. Then, we can rotate by θ about the z-axis, after which we can undo the two rotations that did the aligning. Our final rotation matrix will be of the form

$$\mathbf{R} = \mathbf{R}_x(-\theta_x)\mathbf{R}_y(-\theta_y)\mathbf{R}_z(\theta)\mathbf{R}_y(\theta_y)\mathbf{R}_x(\theta_x).$$

This sequence of rotations is shown in Figure 4.56. The difficult part of the process is determining θ_x and θ_y.

We proceed by looking at the components of $\mathbf{v}$. Because $\mathbf{v}$ is a unit-length vector,

$$\alpha_x^2 + \alpha_y^2 + \alpha_z^2 = 1.$$

We draw a line segment from the origin to the point $(\alpha_x, \alpha_y, \alpha_z)$. This line segment has unit length and the orientation of $\mathbf{v}$. Next, we draw the perpendiculars

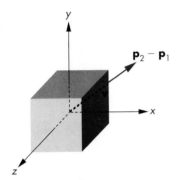

Figure 4.55 Movement of the fixed point to the origin.

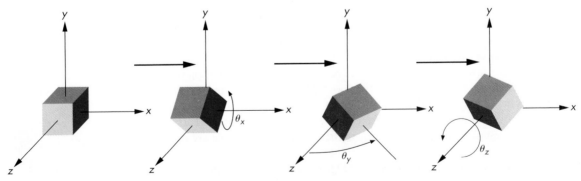

Figure 4.56 Sequence of rotations.

from the point $(\alpha_x, \alpha_y, \alpha_z)$ to the coordinate axes, as shown in Figure 4.57. The three **direction angles**—ϕ_x, ϕ_y, ϕ_z—are the angles between the line segment (or **v**) and the axes. The **direction cosines** are given by

$$\cos \phi_x = \alpha_x,$$
$$\cos \phi_y = \alpha_y,$$
$$\cos \phi_z = \alpha_z.$$

Only two of the direction angles are independent, because

$$\cos^2 \phi_x + \cos^2 \phi_y + \cos^2 \phi_z = 1.$$

We can now compute θ_x and θ_y using these angles. Consider Figure 4.58. It shows that the effect of the desired rotation on the point $(\alpha_x, \alpha_y, \alpha_z)$ is to rotate the line segment into the plane $y = 0$. If we look at the projection of the line segment (before the rotation) on the plane $x = 0$, we see a line segment of length d on this plane. Another way to envision this figure is to think of the plane $x = 0$ as a wall, and to consider a distant light source located far down the positive x-axis. The line that we see on the wall is the shadow of the line segment from the origin to $(\alpha_x, \alpha_y, \alpha_z)$. Note that the length of the shadow is less than the length of the line segment. We can say the line segment has been **foreshortened** to $d = \sqrt{\alpha_y^2 + \alpha_z^2}$. The desired angle of rotation is determined by the angle that this shadow makes with the z-axis. However, the rotation matrix is determined by the sine and cosine of θ_x; thus, we never need to compute θ_x; rather, we need to compute only

$$\mathbf{R}_x(\theta_x) = \begin{bmatrix} 1 & 0 & 0 & 0 \\ 0 & \alpha_z/d & -\alpha_y/d & 0 \\ 0 & \alpha_y/d & \alpha_z/d & 0 \\ 0 & 0 & 0 & 1 \end{bmatrix}.$$

We compute $\mathbf{R}_y$ in a similar manner. Figure 4.59 shows the rotation. Note that this angle is clockwise about the y-axis, and we have to be careful of the sign of the sine terms in the matrix, which is

$$\mathbf{R}_y(\theta_y) = \begin{bmatrix} d & 0 & -\alpha_x & 0 \\ 0 & 1 & 0 & 0 \\ \alpha_x & 0 & d & 0 \\ 0 & 0 & 0 & 1 \end{bmatrix}.$$

Finally, we concatenate all the matrices to find

$$\mathbf{M} = \mathbf{T}(\mathbf{p}_0)\mathbf{R}_x(-\theta_x)\mathbf{R}_y(-\theta_y)\mathbf{R}_z(\theta)\mathbf{R}_y(\theta_y)\mathbf{R}_x(\theta_x)\mathbf{T}(-\mathbf{p}_0).$$

Let us look at a specific example. Suppose that we wish to rotate an object by 45 degrees about the line passing through the origin and the point $(1, 2, 3)$. We leave the fixed point at the origin. The first step is to find the point along

Figure 4.57 Direction angles.

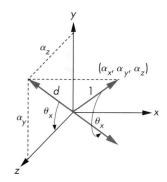
Figure 4.58 Computation of the x rotation.

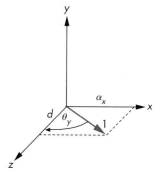
Figure 4.59 Computation of the y rotation.

the line that is a unit distance from the origin. We obtain it by normalizing $(1, 2, 3)$ to $(1/\sqrt{14}, 2/\sqrt{14}, 3/\sqrt{14})$, or $(1/\sqrt{14}, 2/\sqrt{14}, 3/\sqrt{14}, 1)$, in homogeneous coordinates. The first part of the rotation takes this point to $(0, 0, 1, 1)$. We first rotate about the x-axis by the angle $\cos^{-1} \frac{3}{\sqrt{13}}$. This matrix carries $(1/\sqrt{14}, 2/\sqrt{14}, 3/\sqrt{14}, 1)$ to $(1/\sqrt{14}, 0, \sqrt{13/14}, 1)$, which is in the plane $y = 0$. The y rotation must be by the angle $\cos^{-1}(\sqrt{13/14})$. This rotation aligns the object with the z-axis, and now we can rotate about the z-axis by the desired 45 degrees. Finally, we undo the first two rotations. If we concatenate these five transformations into a single rotation matrix $\mathbf{R}$, we find that

$$
\mathbf{R} = \mathbf{R}_x \left(-\cos^{-1} \frac{3}{\sqrt{13}} \right) \mathbf{R}_y \left(-\cos^{-1} \sqrt{\frac{13}{14}} \right) \mathbf{R}_z(45)\mathbf{R}_y \left(\cos^{-1} \sqrt{\frac{13}{14}} \right)
$$

$$
\mathbf{R}_x \left(\cos^{-1} \frac{3}{\sqrt{13}} \right)
$$

$$
= \begin{bmatrix} \frac{2+13\sqrt{2}}{28} & \frac{2-\sqrt{2}-3\sqrt{7}}{14} & \frac{6-3\sqrt{2}+4\sqrt{7}}{28} & 0 \\ \frac{2-\sqrt{2}+3\sqrt{7}}{14} & \frac{4+5\sqrt{2}}{14} & \frac{6-3\sqrt{2}-\sqrt{7}}{14} & 0 \\ \frac{6-3\sqrt{2}-4\sqrt{7}}{28} & \frac{6-3\sqrt{2}+\sqrt{7}}{14} & \frac{18+5\sqrt{2}}{28} & 0 \\ 0 & 0 & 0 & 1 \end{bmatrix}.
$$

This matrix does not change any point on the line passing through the origin and the point $(1, 2, 3)$. If we want a fixed point other than the origin, we form the matrix

$$
\mathbf{M} = \mathbf{T}(\mathbf{p}_f)\mathbf{R}\mathbf{T}(-\mathbf{p}_f).
$$

This example is not simple. It illustrates the powerful technique of applying many simple transformations to get a complex one. The problem of rotation about an arbitrary point or axis arises in many applications. The major variants lie in the manner in which the axis of rotation is specified. However, we can usually employ techniques similar to the ones that we have used here to determine direction angles or direction cosines.

4.9 OpenGL Transformation Matrices

We can now focus on the implementation of a homogeneous-coordinate transformation package and of that package's interface to the user. In OpenGL, there are three matrices that are part of the state. We shall use only the model-view matrix in this chapter. All three types are manipulated by a common set of functions, and we use the `glMatrixMode` function to select the matrix to which the operations apply.

Figure 4.60 Current transformation matrix (CTM).

4.9.1 The Current Transformation Matrix

The generalization common to most graphics systems is the **current transformation matrix** (**CTM**). It is the matrix that is applied to any vertex that is defined subsequent to its setting. If we change the CTM, we change the state of the system. The CTM is part of the pipeline (Figure 4.60); thus, if **p** is a vertex, the pipeline produces **Cp**. The CTM is a 4×4 matrix; it can be altered by a set of functions provided by the graphics package.[8]

Let **C** denote the CTM. Initially, it is set to the 4×4 identity matrix; it can be reinitialized as needed. If we use the symbol ← to denote replacement, we can write this initialization operation as

$$\mathbf{C} \leftarrow \mathbf{I}.$$

The functions that alter **C** are of two forms: those that reset it to some matrix, and those that modify it by premultiplication or postmultiplication by a matrix.[9] The three transformations supported in most systems are translation, scaling with a fixed point of the origin, and rotation with a fixed point of the origin. Symbolically, we can write these operations in postmultiplication form as

$$\mathbf{C} \leftarrow \mathbf{CT},$$
$$\mathbf{C} \leftarrow \mathbf{CS},$$
$$\mathbf{C} \leftarrow \mathbf{CR},$$

and in set form as

$$\mathbf{C} \leftarrow \mathbf{T},$$
$$\mathbf{C} \leftarrow \mathbf{S},$$
$$\mathbf{C} \leftarrow \mathbf{R}.$$

---

8. In OpenGL, the model-view matrix normally is an affine-transformation matrix and has only 12 degrees of freedom, as discussed in Section 4.5. The projection matrix, as we shall see in Chapter 5, is also a 4×4 matrix, but it is not affine.

9. OpenGL uses only postmultiplication. PHIGS allows both premultiplication and postmultiplication.

Most systems allow us to set directly, or to load, the CTM with an arbitrary matrix, or to postmultiply by an arbitrary matrix **M**:

$$\mathbf{C} \leftarrow \mathbf{M},$$

$$\mathbf{C} \leftarrow \mathbf{CM}.$$

4.9.2 Rotation, Translation, and Scaling

In OpenGL, the matrix that is applied to all primitives is the product of the model-view matrix (GL_MODELVIEW) and the projection matrix (GL_PROJECTION). We can think of the CTM as the product of these matrices (Figure 4.61), and we can manipulate each individually by selecting the desired matrix by glMatrixMode. We can load a matrix with the function

```
glLoadMatrixf(pointer_to_matrix);
```

or a set a matrix to the identity matrix with the function

```
glLoadIdentity();
```

Arbitrary 4 × 4 matrices can be specified by a pointer to a one-dimensional array of 16 entries organized by the *columns* of the desired matrix. We can alter the selected matrix with glMultMatrixf(pointer_to_matrix). Rotation, translation, and scaling are provided through the three functions

```
glRotatef(angle, vx, vy, vz);
glTranslatef(dx, dy, dz);
glScalef(sx ,sy, sz);
```

All three alter the selected matrix by postmultiplication. For rotation, the angle is specified in degrees, and the variables vx, vy, and vz are the components of a vector about which we wish to rotate. In the translation function, the variables are the components of the displacement vector; for scaling, the variables determine the scale factors along the coordinate axes.

Figure 4.61 Model-view and projection matrices.

4.9.3 Rotation About a Fixed Point in OpenGL

In Section 4.8, we showed that we can perform a rotation about a fixed point, other than the origin, by first moving the fixed point to the origin, then rotating about the origin, and finally moving the fixed point back to its original location. The following sequence sets the matrix mode, then forms the required matrix for a 45-degree rotation about the line through the origin and the point $(1, 2, 3)$ with a fixed point of $(4, 5, 6)$:

```
glMatrixMode(GL_MODELVIEW);
glLoadIdentity();
glTranslatef(4.0, 5.0, 6.0);
glRotatef(45.0, 1.0, 2.0, 3.0);
glTranslatef(-4.0, -5.0, -6.0);
```

Note that we do not have to form the rotation matrix about an arbitrary axis, as we did in Section 4.8, although you might test your skill with transformations by doing so, forming the same matrix by concatenation of rotations about the three axes.

4.9.4 Order of Transformations

You might be bothered by what appears to be a reversal of the required function calls. The rule in OpenGL is this: *The transformation specified last is the one applied first.* A little examination shows why this order is correct and is a consequence of multiplying the CTM on the right by the specified affine transformation. The sequence of operations that we specified was

$$\mathbf{C} \leftarrow \mathbf{I},$$
$$\mathbf{C} \leftarrow \mathbf{CT}(4.0, 5.0, 6.0),$$
$$\mathbf{C} \leftarrow \mathbf{CR}(45.0, 1.0, 2.0, 3.0),$$
$$\mathbf{C} \leftarrow \mathbf{CT}(-4.0, -5.0, -6.0).$$

In each step, we postmultiply at the end of the existing CTM, forming the matrix

$$\mathbf{C} = \mathbf{T}(4.0, 5.0, 6.0)\mathbf{R}(45.0, 1.0, 2.0, 3.0)\mathbf{T}(-4.0, -5.0, -6.0),$$

which is the matrix that we expect from Section 4.8. Each vertex $\mathbf{p}$ that is specified *after* the model-view matrix has been set will be multiplied by $\mathbf{C}$, thus forming the new vertex

$$\mathbf{q} = \mathbf{Cp}.$$

There are other ways to think about the order of operations. One way is in terms of a stack. Altering the CTM is similar to pushing matrices onto a stack; when we apply the final transformation, the matrices are popped off the stack in the reverse of the order they were placed there. The analogy is conceptual, rather than exact, because, when we call a transformation function in OpenGL, the matrix is altered immediately. However, OpenGL provides stacks to store matrices. When we discuss hierarchical modeling in Chapter 9, we shall need the operations

```
glPushMatrix();
glPopMatrix();
```

to traverse our data structures. In addition, as we did when we used the pushing and popping attributes in Chapter 3, we shall often find it helpful to bracket changes in state with a push and a pop of the matrix.

4.9.5 Spinning of the Cube

In this program, we take the cube that we defined in Section 4.4, and we rotate it using the three buttons of the mouse. We shall define three callback functions:

```
glutDisplayFunc(display);
glutIdleFunc(spincube);
glutMouseFunc(mouse);
```

The function display first sets a model-view matrix using the values of three angles determined by the mouse callback. It then draws a cube, using the colorcube function from Section 4.4. This example uses double buffering. Each time that display is called, it starts by clearing the frame buffer and the depth buffer—for hidden-surface removal; it finishes with a buffer swap.

```
void  display(void)
{
   glClear(GL_COLOR_BUFFER_BIT | GL_DEPTH_BUFFER_BIT);
   glLoadIdentity();
   glRotatef(theta[0], 1.0, 0.0, 0.0);
   glRotatef(theta[1], 0.0, 1.0, 0.0);
   glRotatef(theta[2], 0.0, 0.0, 1.0);
   colorcube();
   glutSwapBuffers();
}
```

The mouse callback selects the axis for rotation:

```
void mouse(int btn, int state, int x, int y)
{
    if(btn==GLUT_LEFT_BUTTON && state == GLUT_DOWN) axis = 0;
    if(btn==GLUT_MIDDLE_BUTTON && state == GLUT_DOWN) axis = 1;
    if(btn==GLUT_RIGHT_BUTTON && state == GLUT_DOWN) axis = 2;
}
```

The idle callback increments the angle associated with the chosen axis by 2 degrees each time:

```
void spinCube()
{
   theta[axis] += 2.0;
   if( theta[axis] > 360.0 ) theta[axis] -= 360.0;
   glutPostRedisplay();
}
```

We can terminate the program using the keyboard with the simple keyboard callback

```
void mykey(char key, int mousex, int mousey)
{
   if(key=='q'||key=='Q') exit();
}
```

We shall not discuss hidden-surface removal until Chapter 5, but we note here that using it in OpenGL is almost trivial. We need only to clear the depth buffer and to enable the function by `glEnable(GL_DEPTH_TEST)`. For the complete program, see Appendix A.

4.9.6 Loading, Pushing, and Popping Matrices

For most purposes, we can use rotation, translation, and scaling to form a desired transformation matrix. In some circumstances, however, such as with forming a shear matrix, it is easier to set up the matrix directly. Just as we load an identity matrix, we can load a 4 × 4 homogeneous-coordinate matrix as the current matrix by

```
glLoadMatrixf(myarray)
```

We can also multiply on the right of the current matrix by a user-defined matrix using the function

```
glMultMatrixf(myarray)
```

The array `myarray` is a one-dimensional array of 16 elements arranged by *columns*. Thus, if we want the 4 × 4 matrix **M**, then we can form `myarray` by

```
GLfloat myarray[16];

for(i=0;i<3;i++)for(j=0;j=3;j++)
   myarray[4*j+i]= m[i][j];
```

Sometimes we want to perform a transformation and then return to the same state as before its execution. This situation occurs when we execute an instance transformation that applies to a particular object and does not apply to the following objects in the code. Rather than recompute the transformation that existed before the instance transformation, we can push the transformation matrix on a stack with glPushMatrix before we multiply by the instance transformation and recover it later with glPopMatrix. Thus, we often see the sequence

```
glPushMatrix();
glTranslatef(....);
glRotatef(.....);
glScalef(.....);

/* draw object here */

glPopMatrix();
```

One place where pushing and popping of matrices and of attributes is extremely important is encountered when we use display lists. By pushing state variables on their stacks when we begin a display list and popping them at the end of the display list, we avoid any subsequent side affects due to state changes in the display list.

4.10 Interfaces to Three-Dimensional Applications

In Section 4.9 we used a three-button mouse to control the direction of rotation of our cube. This interface is limited. Rather than use all three mouse buttons to control rotation, we might want to use the mouse to control functions, such as exiting the program, that we would have had to assign to keys in our previous example.

We noted in Section 4.8 that there were many ways to obtain a given orientation. Rather than do rotations about the x-, y-, and z-axes in that order, we could do a rotation about the x-axis, followed by a rotation about the y-axis, and finish with another rotation about the x-axis. If we do our orientation this way, we can obtain our desired orientation using only two mouse buttons. There is still a problem, however: Our rotations are in a single direction. It would be easier to orient an object if we could rotate either forward or backward about an axis, and could stop the rotation once we reached a desired orientation.

GLUT allows us to use the keyboard in combination with the mouse. We could, for example, use the left mouse button for a forward rotation about the x-axis and the control key in combination with the left mouse button for a backward rotation about the x-axis.

There are other options that provide a more interesting interaction. We consider two of them.

4.10.1 Using Areas of the Screen

Suppose that we want to use one mouse button for orienting an object, one for getting closer to or farther from the object, and one for translating the object to the left or right. We can use the motion callback to achieve all these functions. The callback returns which button has been activated and where the mouse is located. We can use the location of the mouse to control how fast and in which direction we rotate or translate, and to move in or out.

As we just noted, we need the ability to rotate about only two axes to achieve any orientation. We could then use the left mouse button and the mouse position to control orientation. We can use the distance from the center of the screen to control the x and y rotations. Thus, if the left mouse button is held down but the mouse is located in the center of the screen, there will be no rotation; if the mouse is moved up, the object will be rotated about the y-axis in a clockwise manner; if the mouse is moved down, the object will be rotated about the y-axis in a counterclockwise manner. Likewise, motion to the right or left will cause rotation about the x-axis. The distance from the center can control the speed of rotation. Motion toward the corners can cause simultaneous rotations about the x- and y-axes.

Using the right mouse button in a similar manner, we can translate the object right to left and up to down. We might use the middle mouse button to move the object toward or away from the viewer by having the mouse position control a translation in the z direction.

The code for such an interface is straightforward in GLUT; we leave it as an exercise (Exercise 4.19).

4.10.2 A Virtual Trackball

The use of the mouse position to control rotation about two axes provides us with most of the functionality of a trackball (Section 3.2). We can go one step further and create a graphical or virtual trackball using our mouse and the screen. One of the benefits of such a device is that we can create a frictionless trackball that, once we start it rotating, will continue to rotate until stopped by the user. Thus, the device will support continuous rotations of objects but will still allow changes in the speed and orientation of the rotation. We could also do the same for translation and other parameters that we can control from the mouse.

We start by mapping the position of a trackball to that of a mouse. Consider the trackball in Figure 4.62. We assume that the ball has a radius of 1 unit. We can map a position on its surface to the plane $y = 0$ by doing an orthogonal projection to the plane, as shown in Figure 4.63. The position (x, y, z) on the surface of the ball is mapped to $(x, 0, z)$ on the plane. This projection is reversible because we know that the three-dimensional point that is projected to the point on the plane must satisfy the equation of the sphere

$$x^2 + y^2 + z^2 = 1.$$

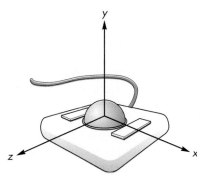

Figure 4.62 Trackball frame.

Thus, given the point on the plane $(x, 0, z)$, the corresponding point on the hemisphere must be (x, y, z), where

$$y = \sqrt{1 - x^2 - z^2}.$$

We can compute the three-dimensional information and track it as the mouse moves. Suppose we have two positions on the hemisphere $\mathbf{p}_1$ and $\mathbf{p}_2$; then, the vectors from the origin to these points determine the orientation of a plane, as in Figure 4.64, whose normal is defined by their cross product

$$\mathbf{n} = \mathbf{p}_1 \times \mathbf{p}_2.$$

The motion of the trackball that moves from $\mathbf{p}_1$ to $\mathbf{p}_2$ can be achieved by a rotation about $\mathbf{n}$. The angle of rotation is the angle between the vectors $\mathbf{p}_1$ and $\mathbf{p}_2$, which we can compute using the magnitude of the cross product. Because both $\mathbf{p}_1$ and $\mathbf{p}_2$ have unit length,

$$|\sin \theta| = |\mathbf{n}|.$$

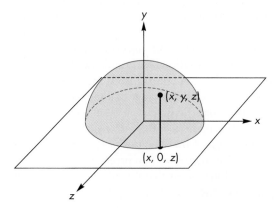

Figure 4.63 Projection of the trackball position to the plane.

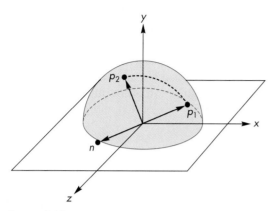

Figure 4.64 Computation of the plane of rotation.

If we are tracking the mouse at a high rate, then the change in positions that we detect will be small; rather than use an inverse trigonometric function to find θ, we can use an approximation, such as

$$\sin \theta \approx \theta.$$

We can implement the virtual trackball through use of the idle, motion, and mouse callbacks in GLUT. We can think of the process in terms of three logical variables or flags that control the tracking of the mouse and of the display redrawing. These are set initially as[10]

```
bool trackingMouse = false;
bool trackballMove = false;
bool redrawContinue = false;
```

If redrawContinue is true, the idle function posts a redisplay. If trackingMouse is true, we update the trackball position as part of the motion callback. If trackballMove is true, we update the rotation matrix that we use in our display routine.

The changes in these variables are controlled through the mouse callback. When we push a mouse button—either a particular button or any button depending on exactly what we want—then we start updating the trackball position by initializing it, then letting the motion callback update it and post redisplays in response to changes in the position of the mouse. When the mouse button is released, we stop tracking the mouse. We can use the most recent two mouse positions to define a velocity vector so that we can continually update the rotation matrix. Thus, once the mouse button is released, the object will

10. If the compiler does not support the Boolean type, we can use #define bool int and then define true and false as 1 and 0, respectively.

continue to rotate at a constant velocity—an effect that we could achieve with an ideal frictionless trackball, but not directly with either a real mouse or a real trackball.

The code for the rotating cube with a virtual trackball is in trackball.c. This code has a few simple approximations to speed it up; it also takes care of a few problems, such as what happens if the mouse position is not directly below the hemisphere of the trackball—for example, when it is located in the corner of the window.

4.10.3 Smooth Rotations

The trackball example illustrates a problem with our method of computing rotations. Our approach to orienting objects is based on angles (the Euler angles) measured with respect to the three coordinate axes. This perspective led to our forming rotation matrices by concatenating simple rotations about the x-, y-, and z-axes to obtain a desired rotation about an arbitrary axis. Although OpenGL allows us to rotate about an arbitrary axis, we usually employ our concatenation strategy to determine this axis and the corresponding angle of rotation.

Consider what happens if we wish to move between two orientations as part of an animation. In principle, we can determine an appropriate rotation matrix as the product of rotations about the three axes,

$$\mathbf{R}(\theta) = \mathbf{R}_x(\theta_x)\mathbf{R}_y(\theta_y)\mathbf{R}_z(\theta_z).$$

If we want to create a sequence of images that move between the two orientations, we can change the individual angles in small increments, either individually or simultaneously. Such a sequence would not appear smooth to a viewer; she would detect the individual rotations about each of the three axes.

With the trackball, we saw that we could rotate the cube directly from one orientation to another in a smooth manner. We did so by exploiting the equivalence between the two orientations of the cube and two points on a unit circle. A smooth rotation between the two orientations corresponds to a great circle on the surface of a sphere. This circle corresponds to a single rotation about a suitable axis that is the normal to the plane determined by the two points on the sphere and that sphere's center. If we increase this angle smoothly, our viewer will see a smooth rotation.

In one sense, what has failed us is our mathematical formulation, which relies on the use of coordinate axes. However, a deeper and less axis-dependent method is embedded within the matrix formulation. Suppose that we start with an arbitrary rotation matrix $\mathbf{R}$. All points on a line in the direction $\mathbf{d}$ are unaffected by the rotation. Thus, for any such point $\mathbf{p}$,

$$\mathbf{R}\mathbf{p} = \mathbf{p}.$$

In terms of the matrix $\mathbf{R}$, the column matrix $\mathbf{p}$ is an **eigenvector** of the matrix corresponding to the **eigenvalue** 1 (see Appendix C). In addition, for the direction $\mathbf{d}$

$$\mathbf{R}\mathbf{d} = \mathbf{d},$$

so that its direction is unaffected by the rotation. Consequently, $\mathbf{d}$ is also an eigenvector of $\mathbf{R}$ corresponding to another eigenvalue of 1. The point $\mathbf{p}$ must be the fixed point of the rotation, and the vector $\mathbf{d}$ must be the normal to a plane perpendicular to the direction of rotation. In terms of the trackball, computing the axis of rotation was equivalent to finding a particular eigenvector of the desired rotation matrix. We could also go the other way. Given an arbitrary rotation matrix, by finding its eigenvalues and eigenvectors, we also determine the axis of rotation and the fixed point.

4.10.4 Incremental Rotation

Suppose that we are given two orientations of an object such as a camera and we want to go smoothly from one to the other. One approach is to find the great circle path as we did with the virtual trackball and make incremental changes in the angle that rotates us along this path. Thus, we start with the axis of rotation, a start angle, a final angle, and a desired increment in the angle determined by the number of steps we wish to take. The main loop in the code will be of the form

```
for(i=0, i<imax; i++)
{
    glRotatef(dx, dy, dz, delta_theta);
    draw_object()
}
```

One problem with this approach is that the calculation of the rotation matrix requires the evaluation of the sines and cosines of three angles. We would do better if we compute the rotation matrix once and reuse it through code such as

```
GLfloat m[16];
glRotatef(dx, dy, dz, delta_theta);
glGetFloatv(GL_MODELVIEW, m);

for(i=0, i<imax; i++)
{
    glMultMatrixf(m);
    draw_object()
}
```

We could also use the small angle approximations

$$\sin \theta \approx \theta,$$

$$\cos \theta \approx 1.$$

If we form an arbitrary rotation matrix through the Euler angles

$$\mathbf{R} = \mathbf{R}_z(\psi)\mathbf{R}_y(\phi)\mathbf{R}_x(\theta),$$

then we can use the approximations to write $\mathbf{R}$ as

$$\mathbf{R} = \begin{bmatrix} \cos\psi & -\sin\psi & 0 & 0 \\ \sin\psi & \cos\psi & 0 & 0 \\ 0 & 0 & 1 & 0 \\ 0 & 0 & 0 & 1 \end{bmatrix} \begin{bmatrix} \cos\phi & 0 & \sin\psi & 0 \\ 0 & 1 & 0 & 0 \\ -\sin\psi & 0 & \cos\psi & 0 \\ 0 & 0 & 0 & 1 \end{bmatrix}$$

$$\begin{bmatrix} 1 & 0 & 0 & 0 \\ 0 & \cos\theta & -\sin\theta & 0 \\ 0 & \sin\theta & \cos\theta & 0 \\ 0 & 0 & 0 & 1 \end{bmatrix}$$

$$\approx \begin{bmatrix} 1 & \psi & -\phi & 0 \\ -\psi & 1 & -\theta & 0 \\ \phi & \theta & 1 & 0 \\ 0 & 0 & 0 & 1 \end{bmatrix}.$$

4.11 Quaternions

Quaternions are an extension of complex numbers that provide an alternative method for describing and manipulating rotations. Although less intuitive than our original approach, quaternions provide advantages for animation and hardware implementation of rotation.

4.11.1 Complex Numbers and Quaternions

In two dimensions, the use of complex numbers to represent operations such as rotation is well known to most students of engineering and science. For example, suppose that we let $\mathbf{i}$ denote the pure imaginary number such that $\mathbf{i}^2 = -1$. Recalling Euler's identity

$$e^{i\theta} = \cos\theta + \mathbf{i}\sin\theta,$$

we can write the polar representation of a complex number $\mathbf{c}$ as

$$\mathbf{c} = a + \mathbf{i}b = re^{i\theta},$$

where $r = \sqrt{a^2 + b^2}$ and $\theta = \tan^{-1} b/a$. If we rotate $\mathbf{c}$ about the origin by ϕ to

$\mathbf{c}'$, we can find $\mathbf{c}'$ using a rotation matrix, or we can use the polar representation to write

$$\mathbf{c}' = re^{i(\theta+\phi)} = re^{i\theta} e^{i\phi}.$$

Thus $e^{i\phi}$ is a rotation operator in the complex plane and provides an alternative to using transformations that may prove more efficient in practice.

However, we are really interested in rotations in a three-dimensional space. In three dimensions, the problem is more difficult because to specify a rotation about the origin we need to specify both a direction (a vector) and the amount of rotation about it (a scalar). One solution is use a representation that consists of both a vector and a scalar. Usually, this representation is written as the **quaternion**

$$a = (q_0, q_1, q_2, q_3) = (q_0, \mathbf{q}),$$

where $\mathbf{q} = (q_1, q_2, q_3)$. The operations among quaternions are based on the use of three "complex" numbers $\mathbf{i}$, $\mathbf{j}$, and $\mathbf{k}$ with the properties

$$\mathbf{i}^2 = \mathbf{j}^2 = \mathbf{k}^2 = \mathbf{ijk} = -1$$

These numbers are analogous to the unit vectors in three dimensions, and we can write $\mathbf{q}$ as

$$\mathbf{q} = q_1\mathbf{i} + q_2\mathbf{j} + q_3\mathbf{k}.$$

Now we can use the relationships among $\mathbf{i}$, $\mathbf{j}$, and $\mathbf{k}$ to derive quaternion addition and multiplication. If the quaternion b is given by

$$b = (p_0, \mathbf{p}),$$

then, using the dot and cross products for vectors,

$$a + b = (p_0 + q_0, \mathbf{p} + \mathbf{q}),$$
$$ab = (p_0 q_0 - \mathbf{p} \cdot \mathbf{q}, q_0\mathbf{p} + p_0\mathbf{q} + \mathbf{q} \times \mathbf{p}).$$

We can also define a magnitude for quaternions in the normal manner as

$$|a|^2 = q_0^2 + q_1^2 + q_2^2 + q_3^2 = q_0^2 + \mathbf{q} \cdot \mathbf{q}.$$

Quaternions have a multiplicative identity, the quaternion $(1, \mathbf{0})$, and it is easy to verify that the inverse of a quaternion is given by

$$a^{-1} = \frac{1}{|a|^2}(q_0, -\mathbf{q}).$$

4.11.2 Quaternions and Rotation

So far we have only defined a new mathematical object. For it to be of use to us, we must relate it to the our geometric entities and show how it can be used to carry out operations such as rotation. Suppose that we use the vector part of a quaternion to represent a point in space

$$p = (0, \mathbf{p}).$$

Thus, the components of $\mathbf{p} = (x, y, z)$ give the location of the point. Consider the quaternion

$$r = \left(\cos \frac{\theta}{2}, \sin \frac{\theta}{2} \mathbf{v} \right),$$

where $\mathbf{v}$ has unit length. We can then show that the quaternion r is a unit quaternion ($|r| = 1$), and therefore

$$r^{-1} = \left(\cos \frac{\theta}{2}, - \sin \frac{\theta}{2} \mathbf{v} \right).$$

If we consider the quaternion product of the quaternion p that represents a point with r, we obtain the quaternion

$$p' = rpr^{-1},$$

This quaternion has the form $(0, \mathbf{p}')$, where

$$\mathbf{p}' = \cos^2 \frac{\theta}{2} \mathbf{p} + \sin^2 \frac{\theta}{2} (\mathbf{p} \cdot \mathbf{v}) \mathbf{v} + 2 \sin \frac{\theta}{2} \cos \frac{\theta}{2} (\mathbf{v} \times \mathbf{p})$$

and thus p' is the representation of a point. What is less obvious is that p' is the result of rotating the point $\mathbf{p}$ by θ degrees about the vector $\mathbf{v}$. However, we can verify that this indeed is the case by comparing terms in p' with those of the general rotation. Before doing so, consider the implication of this result. As we get the same result, the quaternion product formed from r and p is an alternate to transformation matrices as a representation of rotation with a fixed point of the origin about an arbitrary axis. If we count operations, quaternions are faster and have been built into both hardware and software implementations.

Let us consider a few examples. Suppose that we consider the rotation about the z axis by θ with a fixed point at the origin. The desired unit vector v is $(0,0,1)$ yielding the quaternion

$$r = \cos \frac{\theta}{2} + \sin \frac{\theta}{2} (0, 0, 1).$$

The rotation of an arbitrary point $\mathbf{p} = (x, y, z)$ yields the quaternion

$$p' = rpr^{-1} = r(0, \mathbf{p})r^{-1} = (0, \mathbf{p}'),$$

where

$$\mathbf{p}' = (x \cos \theta - y \sin \theta, x \sin \theta + y \cos \theta, z).$$

Thus, we get the expected result but with fewer operations. If we consider a sequence of rotations about the coordinate axes that in matrix form yields the matrix $\mathbf{R} = \mathbf{R}_x(\theta_x)\mathbf{R}_y(\theta_y)\mathbf{R}_z(\theta_z)$, we instead can use the product of the corresponding quaternions to form $r_x r_y r_z$.

Returning to the rotation about an arbitrary axis, in Section 4.8.4, we derived a matrix of the form

$$\mathbf{M} = \mathbf{T}(\mathbf{p}_0)\mathbf{R}(-\theta_x)\mathbf{R}(-\theta_y)\mathbf{R}(\theta_z)\mathbf{R}(\theta_y)\mathbf{R}(\theta_x)\mathbf{T}(-\mathbf{p}_0).$$

Because of the translations at the beginning and end, we cannot use quaternions for the entire operation. We can, however, recognize that the elements of $p' = rpr^{-1}$ can be used to find the elements of the homogeneous coordinate rotation matrix embedded in $\mathbf{M}$. Thus, if again $r = (\cos\frac{\theta}{2}, \sin\frac{\theta}{2}\mathbf{v})$, then

$$\mathbf{R} = \begin{bmatrix} 1 - 2\sin^2\frac{\theta}{2}(v_y^2 + v_z^2) & 2\sin^2\frac{\theta}{2}v_x v_y - 2\cos\frac{\theta}{2}\sin\frac{\theta}{2}v_z \\ 2\sin^2\frac{\theta}{2}v_x v_y + 2\cos\frac{\theta}{2}\sin\frac{\theta}{2}v_z & 1 - 2\sin^2\frac{\theta}{2}(v_x^2 + v_z^2) \\ 2\sin^2\frac{\theta}{2}v_x v_z - 2\cos\frac{\theta}{2}\sin\frac{\theta}{2}v_y & 2\sin^2\frac{\theta}{2}v_y v_z + 2\cos\frac{\theta}{2}\sin\frac{\theta}{2}v_x \\ 0 & 0 \end{bmatrix}$$

$$\begin{matrix} 2\sin^2\frac{\theta}{2}v_x v_z + 2\cos\frac{\theta}{2}\sin\frac{\theta}{2}v_y & 0 \\ 2\sin^2\frac{\theta}{2}v_y v_z - 2\cos\frac{\theta}{2}\sin\frac{\theta}{2}v_a & 0 \\ 1 - 2\sin^2\frac{\theta}{2}(v_x^2 + v_y^2) & 0 \\ 0 & 1 \end{matrix}.$$

This matrix can be made to look more familiar if we use the trigonometric identities

$$\cos\theta = \cos^2\frac{\theta}{2} - \sin^2\frac{\theta}{2} = 1 - 2\sin^2\frac{\theta}{2},$$

$$\sin\theta = 2\cos\frac{\theta}{2}\sin\frac{\theta}{2},$$

and recall that $\mathbf{v}$ is a unit vector, so that

$$v_x^2 + v_y^2 + v_z^2 = 1.$$

Thus, we can use quaternion products to form r and then form the rotation part of $\mathbf{M}$ by matching terms between $\mathbf{R}$ and r. We then use our normal transformation operations to add in the effect of the two translations.

In addition to the efficiency of using quaternions instead of rotation matrices, quaternions can be interpolated to obtain smooth sequences of rotations for animation. We shall see additional examples that require smooth rotation in Chapter 9.

4.12 Summary and Notes

In this chapter, we have presented two different—but ultimately complementary—points of view regarding the mathematics of computer graphics. One is that mathematical abstraction of the objects with which we work in computer graphics is necessary if we are to understand the operations that we carry out in our programs. The other is that transformations—and the techniques for carrying them out, such as the use of homogeneous coordinates—are the basis for implementations of graphics systems.

Our mathematical tools come from the study of vector analysis and linear algebra. For computer-graphics purposes, however, the order in which we have chosen to present these tools is the reverse of the order that most students learn. In particular, linear algebra is studied first, then vector-space concepts are linked to the study of n-tuples in $\mathbf{R}^n$. In contrast, our study of representation in mathematical spaces led to our use of linear algebra as a tool for implementing abstract types.

We pursued a coordinate-free approach for two reasons. First, we wanted to show that all the basic concepts of geometric objects and of transformations are independent of the ways the latter are represented. Second, as object-oriented languages become more prevalent, application programmers will work directly with the objects, instead of with those objects' representations. The references in Section 4.13 contain examples of geometric programming systems that illustrate the potential of this approach.

Homogeneous coordinates provided a wonderful example of the power of mathematical abstraction. By going to an abstract mathematical space—the affine space—we were able to find a tool that led directly to efficient software and hardware methods.

Finally, we provided the set of affine transformations supported in OpenGL and discussed ways that we could concatenate them to provide all affine transformations. The strategy of combining a few simple types of matrices to build a desired transformation is a powerful one; you should use it for a few of the exercises at the end of this chapter. In Chapter 5, we build on these techniques to develop viewing for three-dimensional graphics; in Chapter 9 we use our transformations to build hierarchical models.

4.13 Suggested Readings

There are many texts on vector analysis and linear algebra, although most treat the two topics separately. Within the geometric-design community the vector-space approach of coordinate-free descriptions of curves and surfaces has been popular; see the book by Faux and Pratt [Fau80]. See DeRose [DeR89, DeR90] for an introduction to geometric programming. Homogeneous coordinates arose in geometry [Max51], and were later discovered by the graphics community [Rie81]. Their use in hardware started with the Silicon Graphics Geometry Engine [Cla82]. Modern hardware architectures use application specific integrated circuits (ASICs) that include homogeneous coordinate transformations.

Quaternions were introduced to computer graphics by Shoemaker [Sho85] for use in animation. See the book by Kuipers [Kui99] for many examples of the use of rotation matrices and quaternions.

Software tools such as Mathematica [Wol91] and MATLAB [Mat95] are excellent aids for learning to manipulate transformation matrices.

Exercises

4.1 Consider the solution of either constant-coefficient linear differential or difference equations (recurrences). Show that the solutions of the homogeneous equations form a vector space. Relate the solution for a particular inhomogeneous equation to an affine space.

4.2 Show that the following sequences commute:
a. A rotation and a uniform scaling
b. Two rotations about the same axis
c. Two translations

4.3 Write a library of functions that will allow you to do geometric programming. Your library should contain functions for manipulating the basic geometric types (points, lines, vectors) and operations on those types, including dot and cross products. It should allow you to change frames. You can also create functions to interface with OpenGL, so that you can display the results of geometric calculations.

4.4 If we are interested in only two-dimensional graphics, we can use three-dimensional homogeneous coordinates by representing a point as $\mathbf{p} = [x\, y\, 1]^T$ and a vector as $\mathbf{v} = [a\, b\, 0]^T$. Find the 3×3 rotation, translation, scaling, and shear matrices. How many degrees of freedom are there in an affine transformation for transforming two-dimensional points?

4.5 We can specify an affine transformation by considering the location of a small number of points both before and after these points have been transformed. In three dimensions, how many points must we consider to specify the transformation uniquely? How does the required number of points change when we work in two dimensions?

4.6 How must we change the rotation matrices if we are working in a left-handed system and we retain our definition of a positive rotation?

4.7 Show that any sequence of rotations and translations can be replaced by a single rotation about the origin, followed by a translation.

4.8 Derive the shear transformation from the rotation, translation, and scaling transformations.

4.9 In two dimensions, we can specify a line by the equation $y = mx + h$. Find an affine transformation to reflect two-dimensional points about this line. Extend your result to reflection about a plane in three dimensions.

4.10 In Section 4.8 we showed that an arbitrary rotation matrix could be composed from successive rotations about the three axes. How many ways can we compose a given rotation if we can do only three simple rotations? Are all three of the simple rotation matrices necessary?

4.11   Add shear to the instance transformation. Show how to use this expanded instance transformation to generate parallelepipeds from a unit cube.

4.12   Find a homogeneous-coordinate representation of a plane.

4.13   Determine the rotation matrix formed by glRotate. That is, assume that the fixed point is the origin and that the parameters are those of the function.

4.14   Write a program to generate a Sierpinski gasket as follows. Start with a white triangle. At each step, use transformations to generate three similar triangles that are drawn over the original triangle, leaving the center of the triangle white and the three corners black.

4.15   Start with a cube centered at the origin and aligned with the coordinate axes. Find a rotation matrix that will orient the cube symmetrically, as shown in Figure 4.65.

4.16   We have used vertices in three dimensions to define objects such as three-dimensional polygons. Given a set of vertices, find a test to determine whether the polygon that they determine is planar.

4.17   Three vertices determine a triangle if they do not lie in the same line. Devise a test for collinearity of three vertices.

4.18   We defined an instance transformation as the product of a translation, a rotation, and a scaling. Can we accomplish the same effect by applying these three types of transformations in a different order?

4.19   Write a program that allows you to orient the cube with one mouse button, to translate it with a second, and to zoom in and out with a third.

4.20   Given two nonparallel three-dimensional vectors u and v, how can we form an orthogonal coordinate system in which u is one of the basis vectors?

4.21   An incremental rotation about the z-axis is determined by the matrix

$$\begin{bmatrix} 1 & -\theta & 0 & 0 \\ \theta & 1 & 0 & 0 \\ 0 & 0 & 1 & 0 \\ 0 & 0 & 0 & 1 \end{bmatrix}.$$

What negative aspects are there if we use this matrix for a large number of steps? Hint: consider points a distance of 1 from the origin. Can you suggest a remedy?

4.22   Find the quaternions for 90-degree rotations about the x- and y-axes. Determine their product.

Figure 4.65 Symmetric orientation of cube.

4.23 Determine the rotation matrix $\mathbf{R} = \mathbf{R}(\theta_x)\mathbf{R}(\theta_y)\mathbf{R}(\theta_z)$. Find the corresponding quaternion.

4.24 Redo the trackball program using quaternions instead of rotation matrices.

4.25 Implement a simple package in C++ that can do the required mathematical operations for transformations. Such a package might include matrices, vectors, and frames.

Viewing

We have completed our discussion of the first half of the synthetic camera model—specifying objects in three dimensions. We now investigate the multitude of ways in which we can describe our virtual camera. Along the way, we examine related topics, such as the relationship between classical viewing techniques and computer viewing.

There are three parts to our approach. First, we look at the types of views that we can create and why we need more than one type of view. Then we examine how an application viewer can create a particular view within OpenGL. We shall see that the viewing process has two parts. In the first, we use the model-view matrix to switch from the world frame in which we defined our objects to their representation in a frame in which the camera is at the origin. This representation of the geometry will allow us to use canonical viewing procedures. The second part of the process deals with the type of projection we prefer (parallel or perspective) and the part of the world we wish to image (the clipping or view volume). These specifications will allow us to form a projection matrix that is concatenated with the model-view matrix. Once more, we use a simple example program to demonstrate how the OpenGL API handles viewing. Finally, we derive the projection matrices that describe the most important parallel and perspective views.

5.1 Classical and Computer Viewing

Before looking at the interface between computer-graphics systems and application programmers for three-dimensional viewing, we take a slight diversion to consider classical viewing. There are two reasons for examining classical viewing. First, many of the jobs that were formerly done by hand drawing—such as animation in movies, architectural rendering, drafting, and mechanical-parts design—are now done routinely with the aid of computer graphics. Practitioners of these fields need to be able to produce classical views—such as isometrics, elevations, and various perspectives—and thus must be able to use the computer system to produce such renderings. Second, the relationships between classical and computer viewing show many advantages of, and a few difficulties with, the approach used by most APIs.

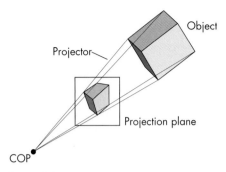

Figure 5.1 Viewing.

When we introduced the synthetic-camera model in Chapter 1, we pointed out the similarities between classical and computer viewing. The basic elements in both cases are the same. We have objects, a viewer, projectors, and a projection plane (Figure 5.1). The projectors meet at the **center of projection** (**COP**). The COP corresponds to the center of the lens in the camera or in the eye, and, in a computer-graphics systems, it is the origin of the **camera frame**. All standard graphics systems follow the model that we described in Chapter 1, which is based on geometric optics. The projection surface is a plane, and the projectors are straight lines. This situation not only is the one usually encountered, but also is the one that is easiest to implement, especially with our pipeline model.

Both classical and computer graphics allow the viewer to be an infinite distance from the objects. Note that, as we move the COP to infinity, the projectors become parallel, and the COP can be replaced by a **direction of projection** (**DOP**), as shown in Figure 5.2. Note also that, as the COP moves to infinity, the size of the image remains about the same, even though the viewer is infinitely far from the objects. Views with a finite COP are called **perspective views**; views with a COP at infinity are called **parallel views**.

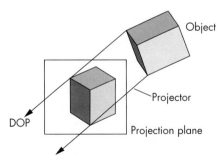

Figure 5.2 Movement of the center of projection (COP) to infinity.

Color Plates 9 and 10 show a parallel and a perspective rendering, respectively. These plates illustrate the importance of having both types of view available in applications such as architecture; in an API that supports both types of viewing, the user can switch easily between various viewing modes. Most modern APIs support both parallel and perspective viewing. The class of projections produced by these systems is known as **planar geometric projections**, because the projection surface is a plane and the projectors are lines. Both perspective and parallel projections preserve lines; they do not, in general, preserve angles. Although the parallel views are the limiting case of perspective viewing, both classical and computer viewing usually treat them as separate cases. For classical views, the techniques that people use to construct the two types by hand are different, as anyone who has taken a drafting class surely knows. From the computer perspective, there are differences in how we specify the two types of views. In addition, parallel views are considerably easier to implement,[1] if, rather than looking at them as the limit of the perspective view, we derive the limiting equations and use those equations directly.

Although computer graphics systems have two fundamental types of viewing (parallel and perspective), classical graphics appears to permit a host of different views, ranging from multiview orthographic projections to one-, two-, and three-point perspectives. This seeming discrepancy arises in classical graphics as a result of the desire to show a specific relationship among an object, the viewer, and the projection plane, as opposed to the computer graphics approach of complete independence of all specifications.

5.1.1 Classical Viewing

When an architect draws an image of a building, she knows which side she wishes to display, and thus where she should place the viewer in relationship to the building. Each classical view is determined by a specific relationship between the objects and the viewer.

In classical viewing, there is the underlying notion of a **principal face**. The types of objects viewed in real-world applications, such as architecture, tend to be composed of a number of planar faces, each of which can be thought of as a principal face. For a rectangular object, such as a building, there are natural notions of the front, back, top, bottom, right, and left faces. In addition, many real-world objects have faces that meet at right angles; thus, such objects often have three orthogonal directions associated with them.

---

1. In modern pipeline architectures, this statement may not always be true, because usually there is only a single geometric pipeline that does both types of viewing. Software implementation of parallel viewing requires fewer operations than does that of perspective viewing.

Front elevation   Elevation oblique   Plan oblique

Isometric   One-point perspective   Three-point perspective

Figure 5.3 Classical views.

Figure 5.3 shows some of the main types of views. We start with the most restrictive view for each of the parallel and perspective types, then move to the less restrictive conditions.

5.1.2 Orthographic Projections

Our first classical view is the **orthographic projection** shown in Figure 5.4. In all orthographic (or orthogonal) views, the projectors are perpendicular to the projection plane. In a **multiview orthographic projection**, the projection plane is parallel to one of the principal faces of the object. Usually, we display at least three views—such as the front, top, and right—to display the object. The reason that we produce multiple views should be clear from Figure 5.5. For a boxlike

Figure 5.4 Orthographic projections.

Figure 5.5 Temple and three multiview orthographic projections.

object, only the faces parallel to the projection plane appear in the image. A viewer usually needs more than two views to visualize what an object looks like from its multiview orthographic projections. Visualization from these images can take skill on the part of the viewer. The importance of this type of view is that the view preserves both distances and angles, and, because there is no distortion of either distance or shape, multiview orthographic projections are well suited for working drawings.

5.1.3 Axonometric Projections

If we want to see more principal faces of our boxlike object in a single view, we must remove one of our restrictions. In **axonometric** views, the projectors are still orthogonal to the projection plane, as they are in Figure 5.6, but the projection plane can have any orientation with respect to the object. If the projection plane is placed symmetrically with respect to the three principal faces that meet at a corner of our rectangular object, we have an **isometric** view. If the projection plane is placed symmetrically with respect to two of the principal faces, the view is **dimetric**. The general case is a **trimetric** view. These views are shown in Figure 5.7. Note that in an isometric view, a line segment's length in the image space is shorter than its length measured in the object space. This **foreshortening** of distances is the same in the three principal directions, so we can still make distance measurements. In the dimetric view, however, there are two different foreshortening ratios; in the trimetric view, there are three. Also, although parallel lines are preserved in the image, angles are not. A circle is projected into an ellipse. This distortion is the price we pay for the ability to

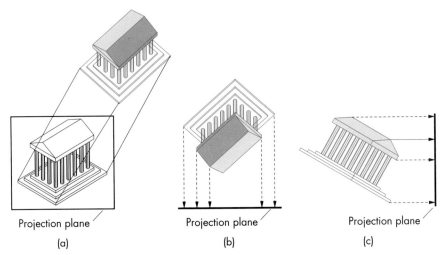

Figure 5.6 Axonometric projections. (a) Construction of trimteric-view projections. (b) Top view. (c) Side view.

see more than one principal face in a view that can be produced easily either by hand or by computer. Axonometric views are used extensively in architectural and mechanical design.

5.1.4 Oblique Projections

The **oblique** views are the most general parallel views. We allow the projectors to make an arbitrary angle with the projection plane, as shown in Figure 5.8. In an oblique projection, angles in planes parallel to the projection plane are preserved. A circle in a plane parallel to the projection plane is projected into a circle, yet we can see more than one principal face of the object. Oblique views are the most difficult to construct by hand. They are also somewhat unnatural. Most physical viewing devices, including the human visual system, have a lens that is in a fixed relationship with the image plane—usually, the lens is parallel to

Dimetric   Trimetric   Isometric

Figure 5.7 Axonometric views.

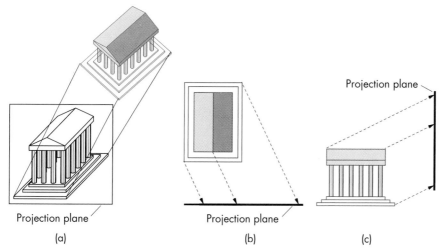

Figure 5.8 Oblique view. (a) Construction. (b) Top view. (c) Side view.

the plane. Although these devices produce perspective views, if the viewer is far from the object, the views are approximately parallel, but orthogonal, because the projection plane is parallel to the lens. The bellows camera that we used to develop the synthetic-camera model in Section 1.6 has the flexibility to produce approximations to parallel oblique views.

From the application programmer's point of view, there is no significant difference among the different parallel views. The application programmer specifies a type of view—parallel or perspective—and a set of parameters that describe the camera. The problem for the application programmer is how to specify these parameters in the viewing procedures so as best to view an object or to produce a specific classical view.

5.1.5 Perspective Viewing

All perspective views are characterized by **diminution** of size. When objects are moved farther from the viewer, their images become smaller. This size change gives perspective views their natural appearance; however, because the amount by which a line is foreshortened depends on how far the line is from the viewer, we cannot make measurements from a perspective view. Hence, the major use of perspective views is in applications such as architecture and animation, where it is important to achieve real-looking images.

In the classical perspective views, the viewer is located symmetrically with respect to the projection plane, as shown in Figure 5.9. Thus, the pyramid determined by the window in the projection plane and the center of projection is a symmetric or right pyramid. This symmetry is caused by the fixed relationship between the back and lens of the eye for human viewing, or between the back and

Figure 5.9 Perspective viewing.

lens of a camera for standard cameras, and by similar fixed relationships in most physical situations. Some cameras, such as the bellows camera, have movable film backs and can produce general perspective views. The model used in computer graphics includes this general case.

The classical perspective views are usually known as **one-**, **two-**, and **three-point perspectives**. The differences among the three cases are based on how many of the three principal directions in the object are parallel to the projection plane. Consider the three perspective projections of the building in Figure 5.10. Any corner of the building includes the three principal directions. In the most general case—the three-point perspective—parallel lines in all three principal directions converge at three **vanishing points** (Figure 5.10a). If we allow one of the principal directions to become parallel to the projection plane, we have a two-point projection (Figure 5.10b), in which lines in only two of the principal directions converge. Finally, in the one-point perspective (Figure 5.10c), two of the principal directions are parallel to the projection plane, and we have only a single vanishing point. As with parallel viewing, it should be apparent from the

(a)   (b)   (c)

Figure 5.10 Classical perspective views: The (a) three-, (b) two-, and (c) one-point perspectives.

programmer's point of view that the three situations are merely special cases of general perspective viewing, which we implement in Section 5.4.

5.2 Viewing with a Computer

We can now return to three-dimensional graphics from a computer perspective. Because viewing in computer graphics is based on the synthetic camera model, we should be able to construct any of the classical views. However, there is a fundamental difference. All the classical views were based on a particular relationship between the objects, the viewer, and the projectors. In computer graphics, we stress the independence of the object specifications and camera parameters. In OpenGL, we shall have the choice of a perspective camera or an orthogonal camera. Whether a perspective view is a one-, two- or three-point perspective is not something that is understood by OpenGL, as it would require knowing the relationships between objects and the camera. On balance, we prefer this independence, but if an application needs a particular type of view, the application programmer may well have to determine where to place the camera.

In terms of the pipeline architecture, viewing consists of two fundamental operations. First, we must position the camera. This operation is the job of the model-view transformation. After vertices pass through this transformation, they are represented in camera coordinates. The second step is the application of the projection transformation. This step applies the specified projection—orthographic or perspective—to the vertices and puts objects within the specified clipping volume in a normalized clipping volume. We shall examine these steps in detail in the next few sections, but at this point it would help to review the default camera, that is, the camera that OpenGL uses if we do not specify any viewing functions.

OpenGL starts with the camera at the origin, pointing in the negative z direction. This camera is set up for orthogonal views and has a viewing volume that is a cube, centered at the origin and with sides of length 2. Thus, objects within this box are visible and projected as in Figure 5.11. Until now, we were able to ignore any complex viewing procedures by exploiting our knowledge of this camera. Thus, we were able to define objects in the application programs that fit inside this cube and knew that they would be visible. In this approach, both the model-view and projection matrices were left as the default identity matrices.

Subsequently, we altered the model-view matrix, initially an identity matrix, by rotations and translations, so as to place the camera where we desired. We also saw that the parameters in glOrtho altered the projection matrix, also initially an identity matrix, so as to allow us to see objects inside an arbitrary right parallelepiped. In this chapter, we shall generate a wider variety of views by using the model-view matrix to position the camera and the projection matrix to produce both orthographic and perspective views.

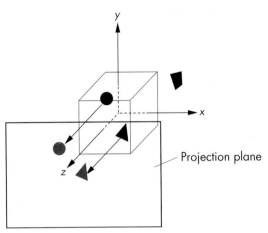

Figure 5.11 Imaging using the default camera.

5.3 Positioning of the Camera

We shall focus on the API that OpenGL provides for three-dimensional graphics. In this section, we deal with positioning the camera; in Section 5.4 we discuss how we specify the desired projection. We also see how other APIs specify a camera.

In OpenGL, the model-view and projection matrices are concatenated together to form the matrix that applies to geometric entities such as vertices. We have seen one use of the model-view matrix—to position objects in space. The other is to convert from the reference frame used for modeling to the frame of the camera.

5.3.1 Positioning of the Camera Frame

As we saw in Chapter 4, we can specify vertices in any units we choose, and we can define a model-view matrix by a sequence of affine transformations that repositions these vertices. We can also view this operation as changing the frame, and the result of applying the model-view transformation as giving the locations of the vertices in a different frame. In other words, we define objects in a reference frame, and the modeling part of the model-view matrix converts from the modeling frame to the world or user frame. In certain other APIs, objects are said to be modeled in **master** or **modeling coordinates**, and the instance transformation brings them into the world frame.

We model our objects independently from the viewing, and thus from the location of the camera. OpenGL places a camera at the origin of the world frame pointing in the negative z direction (Figure 5.12). Hence, if the model-view

Figure 5.12 Initial camera position.

matrix is an identity matrix, then the camera frame and the world frame are identical.

In most applications, we model our objects as being located around the origin, so a camera located at the default position with the default orientation does not see all the objects in the scene. Thus, either we must move the camera away from the objects that we wish to have in our image, or the objects must be moved in front of the camera. These are equivalent operations, as either can be looked at as positioning the frame of the camera with respect to the frame of the objects.

It might help to think of a scene in which we have defined several objects initially, with the model-view matrix as the identity, by specifying all vertices through glVertex. Subsequent changes to the model-view move the world frame relative to the camera, and affect the camera's view of all objects defined *afterward*, as their vertices are specified relative to the repositioned world frame. Equivalently, in terms of the flow of an application program, the projection and model-view matrices are part of the state; when a primitive is defined, the system uses the present state to obtain the matrices that apply to it.

Consider the sequence in Figure 5.13. In Figure 5.13(a), we have the initial configuration. A vertex specified at **p** has the same representation in both frames. In Figure 5.13(b), we have changed the model-view matrix to **C** by a sequence of transformations. The two frames are no longer the same, although **C** contains the information to move from the camera frame to the world frame, or, equivalently, contains the information that moves the camera away from its initial position at the origin of the world frame. A vertex specified at **q** through glVertex, *after* the

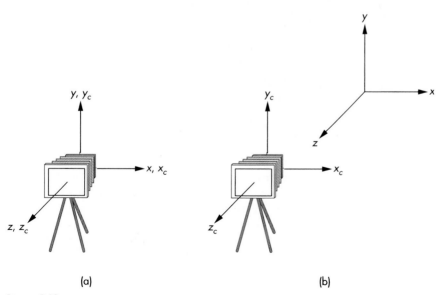

Figure 5.13 Movement of the camera and world frames. (a) Initial configuration. (b) Configuration after change in the model-view matrix.

change to the model-view matrix, is at **q** in the world frame. However, its position in the camera frame is **Cq** and is known internally to OpenGL; OpenGL converts positions to the camera frame through the viewing pipeline. The equivalent view is that the camera is still at the origin of its own frame, and the model-view matrix is applied to primitives specified in this system. In practice, you can use either view. But be sure to take great care regarding where in the program the primitives are specified relative to changes in the model-view matrix.

At any given time, the state of the model-view matrix encapsulates the relationship between the camera frame and the world frame. Although combining the modeling and viewing transformations into a single matrix may initially cause confusion, on closer examination this approach is a good one. If we regard the camera as an object with geometric properties, then transformations that alter the position and orientation of objects should also affect the position and orientation of the camera relative to these objects.

The obvious next problems are how we specify the desired position of the camera and how we implement camera positioning in OpenGL. Here, we find it convenient to think in terms of moving the default camera relative to the world frame. We outline three approaches, one in this section and two in Section 5.3.2. Two others are given as exercises (Exercises 5.2 and 5.3).

Our first approach is to specify the position indirectly by applying a sequence of rotations and translations to the model-view matrix. This approach is a direct application of the instance transformation that we presented in Chapter 4, but we must be careful for two reasons. First, we usually want to define the camera *before* we position any objects in the scene.[2] Second, transformations on the camera may appear to be backward from what you might expect.

Consider object centered at the origin. The camera is in its initial position, also at the origin, pointing down the negative z-axis. Suppose that we want an image of the faces of the object that point in the positive x direction. We must move the camera *away* from the origin. If we allow the camera to remain pointing in the negative z direction, then we want to move the camera backward along the positive z-axis, and the proper transformation is

```
glTranslatef(0.0, 0.0, -d);
```

where d is a positive number.

Many people find it helpful to interpret this operation as moving the camera frame relative to the world frame. This point of view has a basis in classical viewing. In computer graphics, we usually think of objects as being positioned in a fixed frame, and it is the viewer who must move to the right position to achieve the desired view. In classical viewing, the viewer dominates. Conceptually, we do

---

2. In an animation, where in the program we define the position of the camera depends on whether we wish to attach the camera to a particular object or to place the camera in a fixed position in the scene; see Exercise 5.3.

viewing by picking up the object, orienting it as desired, and bringing it to the desired location. One consequence of the classical approach is that distances are measured from the viewer to the object, rather than—as in most physically based systems—from the object to the viewer. Classical viewing thus results in a left-handed camera frame. Many graphics systems follow this view by having modeling in right-handed coordinates and viewing in left-handed coordinates—a decision that, although technically correct, can cause confusion among users. In OpenGL, clipping distances—such as in glOrtho—are measured *from* the camera, a choice equivalent to using a left-handed camera frame.

Suppose that we want to look at the same object from the positive *x*-axis. Now we not only have to move away from the object, but also have to rotate the camera about the *y* axis, as shown in Figure 5.14. We must do the translation after we rotate the camera by 90 degrees about the *y* axis. In the program, the calls must be in the reverse order, as we discussed in Section 4.8, so we expect to see code like the following:

```
glMatrixMode(GL_MODELVIEW);
glLoadIdentity();
glTranslatef(0.0, 0.0, -d);
glRotatef(-90.0, 0.0, 1.0, 0.0);
```

Figure 5.14 Positioning of the camera.

In terms of the two frames, we first rotate the world frame relative to the camera frame; then we move the two frames apart.

In Chapters 2 and 4, we were able to show simple three-dimensional examples by using the default projection matrix. The projection matrix, which we study in detail in Section 5.4, is set initially to an identity matrix. The default setting has the effect of creating an orthographic projection with the camera at the origin, pointed in the negative *z* direction. In our cube example in Chapter 4, we rotated the cube to see the desired faces. As we just discussed, rotating the cube is equivalent to rotating the frame of the cube with respect to the frame of the camera; we could have achieved the same view by rotating the camera relative to the cube. We can extend this strategy of translating and rotating the camera to create other orthographic views. Perspective views require changes to the projection matrix.

Consider creating an isometric view of the cube. Suppose that we again start with a cube centered at the origin and aligned with the axes. As the default camera is in the middle of the cube, we eventually want to move the camera away from the cube by a translation. We have an isometric view when the camera is located symmetrically with respect to three adjacent faces of the cube. We can rotate the cube to achieve this orientation, and then move the camera away.

Even though we have yet to move the default camera, suppose that we are now looking at the cube from somewhere on the positive *z*-axis. We can obtain one of the eight isometric views—there is one for each vertex—by first rotating the cube about the *y*-axis until we see the two faces symmetrically, as in Figure 5.15(a). Clearly, we obtain this view by rotating the cube by 45 degrees. The second

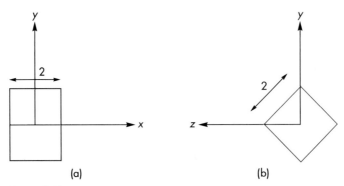

Figure 5.15 Cube after rotation about x-axis. (a) View from positive z-axis. (b) View of y, z plane.

rotation is about the x-axis. We rotate the cube down until we get the desired isometric. The required angle of rotation is -35.26 degrees about the x-axis. This second angle of rotation may not seem obvious. Consider what happens to the cube after the first rotation. From our position on the positive z-axis, the cube appears as in Figure 5.15(a). The original corner vertex at $(-1, 1, 1)$ has been transformed to $(0, 1, \sqrt{2})$. If we look at the cube from the x-axis as in Figure 5.15(b), we see that we want to rotate the top-right vertex to the y-axis. The right triangle that determines this angle has sides of 1 and $\sqrt{2}$, which correspond to an angle of 35.26 degrees. However, we need a clockwise rotation, so the angle must be negative. Finally, we move the camera away from the origin. Thus, our strategy is to first rotate the frame of the camera relative to the frame of the object, and then to separate the two frames; the model-view matrix is of the form

$$\mathbf{M} = \mathbf{T}\mathbf{R}_x\mathbf{R}_y.$$

We obtain this model-view matrix for an isometric by multiplying the matrices in homogeneous coordinates. The concatenation of the rotation matrices yields

$$\mathbf{R} = \mathbf{R}_x\mathbf{R}_y = \begin{bmatrix} 1 & 0 & 0 & 0 \\ 0 & \sqrt{6}/3 & -\sqrt{3}/3 & 0 \\ 0 & \sqrt{3}/3 & \sqrt{6}/3 & 0 \\ 0 & 0 & 0 & 1 \end{bmatrix} \begin{bmatrix} \sqrt{2}/2 & 0 & \sqrt{2}/2 & 0 \\ 0 & 1 & 0 & 0 \\ -\sqrt{2}/2 & 0 & \sqrt{2}/2 & 0 \\ 0 & 0 & 0 & 1 \end{bmatrix}$$

$$= \begin{bmatrix} \sqrt{2}/2 & 0 & \sqrt{2}/2 & 0 \\ \sqrt{6}/6 & \sqrt{6}/3 & -\sqrt{6}/6 & 0 \\ -\sqrt{3}/3 & \sqrt{3}/3 & \sqrt{3}/3 & 0 \\ 0 & 0 & 0 & 1 \end{bmatrix}.$$

It is simple to verify that the original vertex $(-1, 1, 1)$ is correctly transformed to $(0, 0, \sqrt{3})$ by this matrix. If we concatenate in the translation by $(0, 0, -d)$,

the matrix becomes

$$\mathbf{TR} = \begin{bmatrix} \sqrt{2}/2 & 0 & \sqrt{2}/2 & 0 \\ \sqrt{6}/6 & \sqrt{6}/3 & -\sqrt{6}/6 & 0 \\ -\sqrt{3}/3 & \sqrt{3}/3 & \sqrt{3}/3 & -d \\ 0 & 0 & 0 & 1 \end{bmatrix}.$$

In OpenGL, the code for setting the model-view matrix is thus

```
glMatrixMode(GL_MODELVIEW);
glLoadIdentity();
glTranslatef(0.0, 0.0, -d);
glRotatef(35.26, 1.0, 0.0, 0.0);
glRotatef(45.0, 0.0, 1.0, 0.0);
```

Note that the clipping volume as set by glOrtho is relative to the camera frame. Thus, for an orthographic view, the translation of the camera does not affect the size of the image, but it can affect whether or not objects are clipped.

5.3.2 Two Viewing APIs

The construction of the model-view matrix for an isometric view is a little unsatisfying. Although the approach was intuitive, an interface that requires us to compute the individual angles before specifying the transformations is a poor one for an application program. We can take a different approach to positioning the camera—an approach that is similar to that used by PHIGS and GKS-3D, two of the original standard APIs for three-dimensional graphics. Our starting point is again the world frame. We describe the camera's position and orientation in this frame. The precise type of image that we wish to obtain—perspective or parallel—is determined separately by the specification of the equivalent of the projection matrix in OpenGL. This part of the viewing process is often called the **normalization transformation**. We approach this problem as one of a change in frames. We again think of the camera as positioned initially at the origin, pointed in the negative z direction. Its desired location is centered at a point called the **view-reference point** (**VRP**; Figure 5.16), whose position is given in the world frame. The user executes a function such as

```
set_view_reference_point(x, y, z);
```

to specify this position. Next, we want to specify the orientation of the camera. We can divide this specification into two parts: specification of the **view-plane normal** (**VPN**), and specification of the **view-up vector** (**VUP**). The VPN (**n** in Figure 5.16) gives the orientation of the projection plane or back of the camera. The orientation of a plane is determined by that plane's normal, and thus part of the API is a function

```
set_view_plane_normal(nx, ny, nz);
```

Figure 5.16 Camera frame.

The orientation of the plane does not specify what direction is up from the camera's perspective. Given only the VPN, we can rotate the camera with its back in this plane. The specification of the VUP fixes the camera and is performed by

```
set_view_up(vup_x, vup_y, vup_z);
```

We project the VUP vector on the view plane to obtain the up-direction vector $\mathbf{v}$ (Figure 5.17). Use of the projection allows the user to specify any vector not parallel to $\mathbf{v}$, rather than being forced to compute a vector lying in the projection plane. The vector $\mathbf{v}$ is orthogonal to $\mathbf{n}$. We can use the cross product to obtain a third orthogonal direction $\mathbf{u}$. This new orthogonal coordinate system usually is referred to as either the **viewing-coordinate system** or the **u-v-n system**. With the addition of the VRP, we have the desired camera frame. The matrix that does the change of frames is the **view-orientation matrix**.

We can derive this matrix using rotations and translations in homogeneous coordinates. We start with the specifications of the view-reference point,

Figure 5.17 Determination of the view-up vector.

$$\mathbf{p} = \begin{bmatrix} x \\ y \\ z \\ 1 \end{bmatrix},$$

the view-plane normal,

$$\mathbf{n} = \begin{bmatrix} n_x \\ n_y \\ n_z \\ 0 \end{bmatrix},$$

and the view-up vector,

$$\mathbf{v}_{up} = \begin{bmatrix} v_{up_x} \\ v_{up_y} \\ v_{up_z} \\ 0 \end{bmatrix}.$$

We construct a new frame with the view-reference point as its origin, the view-plane normal as one coordinate direction, and two other orthogonal directions that we call $\mathbf{u}$ and $\mathbf{v}$. Our default is that the original x, y, z axes become u, v, n, respectively. This choice corresponds to the default model-view matrix in OpenGL. The view-reference point can be handled through a simple translation $\mathbf{T}(-x, -y, -z)$ from the viewing frame to the original origin. The rest of model-view matrix is determined by a rotation so that the model-view matrix $\mathbf{V}$ is of the form

$$\mathbf{V} = \mathbf{TR}.$$

The direction $\mathbf{v}$ must be orthogonal to $\mathbf{n}$; hence,

$$\mathbf{n} \cdot \mathbf{v} = 0.$$

Figure 5.17 shows that $\mathbf{v}$ is the projection of $\mathbf{v}_{up}$ into the plane formed by $\mathbf{n}$ and $\mathbf{v}_{up}$ and thus must be a linear combination of these two vectors,

$$\mathbf{v} = \alpha\mathbf{n} + \beta\mathbf{v}_{up}.$$

If we temporarily ignore the length of the vectors, we can set $\beta = 1$ and solve for

$$\alpha = -\frac{\mathbf{v}_{up} \cdot \mathbf{n}}{\mathbf{n} \cdot \mathbf{n}}$$

and

$$\mathbf{v} = \mathbf{v}_{up} - \frac{\mathbf{v}_{up} \cdot \mathbf{n}}{\mathbf{n} \cdot \mathbf{n}}\,\mathbf{n}.$$

We can find the third orthogonal direction by taking the cross product

$$\mathbf{u} = \mathbf{v} \times \mathbf{n}.$$

These vectors do not generally have unit length. We can normalize each independently, obtaining three unit-length vectors $\mathbf{u}'$, $\mathbf{v}'$, and $\mathbf{n}'$. The matrix

$$\mathbf{M} = \begin{bmatrix} u'_x & v'_x & n'_x & 0 \\ u'_y & v'_y & n'_y & 0 \\ u'_z & v'_z & n'_z & 0 \\ 0 & 0 & 0 & 1 \end{bmatrix}$$

is a rotation matrix that orients a vector in the $\mathbf{u}'\mathbf{v}'\mathbf{n}'$ system with respect to the original system. However, we really want to go in the other direction, to get the representation of vectors in the original system in the $\mathbf{u}'\mathbf{v}'\mathbf{n}'$ system. We want $\mathbf{M}^{-1}$, but because $\mathbf{M}$ is a rotation matrix, the desired matrix $\mathbf{R}$ is

$$\mathbf{R} = \mathbf{M}^{-1} = \mathbf{M}^{T}.$$

Finally, multiplying by the translation matrix $\mathbf{T}$, we have

$$\mathbf{V} = \mathbf{RT} = \begin{bmatrix} u'_x & u'_y & u'_z & -xu'_x - yu'_y - zu'_z \\ v'_x & v'_y & v'_z & -xv'_x - yv'_y - zv'_z \\ n'_x & n'_y & n'_z & -xn'_x - yn'_y - zn'_z \\ 0 & 0 & 0 & 1 \end{bmatrix}.$$

Note that, in this case, the translation matrix is on the right, whereas in our first derivation it was on the left. One way to interpret this difference is that in our first derivation, we rotated the frames and then pushed them apart in a direction represented in the camera frame. In the second derivation, the camera position was specified in the world frame. Another way to understand this difference is to note that the matrices $\mathbf{RT}$ and $\mathbf{TR}$ have similar forms. The rotation parts of the product—the upper-left 3×3 submatrices—are identical, as are the bottom rows. The top three elements in the right column differ because the frame of the rotation affects the translation coefficients in **TR** and does not affect them in **RT**. For our isometric example,

$$\mathbf{n} = \begin{bmatrix} -1 \\ 1 \\ 1 \\ 0 \end{bmatrix},$$

$$\mathbf{v}_{up} = \begin{bmatrix} 0 \\ 1 \\ 0 \\ 0 \end{bmatrix}.$$

The camera position must be along a diagonal in the original frame. If we use

$$\mathbf{p} = \frac{\sqrt{3}}{3} \begin{bmatrix} -d \\ d \\ d \\ 1 \end{bmatrix},$$

we obtain the same model-view matrix that we derived in Section 5.3.1.

5.3.3 The Look-At Function

The use of the VRP, VPN, and VUP is but one way to provide an API for specifying the position of a camera. In many situations, a more direct method is appropriate. Consider the situation in Figure 5.18. Here, a camera is located at a point **e** called the **eye point**, specified in the world frame, and it is pointed at a second point **a**, called the **at point**. These points determine a VPN and a VRP. The VPN is given by the vector formed by point subtraction between the eyepoint and the at point

$$\mathbf{vpn} = \mathbf{e} - \mathbf{a}.$$

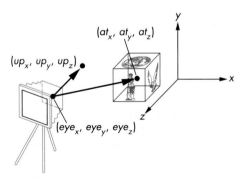

Figure 5.18 Look-at positioning.

The view-reference point is the eyepoint. Hence, we need only to add the desired up direction for the camera. The OpenGL utility function

```
gluLookAt(eyex, eyey, eyez, atx, aty, atx, upx, upy, upz);
```

alters the model-view matrix for a camera pointed along this line. Thus, we usually use the sequence

```
glMatrixMode(GL_MODELVIEW);
glLoadIdentity();
gluLookAt(eyex,eyey,eyez, atx, aty, atx, upx, upy, upz);

/* define objects here */
```

Note that we can use the standard rotations, translations, and scalings as part of defining our objects. Although these transformations will also alter the model-view matrix, it is often helpful conceptually to consider the use of gluLookAt as positioning the objects and subsequent operations that affect the model-view matrix as positioning the objects.

5.3.4 Other Viewing APIs

In many applications, neither of the viewing interfaces that we have presented is appropriate. Consider a flight-simulation application. The pilot using the simulator usually uses three angles—**roll**, **pitch**, and **yaw**—to specify her orientation. These angles are specified relative to the center of mass of the vehicle and to a coordinate system aligned along the axes of the vehicle, as shown in Figure 5.19. Hence, the pilot sees an object in terms of the three angles and of the distance from the object to the center of mass of her vehicle. A viewing transformation can be constructed (Exercise 5.2) from these specifications from a translation and three simple rotations.

Viewing in many applications is most naturally specified in polar— rather than rectilinear—coordinates. Applications involving objects that rotate about other

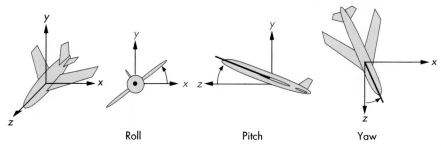

Roll   Pitch   Yaw

Figure 5.19 Roll, pitch, and yaw.

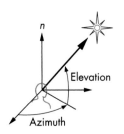

Figure 5.20 Elevation and azimuth.

objects fit this category. For example, consider the specification of a star in the sky. Its direction from a viewer is given by its elevation and azimuth (Figure 5.20). The **elevation** is the angle above the plane of the viewer at which the star appears. Note that, by defining a normal at the point that the viewer is located and using this normal to define a plane, we define the elevation, regardless of whether or not the viewer is actually standing on a plane. We can form two other axes in this plane, creating a viewing-coordinate system. The **azimuth** is the angle measured from an axis in this plane to the projection onto the plane of the line between the viewer and the star. The camera can still be rotated about the direction it is pointed by a **twist angle**.

5.4 Simple Projections

With a real camera, once we position it, we still must select a lens. As we saw in Chapter 1, it is the combination of the lens and the size of the film (or of the back of the camera) that determines how much of the world in front of a camera appears in the image. In computer graphics, we make an equivalent choice when we select the type of projection and the viewing parameters.

With a physical camera, a wide-angle lens gives the most dramatic perspectives, with objects near the camera appearing large compared to objects far from the lens. A telephoto lens gives an image that appears flat and is close to a parallel view. Most APIs distinguish between parallel and perspective views by providing different functions for the two cases. OpenGL does the same, even though the implementation of the two can use the same pipeline, as we shall see in Sections 5.9 and 5.10.

Just as we did with the model-view matrix, we can set the projection matrix with the glLoadMatrix function. Alternatively, we can use OpenGL functions for the most common viewing conditions. First, we consider the mathematics of projection. We can extend our use of homogeneous coordinates to the projection process, which allows us to characterize a particular projection with a 4×4 matrix.

5.4.1 Perspective Projections

Suppose that we are in the camera frame with the camera located at the origin, pointed in the negative z direction. Figure 5.21 shows two possibilities. In Figure 5.21(a), the back of the camera is orthogonal to the z direction and is parallel to the lens. This configuration corresponds to most physical situations, including those of the human visual system and of simple cameras. The situation in Figure 5.21(b) is more general; the back of the camera can have any orientation with respect to the front. We consider the first case in detail because it is simpler. However, the derivation of the general result follows the same steps and should be a direct exercise (Exercise 5.6).

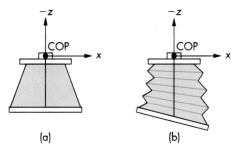

Figure 5.21 Two cameras.

As we saw in Chapter 1, we can place the projection plane in front of the center of projection. If we do so for the configuration of Figure 5.21(a), we get the views shown in Figure 5.22. A point in space (x, y, z) is projected along a projector into the point (x_p, y_p, z_p). All projectors pass through the origin and, because the projection plane is perpendicular to the z-axis,

$$z_p = d.$$

Because the camera is pointing in the negative z direction, the projection plane is in the negative half-space $z < 0$, and the value of d is negative.

From the top view of Figure 5.22(b), we see two similar triangles whose tangents must be same. Hence,

$$\frac{x}{z} = \frac{x_p}{d},$$

and

$$x_p = \frac{x}{z/d}.$$

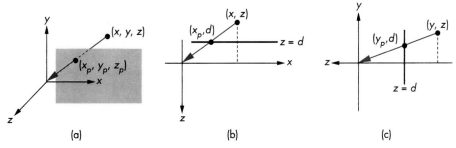

Figure 5.22 Three views of perspective projection. (a) Three-dimensional view. (b) Top view. (c) Side view.

Using the side view, we obtain a similar result for y_p,

$$y_p = \frac{y}{z/d}.$$

These equations are nonlinear. The division by z describes **nonuniform fore-shortening**: The images of objects farther from the center of projection are reduced in size (diminution) compared to the images of objects closer to the COP.

We can look at the projection process as a transformation that takes points (x, y, z) to other points (x_p, y_p, z_p). Although this **perspective transformation** preserves lines, it is not affine. It is also irreversible: Because all points along a projector project into the same point, we cannot recover a point from its projection.[3] We can, however, modify slightly our use of homogeneous coordinates to handle projections.

When we introduced homogeneous coordinates, we represented a point in three dimensions (x, y, z) by the point $(x, y, z, 1)$ in four dimensions. Suppose that, instead, we replace (x, y, z) by the four-dimensional point

$$\mathbf{p} = \begin{bmatrix} wx \\ wy \\ wz \\ w \end{bmatrix}.$$

As long as $w \neq 0$, we can recover the three-dimensional point from its four-dimensional representation by dividing the first three components by w. In this new homogeneous-coordinate form, points in three dimensions become lines in four dimensions. Transformations are again represented by 4×4 matrices, but now the final row of the matrix can be altered—and thus w can be changed by such a transformation.

Obviously, we would prefer to keep $w = 1$ to avoid the divisions otherwise necessary to recover the three-dimensional point. However, by allowing w to change, we can represent a broader class of transformations, including perspective projections. Consider the matrix

$$\mathbf{M} = \begin{bmatrix} 1 & 0 & 0 & 0 \\ 0 & 1 & 0 & 0 \\ 0 & 0 & 1 & 0 \\ 0 & 0 & 1/d & 0 \end{bmatrix}.$$

---

3. In Sections 5.8 and 5.9 we shall see the advantages of OpenGL's use of an invertible variant of the projection transformation.

The matrix $\mathbf{M}$ transforms the point

$$\mathbf{p} = \begin{bmatrix} x \\ y \\ z \\ 1 \end{bmatrix}$$

to the point

$$\mathbf{q} = \begin{bmatrix} x \\ y \\ z \\ z/d \end{bmatrix}.$$

At first glance, $\mathbf{q}$ may not seem sensible; but, when we remember that we have to divide the first three components by the fourth to return to our original three-dimensional space, we obtain the results

$$x_p = \frac{x}{z/d},$$

$$y_p = \frac{y}{z/d},$$

$$z_p = \frac{z}{z/d} = d,$$

which are the equations for a simple perspective projection. In homogeneous coordinates, dividing $\mathbf{q}$ by its w component replaces $\mathbf{q}$ by the equivalent point

$$\mathbf{q}' = \begin{bmatrix} \frac{x}{z/d} \\ \frac{y}{z/d} \\ d \\ 1 \end{bmatrix} = \begin{bmatrix} x_p \\ y_p \\ z_p \\ 1 \end{bmatrix}.$$

We have shown that we can do at least a simple perspective projection, by defining a 4×4 projection matrix that we apply after the model-view matrix. However, we must perform a **perspective division** at the end. This division can be made part of the pipeline, as shown in Figure 5.23.

5.4.2 Orthogonal Projections

Orthogonal or **orthographic** projections are a special case of parallel projections, in which the projectors are perpendicular to the view plane. In terms of a camera, orthogonal projections correspond to a camera with a back plane parallel to the

Figure 5.23 Projection pipeline.

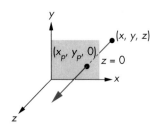

Figure 5.24 Orthogonal projection.

lens, which has an infinite focal length. However, rather than using limiting relations as the COP moves to infinity, we can derive the projection equations directly. Figure 5.24 shows an orthogonal projection with the projection plane $z = 0$. As points are projected into this plane, they retain their x and y values, and the equations of projection are

$$x_p = x,$$
$$y_p = y,$$
$$z_p = 0.$$

We can write this result using our original homogeneous coordinates:

$$\begin{bmatrix} x_p \\ y_p \\ z_p \\ 1 \end{bmatrix} = \begin{bmatrix} 1 & 0 & 0 & 0 \\ 0 & 1 & 0 & 0 \\ 0 & 0 & 0 & 0 \\ 0 & 0 & 0 & 1 \end{bmatrix} \begin{bmatrix} x \\ y \\ z \\ 1 \end{bmatrix}.$$

In this case, a division is unnecessary, although, in hardware implementations, we can use the same pipeline for both perspective and orthogonal transformations.

We can expand both our simple projections to general perspective and parallel projections by preceding the projection by a sequence of transformations that converts the general case to one of the two cases that we know how to apply. First, we examine the API that the application programmer uses in OpenGL to specify a projection.

5.5 Projections in OpenGL

The projections that we developed in Section 5.4 did not take into account the properties of the camera—the focal length of its lens or the size of the film plane. Figure 5.25 shows the **angle of view** for a simple pinhole camera, like the one

Figure 5.25 Definition of a view volume.

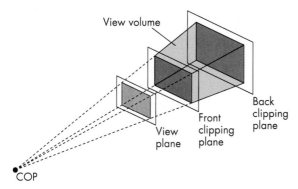

Figure 5.26   Front and back clipping planes.

that we discussed in Chapter 1. Only those objects that fit within the angle of view of the camera appear in the image. If the back of the camera is rectangular, only objects within a semi-infinite pyramid—the **view volume**— whose apex is at the COP can appear in the image. Objects not within the view volume are said to be **clipped** out of the scene. Hence, our description of simple projections has been incomplete; we did not include the effects of clipping.

Most graphics APIs define clipping parameters through the specification of a projection. In a computer-graphics system, we allow a finite clipping volume by specifying front and back clipping planes, in addition to the angle of view, as shown in Figure 5.26. The resulting view volume is a **frustum**—a truncated pyramid. We have fixed only one parameter: We have specified that the COP is at the origin in the camera frame. We should be able to define each of the six sides of the frustum to have almost any orientation and position. If we did so, however, we would make it difficult to specify a view, and rarely do we need this flexibility. We examine the OpenGL API. Other APIs differ in their function calls, but incorporate similar restrictions.

5.5.1 Perspective in OpenGL

In OpenGL, we have two functions for specifying perspective views and one for specifying parallel views. Alternatively, we can form the projection matrix directly, either by loading it, or by applying rotations, translations, and scalings to an initial identity matrix. We can specify our camera view by the function

```
glFrustum(xmin, xmax, ymin, ymax, near, far)
```

These parameters are shown in Figure 5.27. The near and far distances must be positive and are measured from the COP to these planes, both of which are parallel to the plane $z = 0$. Note that, because the camera is pointing in the

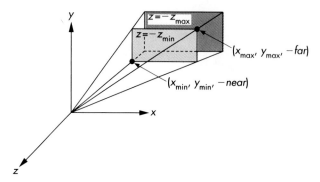

Figure 5.27 Specification of a frustum.

negative z direction, the front (near) clipping plane is the plane $z = -near$, and the back (far) clipping plane is the plane $z = -far$.[4] The plane $x = x_{min}$ is to the left of the camera as viewed from the COP in the direction of the camera. Similar statements hold for xmax, ymin, and ymax. Consequently, the function glFrustum is often written as

```
glFrustum(left, right, bottom, top, near, far)
```

Because the projection matrix determined by these specifications multiplies the present matrix, we must first select the matrix mode. A typical sequence is

```
glMatrixMode(GL_PROJECTION);
glLoadIdentity();
glFrustum(xmin, xmax, ymin, ymax, near, far);
```

Note that none of the left (xmin), right (xmax), top (ymax), and bottom (ymin) specifications have to be symmetric with respect to the z-axis, and that the resulting frustum also does not have to be symmetric (a right frustum). In Section 5.9, we show how the projection matrix for this projection can be derived from the simple perspective-projection matrix of Section 5.4.

In many applications, it is natural to specify the angle or field of view. However, if the projection plane is rectangular, rather than square, then we see a different angle of view in the top and side views (Figure 5.28). The angle *fov* is the angle between the top and bottom planes of the clipping volume. The OpenGL utility function

```
gluPerspective(fovy, aspect, near, far)
```

---

4. Measuring distances from the camera to the objects is equivalent to switching from the right-handed world frame that we used for specifying our objects to a left-handed camera frame.

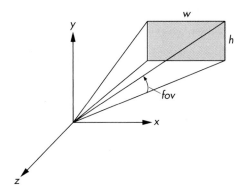

Figure 5.28 Specification using the field of view.

allows us to specify the angle of view in the up (y) direction, as well as the aspect ratio—width divided by height—of the projection plane. The near and far planes are specified as in glFrustum. This matrix also alters the present matrix, so we must again select the matrix mode, and usually must load an identity matrix, before invoking this function.

5.5.2 Parallel Viewing in OpenGL

The only parallel-viewing function provided by OpenGL is the orthogonal (orthographic) viewing function

glOrtho(xmin, xmax, ymin, ymax, near, far)

or

glOrtho(left, right, bottom, top, near, far)

Its parameters are identical to those of glFrustum. The view volume is a right parallelepiped, as shown in Figure 5.29. The near and far clipping planes are again at $z = -near$ and $z = -far$, respectively.

In perspective viewing, we require the distances to both the near and far planes to be positive, because all projectors pass through the COP at the origin, and objects behind the COP are projected upside down, as compared with objects in front of the COP. Points in the plane $z = 0$ cannot be projected at all, and lead to division by zero. This problem does not exist in parallel viewing, and there are thus no restrictions on the sign of the near and far distances in glOrtho.

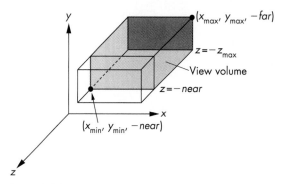

Figure 5.29 Orthographic viewing.

5.6 Hidden-Surface Removal

We can now return to our rotating-cube program of Section 4.9 and add perspective viewing and movement of the camera. First, we can use our development of viewing to understand the hidden-surface–removal process that we used in our first version of the program. When we look at a cube that has opaque sides, we see only its three front-facing sides. From the perspective of our basic viewing model, we can say that we see only these faces because they block the projectors from the COP from reaching any other surfaces.

From the perspective of computer graphics, however, all the faces of the cube have been specified and travel down the graphics pipeline; thus, the graphics system must be careful about which surfaces it displays. Conceptually, we seek algorithms that either remove those surfaces that should not be visible to the viewer, called **hidden-surface–removal algorithms**, or find which surfaces are visible, called **visible-surface algorithms**. There are many approaches to the problem, several of which we investigate in Chapter 8. OpenGL has a particular algorithm associated with it, the **z-buffer algorithm**, to which we can interface through three function calls. Hence, we introduce that algorithm here, and we return to the topic in Chapter 8.

Hidden-surface–removal algorithms can be divided into two broad classes. **Object-space algorithms** attempt to order the surfaces of the objects in the scene such that drawing surfaces in a particular order provides the correct image. For example, for our cube, if we were to draw the back-facing surfaces first, we could "paint" over them with the front surfaces and would produce the correct image. This class of algorithms does not work well with pipeline architectures in which objects are passed down the pipeline in an arbitrary order. In order to decide on a proper order in which to render the objects, the graphics system must have all the objects available so it can sort them into the desired order.

Image-space algorithms work as part of the projection process and seek to determine the relationship among object points on each projector. The z-buffer

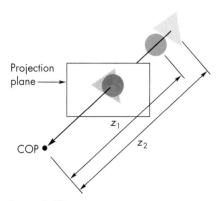

Figure 5.30 The z-buffer algorithm.

algorithm is of the latter type and fits in well with the rendering pipeline in most graphics systems because we can save partial information as each object is rendered.

The basic idea of the z-buffer algorithm is shown in Figure 5.30. A projector from the COP passes through two surfaces. Because the circle is closer to the viewer than the triangle, it is the circle's color that determines the color that is placed in the color buffer at the location corresponding to where the projector pierces the projection plane. The difficulty is determining how we can make this idea work regardless of the order in which the triangle and the circle pass through the pipeline.

Let's assume that all the objects are polygons. If, as the polygons are rasterized, we can keep track of the distance from the COP to the closest point on each projector, then we can update this information as successive polygons are projected and filled. Ultimately, we display only the closest point on each projector. The algorithm requires a **depth** or **z buffer** to store the necessary depth information as polygons are rasterized. Because we must keep depth information for each pixel in the color buffer, the z buffer has the same spatial resolution as the color buffers. Its depth corresponds to the amount of depth resolution that is supported, usually 16, 24, or 32 bits. This buffer can come from the standard memory in the system, or special memory can be added at the end of a hardware pipeline. In OpenGL, the z buffer is one of the buffers that constitute the frame buffer.

The depth buffer is initialized to a value that corresponds to the farthest distance from the viewer. When each polygon that is inside the clipping volume is rasterized, the depth of each pixel—how far the corresponding point on the polygon is from the viewer—is calculated. If this distance is greater than the value at that pixel's location in the depth buffer, then a polygon that has already been rasterized is closer to the viewer along the projector corresponding to the pixel. Hence, for this pixel we ignore the color of the polygon and go on to the next pixel for this polygon, where we make the same test. If, however, the depth is less than what is already in the z buffer, then along this projector the polygon being rendered is closer than any one we have seen so far. Thus, we use the color of the polygon to replace the color of the pixel in the color buffer and update the depth in the z buffer.

For the example in Figure 5.30, we see that if the triangle passes through the pipeline first, its colors and depths will be placed in the color and z buffers. When the circle passes through the pipeline, its colors and depths will replace the colors and depths of the triangle where they overlap. If the circle is rendered first, its colors and depths will be placed in the buffers. When the triangle is rendered, in the areas where there is overlap, the depths of the triangle are greater than the depth of the circle, and at the corresponding pixels no changes will be made to the frame or z buffers.

Major advantages of this algorithm are that its worst-case complexity is proportional to the number of polygons and that it can be implemented with a small number of additional calculations over what we have to do anyway to project and display polygons. We shall return to this issue in Chapter 8.

From the application programmer's perspective, she must initialize the depth buffer and enable hidden-surface removal by using

```
glutInitDisplayMode(GLUT_DOUBLE | GLUT_RGB | GLUT_DEPTH);
glEnable(GL_DEPTH_TEST);
```

Here we use the GLUT library for the initialization and specify a depth buffer in addition to our usual RGB color and double buffering. The programmer can clear the buffer as necessary for a new rendering by using

```
glClear(GL_DEPTH_BUFFER_BIT);
```

5.6.1 Culling

For a convex object, such as the cube, we could simply remove all the faces pointing away from the viewer, and we could render only the ones facing the viewer. We consider this special case further in Chapter 8. We can turn on culling in OpenGL by simply enabling it

```
glEnable(GL_CULL);
```

However, culling works only if we have a convex object. Often we can use culling in addition to the z-buffer algorithm (which works with any collection of polygons). For example, suppose that we have a scene composed of a collection of n cubes. If we use only the z-buffer algorithm, we pass $6n$ polygons through the pipeline. If we enable culling, half the polygons can be eliminated early in the pipeline, and thus only $3n$ polygons can pass through all stages of the pipeline.

5.7 Walking Through a Scene

In the color-cube program in Chapter 4, the cube rotated about the origin. We used an orthographic projection, and we did not have to worry about pointing the camera in any but the default direction, or about defining the relationship between the object and the center of projection.

In this version, we use perspective viewing, and we allow the viewer to move the camera by depressing the x, X, y, Y, z, and Z keys on the keyboard, but we have the camera always pointing at the center of the cube. The gluLookAt function provides a simple way to reposition and reorient the camera.

The changes that we have to make to our previous program (Section 4.9) are minor. We define an array viewer[3] to hold the camera position. Its contents are altered by the keyboard callback function keys

```
void keys(unsigned char key, int x, int y)
{
   if(key == 'x') viewer[0]-= 1.0;
   if(key == 'X') viewer[0]+= 1.0;
   if(key == 'y') viewer[1]-= 1.0;
   if(key == 'Y') viewer[1]+= 1.0;
   if(key == 'z') viewer[2]-= 1.0;
   if(key == 'Z') viewer[2]+= 1.0;
   glutPostRedisplay();
}
```

The display function calls LookAt using viewer for the camera position, and uses the origin for the "at" position. The cube is rotated, as before, based on the mouse input. Note the order of the function calls in display that alter the model-view matrix:

```
void display(void)
{

   glClear(GL_COLOR_BUFFER_BIT | GL_DEPTH_BUFFER_BIT);
   glLoadIdentity();
   gluLookAt(viewer[0],viewer[1],viewer[2], 0.0, 0.0, 0.0,
                                0.0, 1.0, 0.0);
   glRotatef(theta[0], 1.0, 0.0, 0.0);
   glRotatef(theta[1], 0.0, 1.0, 0.0);
   glRotatef(theta[2], 0.0, 0.0, 1.0);

   colorcube();

   glFlush();
   glutSwapBuffers();
}
```

We can invoke glFrustum from the reshape callback to specify the camera lens through the following code:

```
void myReshape(int w, int h)
{
    glViewport(0, 0, w, h);
    glMatrixMode(GL_PROJECTION);
    glLoadIdentity();
    if(w<=h) glFrustum(-2.0, 2.0, -2.0 * (GLfloat) h/ (GLfloat)
        w,2.0* (GLfloat) h / (GLfloat) w, 2.0, 20.0);
    else glFrustum(-2.0, 2.0, -2.0 * (GLfloat) w/ (GLfloat) h,
        2.0* (GLfloat) w / (GLfloat) h, 2.0, 20.0);
    glMatrixMode(GL_MODELVIEW);
}
```

Note that we chose the values of the parameters in glFrustum based on the aspect ratio of the window. Other than the added specification of a keyboard callback function in main, the rest of the program is the same as the program in Section 4.9. The complete program is given in Appendix A. If you run this program, you should note the effects of moving the camera, the lens, and the sides of the viewing frustum. Note what happens as you move toward the cube. You should also consider the effect of always having the viewer look at the center of the cube as she is moving.

There are various ways to move around the scene using an interactive device. Suppose we did not use the mouse to rotate the cube. Then we could use the mouse buttons to move the user forward, or to turn her right or left (see Exercise 5.14). In this example, we are using direct positioning of the camera through gluLookAt. There are other possibilities. One is to use rotation and translation matrices to alter the model-view matrix incrementally. If we want to move the viewer through the scene without having her looking at a fixed point, this option may be more appealing. We could also keep a position variable in the program, and change it as the viewer moves. In this case, the model-view matrix would be computed from scratch, rather than changed incrementally. Which option we choose depends on the particular application, and often on other factors, such as the possibility that numerical errors might accumulate if we were to change the model-view matrix incrementally many times.

5.8 Parallel-Projection Matrices

The OpenGL projection matrices are not quite as simple as the projection matrices that we derived in Section 5.4. In this section and the next, we derive the OpenGL projection matrices. Because projections are such a key part of three-dimensional computer graphics, understanding projections is crucial both for writing user applications and for implementing a graphics system. Furthermore, although the OpenGL projection functions that we introduced are sufficient for most viewing situations, views such as parallel oblique are not provided directly

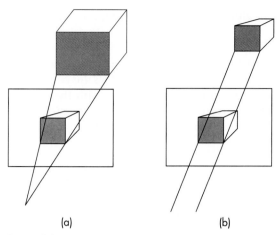

(a)   (b)

Figure 5.31 Predistortion of objects. (a) Perspective
view. (b) Orthographic projection of distorted object.

by the OpenGL API. We can obtain such views by setting up a projection matrix
from scratch, or by modifying one of the standard views. We can apply either of
these approaches using the matrices that we derive.

5.8.1 Projection Normalization

Our approach is based on a technique called **projection normalization**, which
converts all projections into orthogonal projections by first distorting the objects
such that the orthogonal projection of the distorted objects is the same as the
desired projection of the original objects. This technique is shown in Figure 5.31.
However, because the distortion of the objects is described by a homogeneous-
coordinate matrix, we can, rather than distorting the objects, concatenate this
matrix with a simple orthogonal-projection matrix to form the desired projection
matrix, as shown in Figure 5.32.

5.8.2 Orthogonal-Projection Matrices

Although parallel viewing is a special case of perspective viewing, we start with
orthogonal parallel viewing, and extend the normalization technique to perspective viewing. We have shown that projection converts points in three-dimensional
space to points on the projection plane, and that the transformation that does

Figure 5.32 Normalization transformation.

this operation is singular. All points along a projector project into the same point on the projection plane.

Our development breaks projection into two parts. The first converts the specified viewing volume to standard volume by a nonsingular homogeneous-coordinate transformation. We apply the transformation that does this conversion to all our objects by concatenating the transformation matrix with the model-view matrix. Objects are distorted in a manner that yields the desired projection through the second step, which is an orthogonal projection on the transformed objects and volume

$$x_p = x,$$
$$y_p = y,$$
$$z_p = 0.$$

Note that carrying out this orthographic projection requires only setting the z value to zero, or equivalently just neglecting it, because it is not needed. The real work in the projection process is in the first transformation. The reasons for separating the projection process into two parts have to do with many of the other tasks that we do as part of the viewing pipeline. In particular, we shall see in Chapter 8 that clipping must be done in three dimensions, and that the use of the nonsingular transformation matrix allows us to retain depth information along projectors that is necessary for hidden-surface removal and shading (Chapter 6). The first part of the process defines what most systems, including OpenGL, call the **projection matrix**. OpenGL also distinguishes between *screen coordinates*, which are two-dimensional and lack depth information, and *window coordinates*, which are three-dimensional and retain the depth information. In OpenGL, the projection matrix and the subsequent perspective division convert vertices to window coordinates.

For orthographic projections, the simplest clipping volume to deal with is a cube whose center is at the origin and whose sides are given by the six planes

$$x = \pm 1,$$
$$y = \pm 1,$$
$$z = \pm 1.$$

This cube is the default OpenGL view volume; equivalently, we can use the function calls

```
glMatrixMode(GL_PROJECTION);
glLoadIdentity();
glOrtho(-1.0, 1.0, -1.0, 1.0, -1.0, 1.0);
```

We call this volume the **canonical view volume**. The final two parameters in glOrtho are distances to the near and far planes measured from a camera at the origin pointed in the negative z direction. The near plane is at $z = 1.0$, which is behind the camera; the far plane is at $z = -1.0$, which is in front of the camera. Although the projectors are parallel and an orthographic projection is conceptually akin to having a camera with a long telephoto lens located far from the objects, the importance of the near and far distances in glOrtho is that they determine which objects are clipped out.

Now suppose that, instead, we set the glOrtho parameters by the function call

```
glOrtho(xmin, xmax, ymax, ymin, near, far);
```

We now have specified a right parallelepiped view volume whose right side (relative to the camera) is the plane $x = x_{max}$, whose left side is the plane $x = x_{min}$, whose top is the plane $y = y_{max}$, and whose bottom is the plane $y = y_{min}$. The front is the near clipping plane $z = -near$, and the back is the far clipping plane $z = -far$. The projection matrix that OpenGL sets up is the matrix that transforms this volume to the cube centered at the origin with sides of length 2 shown in Figure 5.33, where $z_{max} = -near$ and $z_{min} = -far$. This matrix converts the vertices that specify our objects, such as through calls to glVertex, to vertices within this canonical view volume, by scaling and translating them. Consequently, vertices are transformed such that vertices within the specified view volume are transformed to vertices within the canonical view volume, and vertices outside the specified view volume are transformed to vertices outside the canonical view volume. Putting everything together, we see that the projection matrix is determined by the type of view and the view volume specified in glOrtho, and that these specifications are relative to the camera. The positioning and orientation of the camera are determined by the model-view matrix. These two matrices are concatenated together, and objects have their vertices transformed by this matrix product.

We can use our knowledge of affine transformations to find this projection matrix. There are two tasks that we need to do. First, we must move the center of the specified view volume to the center of the canonical view volume (the origin) by doing a translation. Second, we must scale the sides of the specified view volume to each have a length of 2 (Figure 5.34). Hence, the two transformations

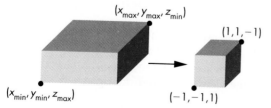

Figure 5.33 Mapping a view volume to the canonical view volume.

Figure 5.34 Affine transformations for normalization.

are $\mathbf{T}(-(x_{max}+x_{min})/2, -(y_{max}+y_{min})/2, -(z_{max}+z_{min})/2)$ and $\mathbf{S}(2/(x_{max}-x_{min}), 2/(y_{max}-y_{min}), 2/(z_{max}-z_{min}))$, and can be concatenated together to form the projection matrix

$$\mathbf{P} = \mathbf{ST} = \begin{bmatrix} \frac{2}{x_{max}-x_{min}} & 0 & 0 & -\frac{x_{max}+x_{min}}{x_{max}-x_{min}} \\ 0 & \frac{2}{y_{max}-y_{min}} & 0 & -\frac{y_{max}+y_{min}}{y_{max}-y_{min}} \\ 0 & 0 & \frac{2}{z_{max}-z_{min}} & -\frac{z_{max}+z_{min}}{z_{max}-z_{min}} \\ 0 & 0 & 0 & 1 \end{bmatrix}.$$

Because the camera is pointing in the negative z direction, the projectors are directed from infinity on the negative z-axis toward the origin. In terms of the near and far distances in glOrtho, the projection matrix can be written as

$$\mathbf{P} = \begin{bmatrix} \frac{2}{x_{max}-x_{min}} & 0 & 0 & -\frac{x_{max}+x_{min}}{x_{max}-x_{min}} \\ 0 & \frac{2}{y_{max}-y_{min}} & 0 & -\frac{y_{max}+y_{min}}{y_{max}-y_{min}} \\ 0 & 0 & -\frac{2}{far-near} & \frac{far+near}{far-near} \\ 0 & 0 & 0 & 1 \end{bmatrix}.$$

5.8.3 Oblique Projections

OpenGL provides through glOrtho a limited class of parallel projections—namely, only those for which the projectors are orthogonal to the projection plane. As we saw earlier in this chapter, oblique parallel projections are useful in many fields.[5] We could develop an oblique projection matrix directly; instead, however, we follow the process that we used for the general orthogonal projection. We convert the desired projection to a canonical orthogonal projection of distorted objects.

An oblique projection can be characterized by the angle that the projectors make with the projection plane, as shown in Figure 5.35. In APIs that support general parallel viewing, the view volume for an oblique projection has the near and far clipping planes parallel to the view plane, and the right, left, top, and

---

5. Note that without oblique projections we cannot draw coordinate axes in the way that we have been doing in this book; see Exercise 5.15.

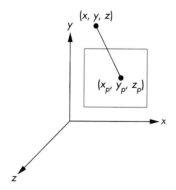

Figure 5.35 Oblique projection.

bottom planes parallel to the direction of projection, as shown in Figure 5.36. We can derive the equations for oblique projections by considering the top and side views in Figure 5.37, which shows a projector and the projection plane $z = 0$. The angles θ and ϕ characterize the degree of obliqueness. In drafting, projections such as the cavalier and cabinet projections are determined by specific values of these angles. However, these angles are not the only possible interface (see Exercises 5.9 and 5.10).

If we consider the top view, we can find x_p by noting that

$$\tan \theta = \frac{z}{x - x_p},$$

and thus

$$x_p = x - z \cot \theta.$$

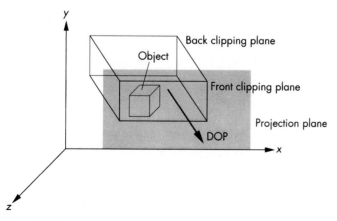

Figure 5.36 Oblique clipping volume.

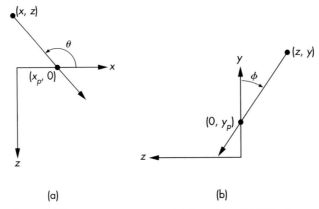

figure 5.37 Oblique projection. (a) Top view. (b) Side view.

Likewise,

$$y_p = y - z \cot \phi.$$

Using the equation for the projection plane

$$z_p = 0,$$

we can write these results in terms of a homogeneous-coordinate matrix

$$\mathbf{P} = \begin{bmatrix} 1 & 0 & -\cot\theta & 0 \\ 0 & 1 & -\cot\phi & 0 \\ 0 & 0 & 0 & 0 \\ 0 & 0 & 0 & 1 \end{bmatrix}.$$

Following our strategy of the previous example, we can break $\mathbf{P}$ into the product

$$\mathbf{P} = \mathbf{M}_{\text{orth}}\mathbf{H}(\theta, \phi) = \begin{bmatrix} 1 & 0 & 0 & 0 \\ 0 & 1 & 0 & 0 \\ 0 & 0 & 0 & 0 \\ 0 & 0 & 0 & 1 \end{bmatrix}\begin{bmatrix} 1 & 0 & -\cot\theta & 0 \\ 0 & 1 & -\cot\phi & 0 \\ 0 & 0 & 1 & 0 \\ 0 & 0 & 0 & 1 \end{bmatrix},$$

where $\mathbf{H}(\theta, \phi)$ is a shearing matrix. Thus, we can implement an oblique projection by first doing a shear of the objects by $\mathbf{H}(\theta, \phi)$, and then doing an orthographic projection. Figure 5.38 shows the effect of $\mathbf{H}(\theta, \phi)$ on an object—a cube—inside an oblique view volume. The sides of the clipping volume become orthogonal to the view plane, but the sides of the cube become oblique as they are affected by the same shear transformation. However, the orthographic projection of the distorted cube is identical to the oblique projection of the undistorted cube.

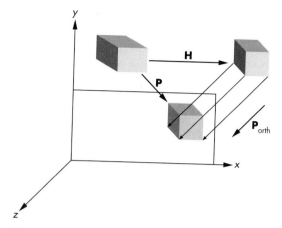

Figure 5.38 Effect of shear transformation.

We are not finished, because the view volume created by the shear is not our canonical view volume. We have to apply the same scaling and translation matrices that we used in Section 5.8.1. Hence, the transformation

$$\mathbf{ST} = \begin{bmatrix} \dfrac{2}{x_{max}-x_{min}} & 0 & 0 & -\dfrac{x_{max}+x_{min}}{x_{max}-x_{min}} \\ 0 & \dfrac{2}{y_{max}-y_{min}} & 0 & -\dfrac{y_{max}+y_{min}}{y_{max}-y_{min}} \\ 0 & 0 & \dfrac{2}{z_{max}-z_{min}} & -\dfrac{z_{max}+z_{min}}{z_{max}-z_{min}} \\ 0 & 0 & 0 & 1 \end{bmatrix}$$

must be inserted after the shear and before the final orthographic projection, so the final matrix is

$$\mathbf{P} = \mathbf{M}_{orth}\mathbf{STH}.$$

The values of x_{min}, x_{max}, y_{min}, and y_{max} are the vertices of the right parallelepiped view volume created by the shear. These values depend on how the sides of the original view volume are communicated through the application program; they may have to be determined from the results of the shear to the corners of the original view volume.

5.9 Perspective-Projection Matrices

For perspective projections, we follow a path similar to the one that we used for parallel projections: We find a transformation that, by distorting the vertices of our objects, allows us to do a simple canonical projection to obtain the desired image. Our first step is to decide what this canonical viewing volume should be. We then introduce a new transformation, the **perspective-normalization**

transformation, that converts a perspective projection to an orthogonal projection. Finally, we derive the perspective-projection matrix used in OpenGL.

5.9.1 Perspective Normalization

In Section 5.4 we introduced a simple perspective-projection matrix that, for the projection plane at $z = -1$ and the center of projection at the origin, is

$$
\mathbf{M} = \begin{bmatrix} 1 & 0 & 0 & 0 \\ 0 & 1 & 0 & 0 \\ 0 & 0 & 1 & 0 \\ 0 & 0 & -1 & 0 \end{bmatrix}.
$$

Suppose that to form an image, we also need to specify a clipping volume. Suppose that we fix the angle of view at 90 degrees by making the sides of the viewing volume intersect the projection plane at a 45-degree angle. Equivalently, the view volume is the semi-infinite view pyramid formed by the planes

$$x = \pm z,$$

$$y = \pm z,$$

shown in Figure 5.39. We can make the volume finite by specifying the near plane to be $z = z_{max}$ and the far plane to be $z = z_{min}$, where both these values are negative and

$$z_{max} > z_{min}.$$

Consider the matrix

$$
\mathbf{N} = \begin{bmatrix} 1 & 0 & 0 & 0 \\ 0 & 1 & 0 & 0 \\ 0 & 0 & \alpha & \beta \\ 0 & 0 & -1 & 0 \end{bmatrix},
$$

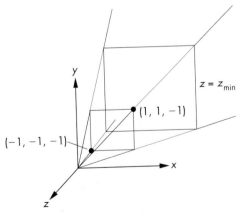

Figure 5.39 Simple perspective projection.

which is similar to **M** but is nonsingular. For now, we leave α and β unspecified (but nonzero). If we apply **N** to the homogeneous-coordinate point $\mathbf{p} = [\, x \quad y \quad z \quad 1 \,]^T$, we obtain the new point $\mathbf{q} = [\, x' \quad y' \quad z' \quad w' \,]^T$, where

$$x' = x,$$

$$y' = y,$$

$$z' = \alpha z + \beta,$$

$$w' = -z.$$

After dividing by w', we have the three-dimensional point

$$x'' = -\frac{x}{z},$$

$$y'' = -\frac{y}{z},$$

$$z'' = -\left(\alpha + \frac{\beta}{z} \right).$$

If we apply an orthographic projection along the z-axis to **N**, we obtain the matrix

$$\mathbf{M}_{\text{orth}}\mathbf{N} = \begin{bmatrix} 1 & 0 & 0 & 0 \\ 0 & 1 & 0 & 0 \\ 0 & 0 & 0 & 0 \\ 0 & 0 & -1 & 0 \end{bmatrix},$$

which is a simple perspective-projection matrix, and the projection of the arbitrary point **p** is

$$\mathbf{p}' = \mathbf{M}_{\text{orth}}\mathbf{N}\mathbf{p} = \begin{bmatrix} x \\ y \\ 0 \\ -z \end{bmatrix}.$$

After we do the perspective division, we obtain the desired values for x_p and y_p:

$$x_p = -\frac{x}{z},$$

$$y_p = -\frac{y}{z}.$$

We have shown that we can apply a transformation **N** to points, and, after an orthogonal projection, we obtain the same result as we would have for a perspective projection. This process is similar to how we converted oblique projections to orthogonal projections by first shearing the objects.

The matrix **N** is nonsingular and transforms the original viewing volume into a new volume. We choose α and β such that the new volume is the canonical clipping volume. Consider the sides

$$x = \pm z.$$

They are transformed by $x'' = -x/z$ to the planes

$$x'' = \pm 1.$$

Likewise, the sides $y = \pm z$ are transformed to

$$y'' = \pm 1.$$

The front of the view volume $z = z_{max}$ is transformed to the plane

$$z'' = -\left(\alpha + \frac{\beta}{z_{max}}\right).$$

Finally, the far plane $z = z_{min}$ is transformed to the plane

$$z'' = -\left(\alpha + \frac{\beta}{z_{min}}\right).$$

If we select

$$\alpha = \frac{z_{max} + z_{min}}{z_{max} - z_{min}},$$

$$\beta = -\frac{2 z_{max} z_{min}}{z_{max} - z_{min}},$$

then the plane $z = z_{min}$ is mapped to the plane $z'' = -1$, the plane $z = z_{max}$ is mapped to the plane $z'' = 1$, and we have our canonical clipping volume. Figure 5.40 shows this transformation and the distortion to a cube within the volume. Thus, $\mathbf{N}$ has transformed the viewing frustum to a right parallelepiped, and an orthographic projection in the transformed volume yields the same image as does the perspective projection. The matrix $\mathbf{N}$ is called the **perspective-normalization matrix**. The mapping

$$z'' = -\left(\alpha + \frac{\beta}{z}\right)$$

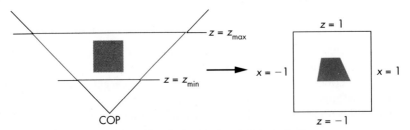

figure 5.40 Perspective normalization of view volume.

is nonlinear but preserves the ordering of depths. Thus, if z_1 and z_2 are the depths of two points within the original viewing volume and

$$z_1 > z_2,$$

then their transformations satisfy

$$z_1'' > z_2''.$$

Consequently, hidden-surface removal works in the normalized volume, although the nonlinearity of the transformation can cause numerical problems because the depth buffer has a limited resolution, usually 24 or 32 bits. Note that, although the original projection plane we placed at $z = -1$ has been transformed by $\mathbf{N}$ to the plane $z'' = \beta - \alpha$, there is little consequence to this result because we follow $\mathbf{N}$ by an orthographic projection.

Although we have shown that both perspective and parallel transformations can be converted to orthographic transformations, the effects of this conversion are greatest in implementation. As long as we can put a carefully chosen projection matrix in the pipeline before the vertices are defined, we need only one viewing pipeline for all possible views. In Chapter 8, where we discuss implementation in detail, we shall see how converting all view volumes to right parallelepipeds by our normalization process simplifies both clipping and hidden-surface removal.

5.9.2 OpenGL Perspective Transformations

The OpenGL function glFrustum does not restrict the view volume to a symmetric (or right) frustum. The parameters are as shown in Figure 5.41. We can form the OpenGL perspective matrix by first converting this frustum to the symmetric frustum with 45-degree sides (see Figure 5.39). The process is similar to the conversion of an oblique parallel view to an orthogonal view. First, we do a shear to convert the asymmetric frustum to a symmetric one. Figure 5.41 shows the desired transformation. The shear angle is determined by our desire

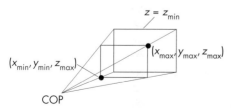

Figure 5.41 OpenGL perspective.

to skew (shear) the point $((x_{min} + x_{max})/2, (y_{max} + y_{min})/2, z_{min})$ to $(0, 0, z_{min})$. The required shear matrix is

$$\mathbf{H}(\theta, \phi) = \mathbf{H}\left(\cot^{-1}\left(\frac{x_{min} + x_{max}}{2z_{max}}\right), \cot^{-1}\left(\frac{y_{max} + y_{min}}{2z_{max}}\right)\right).$$

The resulting frustum is described by the planes

$$x = \pm\frac{x_{max} - x_{min}}{2z_{max}},$$

$$y = \pm\frac{y_{max} - y_{min}}{2z_{max}},$$

$$z = z_{min},$$

$$z = z_{max}.$$

The next step is to scale the sides of this frustum to

$$x = \pm z,$$

$$y = \pm z,$$

without changing either the near plane or the far plane. The required scaling matrix is $\mathbf{S}(2z_{max}/(x_{max} - x_{min}), 2z_{max}/(y_{max} - y_{min}), 1)$. Note that this transformation is determined uniquely without reference to the location of the far plane $z = z_{min}$, because, in three dimensions, an affine transformation is determined by the results of the transformation on four points. In this case, these points are the four vertices where the sides of the frustum intersect the near plane.

To get the far plane to the plane $z = -1$ and the near plane to $z = 1$ after applying a projection normalization, we use the projection-normalization matrix $\mathbf{N}$:

$$\mathbf{N} = \begin{bmatrix} 1 & 0 & 0 & 0 \\ 0 & 1 & 0 & 0 \\ 0 & 0 & \alpha & \beta \\ 0 & 0 & -1 & 0 \end{bmatrix},$$

with α and β as in Section 5.9.1. The resulting projection matrix is

$$\mathbf{P} = \mathbf{NSH} = \begin{bmatrix} \dfrac{2z_{min}}{x_{max} - x_{min}} & 0 & \dfrac{x_{max} + x_{min}}{x_{max} - x_{min}} & 0 \\[2ex] 0 & \dfrac{2z_{min}}{y_{max} - y_{min}} & \dfrac{y_{max} + y_{min}}{y_{max} - y_{min}} & 0 \\[2ex] 0 & 0 & -\dfrac{z_{max} + z_{min}}{z_{max} - z_{min}} & \dfrac{2z_{max}z_{min}}{z_{max} - z_{min}} \\[2ex] 0 & 0 & -1 & 0 \end{bmatrix},$$

or, in terms of the near and far distances,

$$
P = NSH = \begin{bmatrix} \dfrac{2z_{min}}{x_{max}-x_{min}} & 0 & \dfrac{x_{max}+x_{min}}{x_{max}-x_{min}} & 0 \\[2ex] 0 & \dfrac{2z_{min}}{y_{max}-y_{min}} & \dfrac{y_{max}+y_{min}}{y_{max}-y_{min}} & 0 \\[2ex] 0 & 0 & -\dfrac{far+near}{far-near} & -\dfrac{2far*near}{far-near} \\[2ex] 0 & 0 & -1 & 0 \end{bmatrix}.
$$

5.10 Projections and Shadows

The creation of simple shadows is an interesting application of projection matrices. Although shadows are not geometric objects, they are important components of realistic images and give many visual clues to the spatial relationships among the objects in a scene. Starting from a physical point of view, shadows require one or more light sources to be present. A point is in shadow if it is not illuminated by any light source, or equivalently if a viewer at that point cannot see any light sources. However, if the only light source is at the center of projection, there are no visible shadows, because any shadows are behind visible objects. This lighting strategy has been called the "flashlight in the eye" model and corresponds to the simple lighting we have used thus far.

To add physically correct shadows, we must understand the interaction between light and materials, a topic that we investigate in Chapter 6. There, we show that such calculations are difficult; normally, they cannot be done in real time.

Nevertheless, the importance of shadows in applications such as flight simulators led to a number of special approaches that can be used in many circumstances. Consider the shadow generated by the point source in Figure 5.42. We assume for simplicity that the shadow falls on the ground or the surface

$$y = 0.$$

Not only is the shadow a flat polygon, called a **shadow polygon**, but also it is the projection of the original polygon onto the surface. Specifically, the shadow polygon is the projection of the polygon onto the surface with the center of projection at the light source. Thus, if we do a projection from a frame in which the light source is at the origin, we obtain the vertices of the shadow polygon. These vertices must then be converted back to a representation in the world frame. Rather than do the work as part of an application program, we can find a suitable projection matrix and use OpenGL to compute the vertices of the shadow polygon.

Suppose that we start with a light source at (x_l, y_l, z_l), as in Figure 5.43(a). If we reorient the figure such that the light source is at the origin, as in Figure 5.43(b), by a translation matrix $T(-x_l, -y_l, -z_l)$, then we have a simple

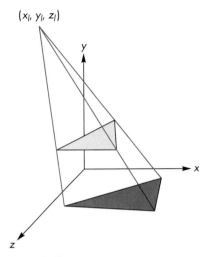

(x_l, y_l, z_l)

Figure 5.42 Shadow from a single polygon.

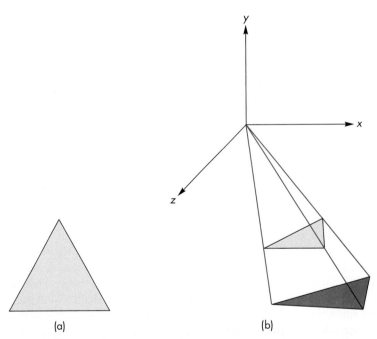

(a)

(b)

Figure 5.43 Shadow polygon projection (a) from a light source, and (b) with source moved to the origin.

perspective projection through the origin. The projection matrix is

$$\mathbf{M} = \begin{bmatrix} 1 & 0 & 0 & 0 \\ 0 & 1 & 0 & 0 \\ 0 & 0 & 1 & 0 \\ 0 & \frac{1}{-y_l} & 0 & 0 \end{bmatrix}.$$

Finally, we translate everything back with $\mathbf{T}(x_l, y_l, z_l)$. The concatenation of this matrix and the two translation matrices projects the vertex (x, y, z) to

$$x_p = x_l - \frac{x - x_l}{(y - y_l)/y_l},$$

$$y_p = 0,$$

$$z_p = z_l - \frac{z - z_l}{(y - y_l)/y_l}.$$

However, with an OpenGL program, we can alter the model-view matrix to form the desired polygon,

```
GLfloat m[16];                   /* Shadow Projection Matrix */
for(i=0;i<15;i++) m[i]=0.0;
m[0]=m[5]=m[10]=1.0;
m[7]= -1.0/yl;

glColor3fv(polygon_color)
glBegin(GL_POLYGON)
    .
    .                            /* Draw the polygon normally */
    .
glEnd();
glMatrixMode(GL_MODELVIEW);
glPushMatrix();                  /* Save state */
glTranslatef(xl,yl,zl);          /* Translate back */
glMultMatrixf(m);                /* Project */
glTranslate(-xl,-yl,-zl);        /* Move light to origin */
glColor3fv(shadow_color);
glBegin(GL_POLYGON);
    .
    .                            /* Draw the polygon again */
    .
glEnd();
glPopMatrix();                   /* Restore state */
```

Note that although we are performing a projection with respect to the light source, the matrix that we use is the model-view matrix. We render the same polygon twice: the first time as usual and the second time with an altered model-view matrix that transforms the vertices. The same viewing conditions are applied to both the polygon and its shadow polygon. The results of computing shadows for the cube are shown in Back Plate 3. The code is in the program cubes.c.

For a simple environment, such as an airplane flying over terrain casting a single shadow, this technique works well. It is also easy to convert from point sources to distant (parallel) light sources (see Exercise 5.17). However, when objects can cast shadows on other objects, this method becomes impractical. In Chapter 13 we address more general, but slower, rendering methods that will create shadows automatically as part of the rendering process.

5.11 Summary and Notes

We have come a long way. We can now write complete, nontrivial, three-dimensional applications. Probably the most instructive activity that you can do now is to write such an application. Facility with manipulating the model-view and projection functions takes practice.

We have presented the mathematics of the standard projections. Although most APIs obviate the user from writing projection functions, understanding the mathematics leads to understanding a pipeline implementation based on concatenation of 4×4 matrices. Until recently, user programs had to do the projections within the applications, and most hardware systems did not support perspective projections.

There are three major themes in the remainder of this book. First, we explore modeling further by expanding our basic set of primitives. In Chapter 9, we incorporate more complex relationships between simple objects through hierarchical models. In Chapter 10, we leave the world of flat objects, adding curves and curved surfaces. These objects are defined by vertices, and we can implement them by breaking them into small flat primitives, so we can use the same viewing pipeline. Then, in Chapter 11, we explore approaches to modeling that do not force us to describe objects through procedures rather than as geometric objects. This approach allows us to model objects with only as much detail as is needed, to incorporate physical laws into our models, and to model natural phenomena that cannot be described by polygons.

The second major theme is realism. Although more complex objects allow us to build more realistic models, we also explore more complex rendering options. In Chapter 6 we consider the interaction of light with the materials that characterize our objects. We look more deeply at hidden-surface–removal methods, at shading models, and, in Chapter 7, at techniques such as texture mapping that allow us to create complex images from simple objects using advanced rendering techniques.

Third, we look more deeply at implementation in Chapter 8. At this point, we have introduced the major functional units of the graphics pipeline. We discuss the details of the algorithms used in each unit. We shall also see additional possibilities for creating images by working directly in the frame buffer.

After reading Chapter 6, you should be able to read the remaining chapters in any order.

5.12 Suggested Readings

Carlbom and Paciorek [Car78] discuss the relationships between classical and computer viewing. Rogers and Adams [Rog90] give many examples of the projection matrices corresponding to the standard views used in drafting. Foley [Fol90], Watt [Wat00], and Hearn and Baker [Hea94] derive canonical projection transformations. All follow a PHIGS orientation, so the API is slightly different from the one used here, although Foley derives the most general case. The references differ in whether they use column or row matrices, in where the COP is located, and in whether the projection is in the positive or negative z direction. See the *OpenGL Programmer's Guide* [Ope01a] for a further discussion of the use of the model-view and projection matrices in OpenGL.

Exercises

5.1 Not all projections are planar geometric projections. Give an example of a projection in which the projection surface is not a plane, and another in which the projectors are not lines.

5.2 Consider an airplane whose position is specified by the roll, pitch, and yaw, and by the distance from an object. Find a model-view matrix in terms of these parameters.

5.3 Consider a satellite rotating around the earth. Its position above the earth is specified in polar coordinates. Find a model-view matrix that keeps the viewer looking at the earth. Such a matrix could be used to show the earth as it rotates.

5.4 Show how to compute u and v directions from the VPN, VRP, and VUP using only cross products.

5.5 Can we obtain an isometric of the cube by a single rotation about a suitably chosen axis? Explain your answer.

5.6 Derive the perspective-projection matrix when the COP can be at any point and the projection plane can be at any orientation.

5.7 Show that perspective projection preserves lines.

5.8 Any attempt to take the projection of a point in the same plane as the COP will lead to a division by zero. What is the projection of a line segment that has endpoints on either side of the projection plane?

5.9 Define one or more APIs to specify oblique projections. You do not need write the functions; just decide which parameters the user must specify.

5.10 Derive an oblique-projection matrix from specification of front and back clipping planes, and top-right and bottom-left intersections of the sides of the clipping volume with the front clipping plane.

5.11   Our approach of normalizing all projections seems to imply that we could predistort all objects and support only orthographic projections. Explain any problems we would face if we took this approach to building a graphics system.

5.12   How do the OpenGL projection matrices change if the COP is not at the origin? Assume that the COP is at $(0, 0, d)$ and the projection plane is $z = 0$.

5.13   We can create an interesting class of three-dimensional objects by extending two-dimensional objects into the third dimension by extrusion. For example, a circle becomes a cylinder, a line becomes a quadrilateral, and a quadrilateral in the plane becomes a parallelepiped. Use this technique to convert the two-dimensional maze from Exercise 2.8 to a three-dimensional maze.

5.14   Extend the maze program of Exercise 5.13 to allow the user to walk through the maze. A click on the middle mouse button should move the user forward; a click on the right or left button should turn the user 90 degrees to the right or left, respectively.

5.15   If we were to use orthogonal projections to draw the coordinate axes, the x- and y-axes would lie in the plane of the paper, but the z-axis would point out of the page. Instead, we can draw the x- and y-axes as meeting at a 90-degree angle, with the z-axis going off at -135 degrees from the x-axis. Find the matrix that projects the original orthogonal-coordinate axes to this view.

5.16   Write a program to display a rotating cube in a box with three light sources. Each light source should project the cube onto one of the three visible sides of the box.

5.17   Find the projection of a point onto the plane $ax + by + cz + d = 0$ from a light source located at infinity in the direction (d_x, d_y, d_z).

5.18   Using one of the three-dimensional interfaces discussed in Chapter 4, write a program to move the camera through a scene composed of simple objects.

5.19   In animation, often we can save work by working with two-dimensional patterns that are mapped onto flat polygons that are always parallel to the camera. Write a program that will keep a simple polygon facing the camera as the camera moves.

5.20   Stereo images are produced by creating two images with the viewer in two slightly different positions. Consider a viewer who is at the origin but whose eyes are separated by Δx units. What are the appropriate viewing specifications to create the two images?

Shading

We have learned to build three-dimensional graphical models and to display them. However, if you render one of our models, you might be disappointed to see images that look flat and thus fail to show the three-dimensional nature of the model. This appearance is a consequence of our unnatural assumption that each surface is lit such that it appears to a viewer in a single color. Under this assumption, the orthographic projection of a sphere is a uniformly colored circle, and a cube appears as a flat hexagon. If we look at a photograph of a lit sphere, we see not a uniformly colored circle but rather a circular shape with many gradations or **shades** of color. It is these gradations that give two-dimensional images the appearance of being three-dimensional.

What we have left out is the interaction between light and the surfaces in our models. This chapter fills that gap. We develop separate models of light sources and of the most common light–material interactions. Our aim is to add shading to a fast pipeline graphics architecture, so we develop only a local lighting model. Such models, as opposed to global lighting models, allow us to compute the shade to assign to a point on a surface, independent of any other surfaces in the scene. The calculations depend on only the material properties assigned to the surface, the local geometry of the surface, and the locations and properties of the light sources.

Following our previous development, we investigate how we can apply shading to polygonal models. We develop a recursive approximation to a sphere that will allow us to test our shading algorithms. We then discuss how light and material properties are specified in OpenGL and can be added to our sphere-approximating program.

We conclude the chapter with a short discussion of the two most important methods for handling global lighting effects: ray tracing and radiosity.

6.1 Light and Matter

In Chapters 1 and 2 we presented the rudiments of human color vision, delaying until now any discussion of the interaction between light and surfaces. Perhaps the most general approach to rendering is based on physics, where we use principles such as conservation of energy to derive equations that describe how light is reflected from surfaces.

From a physical perspective, a surface can either emit light by self-emission, as a light bulb does, or reflect light from other surfaces that illuminate it. Some surfaces may both reflect light and emit light from internal physical processes. When we look at a point on an object, the color that we see is determined by multiple interactions among light sources and reflective surfaces. These interactions can be viewed as a recursive process. Consider the simple scene in Figure 6.1. Some light from the source that reaches surface A is reflected. Some of this reflected light reaches surface B, and some of it is then reflected back to A, where some of it is again reflected back to B, and so on. This recursive reflection of light between surfaces accounts for subtle shading effects, such as the bleeding of colors between adjacent surfaces. Mathematically, this recursive process results in an integral equation, the **rendering equation**, that, in principle, we could use to find the shading of all surfaces in a scene. Unfortunately, this equation cannot be solved in general, even by numerical methods. There are various approximate approaches, such as radiosity and ray tracing, each of which is an excellent approximation to the rendering equation for particular types of surfaces. Unfortunately, neither ray tracing nor radiosity can yet be used to render scenes at the rate at which we can pass polygons through the modeling-projection pipeline. Consequently, we focus on a simpler rendering model, based on the Phong reflection model, that provides a compromise between physical correctness and efficient calculation. We shall consider the rendering equation, radiosity, and ray tracing in greater detail in Chapter 13.

Rather than looking at a global energy balance, we follow rays of light from light-emitting (or self-luminous) surfaces, which we call **light sources**. We then model what happens to these rays as they interact with reflecting surfaces in the scene. This approach is similar to ray tracing, but we consider only single interactions between light sources and surfaces. There are two independent parts of the problem. First, we must model the light sources in the scene. Then, we

Figure 6.1 Reflecting surfaces.

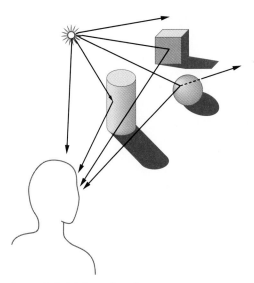

Figure 6.2 Light and surfaces.

must build a reflection model that deals with the interactions between materials and light.

To get an overview of the process, we can start following rays of light from a point source, as shown in Figure 6.2. As we noted in Chapter 1, our viewer sees only the light that leaves the source and reaches her eyes—perhaps through a complex path and multiple interactions with objects in the scene. If a ray of light enters her eye directly from the source, she sees the color of the source. If the ray of light hits a surface that is visible to our viewer, the color she sees is based on the interaction between the source and the surface material: She sees the color of the light reflected from the surface toward her eyes.

In terms of computer graphics, we replace the viewer by the projection plane, as shown in Figure 6.3. Conceptually, the clipping window in this plane is mapped to the screen; thus, we can think of the projection plane as ruled into rectangles, each corresponding to a pixel. The color of the light source and of the surfaces determines the color of one or more pixels in the frame buffer.

We need to consider only those rays that leave the source and reach the viewer's eye, either directly or through interactions with objects. In the case of computer viewing, these are the rays that reach the COP after passing through the clipping rectangle. Note that most rays leaving a source do not contribute to the image and are thus of no interest to us. We make use of this observation in Section 6.10.

Figure 6.2 shows both single and multiple interactions between rays and objects. It is the nature of these interactions that determines whether an object appears red or brown, light or dark, dull or shiny. When light strikes a surface, some of it is absorbed, and some of it is reflected. If the surface is opaque, reflection and absorption account for all the light striking the surface. If the

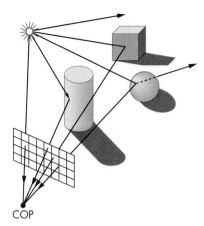

COP

Figure 6.3 Light, surfaces, and computer imaging.

surface is translucent, some of the light is transmitted through the material and emerges to interact with other objects. These interactions depend on wavelength. An object illuminated by white light appears red because it absorbs most of the incident light but reflects light in the red range of frequencies. A shiny object appears so because its surface is smooth. Conversely, a dull object has a rough surface. The shading of objects also depends on the orientation of their surfaces, a factor that, as we shall see, is characterized by the normal vector at each point. These interactions between light and materials can be classified into the three groups shown in Figure 6.4.

1. **Specular surfaces** appear shiny because most of the light that is reflected is **scattered** in a narrow range of angles close to the angle of reflection. Mirrors are **perfectly specular surfaces**; the light from an incoming light ray may be partially absorbed, but all reflected light emerges at a single angle, obeying the rule that the angle of incidence is equal to the angle of reflection.

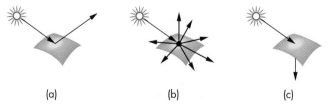

(a)   (b)   (c)

Figure 6.4 Light–material interactions. (a) Specular surface. (b) Diffuse surface. (c) Translucent surface.

2. **Diffuse surfaces** are characterized by reflected light being scattered in all directions. Walls painted with matte or flat paint are diffuse reflectors, as are many natural materials, such as terrain viewed from an airplane or a satellite. **Perfectly diffuse surfaces** scatter light equally in all directions and thus appear the same to all viewers.
3. **Translucent surfaces** allow some light to penetrate the surface and to emerge from another location on the object. This process of **refraction** characterizes glass and water. Some incident light may also be reflected at the surface.

We shall model all these surfaces in Section 6.3. First, we consider light sources.

6.2 Light Sources

Light can leave a surface through two fundamental processes: self-emission and reflection. We usually think of a light source as an object that emits light only through internal energy sources. However, a light source, such as a light bulb, can also reflect some light that is incident on it from the surrounding environment. We neglect this term in our simple models. When we discuss OpenGL lighting in Section 6.7, we shall see that we can easily simulate a self-emission term.

If we consider a source such as the one in Figure 6.5, we can look at it as an object with a surface. Each point (x, y, z) on the surface can emit light that is characterized by the direction of emission (θ, ϕ) and the intensity of energy emitted at each wavelength λ. Thus, a general light source can be characterized by a six-variable **illumination function** $I(x, y, z, \theta, \phi, \lambda)$. Note that we need two angles to specify a direction, and that we are assuming that each frequency can be considered independently. From the perspective of a surface that is illuminated by this source, we can obtain the total contribution of the source (Figure 6.6) by integrating over the surface of the source, a process that accounts for the emission angles that reach the surface under consideration and that also must account for the distance between the source and the surface. For a distributed light source, such as a light bulb, the evaluation of this integral is difficult, whether we use

Figure 6.5 Light source.

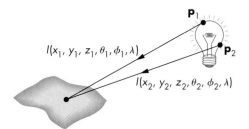

Figure 6.6 Adding the contribution from a source.

analytic or numerical methods. Often, it is easier to model the distributed source with polygons, each of which is a simple source, or with an approximating set of point sources.

We consider four basic types of sources: ambient lighting, point sources, spotlights, and distant light. These four lighting types are sufficient for rendering most simple scenes.

6.2.1 Color Sources

Not only do light sources emit different amounts of light at different frequencies, but also their directional properties can vary with frequency. Consequently, a physically correct model can be complex. However, our model of the human visual system is based on three-color theory that says we perceive three primaries, rather than a full color distribution. For most applications, we can thus model light sources as having three components—red, green, and blue—and can use each of the three color sources to obtain the corresponding color component that a human observer sees.

We describe a source through a three-component intensity or **luminance** function

$$\mathbf{I} = \begin{bmatrix} I_r \\ I_g \\ I_b \end{bmatrix},$$

each of whose components is the intensity of the independent red, green, and blue components. Thus, we use the red component of a light source for the calculation of the red component of the image. Because color–light computations involve three similar but independent calculations, we tend to present a single scalar equation, with the understanding that it can represent any of the three color components.

6.2.2 Ambient Light

In some rooms, such as in certain classrooms or kitchens, the lights have been designed and positioned to provide uniform illumination throughout the room. Often, such illumination is achieved through large sources that have diffusers whose purpose is to scatter light in all directions. We could create an accurate simulation of such illumination, at least in principle, by modeling all the distributed sources, and then integrating the illumination from these sources at each point on a reflecting surface. Making such a model and rendering a scene with it would be a daunting task for a graphics system, especially one for which real-time performance is desirable. Alternatively, we can look at the desired effect of the sources: to achieve a uniform light level in the room. This uniform lighting is called **ambient light**. If we follow this second approach, we can postulate an ambient intensity at each point in the environment. Thus, ambient illumination is characterized by an intensity, $\mathbf{I}_a$, that is identical at every point in the scene.

Our ambient source has three color components:

$$\mathbf{I}_a = \begin{bmatrix} I_{ar} \\ I_{ag} \\ I_{ab} \end{bmatrix}.$$

We use the *scalar* I_a to denote any one of the red, green, or blue components of $\mathbf{I}_a$. Although every point in our scene receives the same illumination from $\mathbf{I}_a$, each surface can reflect this light differently.

6.2.3 Point Sources

An ideal **point source** emits light equally in all directions. We can characterize a point source located at a point $\mathbf{p}_0$ by a three-component color matrix:

$$\mathbf{I}(\mathbf{p}_0) = \begin{bmatrix} I_r(\mathbf{p}_0) \\ I_g(\mathbf{p}_0) \\ I_b(\mathbf{p}_0) \end{bmatrix}.$$

The intensity of illumination received from a point source is proportional to the inverse square of the distance between the source and surface. Hence, at a point $\mathbf{p}$ (Figure 6.7), the intensity of light received from the point source is given by the matrix

$$\mathbf{i}(\mathbf{p}, \mathbf{p}_0) = \frac{1}{|\mathbf{p} - \mathbf{p}_0|^2} \mathbf{I}(\mathbf{p}_0).$$

As we did with ambient light, we use $I(\mathbf{p}_0)$ to denote any of the components of $\mathbf{I}(\mathbf{p}_0)$.

The use of point sources in most applications is determined more by their ease of use than by their resemblance to physical reality. Scenes rendered with only point sources tend to have high contrast; objects appear either bright or dark. In the real world, it is the large size of most light sources that contributes to softer

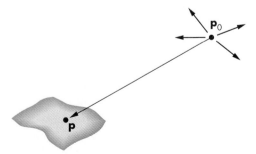

figure 6.7   Point source illuminating a surface.

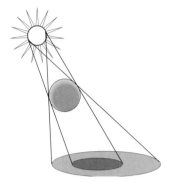

Figure 6.8 Shadows created by finite-size light source.

Figure 6.9 Spotlight.

Figure 6.10 Attenuation of a spotlight.

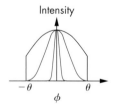

Figure 6.11 Spotlight exponent.

scenes, as we can see from Figure 6.8, which shows the shadows created by a source of finite size. Some areas are fully in shadow, or in the **umbra**, whereas others are in partial shadow, or in the **penumbra**. We can mitigate the high-contrast effect from point-source illumination by adding ambient light to a scene.

The distance term also contributes to the harsh renderings with point sources. Although the inverse-square distance term is correct for point sources, in practice it is usually replaced by a term of the form $(a + bd + cd^2)^{-1}$, where d is the distance between $\mathbf{p}$ and $\mathbf{p}_0$. The constants a, b, and c can be chosen to soften the lighting. Note that if the light source is far from the surfaces in the scene, the intensity of the light from the source is sufficiently uniform that the distance term is constant over the surfaces.

6.2.4 Spotlights

Spotlights are characterized by a narrow range of angles through which light is emitted. We can construct a simple spotlight from a point source by limiting the angles at which light from the source can be seen. We can use a cone whose apex is at $\mathbf{p}_s$, which points in the direction $\mathbf{l}_s$, and whose width is determined by an angle θ, as shown in Figure 6.9. If $\theta = 180$, the spotlight becomes a point source.

More realistic spotlights are characterized by the distribution of light within the cone—usually with most of the light concentrated in the center of the cone. Thus, the intensity is a function of the angle ϕ between the direction of the source and a vector $\mathbf{s}$ to a point on the surface (as long as this angle is less than θ; Figure 6.10). Although this function could be defined in many ways, it is usually defined by $\cos^e \phi$, where the exponent e (Figure 6.11) determines how rapidly the light intensity drops off. As we shall see throughout this chapter, cosines are convenient functions for lighting calculations. If both $\mathbf{s}$ and $\mathbf{l}$ are unit-length vectors, we can compute the cosine with the dot product

$$\cos \phi = \mathbf{s} \cdot \mathbf{l},$$

a calculation that requires only three multiplications and two additions.

6.2.5 Distant Light Sources

Most shading calculations require the direction from the point on the surface to the light source. As we move across a surface, calculating the intensity at each point, we should recompute this vector repeatedly—a computation that is a significant part of the shading calculation. However, if the light source is far from the surface, the vector does not change much as we move from point to point, just as the light from the sun strikes all objects that are in close proximity to one another at the same angle. Figure 6.12 illustrates that we are effectively replacing a point source of light with a source that illuminates objects with parallel rays of light—a parallel source. In practice, the calculations for distant light sources are similar to the calculations for parallel projections; they replace the *location* of the light source with the *direction* of the light source. Hence, in homogeneous coordinates, a point light source at $\mathbf{p}_0$ is represented internally as a four-dimensional column matrix:

$$\mathbf{p}_0 = \begin{bmatrix} x \\ y \\ z \\ 1 \end{bmatrix},$$

Figure 6.12 Parallel light source.

In contrast, the distant light source is decribed by a direction vector whose representation in homogeneous coordinates is the matrix

$$\mathbf{p}_0 = \begin{bmatrix} x \\ y \\ z \\ 0 \end{bmatrix}.$$

The graphics system can carry out rendering calculations more efficiently for distant light sources than for near ones. Of course, a scene rendered with distant light sources looks different from a scene rendered with near sources. Fortunately, OpenGL allows both types of sources.

6.3 The Phong Reflection Model

Although we could approach light–material interactions through physical models, we have chosen to use a model that leads to efficient computations, especially when we use it with our pipeline rendering model. The reflection model that we present was introduced by Phong. It has proved to be efficient, and to be a close enough approximation to physical reality to produce good renderings under a variety of lighting conditions and material properties.

The model uses the four vectors shown in Figure 6.13 to calculate a color for an arbitrary point $\mathbf{p}$ on a surface. If the surface is curved, all four vectors can change as we move from point to point. The vector $\mathbf{n}$ is the normal at $\mathbf{p}$; we discuss its calculation in Section 6.4. The vector $\mathbf{v}$ is in the direction from $\mathbf{p}$ to the viewer or COP. The vector $\mathbf{l}$ is in the direction of a line from $\mathbf{p}$ to an arbitrary point on the source for a distributed light source, or, as we are assuming for now, to the point light source. Finally, the vector $\mathbf{r}$ is in the direction that a perfectly reflected ray from $\mathbf{l}$ would take. Note that $\mathbf{r}$ is determined by $\mathbf{n}$ and $\mathbf{l}$. We calculate it in Section 6.4.

The Phong model supports the three types of material–light interactions— ambient, diffuse, and specular—that we introduced in Section 6.1. Suppose that we have a set of point sources. We assume that each source can have separate ambient, diffuse, and specular components for each of the three primary colors. Although this assumption may appear unnatural, remember that our goal is to create realistic shading effects in as close to real time as possible. We use a

Figure 6.13 Vectors used by the Phong model.

local model to simulate effects that can be global in nature. Thus, our light-source model has ambient, diffuse, and specular terms. We need 9 coefficients to characterize these terms at any point $\mathbf{p}$ on the surface. We can place these 9 coefficients in a 3×3 illumination matrix for the ith light source:

$$\mathbf{L}_i = \begin{bmatrix} L_{ira} & L_{iga} & L_{iba} \\ L_{ird} & L_{igd} & L_{ibd} \\ L_{irs} & L_{igs} & L_{ibs} \end{bmatrix}.$$

The first row contains the ambient intensities for the red, green, and blue terms from source i. The second row contains the diffuse terms; the third contains the specular terms. We assume that any distance-attenuation terms have not yet been applied.

We construct the model by assuming that we can compute how much of each of the incident lights is reflected at the point of interest. For example, for the red diffuse term from source i, L_{ird}, we can compute a reflection term R_{ird}, and the latter's contribution to the intensity at $\mathbf{p}$ is $R_{ird}L_{ird}$. The value of R_{ird} depends on the material properties, the orientation of the surface, the direction of the light source, and the distance between the light source and the viewer. Thus, for each point, we have 9 coefficients that we can place in a matrix of reflection terms of the form

$$\mathbf{R}_i = \begin{bmatrix} R_{ira} & R_{iga} & R_{iba} \\ R_{ird} & R_{igd} & R_{ibd} \\ R_{irs} & R_{igs} & R_{ibs} \end{bmatrix}.$$

We can then compute the contribution for each color source by adding the ambient, diffuse, and specular components. For example, the red intensity that we see at $\mathbf{p}$ from source i is

$$\begin{aligned} I_{ir} &= R_{ira}L_{ira} + R_{ird}L_{ird} + R_{irs}L_{irs} \\ &= I_{ira} + I_{ird} + I_{irs}. \end{aligned}$$

We obtain the total intensity by adding the contributions of all sources and, possibly, a global ambient term. Thus, the red term is

$$I_r = \sum_i (I_{ira} + I_{ird} + I_{irs}) + I_{ar},$$

where I_{ar} is the red component of the global ambient light.

We can simplify our notation by noting that the necessary computations are the same for each source and for each primary color. They differ depending on whether we are considering the ambient, diffuse, or specular terms. Hence, we can omit the subscripts i, r, g, and b. We write

$$I = I_a + I_d + I_s = L_a R_a + L_d R_d + L_s R_s,$$

with the understanding that the computation will be done for each of the primaries and each source; the global ambient term can be added at the end.

6.3.1 Ambient Reflection

The intensity of ambient light L_a is the same at every point on the surface. Some of this light is absorbed, and some is reflected. The amount reflected is given by the ambient reflection coefficient, $R_a = k_a$. Because only a positive fraction of the light is reflected, we must have

$$0 \le k_a \le 1,$$

and thus

$$I_a = k_a L_a.$$

Here, L_a can be any of the individual light sources, or it can be a global ambient term.

A surface has, of course, three ambient coefficients—k_{ar}, k_{ag}, and k_{ab}—and they can differ. Hence, for example, a sphere appears yellow under white ambient light if its blue ambient coefficient is small and its red and green coefficients are large.

6.3.2 Diffuse Reflection

A perfectly diffuse reflector scatters the light that it reflects equally in all directions. Hence, such a surface appears the same to all viewers. However, the amount of light reflected depends both on the material, because some of the incoming light is absorbed, and on the position of the light source relative to the surface. Diffuse reflections are characterized by rough surfaces. If we were to magnify a cross section of a diffuse surface, we might see an image like that shown in Figure 6.14. Rays of light that hit the surface at only slightly different angles are reflected back at markedly different angles. Perfectly diffuse surfaces are so rough that there is no preferred angle of reflection. Such surfaces, sometimes called **Lambertian surfaces**, can be modeled mathematically with Lambert's law.

Figure 6.14 Rough surface.

Consider a diffuse planar surface, as shown in Figure 6.15, illuminated by the sun. The surface is brightest at noon and dimmest at dawn and dusk because, according to Lambert's law, we see only the vertical component of the incoming light. One way to understand this law is to consider a small parallel light source striking a plane, as shown in Figure 6.16. As the source is lowered in the (artificial) sky, the same amount of light is spread over a larger areas, and the surface appears dimmer. Returning to the point source of Figure 6.15, we can characterize diffuse reflections mathematically. Lambert's law states that

$$R_d \propto \cos \theta,$$

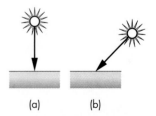

(a)   (b)

Figure 6.15 Illumination of a diffuse surface. (a) At noon. (b) In the afternoon.

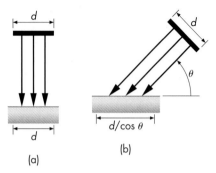

Figure 6.16 Vertical contributions by Lambert's law. (a) At noon. (b) In the afternoon.

where θ is the angle between the normal at the point of interest $\mathbf{n}$ and the direction of the light source $\mathbf{l}$. If both $\mathbf{l}$ and $\mathbf{n}$ are unit-length vectors,[1] then

$$\cos \theta = \mathbf{l} \cdot \mathbf{n}.$$

If we add in a reflection coefficient k_d that represents the fraction of incoming diffuse light that is reflected, we have the diffuse reflection term:

$$I_d = k_d (\mathbf{l} \cdot \mathbf{n}) L_d.$$

If we wish to incorporate a distance term, to account for attenuation as the light travels a distance d from the source to the surface, we can again use the quadratic attenuation term:

$$I_d = \frac{k_d}{a + bd + cd^2} (\mathbf{l} \cdot \mathbf{n}) L_d.$$

6.3.3 Specular Reflection

If we employ only ambient and diffuse reflections, our images will be shaded and will appear three-dimensional, but all the surfaces will look dull, somewhat like chalk. What we are missing is the highlights that we see reflected from shiny objects. These highlights usually show a color different from the color of the reflected ambient and diffuse light. For example, a red ball, viewed under white light, has a white highlight that is the reflection of some of the light from the source in the direction of the viewer (Figure 6.17).

Figure 6.17 Specular highlights.

---

1. Direction vectors, such as $\mathbf{l}$ and $\mathbf{n}$, are used repeatedly in shading calculations through the dot product. In practice, both the programmer and the graphics software should seek to normalize all such vectors as soon as possible.

Whereas a diffuse surface is rough, a specular surface is smooth. The smoother the surface is, the more it resembles a mirror; Figure 6.18 shows that as the surface gets smoother, the reflected light is concentrated in a smaller range of angles, centered about the angle of a perfect reflector—a mirror or a perfectly specular surface. Modeling specular surfaces realistically can be complex, because the pattern by which the light is scattered is not symmetric. It depends on the wavelength of the incident light, and it changes with the reflection angle.

Figure 6.18 Specular surface.

Phong proposed an approximate model that can be computed with only a slight increase over the work done for diffuse surfaces. The model adds a term for specular reflection. Hence, we consider the surface as being rough for the diffuse term and smooth for the specular term. The amount of light that the viewer sees depends on the angle ϕ between $\mathbf{r}$, the direction of a perfect reflector, and $\mathbf{v}$, the direction of the viewer. The Phong model uses the equation

$$I_s = k_s L_s \cos^{\alpha} \phi.$$

The coefficient k_s ($0 \le k_s \le 1$) is the fraction of the incoming specular light that is reflected. The exponent α is a **shininess** coefficient. Figure 6.19 shows how, as α is increased, the reflected light is concentrated in a narrower region, centered on the angle of a perfect reflector. In the limit, as α goes to infinity, we get a mirror; values in the range 100 to 500 correspond to most metallic surfaces, and smaller values (< 100) correspond to materials that show broad highlights.

The computational advantage of the Phong model is that, if we have normalized $\mathbf{r}$ and $\mathbf{n}$ to unit length, we can again use the dot product, and the specular term becomes

$$I_s = k_s L_s (\mathbf{r} \cdot \mathbf{v})^{\alpha}.$$

We can add a distance term, as we did with diffuse reflections. What is referred to as the **Phong model**, including the distance term, is written

$$I = \frac{1}{a + bd + cd^2}(k_d L_d \mathbf{l} \cdot \mathbf{n} + k_s L_s (\mathbf{r} \cdot \mathbf{v})^{\alpha}) + k_a L_a.$$

This formula is computed for each light source and for each primary.

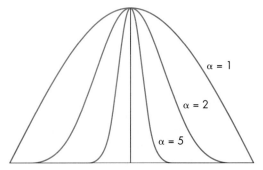

Figure 6.19 Effect of shininess coefficient.

It might seem to make little sense either to associate a different amount of ambient light with each source, or to allow the components for specular and diffuse lighting to be different. Because we cannot solve the full rendering equation, we must use various tricks in an attempt to obtain realistic renderings. Consider, for example, an environment with many objects. When we turn on a light, some of that light hits a surface directly. These contributions to the image can be modeled with specular and diffuse components of the source. However, much of the rest of the light from the source is scattered from multiple reflections from other objects and makes a contribution to the light received at the surface under consideration. We can approximate this term by having an ambient component associated with the source. The shade that we should assign to this term depends on *both* the color of the source and the color of the objects in the room—an unfortunate consequence of our use of approximate models. To some extent, the same analysis holds for diffuse light. Diffuse light reflects among the surfaces, and the color that we see on a particular surface depends on other surfaces in the environment. Again, by using carefully chosen diffuse and specular components with our light sources, we can approximate a global effect with local calculations.

Color Plate 25 shows a group of Utah teapots (Section 10.10) that have been rendered in OpenGL using the Phong model. Note that it is only our ability to control material properties that makes the teapots appear different from one another. The various teapots demonstrate how the Phong model can create a variety of surface effects, ranging from dull surfaces to highly reflective surfaces that look like metal.

We have developed the Phong model in object space. The actual shading, however, is not done until the objects have passed through the model-view and projection transformations. These transformations can affect the cosine terms in the model (see Exercise 6.20). Consequently, to make a correct shading calculation, we must either preserve the correct relationships as vertices and vectors pass through the pipeline, perhaps by sending additional information through the pipeline from object space, or go backward through the pipeline to obtain the required information when a shade needs to be determined.

6.4 Computation of Vectors

The illumination and reflection models that we have derived are sufficiently general that they can be applied to either curved or flat surfaces, to parallel or perspective views, and to distant or near surfaces. Most of the calculations for rendering a scene involve the determination of the required vectors and dot products. For each special case, simplifications are possible. For example, if the surface is a flat polygon, the normal is the same at all points on the surface. If the light source is far from the surface, the light direction is the same at all points.

In this section we examine how the vectors are computed for the general case. In Section 6.5 we see what additional techniques can be applied when our objects are composed of flat polygons. This case is especially important, because most renderers, including OpenGL, render curved surfaces by approximating those surfaces with many small flat polygons.

6.4.1 Normal Vectors

For smooth surfaces, the vector normal to the surface exists at every point and gives the local orientation of the surface. Its calculation depends on how the surface is represented mathematically. Two simple cases—the plane and the sphere—illustrate both how we compute normals and where the difficulties lie.

A plane can be described by the equation

$$ax + by + cz + d = 0.$$

As we saw in Chapter 4, this equation could also be written in terms of the normal to the plane, $\mathbf{n}$, and a point, $\mathbf{p}_0$, known to be on the plane as

$$\mathbf{n} \cdot (\mathbf{p} - \mathbf{p}_0) = 0,$$

where $\mathbf{p}$ is any point (x, y, z) on the plane. Comparing the two forms, we see that the vector $\mathbf{n}$ is given by

$$\mathbf{n} = \begin{bmatrix} a \\ b \\ c \end{bmatrix},$$

or, in homogeneous coordinates,

$$\mathbf{n} = \begin{bmatrix} a \\ b \\ c \\ 0 \end{bmatrix}.$$

However, suppose that instead we are given three noncollinear points—$\mathbf{p}_0$, $\mathbf{p}_1$, $\mathbf{p}_2$—that are in this plane and thus are sufficient to determine it uniquely. The vectors $\mathbf{p}_2 - \mathbf{p}_0$ and $\mathbf{p}_1 - \mathbf{p}_0$ are parallel to the plane, and we can use their cross product to find the normal

$$\mathbf{n} = (\mathbf{p}_2 - \mathbf{p}_0) \times (\mathbf{p}_1 - \mathbf{p}_0).$$

We must be careful about the order of the vectors in the cross product: Reversing the order changes the surface from outward pointing to inward pointing, and that reversal can affect the lighting calculations. Some graphics systems use the first three vertices in the specification of a polygon to determine the normal automatically. OpenGL does not do so, but, as we shall see in Section 6.5, forcing users to compute normals creates more flexibility in how we apply our lighting model.

For curved surfaces, how we compute normals depends on how we represent the surface. In Chapter 10, we discuss three different methods for representing curves and surfaces. We can see a few of the possibilities by considering how we represent a unit sphere centered at the origin. The usual equation for this sphere is the **implicit equation**

$$f(x, y, z) = x^2 + y^2 + z^2 - 1 = 0,$$

or, in vector form,

$$f(\mathbf{p}) = \mathbf{p} \cdot \mathbf{p} - 1 = 0.$$

The normal is given by the **gradient vector**, which is defined by the column matrix

$$\mathbf{n} = \begin{bmatrix} \frac{\partial f}{\partial x} \\ \frac{\partial f}{\partial y} \\ \frac{\partial f}{\partial z} \end{bmatrix} = \begin{bmatrix} 2x \\ 2y \\ 2z \end{bmatrix} = 2\mathbf{p}.$$

The sphere could also be represented in **parametric form**. In this form, the x, y, and z values of a point on the sphere are represented independently in terms of two parameters u and v:

$$x = x(u, v),$$
$$y = y(u, v),$$
$$z = z(u, v).$$

As we shall see in Chapter 10, this form is preferable in computer graphics, especially for representing curves and surfaces, although, for a particular surface, there may be multiple parametric representations. One parametric representation for the sphere is

$$x(u, v) = \cos u \sin v,$$
$$y(u, v) = \cos u \cos v,$$
$$z(u, v) = \sin u.$$

As u and v vary in the range $-\pi/2 < u < \pi/2$, $-\pi < v < \pi$, we get all the points on the sphere. When we are using the parametric form, we can obtain the normal from the **tangent plane**, shown in Figure 6.20, at a point $\mathbf{p}(u, v) = [\, x(u, v) \quad y(u, v) \quad z(u, v) \,]^T$ on the surface. The tangent plane gives the local orientation of the surface at a point; we can derive it by taking the linear terms of the Taylor series expansion of the surface at $\mathbf{p}$. The result is that, at $\mathbf{p}$, lines in the directions of the vectors represented by

Figure 6.20 Tangent plane to sphere.

$$\frac{\partial \mathbf{p}}{\partial u} = \begin{bmatrix} \frac{\partial x}{\partial u} \\ \frac{\partial y}{\partial u} \\ \frac{\partial z}{\partial u} \end{bmatrix}, \qquad \frac{\partial \mathbf{p}}{\partial v} = \begin{bmatrix} \frac{\partial x}{\partial v} \\ \frac{\partial y}{\partial v} \\ \frac{\partial z}{\partial v} \end{bmatrix}$$

lie in the tangent plane. We can use their cross product to obtain the normal

$$\mathbf{n} = \frac{\partial \mathbf{p}}{\partial u} \times \frac{\partial \mathbf{p}}{\partial v}.$$

For our sphere, we find that

$$\mathbf{n} = \cos u \begin{bmatrix} \cos u \sin v \\ \cos u \cos v \\ \sin u \end{bmatrix} = (\cos u)\mathbf{p}.$$

We are interested in only the direction of $\mathbf{n}$; thus, we can divide by $\cos u$ to obtain the unit normal to the sphere

$$\mathbf{n} = \mathbf{p}.$$

In Section 6.9 we use this result to shade a polygonal approximation to a sphere.

Within a graphics system, we usually work with a collection of vertices, and the normal vector must be approximated from some set of points close to the point where the normal is needed. The pipeline architecture of real-time graphics systems makes this calculation difficult, because we process one vertex at a time, and thus the graphics system may not have the information available to compute the approximate normal at a given point. Consequently, graphics systems often leave the computation of normals to the user program.

In OpenGL, we can associate a normal with a vertex through functions such as

```
glNormal3f(nx, ny, nz);
glNormal3fv(pointer_to_normal);
```

Normals are modal variables. If we define a normal before a sequence of vertices through glVertex calls, this normal is associated with all the vertices, and is used for the lighting calculations at all the vertices. The problem remains, however, that we have to determine these normals ourselves.

6.4.2 Angle of Reflection

Once we have calculated the normal at a point, we can use this normal and the direction of the light source to compute the direction of a perfect reflection. An ideal mirror is characterized by the following statement: *The angle of incidence is equal to the angle of reflection*. These angles are as pictured in Figure 6.21. The **angle of incidence** is the angle between the normal and the light source (assumed to be a point source); the **angle of reflection** is the angle between the normal and the direction in which the light is reflected. In two dimensions, there is but a single angle satisfying the angle condition. In three dimensions, however, our statement is insufficient to compute the required angle: There is an infinite number of angles satisfying our condition. We must add the following statement: *At a point* $\mathbf{p}$ *on the surface, the incoming light ray, the reflected light ray, and the normal at the point must all lie in the same plane*. These two conditions

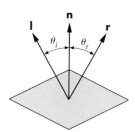

Figure 6.21 A mirror.

are sufficient for us to determine $\mathbf{r}$ from $\mathbf{n}$ and $\mathbf{l}$. Our primary interest is the direction, rather than the magnitude, of $\mathbf{r}$. However, many of our rendering calculations will be easier if we deal with unit-length vectors. Hence, we assume that both $\mathbf{l}$ and $\mathbf{n}$ have been normalized such that

$$|\mathbf{l}| = |\mathbf{n}| = 1.$$

We also want

$$|\mathbf{r}| = 1.$$

If $\theta_i = \theta_r$, then

$$\cos \theta_i = \cos \theta_r.$$

Using the dot product, the angle condition is

$$\cos \theta_i = \mathbf{l} \cdot \mathbf{n} = \cos \theta_r = \mathbf{n} \cdot \mathbf{r}.$$

The coplanar condition implies that we can write $\mathbf{r}$ as a linear combination of $\mathbf{l}$ and $\mathbf{n}$:

$$\mathbf{r} = \alpha\mathbf{l} + \beta\mathbf{n}.$$

Taking the dot product with $\mathbf{n}$, we find that

$$\mathbf{n} \cdot \mathbf{r} = \alpha\mathbf{l} \cdot \mathbf{n} + \beta = \mathbf{l} \cdot \mathbf{n}.$$

We can get a second condition between α and β from our requirement that $\mathbf{r}$ also be of unit length; thus,

$$1 = \mathbf{r} \cdot \mathbf{r} = \alpha^2 + 2\alpha\beta\mathbf{l} \cdot \mathbf{n} + \beta^2.$$

Solving these two equations, we find that

$$\mathbf{r} = 2(\mathbf{l} \cdot \mathbf{n})\mathbf{n} - \mathbf{l}.$$

6.4.3 Use of the Halfway Vector

If we use the Phong model with specular reflections in our rendering, the dot product $\mathbf{r} \cdot \mathbf{v}$ should be recalculated at every point on the surface. We can obtain an interesting approximation by using the unit vector halfway between the viewer vector and the light-source vector:

$$\mathbf{h} = \frac{\mathbf{l} + \mathbf{v}}{|\mathbf{l} + \mathbf{v}|}.$$

Figure 6.22 shows all five vectors. Here we have defined ψ as the angle between $\mathbf{n}$ and $\mathbf{h}$, the **half-angle**. When $\mathbf{v}$ lies in the same plane as do $\mathbf{l}$, $\mathbf{n}$, and $\mathbf{r}$, we can show (Exercise 6.7) that

$$2\psi = \phi.$$

Figure 6.22 Determination of the halfway vector.

If we replace $\mathbf{r} \cdot \mathbf{v}$ with $\mathbf{n} \cdot \mathbf{h}$, we avoid calculation of $\mathbf{r}$. However, the halfway angle ψ is smaller than ϕ, and if we use the same exponent e in $(\mathbf{n} \cdot \mathbf{h})^e$ that we used in $(\mathbf{r} \cdot \mathbf{v})^e$, then the size of the specular highlights will be smaller. We can mitigate this problem by replacing the value of the exponent e with a value e', so that $(\mathbf{n} \cdot \mathbf{h})^{e'}$ is closer to $(\mathbf{r} \cdot \mathbf{v})^e$. It is clear that avoiding recalculation of $\mathbf{r}$ is desirable. However, to appreciate fully where savings can be made, you should consider all the cases of flat and curved surfaces, near and far light sources, and near and far viewers; see Exercise 6.8.

6.4.4 Transmitted Light

Similar shading calculations apply if our model allows for transmitted light (as will our simple ray tracer in Chapter 13). Consider a surface that transmits all the light that strikes it, as shown in Figure 6.23. If the speed of light differs in the two materials, the light is bent at the surface. Let η_l and η_t be the **indices of refraction**—a measure of the relative speed of light in the two materials on the two sides of the surface. **Snell's law** (see Exercise 6.13) states that

$$\frac{\sin \theta_l}{\sin \theta_t} = \frac{\eta_t}{\eta_l}.$$

We can find the direction of the transmitted light $\mathbf{t}$ as follows. We know $\cos \theta_l$ from $\mathbf{n}$ and $\mathbf{l}$; if they have been normalized, it is simply their dot product. Given $\cos \theta_t$, we can find $\sin \theta_t$, and from it $\sin \theta_l$. Letting $\eta = \eta_t/\eta_l$, we have

$$\cos \theta_t = \left(1 - \frac{1}{\eta^2}(1 - \cos^2 \theta_l)\right)^{\frac{1}{2}}.$$

Figure 6.23 Perfect light transmission.

Just as in the computation of the reflected light, the three vectors must be coplanar; thus,

$$\mathbf{t} = \alpha \mathbf{n} + \beta \mathbf{l}.$$

If we further impose the condition that $\mathbf{t}$ have unit length, we can do a derivation, similar to that for the reflected vector, to find

$$\mathbf{t} = -\frac{1}{\eta}\mathbf{l} - \left(\cos \theta_t - \frac{1}{\eta}\cos \theta_l\right)\mathbf{n}.$$

The first two negative signs in this equation are a consequence of $\mathbf{t}$ pointing away from the back side of the surface. The angle for which the square-root term in the expression for $\cos \theta_t$ becomes zero ($\sin \theta_l = \eta$) is known as the **critical angle**. If light strikes the surface at this angle, the transmitted light is in a direction along the surface. If θ_l is increased further, all light is reflected, and none is transmitted.

A more general expression for what happens at a transmitting surface corresponds to Figure 6.24. Some light is transmitted, some is reflected, and the rest is absorbed. Of the transmitted light, some is scattered in a manner similar to specular reflections, except that here the light is concentrated in the direction

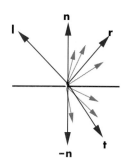

Figure 6.24 Light interaction at surface.

Figure 6.25 Polygonal mesh.

of **t**. Thus, a transmission model might include a term proportional to $\mathbf{t} \cdot \mathbf{v}$ for viewers on the transmitted side of the surface. We can also use the analogy of a half-angle to simplify calculation of this term (see Exercise 6.15).

6.5 Polygonal Shading

Assuming that we can compute normal vectors, given a set of light sources and a viewer, both the lighting and illumination models that we have developed can be applied at every point on a surface. Unfortunately, even if we have simple equations to determine normal vectors, as we did in our example of a sphere (Section 6.4), the amount of computation required can be large. We have already seen many of the advantages of using polygonal models for our objects. A further advantage is that, for flat polygons, we can significantly reduce the work required for shading. Most graphics systems, including OpenGL, exploit the efficiencies possible for rendering flat polygons by decomposing curved surfaces into many small flat polygons.

Consider a polygonal mesh, such as is shown in Figure 6.25, where each polygon is flat and thus has a well-defined normal vector. We consider three ways to shade the polygons: flat shading, interpolative or Gouraud shading, and Phong shading.

6.5.1 Flat Shading

The three vectors—**l**, **n**, and **v**—can vary as we move from point to point on a surface. For a flat polygon, however, **n** is constant. If we assume a distant viewer,[2] **v** is constant over the polygon. Finally, if the light source is distant, **l** is constant. Here, *distant* could be interpreted in the strict sense of meaning that the source is at infinity. The necessary adjustments, such as changing the *location* of the source to the *direction* of the source, could then be made to the shading equations and to their implementation. *Distant* could also be interpreted in terms of the size of the polygon relative to how far the polygon is from the source or viewer,

---

2. We can make this assumption in OpenGL by setting the near viewer flag to false.

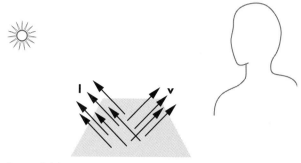

Figure 6.26 Distant source and viewer.

as shown in Figure 6.26. Graphics systems or user programs often exploit that definition.

If the three vectors are constant, then the shading calculation needs to be carried out only once for each polygon, and each point on the polygon is assigned the same shade. This technique is known as **flat** or **constant shading**. In OpenGL, we specify flat shading through

```
glShadeModel(GL_FLAT);
```

If flat shading is in effect, OpenGL uses the normal associated with the first vertex of a single polygon for the shading calculation. For primitives such as a triangle strip, OpenGL uses the normal of the third vertex for the first triangle, the normal of the fourth for the second, and so on. Similar rules hold for other primitives, such as quadrilateral strips.

Flat shading will show differences in shading for the polygons in our mesh. If the light sources and viewer are near the polygon, the vectors $\mathbf{l}$ and $\mathbf{v}$ will be different for each polygon. However, if our polygonal mesh has been designed to model a smooth surface, flat shading will almost always be disappointing, because we can see even small differences in shading between adjacent polygons, as shown in Figure 6.27. The human visual system has a remarkable sensitivity to

Figure 6.27 Flat shading of polygonal mesh.

Figure 6.28 Step chart.

Figure 6.29 Perceived and actual intensities at an edge.

small differences in light intensity, due to a property known as **lateral inhibition**. If we see an increasing sequence of intensities, as is shown in Figure 6.28, we perceive the increases in brightness as overshooting on one side of an intensity step and undershooting on the other, as shown in Figure 6.29. We see stripes, known as **Mach bands**, along the edges. This phenomenon is a consequence of how the cones in the eye are connected to the optic nerve, and there is little that we can do to avoid it, other than to look for smoother shading techniques that do not produce large differences in shades at the edges of polygons.

6.5.2 Interpolative and Gouraud Shading

In our rotating-cube example of Section 4.9, we saw that OpenGL interpolates colors assigned to vertices across a polygon. If we set the shading model to be smooth via

```
glShadeModel(GL_SMOOTH);
```

then OpenGL interpolates colors for other primitives such as lines. Suppose that we have enabled both smooth shading and lighting, and that we assign to each vertex the normal of the polygon being shaded. The lighting calculation is made at each vertex, determining a vertex color, using the material properties and the vectors $\mathbf{v}$ and $\mathbf{l}$ computed for each vertex. Note that if the light source is distant, and either the viewer is distant or there are no specular reflections, then interpolative shading shades a polygon in a constant color.

If we consider our mesh, the idea of a normal existing at a vertex should cause concern to anyone worried about mathematical correctness. Because multiple polygons meet at interior vertices of the mesh, each of which has its own normal, the normal at the vertex is discontinuous. Although this situation might complicate the mathematics, Gouraud realized that the normal at the vertex could be *defined* in such a way as to achieve smoother shading through interpolation. Consider an interior vertex, as shown in Figure 6.30, where four polygons meet. Each has its own normal. In **Gouraud shading**, we define the normal at a vertex to be the normalized average of the normals

Figure 6.30 Normals near interior vertex.

of the polygons that share the vertex. For our example, the **vertex normal** is given by

$$\mathbf{n} = \frac{\mathbf{n}_1 + \mathbf{n}_2 + \mathbf{n}_3 + \mathbf{n}_4}{|\mathbf{n}_1 + \mathbf{n}_2 + \mathbf{n}_3 + \mathbf{n}_4|}.$$

From an OpenGL perspective, Gouraud shading is deceptively simple. We need only to set the vertex normals correctly. Often, the literature makes no distinction between interpolative and Gouraud shading. However, the lack of a distinction causes a problem: How do we find the normals that we should average together? If our program is linear, specifying a list of vertices (and other properties), we do not have the necessary information about which polygons share a vertex. What we need, of course, is a data structure for representing the mesh. Traversing this data structure can generate the vertices with the averaged normals. Such a data structure should contain, minimally, polygons, vertices, normals, and material properties. One possible structure is the one shown in Figure 6.31. The key information that must be represented in the data structure is which polygons meet at each vertex.

Color Plates 4 and 5 show the shading effects available in OpenGL. In Color Plate 4, there is a single light source, but each polygon has been rendered with a single shade (constant shading), computed using the Phong model. In Color Plate 5, normals have been assigned to all the vertices. OpenGL has then computed shades for the vertices and has interpolated these shades over the faces of the polygons.

Color Plate 21 contains another illustration of the smooth shading provided by OpenGL. We used this color cube as an example in both Chapter 2 and Chapter 3, and the programs are in Appendix A. The eight vertices are colored black, white, red, green, blue, cyan, magenta, and yellow. Once smooth shading is enabled, OpenGL interpolates the colors across the faces of the polygons automatically.

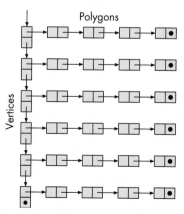

Figure 6.31 Mesh data structure.

Figure 6.32 Edge normals.

6.5.3 Phong Shading

Even the smoothness introduced by Gouraud shading may not prevent the appearance of Mach bands. Phong proposed that, instead of interpolating vertex intensities, as we do in Gouraud shading, we interpolate normals across each polygon. Consider a polygon that shares edges and vertices with other polygons in the mesh, as shown in Figure 6.32. We can compute vertex normals by interpolating over the normals of the polygons that share the vertex. Next, we can use bilinear interpolation, as we did in Chapter 4, to interpolate the normals over the polygon. Consider Figure 6.33. We can use the interpolated normals at vertices A and B to interpolate normals along the edge between them:

$$\mathbf{n}(\alpha) = (1 - \alpha)\mathbf{n}_A + \alpha\mathbf{n}_B.$$

We can do a similar interpolation on all the edges. The normal at any interior point can be obtained from points on the edges by

$$\mathbf{n}(\alpha, \beta) = (1 - \beta)\mathbf{n}_C + \beta\mathbf{n}_D.$$

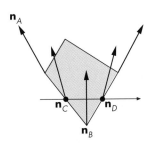

Figure 6.33 Interpolation of normals in Phong shading.

Once we have the normal at each point, we can make an independent shading calculation. Usually, this process can be combined with the scan conversion of the polygon, so that the line between C and D projects to a scan line in the frame buffer. We examine such issues in Chapter 8.

Phong shading produces renderings smoother than those of Gouraud shading, but at a significantly greater computational cost; see Exercise 6.21. There are various hardware implementations for Gouraud shading, and they require only a slight increase in the time required for rendering; neither is true, however, for Phong shading. Consequently, Phong shading is almost always done off line.

6.6 Approximation of a Sphere by Recursive Subdivision

We have used the sphere as an example curved surface to illustrate shading calculations. However, the sphere is not an object that is supported within OpenGL. Both the GL utility library (GLU) and the GL Utility Toolkit (GLUT) contain spheres, the former by supporting quadric surfaces, a topic that we discuss in Chapter 10, and the latter through a polygonal approximation.

We develop our own polygonal approximation to a sphere. It provides a basis for us to write simple programs that illustrate the interactions between shading parameters and polygonal approximations to curved surfaces. We introduce **recursive subdivision**, a powerful technique for generating approximations to curves and surfaces to any desired level of accuracy.

Our starting point is a tetrahedron, although we could start with any regular polyhedron whose facets could be divided initially into triangles.[3] The regular tetrahedron is composed of four equilateral triangles, determined by four vertices. We start with the four vertices $(0, 0, 1)$, $(0, 2\sqrt{2}/3, -1/3)$, $(-\sqrt{6}/3, -\sqrt{2}/3, -1/3)$, $(\sqrt{6}/3, -\sqrt{2}/3, -1/3)$. All four lie on the unit sphere, centered at the origin. Exercise 6.6 suggests one method for finding these points.

We get a first approximation by drawing a wireframe for the tetrahedron. We define the four vertices globally using our point type from Chapter 4,

```
point3 v[4]={{0.0, 0.0, 1.0}, {0.0, 0.942809, -0.333333},
 {-0.816497, -0.471405, -0.333333},
 {0.816497, -0.471405, -0.333333}};
```

We can draw triangles using the function

```
void triangle( point3 a, point3 b, point3 c)
{
  glBegin(GL_LINE_LOOP);
    glVertex3fv(a);
    glVertex3fv(b);
    glVertex3fv(c);
  glEnd();
}
```

The tetrahedron can be drawn by

```
void tetrahedron()
{
    triangle(v[0], v[1], v[2] );
```

---

3. The regular icosahedron is composed of 12 equilateral triangles; it makes a nice starting point for generating spheres; see [Ope01a].

```
    triangle(v[3], v[2], v[1] );
    triangle(v[0], v[3], v[1] );
    triangle(v[0], v[2], v[3] );
}
```

Figure 6.34 Tetra-
hedron.

The order of vertices obeys the right-hand rule, so we can convert the code to draw shaded polygons with little difficulty. If we add the usual code for initialization, our program will generate an image such as that in Figure 6.34: a simple regular polyhedron, but a poor approximation to a sphere.

We can get a closer approximation to the sphere by subdividing each facet of the tetrahedron into smaller triangles. Subdividing into triangles will ensure that all the new facets will be flat. There are at least three ways to do the subdivision, as shown in Figure 6.35. We can bisect each of the angles of the triangle, and draw the three bisectors, which meet at a common point, thus generating three new triangles. We can also compute the center of mass (centrum) of the vertices by simply averaging them, and then drawing lines from this point to the three vertices, again generating three triangles. However, these techniques do not preserve the equilateral triangles that make up the regular tetrahedron. Instead— recalling a construction for the Sierpinski gasket of Chapter 2—we can connect the bisectors of the sides of the triangle, forming four equilateral triangles, as shown in Figure 6.35(c). We use this technique for our example.

After we have subdivided a facet as just described, the four new triangles will still be in the same plane as the original triangle. We can move the new vertices that we created by bisection to the unit sphere by normalizing each bisected vertex, using a simple normalization function such as

```
void normal(point3 p)
{
    double d=0.0;
    int i;
    for(i=0; i<3; i++) d+=p[i]*p[i];
    d=sqrt(d);
    if(d > 0.0) for(i=0; i<3; i++) p[i]/=d;
}
```

(a)   (b)   (c)

Figure 6.35 Subdivision of a triangle by (a) bisecting angles, (b) computing the centrum, and (c) bisecting sides.

We can now subdivide a single triangle, defined by the vertices numbered a, b, and c, by the code

```
point3 v1, v2, v3;
int j;
for(j=0; j<3; j++) v1[j]=v[a][j]+v[b][j];
normal(v1);
for(j=0; j<3; j++) v2[j]=v[a][j]+v[c][j];
normal(v2);
for(j=0; j<3; j++) v3[j]=v[c][j]+v[b][j];
normal(v3);
triangle(v[a], v2, v1);
triangle(v[c], v3, v2);
triangle(v[b], v1, v3);
triangle(v1, v2, v3);
```

We can use this code in our tetrahedron routine to generate 16 triangles rather than 4, but we would rather be able to repeat the subdivision process *n* times to generate successively closer approximations to the sphere. By calling the subdivision routine recursively, we can control the number of subdivisions.

First, we make the tetrahedron routine depend on the depth of recursion by adding an argument n:

```
void tetrahedron(int n)
{
    divide_triangle(v[0], v[1], v[2] , n);
    divide_triangle(v[3], v[2], v[1], n );
    divide_triangle(v[0], v[3], v[1], n );
    divide_triangle(v[0], v[2], v[3], n );
}
```

The divide_triangle function calls itself to subdivide further if n is greater than zero, but generates triangles if n has been reduced to zero. Here is the code:

```
divide_triangle(point3 a, point3 b, point3 c, int n)
{
 point3 v1, v2, v3;
 int j;
 if(n>0)
 {
   for(j=0; j<3; j++) v1[j]=a[j]+b[j];
   normal(v1);
   for(j=0; j<3; j++) v2[j]=a[j]+c[j];
   normal(v2);
   for(j=0; j<3; j++) v3[j]=c[j]+b[j];
   normal(v3);
   divide_triangle(a ,v2, v1, n-1);
   divide_triangle(c ,v3, v2, n-1);
```

```
    divide_triangle(b ,v1, v3, n-1);
    divide_triangle(v1 ,v2, v3, n-1);
  }
  else triangle(a, b, c);
}
```

Figure 6.36 shows an approximation to the sphere drawn with this code. We now turn to adding lighting and shading to our sphere approximation. First, we must examine how lighting and shading are handled by the OpenGL API.

Figure 6.36 Sphere approximations using subdivision.

6.7 Light Sources in OpenGL

OpenGL supports the four types of light sources that we just described, and allows at least eight light sources in a program. Each must be individually specified and enabled. Although there are many parameters that must be specified, they are exactly the parameters required by the Phong model. The OpenGL functions

```
glLightfv(source, parameter, pointer_to_array);
glLightf(source, parameter, value);
```

allow us to set the required vector and scalar parameters, respectively. There are four vector parameters that we can set: the position (or direction) of the light source and the amount of ambient, diffuse, and specular light associated with the source.

For example, suppose that we wish to specify the first source GL_LIGHT0, and to locate it at the point $(1.0, 2.0, 3.0)$. We store its position as a point in homogeneous coordinates:

```
GLfloat light0_pos[]={1.0, 2.0, 3.0, 1.0};
```

With the fourth component set to zero, the point source becomes a distant source with direction vector

```
GLfloat light0_dir[]={1.0, 2.0, 3.0, 0.0};
```

For our single light source, if we want a white specular component, and red ambient and diffuse components, we can use the code

```
GLfloat diffuse0[]={1.0, 0.0, 0.0, 1.0};
GLfloat ambient0[]={1.0, 0.0, 0.0, 1.0};
GLfloat specular0[]={1.0, 1.0, 1.0, 1.0};

glEnable(GL_LIGHTING);
glEnable(GL_LIGHT0);
```

```
glLightfv(GL_LIGHT0, GL_POSITION, light0_pos);
glLightfv(GL_LIGHT0, GL_AMBIENT, ambient0);
glLightfv(GL_LIGHT0, GL_DIFFUSE, diffuse0);
glLightfv(GL_LIGHT0, GL_SPECULAR, specular0);
```

Note that we must enable both lighting and the particular source.

We can also add a global ambient term that is independent of any of the sources. For example, if we want a small amount of white light, we can use the code

```
GLfloat global_ambient[]={0.1, 0.1, 0.1, 1.0};

glLightModelfv(GL_LIGHT_MODEL_AMBIENT, global_ambient);
```

The distance terms are based on the distance-attenuation model,

$$f(d) = \frac{1}{a + bd + cd^2}$$

which contains constant, linear, and quadratic terms. These terms are set individually via glLightf; for example,

```
glLightf(GL_LIGHT0, GL_CONSTANT_ATTENUATION, a);
```

We can convert a positional source to a spotlight by choosing the spotlight direction (GL_SPOT_DIRECTION), the exponent (GL_SPOT_EXPONENT), and the angle (GL_SPOT_CUTOFF). All three are specified by glLightf and glLightfv.

There are two other light parameters provided by OpenGL that we should mention: GL_LIGHT_MODEL_LOCAL_VIEWER and GL_LIGHT_MODEL_TWO_SIDE. Lighting calculations can be time-consuming. If the viewer is assumed to be an infinite distance from the scene, then the calculation of reflections is easier, because the direction to the viewer from any point in the scene is unchanged. The default in OpenGL is to make this approximation, because its effect on many scenes is minimal. If you prefer that the full light calculation be made, using the true position of the viewer, you can change the model by using

```
glLightModeli(GL_LIGHT_MODEL_LOCAL_VIEWER, GL_TRUE);
```

In Chapter 4 we saw that a surface has both a front face and a back face. For polygons, we determine front and back by the order in which the vertices are specified, using the right-hand rule. For most objects, we see only the front faces, so we are not concerned with how OpenGL shades the back-facing surfaces. For example, for convex objects, such as a sphere or a parallelepiped (Figure 6.37), the viewer can never see a back face, regardless of where she is positioned. However, if we remove a side from a cube, or slice the sphere, as shown in Figure 6.38, a properly placed viewer may see a back face; thus, we must shade

Figure 6.37 Shading of convex objects.

Figure 6.38 Visible back surfaces.

both the front and back faces correctly. We can ensure that OpenGL handles both faces correctly by invoking the function

```
glLightModeli(GL_LIGHT_MODEL_TWO_SIDED, GL_TRUE);
```

Light sources are objects, just like polygons and points. Hence, light sources are affected by the OpenGL model-view transformation. We can define them at the desired position, or define them in a convenient position and move them to the desired position by the model-view transformation. The basic rule governing object placement is that vertices are converted to eye coordinates by the model-view transformation that is in effect at the time the vertices are defined. Thus, by careful placement of the light-source specifications relative to the definition of other geometric objects, we can create light sources that remain stationary while the objects move, light sources that move while objects remain stationary, and light sources that move with the objects.

6.8 Specification of Materials in OpenGL

Material properties in OpenGL match up directly with the supported light sources and with the Phong reflection model. We can also specify different material properties for the front and back faces of a surface. All our reflection parameters are specified through the functions

```
glMaterialfv(face, type, pointer_to_array);
glMaterialf(face, value);
```

For example, we might define ambient, diffuse, and specular reflectivity coefficients (k_a, k_d, k_s) for each primary color through three arrays:

```
GLfloat ambient[] = {0.2, 0.2, 0.2, 1.0};
GLfloat diffuse[] = {1.0, 0.8, 0.0, 1.0};
GLfloat specular[]={1.0, 1.0, 1.0, 1.0};
```

Here, we have defined a small amount of white ambient reflectivity, yellow diffuse properties, and white specular reflections. We set the material properties for the front and back faces by the calls

```
glMaterialfv(GL_FRONT_AND_BACK, GL_AMBIENT, ambient);
glMaterialfv(GL_FRONT_AND_BACK, GL_DIFFUSE, diffuse);
glMaterialfv(GL_FRONT_AND_BACK, GL_SPECULAR, specular);
```

Note that if both the specular and diffuse coefficients are the same (as is often the case), we can specify both by using GL_DIFFUSE_AND_SPECULAR for the type parameter. To specify different front- and back-face properties, we use GL_FRONT and GL_BACK. The shininess of a surface—the exponent in the specular-reflection term—is specified by glMaterialf; for example,

```
glMaterialf(GL_FRONT_AND_BACK, GL_SHININESS, 100.0);
```

OpenGL also allows us to define surfaces that have an emissive component that characterizes self-luminous sources. That method is useful if you want a light source to appear in your image. This term is unaffected by any of the light sources, and it does not affect any other surfaces. It adds a fixed color to the surfaces and is specified in a manner similar to other material properties. For example,

```
GLfloat emission[]={0.0, 0.3, 0.3, 1.0};
```

```
glMaterialfv(GL_FRONT_AND_BACK, GL_EMISSION, emission);
```

defines a small amount of blue–green (cyan) emission.

Material properties are modal: Their values remain the same until changed, and, when changed, affect only surfaces defined after the change. If we are using multiple materials, we can incur significant overhead if we have to change material properties each time that we begin a new polygon. OpenGL contains a method, glColorMaterial, that you can use to change a single material property. It is more efficient for changing a single color material property, but is less general than the method using glMaterial.

From an application programmer's perspective, we would like to have material properties that we can specify with a single function call, rather than having to make a series of calls to glMaterial for each polygon. We can achieve this goal by defining material objects in the application using structs or classes. For example, consider the typedef

```
typedef struct materialStruct
    GLfloat ambient[4];
    GLfloat diffuse[4];
    GLfloat specular[4];
    GLfloat shininess;
 materialStruct;
```

We can now define materials by code such as

```
material StructbrassMaterials =
{
    0.33, 0.22, 0.03, 1.0,
    0.78, 0.57, 0.11, 1.0,
    0.99, 0.91, 0.81, 1.0,
    27.8
;
}
```

and access this code through a pointer

```
currentMaterials=&brassMaterials;
```

which allows us to set material properties through a function

```
void materials( materialStruct *materials)
glMaterialfv(GL_FRONT, GL_AMBIENT, materials->ambient);
glMaterialfv(GL_FRONT, GL_DIFFUSE, materials->diffuse);
glMaterialfv(GL_FRONT, GL_SPECULAR, materials->specular);
glMaterialf(GL_FRONT, GL_SHININESS, materials->shininess);
```

6.9 Shading of the Sphere Model

We can now shade our spheres. Here, we omit our standard OpenGL initialization; the complete program is given in Appendix A.

If we are to shade our approximate spheres with OpenGL's shading model, we must assign normals. One simple, but illustrative, choice is to flat shade each triangle, using the three vertices to determine a normal, and then to assign this normal to the first vertex. Following our approach of Section 6.6, we use the cross product, and then normalize the result. A cross-product function is

```
cross(point3 a, point3 b, point3 c, point3 d);
{
    d[0]=(b[1]-a[1])*(c[2]-a[2])-(b[2]-a[2])*(c[1]-a[1]);
    d[1]=(b[2]-a[2])*(c[0]-a[0])-(b[0]-a[0])*(c[2]-a[2]);
    d[2]=(b[0]-a[0])*(c[1]-a[1])-(b[1]-a[1])*(c[0]-a[0]);
    normal(d);
}
```

Assuming that light sources have been defined and enabled, we can change the triangle routine to produce shaded spheres:

```
void triangle( point3 a, point3 b, point3 c)
{
    point3 n;
    cross(a, b, c, n);
    glBegin(GL_POLYGON);
    glNormal3fv(n);
    glVertex3fv(a);
    glVertex3fv(b);
    glVertex3fv(c);
    glEnd();
}
```

Figure 6.39 Flat-shaded sphere.

The result of flat shading our spheres is shown in Figure 6.39. Note that even as we increase the number of subdivisions so that the interior of the spheres appears smooth, we can still see edges of polygons around the outside of the sphere image. This type of outline is called a **silhouette edge**.

We can easily apply interpolative shading to the sphere models, because we know that the normal at each point **p** on the surface is in the direction from the origin to **p**. We can then assign the true normal to each vertex, and OpenGL will interpolate the shades at these vertices across each triangle. Thus, we change triangle to

```
void triangle( point3 a, point3 b, point3 c)
{
    point3 n;
    int i;
    glBegin(GL_POLYGON);
        for(i=0;i<3;i++) n[i]=a[i];
        normal(n);
        glNormal3fv(n);
        glVertex3fv(a);
        for(i=0;i<3;i++) n[i]=b[i];
        normal(n);
        glNormal3fv(n);
        glVertex3fv(b);
        for(i=0;i<3;i++) n[i]=c[i];
        normal(n);
        glNormal3fv(n);
        glVertex3fv(c);
    glEnd();
}
```

The results of this definition of the normals are shown in Figure 6.40 and in Back Plate 2.

Although using the true normals produces a rendering more realistic than flat shading, the example is not general, because we have used normals that are known analytically. We also have not provided a true Gouraud-shaded image. Suppose we want a Gouraud-shaded image of our approximate sphere. At each vertex we need to know the normals of all polygons incident at the vertex. Our code does not have a data structure that contains the required information. Try Exercises 6.9 and 6.10, in which you construct such a structure. Note that six polygons meet at a vertex created by subdivision, whereas only three polygons meet at the original vertices of the tetrahedron.

Figure 6.40 Shading of the sphere with the true normals.

6.10 Global Rendering

There are limitations imposed by the local lighting model that we have used. Consider, for example, an array of spheres illuminated by a distant source, as shown in Figure 6.41(a). The spheres close to the source block some of the light from the source from reaching the other spheres. However, if we use our

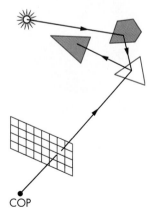

Figure 6.41 Array of shaded spheres. (a) Global lighting model. (b) Local lighting model.

local model, each sphere is shaded independently; all appear the same to the viewer (Figure 6.41b). In addition, if these spheres are specular, some light is scattered among spheres. Thus, if the spheres were very shiny, we should see the reflection of multiple spheres in some of the spheres and possibly even see the multiple reflections of some spheres in themselves. Our lighting model cannot handle this situation. Nor can it produce shadows, except by using the tricks for some special cases, as we saw in Chapter 5.

All of these phenomena—shadows, reflections, blockage of light—are global effects and require a global lighting model to explain. Although such models exist and can be quite elegant, in practice, they are incompatible with the pipeline model. With the pipeline model, we must render each polygon independently of the other polygons, and we want our image to be the same regardless of the order in which the application produces the polygons. Although this restriction limits the lighting effects that we can simulate, we can render scenes very rapidly.

In Chapter 13, we shall consider two alternative rendering strategies—ray tracing and radiosity—which can handle global effects. Each is best at different lighting conditions. Ray tracing starts with the synthetic camera model but for each projector that strikes a polygon, determines if that point is indeed illuminated by one or more sources before computing the local shading at each point. Thus, in Figure 6.42 we see three polygons and a light source. The projector shown intersects one of the polygons. A local renderer would use the Phong model to compute the shade at the point of intersection. The ray tracer would find that the light source cannot strike the point of intersection directly but that light from the source is reflected from the third polygon and this reflected light illuminates the point of intersection. In Chapter 13, we shall show how to find this information and make the required calculations.

A radiosity renderer is based upon energy considerations. From a physical point of view, all the light energy in a scene is conserved. Consequently, there is an energy balance that accounts for all the light that radiates from sources and is reflected by various surfaces in the scene. A radiosity calculation thus requires the solution of a large set of equations involving all the surfaces. As we shall see in Chapter 13, a ray tracer is best suited to a scene consisting of highly reflective

COP

Figure 6.42 Polygon blocked from light source.

surfaces, while a radiosity renderer is best suited for a scene in which all the surfaces are perfectly diffuse.

Although a pipeline renderer cannot take into account many global phenomena exactly, this observation does not mean we cannot produce realistic imagery with OpenGL or another API that is based upon a pipeline architecture. What we can do is use our knowledge of OpenGL and of the effects that global lighting produces to approximate what a global renderer would do. For example, our use of projective shadows in Chapter 5 shows that we can produce simple shadows. Many of the most exciting advances in computer graphics over the past few years have been in the use of pipeline renderers for global effects. We shall study many such techniques in the next few chapters, including mapping methods, multirendering, and transparency.

6.11 Summary and Notes

We have developed a lighting model that fits well with our pipeline approach to graphics. With it, we can create a variety of lighting effects, and we can employ different types of light sources. Although we cannot create the global effects of a ray tracer, a good graphics workstation can render a polygonal scene using the Phong reflection model and interpolative shading in the same amount of time as it can render a scene without shading. From the perspective of a user program, adding shading requires only setting parameters that describe the light sources and materials. In spite of the limitations of the local lighting model that we have introduced, our simple renderer performs remarkably well; it is the basis of the reflection model supported by most APIs, including OpenGL.

The recursive-subdivision technique that we used to generate an approximation to a sphere is a powerful one that will reappear in various guises in Chapters 10 and 11, where we use variants of this technique to render curves and surfaces. It will also arise when we introduce modeling techniques that rely on the self-similarity of many natural objects.

This chapter concludes our development of polygonal-based graphics. You should now be able to generate scenes with lighting and shading. Techniques for creating even more sophisticated images, such as texture mapping and compositing, involve using the pixel-level capabilities of graphics systems—topics that we consider in Chapter 7.

Now is a good time for you to write an application program. Experiment with various lighting and shading parameters. Try to create light sources that move, either independently or with the objects in the scene. You will probably face difficulties in producing shaded images that do not have small defects, such as cracks between polygons through which light can enter. Many of these problems are artifacts of small numerical errors in rendering calculations. There are many tricks of the trade for mitigating the effects of these errors. Some you will discover on your own; others are given in the suggested readings for this chapter.

We turn to implementation issues in Chapter 8. Although we have seen some of the ways in which the different modules in the rendering pipeline function, we have not yet seen the details. As these details are developed in Chapter 8, you will see how the pieces fit together such that each successive step in the pipeline requires only a small increment of work.

6.12 Suggested Readings

The use of lighting and reflection in computer graphics has followed two parallel paths: the physical and the computational. From the physical perspective, Kajiya's rendering equation [Kaj86] describes the overall energy balance in an environment and requires knowledge of the reflectivity function for each surface. Reflection models, such as the Torrance–Sparrow model [Tor67] and Cook–Torrance model [Coo82], are based on modeling a surface with small planar facets. See Hall [Hal89] and Foley [Fol90] for discussions of such models.

Phong [Pho75] is credited with putting together a computational model that included ambient, diffuse, and specular terms. The use of the halfway vector was first suggested by Blinn [Bli77]. The basic model of transmitted light was used by Whitted [Whi80]. It was later modified by Heckbert and Hanrahan [Hec84]. Gouraud [Gou71] introduced interpolative shading.

The *OpenGL Programmer's Guide* [Ope01a] contains many good hints on effective use of OpenGL's rendering capability.

Exercises

6.1   Most graphics systems and APIs use the simple lighting and reflection models that we introduced for polygon rendering. Describe the ways in which each of these models is incorrect. For each defect, give an example of a scene in which you would notice the problem.

6.2   Often, when a large polygon is shaded by OpenGL, it is rendered brightly in one area and more dimly in others. Explain why the image is uneven. Describe how you can avoid this problem.

6.3   In the development of the Phong reflection model, why do we not consider light sources being obscured from the surface by other surfaces in our reflection model?

6.4   How should the distance between the viewer and the surface enter the rendering calculations?

6.5   We have postulated an RGB model for the material properties of surfaces. Give an argument for using a subtractive color model instead.

6.6   Find four points equidistant from one another on a unit sphere. These points determine a tetrahedron. *Hint:* You can arbitrarily let one of the points be at $(0,1,0)$, and let the other three be in the plane $y = -d$ for some positive value of d.

6.7 Show that if $\mathbf{v}$ lies in the same plane as $\mathbf{l}$, $\mathbf{n}$, and $\mathbf{r}$, then the half-angle satisfies

$$2\psi = \phi.$$

What relationship is there between the angles if $\mathbf{v}$ is not coplanar with the other vectors?

6.8 Consider all the combinations of near or far viewers, near or far light sources, flat or curved surfaces, and diffuse and specular reflections. For which cases can you simplify the shading calculations? In which cases does the use of the halfway vector help? Explain your answers.

6.9 Construct a data structure for representing the subdivided tetrahedron. Traverse the data structure such that you can Gouraud shade the approximation to the sphere based on subdividing the tetrahedron.

6.10 Repeat Exercise 6.9, but start with an icosahedron instead of a tetrahedron.

6.11 Construct a data structure for representing meshes of quadrilaterals. Write a program to shade the meshes represented by your data structure.

6.12 Write a program that does recursive subdivisions on quadrilaterals and quadrilateral meshes.

6.13 Consider two materials that meet along a planar boundary. Suppose that the speed of light in the two materials is v_1 and v_2. Show that Snell's law is a statement that light travels from a point in one material to a point in the second material in the minimum time.

6.14 Show that the halfway vector $\mathbf{h}$ is at the angle at which a surface must be oriented so that the maximum amount of reflected light reaches the viewer.

6.15 For transmitted light, find a vector $\mathbf{h}'$ such that if the surface were oriented at this angle, the maximum amount of transmitted light would be in the direction of the viewer.

6.16 Although we have yet to discuss frame-buffer operations, you can start constructing a ray tracer using a single routine of the form write_pixel(x, y, color) that places the value of color (either an RGB color or an intensity) at the pixel located at (x, y) in the frame buffer. Write a pseudocode routine ray that recursively traces a cast ray. You can assume that you have a function available that will intersect a ray with an object. Consider how to limit how far the original ray will be traced.

6.17 If you have a pixel-writing routine available on your system, write a ray tracer that will ray trace a scene composed of only spheres. Use the mathematical equations for the spheres, rather than a polygonal approximation.

6.18 Add light sources and shading to the maze program in Exercise 5.13.

6.19 Using the sphere-generation program in Appendix A as a starting point, construct an interactive program that will allow you to position one or more light sources and to alter material properties. Use your program to try to generate images of surfaces that match familiar materials, such as various metals, plastic, and carbon.

6.20 As geometric data pass through the viewing pipeline, a sequence of rotations, translations, scalings, and a projection transformation is applied to the vectors that determine the cosine terms in the Phong reflection model. Which, if any, of these operations preserve the angles between the vectors? What are the implications of your answer for implementation of shading?

6.21 Estimate the amount of extra calculations required for Phong shading as compared to Gouraud shading. Take into account the results of Exercise 6.20.

6.22 Generalize the shadow-generation algorithm (Section 5.10) to handle flat surfaces at arbitrary orientations.

6.23 Convert the shadow-generation algorithm (Section 5.10) to an algorithm for distant sources. *Hint:* The perspective projection should become a parallel projection.

6.24 Compare the shadow-generation algorithm of Section 5.10 to the generation of shadows by a global-rendering method. What types of shadows can be generated by one method but not the other?

Discrete Techniques

For many years, computer graphics dealt exclusively with geometric objects, such as lines, polygons, and polyhedra. Raster systems have been in existence for more than 30 years, but, until recently, application programmers have had only indirect access to the frame buffer. Although lines and polygons were rasterized into the frame buffer, application programmers had no functions in the API that would allow them to read or write individual pixels. Many of the most exciting methods that have evolved over the past decade rely on interactions among the various buffers that make up the frame buffer. Texture mapping, antialiasing, compositing, and alpha blending are only a few of the techniques that become possible when the API allows us to work with discrete buffers. This chapter introduces these techniques, focusing on those that are supported by OpenGL and by similar APIs.

We start by looking at the frame buffer in more detail and how we can read and write to it. We shall learn to work with arrays of pixels that form digital images. We then consider mapping methods. These techniques are applied during the rendering process, and they enable us to give the illusion of a surface of great complexity, although the surface might be a single polygon. All these techniques use arrays of pixels to define how the rendering process that we studied in Chapter 6 is modified to create these illusions. We shall then look at some of the other buffers that are supported by the OpenGL API and how these buffers can be used for new applications. In particular, we examine techniques for combining or compositing images. Here we use the fourth "color" in RGBA mode, and we shall see that we can use this channel to blend images and to create effects such as transparency. We conclude with a discussion of the aliasing problems that arise whenever we work with discrete elements.

7.1 Buffers

We have already used two types of standard buffers: color buffers and depth buffers. Later, we introduce others. What all buffers have in common is that they are inherently discrete: They have limited resolution, both spatially and in

Figure 7.1 Buffer.

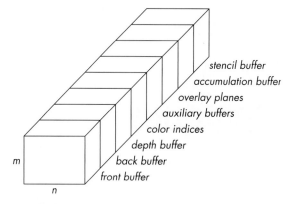

Figure 7.2 OpenGL frame buffer.

depth. We can define a (two-dimensional)[1] **buffer** as a block of memory with a spatial resolution of $n \times m$ k-bit elements (Figure 7.1).

As we have seen, OpenGL defines the frame buffer as consisting of a variety of buffers, including the front and back color buffers, the depth buffer, and other buffers that we shall introduce in the this chapter. Thus at a given spatial location, the k bits in the frame buffer can include bits for an index, such as an 8-bit pointer into a color table, 32-bit RGB colors, integers representing depths, or even floating point numbers. Figure 7.2 shows the OpenGL frame buffer and some of its constituent parts. If we consider the whole frame buffer, the resolution of the frame buffer, n and m, matches the spatial resolution of the display. The depth of the frame buffer—the value of k—can exceed a few hundred bits. Even for the simple cases that we have seen so far, we have 64 bits for the front and back color buffer, 32 bits for the depth buffer, and 8 bits for color indices.

When we work with the frame buffer, we usually work with one constituent buffer at a time. Thus, we shall use the term *buffer* in what follows to mean a particular buffer within the frame buffer. Each of these buffers is $n \times m$ and is k bits deep. However, k can be different for different buffers. For a color buffer, its k is determined by how many colors the system can display, usually 24 for RGB displays and 32 for RGBA displays. For the depth buffer, its k is determined by the depth resolution that the system can support, often 32 bits to match the size of a floating point number or an integer. We use the term **bitplane** to refer to any of the k $n \times m$ planes in a buffer, and **pixel** to refer to all k of the elements at a particular spatial location. With this definition, a pixel can be a byte, an integer, or even a floating-point number, depending on which buffer is used and how we choose to store the information.

-----

1. We can also have one-, three-, and four-dimensional buffers.

The applications programmer generally will not know how information is stored in the frame buffer because the frame buffer is inside the implementation which the programmer sees as a black box. Thus, the application program sends (writes) information into the frame buffer or obtains (reads) information from the frame buffer through OpenGL functions. When the application program reads or writes pixels, not only are data transferred between ordinary processor memory and the implementation, but usually these data must be reformatted to be compatible with the frame buffer. Consequently, what are ordinarily thought of as digital images, for example JPEG-, GIF-, or TIFF-formatted images, exist only on the application side of the process. Not only must the application programmer worry how to interpret particular formats so they can be sent to the frame buffer through OpenGL functions, but the programmer also must be aware of the time that is spent in the movement of digital data between processor memory and the frame buffer.

7.2 Digital Images

Before we look at how the graphics system can work with digital images through pixel and bit operations, let's first examine what we mean by a digital image.[2] Within our programs, we generally work with images that are arrays of pixels. These images can be of a variety of sizes and data types, depending on the type of image with which we are working. For example, if we are working with RGB images, we usually represent each of the color components with one byte whose values range from 0 to 255. Thus, we might define a 512×512 image in our program as

```
myimage[512][512][3];
```

If we are working with monochromatic or **luminance** images, each pixel represents a gray level from black (0) to white (255), so we would use

```
GLubyte myimage[512][512];
```

If we are working with color-index mode images, each pixel is a pointer into a table of colors, so that we might use unsigned bytes for the image plus three color tables

```
GLubyte myimage[512][512], red[256], green[256], blue[255];
```

---

2. Most references often use the term *image* instead of *digital image*. This terminology can be confused with using the term *image* to refer to the result of combining geometric objects and a camera, through the projection process, to obtain what we have called an image. In this chapter, the context should be clear so that there should not be any confusion.

Thus, for example, the red for a given index is `red[myimage[i][j]]`. One way to form digital images is through code in the application program. For example, suppose that we want to create a 512×512 image that consists of 8×8 checkerboard of alternating red and black squares, such as we might use for a game. The following code will work:

```
GLubyte check[512][512];
int i,j;
for (i=0; i<512; i++)
for(j=0; j<512; j++)
 {
    for(k=0;k<3;k++) check[i][j][k]=0;
    if((8*i+j/64)%64) check[i][j][0]=255;
}
```

Usually, writing code to form images is limited to images that contain regular patterns. More often, we obtain images directly from data. For example, if we have an array of real numbers that we have obtained from an experiment or a simulation, we can scale them to go over the range 0 to 255 and then convert these data to unsigned bytes to form a luminance image.

There is a third method of obtaining images that has become much more prevalent because of the influence of the Internet. Images are produced by scanning continuous images, such as photographs, or produced directly using digital cameras. Each image is in one of many possible "standard" formats. Some of the most popular formats are GIF, TIFF, PS, EPS, and JPEG. These formats include direct coding of the values in some order, compressed but lossless coding, and compressed lossy coding. Each format arose from the particular needs of a group of applications. For example, Postscript (PS) images are defined as part of the Postscript language used to control printers. These images are an exact encoding of the image data—either RGB or luminance—into the 7-bit ASCII character set. Consequently, Postscript images can be understood by a large class of printers and other devices but tend to be very large. Encapsulated Postscript (EPS) are similar but include additional information that is useful for previewing images. GIF images are color index images and thus store a color table and an array of indices for the image.

TIFF images can have two forms. In one form, all the image data are coded directly. A header describes how the data are arranged. In the second form, the data are compressed. Compression is possible because most images contain much redundant data. For example, large areas of most images show very little variation in color or intensity. This redundancy can be removed by algorithms that result in a compressed version of the original image that requires less storage. Compressed TIFF images are formed by the Lempel-Ziv algorithm that provides optimal lossless compression that allows the original image to be compressed and recovered exactly. JPEG images are compressed by an algorithm that allows small errors in the reconstruction of the image from the compressed data. Consequently, JPEG images have very high **compression ratios**, that is, the ratio of the number of bits in the original file to the number of bits in the compressed data file, with little or no visible distortion. Figure 7.3 shows three versions of a single 1200×1200 luminance image: uncompressed, as a TIFF image (a); and as two JPEG images, compressed with different ratios (b and c). The corresponding file sizes are 1,440,198, 80,109, and 38,962 bytes, respectively. Thus, the TIFF image has one byte for each pixel plus 198 bytes of header and trailer information. For the JPEG images, the compression ratios are approximately 18 and 37. Even with the higher compression ratio there is little visible distortion in the image. If we store the original image as a Postscript image, the file will be approximately twice as large as the TIFF image because each byte will be converted into two 7-bit ASCII characters, each pair requiring 2 bytes of storage. If we store the image as a compressed TIFF file, we need only about one-half of the storage. Using a zip file—a popular format used for compressing arbitrary files—would give about

(a)   (b)

(c)

Figure 7.3 (a) Original TIFF luminance image. (b) JPEG image compressed by a factor of 18. (c) JPEG image compressed by a factor of 37.

the same result. This amount of compression is image-dependent. Although this compression method is lossless, the compression ration is far worse than is obtainable with lossy JPEG images, which are visibly almost indistinguishable from the original. This closeness accounts for the popularity of the JPEG format for sending images over the Internet.

The large number of image formats poses problems for a graphics API. Although some are simple, others are quite complex. The OpenGL API avoids the problem by not including any image formats. As we shall see in the next section, while OpenGL can work with images that are arrays of standard data types in memory, it is the application programmer's responsibility to read any formatted images into processor memory and write them out as formatted files. We shall not deal with these issues here, as any discussion would require us to discuss the details of particular image formats. The necessary information can be found in the references at the end of the chapter.

We can also obtain digital images directly from our graphics system by forming images of three-dimensional scenes using the geometric pipeline and then reading these images back. We shall see how to do the required operations later in the chapter.

7.3 Writing into Buffers

In a modern graphics system, a user program can both write into and read from the buffers. There are two factors that make these operations different from the usual reading and writing into computer memory. First, we only occasionally want to read or write a single pixel or bit. Rather, we tend to read and write rectangular blocks of pixels (or bits), known as **bit blocks**. For example, we rasterize an entire scan line at a time when we fill a polygon; we write a small block of bits when we display a raster character; we change the values of all pixels in a buffer when we do a clear operation. Hence, it is important to have both the hardware and software support a set of operations that work on rectangular blocks of pixels, known as **bit-block transfer** (**bitblt**) operations, as efficiently as possible. These operations are also known as **raster operations** (**raster-ops**).

Suppose that we want to take an $n \times m$ block of pixels from one of our buffers, the **source buffer**, and to copy it into either the same buffer or another buffer, the **destination buffer**. This transfer is shown in Figure 7.4. A typical form for a bitblt write operation is

```
write_block(source, n, m, x, y, destination, u, v);
```

where `source` and `destination` are the buffers. The operation writes an n × m source block whose lower-left corner is at (x,y) to the destination buffer starting at a location (u,v). Although there are numerous details that we must consider, such as what happens if the source block goes over the boundary of the destination block, the essence of bitblt is that a single function call alters

Figure 7.4 Writing of a block.

the entire destination block. Note that, from the hardware perspective, the type of processing involved has none of the characteristics of the processing of geometric objects. Consequently, the hardware that optimizes bitblt operations has a completely different architecture from the pipeline hardware that we use for geometric operations. Thus, the OpenGL architecture contains both a geometric pipeline and a pixel pipeline, each of which usually is implemented separately.

7.3.1 Writing Modes

A second difference between normal writing into memory and bitblt operations is the variety of ways we can write into the buffers. In Chapter 3, we introduced logic operations so that we could use the XOR write mode to draw rubber-band lines. OpenGL supports 16 different modes. To understand the full range of possibilities, let's consider how we might write into a buffer.

The usual concept of a write-to memory is replacement. The execution of a statement in a C program such as

y=x;

results in the value at the location where y is stored being replaced with the value at the location of x.

There are other possibilities. Suppose that we can work 1 bit at a time in our buffers. Consider the writing model in Figure 7.5. The bit that we wish to place in memory, perhaps in an altered form, is called the **source bit**, **s**; the place in memory where we want to put it is called the **destination bit**, **d**. If, as in Chapter 3, we are allowed to read before writing, as depicted in Figure 7.4, then writing can be described by a replacement function f such that

$$d \leftarrow f(d, s).$$

For a 1-bit source and destination, there are only 16 possible ways to define the function f—namely, the 16 logical operations between two bits. These

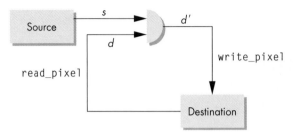

Figure 7.5 Writing model.

operations are shown in Figure 7.6, where each of the 16 columns on the right corresponds to one possible f. We can use the binary number represented by each column to denote a **writing mode**; equivalently, we can denote writing modes by the logical operation defined by the column. Suppose that we think of the logical value "1" as corresponding to a background color (say, black) and "0" as corresponding to a foreground color (say, white). We can examine the effects of various choices of f. Writing modes 0 and 15 are clear operations that change the value of the destination to either the foreground or the background color. The new value of the destination bit is independent of both the source and the destination values. Modes 3 and 7 are the normal writing modes. Mode 3 is the function

$$d \leftarrow s.$$

It simply replaces the value of the destination bit with the source. Mode 7 is the logical OR operation:

$$d \leftarrow s + d.$$

Figure 7.7 shows that these two writing modes can have different effects on the contents of the frame buffer. Both modes write the foreground color over the background color, but they differ if we try to write the background color over the foreground color. Which mode should be used depends on what effect the application programmer wishes to create.

s	d	0	1	2	3	4	5	6	7	8	9	10	11	12	13	14	15
0	0	0	0	0	0	0	0	0	0	1	1	1	1	1	1	1	1
0	1	0	0	0	0	1	1	1	1	0	0	0	0	1	1	1	1
1	0	0	0	1	1	0	0	1	1	0	0	1	1	0	0	1	1
1	1	0	1	0	1	0	1	0	1	0	1	0	1	0	1	0	1

Figure 7.6 Writing modes.

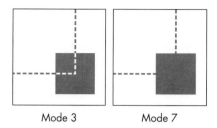

Mode 3   Mode 7

Figure 7.7 Writing in modes 3 and 7.

7.3.2 Writing with XOR

Mode 6 is the exclusive-or operation XOR, denoted by $\oplus$; it is the most interesting of the writing modes. Unlike modes 3 and 7, mode 6 cannot be implemented without a read of the destination bit. The power of the XOR write mode comes from the property that, if s and d are binary variables, then

$$d = (d \oplus s) \oplus s.$$

Thus, if we apply XOR twice to a bit, we return that bit to its original state.

The most important applications of this mode involve interaction. In Chapter 3, we used XOR mode for rubberbanding. We can also use this mode to implement other operations that require the redrawing of parts of the display.

Consider what happens when we use menus in an interactive application, such as in our painting program from Chapter 3. In response to a mouse click, a menu appears, covering a portion of the screen. After the user indicates an action from the menu, the menu disappears, and the area of the screen that it covered is returned to that area's original state. What has transpired involves the use of off-screen memory, known as **backing store**. Suppose that the menu has been stored off-screen as an array of bits, M, and that the area of the screen where the menu appears is an array of bits, S. Consider the sequence of operations

$$S \leftarrow S \oplus M,$$
$$M \leftarrow S \oplus M,$$
$$S \leftarrow S \oplus M,$$

where we assume that the XOR operation is applied to corresponding bits in S and M. If we substitute the result of the first equation in the second, and the result of the second in the third, we find that, at the end of three operations, the menu appears on the screen. The original contents of the screen, where the menu is now located, are now off-screen, where the menu was originally. We have swapped the menu with an area of the screen using three bitblt operations. This method of swapping is considerably different from the normal mode of swapping, which uses replacement-mode writing, but requires temporary storage to effect the swap.

There are numerous variants of this technique. One is to move a cursor around the screen without affecting the area under it. Another is filling polygons with a solid color as part of scan conversion. Note that, because many APIs trace their backgrounds to the days before raster displays became the norm, the XOR-write mode is not always available.

7.4 Bit and Pixel Operations in OpenGL

Digital images consist of k-bit pixels, where k can be any number from 1, for binary images, to 32, for RGBA images, to even greater numbers, for high-resolution color applications. Although, in principle, a 1-bit image, or **bitmap**, is the same type of entity as an 8-bit (1-byte) or 24-bit (3-byte) image, hardware and software often treat them differently. From the hardware perspective, bitmaps involve implementation of only logical operations, and they work one plane at a time in a buffer. From the software perspective, bitmaps are used differently from multibit images, even though both might use the same physical memory. Typically, bitmaps are used for fonts, masks, and patterns. OpenGL allows the user to work with either bitmaps or images of multibit pixels through two different sets of operations.

Bitblt operations make sense when we are working with 1-bit pixels, such as those used for fonts and cursors. It is less clear how to use these operations for multibit pixels and colors, because the bitwise result of the 16 operations does not usually translate into a visually sensible image, even though OpenGL allows us to use logic operations with any primitives. OpenGL supports logic operations through the `glLogicOp` functionality that we saw in Chapter 3.

Not only does OpenGL support a separate pixel pipeline and a variety of buffers, but also data can be moved among these buffers and between buffers and the processor memory. Depending on which buffer we are using, we can store information ranging from indices to color components to depths. In addition, we can store information in the processor memory in the standard data types (bytes, integers, and floats). This plethora of formats and types can make writing efficient code for dealing with bits and pixels a difficult task. We shall not discuss what the details are, but instead shall look at what capabilities are supported.

7.4.1 OpenGL Buffers and the Pixel Pipeline

OpenGL can support various buffers, including the following:

- Color buffers
- Depth buffer
- Accumulation buffer
- Stencil buffer

The color buffers include the buffer whose contents are displayed on our output device, but, as we saw in our discussion of double buffering in Chapter 3, the color buffers can include separate buffers for reading and writing. In double buffering, these color buffers are referred to as the **front** and **back buffers**. We may also want to produce stereo pairs of images, using **right** and **left buffers**, that contain the image as seen by the right and left eyes, respectively. For stereoscopic animations, we may want to employ four color buffers. Generally, we render geometric objects into the color buffers, but we can also write pixels directly into, and can read pixels from, the buffers. Only color buffers can be made visible.

The depth buffer normally is used for hidden-surface removal, but we can also read data from it and write data to it. In Section 7.10, we show how the accumulation buffer can be used for a variety of operations that involve combining multiple images. The stencil buffer often is used for masking operations. For example, we can use the values in this buffer as a mask to determine whether a pixel in the color buffer should be written to the screen.

For now, we assume that we are working in a color buffer—typically the back buffer—although many of these operations can be applied to other buffers. Note that a given implementation may support only some of these buffers, and that the depth of a buffer is implementation-dependent.

OpenGL maintains a **raster position**. We can think of this position as defining an internal cursor, in window coordinates, from which writing of raster primitives is measured. The raster position can be set by the variants of the function glRasterPos. For example, the function

```
glRasterPos3f(x, y, z);
```

describes a position by three floats that is subject to both the model-view and projection transformations before conversion to screen coordinates. This position is stored, like any other geometric entity, in four-dimensional homogeneous coordinates. However, once this position is transformed by the viewing pipeline to a position in screen coordinates, writing of pixels or bits takes place in raster units (integers), with the pixel centers located halfway between integers.

In OpenGL there is a **present drawing buffer** where pixel data from the user program are placed by write operations and a **present read buffer** from which any pixel-read operation gets its data. Either could be any of the supported buffers. By default, they are both the back buffer in double buffer mode but can be changed by glDrawBuffer and glReadBuffer functions.

As pixels make their way from processor memory—where they have been generated by the application—to the one of the buffers in the frame buffer, a sequence of operations takes place. This sequence defines the pixel pipeline described in Figure 7.8. The first operation, **unpacking**, converts pixels from the format in the user program to the format used internally by OpenGL. These new pixels can also be mapped into new values through user-defined lookup tables. The resulting pixels then pass through a series of tests that determine whether

Figure 7.8 The OpenGL pixel pipeline.

the pixel should be written into the frame buffer and, if it should be written, how it should be written. For example, we can mask out regions where no drawing will take place and use our logic operations to determine how to combine pixels with what is already in the buffer. If we read information from a buffer back to processor memory, we must convert (**pack**) the data from OpenGL's internal format to whatever format we want to use in our application.

7.4.2 Bitmaps

OpenGL treats arrays of one-bit pixels (bitmaps) differently from multibit pixels (pixelmaps) and provides different programming interfaces for the two cases. Bitmaps are used for fonts and for displaying cursors, often making use of the XOR writing mode. Both of these examples rely on the use of the present raster position to position the bitmap. Thus, once the bitmap is located in the present buffer, each bit in the bitmap corresponds to a pixel in this buffer. The bits in the bitmap are used as **masks** that determine whether the color of the pixel at that location is to be altered. If a bit is 0, then the pixel is unchanged. If it is 1, then the pixel is changed based on the **raster color** and the drawing mode. The raster color is set by glColor and is the same as the drawing color used for geometric primitives, except that the raster color is fixed by the last invocation of glRasterPos. Thus, suppose that a bit is positioned over a pixel that is red and the present raster color is green. If the bit has a value of 0, the pixel will remain red. If the bit has a value of 1 and we are in the default replacement write mode, then the red pixel will be changed to green. If, however, we were in XOR write mode, the new pixel color would be yellow, which is result of the bitwise XOR between the 24-bit representations of the RGB colors red and green.

We place an array bitmap at the current raster position (assuming that this position is a valid location in the buffer) with the function

```
glBitmap(width, height, xo, yo, xi,yi, bitmap);
```

The width and height are in bits. The floating-point numbers xo and yo give an offset relative to the current raster position, and give the position where the lower-left corner of the bitmap is to start (Figure 7.9); xi and yi are floating-point numbers used to increment the raster position after the bitmap is drawn.

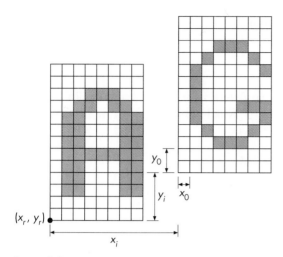

Figure 7.9 Outputting of a bitmap.

7.4.3 Raster Fonts

Raster fonts demonstrate the use of the raster position. In Chapter 3, we observed that raster text is much faster to render than is stroke text. In general, a **font** or **typeface** defines a set of characters of a particular family, such as Times, Courier, or Computer Modern. Each font can have various sizes, such as 10-point or 24-point,[3] and styles, such as bold or italic. However, we use the term *font* with *raster* to denote a set of characters of a particular size and style. Hence, an 8 × 13 font, as provided by the GLUT library, is denoted by GLUT_BITMAP_8_BY_13; a 10-point proportional font[4] is GLUT_BITMAP_TIMES_ROMAN_10. A typical font has 128 or 256 characters. Each character in a raster font is defined by a pattern of bits, as shown in Figure 7.10. Note that when we define a font as a pattern of bits, the size of text on the screen depends on the resolution of the screen—a relation that does not hold for the rendering of geometric objects.

Bitmapped fonts are designed both to fit in a certain space and to be readable. Thus, as we can see from Figure 7.10, in all but the smallest fonts, we must allow for vertical and horizontal spacing between characters; for room for descenders, as in the lowercase letters g and y; and for the size differences between uppercase and lowercase letters. Once we have designed a font, we can store it in an array

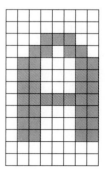

Figure 7.10 Definition of a character.

---

3. There are 72 points to 1 inch.
4. A *proportional font* is a font in which not all characters have the same width. In a *monotype font*, all characters have the same width.

as bits. For example, if we wish to define a 128-character 8 × 13 font, we can use an array

```
GLubyte my_font[128][13];
```

As we did in Chapter 3, we can define a font using a display list for each character. Assuming that the array my_font has been defined, these display lists can be generated by the code (see Section 3.4)[5]

```
base=glGenLists(128); for(i=0; i<127; i++)
{
    glNewList(base+i, GL_COMPILE);
    glBitMap(8, 13, 0.0, 2.0, 10.0, 0.0, my_font[i]);
    glEndList();
}
```

In this example, note that each character is started 2 bits up from the current raster position, and the raster position is shifted 2 additional bits after the character is drawn, leaving a 2-bit horizontal and vertical separation between characters.

7.4.4 Pixels and Images

In OpenGL, so that we can accommodate different types of images, pixels can be handled as groups of 8-bit bytes in a variety of formats. For example, we can work with RGB images, where the value of each color component is stored as a single byte, or we can work with a monochrome (luminance) image in which each pixel is a single floating-point number.

There are three functions for moving images in OpenGL:

```
glReadPixels(x, y, width, height, format, type, image);
glDrawPixels(width, height, format, type, image);
glCopyPixels(x,y, width, height,type);
```

The functions glReadPixels and glDrawPixels read and write rectangles of pixels between an OpenGL buffer and an array image in processor memory, whereas glCopyPixels reads and writes from one area of a color buffer to another area of the same buffer. In glReadPixels, we can specify an offset (x, y) in the frame buffer where reading of the block of dimensions width and height should begin. Although, in most applications, we use the back color buffer, which is selected by default, we can use the functions glReadBuffer and glDrawBuffer to select any of OpenGL's buffers for reading and writing.

---

5. We are, perhaps, wasting space by allocating memory for the first 32 ASCII characters. These characters are usually nonprinting characters, used only for control, and do not generate any visible output.

The format and type parameters describe the image in processor memory. Its format describes the kind of image (RGB, RBGA, color index), and its type is the data type used by the application (int, float). Thus, for the image we defined in Section 7.2, we had

```
GLubyte myimage[512][512][3]
```

to describe an RGB image. We could write this image into the present draw buffer by

```
glDrawPixels(xstart, ystart, 512, 512, GL_RGB,
    GL_UNSIGNED_BYTE, myimage);
```

There is another vexing problem that you may encounter. Different processors often have different methods for arranging information in memory. For example, processors differ as to which byte in a multibyte data type, such as an int, is the most significant byte. Some processors only allow information to begin only on 4-byte boundaries. Consequently, the storage of an array such as myimage might differ on different computers. Such system-dependent features can affect OpenGL programs, especially when reading and writing pixels. OpenGL provides a function, glPixelStore, that allows the application program to describe how data should be packed and unpacked. Normally, the defaults in a system are set so that you will not need this function, but that is not always the case, especially if you try to run code developed on one system on another.

7.4.5 Lookup Tables

In OpenGL, all colors can be modified by lookup tables as they are placed into buffers. Suppose that a buffer contains 8-bit components. Then, each component can have 256 possible values, and we can regard each of these values as an index into a 256-entry lookup table, as shown in Figure 7.11. If each value in the table is also 8 bits, then the index into the table selects a new value for the component. The tables are defaulted to provide an identity mapping of input values to output values. The function glPixelMap allows us to load user-defined maps.

These maps are essentially the same as the color lookup tables that we introduced in Chapter 2. If we make a correspondence between the color indices and

Figure 7.11 Lookup table for RGB.

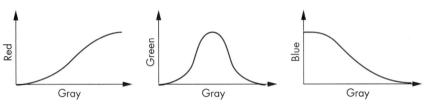

Figure 7.12 Thermal color map.

the gray levels of a monochromatic (luminance) image, we can use these maps to enhance a display by converting gray levels to colors. An image colored in such a manner is called a **pseudocolor** image. We demonstrate this technique to assign colors to points in the Mandelbrot set in Chapter 11.

The major problem for the user is how to select the palette of 256 colors from the (typically) 2^{24} available RGB colors. One popular choice is based on a thermal scale, using hot colors (red, white, and yellow) for important values, and cool colors (blues and greens) for unimportant values. For example, suppose that our gray-scale image is such that the low values are least important and the high values are most important. Figure 7.12 shows a possible map of the gray levels to RGB that forms such a thermal scale. Color Plate 19 shows the use of a thermal scale in a scientific visualization. Here, the colors represent temperatures in the mantle of the earth as generated by a computer model.

Another use of lookup tables is for color conversion and brightness adjustments. For example, the shading models that we use in computer graphics often generate images that are dark and lack contrast. If we were to plot the distribution of luminance values as a graph called a **histogram**, we might see a plot like the one shown in Figure 7.13, which shows that the majority of the values are in the lower ranges. If we apply the lookup table in Figure 7.14 to each color, we map lower gray levels to higher (brighter) values, and lighten the image. The distribution of levels for the resulting image is more uniform yet still spans the full range of luminance values, thus improving the contrast of the original image.

Figure 7.13 Histogram of dark image.

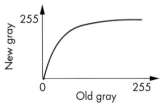

Figure 7.14 Lookup table for lightening of an image.

We can also use these tables for color conversion. In most APIs, including OpenGL, the RGB values do not refer to any particular system. Often, if we photograph the image that is on the screen of a CRT, the resulting photographic print may look noticeably different from the image on the screen, due to the differences in the color properties of the film, the photographic paper, and the CRT, and the perceptual characteristics of the viewer. We can use a lookup table for each of the R, G, and B components to make color adjustments, called **color balancing**, before we take the photograph. The lookup tables thus provide a method of color conversion across different RGB systems.

Operations such as histogram evaluation and using tables for color changes are core to the field of **image processing**. In Section 7.10, we shall investigate these and other imaging operations further and discuss how they can be supported within the OpenGL architecture.

7.4.6 Buffers for Picking

Buffers provide limitless opportunities for constructing and manipulating images. They can also be used interactively, in ways that might not be apparent at first. Consider the problem of picking. In Chapter 3, we introduced the OpenGL mechanism that uses feedback and hit lists to provide the information needed to identify objects on the display. This mechanism, although very general, required a fair amount of code to implement. If there are not too many distinct object identifiers, we can use buffers to provide an alternative picking mechanism, which is simpler to implement.

Suppose that we have no more than 256 identifiers (assuming 8-bit-deep buffers). As we render primitives, we place the identifier of the object being rendered into an extra buffer at a location corresponding to the location in the frame buffer where the fragment is rendered. Thus, the "colors" in this extra buffer are identifiers of objects located at corresponding pixels in the frame buffer. We can use OpenGL's pixel-reading functions to obtain these colors. Picking reduces to reading the value of this buffer at the pixel corresponding to the cursor location. This method will also work with 24-bit colors if we set up a table that maps the colors into object identifiers. If we combine this process with the z-buffer algorithm, then each pixel in this buffer has the identifier of the closest object to the camera along the ray through the pixel.

7.5 Mapping Methods

One of the most powerful uses of buffers is for surface rendering. The process of modeling an object by a set of geometric primitives and then rendering these primitives has its limitations. Consider, for example, the task of creating a virtual orange by computer. Our first attempt might be to start with a sphere. From our discussion in Chapter 6, we know that we can build an approximate sphere out of triangles, and can render these triangles using material properties that match those of a real orange. Unfortunately, such a rendering would be far too regular to look much like an orange. We could instead follow the path that we shall explore in Chapter 10: We could try to model the orange with some sort of curved surface, and then render the surface. This procedure would give us more control over the shape of our virtual orange, but the image that we would produce still would not look right. Although it might have the correct overall properties, such as shape and color, it would lack the fine surface detail of the real orange. Some of the procedural-modeling methods of Chapter 11 might be able to give us more detail, and might incorporate some of the randomness that we see on the surface of a real orange, but they would do so at the cost of generating a model with more polygons than we would like to render.

An alternative is not to attempt to build increasingly more complex models, but rather to build a simple model and to add detail as part of the rendering process. As the implementation renders a surface—be it a polygon or a curved surface—it breaks up the surface into small pieces, called **fragments**, each of which, when projected, is at most the size of one pixel. Fragments smaller than one pixel can be important because, in high-end systems, many surfaces may contribute to the color of a pixel. As part of the rendering process, we must assign a shade or color to each fragment. We start by choosing a shading model from the ones we studied in Chapter 6. The mapping algorithms can be thought of as either modifying the shading algorithm based on a two-dimensional array, the map, or as modifying the shading by using the map to alter surface parameters, such as material properties and normals. There are three major techniques:

- Texture mapping
- Bump mapping
- Environmental mapping

Texture mapping uses a pattern (or texture) to determine the color of a fragment. These patterns could be determined by a fixed pattern, such as the regular patterns often used to fill polygons; by a procedural texture-generation method; or through a digitized image. In all cases, we can characterize the image produced by a mapping of a texture to the surface, as shown in Figure 7.15, as part of the rendering of the surface.

Whereas texture maps give detail by painting patterns onto smooth surfaces, **bump maps** distort the normal vectors during the shading process to make the surface appear to have small variations in shape, such as the bumps on a real orange. **Reflection** or **environmental maps** allow us to create images that have the appearance of ray-traced images without our having to trace reflected rays. In this case, an image of the environment is painted onto the surface as that surface is being rendered.

The three methods have much in common. All three alter the shading of individual pixels and are implemented as part of the rendering process. All rely on the map being stored as a one-, two-, or three-dimensional digital image. All allows to keep the geometric complexity low while creating the illusion of complex geometry. However, all are also subject to aliasing errors.

There are various examples of two-dimensional mappings in the color plates. Color Plate 7 was created using an OpenGL environmental map and shows how

Figure 7.15 Texture mapping a pattern to a surface.

a single texture map can create the illusion of a highly reflective surface while avoiding global calculations. Color Plate 23 uses a texture map for the surface of the table; Color Plate 10 uses texture mapping to create a brick pattern. Much of the detail in Color Plate 15 is from a texture map. In these virtual-reality and visualization simulations, real-time performance is required. When these simulations are executed on workstations with hardware texture mapping, texture mapping allows the detail to be added without significantly degrading the rendering time.

7.6 Texture Mapping

Textures are patterns. They can range from regular patterns, such as stripes and checkerboards, to the complex patterns that characterize natural materials. In the real world, we can distinguish among objects of similar size and shape by their textures. Thus, if we want to create detailed virtual objects, we can extend our present capabilities by placing, or mapping, a texture to the objects that we create. We consider only two-dimensional textures, although the methods we develop are applicable to textures with other dimensions.

Textures can be one, two, three, or four dimensional. For example, a one-dimensional texture might be used to create a pattern for a curve. A three-dimensional texture might describe a solid block of material from which we could sculpt an object. Because the use of surfaces is so important in computer graphics, mapping two-dimensional textures to surfaces is by far the most common use of texture mapping. However, the processes by which we map these entities is much the same regardless of the dimensionality of the texture, and we lose little by concentrating on two-dimensional texture mapping.

7.6.1 Two-Dimensional Texture Mapping

Although there are multiple approaches to texture mapping, all require a sequence of steps that involve mappings among three or four different coordinate systems. At various stages in the process, we shall be working with screen coordinates, where the final image is produced; world coordinates, where we describe the objects upon which the textures will be mapped; texture coordinates, which we use to describe the texture; and parametric coordinates, which we use to help us define curved surfaces. Methods differ according to the types of surfaces we are using and the type of rendering architecture we have. Our approach will be to start with a fairly general discussion of texture, introducing the various mappings, and then to show how texture mapping is handled by a real-time pipeline architecture, such as employed by OpenGL.

In most applications, textures start out as two-dimensional images of the sorts we introduced in Section 7.2. Thus, they might be formed by application programs or scanned in from a photograph, but, regardless of their origin, they are eventually brought into processor memory as arrays. We call the elements of these arrays **texels**, or texture elements, rather than pixels to emphasize how they will be used. However, at this point, we prefer to think of this array as a continuous rectangular two-dimensional texture pattern $T(s, t)$. The independent variables s and t are known as **texture coordinates**.[6] With no loss of generality, we can scale our texture coordinates to vary over the interval $(0,1)$.

A **texture map** associates a unique point of T with each point on a geometric object that is itself mapped to screen coordinates for display. If the object is represented in spatial (geometric) coordinates $[(x, y, z) \text{ or } (x, y, z, w)]$, then there are functions such that

$$x = x(s, t),$$
$$y = y(s, t),$$
$$z = z(s, t),$$
$$w = w(s, t).$$

One of the difficulties we must confront is that although these functions exist conceptually, finding them may not be possible in practice. In addition, we are worried about the inverse problem: having been given a point (x, y, z) or (x, y, z, w) on an object, how do we find the corresponding texture coordinates, or equivalently the "inverse" functions

$$s = s(x, y, z, w),$$
$$t = t(x, y, z, w).$$

If we define the geometric object using parametric (u, v) surfaces, such as we did for the sphere in Section 6.4, there is an additional mapping function that gives world coordinate values, (x, y, z) or (x, y, z, w) in terms of u and v. Although this mapping is known for simple surfaces, such as spheres and triangles, and for the surfaces that we shall discuss in Chapter 10, we also need the mapping from parametric coordinates (u, v) to texture coordinates and sometimes the inverse mapping from texture coordinates to parametric coordinates.

We also have to consider the projection process that take us from world coordinates to screen coordinates. Thus, we can think of a function that takes a texture coordinate pair (s, t) and tells us where on the screen the corresponding value of $T(s, t)$ will make its contribution to the final image, that is, whether (x_s, y_s) is a location on the display

$$x_s = x_s(s, t),$$
$$y_s = y_s(s, t).$$

---

6. In four dimensions, a value of T is for a point in (s, t, r, q) space.

Depending on the algorithm and the rendering architecture, we might also want the function that takes us from a point on the display to the texel that makes a contribution to the color at that point.

One way to think about texture mapping is in terms of two concurrent mappings: the first from texture coordinates to geometric coordinates, and the second from parametric coordinates to geometric coordinates, as shown in Figure 7.16. A third mapping takes us to screen coordinates.

Conceptually, the texture-mapping process is simple. A small area of the texture pattern maps to the area of the geometric surface, corresponding to a pixel in the final image. If we assume that the values of T are RGB color values, we can use these values either to modify the color of the surface or to assign a color to the surface based on only the texture value. This color assignment is carried out as part of the shading calculation.

On closer examination, we face a number of difficulties. First, we must determine the map from texture coordinates to geometric coordinates. A two-dimensional texture usually is defined over a rectangular region in texture space. The mapping from this rectangle to an arbitrary region in three-dimensional space may be a complex function or may have undesirable properties. For example, if we wish to map a rectangle to a sphere, we cannot do so without distortion of shapes and distances. Second, owing to the nature of the rendering process, which works on a pixel-by-pixel basis, we are more interested in the inverse map from screen coordinates to texture coordinates. It is when we are determining the shade of a pixel that we must determine what point in the texture image to use—a calculation that requires us to go

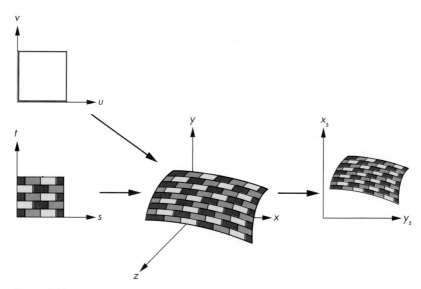

Figure 7.16 Texture maps for a parametric surface.

from screen coordinates to texture coordinates. Third, because we calculate the shade for pixels, each of which generates a color for a small rectangle on the display surface, we are interested in mapping not points to points, but rather areas to areas. Here again is a potential aliasing problem that we must treat carefully if we are to avoid artifacts, such as wavy sinusoidal or moiré patterns.

Figure 7.17 shows several of the difficulties. Suppose that we are computing a color for the square pixel centered at screen coordinates (x_s, y_s). The center (x_s, y_s) corresponds to a point (x, y, z) in object space, but, if the object is curved, the projection of the corners of the pixel backward into object space yields a curved **preimage** of the pixel. In terms of the texture image $T(s, t)$, projecting the pixel back yields a preimage in texture space that is the area of the texture that should contribute to the shading of the pixel.

Let us put aside for a moment the problem of how we find the inverse map, and let us look at the assignment of shades. One possibility is to use the point that we get by back projection of the pixel center to find a texture value. Although this technique is simple, it is subject to serious aliasing problems, which are especially visible if the texture is periodic. Figure 7.18 illustrates the aliasing problem. Here, we have a repeated texture and a flat surface. The back projection of the center of each pixel happens to fall in between the dark lines, and the texture value is always the lighter color. More generally, not taking into account the finite size of a pixel can lead to moiré patterns in the image. A better strategy—but one more difficult to implement—is to assign a texture value based on averaging of the texture map over the preimage. Note that this method is imperfect too. For the example in Figure 7.18, we would assign an average shade, but we would still not get the striped pattern of the texture. Ultimately, we still have aliasing defects due to the limited resolution of both the frame buffer and the texture map. These problems are most visible when there is a regular texture.

Now we can turn to the mapping problem. In computer graphics, most curved surfaces are represented parametrically. A point **p** on the surface is a function of

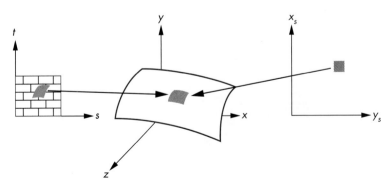

figure 7.17 Preimages of a pixel.

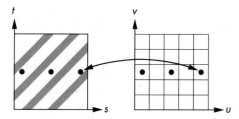

Figure 7.18 Aliasing in texture generation.

two parameters u and v. For each pair of values, we generate the point

$$\mathbf{p}(u, v) = \begin{bmatrix} x(u, v) \\ y(u, v) \\ z(u, v) \end{bmatrix}.$$

In Chapter 10, we study in detail the derivation of such surfaces. Given a parametric surface, we can often map a point in the texture map $T(s, t)$ to a point on the surface $\mathbf{p}(u, v)$ by a linear map of the form

$$u = as + bt + c,$$
$$v = ds + et + f.$$

As long as $ae \neq bd$, this mapping is invertible. Linear mapping makes it easy to map a texture to a group of parametric surface patches. For example, if, as shown in Figure 7.19, the patch determined by the corners (s_{min}, t_{min}) and (s_{max}, t_{max}) corresponds to the surface patch with corners (u_{min}, v_{min}) and (u_{max}, v_{max}), then the mapping is

$$u = u_{min} + \frac{s - s_{min}}{s_{max} - s_{min}}(u_{max} - u_{min}),$$

$$v = v_{min} + \frac{t - t_{min}}{t_{max} - t_{min}}(v_{max} - v_{min}).$$

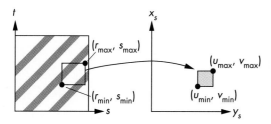

Figure 7.19 Linear texture mapping.

This mapping is easy to apply, but it does not take into account the curvature of the surface. Equal-sized texture patches must be stretched to fit over the surface patch.

Another approach to the mapping problem is to use a two-part mapping. The first step maps the texture to a simple three-dimensional intermediate surface, such as a sphere, cylinder, or cube. In the second step, the intermediate surface containing the mapped texture is mapped to the surface being rendered. This two-step mapping process can be applied to surfaces defined in either geometric or parametric coordinates. The following example is essentially the same in either system.

Suppose that our texture coordinates vary over the unit square, and that we use the surface of a cylinder of height h and radius r as our intermediate object, as shown in Figure 7.20. Points on the cylinder are given by the parametric equations

$$x = r \cos(2\pi u),$$
$$y = r \sin(2\pi u),$$
$$z = v/h,$$

as u and v vary over $(0,1)$. Hence, we can use the mapping

$$s = u,$$
$$t = v.$$

By using only the curved part of the cylinder, and not the top and bottom, we were able to map the texture without distorting its shape. However, if we map to a closed object, such as a sphere, we must introduce shape distortion. This problem is similar to the problem of creating a two-dimensional image of the earth for a map. If you look at the various maps of the earth in an atlas, all distort shapes and distances. Both texture-mapping and map-design techniques must choose among a variety of representations, based on where we wish to place the distortion. For example, the familiar Mercator projection puts the most

Figure 7.20 Texture mapping with a cylinder.

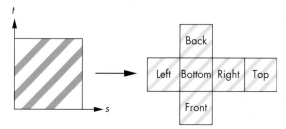

Figure 7.21 Texture mapping with a box.

distortion at the poles. If we use a sphere of radius r as the intermediate surface, a possible mapping is

$$x = r\cos(2\pi u),$$
$$y = r\sin(2\pi u)\cos(2\pi v),$$
$$z = r\sin(2\pi u)\sin(2\pi v).$$

We can also use a rectangular box, as shown in Figure 7.21. Here, we map the texture to a box that can be unraveled, like a cardboard packing box. This mapping often is used with environmental maps (Section 7.7).

The second step is to map the texture values on the intermediate object to the desired surface. Figure 7.22 shows three possible strategies. In Figure 7.22(a), we take the texture value at a point on the intermediate object, go from this point in the direction of the normal until we intersect the object, and then place the texture value at the point of intersection. We could also reverse this method, starting at a point on the surface of the object and going in the direction of the normal at this point until we intersect the intermediate object, where we obtain the texture value, as shown in Figure 7.22(b). A third option, if we know the center of the object, is to draw a line from the center through a point on the object, and to calculate the intersection of this line with the intermediate surface, as shown in Figure 7.22(c). The texture at the point of intersection with the intermediate object is assigned to the corresponding point on the desired object.

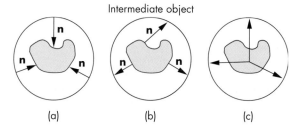

Figure 7.22 Second mapping. (a) Using the normal from the intermediate surface. (b) Using the normal from the object surface. (c) Using the center of the object.

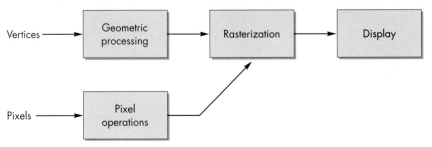

Figure 7.23 Pixel and geometric pipelines.

7.6.2 Texture Mapping in OpenGL

OpenGL supports a variety of texture-mapping options. The first version of OpenGL contained the functionality to map one- and two-dimensional textures to one- through four-dimensional graphical objects. Mapping of three-dimensional textures now is part of OpenGL and is supported in high-end hardware. Because of the many options and parameters, we focus on mapping two-dimensional textures to surfaces.

OpenGL's texture maps rely on its pipeline architecture. We have seen that there are actually two parallel piplines: the geometric pipeline and the pixel pipleine. The pipelines merge during rendering, as shown in Figure 7.23. For texture mapping, the key issue is that any image that emerges from the pixel pipeline can be mapped onto geometric primitives. This architecture determines the type of texture mapping that is supported. In particular, texture mapping is done as primitives are rasterized. This process maps three-dimensional points to locations (pixels) on the display. Each fragment that is generated is tested for visibility (with the z-buffer) and is shaded if visible. We can think of texture mapping as a part of the shading process. Vertices are mapped to texture coordinates, and the required texture values can then be obtained by interpolation in a manner similar to the way that vertex colors are mapped across polygons.

Two-dimensional texture mapping starts with an array of texels. Suppose that we have a 512×512 image my_texels that was generated by our program, or perhaps was read in from a file into an array

```
GLubyte my_texels[512][512];
```

We specify that this array is to be used as a two-dimensional texture (usually as part of our initialization) by

```
glTexImage2D(GL_TEXTURE_2D, 0, 3, 512, 512, 0,
             GL_RGB, GL_UNSIGNED_BYTE, my_texels);
```

More generally, two-dimensional textures are specified through the function

```
glTexImage2D(GL_TEXTURE_2D, level, components, width, height,
             border, format, type, tarray);
```

The texture pattern is stored in the `width` × `height` array `tarray`. The format of this image is described by the next two parameters. The value `components` is the number (1 through 4) of color components (RGBA) that we wish to affect with the map. These parameters are the same as the parameters we used to describe how pixel arrays are stored in processor memory for reading and writing with `glReadPixels` and `glWritePixels`. This similarity is expected as arrays of texels start in processor memory as arrays of pixels that are moved through the pixel pipeline. However, the pixels that move through the pixel pipeline as a result of the execution of the function `glTexImage2D` end up in texture memory, which is not part of the frame buffer. In modern graphics systems, the three types of memory—processor memory, the frame buffer, and texture memory—are often physically separate, each with its own characteristics and limitations.

The parameters `level` and `border` give us fine control over how texture is handled. We defer our discussion of these parameters. We must also enable texture mapping, as we do other options, through

```
glEnable(GL_TEXTURE_2D);
```

The second part of setting up a texture mapping is to specify how the texture is mapped onto a geometric object. OpenGL uses two coordinates, s and t, both of which range over the interval $(0.0, 1.0)$ over the texture image. For our example, the value $(0.0, 0.0)$ corresponds to the point `my_texels[0][0]`, and $(1.0, 1.0)$ corresponds to the point `my_texels[511][511]`, as shown in Figure 7.24. Any values of s and t in the unit interval correspond to a unique texel. OpenGL provides two options for how to deal with values outside the unit interval, which we shall discuss shortly.

OpenGL leaves the mapping of texture coordinates to vertices to the application by having the values of s and t as part of the OpenGL state. These values are assigned by the function

```
glTexCoord2f(s,t);
```

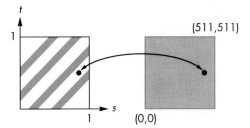

Figure 7.24 Mapping to texture coordinates.

Thus, we use a mechanism similar to what we have used for colors and normal vectors. The renderer uses the present texture coordinates when processing a vertex. If we want to change the texture coordinate assigned to a vertex, we must set the texture coordinate before we specify the vertex. For example, if we want to assign our texture to a quadrilateral, then we use code such as

```
glBegin{GL_QUAD);
 glTexCoord2f(0.0,0.0);
 glVertex2f(x1, y1, z1);
 glTexCoord2f(1.0,0.0);
 glVertex2f(x2, y2, z2);
 glTexCoord2f(1.0,1.0);
 glVertex2f(x3, y3, z3);
 glTexCoord2f(0.0,1.0);
 glVertex2f(x4, y4, z4);
glEnd();
```

We also could set new normals or colors before we specify each vertex. OpenGL then uses bilinear interpolation to find the texture coordinates for the interior points of a polygon, just as it uses bilinear interpolation to determine interior colors from vertex colors.

In the example shown in Figure 7.25(a), we use the whole texture on a rectangle. If we used only part of the range of s and t, for example (0.0, 0.5), we would use only part of my_texels for the texture map, and would get an image like that in Figure 7.25(b). OpenGL interpolates s and t across the quadrilateral, then maps these values back to the appropriate texel in my_texels. The quadrilateral example is simple because there is an obvious map of texture coordinates to vertices. For general polygons, the application programmer must decide how to assign the texture coordinates. Figure 7.26 shows a few of the possibilities with the same texture map. Figures 7.26(a) and (b) use the same triangle but different texture coordinates. Note the effects of the bilinear interpolation and how quadrilaterals are treated as two triangles as they are rendered in Figure 7.26(c).

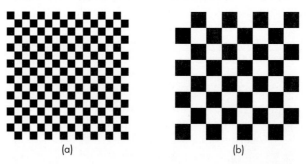

(a)   (b)

figure 7.25 Mapping of a checkerboard texture to a quadrilateral. (a) Using the entire texel array. (b) Using part of the texel array.

Figure 7.26 Mapping of texture to polygons. (a and b) Mapping of a checkerboard texture to a triangle. (c) Mapping of a checkerboard texture to a trapezoid.

The basics of OpenGL texture mapping are simple: Specify an array of colors for the texture values, then assign texture coordinates. Unfortunately, there are a few nasty details that we must discuss before we can use texture effectively. Solving the resulting problems involves making trade-offs between quality of the images and efficiency.

One problem is what happens if we specify a value of s or t outside of the range $(0.0, 1.0)$. Generally, we want the texture either to repeat if we specify values outside this range or to clamp the values to 0.0 or 1.0—that is, we want to use the values at 0.0 and 1.0 for values below and above the interval $(0.0, 1.0)$, respectively. For repeated textures, we set these parameters via

```
glTexParameteri(GL_TEXTURE_WRAP_S, GL_REPEAT);
```

For t, we use GL_TEXTURE_WRAP_T; for clamping, we use GL_CLAMP.

Aliasing is a major problem. When we map texture coordinates to the array of texels, we rarely get a point that corresponds to the center of a texel. One option is to use the value of the texel that is closest to the one computed by the bilinear interpolation. This option is known as **point sampling** but, as we shall see in Section 7.11 is most subject to visible aliasing errors. A better strategy, although one that requires more work, is to use a weighted average of a group of texels in the neighborhood of the texel determined by point sampling. This option is known as **linear filtering**. Thus, in Figure 7.27 we see the location within a texel that is given by bilinear interpolation from the texture coordinates at the vertices and the four texels that would be used to obtain a smoother value. If we are using linear filtering, there is a problem at the edges of the texel array as we need additional texels values outside the array. We can get around this problem by adding a 1-texel-wide border around the the texture and setting border in glTexImage2d to 1. Thus, if there is a border, then the texture array consists of $(2^m + 1) \times (2^n + 1)$ texels.

Figure 7.27 Texels used with linear filtering.

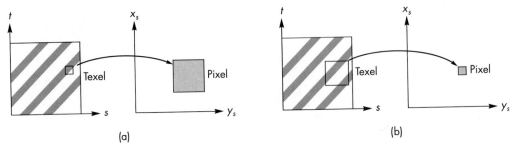

Figure 7.28 Mapping texels to pixels. (a) Magnification. (b) Minification.

There is a further complication, however, in deciding how to use the texels values to obtain a texture value. The size of the pixel that we are trying to color on the screen may be smaller or larger than one texel, as shown in Figure 7.28.

In the first case, the texel is larger than one pixel (**magnification**); in the second, it is smaller (**minification**). In both cases, the fastest strategy is to use the value of the nearest point sampling. We can specify this option for both magnification and minification of textures by

```
glTexParameteri(GL_TEXTURE_2D,GL_TEXTURE_MAG_FILTER,GL_NEAREST);
glTexParameteri(GL_TEXTURE_2D,GL_TEXTURE_MIN_FILTER,GL_NEAREST);
```

Alternatively, we can use filtering to obtain a smoother, less aliased image if we specify GL_LINEAR instead of GL_NEAREST.

OpenGL has another way to deal with the minification problem; it is called **mipmapping**. For objects that project to an area of screen space that is small compared with the size of the texel array, we do not need the resolution of the original texel array. OpenGL allows us to create a series of texture arrays at reduced sizes; it will then automatically use the appropriate size. For a 64×64 original array, we can set up 32×32, 16×16, 8×8, 4×4, 2×2, and 1×1 arrays through the GLU function:

```
gluBuild2DMipmaps(GL_TEXTURE_2D,3,64,64,GL_RGB,GL_UNSIGNED_BYTE,
                                        my_texels);
```

We can also set up the maps directly using the level parameter in glTexImage2D. This parameter is the level in the mipmap hierarchy for the specified texture array. Thus, level 0 refers to the original image, level 1 to the image at half resolution, and so on. However, we can give a pointer to any image in different calls to glTexImage2D and thus can have entirely different images used at different levels of the mipmap hierarchy. These mipmaps are invoked automatically if we specify

```
glTexParameteri(GL_TEXTURE_2D,
    GL_TEXTURE_MIN_FILTER,GL_NEAREST_MIPMAP_NEAREST);
```

This option asks OpenGL to use point sampling with the best mipmap. We can also do filtering within the best mipmap (GL_NEAREST_MIPMAP_LINEAR), point sampling using linear filtering between mipmaps (GL_LINEAR_MIPMAP_NEAREST), or both filters (GL_LINEAR_MIPMAP_LINEAR). Figure 7.29 shows the differences in mapping a texture using the nearest texel, linear filtering, and mipmapping, both with using the nearest texel and with linear filtering. The object is a quadrilateral that appears almost as a triangle when shown in perspective. The texture is a series of black and white lines that is applied so that the lines converge at the far side of the quadrilateral. Note that this texture map, because of its regularity, shows dramatic aliasing effects. The use of the nearest texel shows moiré patterns and jaggedness in the lines. Using linear filtering makes the lines smoother, but there are still clear moiré patterns. The texels between the black and white stripes are

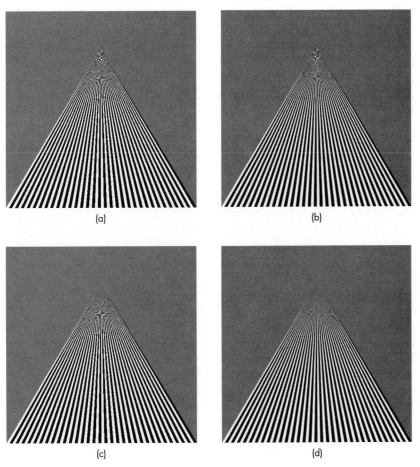

(a)

(b)

(c)

(d)

Figure 7.29 Texture mapping to a quadrilateral using (a) point sampling, (b) linear filtering, (c) mipmapping point sampling, (d) mipmapping linear filtering.

gray because of the filtering. Mipmapping also replaces many of the blacks and whites of the two-color patterns with grays that are the average of the two color values. For the parts of the object that are furthest from the viewer, the texels are gray and blend with the background. The mipmapped texture using the nearest texel in the proper mipmap still shows the jaggedness that is smoothed out when we use linear filtering with the mipmap.

A final issue in using textures in OpenGL is the interaction between texture and shading. For RGB colors, there are two options. The texture can modulate the shade that we would have assigned without texture mapping by multiplying the color components of the texture by the color components from the shader. Modulation is the default mode; it can be set by

```
glTexEnvi(GL_TEX_ENV,GL_TEX_ENV_MODE,GL_MODULATE);
```

If we replace `GL_MODULATE` by `GL_DECAL`, the color of the texture determines the color of the object completely—a technique called **decaling**.

Proper texture mapping also depends on what type of projection is used. Normally, OpenGL uses linear interpolation in screen space to find a texture value. For orthogonal projections the linear map is correct, but it is not correct for perspective projections because of the nonlinear depth scaling. We can ask OpenGL to employ a better interpolation scheme (if one is supported by the implementation) at a time penalty by

```
glHint(GL_PERSPECTIVE_CORRECTION, GL_NICEST);
```

OpenGL provides a number of advanced texture features. OpenGL can also generate texture coordinates automatically with the function `glTexGen`. This function allows a few interesting options. We can form linear maps from geometric coordinates to texture coordinates. One of the important applications of this technique is in terrain generation and mapping. We can map surface features (textures) directly onto a three-dimensional mesh. We can also use a spherical mapping, as we discussed for two-step texture generation. Texture maps can be carried out either in eye or object coordinates, so we can fix the texture to the object, or, in the former case, we can have the texture remain fixed as the object moves, creating the illusion of the object moving through a texture field.

Texture coordinates are stored as four-dimensional arrays, as are vertices, and are transformed by a 4×4 **texture matrix**. This matrix is initially set to an identity matrix and is manipulated in the same manner as the model-view and projection matrices. We first need to select as the matrix to be manipulated by

```
glMatrixMode(GL_TEXTURE);
```

We can use this matrix to scale and orient textures and to create effects in which the texture moves with the object, the camera, or the lights.

7.6.3 Texture Objects

In OpenGL, there is a single *present texture* that is part of the OpenGL state. Thus, if we need multiple textures—for example, if we want to apply different textures to different surfaces in the same scene—we can use `glTexImage2D` each time that another texture is used. This process is very inefficient as each time `glTexImage2D` is executed, another texture image is loaded into texture memory, replacing the texels that were already there. Even if there is sufficient texture memory (and texture mapping can require a great deal of memory), this problem still exists.

OpenGL 1.1 introduced **texture objects** that allow the application program to define objects that consist of the texture array and the various texture parameters that control its application to surfaces. As long as there is sufficient memory to retain them, these objects reside in texture memory even though the present texture changes. If there is not sufficient texture memory, the application can prioritize the texture objects so as to control which ones are removed from memory first.

7.6.4 Multitexturing

Thus far, we have looked at applying a single texture to an object. However, there are many surface rendering effects that can best be implemented by more than a single application of a texture. For example, suppose that we want to apply a shadow, to an object whose surface shades are themselves determined by a texture map. We could use a texture map for the shadow, but if there were only a single texture application, this method would not work.

If, instead, we have multiple texture units as in Figure 7.30, then we can accomplish this task. Each unit acts as an independent texturing stage starting with the results of the previous stage. This facility is supported in recent versions of OpenGL.

7.6.5 Texture Generation

One of the most powerful uses of texture mapping is to provide detail without generating numerous geometric objects. High-end graphics systems can do three-dimensional texture mapping in real time; for every frame, the texture is mapped to objects as part of the rendering process at almost the same rate as non-texture-mapped objects are processed. Graphics boards for personal computers now contain a significant amount of texture memory and allow game developers to use texture mapping to create complex animated environments.

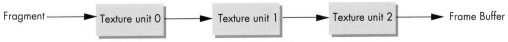

Figure 7.30 Sequence of texture units.

Figure 7.31 Texture generation.

If, for example, we want to simulate grass in a scene, we can texture map an image of grass that we might have obtained by, say, scanning a photograph, faster than we can generate two- or three-dimensional objects that look like grass. In mapping applications, rather than generating realistic surface detail for terrain, we can digitize a real map, and can paint it on a three-dimensional surface model by texture mapping.

We can also look for procedural methods for determining texture patterns. Of particular interest are patterns that we see in nature, such as the textures of sand, grass, or minerals. These textures show both structure (regular patterns) and considerable randomness. Most approaches to generating such textures algorithmically start with a random-number generator and filter its output as shown in Figure 7.31. An ideal random-number generator produces a sequence of values that are statistically uncorrelated, or **white noise**. The filter correlates successive noise values; by controlling the filter, we can simulate various patterns. We can also design random-number generators to create samples of textures directly.

Researchers have applied such random techniques successfully to create three-dimensional textures. Although the generation of a three-dimensional texture field $T(s, t, r)$ is a direct extension of two-dimensional texture-generation techniques, there are practical advantages to using three-dimensional textures. Most important is that, by associating each (s, t, r) value directly with an (x, y, z) point, we can avoid the mapping problem entirely. The user needs only to define a function $T(s, t, r)$ with the desired properties. Conceptually, this process is similar to sculpting the three-dimensional object from a solid block whose volume is colored by the specified texture. This technique has been used to generate objects that look as if they have been carved from solid rock. The texture-generation process defines a function $T(s, t, r)$ that displays the graininess we associate with materials such as marble and granite.

7.7 Environmental Maps

Highly reflective surfaces are characterized by specular reflections that mirror the environment. Consider, for example, a shiny metal ball in the middle of a room. We can see the contents of the room, in a distorted form, on the surface of the ball. Obviously, this is a global effect, as we cannot shade the ball correctly without knowing about the rest of the scene. A physically based rendering method, such as a ray tracer, can produce this kind of image, although

Figure 7.32 Scene with a mirror.

in practice ray-tracing calculations usually are too time-consuming to be practical for real-time applications.

We can extend our mapping techniques to obtain an image that approximates the desired reflection by extending texture maps to **environmental** or **reflection maps**.

The basic idea is simple. Consider the mirror in Figure 7.32, which we can look at as a polygon whose surface is a highly specular material. From the point of view of a renderer, the position of the viewer and the normal to the polygon are known, so that the angle of reflection is given, as in Chapter 6, by

$$\mathbf{r} = 2(\mathbf{v} \cdot \mathbf{n})\mathbf{n} - \mathbf{v}.$$

If we follow along this angle until we intersect the environment, we obtain the shade that is reflected in the mirror. Of course, this shade is the result of a shading process that involves the light sources and materials in the scene. We can obtain an approximately correct value of this shade as part of a two-step rendering pass, similar in some respects to the two-step texture mapping process that we outlined in Section 7.6. In the first pass, we render the scene without the mirror polygon, with the camera placed at the center of the mirror pointed in the direction of the normal of the mirror. Thus, we obtain an image of the objects in the environment as "seen" by the mirror. This image is not quite correct (Exercise 7.3) but is usually good enough. We can then use this image to obtain the shades (texture values) to place on the mirror polygon for the second normal rendering with the mirror placed back in the scene.

There are two difficulties with this approach. First, the images that we obtain in the first pass are not quite correct because they have been formed without one of the objects—the mirror—in the environment. Second, we must confront the mapping issue. Onto what surface should we project the scene in the first pass, and where should we place the camera? Potentially we want all the information in the scene as we may want to do something like have our mirror move so that we should see different parts of the environment on successive frames, and thus a simple projection will not suffice.

There have been a variety of approaches to this projection problem. The classic approach is to project the environment onto a sphere centered at the center of

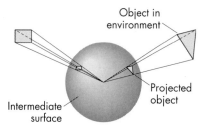

Figure 7.33 Mapping of the environment.

projection. In Figure 7.33, we see some polygons that are outside the sphere and their projections on the sphere. Note that a viewer located at the center of the sphere cannot tell whether she is seeing the polygons in their original positions or their projections on the sphere. This illusion is similar to what we see in a planetarium where the "stars" that appear to be an infinite distance away are actually the projection of lights onto a hemisphere.

In the original version of environmental mapping the surface of the sphere was then converted to a rectangle using lines of longitude and latitude for the mapping. Although conceptually simple, there are problems at the poles where the shape distortion becomes infinite. Computationally, this mapping does not preserve areas very well and requires a lot of computation of trigonometric functions.

OpenGL supports a variation of this method called **spherical mapping**. The application program supplies a circular image that is the orthographic projection of the sphere onto which the environment has been mapped. The advantage of this method is that the mapping from the reflection vector to two-dimensional texture coordinates on this circle is simple and can be implemented in either hardware or software. The difficult part is obtaining the required circular image. It can be approximated by taking a perspective projection with a very wide-angle lens or by remapping some other type of projection, such as the box projection that we discuss next. If we have the image in texture memory through glTexImage2D, OpenGL will generate the texture coordinates automatically by

```
glTexGeni(GL_S, GL_TEXTURE_GEN_MODE, GL_SPHERE_MAP);
glTexGeni(GL_T, GL_TEXTURE_GEN_MODE, GL_SPHERE_MAP);

glEnable(GL_TEXTURE_GEN_S);
glEnable(GL_TEXTURE_GEN_T);
```

If we want to compute an environmental map using the graphics system, we prefer to use the standard projections that are supported by the graphics systems. For an environment such as a room, the natural intermediate object is a box. We compute six projections, corresponding to the walls, floor, and ceiling, using six virtual cameras located at the center of the box, each pointing in a different

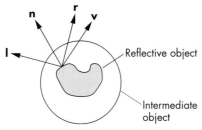

Figure 7.34 Mapping from the intermediate surface.

direction. At this point, we can treat the six images as a single environmental map and derive the textures from it as in Figure 7.34. Color Plate 29 shows one frame from Pixar Animation Studio's Geri's Game. A reflection map was computed on a box (Color Plate 30) and then mapped to Geri's glasses.

We could also compute the six images in our program and use them to compute the circular image required by OpenGL's spherical maps. Note that all these methods can suffer from geometric distortions and aliasing problems. In addition, unless the application recomputes the environmental maps, they are not correct if the viewer moves.

These techniques are one example of **multipass rendering** (or **multirendering**) where in order to compute a single image, we compute multiple images, each using the rendering pipeline. Multipass methods are becoming increasingly more important as the power of graphics cards has increased to the point that we can render a scene multiple times from different perspectives in less time than is needed for reasonable refresh rates. In Section 7.10, we shall introduce the accumulation buffer that supports multirendering and some techniques that use it.

7.8 Bump Maps

Returning to our example of creating an image of an orange, we can take a picture of a real orange, and we can apply it as a texture map to a surface. If we move the lights or rotate the object, however, we immediately notice that we have the image of a model of an orange, rather than the image of a real orange. The problem is that a real orange is characterized primarily by small variations in its surface, rather than by variations in its color, and the former are not captured by texture mapping. The technique of **bump mapping** varies the apparent shape of the surface by perturbing the normal vectors as the surface is rendered; the colors that are generated by shading then show a variation in the surface properties.

We start with the observation that the normal at a point on the surface characterizes the shape of the surface at this point. If we perturb the normal at each point on the surface by a small amount, then we create a surface with small variations. If this perturbation to the normal can be applied only during the rendering, we can use a smooth model of the surface, but we can render it in a way that gives the appearance of a complex surface. Because the perturbations are to the normal vectors, the shading calculations are correct for the altered surface.

We could perturb the normals in many ways; the following procedure for parametric surfaces is an efficient one. Let $\mathbf{p}(u, v)$ be a point on a parametric surface. The unit normal at that point is given by the cross product of the partial derivative vectors:

$$\mathbf{n} = \frac{\mathbf{p}_u \times \mathbf{p}_v}{|\mathbf{p}_u \times \mathbf{p}_v|},$$

where

$$\mathbf{p}_u = \begin{bmatrix} \frac{\partial x}{\partial u} \\ \frac{\partial y}{\partial u} \\ \frac{\partial z}{\partial u} \end{bmatrix}, \qquad \mathbf{p}_v = \begin{bmatrix} \frac{\partial x}{\partial v} \\ \frac{\partial y}{\partial v} \\ \frac{\partial z}{\partial v} \end{bmatrix}.$$

Suppose that we displace the surface in the normal direction by a function called the **bump** or **displacement function**, $d(u, v)$, which is assumed known and small ($|d(u, v)| \ll 1$):

$$\mathbf{p}' = \mathbf{p} + d(u, v)\mathbf{n}.$$

We would prefer not to displace the surface; we just want to make it look as though we have displaced it. We can achieve the desired look by altering the normal $\mathbf{n}$, instead of $\mathbf{p}$, and using the perturbed normal in our shading calculations.

The normal at the perturbed point $\mathbf{p}'$ is given by the cross product

$$\mathbf{n}' = \mathbf{p}'_u \times \mathbf{p}'_v.$$

We can compute the two partial derivatives by differentiating the equation for $\mathbf{p}'$, obtaining

$$\mathbf{p}'_u = \mathbf{p}_u + \frac{\partial d}{\partial u}\mathbf{n} + d(u, v)\mathbf{n}_u,$$

$$\mathbf{p}'_v = \mathbf{p}_v + \frac{\partial d}{\partial v}\mathbf{n} + d(u, v)\mathbf{n}_v.$$

If d is small, we can neglect the term on the right of these two equations, and can take their cross product, noting that $\mathbf{n} \times \mathbf{n} = 0$, to obtain the perturbed normal

$$\mathbf{n}' = \mathbf{n} + \frac{\partial d}{\partial u}\mathbf{n} \times \mathbf{p}_v + \frac{\partial d}{\partial v}\mathbf{n} \times \mathbf{p}_u.$$

This displacement (the difference between the original and perturbed normals) must lie in the tangent plane at $\mathbf{p}$. To apply the bump map, we need two arrays that contain the values of $\partial d / \partial u$ and $\partial d / \partial v$. These arrays can be precomputed by methods similar to those used for texture generation. The normal can then be perturbed during the shading process.

One method to obtain these perturbation arrays is to use an image processing method directly on the function $d(u, v)$. Suppose that we have a sampled version of $d(u, v)$ as an array of pixels $\mathbf{D} = [d_{ij}]$. The required partial derivatives are proportional to the difference between adjacent elements in the array

$$\frac{\partial d}{\partial u} \propto d_{ij} - d_{i-1,j},$$

$$\frac{\partial d}{\partial v} \propto d_{ij} - d_{i,j-1}.$$

These computations can be looked at as taking the differences between an image $\mathbf{D}$ and shifted versions of itself. Although we could do this calculation within the application, many graphics systems support these operations directly in hardware. We can also use a multipass approach to bump mapping called **embossing** that can be done with three renderings. Both these approaches makes use of the accumulation buffer that we shall discuss in Section 7.10.

7.9 Compositing Techniques

In Chapter 6, we developed a model for dealing with transparent surfaces. That model is most appropriate for use with ray tracing, which is a time-consuming rendering technique. OpenGL provides an alternate mechanism, through **alpha (α) blending**, that can, among other effects, create images with transparent objects. The **alpha channel** is the fourth color in RGBA (or RGBα) color mode. Like the other colors, the application program can control the value of A (or α) for each pixel. However, in RGBA mode, if blending is enabled, the value of α controls how the RGB values are written into the frame buffer. Because fragments from multiple objects can contribute to the color of the same pixel, we say that these objects are **blended** or **composited** together.

7.9.1 Opacity and Blending

The **opacity** of a surface is a measure of how much light penetrates through that surface. An opacity of 1 ($\alpha = 1$) corresponds to a completely opaque surface that blocks all light incident on it. A surface with an opacity of 0 is transparent: All light passes through it. The **transparency** or **translucency** of a surface with opacity α is given by $1 - \alpha$.

Consider the three uniformly lit polygons shown in Figure 7.35. Assume that the middle polygon is opaque, and the front polygon, nearest to the viewer, is transparent. If the front polygon were perfectly transparent, the viewer would

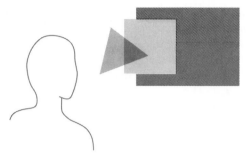

Figure 7.35 Translucent and opaque polygons.

see only the middle polygon. However, if the front polygon is only partially opaque (partially transparent), similar to colored glass, the color that viewer sees is a blending of the colors of the front and middle polygon. Because the middle polygon is opaque, the viewer does not see the back polygon. If the front polygon is red and the middle is blue, she sees magenta, due to the blending of the colors. If we let the middle polygon be only partially opaque, she sees the blending of the colors of all three polygons.

In computer graphics, we usually render polygons one at a time into the frame buffer. Consequently, if we want to use blending or compositing, we need a way to apply opacity as part of the rendering process. We can use the notion of source and destination pixels, just as we used source and destination bits in Section 7.3. As a polygon is processed, pixel-sized fragments are computed and, if they are visible, are assigned colors based on the shading model in use. Until now, we have used the color of a fragment—as computed by the shading model and by any mapping techniques—to replace the color of the pixel in the frame buffer at the location in screen coordinates of the fragment. If we regard the fragment as the source pixel and the frame-buffer pixel as the destination, we can combine these values in various ways. The α channel is one way of controlling the blending on a pixel-by-pixel basis. Combining the colors of polygons is similar to joining two pieces of colored glass into a single piece of glass that has a higher opacity and a color different from either of the original pieces.

If we represent the source and destination pixels with the four-element (RGBα) arrays

$$\mathbf{s} = [\, s_r \quad s_g \quad s_b \quad s_a \,],$$
$$\mathbf{d} = [\, d_r \quad d_g \quad d_b \quad d_a \,],$$

then a compositing operation replaces $\mathbf{d}$ with

$$\mathbf{d}' = [\, b_r s_r + c_r d_r \quad b_g s_g + c_g d_g \quad b_b s_b + c_b d_b \quad b_a s_a + c_a d_a \,].$$

The arrays of constants $\mathbf{b} = [\, b_r \quad b_g \quad b_b \quad b_a \,]$, $\mathbf{c} = [\, c_r \quad c_g \quad c_b \quad c_a \,]$, are the **source** and **destination blending factors**, respectively. As occurs with RGB colors, a value of α over 1.0 is limited (**clamped**) to the maximum of 1.0, and negative values are clamped to 0.0. We can choose both the values of α and the method of combining source and destination values to achieve a variety of effects.

7.9.2 Image Compositing

The most straightforward use of α blending is to combine and display several images that exist as pixel maps, or equivalently, as sets of data that have been rendered independently. In this case, we can regard each image as a radiant object that contributes equally to the final image. Usually, we wish to keep our RGB colors between 0 and 1 in the final image, without having to clamp those values greater than 1. Hence, we can either scale the values of each image or use the source and destination blending factors.

Suppose that we have n images that should contribute equally to the final display. At a given pixel, image i has components $\mathbf{C}_i\alpha_i$. Here, we are using $\mathbf{C}_i$ to denote the color triplet (R_i, B_i, G_i). If we replace $\mathbf{C}_i$ by $\frac{1}{n}\mathbf{C}_i$ and α_i by $\frac{1}{n}$, then we can simply add each image into the frame buffer (assuming the frame buffer is initialized to black with an $\alpha = 0$). Alternately, we can use a source blending factor of $\frac{1}{n}$ by setting the α value for each pixel in each image to be $\frac{1}{n}$, and using 1 for the destination blending factor and α for the source blending factor. Although these two methods produce the same image, if the hardware supports compositing, the second may be more efficient. Note that if n is large, blending factors of the form $\frac{1}{n}$ can lead to significant loss of color resolution. We address this problem in Section 7.10.

7.9.3 Blending and Compositing in OpenGL

The mechanics of blending in OpenGL are straightforward. We enable blending by

```
glEnable(GL_BLEND);
```

Then we set up the desired source and destination factors by

```
glBlendFunc(source_factor, destination factor);
```

OpenGL has a number of blending factors defined, including the values 1 (GL_ONE) and 0 (GL_ZERO), the source α and $1 - \alpha$ (GL_SRC_ALPHA and GL_ONE_MINUS_SRC_ALPHA), and the destination α and $1 - \alpha$ (GL_DST_ALPHA and GL_ONE_MINUS_DST_ALPHA). The application program specifies the desired options and then uses RGBA color.

The major difficulty with compositing is that the order in which we render the polygons affects the image. For example, many applications use the source α

as the source blending factor and $1 - \alpha$ for the destination factor. The resulting color and opacity are

$$(R_{d'}, G_{d'}, B_{d'}, \alpha_{d'}) = (\alpha_s R_s + (1 - \alpha_s) R_d, \alpha_s G + (1 - \alpha_s) G_d, \alpha_s B_s$$
$$+ (1 - \alpha_s) B_d, \alpha_s \alpha_d + (1 - \alpha_s) \alpha_d).$$

This formula ensures that both transparent and opaque polygons are handled correctly and that neither colors nor opacities can saturate. However, the resulting color and α values depend on the order in which the polygons are rendered. Consequently, unlike in most OpenGL programs, where the user does not have to worry about the order in which polygons are rasterized, to get a desired effect we must now control this order within the application.

A more subtle but visibly apparent problem occurs when we combine opaque and translucent objects in a scene. Normally, when we use blending, we do not enable hidden-surface removal because polygons behind any polygon already rendered would not be rasterized and thus would not contribute to the final image. In a scene with both opaque and transparent polygons, any polygon behind an opaque polygon should not be rendered, but translucent polygons in front of opaque polygons should be composited. There is a simple solution to this problem that does not require the application program to order the polygons. We can enable hidden-surface removal as usual and can make the z-buffer read-only for any polygon that is translucent. We do so by

```
glDepthMask(GL_FALSE);
```

When the depth buffer is read-only, a translucent polygon that lies behind any opaque polygon already rendered is discarded. A translucent polygon that lies in front of any polygon that has already been rendered is blended with the color of the polygons of which it is in front. However, because the z-buffer is read-only for this polygon, the depth values in the buffer are unchanged. Opaque polynomials set the depth mask to true and are rendered normally. Note that because the result of compositing depends on the order in which we composite individual elements, we may notice defects in images in which we render translucent polygons in an arbitrary order. If we are willing to sort the translucent polygons, then we can render all the opaque polygons first and then render the translucent polygons in a back-to-front order with the z-buffer in a read-only mode.

7.9.4 Antialiasing

One of the major uses of the α channel is for antialiasing. Because a line must have a finite width to be visible, the default width of a line that is rendered should be one pixel wide. We cannot produce a thinner line. Unless the line is horizontal or vertical, such a line partially covers a number of pixels in the frame buffer, as shown in Figure 7.36. Suppose that, as part of the geometric-processing stage of the rendering process, as we process a fragment, we set the α value for the corresponding pixel to be a number between 0 and 1 that is the amount of that

Figure 7.36 Raster line.

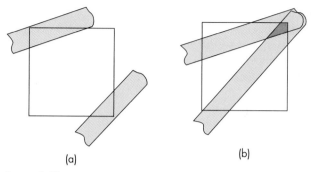

(a)   (b)

Figure 7.37 Fragments. (a) Nonoverlapping. (b) Overlapping.

pixel covered by the fragment. We can then use this α value to modulate the color as we render the fragment to the frame buffer. We can use a destination blending factor of $1 - \alpha$ and a source destination factor of α. However, if there is overlap of fragments within a pixel, then there are numerous possibilities, as we can see from Figure 7.37. In Figure 7.37(a), the fragments do not overlap; in Figure 7.37(b), they do overlap. Consider the problem from the perspective of a renderer that works one polygon a time. For our simple example, suppose that we start with an opaque background, and that the frame buffer starts with the background color C_0. We can set $\alpha_0 = 0$, because no part of the pixel has yet been covered with fragments from polygons. The first polygon is rendered. The color of the destination pixel is set to

$$\mathbf{C}_d = (1 - \alpha_1)\mathbf{C}_0 + \alpha_1\mathbf{C}_1,$$

and its α value is set to

$$\alpha_d = \alpha_1.$$

Thus, a fragment that covers the entire pixel ($\alpha_1 = 1$) will have its color assigned to the destination pixel, and the destination pixel will be opaque. If the background is black, the destination color will be $\alpha_1\mathbf{C}_1$. Now consider the fragment from the second polygon that subtends the same pixel. How we add in its color and α value depends on how we wish to interpret the overlap. If there is no overlap, we can assign the new color by blending the color of the destination with the color of fragment, resulting in the color and α:

$$\mathbf{C}_d = (1 - \alpha_2)((1 - \alpha_1)\mathbf{C}_0 + \alpha_1\mathbf{C}_1) + \alpha_2\mathbf{C}_2,$$
$$\alpha_d = \alpha_1 + \alpha_2.$$

This color is a blending of the two colors and does not need to be clamped. The resulting value of α represents the new fraction of the pixel that is covered. However, the resulting color is affected by the order in which the polygons are rendered. The more difficult questions are what to do if the fragments overlap and how to tell whether there is an overlap. One tactic is to take a probabilistic view. If fragment 1 occupies a fraction α_1 of the pixel, and fragment 2 occupies a fraction α_2 of the same pixel, and we have no other information about the location of the fragments within the pixel, then the average area of overlap is $\alpha_1\alpha_2$. We can represent the average case as shown in Figure 7.38. Hence, the new destination α should be

$$\alpha_d = \alpha_1 + \alpha_2 - \alpha_1\alpha_2.$$

How we should assign the color is a more complex problem, because we have to decide whether the second fragment is in front of the first or the first is in front of the second, or even whether the two should be blended. We can define an appropriate blending for whichever assumption we wish to make. Note that, in a pipeline renderer, polygons can be generated in an order that has nothing to do with their distances from the viewer. However, if we couple α blending with hidden-surface removal, we can use the depth information to make front-versus-back decisions.

In OpenGL, we can invoke antialiasing without having the user program combine α values explicitly if we enable blending and smoothing for points, lines, or polygons; for example, we can use

```
glEnable(GL_POINT_SMOOTH);
glEnable(GL_LINE_SMOOTH);
glEnable(GL_POLYGON_SMOOTH);
glEnable(GL_BLEND);
glBlendFunc(GL_SRC_ALPHA, GL_ONE_MINUS_SRC_ALPHA);
```

to enable all three. There may be a considerable time penalty associated with antialiasing. Color Plate 8 shows OpenGL's antialiasing of polygons.

7.9.5 Back-to-Front and Front-to-Back Rendering

Although using the α channel gives us a way of creating the appearance of translucency, it is difficult to handle transparency in a physically correct manner without taking into account how an object is lit and what happens to rays and projectors that pass through translucent objects. In Figure 7.39 we can see several of the difficulties. We ignore refraction of light through translucent surfaces—an

Figure 7.38 Average overlap.

Figure 7.39 Scene with translucent objects.

effect than cannot be handled easily with a pipeline polygon renderer. Suppose that the rear polygon is opaque, but reflective, and that the two polygons closer to the viewer are translucent. By following various rays from the light source, we can see a number of possibilities. Some rays strike the rear polygon, and the corresponding pixels can be colored with the shade at the intersection of the projector and the polygon. For these rays, we should also distinguish between points illuminated directly by the light source, and points for which the incident light passes through one or both translucent polygons. For rays that pass through only one translucent surface, we have to adjust the color based on the color and opacity of the polygon. We should also add a term that accounts for the light striking the front polygon that is reflected toward the viewer. For rays passing through both translucent polygons, we have to consider their combined effect. For a pipeline renderer, the task is even more difficult—if not impossible—because we have to determine the contribution that each polygon makes as it is passed through the pipeline, rather than considering the contributions of all polygons to a given pixel at the same time.

7.9.6 Depth Cueing and Fog

Depth cueing is one the oldest techniques in three-dimensional graphics. Before raster systems became available, graphics systems could draw only lines. We created the illusion of depth by drawing lines farther from the viewer dimmer than lines closer to the viewer, a technique known as **depth cueing**. We can extend this idea to create the illusion of partially translucent space between the object and the viewer, by blending in a distance-dependent color as each fragment is processed.

Let f denote a **fog factor**, and let z be the distance between a fragment being rendered and the viewer. If the fragment has a color $\mathbf{C}_s$ and the fog is assigned a color $\mathbf{C}_f$, then we can use the color

$$\mathbf{C}_{s'} = f\mathbf{C}_s + (1 - f)\mathbf{C}_f$$

in the rendering. If f varies linearly between some minimum and maximum values, we have a depth-cueing effect. If this factor varies exponentially (Figure 7.40), then we get effects that look more like fog. OpenGL supports linear, exponential, and Gaussian fog densities. For example, in RGBA mode, we can set up a fog-density function $f = e^{-0.5z^2}$ by using the function calls

```
GLfloat fcolor[4] = {...};
glEnable(GL_FOG);
glFogf(GL_FOG_MODE, GL_EXP);
glFogf(GL_FOG_DENSITY, 0.5);
glFogfv(GL_FOG_COLOR, fcolor);
```

Note that the value of z is given in eye coordinates. Color Plate 11 uses fog to give the factory environment a more realistic (and gloomy) feel.

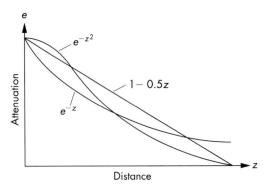

Figure 7.40 Fog density.

7.10 Multirendering and the Accumulation Buffer

There is one other buffer that, if present, is useful for many additional functions. Consider the problem of compositing a set of images each of whose color components is stored as one byte. If we simply add their RGB values into a typical 32-bit RGBA color buffer, many of the color components will overflow the values we can represent with a single byte. If the values in the buffer are clamped at their maximum value, then the resulting image will appear washed out as most of the colors in the composited image will tend toward white. If we try to avoid this problem by scaling the colors before they are added together, we will lose color resolution. Consider, for example, if we want to add together 64 images, each of which has 8 bits of resolution for each of its color components. To prevent limiting, we would have to scale each color component by a factor of 64 or, equivalently, lose 6 bits of accuracy on each color component.

A solution to this problem is to create a buffer, the **accumulation buffer**, that has the same spatial resolution as the frame buffer, but has greater depth resolution. We can think of it as a special type of color buffer whose components are stored as floating-point numbers. We can use the additional resolution to render successive images into one location while retaining numerical accuracy. There are many possible applications.

In OpenGL, we can clear the accumulation buffer as we do any other buffer, and then we can use the function glAccum either to add or to multiply values from the frame buffer into the accumulation buffer, or to copy the contents of the accumulation buffer back to a color buffer. For example, the code

```
glClear(GL_ACCUM_BUFFER_BIT);
for(i=0; i< num_mages; i++)
{
    glClear(GL_COLOR_BUFFER_BIT | GL_DEPTH_BUFFER_BIT);
    display_image(i);
```

```
        glAccum(GL_ACCUM, 1.0/ (float) num_images);
}
glAccum(GL_RETURN, 1.0);
```

uses the user's function `display_images` to generate a sequence of images into the write buffer. Each is added into or accumulated into the accumulation buffer, with a scale factor 1 over the number of images. At the end, the accumulated image is copied back to the write buffer. Note that we could have attempted the same task using blending, but we would have been forced to scale the colors in a lower-resolution buffer to avoid clamping.

7.10.1 Scene Antialiasing

One of the most important uses of the accumulation buffer is for antialiasing. Rather than antialiasing individual lines and polygons, a topic we shall consider in Chapter 8, we can antialias an entire scene using the accumulation buffer. The idea is that if we regenerate the same scene with all the objects, or the viewer, shifted slightly (less than one pixel), then we generate different aliasing artifacts. If we can average together the resulting images, the aliasing effects are smoothed out. In general, it is easier to shift, or **jitter**, the viewer, as we have to change only the parameters in `glPerspective` or `glOrtho`. However, we have to do a calculation in the program to determine how a small change in screen coordinates converts to a corresponding change in camera coordinates. In terms of sampling theory (Section 7.11), we have sampled the world at a finer resolution, or have **supersampled** it, and then have used an averaging filter to reconstruct the world from these samples.

7.10.2 Bump Mapping and Embossing

A surface with bumps has an embossed appearance, because we see shading differences due to the orientation of the bumps with respect to the light source. Surfaces that point toward the light source will appear brighter than surfaces pointing away from the light. The information to alter the surfaces is given by the relationship between the normal to the surface and the light vector. Although we could use the dot product between these two vectors, we can use the displacement matrix $\mathbf{D}$ in combination with the accumulation buffer.

Consider an image that is the difference between $\mathbf{D}$ and a version of it rotated in the direction of the light source. This image will have positive values where faces point toward the light source and negative values where faces point away from the light. We can use this idea as a part of the bump mapping process.

Suppose that we first render the scene into the accumulation buffer, using $\mathbf{D}$ as a texture map. Note that the texture will have a single color because each value of $\mathbf{D}$ has only one component. We then shift $\mathbf{D}$ in the direction of the light source and render the scene again with this rotated image as a texture, this time subtracting the results from the accumulation buffer. Finally, we render the image normally, that is without using $\mathbf{D}$, and add the result to the accumulation buffer.

Note that to do the shift of $\mathbf{D}$ for the second pass, we need the direction of the light source relative to the surface. However, we have the required information to create a homogeneous coordinate matrix that can be applied to each vertex. We use the normal at the vertex—which is part of the state—and one of the two vectors that are used to define the orientation of the displacement function $d(u, v)$. These texture coordinates lie in the plane of the surface and are tangent to the normal. Thus, we can use either one of them and its cross-product with the normal to obtain the three vectors that determine the required rotation matrix.

7.10.3 Image Processing

We can combine use of the accumulation buffer with pixel mapping to perform various image-processing operations. Suppose that we start with a discrete image. Perhaps this image was generated by a rendering, or perhaps we obtained it by digitizing a continuous image using a scanner. We can represent the image with an $N \times M$ matrix,

$$\mathbf{A} = [\, a_{ij} \,],$$

of scalar levels. If we process each color component of a color image independently, we can regard the entries in $\mathbf{A}$ as either individual color components or gray (luminance) levels. A **linear filter** produces a filtered matrix $\mathbf{B}$ whose elements are

$$b_{ij} = \sum_{k=-m}^{m} \sum_{l=-n}^{n} h_{kl}\, a_{i+k,j+l}.$$

We say that $\mathbf{B}$ is the result of **convolving** $\mathbf{A}$ with a filter matrix $\mathbf{H}$. In general, the values of m and n are small, and we can represent $\mathbf{H}$ by a small $(2m + 1 \times 2n + 1)$ **convolution matrix**.

We can view the filtering operation as shown in Figure 7.41 for $m = n = 1$. For each pixel in $\mathbf{A}$, we place the convolution matrix over a_{ij}, and take a weighted average of the surrounding points. The values in the matrix are the weights. For example, for $n = m = 1$, we can average each pixel with its four surrounding neighbors using the 3×3 matrix

$$\mathbf{H} = \frac{1}{5} \begin{bmatrix} 0 & 1 & 0 \\ 1 & 1 & 1 \\ 0 & 1 & 0 \end{bmatrix}.$$

Figure 7.41 Filtering and convolution.

This filter can be used for antialiasing. We can use more points and can weight the center more heavily with

$$\mathbf{H} = \frac{1}{16} \begin{bmatrix} 1 & 2 & 1 \\ 2 & 4 & 2 \\ 1 & 2 & 1 \end{bmatrix}.$$

Note that we must define a border around $\mathbf{A}$ if we want $\mathbf{B}$ to have the same dimensions. Other operations are possible with small matrices. For example, we can use the matrix

$$\mathbf{H} = \begin{bmatrix} 0 & -1 & 0 \\ -1 & 4 & -1 \\ 0 & -1 & 0 \end{bmatrix},$$

to detect changes in value or edges in the image. If the matrix $\mathbf{H}$ is $k \times k$, we can implement a filter by accumulating k^2 images in the accumulation buffer, each time adding in a shifted version of $\mathbf{A}$ using a different filter coefficient in glAccum.

7.10.4 Imaging Extensions

Although we can implement many image-processing operations using the accumulation buffer, if we look closely at the process, we can detect a major efficiency issue. If we are going to be transferring images to and from the accumulation buffer, we will be moving large amounts of data among processor memory, the frame buffer, and texture memory. These transfers will require packing and unpacking of the arrays, further slowing the process.

Our development of accumulation buffer techniques suggests two things. First, it should be fairly simple to add an API that supports standard image-processing operations. Second, it should not require large modifications to the graphics hardware to support imaging operations. In fact, both these issues have been addressed. From an OpenGL perspective, there is an **imaging subset** that defines an API for the most common image-processing operations. These operations are an **OpenGL extension** and are not required to be supported on all implementations. However, of all the OpenGL extensions, the imaging subset is the most commonly supported. Some of the facilities supported include histograms, convolutions (filters), color tables, and color transformations.

On the hardware side, we have seen that graphics hardware supports an imaging pipeline. Typically, this pipeline would be located within the graphics hardware, and this pipeline works on unpacked pixels. Hence, image data would need to be unpacked and transferred from the application only once. Operations such as table lookups, filtering, and color mapping can be accomplished without sending images back to processor memory until any sequence of imaging operations is complete.

7.10.5 Other Multipass Methods

We can also use the accumulation buffer for filtering in time and depth. For example, if we jitter an object and render it multiple times, leaving the positions of the other objects unchanged, we get dimmer copies of the jittered object in the final image. If the object is moved along a path, rather than randomly jittered, we see the trail of the object. This **motion-blur** effect is similar to the result of taking a photograph of a moving object using a long exposure time. We can adjust the constant in glAccum so as to render the final position of the object with greater opacity or to create the impression of speed differences.

We can use filtering in depth to create focusing effects. A real camera cannot produce an image with all objects in focus. Objects within a certain distance from the camera, the camera's **depth of field**, are in focus; objects outside it are out of focus and appear blurred. Computer graphics produces images with an infinite depth of field because we do not have to worry about the limitations of real lenses. Occasionally, however, we want to create an image that looks as though it were produced by a real camera, or to defocus part of a scene so as to emphasize the objects within a desired depth of field. Once more, we can use the accumulation buffer. This time, the trick is to move the viewer in a manner that leaves a particular plane fixed, as shown in Figure 7.42. Suppose that we

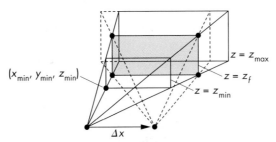

Figure 7.42 Depth-of-field jitter.

wish to keep the plane at $z = z_f$ in focus, and to leave the near ($z = z_{min}$) and far ($z = z_{max}$) clipping distances unchanged. If we use glFrustum, we specify the near clipping rectangle ($x_{min}, x_{max}, y_{min}, y_{max}$). If we move the viewer from the origin in the x direction by Δx, we must change x_{min} to

$$ x'_{min} = x_{min} + \frac{\Delta x}{z_f}(z_f - z_{near}). $$

Similar equations hold for x_{max}, y_{min}, and y_{max}. As we increase Δx and Δy, we create a narrower depth of field.

7.11 Sampling and Aliasing

We have seen a variety of applications in which the conversion from a continuous representation of an entity to a discrete approximation of that entity leads to visible errors in the display. We have used the term *aliasing* to characterize these errors. When we work with buffers, we are always working with digital images, and, if we are not careful, these errors can be extreme. In this section, we examine the nature of digital images and gather facts that will help us to understand where aliasing errors arise and how the effects of these errors can be mitigated.

We start with a continuous two-dimensional image $f(x, y)$. We can regard the value of f as either a gray level in a monochromatic image or the value of one of the primaries in a color image. In the computer, we work with a digital image that is an array of nm pixels arranged as n rows of m pixels. Each pixel has k bits. There are two processes involved in going from a continuous image to a discrete image. First, we must **sample** the continuous image at nm points on some grid to obtain a set of values $\{f_{ij}\}$. Each of these samples of the continuous image is the value of f measured over a small area in the continuous image. Then, we must convert each of these samples into a k-bit pixel by a process known as **quantization.**

7.11.1 Sampling Theory

Suppose that we have a rectangular grid of locations where we wish to obtain our samples of f, as in Figure 7.43. If we assume that the grid is equally spaced, then an ideal sampler would produce a value

$$ f_{ij} = f(x_0 + ih_x, y_0 + jh_y), $$

Figure 7.43 Sampling.

where h_x and h_y are the distances between the grid points in the x and y directions, respectively. Leaving aside for now the fact that no real sampler can make such a precise measurement, there are two important questions. First, what errors have we made in this idealized sampling process? That is, how much of the information in the original image is included in the sampled image? Second, can we go back from the digital image to a continuous image without incurring additional errors? This latter step is called **reconstruction** and describes display processes such as are required in displaying the contents of a frame buffer on the screen of a CRT.

The mathematical analysis of these issues uses Fourier analysis, a branch of applied mathematics particularly well suited for explaining problems of digital signal processing. The essence of Fourier theory is that a function, of either space or time, can be decomposed into a set of sinusoids, at possibly an infinite number of frequencies. This concept is most familiar with sound, where we routinely think of a particular sound in terms of its frequency components or **spectrum**. For a two-dimensional image, we can think of it as being composed of sinusoidal patterns in two spatial frequencies that, when added together, produce the image. Figure 7.44(a) shows a one-dimensional function; Figure 7.44(b) shows the two sinusoids that form it; Figure 7.45 shows two-dimensional periodic functions. Thus, every two-dimensional spatial function $f(x, y)$ has two equivalent representations. One is its spatial form $f(x, y)$; the other is a representation in terms of its spectrum—the frequency-domain representation $g(\xi, \eta)$. The value of g is the contribution to f at the two-dimensional spatial frequency (ξ, η). By using these alternate representations of functions, we find that many phenomena, including sampling, can be explained much more easily in the frequency domain.

We can explain the consequences of sampling, without being overwhelmed by the mathematics, if we accept, without proof, the fundamental theorem known as the Nyquist sampling theorem. There are two parts to the theorem: The first allows us to discuss sampling errors, whereas the second governs reconstruction. We examine the second in Section 7.11.2.

(a)

(b)

Figure 7.44 One-dimensional decomposition. (a) Function. (b) Components.

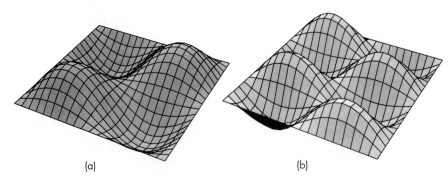

(a)   (b)

Figure 7.45 Two-dimensional periodic functions.

Nyquist sampling theorem (part 1): The ideal samples of a continuous function contain all the information in the original function if and only if the continuous function is sampled at a frequency greater than twice the highest frequency in the function.

Thus, if we are to have any chance of not losing information, we must restrict ourselves to functions that are zero in the frequency domain except in a window of width less than the sampling frequency, centered at the origin. The lowest frequency that cannot be in the data so as to avoid aliasing—one-half of the sampling frequency—is called the **Nyquist frequency**. Functions whose spectra are zero outside of some window are known as **band-limited** functions. For a two-dimensional image, the sampling frequencies are determined by the spacing of a two-dimensional grid with x and y spacing of $1/h_x$ and $1/h_y$, respectively. The theorem assumes an ideal sampling process that gathers an infinite number of samples, each of which is the exact value at the grid point. In practice, we can take only a finite number of samples—the number matching the resolution of our buffer. Consequently, we cannot produce a truly band-limited function. Although this result is a mathematical consequence of Fourier theory, we can observe that there will always be some ambiguity inherent in a finite collection of sampled points, simply because we do not know the function outside the region from which we obtained the samples.[7]

The consequences of violating the Nyquist criteria are aliasing errors. We can see from where the name *aliasing* comes by considering an ideal sampling process. Both the original function and its set of samples have frequency-domain representations. The spectral components of the sampled function are replicas of the spectrum of the original function, with their centers separated by the sampling frequency. Consider the one-dimensional function in Figure 7.46(a), with the samples indicated. Figure 7.46(b) shows its spectrum; in Figure 7.46(c) we have the spectrum of the sampled function, showing the replications of the spectrum in Figure 7.46(b).[8] Because we have sampled at a rate higher than the Nyquist frequency, there is a separation between the replicas.

Now consider the case in Figure 7.47. Here, we have violated the Nyquist criterion, and the replicas overlap. Consider the central part of the plot, which is magnified in Figure 7.48 and shows only the central replica, centered at the origin, and the replica to its right, centered at ξ_s. The frequency ξ_0 is above the Nyquist frequency $\xi_s/2$. There is, however, a replica of ξ_0, generated by the sampling process from the replica on the right, at $\xi_s - \xi_0$, a frequency less

---

7. This statement assumes no knowledge of the underlying function f, other than a set of its samples. If we have additional information, such as knowledge that the function is periodic, knowledge of the function over a finite interval can be sufficient to determine the entire function.

8. We show the magnitude of the spectrum because the Fourier transform produces complex numbers for the frequency-domain components.

$f(x)$ $|g(\xi)|$ $|g_s(\xi)|$

(a)   (b)   (c)

Figure 7.46 Band-limited function. (a) Function and its samples in the spatial domain. (b) Spectrum of the function. (c) Spectrum of the samples.

than the Nyquist frequency. The energy at this frequency can be heard, if we are dealing with digital sound, or seen, if we are considering two-dimensional images. We say that the frequency ξ_0 has an **alias** at $\xi_s - \xi_0$. Note that once aliasing has occurred, we cannot distinguish between information that was at a frequency in the original data and information that was placed at this frequency by the sampling process.

We can demonstrate aliasing and ambiguity without using Fourier analysis by looking at a single sinusoid, as shown in Figure 7.49. If we sample this sinusoid at twice its frequency, we can recover it from two samples. However, these same two samples are samples of a sinusoid of twice this frequency, and can also be samples of sinusoids of other multiples of the basic frequency. All these frequencies are aliases of the same original frequency. If we know that the data were band limited, however, then the samples can describe only the original sinusoid.

If we were to do an analysis of the frequency content of real-world images, we would find that the spectral components of most images are concentrated in the lower frequencies. Consequently, although it is impossible to construct a finite-sized image that is band limited, the aliasing errors often are minimal because there is little content in frequencies above the Nyquist frequency, and little content is aliased into frequencies below the Nyquist frequency. The exceptions to this statement arise when there is regular (periodic) information in the continuous image. In the frequency representation, regularity places most of the information at a few frequencies. If any of these frequencies is above the Nyquist limit, the aliasing effect is noticeable as beat or moiré patterns. Examples that

$|g(\xi)|$

Figure 7.47 Overlapping replicas.

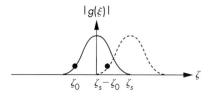

$\zeta_0 \quad \zeta_s - \zeta_0 \ \zeta_s$

Figure 7.48 Aliasing.

you might have noticed include the patterns that appear on video displays when people in the images wear striped shirts or plaid ties, and wavy patterns that arise both in printed (halftoned) figures derived from computer displays and in digital images of farmland with plowed fields.

Often, we can minimize aliasing by prefiltering before we scan an image or by controlling the area of the data that the scanner uses to measure a sample. Figure 7.50 shows two possible ways to scan an image. In Figure 7.50(a) we see an ideal scanner. It measures the value of a continuous image at a point, so the samples are given by

$$f_{ij} = f(x_i, y_i).$$

On the right, we have a more realistic scanner that obtains samples by taking a weighted average over a small interval to produce samples of the form

$$f_{ij} = \int_{x_i-s/2}^{x_i+s/2} \int_{y_i-s/2}^{y_i+s/2} f(x,y) w(x,y) \, dy \, dx.$$

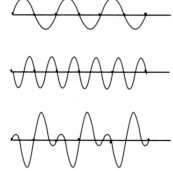

Figure 7.49 Aliasing of sinusoid.

By selecting the size of the window s and the weighting function w, we can attenuate high-frequency components in the image, and thus we can reduce aliasing. Fortunately, real scanners must take measurements over a finite region, called the **sampling aperture**; thus, some antialiasing takes place even if the user has no understanding of the aliasing problem.

(a)   (b)

Figure 7.50 Scanning of an image.
(a) Point sampling. (b) Area averaging.

7.11.2 Reconstruction

Suppose that we have an (infinite) set of samples, the members of which have been sampled at a rate greater than the Nyquist frequency. The reconstruction of a continuous function from the samples is based on part 2 of the Nyquist sampling theorem.

> **Nyquist sampling theorem (part 2):** We can reconstruct a continuous function $f(x)$ from its samples $\{f_i\}$ by the formula

$$f(x) = \sum_{i=-\infty}^{\infty} f_i \operatorname{sinc}(x - x_i).$$

The function $\operatorname{sinc}(x)$ (see Figure 7.51) is defined as

$$\operatorname{sinc}(x) = \frac{\sin \pi x}{\pi x}.$$

The two-dimensional version of the reconstruction formula for a function $f(x, y)$ with ideal samples $\{f_{ij}\}$ is

$$f(x, y) = \sum_{i=-\infty}^{\infty} \sum_{j=-\infty}^{\infty} f_{ij} \operatorname{sinc}(x - x_i) \operatorname{sinc}(y - y_j).$$

These formulas follow from the fact that we can recover an unaliased function in the frequency domain by using a filter that is zero except in the interval $(-\xi_s/2, \xi_s/2)$—a low-pass filter—to obtain a single replica from the infinite number of replicas generated by the sampling process shown in Figure 7.46. The reconstruction of a one-dimensional function is shown in Figure 7.52. In two dimensions, the reconstruction involves use of a two-dimensional sinc, as shown in Figure 7.53. Unfortunately, the sinc function cannot be produced in a physical display, because of its negative side lobes. Consider the display problem for a CRT

Figure 7.51 Sinc function.

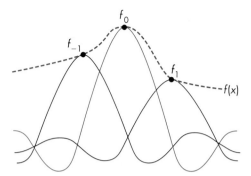

Figure 7.52 One-dimensional reconstruction.

display. We start with a digital image that is a set of samples. For each sample, we can place a spot of light centered at a grid point on the display surface, as shown in Figure 7.54. The value of the sample controls the intensity of the spot, or modulates the beam. We can control the shape of the spot by using techniques such as focusing the beam. The reconstruction formula tells us that the beam should have the shape of a two-dimensional sinc, but because the beam puts out energy, the spot must be nonnegative at all points. Consequently, the display process must make errors. We can evaluate a real display by considering how well its spot approximates the desired sinc. Figure 7.55 shows the sinc and several one-dimensional approximations. The Gaussian-shaped spot corresponds to the shape of many CRT spots, whereas the rectangular spot might correspond to an LCD display with square pixels. Note that we can make either approximation wider or narrower. If we analyze the spot profiles in the frequency domain, we

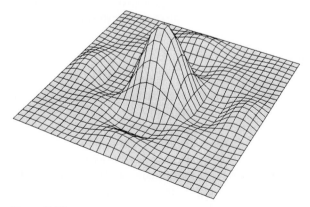

Figure 7.53 Two-dimensional sinc function.

Figure 7.54 Display of a point on CRT.

Figure 7.55 Display spots. (a) Ideal spot. (b) Rectangular approximation. (c) Piecewise-linear approximation. (d) Gaussian approximation.

find that the wider spots are more accurate at low frequencies but are less accurate at higher frequencies. In practice, the spot size that we choose is a compromise. Visible differences across monitors often can be traced to different spot profiles.

7.11.3 Quantization

The mathematical analysis of sampling explains a number of important effects. However, we have not included the effect of each sample being quantized into k discrete levels. Given a scalar function g with values in the range

$$g_{min} \leq g \leq g_{max},$$

a **quantizer** is a function q such that, if $g_i \leq g \leq g_{i+1}$,

$$q(g) = q_i.$$

Figure 7.56 Quantizer.

Thus, for each value of g, we assign it one of k values, as shown in Figure 7.56. In general, designing a quantizer involves choosing the $\{q_i\}$, the quantization levels, and the $\{g_i\}$, the threshold values. If we know the probability distribution for g, $p(g)$, we can solve for the values that minimize the mean square error:

$$e = \int (g - q(g))^2 p(g) \, dg.$$

However, we often design quantizers based on the perceptual issues that we discussed in Chapter 1. A simple rule of thumb is that we should not be able to detect one-level changes, but should be able to detect all two-level changes. Given the threshold for the visual system to detect a change in luminance, we usually need at least 7 or 8 bits (or 128 to 256 levels). We should also consider the logarithmic intensity-brightness response of humans. To do so, we usually distribute the levels exponentially, to give approximately equal perceptual errors as we go from one level to the next.

7.12 Summary and Notes

In the early days of computer graphics, people worked with only three-dimensional geometric objects, whereas those people who were involved with only two-dimensional images were considered to be working in image processing. Advances in hardware have made graphics and image-processing systems practically indistinguishable. For those people involved with synthesizing images—certainly a major part of computer graphics—this merging of fields has brought forth a multitude of new techniques. The idea that a two-dimensional image or texture can be mapped to a three-dimensional surface in no more time than it takes to render the surface with constant shading would have been unthinkable a few years ago. Now, these techniques are routine.

Techniques such as texture mapping have had an enormous effect on real-time graphics. In fields such as animation, virtual reality, and scientific visualization, we use hardware texture mapping to add detail to images without burdening the geometric pipeline. The use of compositing techniques, through the accumulation buffer and the alpha channel, allows the application programmer to perform tasks, such as antialiasing, and to create effects, such as fog and depth of field, that until recently were done on different types of architectures, after the graphics had been created.

Mapping methods provide some of the best examples of the interactions among graphics hardware, software, and applications. Consider texture mapping. Although it was first described and implemented purely as a software algorithm, once people saw its ability to create scenes with great visual complexity, hardware developers started putting large amounts of texture memory in graphics systems. Once texture mapping was implemented in hardware, texture mapping could be done in real time, a development which led to the redesign of many applications, notably computer games.

In this chapter we have concentrated on techniques that are supported by recently available hardware and APIs. Many of the techniques introduced here are new; many more are just appearing in the literature; even more remain to be discovered.

7.13 Suggested Readings

Bump mapping was first suggested by Blinn [Bli77]. Environmental mapping was developed by Blinn and Newell [Bli76]. Texture mapping was first used by Catmull; see the review by Heckbert [Hec86]. Hardware support for texture mapping came with the SGI Reality Engine; see Akeley [Ake93]. Perlin and Hoffert [Per89] designed a noise function to generate two- and three-dimensional texture maps. Many texture synthesis techniques are discussed in Ebert [Ebe98].

The aliasing problem in computer graphics has been of importance since the advent of raster graphics; see Crow [Cro81]. The first concerns were with rasterization of lines, but later other forms of aliasing arose with animations [Mag85] and ray tracing [Gla89]. The image-processing books [Pra78, Gon87, Cas96] provide an introduction to signal processing and aliasing in two dimensions. The books by Glassner [Gla95] and Watt and Policarpo [Wat98] are aimed at practitioners of computer graphics.

Many of the compositing techniques, including use of the α channel, were suggested by Porter and Duff [Por84]. The *OpenGL Programmer's Guide* [Ope01a] contains many examples of how buffers can be used. The recent literature includes many new examples of the use of buffers. See the recent issues of the journals *Computer Graphics* and *IEEE Computer Graphics and Applications*.

Technical details on most of the standard image formats can be found in [Mia99, Mur94].

Exercises

7.1   Show how you can use the XOR writing mode to implement an odd–even fill algorithm.

7.2   What are the visual effects of using XOR to move a cursor around on the screen?

7.3   How is an image produced with an environmental map different from a ray-traced image of the same scene?

7.4   In the movies and television, the wheels of cars and wagons often appear to be spinning in the wrong direction. What causes the effect? Can anything be done to fix this problem? Explain your answer.

7.5   We can attempt to display sampled data by simply plotting the points and letting the human visual system merge the points into shapes. Why is this technique dangerous if the data are close to the Nyquist limit?

7.6   Why do the patterns of striped shirts and ties change as an actor moves across the screen of your television?

7.7   Why should we do antialiasing by preprocessing the data, rather than by postprocessing them?

7.8   Suppose that we have two translucent surfaces characterized by opacities α_1 and α_2. What is the opacity of the translucent material that we create by using the two in series? Give an expression for the transparency of the combined material.

7.9   Assume that we view translucent surfaces as filters of the light passing through them. Develop a blending model based on the complementary colors CMY.

7.10 In Section 7.9 we used $1 - \alpha$ and α for the destination and source blending factors, respectively. What would be the visual difference if we used 1 for the destination factor, and kept α for the source factor?

7.11 Add paintbrushes that add color gradually to image in the paint program in Chapter 3. Also use blending to add erasers that gradually remove images from the screen.

7.12 Devise a method of using texture mapping for the display of three-dimensional arrays of pixels (voxels).

7.13 Show how to use the luminance histogram of an image to derive a lookup table that will make the altered image have a flat histogram.

7.14 When we supersample a scene using jitter, why should we use a random jitter pattern?

7.15 Suppose that a set of objects is texture mapped with regular patterns such as stripes and checkerboards. What is the difference in aliasing patterns that we would see when we switch from parallel to perspective views?

7.16 Consider a scene composed of simple objects, such as parallelepipeds, that are instanced at different sizes. Suppose that you have a single texture map and you are asked to map this texture to all the objects. How would you map the texture so that the pattern would be the same size on each face of each object?

7.17 Write a program using mipmaps in which each mipmap is constructed from a different image. Is there a practical application for such a program?

7.18 Using either your own image-processing code for convolution or the imaging extensions of OpenGL, implement a general 3×3 filtering program for luminance images.

7.19 Take an image from a digital camera or from some other source and apply 3×3 smoothing and sharpening filters repetitively. Pay special attention to what happens at the edges of the filtered images.

7.20 Repeat Exercise 7.19 but first add a small amount of random noise to the image. Describe the differences between the results of the two exercises.

7.21 If your system supports the imaging extensions, compare the performance of filtering using the extensions with filtering done by your own code using processor memory.

7.22 One of the most effective methods of altering the contrast of an image is to allow the user to design a lookup interactively. Consider a graph such as in Figure 7.14 where the curve is approximated with three connected line segments. Write a program that displays an image, allows the user to specify the line segments interactively, and shows the image after it has been altered by the curve.

7.23 In a similar vein to Exercise 7.22, write an interactive program that allows users to design pseudocolor maps.

Implementation of a Renderer

We now turn to implementation. There are three reasons for considering implementation at this point. First, you may be wondering how your programs are processed by the system that you are using: how lines are drawn on the screen, how polygons are filled, and what happens to primitives that lie outside the viewing volumes defined in your program. Second, our contention is that, if we are to use a graphics system efficiently, we need to have an understanding of the implementation process: which steps are easy, and which tax our hardware and software. Third, our discussion of implementation opens the door to new capabilities that are supported by the latest hardware.

Learning implementation involves studying algorithms. As when we study other algorithms, we must be careful to consider such issues as theoretical versus practical performance, hardware versus software implementations, and the specific characteristics of an application. Although we can test whether an OpenGL implementation works correctly, in the sense that it produces the correct pixels on the screen, there are many choices for the algorithms employed. We focus on the basic operations that are necessary to implement a standard API and are required, whether the rendering is done by a pipeline architecture or some other method, such as a ray tracer. Consequently, we present a variety of the basic algorithms for each of the principal tasks in an implementation.

In this chapter, we are concerned with the basic algorithms that are used to implement the rendering pipeline used by OpenGL. Although these algorithms also are used with other rendering strategies, we shall consider the details of other rendering paradigms in Chapter 13.

8.1 Basic Implementation Strategies

Let us begin with a high-level view of the implementation process. In computer graphics, we start with an application program, and we end with an image. We can again consider this process as a black box (Figure 8.1) whose inputs are the objects defined in the program—geometric objects, attributes, transformations—and whose output is an array of colored pixels in the frame buffer.

Within the black box, we must do many tasks, including transformations, clipping, shading, hidden-surface removal, and rasterization of the primitives

Figure 8.1 High-level view of the graphics process.

that appear on the display. These tasks can be organized in a variety of ways, but regardless of the strategy that we adopt, we must always do two things: We must pass every geometric object through the system, and we must assign a color to every pixel in the color buffer that is displayed.

Suppose that we think of what goes into the black box in terms of a single program that performs implementation. This program takes as input a set of vertices specifying geometric objects and produces as output pixels in the frame buffer. Because this program must assign a value to every pixel and must process every geometric primitive (and every light source), we expect this program to contain a number of loops that iterate over these basic variables.

If we wish to write such a program, then we must immediately address the following question: Which variable controls the outer loop? The answer we choose determines the flow of the entire implementation process. There are two fundamental answers. The two strategies that follow are often called the **image-oriented** and the **object-oriented** approaches. These approaches have also been called the **sort-first** and **sort-last** approaches, based on where in the rendering process hidden-surface removal takes place.

In the object-oriented approach, the outer loop is over the objects. We can think of the program as controlled by a loop of this form:

```
for(each_object) render(object);
```

A pipeline renderer fits this description. Vertices are defined by the program and flow through a series of modules that transforms them, colors them, and determines whether they are visible. A polygon might flow through the steps illustrated in Figure 8.2. Note that after a polygon passes through the geometric processing, the rasterization of this polygon potentially can affect any pixels in the frame buffer. Most implementations that follow this approach are based on construction of a rendering pipeline that contains hardware or software modules for each of the tasks. Data (vertices) flow forward through the system.

In the past, the major limitations of the object-oriented approach were the large amount of memory required and the high cost of processing each object independently. Any geometric primitive that emerges from the geometric processing potentially can affect any set of pixels in the frame buffer; thus, the entire frame buffer—and various other buffers, such as the depth buffer used for hidden-surface removal—must be of the size of the display and must be available at all times. Before memory became both cheap and dense, this requirement

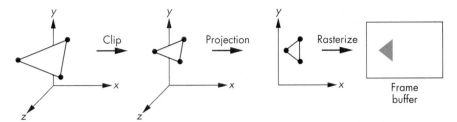

Figure 8.2 Object-oriented approach.

was considered to be a serious problem. Now various pipelined geometric processors are available that can process millions of polygons per second. In fact, precisely because we are doing the same operations on every primitive, the hardware to build an object-based system is fast and relatively cheap, with many of the functions implemented with special-purpose chips.

Today, the main limitation of object-oriented implementations is that they cannot handle most global calculations. Because each geometric primitive is processed independently—and in an arbitrary order—complex shading effects that involve multiple geometric objects, such as reflections, cannot be handled, except by approximate methods. The major exception is hidden-surface removal, where the z-buffer is used to store global information.

Image-oriented approaches loop over pixels, or rows of pixels called **scan lines**, that constitute the frame buffer. In pseudocode, the outer loop of such a program is of the following form:

```
for(each_pixel) assign_a_color(pixel);
```

For each pixel (or scan line), we work backward, trying to determine which geometric primitives can contribute to its color. The advantages of this approach are that we need only limited display memory at any time and that we can hope to generate pixels (or scan lines) at the rate and in the order required to refresh the display. Because the results of most calculations do not differ greatly from pixel to pixel (or scan line to scan line), we can use this coherence in our algorithms by developing incremental forms for many of the steps in the implementation. The main disadvantage of this approach is that, unless we first build a data structure from the geometric data, we do not know which primitives affect which pixels. Such a data structure can be complex and may imply that all the geometric data must be available at all times during the rendering process. For problems with very large databases, even having a good data representation may not avoid memory problems.

We lean toward the object-based approach, although we look at examples of algorithms suited for both approaches.

8.2 Four Major Tasks

There are four major tasks that any implementation must perform to render a geometric entity, such as a three-dimensional polygon, as the latter passes from definition in a user program to possible display on an output device:

- Modeling
- Geometric processing
- Rasterization
- Display

Figure 8.3 shows how these tasks might be organized in a pipeline implementation. Regardless of the approach, all the tasks must be carried out.

8.2.1 Modeling

The usual results of the modeling process are sets of vertices that specify a group of geometric objects supported by the rest of the system. We have seen a few examples that required some modeling by the user, such as the approximation of spheres in Chapter 6. In Chapters 9–11 we explore other modeling techniques.

We can look at the modeler as a black box that produces geometric objects and is usually a user program, yet there are other tasks that the modeler might perform. Consider, for example, clipping: the process of eliminating parts of objects that should not appear on the display. A user can generate geometric objects in her program, and she can hope that the rest of the system can process these objects at the rate at which they are produced; or the modeler can attempt to ease the burden on the rest of the system by minimizing the number of objects that it passes on. This latter approach often means that the modeler may do some of the same jobs as the rest of the system, albeit with different algorithms. In the case of clipping, the modeler, knowing more about the specifics of the application, can often use a good heuristic to eliminate many, if not most, primitives before they are sent on through the standard viewing process.

8.2.2 Geometric Processing

The goals of the geometric processor are to determine which geometric objects appear on the display and to assign shades or colors to these objects. Four related processes are required: normalization, clipping, hidden-surface removal, and

Figure 8.3 Implementation tasks.

shading. Once these processes have been carried out, the projection of the object from three to two dimensions can take place.

The first step in geometric processing usually is to change representations from user coordinates to either camera coordinates or screen coordinates. Regarding the geometric processor as a vertex processor, vertices, represented in homogeneous coordinates, are processed through a sequence of affine transformations so that the desired view is obtained. In most systems, a normalized view volume is created. Not only does the normalization allow us to support only orthographic projections, but in addition, by converting all views to equivalent orthographic views, we simplify the clipping process, as we shall see in Section 8.7.

Geometric objects are transformed by a sequence of transformations that may reshape and move them (modeling) or may change their representations (viewing). Eventually, only those primitives that fit within a specified volume, the **view volume**, appear on the display after rasterization. We cannot, however, simply allow all objects to be rasterized, hoping that the hardware will take care of primitives that lie wholly or partially outside the view volume. The implementation must carry out this task.

Even though an object lies inside the view volume, it will not be displayed if it is obscured by other objects. Algorithms for **hidden-surface removal** (or **visible-surface determination**) are based on the three-dimensional spatial relationships among objects and must be carried out as part of our geometric processing. Our lighting model from Chapter 6 also requires geometric information, such as normals, to compute shading; thus, lighting calculations are another part of geometric processing.

Collectively, these operations constitute what has been called **front-end processing**. All involve three-dimensional calculations, and all require floating-point arithmetic. All generate similar hardware and software requirements.

Geometric calculations require floating-point operations and are generally done on a vertex-by-vertex basis. For example, we compute vertex colors and vertex shades. Texture coordinates are assigned on a per-vertex basis. In an object-oriented renderer, this process usually means that many of the expensive floating-point calculations, including shading, are done before hidden-surface removal.

8.2.3 Rasterization

Once projection takes place, we can work with two-dimensional objects. Although we may have represented our primitives in screen coordinates, what we have is only a description of the object, such as through its vertices. For example, after projection, a line segment that was defined in three dimensions by two vertices becomes a line segment in two dimensions defined by a pair of two-dimensional vertices. To display the object, we must use these vertices to generate a set of pixel values through a process called **rasterization** or **scan conversion**. For line segments, rasterization determines which pixels should be used to approximate a line segment between the projected vertices. For polygons, rasterization determines which pixels lie inside the two-dimensional polygon determined by the projected vertices. The colors that we assign to these pixels can be assigned by the color attributes or obtained by interpolating the shades at the vertices that are computed as in Chapter 6. Objects more complex than line segments and polygons are usually approximated by multiple line segments and polygons, and thus most graphics systems do not have special rasterization algorithms for them. We shall see exceptions to this rule for some special curves and surfaces in Chapter 10.

The separate pixel pipeline (Chapter 7), supported by architectures such as OpenGL, merges with the results of the geometric pipeline at the rasterization stage. Consider what happens when a shaded and texture-mapped polygon is processed. The vertex shades are computed as part of the geometric processing. The texture value is not needed until rasterization when the renderer has determined that a pixel is inside a polygon and is visible. At this point, interpolation of vertex shades and texture coordinates takes place, and the texture parameters determine how to combine the proper texel values and vertex shades to determine the pixel's color.

8.2.4 Display

In most displays, the process of taking the image from the frame buffer and displaying it on a CRT happens automatically and is not of concern to the application program. However, there are numerous problems with the quality of display, such as the jaggedness associated with images on raster displays. We introduce algorithms for reducing this jaggedness, or **aliasing**, and we discuss problems with color reproduction on displays.

8.3 Implementation of Transformations

The use of homogenous coordinates provides the basis for implementing geometric transformations. Our use of 4×4 matrices has allowed us to form arbitrary affine transformations by concatenating a sequence of matrices. In our discussions thus far we have focused on the OpenGL use of model-view and projection matrices. Here, we take a slightly different, but equivalent, approach. We consider the transformations as performing a sequence of coordinate-system changes, where each change can be represented by a homogeneous-coordinate matrix. There are five coordinate systems of interest:

- Object (world) coordinates
- Eye (camera) coordinates
- Clip coordinates
- Normalized device coordinates
- Window (screen) coordinates

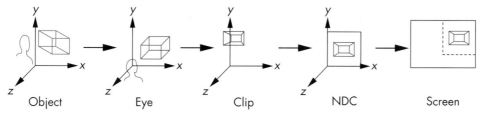

Figure 8.4 Transformation sequence.

Figure 8.4 shows the sequence of transformations acting on a simple object. We first see the box and the viewer in the object coordinate system in which both their positions have been specified. The model-view matrix carries us to eye coordinates, where the viewer is at the origin. The next step in Figure 8.4 is the projection transformation. If our system uses this transformation, we stay in three dimensions, but we normalize the projection, as we did in Chapter 5, into an equivalent orthographic projection of distorted objects. The normalization process maps the view volume—a frustum for perspective views and parallelepiped for parallel views—to a centered cube with sides of length 2.[1] The points are now represented in **clip coordinates**.

Both the model-view and projection transformations are represented by 4×4 matrices in homogeneous coordinates. In hardware implementations, multiplication of four-dimensional vertices by 4×4 matrices is carried out by hardware, often with the matrix-multiplication units implemented at the chip level, allowing the entire matrix multiplication to be done in the same amount of time as a single multiplication.

In many implementations, the next stage is **clipping**, the process of determining which primitives, and parts of primitives, fit within the clipping volume defined by the application program. If the w component of a clipped vertex is not equal to 1, we have to do a perspective division to convert back from homogeneous coordinates to normal three-dimensional coordinates. The result of these steps is that the portions of all primitives that can possibly be displayed—we have yet to apply hidden-surface removal—lie within the cube

$$x = \pm 1,$$
$$y = \pm 1,$$
$$z = \pm 1.$$

This coordinate system is called **normalized device coordinates** because it depends on neither the original application units nor the particulars of the display device, although the information to produce the correct image is retained in this

1. In OpenGL, if the w component is not 1, the sides can be thought of as determined by the planes $x = \pm w$, $y = \pm w$, and $z = \pm w$.

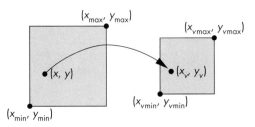

Figure 8.5 Viewport transformation.

coordinate system. Note also that projection has been carried out only partially. We still must do the final orthographic projection:

$$x_p = x,$$
$$y_p = y,$$
$$z_p = 0.$$

Because we have retained the depth information, we can do hidden-surface removal later.

The final transformation converts vertices to units of the display—**window coordinates**. As we saw in Chapter 5, the projection of the clipping volume must appear in the assigned viewport. In OpenGL, this transformation is done after projection and is two-dimensional. The preceding transformations have normalized the view volume such that its sides line up with the sides of the viewport (Figure 8.5), so this transformation is simply

$$x_v = x_{v\min} + (x - x_{\min})\frac{x_{v\max} - x_{v\min}}{x_{\max} - x_{\min}},$$

$$y_v = y_{v\min} + (y - y_{\min})\frac{y_{v\max} - y_{v\min}}{y_{\max} - y_{\min}}.$$

Some APIs allow for three-dimensional viewports, with the final projection being done after this transformation. In this case, we must add the equation

$$z_v = z_{v\min} + (z - z_{\min})\frac{z_{v\max} - z_{v\min}}{z_{\max} - z_{\min}}.$$

OpenGL also defines a two-dimensional coordinate system, **screen coordinates**, which is the same as window coordinates but lacks the depth coordinate.

8.4 Line-Segment Clipping

A **clipper** decides which primitives, or parts of primitives, appear on the display. Primitives that fit within the specified view volume pass through the clipper, or are **accepted**. Primitives that cannot appear on the display are eliminated, or

Figure 8.6 Two-dimensional clipping.

rejected or **culled**. Primitives that are only partially within the view volume must be clipped such that any part lying outside the volume is removed.

Clipping can occur at one or more places in the viewing pipeline. The modeler may clip to limit the primitives that the hardware must handle. The primitives may be clipped after they have been projected from three- to two-dimensional objects. In OpenGL, at least conceptually, primitives are clipped against a three-dimensional view volume before projection and rasterization. We develop a sequence of clippers. For both pedagogic and historic reasons, we start with two two-dimensional line-segment clippers. Both extend directly to three dimensions and to clipping of polygons.

8.4.1 Cohen–Sutherland Clipping

The two-dimensional clipping problem for line segments is shown in Figure 8.6. We can assume for now that this problem arises after three-dimensional line segments have been projected onto the projection plane, and that the window is part of the projection plane that is mapped to the viewport on the display. All values are specified as real numbers. We can see that the entire line segment AB appears on the display, whereas none of CD appears. EF and GH have to be shortened before being displayed. Although a line segment is completely determined by its endpoints, GH shows that, even if both endpoints lie outside the clipping window, part of the line segment may still appear on the display.

We could compute the intersections of the lines of which the segments are parts with the sides of the window, and thus could determine the necessary information for clipping. However, we want to avoid intersection calculations, if possible, because each intersection requires a floating-point division. The Cohen–Sutherland algorithm was the first to seek to replace most of the expensive floating-point multiplications and divisions with a combination of floating-point subtractions and bit operations.

The algorithm starts by extending the sides of the window to infinity, thus breaking up space into the nine regions shown in Figure 8.7. Each region can

1001	1000	1010
0001	0000	0010
0101	0100	0110

$y = y_{max}$

$y = y_{min}$

$x = x_{min}$ $x = x_{max}$

Figure 8.7 Breaking up of space and outcodes.

be assigned a unique 4-bit binary number, or **outcode**, $b_0 b_1 b_2 b_3$, as follows. Suppose that (x, y) is a point in the region; then,

$$b_0 = \begin{cases} 1 & \text{if } y > y_{max}, \\ 0 & \text{otherwise.} \end{cases}$$

Likewise, b_1 is 1 if $y < y_{min}$, and b_2 and b_3 are determined by the relationship between x and the left and right sides of the window. The resulting codes are indicated in Figure 8.7. For each endpoint of a line segment, we first compute the endpoint's outcode, a step that can require eight floating-point subtractions per line segment.

Consider a line segment whose outcodes are given by $o_1 = outcode(x_1, y_1)$ and $o_2 = outcode(x_2, y_2)$. We can now reason on the basis of these outcodes. There are four cases (Figure 8.8):

1. ($o_1 = o_2 = 0$.) Both endpoints are inside the clipping window, as is true for segment AB in Figure 8.8. The entire line segment is inside, and the segment can be sent on to be rasterized.
2. ($o_1 \neq 0, o_2 = 0$; or vice versa.) One endpoint is inside the clipping window; one is outside (see segment CD in Figure 8.8). The line segment must be shortened. The nonzero outcode indicates which edge, or edges, of the window are crossed by the segment. One or two intersections must be computed. Note that after one intersection is computed, we can compute the outcode of the point of intersection to determine whether another intersection calculation is required.
3. (o_1 & $o_2 \neq 0$.) By taking the bitwise AND of the outcodes, we determine whether or not the two endpoints lie on the same outside side of the window. If so, the line segment can be discarded (see segment EF in Figure 8.8).
4. (o_1 & $o_2 = 0$.) Both endpoints are outside, but they are on the outside of different edges of the window. As we can see from segments GH and IJ in Figure 8.8, we cannot tell from just the outcodes whether the segment can be discarded or must be shortened. The best we can do is to intersect with one of the sides of the window, and to check the outcode of the resulting point.

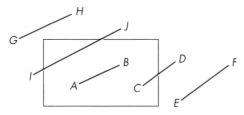

figure 8.8 Cases of outcodes in Cohen–Sutherland algorithm.

All our checking of outcodes requires only Boolean operations. We do intersection calculations only when they are needed, as in the second case, or as in the fourth case, where the outcodes did not contain enough information.

The Cohen–Sutherland algorithm works best when there are many line segments but few are actually displayed. In this case, most of the line segments lie fully outside one or two of the extended sides of the clipping rectangle, and thus can be eliminated on the basis of their outcodes. The other advantage is that this algorithm can be extended to three dimensions. The main disadvantage of the algorithm is that it must be used recursively. Consider line segment GH in Figure 8.8. It must be clipped against both the left and top sides of the clipping window. Generally, the simplest way to do so is to use the initial outcodes to determine the first side of the clipping window to clip against. After this first shortening of the original line segment, a new outcode is computed for the new endpoint created by shortening, and the algorithm is reexecuted.

We have not discussed how to compute any required intersections. The form this calculation takes depends on how we choose to represent the line segment, although only a single division should be required in any case. If we use the standard explicit form of a line,

$$y = mx + h,$$

where m is the slope of the line and h is the line's y intercept, then we can compute m and h from the endpoints. However, vertical lines cannot be represented in this form—a critical weakness of the explicit form. If we were interested in only the Cohen–Sutherland algorithm, it would be fairly simple to program all cases directly, because the sides of the clipping rectangle are parallel to the axes. However, we are interested in more than just clipping; consequently, other representations of the line and line segment are of importance. In particular, parametric representations are almost always used in computer graphics. We have already seen the parametric form of the line in Chapter 4; the parametric representation of other types of curves is considered in Chapter 10.

8.4.2 Liang–Barsky Clipping

If we use the parametric form for lines, we can approach the clipping of line segments in a different—and ultimately more efficient—manner. Suppose that we have a line segment defined by the two endpoints $\mathbf{p}_1 = [x_1, y_1]^T$ and $\mathbf{p}_2 = [x_2, y_2]^T$. We can use these endpoints to define a unique line that we can express parametrically, either in matrix form,

$$\mathbf{p}(\alpha) = (1 - \alpha)\mathbf{p}_1 + \alpha\mathbf{p}_2,$$

or as two scalar equations,

$$x(\alpha) = (1 - \alpha)x_1 + \alpha x_2,$$
$$y(\alpha) = (1 - \alpha)y_1 + \alpha y_2.$$

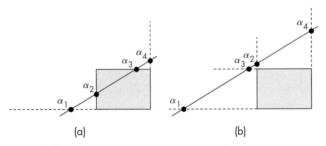

Figure 8.9 Two cases of a parametric line and a clipping window.

Note that this form is robust and needs no changes for horizontal or vertical lines. As the parameter α varies from 0 to 1, we move along the segment from $\mathbf{p}_1$ to $\mathbf{p}_2$. Negative values of α yield points on the line on the other side of $\mathbf{p}_1$ from $\mathbf{p}_2$. Similarly, values of $\alpha > 1$ give points on the line past $\mathbf{p}_2$ going off to infinity.

Consider the line segment and the line of which it is part, as shown in Figure 8.9(a). As long as the line is not parallel to a side of the window (if it is, we can handle that situation with ease), there are four points where the line intersects the extended sides of the window. These points correspond to the four values of the parameter: $\alpha_1, \alpha_2, \alpha_3,$ and α_4. One of these values corresponds to the line entering the window; another corresponds to the line leaving the window. Leaving aside, for the moment, how we compute these intersections, we can order them, and can determine which correspond to intersections that we need for clipping. For the given example,

$$1 > \alpha_4 > \alpha_3 > \alpha_2 > \alpha_1 > 0.$$

Hence, all four intersections are inside the original line segment, with the two innermost (α_2 and α_3) determining the clipped line segment. We can distinguish this case from the case in Figure 8.9(b), which also has the four intersections between the endpoints of the line segment, by noting that the order for this case is

$$1 > \alpha_4 > \alpha_2 > \alpha_3 > \alpha_1 > 0.$$

The line intersects both the top and the bottom of the window before it intersects either the left or the right; thus, the entire line segment must be rejected. Other cases of the ordering of the points of intersection can be argued in a similar way.

Efficient implementation of this strategy requires that we avoid computing intersections until they are needed. Many lines can be rejected before all four intersections are known. We also want to avoid floating-point divisions where possible. If we use the parametric form to determine the intersection with the top of the window, we find the intersection at the value

$$\alpha = \frac{y_{max} - y_1}{y_2 - y_1}.$$

Similar equations hold for the other three sides of the window. Rather than computing these intersections, at the cost of a division for each, we instead write the equation as

$$\alpha(y_2 - y_1) = \alpha \Delta y = y_{max} - y_1 = \Delta y_{max}.$$

All the tests required by the algorithm can be restated in terms of Δy_{max}, Δy, and similar terms can be computed for the other sides of the windows. Thus, all decisions about clipping can be made without floating-point division. Only if an intersection is needed, because a segment has to be shortened, is the division done. The efficiency of this approach, compared to that of the Cohen–Sutherland algorithm, is that we avoid multiple shortening of line segments and the related reexecutions of the clipping algorithm. We forgo discussion of other efficient two-dimensional line-clipping algorithms because, unlike the Cohen–Sutherland and Liang–Barsky algorithms, these algorithms do not extend to three dimensions.

8.5 Polygon Clipping

Polygon clipping arises in a number of ways. Certainly, we want to be able to clip polygons against rectangular windows for display. We may at times want windows that are not rectangular. Other parts of an implementation, such as shadow generation and hidden-surface removal, can require clipping of polygons against other polygons. For example, Figure 8.10 shows the shadow of a polygon that we create by clipping a polygon that is closer to the light source against polygons that are farther away. Many of the antialiasing methods that we shall consider in Section 8.12 rely on the ability to clip polygons against other polygons.

We can generate polygon-clipping algorithms directly from line-clipping algorithms by clipping the edges of the polygon successively. However, we must be careful to remember that a polygon is object, and, depending on the form of the polygon, we can generate more than one polygonal object by clipping. Consider the nonconvex (or **concave**) polygon in Figure 8.11(a). If we clip it against a rectangular window, we get the result shown in Figure 8.11(b). Most viewers looking at this figure would conclude that we have generated three polygons by clipping. Unfortunately, implementing a clipper that can increase the number of objects can be a problem. We could treat the result of the clipper as a single polygon, as shown in Figure 8.12, with edges that overlap along the sides of the window, but this choice might cause difficulties in other parts of the implementation.

Convex polygons do not present such problems. Clipping a convex polygon against a rectangular window can leave at most a single convex polygon (see Exercise 8.3). A graphics system might then either forbid the use of concave

Figure 8.10 Shadow generation by clipping.

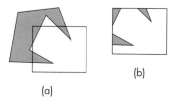

Figure 8.11 Clipping of a concave polygon. (a) Before clipping. (b) After clipping.

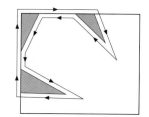

Figure 8.12 Creation of a single polygon.

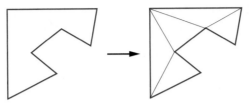

Figure 8.13 Tessellation of a concave polygon.

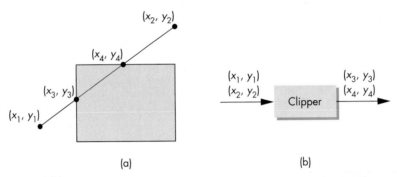

Figure 8.14 Two views of clipping. (a) Clipping against a rectangle. (b) Clipper as a black box.

polygons, or divide (tessellate) a given polygon into a set of convex polygons, as shown in Figure 8.13.[2]

For rectangular clipping regions, both the Cohen–Sutherland and the Liang–Barsky algorithms can be applied to polygons on an edge-by-edge basis. There is another approach, developed by Sutherland and Hodgeman, that fits well with the pipeline architectures that we have discussed.

A line-segment clipper can be envisioned as a black box (Figure 8.14) whose input is the pair of vertices from the segment to be tested and clipped, and whose output either is a pair of vertices corresponding to the clipped line segment, or is nothing if the input line segment lies outside the window.

Rather than considering the clipping window as four line segments, we can consider it as the object created by the intersection of four infinite lines that determine the top, bottom, right, and left sides of the window. We can then subdivide our clipper into a pipeline of simpler clippers, each of which clips against a single line that is the extension of an edge of the window. We can use the black-box view on each of the individual clippers.

---

2. OpenGL includes tessellation functions in the GLU library.

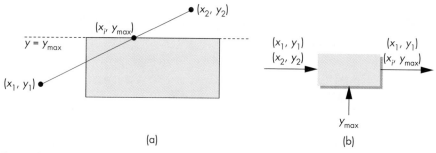

(a)   (b)

Figure 8.15 Clipping against top. (a) Graphically. (b) Black box view.

Suppose we consider clipping against only the top of the window. We can think of this operation as a black box (Figure 8.15) whose input and output are pairs of vertices, with the value of y_{max} as a parameter known to the clipper. Using the similar triangles in Figure 8.16, we see that, if there is an intersection, it lies at

$$x_3 = x_1 + (y_{max} - y_1)\frac{x_2 - x_1}{y_2 - y_1},$$

$$y_3 = y_{max}.$$

Thus, the clipper returns one of three pairs: $\{(x_1, y_1), (x_2, y_2)\}$, $\{(x_1, y_1), (x_i, y_{max})\}$, or $\{(x_i, y_{max}), (x_2, y_2)\}$. We can clip against the bottom, right, and left lines independently, using the same equations with the roles of x and y exchanged as necessary, and the values for the sides of the window inserted. The four clippers can now be arranged in the pipeline of Figure 8.17. If we build this configuration

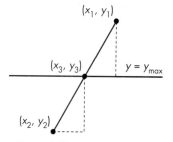

Figure 8.16 Intersection with the top of the window.

(a)

(b)

Figure 8.17 Pipeline clipping. (a) Clipping problem. (b) Pipeline clippers.

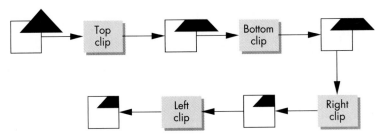

Figure 8.18 Example of pipeline clipping.

in hardware, we have a clipper that is working on four vertices concurrently. Figure 8.18 shows a simple example of the effect of successive clippers on a polygon.

8.6 Clipping of Other Primitives

Our emphasis in Chapters 1–6 was on writing programs in which the objects are built from line segments and flat polygons. We often render the curved objects that we discuss in Chapter 10 by subdividing them into small, approximately flat polygons. In pipeline architectures, we usually find some variant of the clippers that we have presented. Nevertheless, there are situations in which we want either to clip objects before they reach the hardware or to employ algorithms optimized for other primitives.

8.6.1 Bounding Boxes and Volumes

Suppose that we have a many-sided polygon, as shown in Figure 8.19(a). We could apply one of our clipping algorithms, which would clip the polygon by individually clipping all that polygon's edges. However, we can see that the

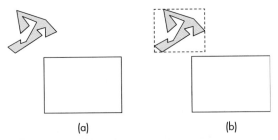

(a)   (b)

Figure 8.19 Using bounding boxes. (a) Polygon and clipping window. (b) Polygon, bounding box, and clipping window.

entire polygon lies outside the clipping window. We can exploit this observation through the use of the **axis-aligned bounding box** or **extent** of the polygon (Figure 8.19b): the smallest rectangle, aligned with the window, that contains the polygon. Calculating the bounding box requires only going through the vertices of the polygon to find the minimum and maximum of both the x and y values.

Once we have the bounding box, we can often avoid detailed clipping. Consider the three cases in Figure 8.20. For the polygon above the window, no clipping is necessary, because the minimum y for the bounding box is above the top of the window. For the polygon inside the window, we can determine that it is inside by comparing the bounding box with the window. Only when we discover that the bounding box straddles the window do we have to carry out detailed clipping, using all the edges of the polygon. The use of extents is such a powerful technique—in both two and three dimensions—that modeling systems often compute a bounding box for each object, automatically, and store the bounding box with the object.

Axis-aligned bounding boxes work in both two and three dimensions. In three dimensions, they can be used in the application to perform clipping to reduce the burden on the pipeline. Other volumes, such as spheres, can also work well. One of the other applications of bounding volumes is in collision detection (Chapter 11). One of the fundamental operations in animating computer games is to determine if two moving entities have collided. For example, consider two animated characters moving in a sequence of images. We need to know when they collide so that we can alter their paths. In a sense, this is a clipping problem, because we want to determine when the volume of one intersects the volume of the other. The complexity of the objects and the need to do these calculations very quickly make this problem difficult. A common approach is to place each object in a bounding volume, either an axis-aligned bounding box or a sphere, and to determine if the volumes intersect. If they do, then detailed calculations can be done.

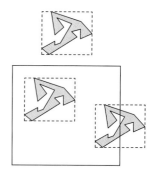

Figure 8.20 Clipping with bounding boxes.

8.6.2 Curves, Surfaces, and Text

The variety of curves and surfaces that we can define mathematically makes it difficult to find general algorithms for processing these objects. The potential difficulties can be seen from the two-dimensional curves in Figure 8.21. For a simple curve, such as a quadratic, we can compute intersections, although at a cost higher than that for lines. For more complex curves, such as the spiral, not only must intersection calculations be computed with numerical techniques, but even determining how many intersections we must compute may be difficult. We can avoid such problems by approximating curves with line segments and surfaces with planar polygons. The use of bounding boxes can also prove helpful, especially in cases such as quadratics where we can compute intersections exactly,

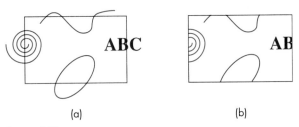

(a)   (b)

Figure 8.21 Curve clipping.

but would prefer to make sure that the calculation is necessary before carrying it out.

The handling of text differs from API to API, with many APIs allowing the user to specify how detailed a rendering of text is required. There are two extremes. On one end, text is stored as bit patterns and is rendered directly by the hardware without any geometric processing. Any required clipping is done in the frame buffer. At the other extreme, text is defined like any other geometric object, and is then processed through the standard viewing pipeline. OpenGL allows both these cases by not having a separate text primitive. The user can choose which mode she prefers by defining either bitmapped characters, using pixel operations, or stroke characters, using the standard primitives. Other APIs, such as PHIGS and GKS, added intermediate options, by having text primitives and a variety of text attributes. In addition to attributes that set the size and color of the text, there are others that allow the user to ask the system to use techniques such as bounding boxes to clip out whole strings of text that cross a clipping boundary.

8.6.3 Clipping in the Frame Buffer

We might also consider delaying clipping until after objects have been projected and converted into screen coordinates. Clipping can be done in the frame buffer through a technique called **scissoring**. However, it is usually better to clip geometric entities before the vertices reach the frame buffer; thus, clipping within the frame buffer generally is required only for raster objects, such as blocks of pixels.

8.7 Clipping in Three Dimensions

In three dimensions, we clip against a bounded volume, rather than against a bounded region in the plane. The simplest extension of two-dimensional clipping to three dimensions is for the right parallelepiped clipping region (Figure 8.22):

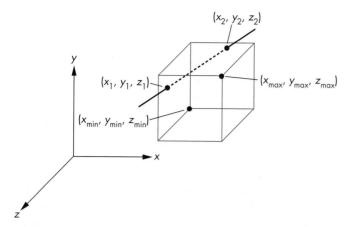

Figure 8.22 Three-dimensional clipping against a right parallelepiped.

$$x_{min} \leq x \leq x_{max},$$
$$y_{min} \leq y \leq y_{max},$$
$$z_{min} \leq z \leq z_{max}.$$

Our three clipping algorithms (Cohen–Sutherland, Liang–Barsky, and Sutherland–Hodgeman) and the use of extents can be extended to three dimensions. For the Cohen–Sutherland algorithm, we replace the 4-bit outcode with a 6-bit outcode. The additional 2 bits are set if the point lies either in front of or behind the clipping volume (Figure 8.23). The testing strategy is virtually identical for the two- and three-dimensional cases.

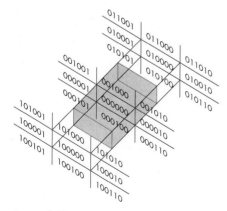

Figure 8.23 Cohen–Sutherland regions in three dimensions.

For the Liang–Barsky algorithm, we add the equation

$$z(\alpha) = (1 - \alpha)z_1 + \alpha z_2$$

to obtain a three-dimensional parametric representation of the line segment. We have to consider six intersections with the surfaces that form the clipping volume, but we can use the same logic as we did in the two-dimensional case. Pipeline clippers add two modules to clip against the front and back of the clipping volume.

The major difference between two- and three-dimensional clippers is that instead of clipping lines against lines, as we do in two dimensions, in three dimensions we are clipping either lines against surfaces or surfaces against surfaces. Consequently, our intersection calculations must be changed. A typical intersection calculation can be posed in terms of a parametric line in three dimensions intersecting a plane (Figure 8.24). If we write the line and plane equations in matrix form (where $\mathbf{n}$ is the normal to the plane and $\mathbf{p}_0$ is a point on the plane), we must solve the equations

$$\mathbf{p}(\alpha) = (1 - \alpha)\mathbf{p}_1 + \alpha \mathbf{p}_2,$$

$$\mathbf{n} \cdot (\mathbf{p}(\alpha) - \mathbf{p}_0) = 0,$$

for the α corresponding to the point of intersection. This value is

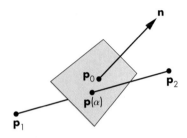

Figure 8.24 Plane–line intersection.

$$\alpha = \frac{\mathbf{n} \cdot (\mathbf{p}_0 - \mathbf{p}_1)}{\mathbf{n} \cdot (\mathbf{p}_2 - \mathbf{p}_1)},$$

and computation of an intersection requires six multiplications and a division. However, if we look at the standard viewing volumes, we see that simplifications are possible. For orthographic viewing (Figure 8.25), the view volume is a right parallelepiped, and each intersection calculation reduces to a single division, as it did for two-dimensional clipping.

When we consider an oblique view (Figure 8.26), we see that the clipping volume no longer is a right parallelepiped. Although you might think that we have to compute dot products to clip against the sides of the volume, here is where the normalization process that we introduced in Chapter 5 pays divi-

Figure 8.25 Clipping for orthographic viewing.

Figure 8.26 Clipping for oblique viewing.

dends. We showed that an oblique projection is equivalent to a shearing of the data followed by an orthographic projection. Although the shear transformation distorts objects, they are distorted such that they project correctly by an orthographic projection. The shear also distorts the clipping volume from a general parallelepiped to a right parallelepiped. Figure 8.27(a) shows a top view of an oblique volume with a cube inside the volume. Figure 8.27(b) shows the volume and object after they have been distorted by the shear. As far as projection is concerned, carrying out the oblique transformation directly or replacing it by a shear transformation and an orthographic projection requires the same amount of computation. When we add in clipping, it is clear that the second approach has a definite advantage, because we can clip against a right parallelepiped. This example illustrates the importance of considering the incremental nature of the steps in an implementation. Analysis of either projection or clipping, in isolation, fails to show the importance of the normalization process.

For perspective projections, the argument for normalization is just as strong. By carrying out the perspective-normalization transformation from Chapter 5, but not the orthographic projection, we again create a rectangular clipping volume and simplify all subsequent intersection calculations.

OpenGL supports additional clipping planes that can be oriented arbitrarily. Hence, if this feature is used in a user program, the implementation must carry out a general clipping routine in software, at a performance cost.

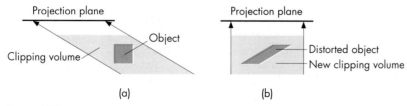

Figure 8.27 Distortion of view volume by shear. (a) Top view before shear. (b) Top view after shear.

8.8 Hidden-Surface Removal

Once vertices have passed through the required geometric transformations, and the objects that they define have been assembled and clipped, we have a set of geometric entities—points, line segments, and polygons—any of which could appear on the display after final projection. But before we rasterize any of these objects, we must solve the problem of hidden-surface removal (or visible-surface determination) to discover whether each object is visible to the viewer or is obscured from the viewer by other objects. We describe a number of techniques for a scene composed purely of planar polygons. This choice is appropriate, as most renderers will have subdivided surfaces into polygons at this point. Line segments can be handled by slight modifications (see Exercise 8.7).

8.8.1 Object-Space and Image-Space Approaches

The study of hidden-surface–removal algorithms clearly illustrates the variety of available algorithms, the differences between working with objects and working with images, and the importance of evaluating the incremental effects of successive algorithms in the implementation process.

Consider a scene composed of k three-dimensional opaque flat polygons, each of which we can consider to be an individual object. We can derive a generic **object-space approach** by considering the objects pairwise, as seen from the center of projection. Consider two such polygons, A and B. There are four possibilities (Figure 8.28):

1. A completely obscures B from the camera; we display only A.
2. B obscures A; we display only B.
3. A and B both are completely visible; we display both A and B.
4. A and B partially obscure each other; we must calculate the visible parts of each polygon.

For complexity considerations, we can regard the determination of which case we have and any required calculation of the visible part of a polygon as a single operation. We proceed iteratively. We pick one of the k polygons and compare it pairwise with the remaining $k - 1$ polygons. After this procedure, we know

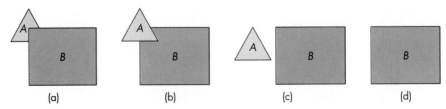

Figure 8.28 Two polygons. (a) B partially obscures A. (b) A partially obscures B. (c) A and B both are visible. (d) B totally obscures A.

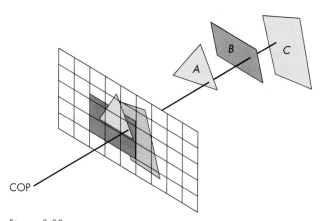

Figure 8.29 Image-space hidden-surface removal.

which part (if any) of this polygon is visible, and we render the visible part. We are now done with this polygon, so we repeat the process with any of the other $k - 1$ polygons. Each step involves comparing one polygon, pairwise, with the other remaining polygons, until we have only two polygons remaining, and we compare them to each other. We can easily determine that the complexity of this calculation is $O(k^2)$. Thus, without deriving any of the details of any particular object-space algorithm, we should suspect that the object-space approach works best for scenes that contain relatively few polygons.

The **image-space approach** follows our viewing and ray-casting model, as shown in Figure 8.29. Consider a ray that leaves the center of projection and passes through a pixel. We can intersect this ray with each of the planes determined by our k polygons, determine for which planes the ray passes through a polygon, and finally, for those rays, find the intersection closest to the center of projection. We color this pixel with the shade of the polygon at the point of intersection. Our fundamental operation is the intersection of rays with polygons. For an $n \times m$ display, we have to carry out this operation nmk times, giving $O(k)$ complexity.[3] Again, without looking at the details of the operations, we were able to get an upper bound. In general, the $O(k)$ bound[4] accounts for the dominance of image-space methods. However, because image-space approaches work at the pixel level, they can create renderings more jagged than those of object-space algorithms.

-----

3. We can use more than one ray for each pixel to increase the accuracy of the rendering.
4. The $O(k)$ bound is a worst-case bound. In practice, image-space algorithms perform much better; see Exercise 8.9.

8.8.2 Sorting and Hidden-Surface Removal

The $O(n^2)$ upper bound for object-oriented hidden-surface removal might remind you of the of the poorer sorting algorithms, such as bubble sort. Any method that involves brute-force comparison of objects by pairs has $O(n^2)$ complexity. But there is a more direct connection that we exploit in the object-oriented sorting algorithms in Section 8.8.5. If we could organize objects by their distances from the camera, we should be able to come up with a direct method of rendering them. It is this analogy that leads to the use of such terms as *sort first* and *sort last* that we used in Section 8.3.

But if we follow the analogy, we know that the complexity of good sorting algorithms is $O(n \log n)$. We should expect the same to be true for object-oriented hidden-surface removal, and, in fact, such is the case. As with sorting, there are multiple algorithms that meet these bounds. In addition, there are related problems involving comparison of objects, such as collision detection, that start off looking as if they are $O(n^2)$ when, in fact, they can be reduced to $O(n \log n)$.

8.8.3 Back-Face Removal

In Chapter 6, we noted that, in OpenGL, we can choose to render only front-facing polygons. For situations where we cannot see back faces, such as scenes composed of convex polyhedra, we can reduce the work required for hidden-surface removal by eliminating all back-facing polygons before we apply any other hidden-surface–removal algorithm. The test for **culling** a back-facing polygon can be derived from Figure 8.30. We see the front of a polygon if the normal, which comes out of the front face, is pointed toward the viewer. If θ is the angle between the normal and the viewer, then the polygon is facing forward if and only if

$$-90 \le \theta \le 90,$$

or, equivalently,

$$\cos \theta \ge 0.$$

The second condition is much easier to test because, instead of computing the cosine, we can use the dot product:

$$\mathbf{n} \cdot \mathbf{v} \ge 0.$$

We can simplify this test even further if we note that usually it is applied after transformation to normalized device coordinates. In this system, all views

Figure 8.30 Back-face test.

are orthographic, with the direction of projection along the z-axis. Hence, in homogeneous coordinates,

$$\mathbf{n} = \begin{bmatrix} 0 \\ 0 \\ 1 \\ 0 \end{bmatrix}.$$

Thus, if the polygon is on the surface

$$ax + by + cz + d = 0$$

in normalized device coordinates, we need only to check the sign of c to determine whether we have a front- or back-facing polygon. This test can be implemented easily in either hardware or software; we must simply be careful to ensure that removing back-facing polygons is correct for our application. In OpenGL, the function `glCullFace` allows us to turn on back-face elimination.

8.8.4 The z-Buffer Algorithm

The z-**buffer algorithm** is the most widely used hidden-surface–removal algorithm. It has the advantages of being easy to implement, in either hardware or software, and of being compatible with pipeline architectures, where it can execute at the speed at which vertices are passing through the pipeline. Although the algorithm works in image space, it loops over the polygons, rather than over pixels, and can be regarded as part of the scan-conversion process that we discuss in Section 8.9.

Suppose that we are in the process of rasterizing one of the two polygons in Figure 8.31. We can compute a color for each point of intersection between a ray from the center of projection and a pixel, using our shading model. In addition, we must check whether this point is visible. It will be visible if it is the closest point of intersection along the ray. Hence, if we are rasterizing B, its shade will

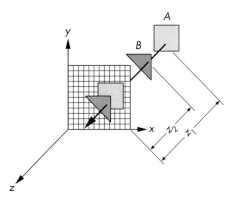

Figure 8.31 The z-buffer algorithm.

appear on the screen if the distance z_2 is less than the distance z_1 to polygon A. Conversely, if we are rasterizing A, the pixel that corresponds to the point of intersection will not appear on the display. Because we are proceeding polygon by polygon, however, we do not have the information on all other polygons as we rasterize any given polygon. However, we can store and update the depth information as we do the scan conversion.

Suppose that we have a buffer, the z buffer, with the same resolution as the frame buffer and with depth consistent with the resolution that we wish to use for distance. For example, if we have a 1024×1280 display and we use single-precision floating-point numbers for the depth calculation, we can use a 1024×1280 z buffer with 32-bit elements. Initially, each element in the depth buffer is initialized to the maximum distance away from the center of projection.[5] The frame buffer is initialized to the background color. At any time during rasterization, each location in the z buffer contains the distance along the ray corresponding to this location of the closest intersection point on any polygon found so far.

The calculation proceeds as follows. We rasterize, polygon by polygon, using one of the methods from Section 8.9. For each point on the polygon corresponding to the intersection of the polygon with a ray through a pixel, we compute the distance from the center of projection. We compare this distance to the value in the z buffer corresponding to this point. If this distance is greater than the distance in the z buffer, then we have already processed a polygon closer to the viewer, and this point is not visible. If the distance is less than the distance in the z buffer,[6] then we have found a point closer to the viewer. We update the distance in the z buffer and place the shade computed for this point at the corresponding location in the frame buffer. Note that for perspective views, the distance we are using in the z-buffer algorithm is the distance that has been altered by the normalization transformation that we discussed in Chapter 5. Although this transformation is nonlinear, it preserves relative distances. However, this nonlinearity can introduce numerical inaccuracies, especially when the distance to the near clipping plane is small.

Unlike other aspects of rendering, where the particular implementation algorithms may unknown to the user, for hidden-surface removal OpenGL, uses the z-buffer algorithm. This exception arises because the application program must initialize the z buffer explicitly every time a new image is to be generated.

The z-buffer algorithm works well with image-oriented approaches to implementation, because the amount of incremental work is small. Suppose that we

---

5. If we have already done perspective normalization, we should replace the center of projection with the direction of projection, because all rays are parallel. However, this change does not affect the z-buffer algorithm, because we can measure distances from any arbitrary plane, such as the plane $z = 0$, rather than from the COP.

6. In OpenGL, we can use the function `glDepthFunc` to decide what do when the distances are equal.

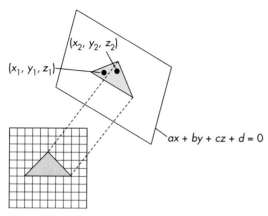

Figure 8.32 Incremental z-buffer algorithm.

are rasterizing a polygon, scan line by scan line—an option we examine in Section 8.9. The polygon is part of a plane (Figure 8.32) that can be represented as

$$ax + by + cz + d = 0.$$

Suppose that (x_1, y_1, z_1) and (x_2, y_2, z_2) are two points on the polygon (and the plane). If

$$\Delta x = x_2 - x_1,$$
$$\Delta y = y_2 - y_1,$$
$$\Delta z = z_2 - z_1,$$

then the equation for the plane can be written in differential form as

$$a\Delta x + b\Delta y + c\Delta z = 0.$$

This equation is in window coordinates, so each scan line corresponds to a line of constant y, and $\Delta y = 0$ as we move across a scan line. On a scan line, we increase x in unit steps, corresponding to moving one pixel in the frame buffer, and Δx is constant. Thus, as we move from point to point across a scan line,

$$\Delta z = -\frac{a}{c}\Delta x.$$

This value is a constant that needs to be computed only once for each polygon.

8.8.5 Depth Sort and the Painter's Algorithm

Depth sort is a direct implementation of the object-space approach to hidden-surface removal. We present the algorithm for a scene composed of planar

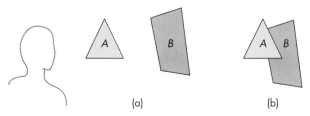

Figure 8.33 Painter's algorithm. (a) Two polygons and viewer are shown. (b) A partially obscures B when viewed.

polygons; extensions to other classes of objects are possible. Depth sort is a variant of an even simpler algorithm known as the **painter's algorithm**.

Suppose that we have a collection of polygons that is sorted based on how far from the viewer the polygons are. For the example in Figure 8.33(a), we have two polygons. To a viewer, they appear as shown in Figure 8.33(b), with the polygon in front partially obscuring the other. To render the scene correctly, we could find the part of the rear polygon that is visible, and could render that part into the frame buffer—a calculation that requires clipping one polygon against the other. Or we could use another approach, analogous to the way an oil painter might render the scene. She probably would paint the farther-back polygon in its entirety, and then would paint the front polygon, in the process painting over the part of the rear polygon not visible to the viewer. Both polygons would be rendered completely, with the hidden-surface removal being done as a consequence of the **back-to-front rendering** of the polygons.[7] The two questions related to this algorithm are how we do the sort, and what we do if polygons overlap. Depth sort addresses both, although in many applications more efficiencies can be found; see, for example, Exercise 8.10.

Suppose we have already computed the extent of each polygon. The next step of depth sort is to order all the polygons by how far away from the viewer their maximum z value is. This step gives the algorithm the name **depth sort**. Suppose that the order is as shown in Figure 8.34, which depicts the z extents of the polygons after the sort. If the minimum depth—the z value—of a given polygon is greater than the maximum depth of the polygon behind the one of interest, we can paint the polygons back to front, and we are done. For example, polygon A in Figure 8.34 is behind all the other polygons and can be painted first. However, the others cannot be painted based solely on the z extents.

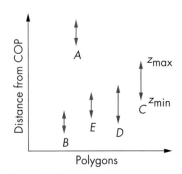

Figure 8.34 The z extents of sorted polygons.

7. Certain application problems can be solved more efficiently with *front-to-back rendering* of polygons.

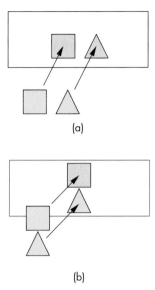

Figure 8.35 Test for overlap in x and y extents. (a) Nonoverlapping x extents. (b) Nonoverlapping y extents.

If the z extents of two polygons overlap, we still may be able to find an order to paint (render) the polygons individually and yield the correct image. The depth-sort algorithm runs a number of increasingly more difficult tests, attempting to find such an ordering. Consider a pair of polygons whose z extents overlap. The simplest test is to check their x and y extents (Figure 8.35). If either of the x or y extents do not overlap,[8] neither polygon can obscure the other, and they can be painted in either order. Even if these tests fail, it may still be possible to find an order in which we can paint the polygons individually. Figure 8.36 shows such a case. All the vertices of one polygon lie on the same side of the plane determined by the other. We can process the vertices (see Exercise 8.12) of the two polygons to determine whether this case exists.

Two troublesome situations remain. If three or more polygons overlap cyclically, as shown in Figure 8.37, there is no correct order for painting. The best we can do is to divide at least one of the polygons into two parts, and to attempt to find an order to paint the new set of polygons. The second problematic case arises

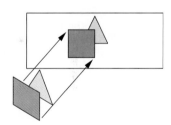

Figure 8.36 Polygons with overlapping extents.

Figure 8.37 Cyclic overlap.

---

8. The x- and y-extent tests apply to only a parallel view. Here is another example of the advantage of working in normalized device coordinates *after* perspective normalization.

Figure 8.38 Piercing polygons.

if a polygon can pierce another polygon, as shown in Figure 8.38. If we want to continue with depth sort, we must derive the details of the intersection—a calculation equivalent to clipping one polygon against the other. If the intersecting polygons have many vertices, we may want to try another algorithm that requires less computation. A performance analysis of depth sort is difficult because the particulars of the application determine how often the more difficult cases arise. For example, if we are working with polygons that describe the surfaces of solid objects, then no two polygons can intersect. Nevertheless, it should be clear that, because of the initial sort, the complexity must be at least $O(n \log n)$, where n is the number of objects.

8.8.6 The Scan-Line Algorithm

Before the reduced cost of memory and the availability of special-purpose graphics chips made pipeline hardware implementations the dominant paradigm, the scan-line method was the most efficient hidden-surface–removal algorithm; it still influences many special-purpose systems. The algorithm combines polygon scan conversion with hidden-surface removal. Although we have yet to discuss the details of scan conversion, we can observe the salient features of the algorithm with the aid of Figure 8.39, which shows two intersecting polygons and their edges. If we rasterize the polygon scan line by scan line, we can use the incremental depth calculation that we derived in this section. However, if we look at the figure, we can observe possibilities for even greater efficiency. As we go from left to right along scan line i, we cross edge a of polygon A. Because we have entered our first polygon on this scan line, there is no reason to carry out a depth calculation. No other polygon can yet affect the colors along this line. When we encounter the next edge, b, we are leaving polygon A, and we color the corresponding pixels with the background color. We next encounter edge c of polygon B; again, having only a single polygon to consider, we can avoid depth calculations. Scan line j shows a more complex situation. First, we encounter edge a again and we can assign colors without a depth calculation. The second edge that we encounter is c; thus, we have two polygons about which to worry. Until we pass edge d, we must carry out depth calculations, and we can make use of our incremental methods.

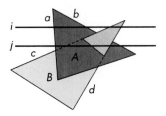

Figure 8.39 Scan-line algorithm.

Although this strategy has elements in common with the z-buffer algorithm, it is fundamentally different because it is working one scan line at a time, rather than one polygon at a time. A good implementation of the algorithm requires a moderately sophisticated data structure for representing which edges are encountered on each scan line. The basic structure is an array of pointers, one for each scan line, each of which points to an incremental edge structure for the scan line.

8.9 Scan Conversion

We are now ready to take the final step in the journey from the specification of geometric entities in an application program to the setting of pixels in a color buffer contained in the frame buffer: rasterization of primitives. We are concerned with only line segments and polygons, both of which are defined by vertices. We can assume that we have clipped the primitives such that each primitive appears on the display. To clarify the discussion, we neglect the effect of hidden-surface removal, and assume that we have objects that can be rasterized individually. We also assume that we have projected all remaining (unclipped) vertices into two dimensions, and that we can work in screen coordinates.

We further assume that the color buffer is an $n \times m$ array of pixels, with $(0, 0)$ corresponding to the lower-left corner. Pixels can be set to a given color by a single function inside the graphics implementation of the form

```
write_pixel(int ix,int iy, int value);
```

The argument `value` can be either an index, in color-index mode, or a pixel value, such as a 32-bit number in RGBA-color mode. On the one hand, a color buffer is inherently discrete; it does not make sense to talk about pixels located at places other than integer values of ix and iy. On the other hand, screen coordinates, which range over the same values as do ix and iy, are real numbers. For example, we can compute a value such as $(63.4, 157.9)$ in screen coordinates, but must realize that the nearest pixel is centered either at $(63, 158)$ or at $(63.5, 157.5)$, depending on how the frame buffer is organized.

Pixels have values that are numbers in the color buffer. Pixels can be displayed in multiple shapes and sizes. We address this matter in Section 8.13. For now, we draw a displayed pixel as a square, whose center is at the location associated with the pixel,[9] and whose side is equal to the distance between pixels. We also assume that a concurrent process reads the contents of the color buffer and creates the display at the required rate. This assumption, which holds in many systems that have dual-ported memory, allows us to treat the rasterization process independently of the display of the contents of the frame buffer.

The simplest scan-conversion algorithm for line segments has become known as the **DDA algorithm**, after the digital differential analyzer, an early electromechanical device for digital simulation of differential equations. Because a line satisfies the differential equation $dy/dx = m$, where m is the slope, generating a line segment is equivalent to solving a simple differential equation numerically.

Suppose that we have a line segment defined by the endpoints (x_1, y_1) and (x_2, y_2). We assume that, because we are working in a color buffer, these values

---

9. In OpenGL, the centers of pixels are located at values halfway between integers. There are some advantages to this choice; see Exercise 8.19.

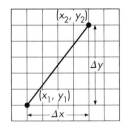

Figure 8.40 Line seg-
ment in window coor-
dinates.

Figure 8.41 Pixels generated
by DDA algorithm.

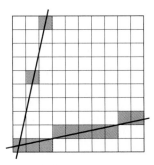

Figure 8.42 Pixels generated
by high- and low-slope lines.

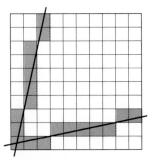

Figure 8.43 Pixels generated
by revised DDA algorithm.

have been rounded to have integer values, so the line segment starts and ends at a known pixel.[10] The slope is given by

$$m = \frac{y_2 - y_1}{x_2 - x_1} = \frac{\Delta y}{\Delta x}.$$

We assume that

$$0 \le m \le 1.$$

We can handle other values of m using symmetry. Our algorithm is based on writing a pixel for each value of ix in write_pixel as x goes from x_1 to x_2. If we are on the line segment, as shown in Figure 8.40, for any change in x equal to Δx, the corresponding changes in y must be

$$\Delta y = m \Delta x.$$

As we move from x_1 to x_2, we increase x by 1 each iteration; thus, we must increase y by

$$\Delta y = m.$$

Although each x is an integer, each y is not, because m is a floating-point number, and we must round it to find the appropriate pixel, as shown in Figure 8.41. Our algorithm, in pseudocode, is

```
for(ix=x1; ix <= x2; ix++)
{
        y+=m;
        write_pixel(x, round(y) , line_color);
}
```

where round is a function that rounds a real to an integer. The reason that we limited the maximum slope to 1 can be seen from Figure 8.42. Our algorithm is of this form: For each x, find the best y. For large slopes, the separation between pixels that are colored can be large, generating an unacceptable approximation to the line segment. If, however, for slopes greater than 1, we swap the roles of x and y, the algorithm becomes this: For each y, find the best x. For the same line segments, we get the approximations in Figure 8.43. Note that the use of symmetry removes any potential problems from either vertical or horizontal line segments. You may want to derive the parts of the algorithm for negative slopes.

Because line segments are determined by vertices, we can use interpolation to assign a different color to each pixel that we generate. We can also generate various dash and dot patterns by changing the color that we use as we generate

---

10. This assumption is not necessary to derive an algorithm. If we use a fixed-point representation for the endpoints and do our calculations using fixed-point arithmetic, then we retain the computational advantages of the algorithm and produce a more accurate rasterization.

pixels. Neither of these effects has much to do with the basic rasterization algorithm, as the latter's job is to determine only which pixels to set, rather than to determine the color that is used.

8.10 Bresenham's Algorithm

The DDA algorithm appears efficient. Certainly it can be coded easily, but it requires a floating-point addition for each pixel generated. Bresenham derived a line-rasterization algorithm that, remarkably, avoids all floating-point calculations and has become the standard algorithm used in hardware and software rasterizers.

We assume, as we did with the DDA algorithm, that the line segment goes between the integer points (x_1, y_1) and (x_2, y_2), and that the slope satisfies

$$0 \leq m \leq 1.$$

This slope condition is crucial for the algorithm, as we can see with aid of Figure 8.44. Suppose that we are somewhere in the middle of the scan conversion of our line segment and have just placed a pixel at $(i + \frac{1}{2}, j + \frac{1}{2})$. We know that the line of which the segment is part can be represented as

$$y = mx + h.$$

At $x = i + \frac{1}{2}$, this line must pass within one-half the length of the pixel at $(i + \frac{1}{2}, j + \frac{1}{2})$;[11] otherwise, the rounding operation would not have generated this pixel. If we move ahead to $x = i + \frac{3}{2}$, the slope condition indicates that we must set the color of one of only two possible pixels: either the pixel at $(i + \frac{3}{2}, j + \frac{1}{2})$, or the pixel at $(i + \frac{3}{2}, j + \frac{3}{2})$. Having reduced our choices to two pixels, we can pose the problem anew in terms of the **decision variable** $d = a - b$, where a and b are the distances between the line and the upper and lower candidate pixels at $x = i + \frac{3}{2}$, as shown in Figure 8.45. If d is positive, the line passes closer to the lower pixel, so we choose the pixel at $(i + \frac{3}{2}, j + \frac{1}{2})$; otherwise, we choose the pixel at $(i + \frac{3}{2}, j + \frac{3}{2})$. Although we could compute d by computing $y = mx + b$, we hesitate to do so because m is a floating-point number.

We obtain the computational advantages of Bresenham's algorithm through two further steps. First, we replace floating-point operations with fixed-point operations. Second, we apply the algorithm incrementally. We start by replacing d with the new decision variable

$$d = (x_2 - x_1)(a - b) = \Delta x(a - b),$$

---

11. We are assuming that the pixels' centers are located halfway between integers.

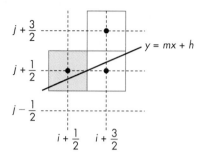

Figure 8.44 Conditions for Bresenham's algorithm.

a change that cannot affect which pixels are drawn, because it is only the sign of
the decision variable that matters. If we substitute for a and b, using the equation
of the line, and noting that

$$m = \frac{y_2 - y_1}{x_2 - x_1} = \frac{\Delta y}{\Delta x},$$

$$h = y_2 - m x_2,$$

then we can see that d is an integer. We have eliminated floating-point calculations, but the direct computation of d requires a fair amount of fixed-point
arithmetic.

Let us take a slightly different approach. Suppose that d_k is the value of d at
$x = k + \frac{1}{2}$. We would like to compute d_{k+1} incrementally from d_k. There are two
situations, depending on whether or not we incremented the y location of the
pixel at the previous step; these situations are shown in Figure 8.46. By observing
that a is the distance between the location of the upper candidate location and
the line, we see that a increases by m only if x was increased by the previous
decision; otherwise, it decreases by $m - 1$. Likewise, b either decreases by $-m$

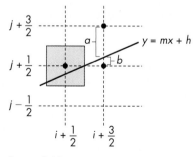

Figure 8.45 Decision variable for
Bresenham's algorithm.

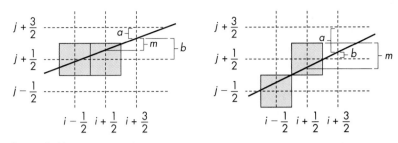

Figure 8.46 Incrementing of the values of a and b.

or increases by $1 - m$ when we increment x. Multiplying by Δx, we find that the possible changes in d are either $-2\Delta y$ or $2(\Delta x - \Delta y)$. We can state this result in the form

$$d_{k+1} = d_k - \begin{cases} 2\Delta y & \text{if } d_k > 0; \\ 2(\Delta y - \Delta x) & \text{otherwise.} \end{cases}$$

The calculation of each successive pixel in the color buffer requires only an addition and a sign test. This algorithm is so efficient that it has been incorporated as a single instruction on graphics chips. See Exercise 8.14 for calculation of the initial value d_0.

8.11 Scan Conversion of Polygons

One of the major advantages that the first raster systems brought to users was the ability to display filled polygons. At that time, coloring each point in the interior of a polygon with a different shade was not possible in real time, and the phrases *rasterizing polygons* and *polygon scan conversion* came to mean filling a polygon with a single color. Unlike scan conversion of lines, where a single algorithm dominates, there are many viable methods for rasterizing polygons. The choice depends heavily on the implementation architecture. We concentrate on methods that fit with our pipeline approach and can also support shading. In Sections 8.11.4–8.11.6, we survey a number of other approaches.

8.11.1 Inside–Outside Testing

Flat simple polygons have well-defined interiors. If they are also convex, they are guaranteed to be rendered correctly by OpenGL and by other graphics systems. More general polygons arise in practice, however, and we can render them in multiple ways. For nonflat polygons, we can work with their projections (Section 8.11.2), or we can use the first three vertices to determine a flat plane to use for the interior. For nonsimple flat polygons, we must decide how to determine whether a given point is inside or outside of the polygon.

Conceptually, the process of filling the inside of a polygon with a color or pattern is equivalent to deciding which points in the plane of the polygon are interior (inside) points.

The **crossing** or **odd–even test** is the most widely used test for making inside–outside decisions. Suppose that **p** is a point inside a polygon. Any ray emanating from **p** and going off to infinity must cross an odd number of edges. Any ray emanating from a point outside the polygon and entering the polygon crosses an even number of edges before reaching infinity. Hence, a point can be defined as being inside if we draw a line through it and if following this line, starting on the outside, we cross an odd number of edges before reaching it. For the star-shaped polygon in Figure 8.47, we obtain the inside coloring shown. Odd–even testing is easy to implement and integrates well with the standard rendering algorithms, Usually, we replace rays through points with scanlines, and we count the crossing of polygon edges to determine inside and outside.

However, we might want our fill algorithm to color the star polygon as shown in Figure 8.48 rather than as shown in Figure 8.47. The **winding** test allows us to make that happen. This test considers the polygon as a knot being wrapped around a point or a line. To implement the test, we consider traversing the edges of the polygon from any starting vertex and going around the edge in a particular direction (which direction does not matter) until we reach the starting point. We illustrate the path by labeling the edges, as shown in Figure 8.48(b). Next we consider an arbitrary point. The **winding number** for this point is the number of times it is encircled by the edges of the polygon. We count clockwise encirclements as positive and counterclockwise encirclements as negative (or vice versa). Thus, points outside the star in Figure 8.48 are not encircled and have a winding number of 0; points that were filled in Figure 8.47 all have a winding number of 1; and points in the center that were not filled by the odd–even test have a winding number of 2. If we change our fill rule to be that a point is inside the polygon if its winding number is not zero, then we fill the inside of the polygon as shown in Figure 8.48(a).

There are several problems with our definition of the winding number. Consider the S-shaped curve in Figure 8.49 that we might approximate with a

Figure 8.47 Filling with the odd–even test.

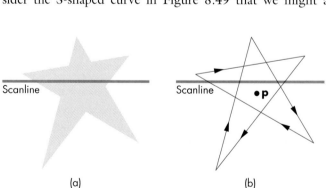

(a)   (b)

Figure 8.48 Fill using the winding number test.

polygon containing many vertices. It is not clear how we should define encirclements for points inside the curve. With a little care, we can modify our odd–even definition to improve the definition for the winding number and to obtain a way of measuring the winding number for an arbitrary point. Consider any line through an interior point **p** that cuts through the polygon completely, as shown in Figure 8.48(b), and that is not parallel to an edge of the polygon. The winding number for this point is the number of edges that cross our line in the downward direction, minus the number of edges that cross our line in the upward direction. If the winding number is not zero, the point is inside the polygon. Note that for this test, it does not matter how we define *up* and *down*.

Figure 8.49 S-shaped curve.

8.11.2 OpenGL and Concave Polygons

Because OpenGL guarantees correct rendering of polygons only if they are convex, we still have the problem of what to do with more general polygons. One approach is to work with the application to ensure that all polygons obey these restrictions. Another is to provide software that can tessellate a given polygon into flat convex polygons, usually triangles. There are many ways to divide a given polygon into triangles. A good tessellation should not produce triangles that are long and thin; it should, if possible, produce sets of triangles that can use supported features, such as triangle strips and triangle fans. There is a tessellator in the GLU library. For a simple polygon without holes, we start by declaring a **tessellator object** and giving it the vertices of the polygons:

```
mytess = gluNewTess();

gluTessBeginPolygon(mytess, NULL);
gluTessBeginContour(mytess);
for(i=0;i<nvertices;i++)
   glTessVertex(mytess,vertex[i],vertex[i]);
gluTessEndContour();
gluTessEndPolygon(mytess);
```

Although there are many parameters that can be set, the basic idea is that we have described a contour, and the tessellating software generates the required triangles and sends them off to be rendered based on the present tessellation parameters.

The use of the winding number is important in OpenGL tessellation algorithms and in trimmed NURBS surfaces (Chapter 10). Here the direction of encirclement of a point by the contours inside the polygon can—based on the tessellation parameters—cause a variety of possible renderings, as in Figure 8.50. The references at the end of the chapter give details of the various tessellation algorithms. From an OpenGL perspective, if tessellators are used, all rendering is done to convex polygons.

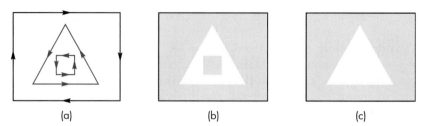

Figure 8.50 Polygon tessellations. (a) Polygon with edges and directions of contours. (b) Tessellation 1. (c) Tessellation 2.

8.11.3 Scan Conversion with the z Buffer

We already have presented most of the essentials of polygon rasterization. In Section 8.11.2, we discussed the odd–even and winding tests for determining whether a point is inside a polygon. In Chapter 6, we learned to shade polygons by interpolation. Here, we have only to put together the pieces and to consider efficiency.

Suppose that we follow the pipeline once more, concentrating on what happens to a single polygon. The vertices and normals pass through the geometric transformations one at a time. The vertices must be assembled into a polygon before the clipping stage. If our polygon is not clipped out, its vertices and normals can be passed on for shading and hidden-surface removal. At this point, although projection normalization has taken place, we still have depth information. If we wish to use an interpolative shading method, we can compute the lighting at each vertex.

Three tasks remain: computation of the final orthographic projection, hidden-surface removal, and shading. Careful use of the z-buffer algorithm can accomplish all three tasks simultaneously. Consider the dual representations of a polygon in Figure 8.51. On the left, the polygon is represented in three-dimensional normalized device coordinates; on the right, it is shown after projection in screen coordinates.

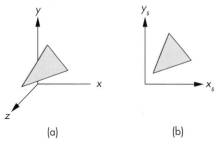

Figure 8.51 Dual representations of a polygon. (a) Normalized device coordinates. (b) Screen coordinates.

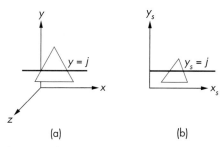

Figure 8.52 Scan line (a) in normalized device coordinates, and (b) in screen coordinates.

The strategy is to process each polygon, one scan line at a time. If we work in terms of the dual representations, we can see that a scan line, projected backward from screen coordinates, corresponds to a line of constant y in normalized device coordinates (Figure 8.52). Suppose that we simultaneously march across this scan line and its back projection. For the scan line in screen coordinates, we move one pixel width each step. We use the normalized-device-coordinate line to determine depths incrementally, and to see whether or not the pixel in screen coordinates corresponds to a visible point on the polygon. Having computed shading for the vertices of the original polygon, we can use bilinear interpolation to obtain the correct color for visible pixels.[12] This process requires little extra effort over the individual steps that we have already discussed. It is controlled, and thus limited, by the rate at which we can send polygons through the pipeline. Modifications such as applying bit patterns, called stipple patterns, or texture to polygons require only slight changes.

8.11.4 Fill and Sort

A different approach to rasterization of polygons starts with the idea of a polygon processor: a black box whose inputs are the vertices for a set of two-dimensional polygons and whose output is a frame buffer with the correct pixels set. Suppose that we consider filling each polygon with a constant color—a choice we make only to clarify the discussion. First, consider a single polygon. The basic rule for filling a polygon is as follows: *If a point is inside the polygon, color it with the inside (fill) color.* This conceptual algorithm indicates that polygon fill is a sorting problem, where we sort all the pixels in the frame buffer into those that are inside the polygon and those that are not. From this perspective, we obtain

---

12. Note that carrying out interpolation of shades in normalized device coordinates yields results different from those of interpolation after projection to screen coordinates.

different polygon-fill algorithms using different ways of sorting the points. We introduce three possibilities:

- Flood fill
- Scan-line fill
- Odd–even fill

8.11.5 Flood Fill

We can display an unfilled polygon by rasterizing its edges into the frame buffer using Bresenham's algorithm. Suppose that we have only two colors: a background color (white) and a foreground, or drawing, color (black). We can use the foreground color to rasterize the edges, resulting in a frame buffer colored as shown in Figure 8.53 for a simple polygon. If we can find an initial point (x, y) inside the polygon—a **seed point**—then we can look at its neighbors recursively, coloring them with the foreground color if they are not edge points. The **flood-fill algorithm** can be expressed in pseudocode, assuming that there is a function read_pixel that returns the color of a pixel:

```
flood_fill(int x, int y)
{
    if(read_pixel(x,y)==WHITE)
    {
        write_pixel(x,y,BLACK);
        flood_fill(x-1,y);
        flood_fill(x+1,y);
        flood_fill(x,y-1);
        flood_fill(x,y+1);
    }
}
```

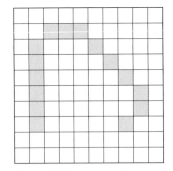

Figure 8.53 Polygon displayed by edges.

We can obtain a number of variants of flood fill by removing the recursion. One way to do so is to work one scan line at a time.

8.11.6 Scan-Line Algorithms

The attraction of a **scan-line algorithm** is that such a method has the potential to generate pixels as they are displayed. Consider the polygon in Figure 8.54, with one scan line shown. If we use our odd–even rule for defining the inside of the polygon, we can see three groups of pixels, or **spans**, on this scan line that are inside the polygon. Note that each span can be processed independently for lighting or depth calculations, a strategy that has been employed in some hardware that has parallel span processors. For our simple example of constant fill, after we have identified the spans, we can color the interior pixels of each span with the fill color.

Figure 8.54 Polygon with spans.

The spans are determined by the set of intersections of polygons with scan lines. The vertices contain all the information that we need to determine these intersections, but the method that we use to represent the polygon determines the order in which these intersections are generated. For example, consider the polygon in Figure 8.55, which has been represented by an ordered list of vertices. The most obvious way to generate scan-line–edge intersections is to process edges defined by successive vertices. Figure 8.55 shows these intersections, indexed in the order in which this method would generate them. Note that this calculation can be done incrementally (see Exercise 8.18). However, as far as fill is concerned, this order is far from the one we want. If we are to fill one scan line at a time, we would like the intersections sorted, first by scan lines, and then by order of x on each scan line, as shown in Figure 8.56. A brute-force approach might be to sort all the intersections into the desired order. However, a large or jagged polygon might intersect so many edges that the n intersections can be large enough—consider, for example, a polygon that spans one-half of the scan lines—that the $O(n \log n)$ complexity of the sort makes the calculation too slow for real-time implementations.

A number of methods avoid the general search. One, originally known as the **y–x algorithm**, creates a bucket for each scan line. As edges are processed, the intersections with scan lines are placed in the proper buckets. Within each bucket, an insertion sort orders the x values along each scan line. The data structure is shown in Figure 8.57. Once again, we see that a properly chosen data structure can speed up the algorithm. We can go even further by reconsidering how to represent polygons. If we do so, we arrive at the scan-line method that was introduced in Section 8.8.

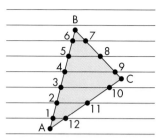

Figure 8.55 Polygon generated by vertex list.

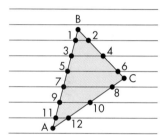

Figure 8.56 Desired order of vertices.

8.11.7 Singularities

We can extend most polygon-fill algorithms to other shapes if we use care (see Exercise 8.17). Polygons have the distinct advantage that the locations of their edges are known exactly. Even polygons can present problems, however, when vertices lie on scan lines. Consider the two cases in Figure 8.58. If we are using an odd–even fill definition, we have to treat these two cases differently. For part (a), we can count the intersection of the scan line with the vertex as either zero

(a)

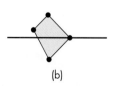

(b)

Figure 8.58 Singularities. (a) Zero or two edge crossings. (b) One edge crossing.

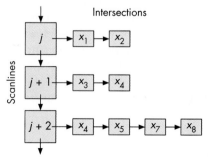

Figure 8.57 Data structure for y–x algorithm.

or two edge crossings; for part (b), the vertex–scan-line intersection must be counted as one edge crossing.

We can fix our algorithm in one of two ways. We can check to see which of the two situations we have, and then count the edge crossings appropriately. Or we can prevent the special case of a vertex lying on an edge—a **singularity**—from ever arising. We rule it out by ensuring that no vertex has an integer y value. If we find one that does, we perturb its location slightly. Another method—one that is especially valuable if we are working in the frame buffer—is to consider a virtual frame buffer of twice the resolution of the real frame buffer. In the virtual frame buffer, pixels are located at only even values of y, and all vertices are located at only odd values of y. Placing pixel centers halfway between integers, as does OpenGL, is equivalent to using this approach.

8.12 Antialiasing

Rasterized line segments and edges of polygons look jagged. Even on a CRT that has a resolution as high as 1024×1280, we can notice these defects in the display. This type of error arises whenever we attempt to go from the continuous representation of an object, which has infinite resolution, to a discrete approximation, which has limited resolution. The name **aliasing** has been given to this effect, because of the tie with aliasing in digital signal processing.

As we saw in Chapter 7, aliasing errors are caused by three related problems with the discrete nature of the frame buffer. First, if we have an $n \times m$ frame buffer, the number of pixels is fixed, and we can generate only certain patterns to approximate a line segment. Many different continuous line segments may be approximated by the same pattern of pixels. We can say that all these segments are **aliased** as the same sequence of pixels. Second, pixel locations are fixed on a uniform grid; regardless of where we would like to place pixels, we cannot place them at other than evenly spaced locations. Third, pixels have a fixed size and shape.

At first glance it might appear that there is little we can do about such problems. Algorithms such as Bresenham's algorithm are optimal in that they choose the closest set of pixels to approximate lines and polygons. However, if we have a display that supports more than two colors, there are other possibilities. Although mathematical lines are one-dimensional entities that have length but not width, rasterized lines must have a width in order to be visible. Suppose that each pixel is a square of width 1 unit, and can occupy a box of 1-unit height and width on the display. Our basic frame buffer can work only in multiples of one pixel;[13] we can think of an idealized line segment in the frame buffer as being one pixel wide, as shown in Figure 8.59. Of course, we cannot draw this

Figure 8.59   Ideal raster line.

---

13. Some frame buffers permit operations in units of less than one pixel through supersampling, a topic that we addressed in Chapter 7.

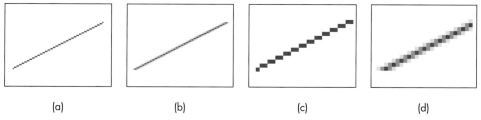

Figure 8.60 Aliased versus antialiased line segments. (a) Aliased line segment. (b) Antialiased line segment. (c) Magnified aliased line segment. (d) Magnified antialiased line segment.

line, because it does not consist of our square pixels. We can view Bresenham's algorithm as a method for approximating the ideal one-pixel-wide line with our real pixels. If we look at the ideal one-pixel-wide line, we can see that it partially covers many pixel-sized boxes. It is our scan-conversion algorithm that forces us, for lines of slope less than 1, to choose exactly one pixel value for each value of x. If, instead, we shade each box by the percentage of the ideal line that crosses it, we get the smoother-appearing image shown in Figure 8.60(b). This technique is known as **antialiasing by area averaging**. The calculation is similar to polygon clipping. There are other approaches to antialiasing, as well as antialiasing algorithms that can be applied to other primitives, such as polygons. Color Plate 8 shows aliased and antialiased versions of a small area of the object in Color Plate 1.

A related problem arises because of the simple way that we are using the z-buffer algorithm. As we have specified that algorithm, the color of a given pixel is determined by the shade of a single primitive. Consider the pixel shared by the three polygons shown in Figure 8.61. If each polygon has a different color, the color assigned to the pixel is the one associated with the polygon closest to the viewer. We could obtain a much more accurate image if we could assign a color based on an area-weighted average of the colors of the three triangles. The accumulation buffer that we introduced in Chapter 7 allows us to implement such techniques.

We have discussed only one type of aliasing: **spatial-domain aliasing**. When we generate sequences of images, such as for animations, we also must be concerned with **time-domain aliasing**. Consider a small object that is moving in front of the projection plane and that has been ruled into pixel-sized units, as shown in Figure 8.62. If our rendering process sends a ray through the center of each pixel and determines what it hits, then sometimes we intersect the object and sometimes, if the projection of the object is small, we miss the object. The viewer will have the unpleasant experience of seeing the object flash on and off the display as the animation progresses. There are several ways to deal with this problem. For example, we can use more than one ray per pixel—a technique common in ray tracing. What is common to all antialiasing techniques is that they require considerably more computation than does rendering without

Figure 8.61 Polygons that share a pixel.

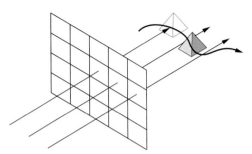

Figure 8.62 Time-domain aliasing.

antialiasing. In practice, for high-resolution images, antialiasing is done off-line, and is done only when a final image is needed.

8.13 Display Considerations

In most interactive applications, the application programmer does not have to worry about how the contents of the frame buffer are displayed. In scan-line–based systems, the display is generated directly by the rasterization algorithms. In the more common approach for workstations, the frame buffer consists of dual-ported memory; the process of writing into the frame buffer is completely independent of the process of reading the frame buffer's contents for display. Thus, the hardware redisplays the present contents of the frame buffer at a rate sufficient to avoid flicker—usually 60 to 85 Hz—and the application programmer worries about only whether or not her program can execute and fill the frame buffer fast enough. As we saw in Chapter 3, the use of double buffering allows the display to change smoothly, even if we cannot push our primitives through the system as fast as we would like.

Numerous other problems affect the quality of the display and often cause users to be unhappy with the output of their programs. For example, two CRT displays may have the same nominal resolution but may display pixels of different sizes (see Exercises 8.22 and 8.23).

8.13.1 Color Systems

Virtually all our discussion of color has been in terms of additive RGB color. Our basic assumption, supported by the three-color theory of human vision, is that the three color values that we determine for each pixel correspond to the tristimulus values that we introduced in Chapter 2. However, there are significant differences across RGB systems. For example, suppose we have a yellow color that OpenGL has represented with the RGB triplet (0.8, 0.6, 0.0). If we use these values to drive both a CRT and a film-image recorder, we will see different colors, even though in both cases the red is 80 percent of maximum, the green is 60 percent of maximum, and the blue is off. The reason is that the film dyes and the CRT phosphors have different color distributions.

The emphasis in the graphics community has been on device-independent graphics; consequently, the real differences among display properties are not addressed by most APIs. Fortunately, the colorimetry literature contains the information we need. The standards for many of the common color systems exist. For example, CRTs are based on the National Television Systems Committee (NTSC) RGB system. We can look at differences in color systems as equivalent to different coordinate systems for representing our tristimulus values. If $\mathbf{C}_1 = [R_1, G_1, B_1]^T$ and $\mathbf{C}_2 = [R_2, G_2, B_2]^T$ are the representations of the same color in two different systems, there is a 3×3 color-conversion matrix $\mathbf{M}$ such that

$$\mathbf{C}_2 = \mathbf{M}\mathbf{C}_1.$$

Whether we determine this matrix from the literature or by experimentation, it allows us to produce similar displays on different output devices.

There are numerous potential problems even with this approach. The color gamuts of the two systems may not be the same. Hence, even after the conversion of tristimulus values, a color may not be producible on one of the systems. Second, the printing and graphic-arts industries use a four-color subtractive system (CMYK) that adds black (K) as a fourth primary. Conversion between RGB and CMYK often requires a great deal of human expertise. Third, there are limitations to our linear color theory. The distance between colors in the color cube is not a measure of how far apart the colors are perceptually. For example, humans are particularly sensitive to color shifts in blue. Color systems such as YUV and Lab have been created to address such issues.

Most RGB color systems are based on the primaries in real systems, such as CRT phosphors and film dyes. None can produce all the colors that we can see. Most color standards are based on a theoretical three-primary system called the **XYZ color system**. Here the Y primary is the luminance of the color. In the XYZ system, all colors can be specified with positive tristimulus values. We use 3×3 matrices to convert from an XYZ color representation to representations in the standard systems. Color researchers often prefer to work with **chromaticity coordinates** rather than tristimulus values. The chromaticity of a color is the three fractions of the color in the three primaries. Thus, if we have the tristimulus values, T_1, T_2, and T_3, for a particular RGB color, its chromaticity coordinates are

$$t_1 = \frac{T_1}{T_1 + T_2 + T_3},$$

$$t_2 = \frac{T_2}{T_1 + T_2 + T_3},$$

$$t_3 = \frac{T_3}{T_1 + T_2 + T_3}.$$

Adding the three equations, we have

$$t_1 + t_2 + t_3 = 1,$$

and thus we can work in the two-dimensional t_1, t_2 space, finding t_3 only when its value is needed. The information that is missing from chromaticity coordinates, which was contained in the original tristimulus values, is the sum $T_1 + T_2 + T_3$, a value related to the intensity of the color. When working with color systems, this intensity is often not important to issues related to producing colors or matching colors across different systems.

Because each color fraction must be nonnegative, the chromaticity values are limited by

$$1 \geq t_i \geq 0.$$

All producible colors must lie inside the triangle in Figure 8.63. Figure 8.64 shows this triangle for the XYZ system and a curve of the representation for each visible spectral line. For the XYZ system, this curve must lie inside the triangle. Figure 8.64 also shows the range (or **gamut**) of colors (in x,y chromaticity coordinates) that are producible on a typical color printer or CRT. If we compare the two figures, we see that the colors inside the curve of pure spectral lines but outside the gamut of the physical display cannot be displayed on the physical device.

One defect of our development of color is that RGB color is based on how color is produced and measured, rather than on how we perceive a color. When we see a given color, we describe it not by three primaries, but rather based on

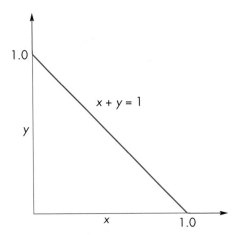

Figure 8.63 Triangle of producible colors in chromaticity coordinates.

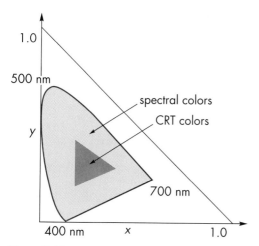

Figure 8.64 Visible colors and color gamut of a display.

other properties, such as the name we give the color and how bright a shade we see. The hue–saturation–lightness (HLS) system is used by artists and some display manufacturers. The **hue** is the name we give to a color: red, yellow, gold. The **lightness** is how bright the color appears. **Saturation** is the color attribute that distinguishes a pure shade of a color from the a shade of the same hue that has been mixed with white, forming a pastel shade. We can relate these attributes to a typical RGB color as shown in Figure 8.65(a). Given a color in the color cube, the lightness is a measure of how far the point is from the origin (black). If we note that all the colors on the principal diagonal of the cube, going from black to white, are shades of gray and are totally unsaturated, then the saturation is a measure of how far the given color is from this diagonal. Finally, the hue is a measure of where the color vector is pointing. HLS colors are usually described in terms of a color cone, as shown in Figure 8.65(b), or through a double cone that also converges at the top. From our perspective, we can look at the HLS system as providing a representation of an RGB color in polar coordinates.

8.13.2 The Color Matrix

One of the OpenGL imaging extensions is a color matrix that simplifies conversion between different color systems. The color matrix is a 4×4 matrix stored as a 16-element array by columns. It operates on RGBA color representations

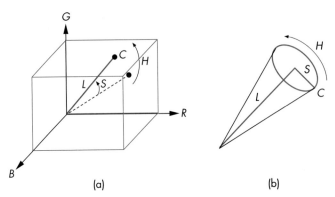

Figure 8.65 Hue–lightness–saturation color. (a) Using the RGB color cube. (b) Using a single cone.

and can be looked at as part of the pipeline that converts a color, $rgba$, to a new color, $r'g'b'a'$, by the matrix multiplication

$$\begin{bmatrix} r' \\ g' \\ b' \\ a' \end{bmatrix} = \mathbf{C} \begin{bmatrix} r \\ g \\ b \\ a \end{bmatrix}.$$

Thus, if we are dealing with opaque surfaces for which $A = 1$, the matrix

$$C = \begin{bmatrix} -1 & 0 & 0 & 1 \\ 0 & -1 & 0 & 1 \\ 0 & 0 & -1 & 1 \\ 0 & 0 & 0 & 1 \end{bmatrix}$$

converts the additive representation of a color to its subtractive representation.

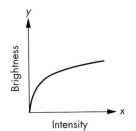

Figure 8.66 Logarithmic brightness.

8.13.3 Gamma Correction

In Chapter 2 we defined brightness as perceived intensity, and observed that the human visual system perceives intensity in a logarithmic manner, as shown in Figure 8.66. One consequence of this property is that if we want the brightness steps to appear to be uniformly spaced, the intensities that we assign to pixels should increase exponentially. These steps can be calculated from the measured minimum and maximum intensities that a display can generate (see Exercise 8.25).

In addition, the intensity I of a CRT is related to the voltage V applied by

$$I \propto V^{\gamma}$$

or

$$\log I = c_0 + \gamma \log V,$$

where the constants γ and c_0 are properties of the particular CRT. One implication of these two results is that two monitors may generate different brightnesses for the same values in the frame buffer. One way to correct for this problem is to have a lookup table, as we discussed in Chapter 7, in the display whose values can be adjusted for the particular characteristics of the monitor—the **gamma correction**.

There is an additional problem with CRTs. It is not possible to have a CRT whose display is totally black when no signal is applied. The minimum displayed intensity is called the **dark field** value and can be problematic, especially when CRT technology is used to project images. In Chapter 13, this problem will arise when we consider creating large images using arrays of projectors.

8.13.4 Dithering and Halftoning

We have specified a color buffer by its spatial resolution (the number of pixels), and by its depth (the number of colors it can display). If we view these separate numbers as fixed, we say that a high-resolution black-and-white laser printer can display only 1-bit pixels. This argument also seems to imply that any black-and-white medium, such as a book, could not display images with multiple shades. We know from experience that that is not the case; the trick is to trade spatial resolution for gray-scale or color resolution. **Halftoning** techniques in the printing industry use photographic means to simulate gray levels by creating patterns of black dots of varying size. The human visual system tends to merge small dots together and sees, not the dots, but rather an intensity proportional to the percentage of black in a small area.

Digital halftones differ because the size and location of displayed pixels are fixed. Consider a 4×4 group of 1-bit pixels, as shown in Figure 8.67. If we look at this pattern from far away, we see not the individual pixels, but rather a gray level based on the number of black pixels. For our 4×4 example, although there are 2^{16} different patterns of black and white pixels, there are only 17 possible shades, corresponding to 0 to 16 black pixels in the array. There are many algorithms for generating halftone, or **dither**, patterns. The simplest picks 17 patterns (for our example) and uses them to create a display with 17 rather than two gray levels, although at the cost of decreasing the spatial resolution by a factor of 4.

Figure 8.67 Digital halftone patterns.

The simple algorithm—always using the same array to simulate a shade—can generate beat or moiré patterns when displaying anything regular. Such patterns arise whenever we image two regular phenomena, as we see the sum and differences of their frequencies. Such effects are closely related to the aliasing problems we discussed in Chapter 7.

Many dithering techniques are based on simply randomizing the least significant bit of the luminance or of each color component. More sophisticated dither algorithms use randomization to create patterns with the correct average properties, but avoid the repetition that can lead to moiré effects (see Exercise 8.26).

Halftoning (or dithering) is often used with color, especially with hard-copy displays, such as ink-jet printers, that can produce only fully on or off colors. Each primary can be dithered to produce more visual colors. OpenGL supports such displays and allows the user to enable dithering (`glEnable(GL_DITHER)`). Color dithering allows color monitors to produce smooth color displays, and normally dithering is enabled. Because dithering is so effective, displays can work well with a limited number of bits per color, allowing frame buffers to have a limited amount of memory. In many applications we need to use the OpenGL inquiry function `glGetIntegerv` to find out how many bits are being used for each color, since this information is important when we use some of the techniques from Chapter 7 that read pixels from the frame buffer. If dithering is enabled and we read pixels out of the frame buffer, pixels that were written with same RGB values may return different values when read. If these small differences are important, dithering should be disabled before reading from the frame buffer.

8.14 Summary and Notes

We have presented an overview of the implementation process, including a sampling of the most important algorithms. Regardless of what the particulars are of an implementation, whether the tasks are done primarily in hardware or in software, whether we are working with a special-purpose graphics workstation or with a simple graphics terminal, and what the API is, the same tasks must be done. These tasks include implementation of geometric transformations, clipping, and rasterization. The relationship among hardware, software, and APIs is an interesting one.

The Geometry Engine that was the basis of many Silicon Graphics workstations is a VLSI chip that performed geometric transformations and clipping through a hardware pipeline. GL, the predecessor of OpenGL, was developed as an API for users of these workstations. Much of the OpenGL literature also follows the pipeline approach. We should keep in mind, however, that OpenGL is an API: It does not say anything about the underlying implementation. In principle, an image defined by an OpenGL program could be obtained from a ray tracer. We should carry away two lessons from our emphasis on pipeline architectures. First, this architecture provides an aid to the applications programmer in understanding the process of creating images. Second, at present, the pipeline view can lead to efficient hardware and software implementations.

The example of the z-buffer algorithm is illustrative of the relationship between hardware and software. A decade ago, many hidden-surface–removal algorithms were used, of which the z-buffer algorithm was only one. The availability of fast cheap memory has made the z-buffer algorithm the dominant one for hidden-surface removal. A related example is that of workstation architectures, where many special-purpose graphics chips have been supplanted by a combination of standard floating-point and signal-processing chips, and special purpose chips (ASICS) for a few specific operations.

So what does the future hold? Certainly, graphics systems will get faster and cheaper. More than any other factor, advances in hardware probably will dictate what future graphics systems will look like. At the present, hardware development is being driven by the games industry. For less than $200 we can purchase a graphics card that exceeds the performance of graphics workstations that a few years ago would have cost more than $100,000. However, the features and performance of these cards are optimized for the needs of the computer game industry. Thus, we do not see uniform speedups in the various graphics functions that we have presented. In addition, new hardware features are appearing far faster than they can be incorporated into standard APIs.

On the software side, the low cost and speed of recent hardware has enabled software developers to produce rendering software that allows users to balance rendering time and quality of rendering. Hence, a user can add some ray-traced objects to a scene, the number depending on how long she is willing to wait for the rendering. The future of standard APIs is much less clear. On one hand, users in the scientific community prefer stable APIs, such as OpenGL, so that application code will have a long lifetime. On the other hand, users want to exploit new hardware features that are not supported on all systems.

Numerous advanced architectures under exploration use massive parallelism. How parallelism can be exploited most effectively for computer graphics is still an open issue. Our two approaches to rendering—object oriented and image oriented—lead to two entirely different ways to develop a parallel renderer that we shall explore further in Chapter 13.

We have barely scratched the surface of implementation. The literature is rich with algorithms for every aspect of the implementation process. The references should help you to explore this topic further.

8.15 References

The books by Rogers [Rog98] and by Foley and colleagues [Fol90] contain many more algorithms than we can present here. Also see the series *Graphic Gems* [Gra90, Gra91, Gra92, Gra 94, Gra95]. Recent books such as Möller and Haines [Mol99] and Eberly [Ebe01] cover the influence of recent advances in hardware.

The Cohen–Sutherland [Sut63] clipping algorithm goes back to the early years of computer graphics, as does Bresenham's algorithm [Bre63, Bre87], which was originally proposed for pen plotters. See [Lia84] and [Sut74a] for the Liang–Barsky and Sutherland–Hogman clippers.

The z-buffer algorithm was developed by Catmull [Cat75]. See Sutherland [Sut74b] for a discussion of various approaches to hidden-surface removal.

Our decision to avoid details of the hardware does not imply that the hardware is either simple or uninteresting. The rate at which a modern graphics processor can display graphical entities requires sophisticated and clever hardware designs [Cla82, Ake88, Ake93]. The discussion by Molnar and Fuchs in Foley and colleagues' volume [Fol90] shows a variety of approaches.

Pratt [Pra78] provides matrices to convert among various color systems. Halftone and dithering are discussing by Jarvis [Jar76] and by Knuth [Knu87].

Exercises

8.1   Consider two line segments represented in parametric form:

$$\mathbf{p}(\alpha) = (1 - \alpha)\mathbf{p}_1 + \alpha\mathbf{p}_2,$$

$$\mathbf{q}(\beta) = (1 - \beta)\mathbf{q}_1 + \beta\mathbf{q}_2.$$

Find a procedure for determining whether the segments intersect, and, if they do, for finding the point of intersection.

8.2   Extend the argument of Exercise 8.1 to find a method for determining whether two flat polygons intersect.

8.3   Prove that clipping a convex object against another convex object results in at most one convex object.

8.4   In what ways can you parallelize the image- and object-oriented approaches to implementation?

8.5   Because normals and vertices can both be represented in homogeneous coordinates, both can be operated on by the model-view transformation. Show that normals may not be preserved by the transformation.

8.6   Derive the viewport transformation. Express it in terms of the three-dimensional scaling and translation matrices used to represent affine transformations in two dimensions.

8.7   Pre–raster-graphics systems were able to display only lines. Programmers produced three-dimensional images using hidden-line–removal techniques. Many current APIs allow us to produce wireframe images, composed of only lines, in which the hidden lines that define nonvisible surfaces have been removed. How does this problem differ from that of the polygon hidden-surface removal that we have considered? Derive a hidden-line–removal algorithm for objects that consist of the edges of planar polygons.

8.8 Often, we display functions of the form $y = f(x, z)$ by displaying a rectangular mesh generated by the set of values $\{f(x_i, z_j)\}$ evaluated at regular intervals in x and z. Hidden-surface removal should be applied, because parts of the surface can be obscured from view by other parts. Derive two algorithms, one using hidden-surface removal and the other using hidden-line removal, to display such a mesh.

8.9 Although we argued that the complexity of the image-space approach to hidden-surface removal is proportional to the number of polygons, performance studies have shown almost constant performance. Explain this result.

8.10 Consider a scene composed of only solid three-dimensional polyhedra. Can you devise an object-space hidden-surface–removal algorithm for this case? How much does it help if you know that all the polyhedra are convex?

8.11 We can look at object-space approaches to hidden-surface removal as analogous to sorting algorithms. However, we argued that the former's complexity is $O(k^2)$. We know that only the worst-performing sorting algorithms have such poor performance, and most are $O(k \log k)$. Does it follow that object-space hidden-surface–removal algorithms have similar complexity? Explain your answer.

8.12 Devise a method for testing whether one planar polygon is fully on one side of another planar polygon.

8.13 What are the differences between our image-space approaches to hidden-surface removal and to ray tracing? Can we use ray tracing as an alternate technique to hidden-surface removal? What are the advantages and disadvantages of such an approach?

8.14 Write a program to generate the locations of pixels along a rasterized line segment using Bresenham's algorithm. Check that your program works for all slopes and all possible locations of the endpoints. What is the initial value of the decision variable?

8.15 Bresenham's algorithm can be extended to circles. Convince yourself of this statement by considering a circle centered at the origin. Which parts of the circle must be generated by an algorithm, and which parts can be found by symmetry? Can you find a part of the circle such that if we know a point generated by a scan-conversion algorithm, we can reduce the number of candidates for the next pixel?

8.16 Show how to use flood fill to generate a maze, like the one you created in Exercise 2.7.

8.17 Suppose that you try to extend flood fill to arbitrary closed curves by scan converting the curve and then applying the same fill algorithm that we used for polygons. What problems can arise if you use this approach?

8.18   Consider the edge of a polygon between vertices at (x_1, y_1) and (x_2, y_2). Derive an efficient algorithm for computing the intersection of all scan lines with this edge. Assume that you are working in window coordinates.

8.19   Vertical and horizontal edges are potentially problematic for polygon-fill algorithms. How would you handle these cases for the algorithms that we have presented?

8.20   In two-dimensional graphics, if two polygons overlap, we can ensure that they are rendered in the same order by all implementations by associating a priority attribute with each polygon. Polygons are rendered in reverse-priority order; that is, the highest-priority polygon is rendered last. How should we modify our polygon-fill algorithms to take priority into account?

8.21   A standard antialiasing technique used in ray tracing is to cast rays not only through the center of each pixel, but also through the pixel's four corners. What is the increase in work compared to casting a single ray through the center?

8.22   Although an ideal pixel is a square of 1 unit per side, most CRT systems generate round pixels that can be approximated as circles of uniform intensity. If a completely full unit square has intensity 1.0, and an empty square has intensity 0.0, how does the intensity of a displayed pixel vary with the radius of the circle?

8.23   Consider a bilevel display with round pixels. Do you think it is wiser to use small circles or large circles for foreground-colored pixels? Explain your answer.

8.24   Why is defocusing the beam of a CRT sometimes called "the poor person's antialiasing"?

8.25   Suppose that a monochrome display has a minimum intensity output of I_{min}—a CRT display is never completely black—and a maximum output of I_{max}. Given that we perceive intensities in a logarithmic manner, how should we assign k intensity levels such that the steps appear uniform?

8.26   Generate a halftone algorithm based on the following idea. Suppose that gray levels vary from 0.0 to 1.0, and that we have a random-number generator that produces random numbers that are uniformly distributed over this interval. If we pick a gray level g, $g/100$ percent of the random numbers generated will be less than g.

8.27   Images produced on displays that support only a few colors or gray levels tend to show contour effects because the viewer can detect the differences between adjacent shades. One technique for avoiding this visual effect is to add a little noise (jitter) to the pixel values. Why does this technique work? How much noise should you add? Does it make sense to conclude that the degraded image created by the addition of noise is of quality higher than that of the original image?

Hierarchical and Object-Oriented Modeling

Models are abstractions of the world—both of the real world in which we live, and of virtual worlds that we create through our programs. We are all familiar with mathematical models that are used in all areas of science and engineering. These models use equations to model the physical phenomena that we wish to study. In computer science, we use abstract data types to model organizations of objects; in computer graphics, we model our worlds with geometric objects. When we build a mathematical model, we choose carefully which type of mathematics fits the phenomena that we wish to model. Although ordinary differential equations may be appropriate for modeling the dynamical behavior of a system of springs and masses, we would probably use partial differential equations to model turbulent fluid flow. We go through analogous processes in computer graphics, choosing which primitives to use in our models and how to show relationships among them. Often, as is true of choosing a mathematical model, there are multiple approaches, so we seek models that can take advantage of the capabilities of our graphics systems.

In this chapter we explore multiple approaches to developing and working with models of geometric objects. We consider models that use a set of simple geometric objects: either the primitives supported by our graphics systems or a set of user-defined objects built from these primitives. We extend the use of transformations from Chapter 4 to include hierarchical relationships among the objects. The techniques that we develop are appropriate for applications, such as robotics and figure animation, where the dynamic behavior of the objects is characterized by relationships among the parts of the model.

The notion of hierarchy is a powerful one and is an integral part of object-oriented methodologies. We extend our hierarchical models of objects to hierarchical models of whole scenes, including cameras, lights, and material properties. Such models allow us to extend our graphics APIs to more object-oriented systems and also give us insight in how to use graphics over networks and distributed environments, such as the World Wide Web.

9.1 Symbols and Instances

Our first concern is how we can store a model that may include many sophisticated objects. There are two immediate issues: how we define an object more complex than the ones we have dealt with until now and how we represent a collection of these objects. Most APIs take a minimalist attitude toward primitives: They contain only a few primitives, leaving it to the user to construct more complex objects from these primitives. Sometimes, additional libraries, such as GLU and GLUT that we have used with OpenGL, provide objects built on top of the basic primitives. We assume that we have available a collection of basic three-dimensional objects provided by these options. In subsequent chapters, we introduce other types of objects, such as curves and surfaces (Chapter 10) and recursively defined objects (Chapter 11).

We can take a nonhierarchical approach to modeling by regarding these objects as **symbols** and by modeling our world as a collection of symbols. Symbols can include geometric objects, fonts, and application-dependent sets of graphical objects, such as the standard symbols used in circuit design. Symbols are usually represented at a convenient size and orientation. For example, a cylinder is usually oriented parallel to one of the axes, as shown in Figure 9.1, often with a unit height and a unit radius, and with its bottom centered at the origin.

Various APIs, including PHIGS and GKS, make a distinction between the frame in which the symbol is defined, sometimes called the **model frame** or **model coordinates**, and the world frame. This distinction can be helpful when the symbols are purely shapes, such as the symbols that we might use for circuit elements in a CAD application, and have no physical units associated with them. In OpenGL, we have to set up the appropriate transformation from the frame of the symbol to the world coordinate frame and to apply it to the model-view matrix before we execute the code for the symbol.

The instance transformation that we introduced in Chapter 4 allows us to place instances of each symbol in the model, with the desired size and orientation, and at the desired location. Thus, the instance transformation

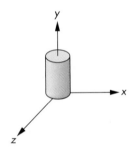

Figure 9.1 Cylinder symbol.

$$\mathbf{M} = \mathbf{T}\mathbf{R}\mathbf{S}$$

is a concatenation of a translation, a rotation, and a scale (and possibly a shear), as shown in Figure 9.2. Consequently, OpenGL programs often contain repetitions of code in the form

```
glMatrixMode(GL_MODELVIEW);
glLoadIdentity();
glTranslatef(...);
glRotatef(...);
glScalef(...);
glutSolidCylinder(...); /* or some other symbol */
```

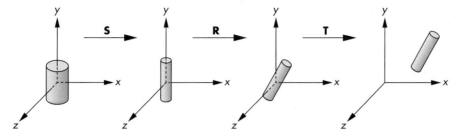

Figure 9.2 Instance transformation.

We can also think of such a model in the form of a table, as shown in Figure 9.3. Here, each symbol is assumed to have a unique numerical identifier. The table shows that this modeling technique contains no information about relationships among objects. However, the table contains all the information that we require to draw the objects and is thus a simple data structure or model for a group of geometric objects. We could search the table for an object, change the instance transformation for an object, and add or delete objects. However, the flatness of the representation limits us.

9.2 Hierarchical Models

Suppose that we wish to build a model of an automobile that we can animate. We can compose the model from five parts—the chassis and the four wheels (Figure 9.4)—each of which we can describe by using our standard graphics primitives. Two frames of a simple animation of the model are shown in Figure 9.5. We could write a program to generate this animation by noting that if each wheel has a radius r, then a 360-degree rotation of a wheel must correspond to the car moving forward (or backward) a distance of $2\pi r$. The program could then contain one function to generate each wheel, and another to generate the

Symbol	Scale	Rotate	Translate
1	s_x, s_y, s_z	$\theta_x, \theta_y, \theta_z$	d_x, d_y, d_z
2			
3			
1			
1			
.			
.			

Figure 9.3 Symbol–instance transformation table.

Figure 9.4 Automobile model.

Figure 9.5 Two frames of animation.

chassis. All these functions could use the same input, such as the desired speed and direction of the automobile. In pseudocode, our program might look like this:

```
main()
{
    float s= ...; /* speed */
    float d[3]={...}; /* direction */
    draw_right_front_wheel(s,d);
    draw_left_front_wheel(s,d);
    draw_right_rear_wheel(s,d);
    draw_left_rear_wheel(s,d);
    draw_chassis(s,d);
}
```

This program is just the kind that we do *not* want to write. It is linear, and it shows none of the relationships among the components of the automobile. There are two types of relationships that we would like to exploit. First, we cannot separate the movement of the car from the movement of the wheels. If the car moves forward, the wheels must turn.[1] Second, we would like to use the fact that all the wheels of the automobile are identical; they are merely located in different places, with different orientations.

We can represent the relationships among parts of the models, both abstractly and visually, with graphs. Mathematically, a **graph** consists of a set of **nodes** (or vertices) and a set of **edges**. Edges connect pairs of nodes, or possibly connect a node to itself. Edges can have a direction associated with them; the graphs we use here are all **directed graphs**, which are graphs that have their edges leaving one node and entering another.

The most important type of graph we use is a tree. A (connected) **tree** is a directed graph without closed paths or loops. In addition, each node, except one—the **root node**—has one edge entering it. Thus, every node, except the root, has a **parent node**, the node from which an edge enters, and can have one or more **child nodes**, nodes to which edges are connected. A node without

---

1. It is not clear whether we should say the wheels move the chassis or the chassis moves the wheels. From a graphics perspective, the latter view is probably more useful.

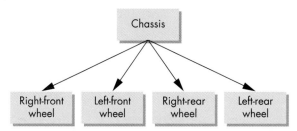

Figure 9.6   Tree structure for automobile.

children is called a **terminal node** or **leaf**. Figure 9.6 shows a tree that represents the relationships in our car model. The chassis is the root node, and all four wheels are its children. Although the mathematical graph is a collection of set elements, in practice, both the edges and nodes can contain additional information. For our car example, each node can contain information defining the geometric objects associated with it. The information about the location and orientation of the wheels can be stored either in their nodes or in the edges connecting them with their parent.

   In most cars the four wheels are identical, so storing the same information on how to draw each one at four nodes is inefficient. We can use the ideas behind the instance transformation to allow us to use a single prototype wheel in our model. If we do so, we can replace the tree structure by the **directed acyclic graph** (**DAG**) in Figure 9.7. In a DAG, although there are loops, we cannot follow directed edges around the loop. Thus, if we follow any path of directed edges from a node, the path terminates at another node, and, in practice, working with DAGs is no more difficult than working with trees. For our car, we can store the information that positions each instance of the single prototype wheel in the chassis node, in the wheel node, or with the edges.

   Both forms—trees and DAGs—are **hierarchical** methods of expressing the relationships in the physical model. In each form, various elements of a model can be related to other parts—their parents and their children. We explore how to express these hierarchies in a graphics program.

Figure 9.7   Directed-acyclic-graph (DAG) model of automobile.

9.3 A Robot Arm

Robotics provides many opportunities for developing hierarchical models. Consider the simple robot arm in Figure 9.8(a). We can model it with three simple objects, or symbols, perhaps using only parallelepipeds and a cylinder. Each of the symbols can be built up from our basic primitives.

   The robot arm consists of the three parts shown in Figure 9.8(b). The mechanism has 3 degrees of freedom, two of which can be described by a **joint angle** between components and the third by an angle the base makes with respect to the ground. In our model, each joint angle determines how to position a

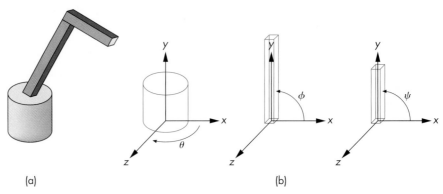

Figure 9.8 Robot arm. (a) Total model. (b) Components.

component with respect to the component to which it is attached, or, in the case of the base, the joint angle positions it relative to the surrounding environment. Each joint angle is measured in each component's own frame. We can rotate the base about its vertical axis by an angle θ. This angle is measured from the x-axis to some fixed point on the bottom of the base. The lower arm of the robot is attached to the base by a joint that allows the arm to rotate in the plane $z = 0$ in the arm's frame. This rotation is specified by an angle ϕ that is measured from the x-axis to the arm. The upper arm is attached to the lower arm by a similar joint, and it can rotate by an angle ψ, measured like that for the lower arm, in its own frame. As the angles vary, we can think of the frames of the upper and lower arms as moving relative to the base. By controlling the three angles, we can position the tip of the upper arm in three dimensions.

Suppose that we wish to write a program to animate our simple robot. Rather than defining each part of the robot, and its motion, independently, we take an incremental approach. The base of the robot can rotate about the y-axis in its frame by the angle θ. Thus, we can describe the motion of any point $\mathbf{p}$ on the base by applying a rotation matrix $\mathbf{R}_y(\theta)$ to it.

The lower arm is rotated about the z-axis in its own frame, but this frame must be shifted to the top of the base by a translation matrix $\mathbf{T}(0, h_1, 0)$, where h_1 is the height above the base, to the point where the joint between the base and the lower arm is located. However, if the base has rotated, then we must also rotate the lower arm, using $\mathbf{R}_y(\theta)$. We can accomplish the positioning of the lower arm by applying $\mathbf{R}_y(\theta)\mathbf{T}(0, h_1, 0)\mathbf{R}_z(\phi)$ to the arm's vertices. We can interpret the matrix $\mathbf{R}_y(\theta)\mathbf{T}(0, h_1, 0)$ as the matrix that positions the lower arm *relative* to the world frame, and $\mathbf{R}_z(\phi)$ as the matrix that positions the lower arm *relative* to the base. Equivalently, we can interpret these matrices as positioning the frames of the lower arm and base relative to some world frame, as shown in Figure 9.9.

Figure 9.9 Movement of robot components and frames.

When we apply similar reasoning to the upper arm, we find that this arm has to be translated by a matrix $\mathbf{T}(0, h_2, 0)$ relative to the lower arm, and then rotated by $\mathbf{R}_z(\psi)$. The matrix that controls the upper arm is thus $\mathbf{R}_y(\theta)\mathbf{T}(0, h_1, 0)\mathbf{R}_z(\phi)\mathbf{T}(0, h_2, 0)\mathbf{R}_z(\psi)$. The form of the display function for an OpenGL program to display the robot as a function of the joint angles shows how we can alter the model-view matrix incrementally to display the various parts of the model efficiently:

```
display()
{
    glRotatef(theta, 0.0, 1.0, 0.0);
    base();
    glTranslatef(0.0, h1, 0.0);
    glRotatef(phi, 0.0, 0.0, 1.0);
    lower_arm();
    glTranslatef(0.0, h2, 0.0);
    glRotatef(psi, 0.0, 0.0, 1.0);
    upper_arm();
}
```

Note that we have described the positioning of the arm independently of the details of the individual parts. As long as the positions of the joints do not change, we can alter the form of the robot by changing only the functions that draw the three parts. This separation makes it possible to write separate programs to describe the components and to animate the robot. Figure 9.10 shows the relationships among the parts of the robot arm as a tree. The program robot.c in Appendix A implements the structure and allows you to animate the robot with the mouse through a menu. It uses a cylinder for the base and parallelepipeds for the arms.

Returning to the tree in Figure 9.10, we can look at it as a tree data structure of nodes and edges—as a graph. If we store all the necessary information in the nodes, rather than in the edges, then each node (Figure 9.11) must store at least three items:

1. A pointer to a function that draws the object represented by the node
2. A homogeneous-coordinate matrix that positions, scales, and orients this node (and its children) relative to the node's parent
3. Pointers to children of the node

Certainly, we can include other information in a node, such as a set of attributes (color, fill pattern, material properties) that applies to the node. Drawing an object described by such a tree requires performing a tree **traversal**. That is, we must visit every node; at each node, we must compute the matrix that applies to the primitives pointed to by the node, and must display these primitives. Our OpenGL program shows an incremental approach to this traversal.

This example is a simple one: There is only a single child for each of the parent nodes in the tree. The next example shows how we handle more complex models.

Figure 9.10 Tree structure for the robot arm in Figure 9.8.

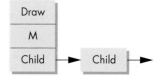

Figure 9.11 Node representation.

9.4 Trees and Traversal

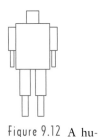

Figure 9.12 A humanoid figure.

Figure 9.12 shows a boxlike representation of a humanoid that might be used for a robot or in a virtual reality application. If we take the torso as the root element, we can represent this figure with a tree, as shown in Figure 9.13. Once we have positioned the torso, the position and orientation of the other parts of the model are determined by the set of joint angles. We can animate the figure by defining the motion of its joints. In a basic model, the knee and elbow joints might each have only a single degree of freedom, like the robot arm, whereas the joint at the neck might have 2 degrees of freedom.

Let us assume that we have functions, such as head and left_upper_arm, that draw the individual parts (symbols) in their own frames. We can now build a set of nodes for our tree by defining matrices that position each part relative to its parent, exactly as we did for the robot arm. If we assume that each body part has been defined at the desired size, each of these matrices is the concatenation of a translation matrix with a rotation matrix. We can show these matrices, as we do in Figure 9.14, by using the matrices to label the edges of the tree. Remember that each matrix represents the incremental change when we go from the parent to the child.

The interesting part of this example is how we do the traversal of the tree to draw the figure. In principle we could use any tree-traversal algorithm, such as a depth-first or breadth-first search. Although, in many applications, it is insignificant which traversal algorithm is used, we shall see that there are good reasons for always using the same algorithm for traversing our graphs. We shall always traverse our trees left to right, depth first. That is, we start with the left branch, follow it to the left as deep as we can go, then go back up to the first right branch, and proceed recursively. This order of traversal is called a **pre-order traversal**.

We can write a tree-traversal function in one of two ways. We can do the traversal explicitly in the code, using stacks to store the required matrices and

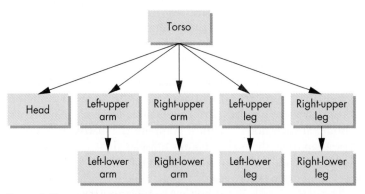

Figure 9.13 Tree representation of Figure 9.12.

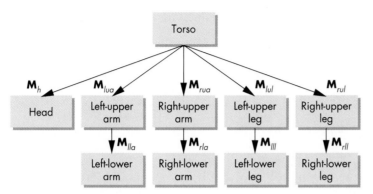

Figure 9.14 Tree with matrices.

attributes as we move through the tree. We can also do the traversal recursively. In this second approach, the code is simpler as the storage of matrices and attributes is done implicitly. We develop both approaches because both are useful and because their development yields further insights into how we can build graphics systems.

9.4.1 A Stack-Based Traversal

Consider the drawing of the figure by a function figure. This function might be called from the display callback or from a mouse callback in an animation that uses the mouse to control the joint angles. The model-view matrix, $\mathbf{M}$, in effect when this function is invoked determines the position of the figure relative to the rest of the scene (and to the camera). The first node that we encounter results in the torso being drawn with $\mathbf{M}$ applied to all the torso's primitives. We then trace the leftmost branch of the tree to the node for the head. There, we invoke the function head with the model-view matrix updated to $\mathbf{M}\mathbf{M}_h$. Next, we back up to the torso node, then go down the subtree defining the left leg. This part looks just like the code for the robot arm; we draw the left-upper leg with the matrix $\mathbf{M}\mathbf{M}_{lul}$, and the left-lower leg with matrix $\mathbf{M}\mathbf{M}_{lul}\mathbf{M}_{lll}$. Then, we move on to the right leg, left arm, and left leg. Each time that we switch limbs, we must back up to the root and recover $\mathbf{M}$.

It is probably easiest to think in terms of the current transformation matrix of Chapter 4—the model-view matrix $\mathbf{C}$ that is applied to the primitives defined at a node. The matrix $\mathbf{C}$ starts out as $\mathbf{M}$, is updated to $\mathbf{M}\mathbf{M}_h$ for the head, and later to $\mathbf{M}\mathbf{M}_{lul}\mathbf{M}_{lll}$, and so on. The user program must manipulate $\mathbf{C}$ before each call to a function defining a part of the figure. In addition to the usual OpenGL functions for rotation, translation, and scaling, the functions glPushMatrix and glPopMatrix are particularly helpful for traversing our tree.

Consider the code (without parameter values) for the beginning of the function `figure`:

```
figure()
{
    glPushMatrix();
    torso();
    glTranslate();
    glRotate3():
    head();
    glPopMatrix();
    glPushMatrix();
    glTranslate();
    glRotate3();
    left_upper_leg();
    glTranslate();
    glRotate3();
    left_lower_leg();
    glPopMatrix();
    glPushMatrix();
    glTranslate();
    glRotate3();
    right_upper_leg();
    glPopMatrix();
    glPushMatrix();

      .
      .
      .
```

The first `glPushMatrix` duplicates the current model-view matrix (assuming that we have done a previous `glMatrixMode(GL_MODELVIEW)`), putting the copy on the top of the model-view-matrix stack. This method of pushing allows us to work immediately with the other transformations that alter the model-view matrix, knowing that we have preserved a copy on the stack. The following calls to `glTranslate` and `glRotate` determine $\mathbf{M}_h$ and concatenate it with the initial model-view matrix. We can then generate the primitives for the head. The subsequent `glPopMatrix` recovers the original model-view matrix. Note that we must do another `glPushMatrix` to leave a copy of the original model-view matrix that we can recover when we come back to draw the right leg. You should be able to complete this function by continuing in a similar manner.

The program `figure` in Appendix A implements this figure with a menu that will allow you to change the various joint angles. The individual parts are implemented using OpenGL quadrics—ellipses and cylinders—and the entire model is shaded as we discussed in Chapter 6.

We have not considered how attributes such as color and material properties are handled by our traversal of a hierarchical model. Attributes are modal variables: Once set, they remain in place until changed again. Hence, we must be careful as we traverse our tree. For example, suppose that within the code for `torso` we set the color to red; then within the code for head we set the color to blue. If there are no other color changes, the color will still be blue as we traverse the rest of the tree, and may remain blue after we leave the code for figure. Here is an example in which the particular traversal algorithm can make a difference, because what will be affected by a change in attributes depends on the order in which the nodes are visited.

This situation may be disconcerting, but there is a solution. OpenGL has the functions glPushAttrib and glPopAttrib that allow us to deal with attributes in a manner similar to our use of the model-view matrix. If we push the attributes on the attribute stack on entrance to the function figure, and pop on exit, we have restored the attributes to their original state. Moreover, we can use additional pushes and pops within figure to control how attributes are handled in greater detail. OpenGL divides its state into groups, and allows a user to push any set of these groups on the attribute stack. The user needs only to set the bits in a mask that is the parameter for glPushAttrib. Attribute groups include lighting, so we can push material properties and lights onto the stack, polygon, and line groups.

In a more complex model, we can apply these ideas recursively. If, for example, we want to use a more detailed model of the head—one incorporating eyes, ears, a nose, and a mouth—then we could model these parts separately. The head would then itself be modeled hierarchically, and its code would include the pushing and popping of matrices and attributes.

Although we have discussed only trees, if two or more nodes call the same function, we really have a DAG. Pushing and popping allow us to isolate the graphics state for different pieces of code. In OpenGL, display lists can call other display lists—so we have another method of creating trees and DAGs.

Color Plates 12, 16, and 22 show hierarchical models of robots and figures used in simulations. These objects were created with high-level interactive software that relies on our ability to traverse hierarchical structures to render the models.

The approach that we used to describe hierarchal objects is workable but has limitations. The code is explicit and relies on the application programmer to push and pop the required matrices and attributes. In reality, we implemented a stack-based representation of a tree. The code was hard-wired for the particular example and thus would be difficult to extend or use dynamically. The code also does not make a clear distinction between building a model and rendering it. Although many application programmers write code in this form, we prefer to use it primarily to illustrate the flow of an OpenGL program that implements tree hierarchies. We now turn to a more general and powerful approach to working with tree-structured hierarchies.

9.5 Use of Tree Data Structures

Our second approach is to use a standard tree data structure to represent our hierarchy and then to render it with a traversal algorithm that is independent of the model. We use a **left-child right-sibling** structure.

(a)

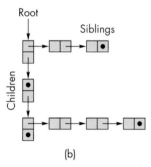

(b)

Figure 9.15 (a) Tree.
(b) Left-child right-sibling
representation.

Consider the alternate representation of a tree in Figure 9.15. It is arranged such that all the elements at the same level are linked left to right. The children of a given node are represented as a second list arranged from the leftmost child to the rightmost. This second list points downward in Figure 9.15. This representation describes the structure of our hierarchical figure, but the structure still lacks the graphical information.

At each node we must store the information necessary to draw the object: a function that defines the object, and the homogeneous coordinate matrix that positions the object relative to its parent. Consider the node structure

```
typedef struct treenode
{
    GLfloat m[16];
    void (*f)();
    struct treenode *sibling;
    struct treenode *child;
}treenode;
```

The array m stores a 4×4 homogeneous coordinate matrix by columns, as is standard in OpenGL. When we render the node, this matrix must first multiply the current model-view matrix; then, the function f, which includes the graphics primitives, is rendered. We also store a pointer to the sibling node on the right and a pointer to the leftmost child. If one or the other does not exist, then we store the null pointer (NULL). For our figure, we define ten nodes corresponding to the ten parts of our model:

```
treenode torso_node, head_node, lua_node, rua_node, lll_node,
        rll_node, lla_node, rla_node, rul_node, lul_node;
```

We can define the nodes either in the main function or in myinit. For example, consider the root of the figure tree—the torso node. It can be oriented by a rotation about the y-axis. We use OpenGL to form the corresponding rotation matrix, then copy the matrix's elements to the m member of the node by the code

```
glLoadIdentity();
glRotatef(theta[0], 0.0, 1.0, 0.0);
glGetFloatv(GL_MODELVIEW_MATRIX,torso_node.m);
```

The function to be executed is the torso function that draws a cylinder. The torso node has no siblings, and its leftmost child is the head node, so the rest of torso node is given by

```
torso_node.f = torso;
torso_node.sibling = NULL;
torso_node.child =  &head_node;
```

The code for the left-upper arm node is

```
glLoadIdentity();
glTranslatef(-(TORSO_RADIUS+UPPER_ARM_RADIUS),
    0.9*TORSO_HEIGHT, 0.0);
glRotatef(theta[3], 1.0, 0.0, 0.0);
glGetFloatv(GL_MODELVIEW_MATRIX,lua_node.m);
lua_node.f = left_upper_arm;
lua_node.sibling =  &rua_node;
lua_node.child = &lla_node;
```

We determine the matrix for this node by shifting the arm's position relative to the torso, and rotating about its joint angle. The translation parameters position the left-upper arm's pivot joint. This node's child is the left-lower arm, and its rightmost sibling is the right-upper arm. The other nodes are defined in a similar manner.

Traversing the tree in the same order (preorder traversal) as in Section 9.4 can be accomplished by the recursive code

```
void traverse(treenode* root)
{
  if(root==NULL) return;
  glPushMatrix();
  glMultMatrixf(root->m);
  root->f();
  if(root->child!=NULL) traverse(root->child);
  glPopMatrix();
  if(root->sibling!=NULL) traverse(root->sibling);
}
```

To render a nonnull node, we first save the graphics state (glPushMatrix). We then use the matrix at the node to modify the model-view matrix (assuming that we already are in the correct matrix mode). We then draw the objects at the node with the function pointed to by f. Finally, we traverse all the children recursively. Note that because we have multiplied the model-view matrix by the local matrix, we are passing this altered matrix to the children. For the siblings, however, we do not want to use this matrix, because each has its own local matrix. Hence, we must return to the original state (glPopMatrix) before traversing the children. If we are changing attributes within nodes, either we can push and pop attributes within the rendering functions, or we can push the attributes when we push the model-view matrix.

One of the nice aspects of this traversal method is that it is completely independent of the particular tree; thus, we can use a generic display callback such as

```
void display(void)
{
  glClear(GL_COLOR_BUFFER_BIT|GL_DEPTH_BUFFER_BIT);
```

```
  glLoadIdentity();
  traverse(&torso_node);
  glutSwapBuffers();
}
```

The complete code is given in figuretree.c. In this code, we again animate the figure by controlling individual joint angles, which are selected from a menu and are incremented and decremented through the mouse buttons. Thus, the dynamics of the program are in the mouse callback, which changes an angle, recomputes the appropriate node matrix, and then posts a redisplay:

```
void mouse(int btn, int state, int x, int y)
{
  if(btn==GLUT_LEFT_BUTTON && state == GLUT_DOWN)
  {
    theta[angle] += 5.0;
    if( theta[angle] > 360.0 ) theta[angle] -= 360.0;
  }
  if(btn==GLUT_RIGHT_BUTTON && state == GLUT_DOWN)
  {
    theta[angle] -= 5.0;
    if( theta[angle] < 360.0 ) theta[angle] += 360.0;
  }
  glPushMatrix();
  switch(angle)
  {
    case 0 :
      glLoadIdentity();
      glRotatef(theta[0], 0.0, 1.0, 0.0);

      glGetFloatv(GL_MODELVIEW_MATRIX,torso_node.m);
      break;

/* other cases */
  }
  glPopMatrix();
  glutPostRedisplay();
}
```

There is one more feature that we can add to show the flexibility of this approach. As the program executes, we can add or remove *dynamic nodes* rather than static nodes. We can create dynamic nodes with the C code[2]

---

2. We shall use C++ syntax for these types starting in Section 9.7 when we discuss objects.

```
typedef treenode* tree_ptr;
tree_ptr torso_ptr;
torso_ptr = malloc(sizeof(treenode));
```

Nodes are defined as before; for example,

```
glLoadIdentity();
glTranslatef(-(TORSO_RADIUS+UPPER_ARM_RADIUS),
   0.9*TORSO_HEIGHT, 0.0);
glRotatef(theta[3], 1.0, 0.0, 0.0);
glGetFloatv(GL_MODELVIEW_MATRIX,lua_ptr->m);
lua_ptr->f = left_upper_arm;
lua_ptr->sibling =  rua_ptr;
lua_ptr->child = lla_ptr;
```

with the traversal by

```
traverse(torso_ptr);
```

For our figure example, there is no particular advantage to the dynamic approach; in a more general setting, however, we can use the dynamic approach to create structures that change interactively. For example, we can use this form to write an application that will let us edit figures, adding and removing parts as desired. This type of implementation is the basis for the scene trees that we discuss in Section 9.8. Back Plate 1 shows one frame of an animation with the figure.

Note that as we have coded our examples, there is a fixed traversal order for the graph. If we applied some other traversal algorithm, we could have produced a different image if we made any state changes within the graph such as changing transformations or attributes. We can avoid some of these potential problems if we are careful to isolate parts of our code by pushing and popping attributes and matrices in each node (although there is a performance penalty for doing so very often). Some APIs, including JAVA 3D, provide tree structures that can be traversed in multiple ways, providing the same image from a given graph, regardless of which traversal algorithm is used.

9.6 Animation

Our two examples—the robot and the figure—are **articulated**: The models consist of rigid parts connected by joints. We can make such models change their positions in time—animate them—by altering the values of a small set of parameters. Hierarchical models allow us to reflect correctly the compound motions incorporating the physical relationships among the parts of the model. What we have not discussed is how to alter the parameters over time so as to achieve the desired motion.

Of the many approaches to animation, a few basic techniques are of particular importance when we work with articulated figures. These techniques arise both from traditional hand animation and from robotics.

In the case of our robot model, consider the problem of moving the tip of the upper arm from one position to another. The model has 3 degrees of freedom—the three angles that we can specify. Although each set of angles has a unique position for the tip, the converse is not true. Given a desired position of the tip of the arm, there may be no set of angles that place the tip as desired, a single set of angles that yields the specified position, or multiple sets of angles that place the tip at the desired position.

Studying **kinematics** involves describing the position of the parts of the model based on only the joint angles. We can use our hierarchical-modeling methods either to determine positions numerically or to find explicit equations that give the position of any desired set of points in the model in terms of the joint angles. Thus, if θ is an array of the joint angles and $\mathbf{p}$ is an array whose elements are the vertices in our model, a kinematic model is of the form

$$\mathbf{p} = f(\theta).$$

Likewise, if we specify the rates of change of the joint angles—the joint velocities—then we can obtain velocities of points on the model.

The kinematic model neglects matters such as the effects of inertia and friction. We could derive more complex differential equations that describe the dynamical behavior of the model in terms of applied forces—a topic that is studied in robotics.

Whereas both kinematics and dynamics are ways of describing the forward behavior of the model, in animation, we are more concerned with **inverse kinematics** and **inverse dynamics**: Given a desired state of the model, how can we adjust the joint angles so as to achieve this position? There are two major concerns. First, given an environment including the robot and other objects, we must determine whether there exists a sequence of angles that achieves the desired state. There may be no single-valued function of the form

$$\theta = g(\mathbf{p}).$$

Not only must we determine whether the final position corresponds to a set of joint angles, but also we must find a way to alter the joint angles so as not to hit any obstacles and not to violate any physical constraints. Although, for a model as simple as our robot, we might be able to find equations that give the joint angles in terms of the position, we cannot do so in general, because the forward equations do not have unique inverses. The figure model, which has 11 degrees of freedom, should give you an idea of how difficult this problem is to solve.

A basic approach to overcoming these difficulties comes from traditional hand-animation techniques. In **key-frame animation**, the animator positions the objects at a set of times—the key frames. In hand animation, animators then can fill in the remaining frames, a process called **inbetweening**. In computer graphics, we can automate inbetweening by interpolating the joint angles between the key frames, or equivalently, using simple approximations to obtain the required dynamic equations between key frames. We can also use the spline curves that we develop in Chapter 10 to give smooth methods of going between key frames. Although we can develop code for the interpolation, both a skillful (human) animator and good interactive methods are crucial if we are to choose the key frames and the positions of objects in these frames.

We can extend these ideas in many ways, as indicated by the suggested readings at the end of the chapter. For example, we can change the shape of an object by giving the shape, in terms of our standard primitives, at different key frames. We can then interpolate between these shapes with a technique known as **morphing**. Here, the major difficulties are to identify which vertices in the first frame correspond to which vertices in the second frame, and to find automated methods that can generate new vertices or eliminate vertices when necessary to interpolate between objects with different numbers of vertices. Again, implementation involves interactive programs and skilled animators. In Chapter 13, we shall introduce rendering techniques that also rely on matching vertices in different images.

9.7 Graphical Objects

Although we have introduced multiple graphics paradigms, our development has been heavily based on a pipeline implementation of the synthetic–camera model. We made this choice because we want to support interactive three-dimensional applications with currently available hardware and software. Consequently, we have emphasized immediate-mode graphics where primitives are rendered to the screen when the code defining them is executed in a user program. Once primitives are rendered, they leave no trace other than their images on the screen. Any changes in attributes or positioning require that we reexecute code in the application program.

In addition, our desire to present the basics of implementation has led us to develop graphics in a manner that was never far from the details of the implementation. For all its benefits, this approach has not let us exploit many high-level alternatives to developing graphical applications.

Now we move to a higher level of abstraction and introduce two major concepts. First, we expand our notion of objects from geometric objects, such as polygons and vectors, to include most of the elements within a graphics program, such as viewers, lights, and material properties. Second, we focus on objects that exist even after their images have been drawn and exist even if we never display them. We have already seen that we can create such objects using display lists; here, we investigate other approaches, such as the use of classes in C++ or structures in C. Although the OpenGL API does not support this approach directly, we do not have to abandon OpenGL. We still use OpenGL for rendering, and we regard what we develop as a software layer on top of OpenGL.

9.7.1 Methods, Attributes, and Messages

Our programs manipulate data. The data may be in many forms, ranging from numbers to strings to the geometric entities that we build in our applications. In traditional imperative programming, the programmer writes code to manipulate the data, usually through functions. The data are passed to a function through the function's parameters. Data are returned in a similar manner. To manipulate the data sent to it, the function must be aware of how those data are organized. Consider, for example, the cube that we have used in many of our previous examples. We have seen that we can model it in various ways, including with vertex pointers, edge lists, and lists of polygon vertices. The application programmer may care little about which model is used and may prefer to regard the cube as an atomic entity or an *object*. In addition, she may care little about the details of how the cube is rendered to the screen: which shading model or which polygon-fill algorithm is used. She can assume that the cube "knows how to render itself," and that, conceptually, the rendering algorithm is tied to the object itself. In some ways, OpenGL supports this view by using the state of the graphics system to control rendering. For example, the color of the cube, its orientation, and the lights that are applied to its surfaces can all be part of the state of the graphics system and may not depend on how the cube is modeled.

However, if we are working with a physical cube, we might find this view a bit strange. The location of a physical cube is tied to the physical object, as are its color, size, and orientation. Although we could use OpenGL to tie some properties to a virtual cube—through pushing and popping various attributes and matrices—the underlying programming model does not support these ideas well. For example, a function that transforms the cube other than by a homogeneous coordinate transformation would have to know exactly how the cube is represented and would work as shown in Figure 9.16.

The application programmer would write a function that would take as its inputs a pointer to the cube's data and the parameters of the transformation. It would then manipulate the data for the cube and return control to the application program (perhaps also returning some values).

Object-oriented design and object-oriented programming look at manipulation of objects in a fundamentally different manner. Even in the early days of object-oriented programming, languages such as Smalltalk recognized that computer graphics provides excellent examples of the power of the object-oriented approach. Recent trends within the software community indicate that we can

Figure 9.16 Imperative programming paradigm.

Figure 9.17 Object-oriented paradigm.

combine our pipeline orientation with an object orientation to build even more powerful graphics systems.

Object-oriented programming languages define **objects** as modules with which we build programs. These modules include the data that define the module, such as the vertices for our cube, properties of the module (**attributes**), and the functions (**methods**) that manipulate the module and its attributes. We send **messages** to objects to invoke a method. This model is shown in Figure 9.17.

The advantage to the writer of the application program is that she now does not need to know how the cube is represented; she needs to know only what functionality the cube object supports—what messages she can send to it.

Although the C struct has some of the properties of objects, the C language does not support the full power of object-oriented approach. In C++, the struct is replaced with the class. C++ classes have two important properties that we can exploit to get the flavor of the object-oriented approach. C programmers should have no trouble understanding these concepts.

9.7.2 A Cube Object

Suppose that we wish to create a cube object in C that has a color attribute and a homogeneous coordinate transformation associated with it. In C, we could use a struct of the form

```
struct  cube
{
    float color[3];
    float matrix[4][4];

/* implementation goes here */

}
```

The implementation part of the structure contains the information on how a cube is actually represented. Typically, a user does not need this information and needs to change only the color or matrix associated with the cube.

Once the struct has been defined, **instances** of the cube object can be created as are other basic data types:

```
cube a, b;
```

Attributes that are part of the class definition can be changed for each instance of the cube. Thus, we can set the color of cube a to red by

```
a.color[0]=1.0;
a.color[1]=a.color[2]=0.0;
```

It should be clear how such a struct can be implemented within an OpenGL system. For example, within the implementation of the cube, we would expect to see a line of code like

```
glColor3fv(color);
```

Although we have created a retained cube object, we are limited in how we can manipulate it or render it. We could write a function that would render the cube through code such as

```
render_cube(a);
```

Or we could rotate the cube by

```
rotate_cube(a, theta, d);
```

where d is the vector about which we wish to rotate.

Although this approach is workable, it has limitations. One is that we need separate rendering and rotation functions for each type of object. A second is that the implementation part of the code is accessible to application programs. C++ classes solve both of these problems. A C++ class can have public, private, and protected members. The **public members** are similar to the members of C struct and can be altered by any function. The **private members** neither are visible to nor can be altered by a function that uses the class. The **protected members** are visible to classes within the same hierarchy. A programmer can also declare classes to be **friends** to give access to specific classes. Thus, in C++, we define the cube as

```
class  cube
{
 public:
   float color[3];
   float matrix[4][4];
 private:

/* implementation goes here */

}
```

thus protecting and hiding the details of the implementation. Furthermore, C++ classes allow us to have members that are functions or methods. Once we add such functions, the object-orientation becomes clearer. Suppose that we add member functions to the public part of the cube class, such as

```
void render();
void translate(float x, float y, float z);
void rotate(float theta, float axis_x, float axis_y,
            float axis_z);
```

Now an application program could create, translate, rotate, and render a cube through the code

```
cube a;
a.rotate(45.0, 1.0, 0.0, 0.0);
a.translate(1.0, 2.0, 3.0);
a.render();
```

Conceptually, this code assumes that an instance of the cube "knows" how to rotate itself, and that, by executing the code a.rotate, we are sending a message to a cube object that we would like it to carry out such a rotation. We could easily write an implementation of the rotation and translation methods that would issue the correct OpenGL transformation function calls.

It is less clear what a function call such as a.render() really does, or how our rotate function relates to the state of the graphics system. One way to understand what this change to an object orientation means is to note that we no longer can work with immediate-mode graphics. Each instance of an object persists and can be altered by further code in the program. OpenGL display lists might be useful as a way of implementing our instances as they continue to exist after the object has been displayed, but there are other possible implementations. What is most important is that we have created an object that continues to exist somewhere in our system in a form unknown to the application program. The attributes of the object are also in the system and can be altered by functions such as rotate. The render function causes the object to be redrawn using the object's rather than the system's present state. In an OpenGL setting, the render step probably involves either executing code such as

```
glBegin(GL_POLYGON);
    glVertex3f(...);
    .
    .
    glVertex3f(...);
glEnd();
```

where the necessary vertex information comes from the implementation part of the structure, or redisplaying a display list corresponding to the instance.

9.7.3 Implementing the Cube Object

As an example of the choices that go into developing the private part of an object, let us consider the cube. One simple implementation would simply use OpenGL polygons or, perhaps, quadrilaterals. Thus, we might base the implementation on a vertex implementation of the form

```
float vertices[6][3]

glBeginGL_POLYGON;
glVertex3f(....
```

But, as we saw in Chapter 4, this implementation requires many more function calls than necessary in the rendering. We could instead use the vertex array data structure that we developed, or we could use OpenGL vertex arrays. We can also use other data structures that may be more efficient depending upon how we intend to use the objects.

We can do far better if we include more information in the implementation. Of particular interest is information that might help in the rendering. Thus, while OpenGL will do hidden-surface removal correctly through the z-buffer algorithm, we often can do much better by eliminating objects earlier through a separate visibility test, as we discussed in Chapter 8. To support this functionality, we might want to include information that determines a bounding volume for the object. For example, we can include the axis-aligned bounding box for objects within the private part of the code. For polygonal objects, we need simply save the minimum and maximum of the x, y, and z of the vertices (after they have been transformed by any transformation matrix stored with the object).

9.7.4 Objects and Hierarchy

One of the major advantages in object-oriented design is the ability to reuse code and to build more sophisticated objects from a small set of simple objects. As in Section 9.4, we can build a figure object from cylinders and have multiple instances of this new object, each with its own color, size, location, and orientation. A class for the figure could refer to the classes for arms and legs; the class for a car could refer to classes for wheels and a chassis. Thus, we would once more have treelike representations like those we developed in Section 9.5.

Often, in object-oriented design, we want the representations to show relationships more complex than the parent–child relationship that characterizes trees. As we have used trees, the structure is such that the highest level of complexity at the root and the relationship between a parent and child is a "has-a" relationship. Thus, the stick figure has two arms and two legs, whereas the car has four wheels and a chassis.

We can look at hierarchy in a different manner, with the simplest objects being the top of the hierarchy and the relationship between parents and children being an "is-a" relationship. This type of hierarchy is typical of taxonomies. A mammal is an animal. A human is a mammal. We used this relationship in describing projections. A parallel projection is a planar geometric projection; an oblique projection is a parallel projection. Has-a relationships allow us to define multiple complex objects from simpler objects and also allow the more complex object to inherit properties from the simpler object. Thus, if we write the code for a parallel projection, the oblique-projection code can use this code and refine only the parts that are necessary to convert the general parallel projection to an oblique one. For geometric objects, we can define base objects with a default set of properties such as their color and material properties. A user could then use these properties or change them in subobjects. These concepts are supported by languages such as C++ that allow for subclasses and inheritance.

9.7.5 Geometric Objects

Suppose that we now want to build an object-oriented graphics system. What objects should we include? Although it is clear that we want to have objects such as points, vectors, polygons, rectangles, and triangles (possibly using subclasses), it is less clear how we should deal with attributes, light sources, and viewers. For example, should a material property be associated with an object such as a cube, or is it a separate object? The answer can be either or both. We could create a cube class in which there is a member for each of the ambient, diffuse, and specular material properties that we introduced with the Phong model in Chapter 6. We could also define a material class using code such as

```
class material
{
 public:
    float specular[3];
    float shininess;
    float diffuse[3];
    float ambient[3];
}
```

We could then assign the material to a geometric object through a member function of the cube class

```
cube a;
material b;
a.setMaterial(b);
```

Light sources are geometric objects—they have position and orientation among their features—and we can easily add a light source object

```
class light
{
  public:
     boolean type;
     boolean near;
     float position[3];
     float orientation[3];
     float specular[3];
     float diffuse[3];
     float ambient[3];
}
```

Once we have built up a collection of geometric objects, we can use it to describe a scene. To take advantage of the hierarchical relationships that we have introduced, we develop a new tree structure called a **scene graph**.

9.8 Scene Graphs

If we think about what goes into describing a scene, we can see that, in addition to our graphical primitives and geometric objects derived from these primitives, we have other objects, such as lights and a camera. These objects may also be defined by vertices and vectors, and may have attributes, such as color, that are similar to the attributes associated with geometric primitives. It is the totality of these objects that describes a scene, and there may be hierarchical relationships among these objects. For example, when a primitive is defined in a program, the camera parameters that exist at that time are used to form the image. If we alter the camera lens between the definition of two geometric objects, we may produce an image in which each object is viewed differently. Although we cannot create such an image with a real camera, the example points out the power of our graphics systems. We can extend our use of tree data structures to describe these relationships among geometric objects, cameras, lights, and attributes.

Knowing that we can write a graphical application program to traverse a graph, we can expand our notion of the contents of a graph to describe an entire scene. One possibility is to use a tree data structure and to include various attributes at each node—in addition to the instance matrix and a pointer to the drawing function. Another possibility is to allow new types of nodes, such as attribute-definition nodes and matrix-transformation nodes. Consider the tree in Figure 9.18. Here, we have set up individual nodes for the colors and for the model-view matrices. Where there are branches at the top can be considered a special type of node, a **separator node** whose function is to isolate the two children. The separator node allows us to preserve the state that exists at the time that we enter a node and thus isolates the state of the subtree beginning at

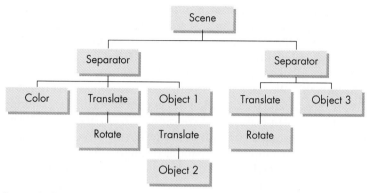

Figure 9.18 Scene tree.

a separator node from the rest of the tree. Using our preorder traversal algorithm, the corresponding OpenGL code is of the form

```
glPushAttrib
glPushMatrix
glColor
glTranslate
glRotate
object1
glTranslate
object2
glPopMatrix
glPushMatrix
glTranslate
glRotate
object3
glPopMatrix
glPopAttrib
```

The separator nodes correspond to the OpenGL push and pop functions. This code preserves and restores both the attributes and the model-view matrix before exiting. It sets a drawing color that applies to the rest of the tree, and traverses the tree in a manner similar to the figure example.

We can go further and note that we can use the attribute and matrix stacks to store the viewing conditions; thus, we can create a camera node in the tree. Although we probably do not want a scene in which individual objects are viewed with different cameras, we may want to view the same set of objects with multiple cameras producing, for example, the multiview orthographic projections and isometric view that are used by architects and engineers. Such images can be created with a scene graph that has multiple cameras.

The scene graph we have just described is equivalent to an OpenGL program in the sense that we can use the tree to generate the program in a totally mechanical fashion. This approach is taken by Open Inventor, an object-oriented API that is built on top of OpenGL. An Inventor program is a description of a scene graph. Execution of the program causes traversal of the scene graph, which in turn executes graphics functions that are written in OpenGL.

The notion of scene graphs couples nicely with the object-oriented paradigm introduced in Section 9.7. We can regard all primitives, attributes, and transformations as software objects, and we can define classes to manipulate these entities. From this perspective, we can make use of concepts such as data encapsulation to build up scenes of great complexity with simple programs that use predefined software objects. We can even support animations through software objects that appear as nodes in the scene graph but cause parameters to change and the scene to be redisplayed. Although, in Open Inventor, the software objects are typically written in OpenGL, the scene graph itself is a database that includes all the elements of the scene. OpenGL enters as the rendering engine that allows the database to be converted to an image, but is not used in the specification of the scene. In this sense, Open Inventor resembles PHIGS: The job of the application program is to place elements in a database. Parts of a PHIGS database can be **posted** or sent to a workstations, and it is the job of the workstation to worry about how the rendering is accomplished.

Graphics software systems are evolving to the configuration shown in Figure 9.19. OpenGL is the rendering engine. It may sit on top of another layer such as Microsoft's DirectX or talk directly to the hardware. Above OpenGL is an object-oriented layer that supports scene graphs and a storage mechanism. User programs can be written for any of the layers, depending on what facilities are required by the application.

Figure 9.19 Modern graphics architecture.

9.9 A Simple Scene Graph API

Although there are a few standard scene graph APIs available, including VRML and JAVA 3D, none have yet become dominant. Rather than discuss one of these, we opt instead to construct our own simple, but extensible, scene graph API. It will include the basics shared by more complex scene graph APIs and will be easy to extend. We start with the public interface that a user can use to define a scene graph and display it. Then we consider a possible implementation using the left-child right-sibling data structure of Section 9.5.

Our design[3] employs two base classes: a node class and a viewer class. We shall use the node class to construct nodes for all our objects including geometric objects, camera objects, material objects, and light source objects. These nodes can then be used to form a tree that is our scene graph. The viewer object provides

---

3. This scene graph API and implementation started as a class project by Ye Cong at the University of New Mexico.

a simple mechanism that will allow us to view the scene graph with an OpenGL program.

9.9.1 The Node Class

Our fundamental node has the public interface:

```
class Node
{
 public:
  Node();
  virtual ~Node();
  virtual void Render();
  void AddChild(Node *);

  friend class GLViewer;

  //private part goes here
};
```

We have both a constructor and destructor for creating and deleting nodes that will enable us to create dynamic scene graphs. We can define a tree hierarchy by having a single method, AddChild, for adding a child to a node. However, as we shall see when we discuss implementation, the order in which we add children can affect the image produced by the scene graph.

As we will have many types of nodes (geometry, camera, materials, lights), each node must have its own render method that will execute when the node is encountered as part of the traversal process.

We can invoke the rendering process from the viewer. The viewer will also let us take care of the standard OpenGL interface with the window system by using GLUT. Here is the public part of the viewer

```
 class GLViewer
{
 public:
  GLViewer();
  ~GLViewer();

  void SetValue(Enum PName, Enum Type);
  void Init(int argc, char **argv);
  void Show(Node *N);

  //private part goes here

};
```

We will be able to have multiple viewers so that we can, for example, display two different views using two different cameras in two OpenGL windows. We could also use different OpenGL windows to view different parts of the same scene graph by passing in different nodes to the Show method. The Show method initiates traversal of a scene graph.

Both the viewer and node classes have many parameters that are used to specify attributes, such as color, line style, and material properties, and rendering options, such as double buffering and hidden-surface removal. We take an approach similar to OpenGL and GLUT by specifying symbolic constants as an enumerated type:

```
enum Enum
{
  PERSPECTIVE, ORTHO, POSITION, AIMAT, UPDIRECTION, ASPECT,
  NEAR, FAR, YANGLE, BLACK, WHITE, RED, GREEN, YELLOW, BLUE,
  MAGENTA, CYAN, GRAY, WIDTH, HEIGHT,DEPTH,
  AMBIENT, DIFFUSE, SPECULAR, SPOT_DIRECTION, DROPOFFRATE,
  CUTOFFANGLE, EMISSION, SHININESS, TRANSLATION, ROTATION, SCALE,
  BUFFER, SINGLE, DOUBLE, RADIUS, STYLE, POINTSIZE, LINEWIDTH,
  FILLED, LINE, POINT, BACKCOLOR
};
```

The following code from a typical application sets up a window on the display and renders a scene graph

```
GLViewer *MyViewer=new GLViewer;

MyViewer->Init(argc, argv);
MyViewer->SetValue(BACKCOLOR, GRAY);
MyViewer->SetValue(BUFFER, DOUBLE);
MyViewer->CreateWin("Working Hard", 500, 500);

MyViewer->Show(Root);
```

We have five major subclasses of our node class: geometry nodes, light nodes, camera nodes, attribute nodes, and transformation nodes. From the OpenGL perspective, there are two types of operations: those that generate primitives and those that change state. However, from the perspective of a scene graph, both types of operations can be initiated from within a node.

9.9.2 Geometry Nodes

Our scene graph allows for both basic objects, such as lines and polygons, and the more complex objects, including cubes, cylinders, triangles, and spheres. Geometry nodes have many properties in common, including color attributes, material properties, and instance matrices that can be applied to them. These properties can be set by a user program, and we have included set methods for them within the geometry class.

```
class Geometry: public Node
{
 public:
  Geometry();
  ~Geometry();

  void SetColor(Enum);
  void SetColor(float, float, float);
  void SetColorv(float *);
  void SetColor(Color *);
  void SetMaterial(Enum, float, float, float, float);
  void SetMaterialv(Enum, float *);
  void SetMaterial(Enum, float);
  void SetMaterial(Material *);
  void SetTransform(Enum, float *, int);
  void SetTransform(Enum, float, float, float, int);
  void SetTransform(Enum, float, float, float, float, int);
  void SetTransform(Transformation *);
  void SetStyle(Enum, Enum);
  void SetStyle(Enum, float);
  void SetStyle(DrawStyle *);
  virtual void Render();

 private:
   //implementation
}
```

Note that a user can set an attribute, such as a color, by setting the attribute directly within a geometry node by using a set method whose parameters are the individual values

```
myObject->SetColor(red, green , blue);
```

or she can first define an attribute object and then attach this object to one or more geometry nodes, as in the code

```
Color *myColor = new Color;
myColor->SetValue(red, green, blue);
myObject->SetColor(myColor);
```

Now we can look at a few of the geometry nodes. The simplest is a line segment that allows us to set the endpoints, either directly or by a pointer to an array of two vertices. Note that in our simple system, we have included only three-dimensional vertices. It is a simple exercise to add two-dimensional vertices. Also, note that we could use a single function SetVertices for all cases, as C++ permits overloading of functions.

```
class Line: public Geometry
{
 public:
  Line();
  void SetVertices(float *, float *);
  void SetVerticesv(float v[][3]);
  void Render();
 private:
   //implementation
};
```

Two other simple geometric objects are a sphere centered at the origin and a cylinder oriented along the y direction with its base lying in the x, z plane.

```
class Sphere: public Geometry
{
 public:
  Sphere();
  Sphere(float R);
  void SetValue(Enum Pname, float v);
  void Render();
 private:
   //implementation
};
```

```
class Cylinder: public Geometry
{
 public:
  Cylinder();
  void SetValue(Enum, float);
  void Render();
 private:
   //implementation
};
```

We also allow for general polygons

```
class Polygon: public Geometry
{
 public:
  Polygon();
  void SetVerticesv(float v[][3], int);
  void Render();
 private:
   //implementation
};
```

9.9.3 Camera Class

The camera class needs only a very simple interface because most of the camera parameters can be specified through a set mechanism. The constructor parameter determines whether the camera is for perspective or orthogonal viewing. The camera orientation can be set by using the same parameters as the OpenGL Lookat function.

```
class Camera: public Node
{
 public:
  Camera(Enum CType);

  void Render();
  void SetValuev(Enum PName, float *v);
  void SetValue(Enum PName, float v1, float v2, float v3);
  void SetValue(Enum PName, float v);
 private:
   //implementation
};
```

Here is an example of specifying a perspective camera:

```
Camera *Camera1=new Camera(PERSPECTIVE);

Camera1->SetValue(POSITION, 2.2, 0.9, 3);
Camera1->SetValue(AIMAT, 0, 0, 0);
Camera1->SetValue(UPDIRECTION, 0, 1, 0);
Camera1->SetValue(ASPECT, 1);
Camera1->SetValue(NEAR, 1);
Camera1->SetValue(FAR, 20);
Camera1->SetValue(YANGLE, 50);
```

From an OpenGL perspective, some of these parameters affect the model-view matrix, whereas others affect the projection matrix. From an object-oriented perspective, these parameters simply describe a virtual camera.

9.9.4 Lights and Materials

Lights and materials have simple public interfaces that allow us to set the standard parameters in the Phong model. Because the scene graph can alter state variables as it is traversed, we want to be able to turn lights on and off within the scene graph. We handle this problem by having a switch object.

```
class Light: public Node
{
 public:
```

```
    Light();
    void Render();

    void SetValue(Enum PName, Enum color);
    void SetValue(Enum PName, float v1, float v2, float v3, float v4 );
    void SetValue(Enum PName, float v1, float v2, float v3);
    void SetValue(Enum PName, float f);
    void SetValuev(Enum PName, float *);
    void TurnOn();
    void TurnOff();

    friend class TurnOff;

 private:
   //implementation
};

class TurnOff: public Node
{
 public:
  TurnOff(Light *L);
  void Render();
 private:
   //implementation
};
```

Thus, if we want to set a light and be able to turn it on and off, we must create both the light and switch object as in the code

```
    Light *Light1=new Light;
    TurnOff *Off1=new TurnOff(Light1);

    Light1->SetValue(POSITION, -2, -3, 1.5, 1);
    Light1->SetValue(SPOT_DIRECTION, 2, 3, -1.5);
    Light1->SetValue(CUTOFFANGLE, 40.0);
    Light1->TurnOn();
```

Material nodes are similar to light nodes and contain a render method and methods to set the standard material parameters.

```
class Material: public Node
{
 public:
  Material();
  void SetValuev(Enum Pname, float *);
  void SetValue(Enum Pname, float v1, float v2, float v3, float v4);
  void SetValue(Enum Pname, float Value);
  void Render();
```

```
private:
   //implementation
};
```

Thus, we might set a material node as

```
Material *myMat = new Material;

myMat->SetValue(DIFFUSE, 0.0, 0.0, 1.0, 1.0);
myMat->SetValue(AMBIENT, 0.0, 0.0, 1.0, 1.0);
myMat->SetValue(SPECULAR, 1.0, 1.0, 1.0, 1.0);
myMat->SetValue(SHININESS, 100.0);
```

and then assign it to an object by

```
myObject->SetMaterial(myMat);
```

9.9.5 Transformations

Transformations include the standard rotation, translation, and scaling matrices whose parameters are set through SetValue methods. The Order member allows us to define a sequence of transformation matrices and the order in which they are multiplied.

```
class Transformation: public Node
{
 public:
  Transformation();
  void SetValuev(Enum Pname, float *, int Order);
  void SetValue(Enum Pname, float x, float y, float z, int Order);
  void SetValue(Enum Pname, float a, float x, float y, float z, int Order);
  void Render();
 private:
   //implementation
};
```

For any of the geometry nodes, we can use the SetTransform method to associate an instance transformation with the object, as in the code

```
Cylinder myCylinder = new Cylinder;
myCylinder->SetTransformation(SCALE, sx, sy, sz, 0);
myCylinder->SetTransformation(TRANSLATION, tx, ty, tz, 2);
myCylinder->SetTransformation(ROTATION, theta, rx, ry, rz, 1);
```

Thus, in the example, the order parameter forces the evaluation order to be scale first, followed by rotation, and then translation.

9.9.6 The Robot Figure

Before discussing the implementation, let us consider a simple example, the robot figure again. The full code is in Appendix A.

```
#include "Scene.h"

int main(int argc, char **argv)

{

  //Define a light

  Light *Light1=new Light;
  TurnOff *Off1=new TurnOff(Light1);

  //Set light parameters here

  //Define a Camera

  Camera *Camera1=new Camera(PERSPECTIVE);

  //set camera parameters

  //Define materials

  Material *RobotMat=new Material;

  //set material parameters

  RobotMat->SetValue(DIFFUSE, 0.0, 0.0, 1.0, 1.0);
  RobotMat->SetValue(AMBIENT, 0.0, 0.0, 1.0, 1.0);
  RobotMat->SetValue(SPECULAR, 1.0, 1.0, 1.0, 1.0);
  RobotMat->SetValue(SHININESS, 100.0);

  //define other materials

  //define robot geometry nodes

  Sphere *Head=new Sphere;

  Cylinder *Torso = new Cylinder;
  Cylinder *UpperArmL=new Cylinder;
  Cylinder *UpperArmR=new Cylinder;
  Cylinder *LowerArmL=new Cylinder;
  Cylinder *LowerArmR=new Cylinder;
  Cylinder *UpperLegL=new Cylinder;
  Cylinder *UpperLegR=new Cylinder;
  Cylinder *LowerLegL=new Cylinder;
```

```
Cylinder *LowerLegR=new Cylinder;

Transformation *HeadTrans=new Transformation;
Transformation *UpArmLTrans=new Transformation;

//transformation for  left upper arm

HeadTrans->SetValue(TRANSLATION, 0, 0, BaseLen+BaseRadius+BaseRadius/3, 0);
UpArmLTrans->SetValue(TRANSLATION, 0, 0, -UpLen, 0);
UpArmLTrans->SetValue(ROTATION, -45, 0, 1, 0, 1);
UpArmLTrans->SetValue(TRANSLATION, 0, BaseRadius+Radius, BaseLen, 2);

//set up other transformation matrices

UpperArmL->SetTransform(UpArmLTrans);
LowerArmL->SetTransform(LowArmTrans);

//assign transformations to nodes

//Set Relationship in Robot:
RobotMat->AddChild(Light1);
Light1->AddChild(Base);

Torso->AddChild(Off1);

Torso->AddChild(UpperArmL);
UpperArmL->AddChild(LowerArmL);
Torso->AddChild(UpperArmR);
UpperArmR->AddChild(LowerArmR);
Torso->AddChild(UpperLegL);
UpperLegL->AddChild(LowerLegL);
Torso->AddChild(UpperLegR);
UpperLegR->AddChild(LowerLegR);

//Transformation Nodes for Robot

Transformation *Trans1=new Transformation;

Trans1->SetValue(TRANSLATION, -0.5, 0, 0, 2);

Trans1->AddChild(RobotMat);

//Root Node:
Node *Root=new Node;

Root->AddChild(Trans1);
Root->AddChild(Camera1);

//set up viewer
```

```
    GLViewer *MyViewer=new GLViewer;

    //Viewer parameters

    //Render

    MyViewer->Show(Root);

    return 0;
}
```

9.9.7 Implementing the Viewer

Let us start our discussion of implementation with the viewer. It initiates the traversal process, and it must interact with the windowing system. We shall make our interface through GLUT so that the viewer will be compatible with everything else we have done. Here is the definition of the viewer, this time including the private members and methods used for its implementation:

```
 class GLViewer
{
 public:
  GLViewer();
  ~GLViewer();

  void SetValue(Enum PName, Enum Type);
  void Init(int argc, char **argv);
  void Show(Node *N);

 private:
  void GLInit();
  int ViewerIndex;
  char *WinName;
  float BackColor[3];

  static Node *Root[3];
  static int ViewerNum;
  static int BufType[3];
  static int WinWidth[3];
  static int WinHeight[3];
  static void Reshape0(int w, int h);
  static void Display0();
  static void Reshape1(int w, int h);
  static void Display1();
  static void Reshape2(int w, int h);
  static void Display2();

};
```

The viewer class has been implemented to allow for up to three independent viewers. The information about these viewers is stored as static members. Each viewer can have its own display and reshape callbacks. We must use a few tricks because we are using GLUT. For example, we must ensure that there is exactly one call to glutMainLoop. The array Root stores the root node for each viewer. The constructor sets up a default window.

```
GLViewer::GLViewer()
{
  int i;

  ViewerIndex=ViewerNum;
  ViewerNum++;

  WinName="";
  BufType[ViewerIndex]=GLUT_SINGLE;
  Root[ViewerIndex]=NULL;
  for(i=0; i<3; i++)
    BackColor[i]=0.0;
}
```

We can set up a nondefault window with Createwin and set parameters with SetValue.

```
GLViewer::~GLViewer()
{
  if(Root[ViewerIndex])
    {
      delete Root[ViewerIndex];
      Root[ViewerIndex]=NULL;
    }
}

void GLViewer::Init(int argc, char **argv)
{
  if(ViewerIndex==0)
    glutInit(&argc, argv);
}

void GLViewer::CreateWin(char *Name, int Width, int Height)
{
  WinName=Name;
  WinWidth[ViewerIndex]=Width;
  WinHeight[ViewerIndex]=Height;

}

void GLViewer::SetValue(Enum PName, Enum Type)
```

```
{
  switch(PName)
    {
    case BUFFER:
      if(Type==DOUBLE)
    BufType[ViewerIndex]=GLUT_DOUBLE;
      else if(Type==SINGLE)
    BufType[ViewerIndex]=GLUT_SINGLE;
      break;
    case BACKCOLOR:
      Root[ViewerIndex]->GetColor(Type, BackColor);
      break;
    default:
      break;
    }
}
```

Because we have done our implementation with OpenGL and GLUT, the traversal mechanism must be part of the display callback. Thus, each viewer has a display callback that starts the traversal at the root node associated with that viewer. The traverse method is a method of the node class.

```
void GLViewer::Show(Node *N)
{
  GLInit();
  Root[ViewerIndex]=N;
  if(ViewerIndex==(ViewerNum-1))
    glutMainLoop();
}

void GLViewer::GLInit()
{
  glutInitDisplayMode(BufType[ViewerIndex] | GLUT_RGB | GLUT_DEPTH);
  glutInitWindowSize(WinWidth[ViewerIndex], WinHeight[ViewerIndex]);
  glutCreateWindow(WinName);
  switch(ViewerIndex)
    {
    case 0:
      glutReshapeFunc(Reshape0);
      glutDisplayFunc(Display0);
      break;
    case 1:
      glutReshapeFunc(Reshape1);
      glutDisplayFunc(Display1);
      break;
    case 2:
      glutReshapeFunc(Reshape2);
      glutDisplayFunc(Display2);
      break;
    default:
```

```
      break;
    }

  glEnable(GL_DEPTH_TEST);
  glClearColor(BackColor[0], BackColor[1], BackColor[2], 1.0);
}

void GLViewer::Display0()
{
  glClear(GL_COLOR_BUFFER_BIT | GL_DEPTH_BUFFER_BIT);
  Root[0]->Traverse();
  if(BufType[0]==GLUT_DOUBLE)
    glutSwapBuffers();
  glFlush();
}

void GLViewer::Reshape0(int w, int h)
{
  glViewport(0, 0, (GLsizei)w, (GLsizei)h);
  WinWidth[0]=w;
  WinHeight[0]=h;
}

// Similar code for other display and reshape functions
```

9.9.8 Implementing a Node

The private part of the node contains its implementation as a left-sibling right-child tree. We have also included a traversal method that is similar to the one that we used for our robot, but we could use any standard traversal algorithm.

There is a protected member, KeepMatrix that can be used to push the present model-view or projection matrix on the stack. This Boolean variable enables us to choose whether or not to pass the present matrix state onto a child and avoids the need for a separator node. Here is a basic traversal:

```
void Node::Traverse()
{
  if(!KeepMatrix)
    glPushMatrix();

  Render();
  if(LeftChild!=NULL)
    LeftChild->Traverse();
  if(!KeepMatrix)
    glPopMatrix();
  if(RightSibling!=NULL)
    RightSibling->Traverse();
}
```

Note that the use of the left-sibling right-child structure implies that children and siblings will be encountered in a predetermined order as the tree is traversed.

What gets drawn on the display depends on each node's render method. These methods will be different for each type of node (geometry, light, material), but all will invoke OpenGL code. Let us look at a few examples. First, returning to the geometry node, we look at all its protected members and see that there are members to store the parameters that can be set by the public methods.

```
class Geometry: public Node
{
 public:
  //public members

 protected:
  Color *ColorNode;
  Material *MatNode;
  Transformation *TransNode;
  DrawStyle *StyleNode;
};
```

Many of the methods for a geometry node are common for all geometry nodes and are similar over the basic parameters. We can can create a geometry node through the constructor

```
Geometry::Geometry()
{
  ColorNode=NULL;
  MatNode=NULL;
  TransNode=NULL;
  StyleNode=NULL;
}
```

and delete through the destructor

```
Geometry::~Geometry()
{
  if(ColorNode)
    {
      delete ColorNode;
      ColorNode=NULL;
    }
// same for other types
```

All the methods for setting parameters are fairly similar. For example, for colors we have

```
void Geometry::SetColor(Enum C)
{
  if(ColorNode==NULL)
    ColorNode=new Color;

  ColorNode->SetValue(C);
}

void Geometry::SetColor(float v1, float v2, float v3)
{
  if(ColorNode==NULL)
    ColorNode=new Color;

  ColorNode->SetValue(v1, v2, v3);
}
```

However, to render each geometry node, we need to have a render method for the particular type. For example, for the polygon, we have the methods and members

```
class Polygon: public Geometry
{
 public:
  Polygon();
  void SetVerticesv(float v[][3], int);
  void Render();

 private:
  float Vertices[1000][3];
  int Size;
};
```

and the simple implementation

```
void Polygon::SetVerticesv(float v[][3], int S)
{
  int i, j;
  Size=S;

  for(i=0; i<S; i++)
    for(j=0; j<3; j++)
      Vertices[i][j]=v[i][j];
}

void Polygon::Render()
{
  int i;
```

```
glPushAttrib(GL_ALL_ATTRIB_BITS);

if(ColorNode)
  ColorNode->Render();
if(MatNode)
  MatNode->Render();
if(TransNode)
  TransNode->Render();
if(StyleNode)
  StyleNode->Render();

glBegin(GL_POLYGON);
for(i=0; i<Size; i++)
  glVertex3fv(Vertices[i]);
glEnd();

glPopAttrib();

}
```

Note the pushing and popping of attributes to isolate state changes made during the rendering of the internal nodes. The internal nodes use the rendering methods from their own classes. For example, color nodes have two private members:

```
class Color: public Node
{
 public:
  Color();
  void SetValuev(float *v);
  void SetValue(float v1, float v2, float v3);
  void SetValue(Enum Type);
  void Render();

 private:
  bool Changed;
  float Color3f[3];
};
```

The Changed flag is set whenever a color is set. Thus, the render method is simply

```
void Color::Render()
{
  if(Changed) glColor3fv(Color3f);
}
```

Although there is fair amount of code required to implement all the nodes that we have described, the implementation is straightforward.

9.10 Other Tree Structures

Tree and DAG structures provide powerful tools to describe scenes; trees are used in a variety of other ways in computer graphics, of which we consider three. The first is the use of expression trees to describe an object hierarchy for solid objects; the other two describe spatial hierarchies that we can use to increase the efficiency of many rendering algorithms.

9.10.1 CSG Trees

The polygonal representation of objects that we have used has many strengths and a few weaknesses. The most serious weakness is that polygons describe only the surfaces that enclose the interior of a three-dimensional object, such as a polyhedron. In CAD applications, this limitation causes difficulties whenever we must employ any volumetric properties of the graphical object, such as its weight or its moment of inertia. In addition, because we display an object by drawing its edges or surfaces, there can be ambiguities in the display. For example, the wire frame in Figure 9.20 can be interpreted either as a cube with a hole through it created by removal of a cylinder or as a solid cube composed of two different materials.

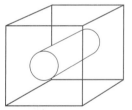

Figure 9.20 Wire frame that has two possible interpretations.

Constructive solid geometry (CSG) avoids these difficulties. Assume that we start with a set of atomic solid geometric entities, such as parallelepipeds, cylinders, and spheres. The attributes of these objects can include surface properties, such as color or reflectivity, but also volumetric properties, such their size and density. In describing scenes of such objects, we consider those points in space that constitute each object. Equivalently, each object is a set of points, and we can use set algebra to form new objects from these solid primitives.

CSG modeling uses three set operations: union, intersection, and set difference. The **union** of two sets A and B, written $A \cup B$, consists of all points that are either in A or in B. The **intersection** of A and B, $A \cap B$, is the set of all points that are in both A and B. The **set difference**, $A - B$, is the set of points that are in A and are not in B. Figure 9.21 shows two objects and possible objects created by the three set operations.

Objects are described by algebraic expressions. The expression $(A - B) \cap (C \cup D)$ might describe an object such as that in Figure 9.22.

Typically, we store and parse algebraic expressions using expression trees, where internal nodes store operations and terminal nodes store operands. For example, the tree in Figure 9.23 is a CSG tree that represents the object $(A - B) \cap (C \cup D)$ in Figure 9.22. We can evaluate or render the CSG tree by a **post-order** traversal; that is, we recursively evaluate the tree to the left of a node and the tree on the right of the node, and finally use these values to evaluate the node itself. Rendering of objects in CSG often is done with a variant of ray tracing; see Exercise 9.10 and Chapter 13.

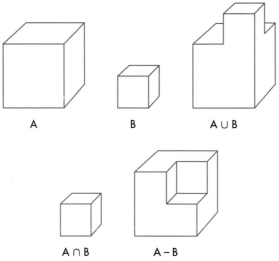

Figure 9.21 Set operations.

9.10.2 Shade Trees

CSG trees are but one application of expression trees to graphics. Shading is another. Consider the simple Phong shading model from Chapter 6, without the distance term

$$I = k_d L_d l \alpha \cdot \mathbf{n} + k_s L_s (\mathbf{r} \cdot \mathbf{v}^\alpha) + k_\alpha L_\alpha I_\alpha.$$

When the renderer computes this expression, $\mathbf{n}$ and $\mathbf{l}$ are known from the state, and $\mathbf{r}$ is computed by

$$\mathbf{r} = 2(\mathbf{l} \cdot \mathbf{n})\mathbf{n} - \mathbf{l}.$$

Both these equations are expressions that involve both arithmetic operations, including exponentiation, and vector operations, such as the dot product. We

Figure 9.22 CSG object.

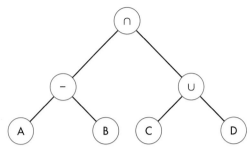

Figure 9.23 CSG tree.

can express them as the trees in Figure 9.24. One obvious use of the tree representation is in implementation, allowing for efficient implementation of Phong shading. But the more interesting application is in designing new shaders. This is the approach taken in the RenderMan shading language. Variables, such as normals and light source parameters, are assumed to be part of the environment and can be combined using a set of scalar and vector operations. As we have seen with our discussion of tree traversals, the evaluation of all these trees can be accomplished with the same simple algorithm. This approach to developing shaders is also supported by some of the latest graphics cards.

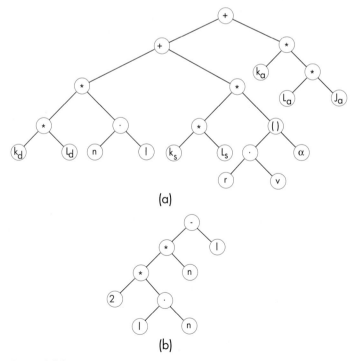

Figure 9.24 (a) Expression trees. (a) For Phong shading. (b) For reflection vector.

9.10.3 BSP Trees

Scene graphs and CSG trees describe hierarchical relationships among the parts of an object. We can also use trees to describe the world object space and encapsulate the spatial relationships among groups of objects. These relationships can lead to fast methods of **visibility testing** to determine which objects might be seen by a camera, thus avoiding processing all objects with tests such as the z-buffer algorithm. These techniques have become very important in real-time animations for computer games.

One approach to spatial hierarchy starts with the observation that a plane divides or partitions three-dimensional space into two parts (half spaces). Successive planes subdivide space into increasingly smaller partitions. In two dimensions, we can use lines to partition space.

Consider the polygons in Figure 9.25, with the viewer located as indicated. Arguing as we did in Chapter 8, there is an order in which to paint these polygons so that the image will be correct. Rather than using a method such as depth sort each time we want to render these polygons, we can store the relative-positioning information in a tree. We start the construction of the tree using the plane of one polygon to separate groups of polygons that are in front of it from those that are behind it. For example, consider a simple world in which all the polygons are parallel and are oriented with their normals parallel to the z-axis. This assumption makes it easier to illustrate the algorithm but does not affect the algorithm as long as the plane of any polygon separates the other polygons into two groups. In this world, the view from the z direction is as shown in Figure 9.26.

Plane A separates the polygons into two groups, one containing B and C, which are in front of A, and the second containing D, E, and F, which are behind A. We use this plane to start a **binary spatial-partition tree** (**BSP tree**) that stores the separating planes and the order in which they are applied. Thus, in the BSP tree in Figure 9.27, A is at the root, B and C are in the left subtree, and D, E, and F are in the right subtree. Proceeding recursively, C is behind the plane of B, so we can complete the left subtree. The plane of D separates E and F, thus completing the right subtree. Note that for a given set of polygons there are multiple possible BSP trees corresponding to the order in which we choose to

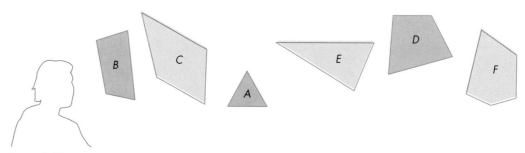

Figure 9.25   Collection of polygons and a viewer.

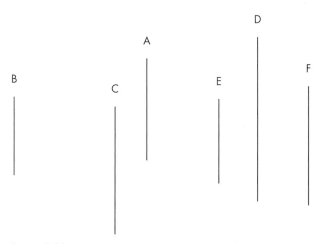

Figure 9.26 Top view of polygons.

make our partitions. In the general case, if a separating plane intersects a polygon, then we can break up the polygon into two polygons, one in front of the plane and one behind it, similar to what we did with overlapping polygons in the depth sort algorithm in Chapter 8.

We can use this tree to paint the polygons by doing a **backward in-order traversal**. That is, we traverse the tree recursively, drawing the right subtree first, followed by the root, and finally by the left subtree. One of the advantages of BSP trees is that we can use the same tree even if the viewer moves by changing the traversal algorithm. If the viewer moves to the back, as in Figure 9.28, then we can paint the polygons using a standard in-order traversal—left subtree, root, right subtree. Also note that we can use the algorithm recursively wherever planes separate sets of polygons or other objects into groups, called **clusters**. Thus, we might group polygons into polyhedral objects, then group these polyhedra into clusters. We can then apply the algorithm within each cluster. In applications such as flight simulators, where the world model does not change but the viewer's

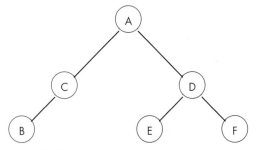

Figure 9.27 Binary spatial-partition (BSP) tree.

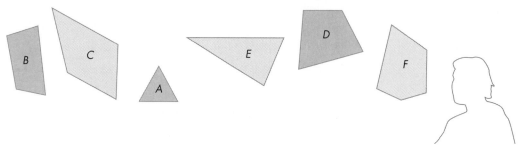

Figure 9.28   Movement of the viewer to back.

position does, the use of BSP trees can be efficient for doing visible surface determination during rendering. The tree contains all the required information to paint the polygons; the viewer's position determines the traversal algorithm.

9.10.4 Quadtrees and Octrees

Figure 9.29   Two-dimensional space of pixels.

One limitation of BSP trees is that the planes that separate polygons can have an arbitrary orientation, so evaluation of points relative to these planes can be costly. Octrees and quadtrees avoid this problem by using separating planes and lines parallel to the coordinate axes.

Consider the two-dimensional picture in Figure 9.29. We assume that this picture is composed of black and white pixels, perhaps formed by the rendering of a three-dimensional scene. If we wish to store the scene, we can save it as a binary array. But notice the great deal of coherence in the picture. Pixels of a each color are clustered together. We can draw two lines as in Figure 9.30, dividing the region into quadrants. Noting that one quadrant is all white, we can assign a single color to it. For the other three, we can subdivide again, and continue subdividing any quadrant that contains pixels of more than a single

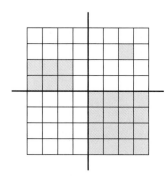

Figure 9.30   First subdivision of space.

Figure 9.31   Quadtree.

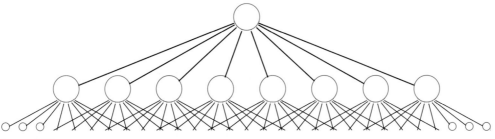

Figure 9.32 Octree.

color. This information can be stored in a tree called a **quadtree**, in which each level corresponds to a subdivision and each node has four children. Thus, the quadtree for our original simple picture is as shown in Figure 9.31.

Because we construct the quadtree by subdividing space with lines parallel to the coordinate axes, formation and traversal of the tree are simpler than are the corresponding operations for a BSP tree. One of the most important advantages of quadtrees is that they can reduce the amount of memory needed to store images.

Quadtrees partition two-dimensional space. They can also be used to partition object space in a manner similar to BSP trees and thus can be traversed in an order depending on the position of the viewer so as to render correctly the objects in each region. In three dimensions, quadtrees extend to **octrees**. The partitioning is done by planes parallel to the coordinate axes, and each step of the partitioning subdivides space into eight octants, as shown in Figure 9.32. Front Plate 4 shows a quadmesh used to represent elevation data.

Octrees are used for representing volume data sets that consist of volume elements called **voxels**, as shown in Figure 9.33. We consider such applications in Chapter 12.

9.11 Graphics and the Web

Figure 9.33 Volume data set.

The World Wide Web has had an enormous effect on virtually all communications and computer applications. It holds the promises of communicating information in a multitude of forms and of allowing new methods of interaction. Inherent in the potential of the web are the needs to move graphical information efficiently, to build applications that are viewable from many locations, and to access resources distributed over many sites. OpenGL and its extensions have had a major influence on the development of net-based three-dimensional applications and standards. We shall take a graphics-oriented approach and see what extensions we need to develop web applications. Some of the concepts will be familiar. We use the client–server model to allow efficient rendering. We also look at how we can implement graphical applications that are independent of the API.

9.11.1 Networks and Protocols

When we discussed networks in the context of client–server graphics in Chapter 3, we were able to ignore the details of how the information was conveyed over the network. Most architectural models of networks are based on a multilevel model such as the one shown in Figure 9.34. The model shown is a simplified version of the standard International Standards Organization (ISO) model. At the lowest level are the physical media that convey the bits. Elements at this level include cables between computers, telephone lines, fiber-optic cables, and any other hardware that can convey binary information between entities on the network. At the next level is a hierarchy of protocols for conveying bits between two entities in a reliable manner. Usually, what we find here is an addressing scheme that allows the information to be sent to and received at the correct location and an error-detection and error-correction method. At the next level are protocols for sending information between a process on one computer and a process on another. Whereas the lower-level protocols are concerned with point-to-point communication, at the higher levels we are concerned with process-to-process communication, in which packets of information may travel through many entities before arriving at their destination. For the millions of computers that form the Internet, the key protocols are the Transmission Control Protocol and Internet Protocol (TCP/IP), both of which are used at this level. One definition of the Internet is that it is the loosely coupled network of computers that use the Internet Protocol. At the highest level, we have applications that communicate over the network. When we use an API such as OpenGL, we are working at this level.

Consider an application that uses the display lists that we discussed in Chapter 3. On one computer there will be a user (client) program that is using a remote graphics server to render graphical entities defined in the application but placed in display lists. At the lowest level, the computers might be connected by means of an Ethernet and use standard Ethernet protocols to communicate. At the middle levels, the two computers can communicate using the TCP/IP protocols. At the next level up, they can exchange graphical information using the X protocols with the OpenGL extensions. From the application program's perspective, we simply use display lists in our program. The levels of communication are illustrated in Figure 9.35.

Stacking protocols gives high-level applications a way to communicate over various standard networks. If we were to have all users write graphical applications in OpenGL, we could do a fair amount of graphics over the web using client–server methods such as display lists. Not all users use the same API, however, and not all machines that support a given API have the same architecture. There

Figure 9.34   Protocol layers.

Figure 9.35   Protocols in OpenGL.

are additional possibilities available. Let us leave aside graphics temporarily and consider a network from a difference perspective—that of gathering information from a variety of resources.

9.11.2 Hypermedia and HTML

As the Internet evolved, a series of standard high-level protocols became widely accepted for transferring mail, files, and other types of information. Systems such as the X Window system allowed users to open windows on remote systems and to transfer basic graphical information. As the Internet grew, however, more and more information become publicly available, and users needed more sophisticated methods to share information that was stored in a distributed way in diverse formats. There are three key elements necessary for sharing such information: (1) an addressing scheme that allows users to identify resources over the network, (2) a method of encoding information in addition to simple text such as pictures and references (or **links**) to other resources, and (3) a method of searching for resources interactively.

The first two needs were addressed by researchers at the European Particle Physics Center (CERN) who created the World Wide Web, a networked hypertext system. Resources—files—are identified by a unique **Uniform Resource Locator** (**URL**) that consists of three parts: the protocol for transferring the document, the server where the document is located, and the location on the server where the document is to be found. For example, the URL for the programs in this text is `ftp://ftp.cs.unm.edu/pub/angel/BOOK`. The first part (`ftp`) indicates that the information will be transferred using the standard file-transfer protocol `ftp`; the second part (`ftp.cs.unm.edu`) identifies the server; and the final part indicates that the information is stored in the directory `pub/angel/BOOK`. The URL for the OpenGL Organization is `http://www.opengl.org`. This URL indicates that this document should be transferred with the hypertext transfer protocol (`http`) and is located at `www.opengl.org`. Because no document is indicated, a default document—the home page—will be returned.

The second contribution of CERN was the **Hypertext Markup Language** (**HTML**), which provided a simple way to describe a document consisting of text, references to other documents (links), and images. HTML documents are text documents, typically in ASCII code or one of the standard extended character sets.

The combination of URL addressing and HTML documents provided a way of making resources available. But until the National Center for SuperComputer Applications (NCSA) came up with its browser, Mosaic, it was not easy for a user to find resources and to search the web. **Browsers** are interactive programs that allow the user to search for and download documents on the web. Mosaic and later Netscape Navigator opened the door to "surfing" the web.

9.11.3 Databases and VRML

HTML provides only limited resources for supporting interactive three-dimensional graphics over the web. The main problem is that HTML recognizes images—arrays of pixels—in only two common formats (GIF and JPEG). HTML lacks any concept of a geometric object, even in two dimensions. This limitation was recognized by the user community, and various proposals for a new language were considered, resulting in the **Virtual Reality Modeling Language** (**VRML**).

There are many ways to convey graphics over a network. We can simply send images as does HTML, but there are obvious limitations to this approach. A second method is to send source code in a common language such as OpenGL. There are clear advantages to this strategy, and they provide arguments in favor of graphics standards. However, using source code would force users to compile programs on the client end of the network—for example, in the browser. A third approach is to use the client–server model, as in OpenGL. However, we have to agree on a single API and on a common format to transmit display lists. JAVA uses this philosophy.

There is a fourth approach that gives us considerably more flexibility in how graphics are created, stored, and transmitted. We can create a database that describes a scene, including the geometric objects, lights, materials, and other properties. This database can be stored in a standard text format and then conveyed over a network easily. The receiver of the database can then render the scene with whatever hardware and software are available locally. VRML employs this approach.

The design of the database involves many of the same concerns that we discussed in Chapter 2 in relation to what functionality is supported by an API. Because many questions, such as which primitives to support, are the same, it made sense to choose database elements related to a commonly accepted API that was supported on a variety of architectures. OpenGL was an obvious candidate, but it lacked the object orientation necessary to describe complex scenes whose components could be distributed over the web. VRML chose to start with the Open Inventor database. As we noted in Section 9.8, Open Inventor is built on top of OpenGL and adds, among other functions, scene graphs. Open Inventor allows the user to store scenes as text files. Once we add links to the database, we have most of what we need to describe three-dimensional scenes whose constituent parts can be located over a network.

VRML is tightly coupled to OpenGL. VRML gives us a way to describe distributed three-dimensional worlds, and a VRML browser can obtain the scene from the web. The browser must also be able to render the scene for the viewer. Consequently, there is an intimate tie between OpenGL and VRML. Although, in principle, the browser could use a rendering engine based on any of our models—pipeline, ray tracing, or radiosity—the fact that the underlying database is based on Open Inventor biases the choice toward an OpenGL-based VRML browser.

9.11.4 Java and Applets

Interaction over the web can be problematic when we use the models and tools that we have discussed. VRML databases are in text format and thus require that the client render whatever is in the database. Thus, a user cannot develop code on one end and know that that code will be executed on the other, because the two machines may be entirely different.

Java solves a portion of this problem by creating a machine in software that can be implemented on any computer. Java programs are compiled into **byte code** that can be run on any Java machine, regardless of what the underlying hardware is. Thus, the client and server exchange byte code over the web. Small programs in byte code, called **applets**, are understood by the standard web browsers and have added a tremendous amount of dynamic behavior to the web.

Java initially included only two-dimensional graphics. There is a new version, Java3D, that allows the creation and rendering of scene graphs although it remains to be seen if it will realize its potential. Within the next few years, we hope to see a convergence of the various approaches. What we hope will emerge is a universal way of conveying graphics over the web—one that can make use of the interactive and rendering capabilities of OpenGL and the object orientation of Open Inventor, Java3D, and DirectX.

9.12 Summary and Notes

The speed at which modern hardware can render geometric objects has opened up the possibilities of a variety of modeling systems. As users of computer graphics, we need a large arsenal of techniques if we are to make full use of our graphics systems. We have introduced hierarchical modeling. Not only are there the many other forms that we investigate in Chapters 10 and 11, but also we can combine these techniques to generate new ones. The suggested readings will help you to explore modeling methods.

We have presented basic themes that apply to most approaches to modeling. One is the use of hierarchy to incorporate relationships among objects in a scene. We have seen that we can use fundamental data structures, such as trees and DAGs, to represent such relationships; traversing these data structures becomes part of the rendering process. The use of scene graphs in Open Inventor, VRML, and Java3D allows the user to build complex animated scenes from a combination of predefined and user-defined software modules. Tree-structured models are also used in the RenderMan Shading Language. Using this language, we can describe complex shaders that involve the interaction of light sources, material properties, atmospheric effects, and a variety of local reflection models. In a manner similar to the way that multiple lights are used in the movie industry, a shader can be associated with a particular surface, an object, or a collection of objects. Certain renderers extend this idea to allow different rendering algorithms to be used on different objects in the same scene.

Object-oriented approaches hold even more promise for complex applications and for applications that are distributed over networks. Despite all the benefits of such high-level approaches, however, the actual rendering in most high-end systems is done at the OpenGL level, because the closeness of this API to the hardware makes for efficient use of the hardware. Consequently, both application programmers and system developers need to be familiar with multiple levels of APIs.

9.13 Suggested Readings

Hierarchical transformations through the use of a matrix stack were described in the graphics literature almost 30 years ago [New73]. The PHIGS API [ANSI88] was the first to incorporate them as part of a standard package. See Watt [Wat93] for an introduction to the use of articulated figures in animation. The paper by Lassiter [Las87] shows the relationship between traditional animation techniques as practiced in the movie industry and animation in computer graphics.

BSP trees were first proposed by Fuchs, Kedem, and Naylor [Fuc80] for use for visibility testing and were later used in many other applications such as CSG. See [Mol99] for other applications.

Scene graphs are the heart of Open Inventor [Wer94]. The Open Inventor database format was the basis of VRML [Har96]. Most recent APIs, such as Java3D [Rus97] and DirectX [Kov97], are object oriented. For a discussion of Java and applets, see the books [Cha98, Arn96]. Trees are integral to the RenderMan Shading Language [Ups89], where they are used to construct shaders. Modeling systems, such as Maya, allow the user to specify different shaders and rendering algorithms for different objects. Recent commodity graphics cards, such as the Nvidia GForce3 [Lin01], support user-defined renderers.

Many applications of visibility testing can be found in [Mol99].

Exercises

9.1   For our simple robot model, describe the set of points that can be reached by the tip of the upper arm.

9.2   Find equations for the position of any point on the simple robot in terms of the joint angles. Can you determine the joint angles from the position of the tip of the upper arm? Explain your answer.

9.3   Given two points in space that are reachable by the robot, describe a path between them in terms of the joint angles.

9.4   Write a simple circuit-layout program in terms of a symbol–instance transformation table. Your symbols should include the shapes for circuit elements—such as resistors, capacitors, and inductors for electrical circuits—or the shapes for various gates (AND, OR, NOT) for logical circuits.

9.5 We can write a description of a binary tree, such as we might use for a search, as a list of nodes with pointers to its children. Write an OpenGL program that will take such a description and display the tree graphically.

9.6 Robotics is only one example in which the parts of the scene show compound motion, where the movement of some objects depends on the movement of other objects. Other examples include bicycles (with wheels), airplanes (with propellers), and merry-go-rounds (with horses). Pick an example of compound motion. Write a graphics program to simulate your selection.

9.7 Given two polygons with the same number of vertices, write a program that will generate a sequence of images that converts one polygon into the other.

9.8 Starting with the tree node in Section 9.5, add an attribute to the node and make any required changes to the traversal algorithm.

9.9 Build a simple scene graph system that includes polygons, materials, a viewer, and light sources.

9.10 Why is ray tracing or ray casting a good strategy for rendering a scene described by a CSG tree?

9.11 Show how quadtrees can be used to draw an image at different resolutions.

9.12 Write a program that will allow the user to construct simple articulated figures from a small collection of basic shapes. Your program should allow the user to place the joints, and it should animate the resulting figures.

9.13 Is it possible to design a scene graph structure that is independent of the traversal algorithm?

9.14 Using the scene graph we developed in this chapter, add the ability to store scene graphs in text format and to read them in from files.

9.15 Add the ability to animate objects to our scene graph.

9.16 Starting with the robot in Section 9.3, add a hand or "gripper" to the end of the arm.

9.17 Add wheels to the robot of Section 9.3 and thus the ability to have it move over a flat surface.

9.18 BSP trees can be made more efficient if they are used hierarchically with objects grouped in clusters. Visibility checking is then done using the bounding volumes of the clusters. Implement such an algorithm, and use it with a scene graph renderer.

Curves and Surfaces

That the world is not flat has been generally accepted since 1492. Nevertheless, in computer graphics, we continue to populate our virtual worlds with flat objects. We have a good reason for such persistence. Graphics systems can render flat three-dimensional polygons at high rates, including doing hidden-surface removal, shading, and texture mapping. We could take the approach that we took with our sphere model, and define curved objects that are, in (virtual) reality, collections of flat polygons. Alternatively, as we shall do here, we can provide the user with the means to work with curved objects in her program, leaving the eventual rendering of these objects to the implementation.

We introduce three ways to model curves and surfaces, paying most attention to the parametric polynomial forms. We also discuss how curves and surfaces can be rendered on current graphics systems, a process that usually involves subdividing the curved objects into collections of flat primitives. From the application programmer's perspective, this process is transparent, because it is part of the implementation. It is important to understand the work involved, however, so that we can appreciate the practical limitations we face in using curves and surfaces.

10.1 Representation of Curves and Surfaces

Before proceeding to our development of parametric polynomial curves and surfaces, we pause to summarize our knowledge of the three major types of object representation—explicit, implicit, and parametric—and to observe the advantages and disadvantages of each form. We can illustrate the salient points using only lines, circles, planes, and spheres.

10.1.1 Explicit Representation

The **explicit form** of a curve in two dimensions gives the value of one variable, the **dependent variable**, in terms of the other, the **independent variable**. In x, y space, we might write

$y = f(x),$

or, if we are fortunate, we might be able to invert the relationship and express x as a function of y:

$$x = g(y).$$

There is no guarantee that either form exists for a given curve. For the line, we usually write the equation

$$y = mx + h,$$

in terms of its slope m and y-intercept h, even though we know that this equation does not hold for vertical lines. This problem is one of many coordinate-system–dependent effects that cause problems for graphics systems and, more generally, for all fields where we work with design and manipulation of curves and surfaces. Lines and circles exist independently of any representation, and any representation that fails for certain orientations, such as vertical lines, has serious deficiencies.

Circles provide an even more illustrative example. Consider a circle of radius r centered at the origin. A circle has constant **curvature**—a measure of how rapidly a curve is bending at a point. No closed two-dimensional curve can be more symmetric than the circle. However, the best we can do, using an explicit representation, is to write one equation for half of it,

$$y = \sqrt{r^2 - x^2},$$

and a second equation

$$y = -\sqrt{r^2 - x^2},$$

for the other half. In addition, we must also specify that these equations hold only if

$$0 \le |x| \le r.$$

In three dimensions, the explicit representation of a curve requires two equations. For example, if x is again the independent variable, we have two dependent variables:

$$y = f(x),$$
$$z = g(x).$$

A surface requires two independent variables, and a representation might take the form

$$z = f(x, y).$$

As is true in two dimensions, a curve or surface may not have an explicit representation. For example, the equations

$$y = ax + b,$$
$$z = cx + d,$$

describe a line in three dimensions, but these equations cannot represent a line in a plane of constant x. Likewise, a surface represented by an equation of the form $z = f(x, y)$ cannot represent a sphere, because a given x and y can generate zero, one, or two points on the sphere.

10.1.2 Implicit Representations

Most of the curves and surfaces with which we work have implicit representations. In two dimensions, an **implicit curve** can be represented by the equation

$$f(x, y) = 0.$$

Our two examples—the line and the circle centered at the origin—have the respective representations

$$ax + by + c = 0,$$
$$x^2 + y^2 - r^2 = 0.$$

The function f, however, is really a testing, or **membership**, function that divides space into those points that belong to the curve and those that do not. It allows us to take an x, y pair and to evaluate f to determine whether this point lies on the curve. In general, however, it gives us no analytic way to find a value y on the curve that corresponds to a given x, or vice versa. The implicit form is less coordinate-system–dependent than is the explicit form, however, in that it does represent all lines and circles.

In three dimensions, the implicit form

$$f(x, y, z) = 0$$

describes a surface. For example, any plane can be written as

$$ax + by + cz + d = 0$$

for constants a, b, c, and d, and a sphere of radius r centered at the origin can be described by

$$x^2 + y^2 + z^2 - r^2 = 0.$$

Curves in three dimensions are not as easily represented in implicit form. We can represent a curve as the intersection, if it exists, of the two surfaces:

$$f(x, y, z) = 0,$$
$$g(x, y, z) = 0.$$

Thus, if we test a point (x, y, z) and it is on both surfaces, then it must lie on their intersection curve. In general, most of the curves and surfaces that arise in real applications have implicit representations. Their use is limited by the difficulty in obtaining points on them.

Algebraic surfaces are those for which the function $f(x, y, z)$ is the sum of polynomials in the three variables. Of particular importance are the **quadric** surfaces, where each term in f can have degree up to 2.[1] Quadrics are of interest not only because they include useful objects (such as spheres, disks, and cones), but also because when we intersect these objects with lines, at most two intersection points are generated. We shall use this characteristic to render quadrics in Section 10.9 and for use in ray tracing in Chapter 13.

10.1.3 Parametric Form

The **parametric form** of a curve expresses the value of each spatial variable for points on the curve in terms of an independent variable, u: the **parameter**. In three dimensions, we have three explicit functions:

$$x = x(u),$$
$$y = y(u),$$
$$z = z(u).$$

One of the advantages of the parametric form is that it is the same in two and three dimensions. In the former case, we simply drop the equation for z. A useful interpretation of the parametric form is to visualize the locus of points $\mathbf{p}(u) = [\, x(u) \quad y(u) \quad z(u) \,]^T$ being drawn as u varies, as shown in Figure 10.1. We can think of the derivative

$$\frac{d\mathbf{p}(u)}{du} = \begin{bmatrix} \frac{dx(u)}{du} \\ \frac{dy(u)}{du} \\ \frac{dz(u)}{du} \end{bmatrix}$$

as the velocity with which the curve is traced out and points in the direction tangent to the curve.

Parametric surfaces require two parameters. We can describe a surface by three equations of the form

$$x = x(u, v),$$
$$y = y(u, v),$$
$$z = z(u, v),$$

or we can use the column matrix

$$\mathbf{p}(u, v) = \begin{bmatrix} x(u, v) \\ y(u, v) \\ z(u, v) \end{bmatrix}.$$

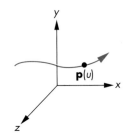

Figure 10.1 Parametric curve.

---

1. Degree is measured as the sum of the powers of the individual terms, so x, yz, or z^2 can be in a quadric, but xy^2 cannot be.

As u and v vary over some interval, we generate all the points $\mathbf{p}(u, v)$ on the surface. As we saw with our sphere example in Chapter 6, the vectors given by the column matrices

$$\frac{\partial \mathbf{p}}{\partial u} = \begin{bmatrix} \frac{\partial x(u,v)}{\partial u} \\ \frac{\partial y(u,v)}{\partial u} \\ \frac{\partial z(u,v)}{\partial u} \end{bmatrix},$$

and

$$\frac{\partial \mathbf{p}}{\partial v} = \begin{bmatrix} \frac{\partial x(u,v)}{\partial v} \\ \frac{\partial y(u,v)}{\partial v} \\ \frac{\partial z(u,v)}{\partial v} \end{bmatrix},$$

determine the tangent plane at each point on the surface. In addition, as long as these vectors are not parallel, their cross product gives the normal (Figure 10.2) at each point; that is,

$$\mathbf{n} = \partial \mathbf{p}/\partial u \times \partial \mathbf{p}/\partial v.$$

The parametric form of curves and surfaces is the most flexible and robust for computer graphics. We could still argue that we have not fully removed all dependencies on a particular coordinate system or frame, because we are still using the x, y, and z for a particular representation. It is possible to develop a system solely on the basis of $\mathbf{p}(u)$ for curves and $\mathbf{p}(u, v)$ for surfaces. For example, the Frenet frame is often used for describing curves in three-dimensional space, and it is defined starting with the tangent and the normal at each point on the curve. However, this frame changes for each point on the curve. For our purposes, the parametric form for x, y, z within a particular frame is sufficiently robust.

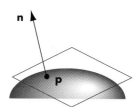

Figure 10.2 Tangent plane and normal at a point on an parametric surface.

10.1.4 Parametric Polynomial Curves

Parametric forms are not unique. A given curve or surface can be represented in many ways, but we shall find that parametric forms in which the functions are polynomials in u for curves, and polynomials in u and v for surfaces, are of most use in computer graphics. Many of the reasons will be summarized in Section 10.2.

Consider a curve of the form[2]

$$\mathbf{p}(u) = \begin{bmatrix} x(u) \\ y(u) \\ z(u) \end{bmatrix}.$$

---

2. At this point there is no need to work in homogeneous coordinates; in Section 10.8 we shall work in them to derive NURBS curves.

A polynomial parametric curve of degree[3] n is of the form

$$\mathbf{p}(u) = \sum_{k=0}^{n} u^k \mathbf{c}_k,$$

where each $\mathbf{c}_k$ has independent x, y, and z components; that is,

$$\mathbf{c}_k = \begin{bmatrix} c_{xk} \\ c_{yk} \\ c_{zk} \end{bmatrix}.$$

The $n + 1$ column matrices $\{\mathbf{c}_k\}$ are the coefficients of $\mathbf{p}$; they give us $3(n + 1)$ degrees of freedom in how we choose the coefficients of a particular $\mathbf{p}$. There is no coupling, however, among the x, y, and z components, so we can work with three independent equations, each of the form

$$p(u) = \sum_{k=0}^{n} u^k c_k,$$

where p is any one of x, y, or z. There are $n + 1$ degrees of freedom in $p(u)$. We can define our curves for any range interval of u:

$$u_{\min} \leq u \leq u_{\max};$$

but, with no loss of generality (see Exercise 10.3), we can assume that $0 \leq u \leq 1$. As the value of u varies over its range, we define a **curve segment**, as shown in Figure 10.3.

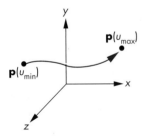

Figure 10.3 Curve segment.

10.1.5 Parametric Polynomial Surfaces

We can define a parametric polynomial surface as

$$\mathbf{p}(u, v) = \begin{bmatrix} x(u, v) \\ y(u, v) \\ z(u, v) \end{bmatrix} = \sum_{i=0}^{n} \sum_{j=0}^{m} \mathbf{c}_{ij} u^i v^j.$$

We must specify $3(n + 1)(m + 1)$ coefficients to determine a particular surface $\mathbf{p}(u, v)$. We shall always take $n = m$, and let u and v vary over the rectangle $0 \leq u, v \leq 1$, defining a **surface patch**, as shown in Figure 10.4. Note that any surface patch can be viewed as the limit of a collection of curves that we generate by holding either u or v constant and varying the other. Our strategy shall be to define parametric polynomial curves and to use the curves to generate surfaces with similar characteristics.

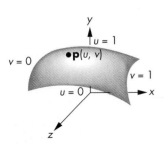

Figure 10.4 Surface patch.

---

3. OpenGL often uses the term *order* to mean 1 greater than the degree.

Color Plate 1
Image of sun object created using NURBS surfaces and rendered with bump mapping.

(Courtesy of Full Dome Project, University of New Mexico.)

Color Plate 2
Wire-frame representation of sun object surfaces.

(Courtesy of Full Dome Project, University of New Mexico.)

Color Plate 3
Flat-shaded polygonal rendering of
sun object.

*(Courtesy of Full Dome Project,
University of New Mexico.)*

Color Plate 4
Smooth-shaded polygonal rendering
of sun object.

*(Courtesy of Full Dome Project,
University of New Mexico.)*

Color Plate 5
Wire-frame of NURBS representation of sun object showing the high number of polygons used in rendering the NURBS surfaces.

(Courtesy of Full Dome Project, University of New Mexico.)

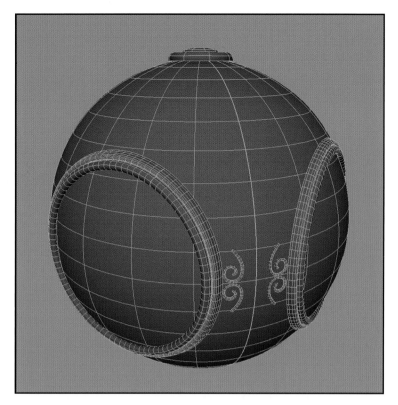

Color Plate 6
Rendering of sun object showing bump map.

(Courtesy of Full Dome Project, University of New Mexico.)

Color Plate 7
Rendering of sun object with an environmental map.

(Courtesy of Full Dome Project, University of New Mexico.)

Color Plate 8
Rendering of a small part of the sun object with an environmental map.

(Courtesy of Full Dome Project, University of New Mexico.)

(a) Without antialiasing.

(b) With antialiasing.

Color Plate 9
Axonometric view from outside
of temple.

*(Courtesy of Richard Nordhaus,
Architect, Albuquerque, NM.)*

Color Plate 10
Perspective view of interior of
temple.

*(Courtesy of Richard Nordhaus,
Architect, Albuquerque, NM.)*

Color Plate 11
Factory environment from video, *I Thought, Therefore I Was.*

(Courtesy of James Pinkerton, Thomas Keller, Brian Jones, John Bell, University of New Mexico and Sandia National Laboratories.)

Color Plate 12
Robot "Ed" from video, *I Thought, Therefore I Was.*

(Courtesy of James Pinkerton, Thomas Keller, Brian Jones, John Bell, University of New Mexico and Sandia National Laboratories.)

Color Plate 13
Welding scene from video,
I Thought, Therefore I Was.

(Courtesy of James Pinkerton,
Thomas Keller, Brian Jones,
John Bell, University of New Mexico
and Sandia National Laboratories.)

Color Plate 14
User interface to an OpenGL
CAD program showing a variety
of interactive modes including
buttons, slide bars, tool bars,
and text boxes

(Courtesy of Brian Jones,
University of New Mexico.)

Color Plate 15
Ocean temperature distribution during El Niño. Data texture mapped to earth model.

(Courtesy of Allen McPherson, Advanced Computing Laboratory, Los Alamos National Laboratory.)

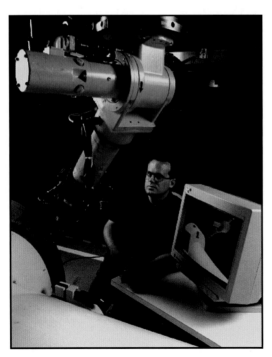

Color Plate 16
Physical robot and its graphical model. The graphical model is used for design, path planning, and simulation.

(Courtesy of Sandia National Laboratories.)

Color Plate 17

(a) NURBS surface representing surface of water and particles used to pull the NURBS control points to create successive images of moving water.

(Courtesy of Saty Raghavachary,
© DreamWorks Feature Animation.)

(b) Rendering of NURBS surface showing static water surface.

(Courtesy of Saty Raghavachary,
© DreamWorks Feature Animation.)

Color Plate 18
Rendering using particles showing moving water from "Spirit-Stallion of the Cimarron."

(Courtesy of Saty Raghavachary,
© DreamWorks Feature Animation.)

Color Plate 19
Fluid dynamics of the mantle of the
Earth. Pseudocolor mapping of
temperatures and isotemperature surface.

(Courtesy of James Painter,
Advanced Computing Laboratory,
Los Alamos National Laboratory.)

Color Plate 20
Volume-rendered image of head by
parallel ray casting. Skin rendered as
transparent, muscle rendered as opaque.

(Courtesy of Kwan-Liu Ma,
James Painter, University of Utah;
Charles Hansen, Mike Krogh,
Advanced Computing Laboratory,
Los Alamos National Laboratory.)

Color Plate 21
RGB color cube.

(Courtesy of University of New Mexico.)

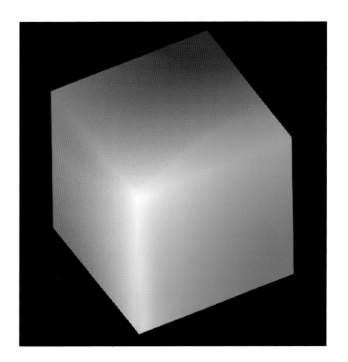

Color Plate 22
Avatar representing a patient who is being diagnosed and treated by a remotely located health professional (inset).

(Courtesy of Tom Caudell, Visualization Laboratory, Albuquerque High Performance Computing Center, University of New Mexico.)

Color Plate 23
Rendering using ray tracer.

*(Courtesy of Patrick McCormick, University of New Mexico
and Los Alamos National Laboratory.)*

Color Plate 24
Radiosity rendering showing soft
shadows and diffuse-diffuse reflections.

*(Courtesy of A. Van Pernis, K. Rasche,
R. Geist, Clemson University.)*

Color Plate 25
Array of Utah teapots with different material properties.

(Courtesy of Silicon Graphics, Inc.)

Color Plate 26
Isosurfaces computed using Marching Cubes from lobster data set (120 × 120 × 34 voxels).

(Courtesy of Patricia Crossno, University of New Mexico and Sandia National Laboratories.)

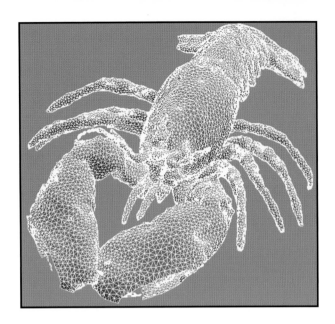

Color Plate 27
Isosurface mesh for lobster data set computed by a particle system of 40,000 particles.

(Courtesy of Patricia Crossno, University of New Mexico and Sandia National Laboratories.)

Color Plate 28
Volume rendering of lobster data set using spatting.

(Courtesy of Lee Ann Fisk, University of New Mexico and Sandia National Laboratories.)

Color Plate 29
One frame from Pixar's *Geri's Game* showing refraction through reflections on Geri's glasses.

(Courtesy of Pixar Animation Studios.)

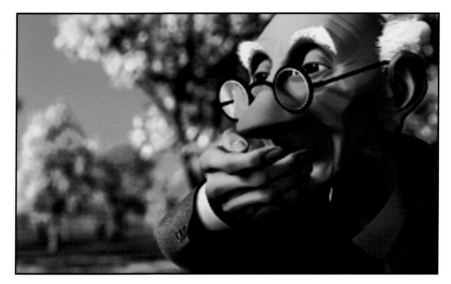

Color Plate 30
Reflection map from environment computed from the center of the lens on Geri's glasses. The reflection map is then mapped to the glasses as part of the rendering process.

(Courtesy of Pixar Animation Studios.)

Color Plate 31
Particle system.   *(Courtesy of Lexus and Rhythm and Hues.)*

(a) Mesh of particles.

(b) Model of Lexus
with surface.

(c) Wind blowing mesh
off Lexus.

(d) Mesh blown away from Lexus.

10.2 Design Criteria

The way curves and surfaces are used in computer graphics and computer-aided design is often different from the way they are used in other fields, and from the way you may have seen them used previously. There are many considerations that determine why we prefer to use parametric polynomials of low degree, including

- Local control of shape
- Smoothness and continuity
- Ability to evaluate derivatives
- Stability
- Ease of rendering

Figure 10.5 Model airplane.

We can understand these criteria with the aid of a simple example. Suppose that we want to build a model airplane, using flexible strips of wood for the structure. We can build the body of the model by constructing a set of cross sections, and then connecting them with longer pieces, as shown in Figure 10.5. To design our cross sections, we might start with a picture of a real airplane, or sketch a desired curve. One such cross section might be like that shown in Figure 10.6. We could try to get a single global description of this cross section, but that description probably would not be what we want. Each strip of wood can be bent to only a certain shape before breaking, and can bend in only a smooth way. Hence, we can regard the curve in Figure 10.6 as only an approximation to what we actually build, which might be more like Figure 10.7. In practice, we probably will make our cross section out of a number of wood strips, each of which will become a curve segment for the cross section. Thus, not only will each segment have to be smooth, but also we want a degree of smoothness where the segments meet at **join points**.

Figure 10.6 Cross-section curve.

Note that, although we might be able ensure that a curve segment is smooth, we have to be particularly careful at the join points. Figure 10.8 shows an example in which, although the two curve segments are smooth, at the join point the derivative is discontinuous. The usual definition of **smoothness** is given in terms of the derivatives along the curve. A curve with discontinuities is of little interest to us. Generally, a curve with a continuous first derivative is smoother than a curve whose first derivative has discontinuities (and so on for the higher derivatives). These notions become more precise in Section 10.3. For now, it should be clear that, for a polynomial curve

Figure 10.7 Approximation of cross-section curve.

$$\mathbf{p}(u) = \sum_{k=0}^{n} \mathbf{c}_k u^k,$$

all derivatives exist and can be computed analytically. Consequently, the only places where we can encounter continuity difficulties are at the join points.

We would like to design each segment individually, rather than designing all the segments by a single global calculation. One reason for this desire is that we would like to work interactively with the shape, carefully molding it to meet

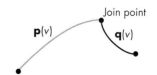

Figure 10.8 Derivative discontinuity at join point.

our specifications. When we make a change, this change will affect the shape in only the area where we are working. This sort of local control is but one aspect of a more general stability principle: *Small changes in the values of input parameters should cause only small changes in output variables.* Another statement of this principle is: *Small changes in independent variables should cause only small changes in dependent variables.*

Working with our piece of wood, we might be able to bend it to approximate the desired shape by comparing it to the entire curve. More likely, we would consider data at a small number of **control** or **data points**, and would use only those data to design our shape. Figure 10.9 shows a possible curve segment and a collection of control points. Note that the curve passes through, or **interpolates**, some of the control points, but only comes close to others. As we shall see throughout this chapter, in computer graphics and CAD, we are usually satisfied if the curve passes close to the control-point data, as long as it is smooth.

This example shows many of the reasons for working with polynomial parametric curves. In fact, the spline curves that we discuss in Sections 10.7 and 10.8 derive their name from a flexible wood or metal device that shipbuilders used to design the shape of hulls. Each spline was held in place by pegs, and the bending properties of the material gave the curve segment a polynomial shape.

Returning to computer graphics, remember that we need methods for rendering curves (and surfaces). A good mathematical representation may be of limited value if we cannot display the resulting curves and surfaces easily. We would like to display whatever curves and surfaces we choose with techniques similar to those used for flat objects, including color, shading, and texture mapping.

Figure 10.9 Curve segment and control points.

10.3 Parametric Cubic Polynomial Curves

Once we have decided to use parametric polynomial curves, we must choose the degree of the curve. On one hand, if we choose a high degree, we will have many parameters that we can set to form the desired shape, but evaluation of points on the curve will be costly. In addition, as the degree of a polynomial curve becomes higher, there is more danger that the curve will become rougher. On the other hand, if we pick too low a degree, we may not have enough parameters with which to work. However, if we design each curve segment over a short interval, we can achieve many of our purposes with low-degree curves. Although there may be only a few degrees of freedom, these few may be sufficient to allow us to produce the desired shape in a small region. For this reason, most designers, at least initially, work with cubic polynomial curves.

We can write a cubic parametric polynomial using a row and column matrix as

$$\mathbf{p}(u) = \mathbf{c}_0 + \mathbf{c}_1 u + \mathbf{c}_2 u^2 + \mathbf{c}_3 u^3 = \sum_{k=0}^{3} \mathbf{c}_k u^k = \mathbf{u}^T \mathbf{c},$$

where

$$\mathbf{c} = \begin{bmatrix} \mathbf{c}_0 \\ \mathbf{c}_1 \\ \mathbf{c}_2 \\ \mathbf{c}_3 \end{bmatrix}, \qquad \mathbf{u} = \begin{bmatrix} 1 \\ u \\ u^2 \\ u^3 \end{bmatrix}, \qquad \mathbf{c}_k = \begin{bmatrix} c_{kx} \\ c_{ky} \\ c_{xz} \end{bmatrix}.$$

Thus, $\mathbf{c}$ is a column matrix containing the coefficients of the polynomial; it is what we wish to determine from the control-point data. We shall derive a number of types of cubic curves. The types will differ in how they use the control-point data. We seek to find 12 equations in 12 unknowns for each type, but, because x, y, and z are independent, we can group these equations into three independent sets of four equations in four unknowns.

The design of a particular type of cubic will be based on data given at some values of the parameter u. These data might take the form of interpolating conditions in which the polynomial must agree with the data at some points. The data may also require the polynomial to interpolate some derivatives at certain values of the parameter. We might also have smoothness conditions that enforce various continuity conditions at the join points that are shared by two curve segments. Finally, we may have conditions that are not as strict, requiring only that the curve pass close to several known data points. Each type of condition will define a different type of curve, and, depending on how we use some given data, the same data can define more than a single curve.

10.4 Interpolation

Our first example of a cubic parametric polynomial is the cubic **interpolating polynomial**. Although we rarely use interpolating polynomials in computer graphics, the derivation of this familiar polynomial illustrates the steps we must follow for our other types, and the analysis of the interpolating polynomial illustrates many of the important features by which we evaluate a particular curve or surface.

Suppose that we have four control points in three dimensions: $\mathbf{p}_0$, $\mathbf{p}_1$, $\mathbf{p}_2$, and $\mathbf{p}_3$. Each is of the form

$$\mathbf{p}_k = \begin{bmatrix} x_k \\ y_k \\ z_k \end{bmatrix}.$$

We seek the coefficients $\mathbf{c}$ such that the polynomial $\mathbf{p}(u) = \mathbf{u}^T \mathbf{c}$ passes through, or interpolates, the four control points. The derivation should be easy. We have four three-dimensional interpolating points; hence, we have 12 conditions and 12 unknowns. First, however, we have to decide at which values of the parameter u the interpolation takes place. Lacking any other information, we can take these values to be the equally spaced values $u = 0, \frac{1}{3}, \frac{2}{3}, 1$—remember that we have decided to let u always vary over the interval $[0, 1]$. The four conditions are thus

$$\mathbf{p}_0 = \mathbf{p}(0) = \mathbf{c}_0,$$

$$\mathbf{p}_1 = \mathbf{p}\left(\frac{1}{3}\right) = \mathbf{c}_0 + \frac{1}{3}\mathbf{c}_1 + \left(\frac{1}{3}\right)^2 \mathbf{c}_2 + \left(\frac{1}{3}\right)^3 \mathbf{c}_3,$$

$$\mathbf{p}_2 = \mathbf{p}\left(\frac{2}{3}\right) = \mathbf{c}_0 + \frac{2}{3}\mathbf{c}_1 + \left(\frac{2}{3}\right)^2 \mathbf{c}_2 + \left(\frac{2}{3}\right)^3 \mathbf{c}_3,$$

$$\mathbf{p}_3 = \mathbf{p}(1) = \mathbf{c}_0 + \mathbf{c}_1 + \mathbf{c}_2 + \mathbf{c}_3.$$

We can write these equations in matrix form as

$$\mathbf{p} = \mathbf{Ac},$$

where

$$\mathbf{p} = \begin{bmatrix} \mathbf{p}_0 \\ \mathbf{p}_1 \\ \mathbf{p}_2 \\ \mathbf{p}_3 \end{bmatrix}$$

and

$$\mathbf{A} = \begin{bmatrix} 1 & 0 & 0 & 0 \\ 1 & \frac{1}{3} & \left(\frac{1}{3}\right)^2 & \left(\frac{1}{3}\right)^3 \\ 1 & \frac{2}{3} & \left(\frac{2}{3}\right)^2 & \left(\frac{2}{3}\right)^3 \\ 1 & 1 & 1 & 1 \end{bmatrix}.$$

The matrix form here has to be interpreted carefully. If we interpret $\mathbf{p}$ and $\mathbf{c}$ as column matrices of 12 elements, the rules of matrix multiplication are violated. Instead, we view $\mathbf{p}$ and $\mathbf{c}$ each as a four-element column matrix whose elements are three-element row matrices. Hence, multiplication of an element of $\mathbf{A}$, a scalar, by an element of $\mathbf{c}$, a three-element column matrix, yields a three-element column matrix, which is the same type as an element of $\mathbf{p}$.[4] We can show that $\mathbf{A}$ is nonsingular, and can invert it to obtain the **interpolating geometry matrix**

$$\mathbf{M}_I = \mathbf{A}^{-1} = \begin{bmatrix} 1 & 0 & 0 & 0 \\ -5.5 & 9 & -4.5 & 1 \\ 9 & -22.5 & 18 & -4.5 \\ -4.5 & 13.5 & -13.5 & 4.5 \end{bmatrix}$$

---

4. We could use row matrices for the elements of $\mathbf{p}$ and $\mathbf{c}$: in that case, ordinary matrix multiplications would work, because we would have a 4×4 matrix multiplying a 4×3 matrix. However, this method would fail for surfaces. The real difficulty is that we should be using *tensors* to carry out the mathematics—a topic beyond the scope of this book.

Figure 10.10 Joining of interpolating segments.

and the desired coefficients

$$\mathbf{c} = \mathbf{M}_I \mathbf{p}.$$

Suppose that we have a sequence of control points $\mathbf{p}_0, \mathbf{p}_1, \ldots, \mathbf{p}_m$. Rather than defining a single interpolating curve of degree m for all the points—a calculation we could do by following a similar derivation to the one for cubic polynomials— we can define a set of cubic interpolating curves, each defined by a group of four control points, and each valid over a short interval in u. We can achieve continuity at the join points by using the control point defining the right side of one segment as the first point for the next segment (Figure 10.10). Thus, we use $\mathbf{p}_0, \mathbf{p}_1, \mathbf{p}_2, \mathbf{p}_3$ to define the first segment; we use $\mathbf{p}_3, \mathbf{p}_4, \mathbf{p}_5, \mathbf{p}_6$, for the second; and so on. Note that if each segment is defined for the parameter u varying over the interval $(0, 1)$, then the matrix $\mathbf{M}_I$ is the same for each segment. Although we have achieved continuity for the sequence of segments, derivatives at the join points will not be continuous.

10.4.1 Blending Functions

We can obtain additional insights into the smoothness of the interpolating polynomial curves by rewriting our equations in a slightly different form. We can substitute the interpolating coefficients into our polynomial; we obtain

$$\mathbf{p}(u) = \mathbf{u}^T \mathbf{c} = \mathbf{u}^T \mathbf{M}_I \mathbf{p},$$

which we can write as

$$\mathbf{p}(u) = \mathbf{b}(u)^T \mathbf{p},$$

where

$$\mathbf{b}(u) = \mathbf{M}_I^T \mathbf{u}$$

is a column matrix of the four **blending polynomials**

$$\mathbf{b}(u) = \begin{bmatrix} b_0(u) \\ b_1(u) \\ b_2(u) \\ b_3(u) \end{bmatrix}.$$

Each blending polynomial is a cubic. If we express $\mathbf{p}(u)$ in terms of these blending polynomials as

$$\mathbf{p}(u) = b_0(u)\mathbf{p}_0 + b_1(u)\mathbf{p}_1 + b_2(u)\mathbf{p}_2 + b_3(u)\mathbf{p}_3 = \sum_{i=0}^{3} b_i(u)\mathbf{p}_i,$$

then we can see that the polynomials blend together the individual contributions of each control point and enable us to see the effect of a given control point on the entire curve. These blending functions for the cubic interpolating polynomial are shown in Figure 10.11 and are given by the equations

$$b_0(u) = -\frac{9}{2}\left(u - \frac{1}{3}\right)\left(u - \frac{2}{3}\right)(u - 1),$$

$$b_1(u) = \frac{27}{2}u\left(u - \frac{2}{3}\right)(u - 1),$$

$$b_2(u) = -\frac{27}{2}u\left(u - \frac{1}{3}\right)(u - 1),$$

$$b_3(u) = \frac{9}{2}u\left(u - \frac{1}{3}\right)\left(u - \frac{2}{3}\right).$$

Because all the zeros of the blending functions lie in the closed interval $[0, 1]$, the blending functions must vary substantially over this interval and are not particularly smooth. This lack of smoothness is a consequence of the interpolating requirement that the curve must pass through the control points, rather than just come close to them. This characteristic is even more pronounced for interpolating polynomials of higher degree. This problem and the lack of derivative continuity at the join points account for limited use of the interpolating polynomial in computer graphics. However, the same derivation and analysis process will allow us to find smoother types of cubic curves.

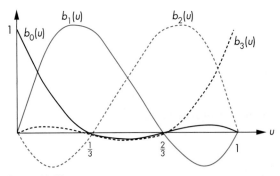

Figure 10.11 Blending polynomials for interpolation.

10.4.2 The Cubic Interpolating Patch

There is a natural extension of the interpolating curve to an interpolating patch. A **bicubic surface patch** can be written in the form

$$\mathbf{p}(u, v) = \sum_{i=0}^{3} \sum_{j=0}^{3} u^i v^j \mathbf{c}_{ij},$$

where $\mathbf{c}_{ij}$ is a three-element column matrix of the x, y, and z coefficients for the ijth term in the polynomial. If we define a 4×4 matrix whose elements are three-element column matrices,

$$\mathbf{C} = [\, \mathbf{c}_{ij} \,],$$

then we can write the surface patch as

$$\mathbf{p}(u, v) = \mathbf{u}^T \mathbf{C} \mathbf{v},$$

where

$$\mathbf{v} = \begin{bmatrix} 1 \\ v \\ v^2 \\ v^3 \end{bmatrix}.$$

A particular bicubic polynomial patch is defined by the 48 elements of $\mathbf{C}$—16 three-element vectors.

Suppose that we have 16 three-dimensional control points $\mathbf{p}_{ij}$, $i = 0, \ldots, 3$, $j = 0, \ldots, 3$. We can use these points to define an interpolating surface patch, as shown in Figure 10.12. If we assume that these data are used for interpolation at the equally spaced values of both u and v of 0, $\frac{1}{3}$, $\frac{2}{3}$, and 1, then we get three

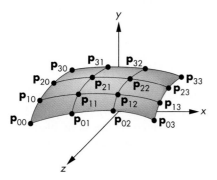

Figure 10.12 Interpolating surface patch.

sets of 16 equations in 16 unknowns. For example, for $u = v = 0$, we get the three independent equations

$$\mathbf{p}_{00} = [\,1 \quad 0 \quad 0 \quad 0\,]\mathbf{C}\begin{bmatrix} 1 \\ 0 \\ 0 \\ 0 \end{bmatrix} = \mathbf{c}_{00}.$$

Rather than writing down and solving all these equations, we can proceed in a more direct fashion. If we consider $v = 0$, we get a curve in u that must interpolate $\mathbf{p}_{00}, \mathbf{p}_{10}, \mathbf{p}_{20}$, and $\mathbf{p}_{30}$. Using our results on interpolating curves, we write this curve as

$$\mathbf{p}(u, 0) = \mathbf{u}^T \mathbf{M}_I \begin{bmatrix} \mathbf{p}_{00} \\ \mathbf{p}_{10} \\ \mathbf{p}_{20} \\ \mathbf{p}_{30} \end{bmatrix} = \mathbf{u}^T \mathbf{C} \begin{bmatrix} 1 \\ 0 \\ 0 \\ 0 \end{bmatrix}.$$

Likewise, the values of $v = \frac{1}{3}, \frac{2}{3}, 1$ define three other interpolating curves, each of which has a similar form. Putting these curves together, we can write all 16 equations as

$$\mathbf{u}^T \mathbf{M}_I \mathbf{P} = \mathbf{u}^T \mathbf{C}\mathbf{A}^T,$$

where $\mathbf{A}$ is the inverse of $\mathbf{M}_I$. We can solve this equation for the desired coefficient matrix

$$\mathbf{C} = \mathbf{M}_I \mathbf{P}\mathbf{M}_I^T,$$

and, substituting into the equation for the surface, we have

$$\mathbf{p}(u, v) = \mathbf{u}^T \mathbf{M}_I \mathbf{P}\mathbf{M}_I^T \mathbf{v}.$$

We can interpret this result in several ways. First, the interpolating surface can be derived from our understanding of interpolating curves—a technique that will enable us to extend other types of curves to surfaces. Second, we can extend our use of blending polynomials to surfaces. By noting that $\mathbf{M}_I^T \mathbf{u}$ describes the interpolating blending functions, we can rewrite our surface patch as

$$\mathbf{p}(u, v) = \sum_{i=0}^{3} \sum_{j=0}^{3} b_i(u)b_j(v)\mathbf{p}_{ij}.$$

Each term $b_i(u)b_j(v)$ describes a **blending patch**. We form a surface by blending together 16 simple patches, each weighted by the data at a control point. The basic properties of the blending patches are determined by the same blending polynomials that arose for interpolating curves; thus, most of the characteristics of surfaces are similar to those of the curves. In particular, the blending patches are not particularly smooth, because the zeros of the functions $b_i(u)b_j(v)$ lie inside the unit square in u, v space. Surfaces formed from curves using this technique are known as **tensor-product surfaces**. Bicubic tensor-product surfaces are a subset of all surface patches that contain up to cubic terms in both parameters. They are an example of **separable surfaces**, which can be written as

$$\mathbf{p}(u, v) = \mathbf{f}(\mathbf{u})\mathbf{g}(v),$$

where $\mathbf{f}$ and $\mathbf{g}$ are suitably chosen row and column matrices, respectively. The advantage of such surfaces is that they allow us to work with functions in u and v independently.

10.5 Hermite Curves and Surfaces

We can use the techniques that we developed for interpolating curves and surfaces to generate various other types of curves and surfaces. The major difference is in the way we use the data at control points.

10.5.1 The Hermite Form

Suppose that we start with only the control points $\mathbf{p}_0$ and $\mathbf{p}_3$,[5] and again insist that our curve interpolate these points at the parameter values $u = 0$ and $u = 1$, respectively. Using our previous notation, we have the two conditions

$$\mathbf{p}(0) = \mathbf{p}_0 = \mathbf{c}_0,$$

$$\mathbf{p}(1) = \mathbf{p}_3 = \mathbf{c}_0 + \mathbf{c}_1 + \mathbf{c}_2 + \mathbf{c}_3.$$

We can get two other conditions if we assume that we know the derivatives of the function at $u = 0$ and $u = 1$. The derivative of the polynomial is simply the parametric quadratic polynomial

$$\mathbf{p}'(u) = \begin{bmatrix} \frac{dx}{du} \\ \frac{dy}{du} \\ \frac{dz}{du} \end{bmatrix} = \mathbf{c}_1 + 2u\mathbf{c}_2 + 3u^2\mathbf{c}_3.$$

If we denote the given values of the two derivatives as $\mathbf{p}'_0$ and $\mathbf{p}'_3$, then our two additional conditions (Figure 10.13) are

$$\mathbf{p}'_0 = \mathbf{p}'(0) = \mathbf{c}_1,$$

$$\mathbf{p}'_3 = \mathbf{p}'(1) = \mathbf{c}_1 + 2\mathbf{c}_2 + 3\mathbf{c}_3.$$

Figure 10.13 Definition of the Hermite cubic.

---

5. We use this numbering to be consistent with our interpolation notation, as well as with the numbering that we use for Bezier curves in Section 10.6.

We can write these equations in matrix form as

$$
\begin{bmatrix} \mathbf{p}_0 \\ \mathbf{p}_3 \\ \mathbf{p}_0' \\ \mathbf{p}_3' \end{bmatrix} = \begin{bmatrix} 1 & 0 & 0 & 0 \\ 1 & 1 & 1 & 1 \\ 0 & 1 & 0 & 0 \\ 0 & 1 & 2 & 3 \end{bmatrix} \mathbf{c}.
$$

Letting $\mathbf{q}$ denote the data matrix

$$
\mathbf{q} = \begin{bmatrix} \mathbf{p}_0 \\ \mathbf{p}_3 \\ \mathbf{p}_0' \\ \mathbf{p}_3' \end{bmatrix},
$$

we can solve the equations to find

$$
\mathbf{c} = \mathbf{M}_H \mathbf{q},
$$

where $\mathbf{M}_H$ is the **Hermite geometry** matrix

$$
\mathbf{M}_H = \begin{bmatrix} 1 & 0 & 0 & 0 \\ 0 & 0 & 1 & 0 \\ -3 & 3 & -2 & -1 \\ 2 & -2 & 1 & 1 \end{bmatrix}.
$$

The resulting polynomial is given by

$$
\mathbf{p}(u) = \mathbf{u}^T \mathbf{M}_H \mathbf{q}.
$$

$\mathbf{p}'(1) = \mathbf{q}'(0)$

$\mathbf{p}(1) = \mathbf{q}(0)$

$\mathbf{p}(0)$

$\mathbf{q}(1)$

Figure 10.14 Hermite form at join point.

We use this method as shown in Figure 10.14, where both the interpolated value and the derivative are shared by the curve segments on the two sides of a join point, and thus both the resulting function and the first derivative are continuous over all segments.

We can get a more accurate idea of the increased smoothness of the Hermite form by rewriting the polynomial in the form

$$
\mathbf{p}(u) = \mathbf{b}(u)^T \mathbf{q},
$$

where the new blending functions are given by

$$
\mathbf{b}(u) = \mathbf{M}_H^T \mathbf{u} = \begin{bmatrix} 2u^3 - 3u^2 + 1 \\ -2u^3 + 3u^2 \\ u^3 - 2u^2 + u \\ u^3 - u^2 \end{bmatrix}.
$$

These four polynomials have none of their zeros inside the interval $(0, 1)$ and are much smoother than are the interpolating polynomial blending functions (see Exercise 10.16).

We can go on and define a bicubic Hermite surface patch through these blending functions,

$$\mathbf{p}(u, v) = \sum_{i=0}^{3} \sum_{j=0}^{3} b_i(u) b_j(v) \mathbf{q}_{ij},$$

where $\mathbf{Q} = [\mathbf{q}_{ij}]$ is the extension of $\mathbf{q}$ to surface data. At this point, however, this equation is just a formal expression. It is not clear what the relationship is between the elements of $\mathbf{Q}$ and the derivatives of $\mathbf{p}(u, v)$. Four of the elements of $\mathbf{Q}$ are chosen to interpolate the corners of the patch, whereas the others are chosen to match certain derivatives at the corners of the patch. In most interactive applications, however, the user enters point data rather than derivative data; consequently, unless we have analytic formulations for the data, usually we do not have these derivatives. However, the approach we took with the Hermite curves and surfaces will lead to the Bezier forms that we introduce in Section 10.6.

10.5.2 Geometric and Parametric Continuity

Before we discuss the Bezier and spline forms, we examine a few issues concerning continuity and derivatives. Consider the join point in Figure 10.15. Suppose that the polynomial on the left is $\mathbf{p}(u)$ and the one on the right is $\mathbf{q}(u)$. We enforce various continuity conditions by matching the polynomials and their derivatives at $u = 1$ for $\mathbf{p}(u)$, with the corresponding values for $\mathbf{q}(u)$ for $u = 0$. If we want the function to be continuous, we must have

Figure 10.15 Continuity at the join point.

$$\mathbf{p}(1) = \begin{bmatrix} p_x(1) \\ p_y(1) \\ p_z(1) \end{bmatrix} = \mathbf{q}(0) = \begin{bmatrix} q_x(0) \\ q_y(0) \\ q_z(0) \end{bmatrix}.$$

All three parametric components must be equal at the join point; we call this property C^0 **parametric continuity.**

When we consider derivatives, we can require, as we did with the Hermite curve, that

$$\mathbf{p}'(1) = \begin{bmatrix} p'_x(1) \\ p'_y(1) \\ p'_z(1) \end{bmatrix} = \mathbf{q}'(0) = \begin{bmatrix} q'_x(0) \\ q'_y(0) \\ q'_z(0) \end{bmatrix}.$$

If we match all three parametric equations and the first derivative, we have C^1 parametric continuity.

If we look at the geometry, however, we can take a different approach to continuity. In three dimensions, the derivative at a point on a curve defines the tangent line at that point. Suppose that instead of requiring matching of the derivatives for the two segments at the join point, we require only that their derivatives be proportional:

$$\mathbf{p}'(1) \propto \mathbf{q}'(0),$$

for some positive number α. If the tangents of the two curves are proportional, then they point in the same direction, but they may have different magnitudes. We call this type of continuity G^1 **geometric continuity**.[6] If the two tangent vectors need only to be proportional, we have only two conditions to enforce, rather than three, leaving 1 extra degree of freedom that we can potentially use to satisfy some other criterion. We can extend this idea to higher derivatives, and can talk about both C^n and G^n continuity.

Although two curves that have only G^1 continuity at the join points have a continuous tangent at the join points, the value of the constant of proportionality—or, equivalently, the relative magnitudes of the tangents on the two sides of the join point—does matter. Curves with the same tangent direction but different magnitudes differ, as shown in Figure 10.16. The curves $\mathbf{p}(u)$ and $\mathbf{q}(u)$ share the same endpoints, and the tangents at the endpoints point in the same direction, but the curves are different. This result is exploited in many painting programs, where the user can interactively change the magnitude, leaving the tangent direction unchanged. However, in other applications, such as animation, where a sequence of curve segments describes the path of an object, G^1 continuity may be insufficient; see Exercise 10.11.

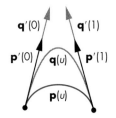

Figure 10.16 Change of magnitude in G^1 continuity.

10.6 Bezier Curves and Surfaces

Comparing the Hermite form to the interpolating form is like comparing apples to oranges; we are comparing forms with some similarities but with significant differences. Both are cubic polynomial curves, but the forms do not use the same data; thus, they cannot be compared on equal terms. We can use the same control-point data that we used to derive the interpolating curves to approximate the derivatives in the Hermite curves. The resulting Bezier curves are excellent approximations to the Hermite curves and are comparable to the interpolating curves because they have been obtained using the same data. In addition, because these curves do not need derivative information, they will be well suited for use in graphics and CAD.

10.6.1 Bezier Curves

Consider again the four control points: $\mathbf{p}_0$, $\mathbf{p}_1$, $\mathbf{p}_2$, and $\mathbf{p}_3$. Suppose that we still insist on interpolating known values at the endpoints with a cubic polynomial $\mathbf{p}(u)$:

$$\mathbf{p}_0 = \mathbf{p}(0),$$

$$\mathbf{p}_3 = \mathbf{p}(1).$$

---

6. G^0 continuity is the same as C^0 continuity.

Bezier proposed that rather than using the other two control points, $\mathbf{p}_2$ and $\mathbf{p}_3$, for interpolation, we use them to approximate the tangents at $u = 0$ and $u = 1$. In parameter space, we can use the linear approximations

$$\mathbf{p}'(0) = \frac{\mathbf{p}_1 - \mathbf{p}_0}{\frac{1}{3}} = 3(\mathbf{p}_1 - \mathbf{p}_0),$$

$$\mathbf{p}'(1) = \frac{\mathbf{p}_3 - \mathbf{p}_2}{\frac{1}{3}} = 3(\mathbf{p}_3 - \mathbf{p}_2),$$

as shown in Figure 10.17. Applying these approximations to the derivatives of our parametric polynomial, $\mathbf{p}(u) = \mathbf{u}^T \mathbf{c}$, at the two endpoints, we have the two conditions

$$3\mathbf{p}_1 - 3\mathbf{p}_0 = \mathbf{c}_1,$$
$$3\mathbf{p}_3 - 3\mathbf{p}_2 = \mathbf{c}_1 + 2\mathbf{c}_2 + 3\mathbf{c}_3,$$

to add to our interpolation conditions

$$\mathbf{p}_0 = \mathbf{c}_0,$$

$$\mathbf{p}_3 = \mathbf{c}_0 + \mathbf{c}_1 + \mathbf{c}_2 + \mathbf{c}_3.$$

Figure 10.17 Approximating tangents.

At this point, we again have three sets of four equations in four unknowns that we can solve, as before, to find

$$\mathbf{c} = \mathbf{M}_B \mathbf{p},$$

where $\mathbf{M}_B$ is the **Bezier geometry matrix**

$$\mathbf{M}_B = \begin{bmatrix} 1 & 0 & 0 & 0 \\ -3 & 3 & 0 & 0 \\ 3 & -6 & 3 & 0 \\ -1 & 3 & -3 & 1 \end{bmatrix}.$$

The cubic Bezier polynomial is thus

$$\mathbf{p}(u) = \mathbf{u}^T \mathbf{M}_B \mathbf{p}.$$

We use this formula exactly as we did for the interpolating polynomial. If we have a set of control points, $\mathbf{p}_0, \dots, \mathbf{p}_n$, we use $\mathbf{p}_0, \mathbf{p}_1, \mathbf{p}_2$, and $\mathbf{p}_3$ for the first curve; $\mathbf{p}_3, \mathbf{p}_4, \mathbf{p}_5$, and $\mathbf{p}_6$ for the second; and so on. It should be clear that we have C^0 continuity, but we have given up the C^1 continuity of the Hermite polynomial because we use different approximations on the left and right of a join point.

We can see important advantages to the Bezier curve by examining the blending functions in Figure 10.18. We write the curve as

$$\mathbf{p}(u) = \mathbf{b}(u)^T \mathbf{p},$$

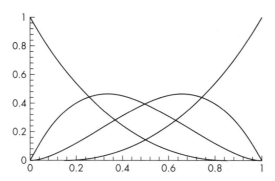

Figure 10.18 Blending polynomials for Bezier cubic.

where

$$\mathbf{b}(u) = \mathbf{M}_B^T \mathbf{u} = \begin{bmatrix} (1-u)^3 \\ 3u(1-u)^2 \\ 3u^2(1-u) \\ u^3 \end{bmatrix}.$$

These four polynomials are one case of the **Bernstein polynomials**,

$$b_{kd}(u) = \frac{d!}{k!(d-k)!} u^k (1-u)^{d-k},$$

which can be shown to have remarkable properties. First, all the zeros of the polynomials are either at $u = 0$ or at $u = 1$. Consequently, for each blending polynomial,

$$0 < b_{id}(u),$$

for $0 < u < 1$. Without any zeros in the interval, each blending polynomial must be smooth. We can also show that, in this interval (see Exercise 10.4),

$$b_{id}(u) \leq 1,$$

and

$$\sum_{i=0}^{d} b_{id}(u) = 1.$$

Under these conditions, the representation of our cubic Bezier polynomial in terms of its blending polynomials,

$$\mathbf{p}(u) = \sum_{i=0}^{3} b_i(u) \mathbf{p}_i,$$

is a convex sum. Consequently, $\mathbf{p}(u)$ must lie in the convex hull of the four control points, as shown in Figure 10.19. Thus, even though the Bezier polynomial does not interpolate all the control points, it cannot be far from them. These two properties, combined with the fact that we are using control-point data, make it easy to work interactively with Bezier curves. A user can enter the four control points to define an initial curve, and then can manipulate the points to control the shape.

Figure 10.19 Convex hull and Bezier polynomial.

10.6.2 Bezier Surface Patches

We can generate the **Bezier surface patches** through the blending functions. If $\mathbf{P}$ is a 4×4 array of control points,

$$\mathbf{P} = \left[\mathbf{p}_{ij} \right],$$

then the corresponding Bezier patch is

$$\mathbf{p}(u, v) = \sum_{i=0}^{3} \sum_{j=0}^{3} b_i(u) b_j(v) \mathbf{p}_{ij} = \mathbf{u}^T \mathbf{M}_B \mathbf{P} \mathbf{M}_B^T \mathbf{v}.$$

The patch is fully contained in the convex hull of the control points (Figure 10.20) and interpolates $\mathbf{p}_{00}$, $\mathbf{p}_{03}$, $\mathbf{p}_{30}$, and $\mathbf{p}_{33}$. We can interpret the other conditions as approximations to various derivatives at the corners of the patch.

Consider the corner for $u = v = 0$. We can evaluate $\mathbf{p}(u)$ and the first partial derivatives to find

$$\mathbf{p}(0, 0) = \mathbf{p}_{00},$$

$$\frac{\partial \mathbf{p}}{\partial u}(0, 0) = 3(\mathbf{p}_{10} - \mathbf{p}_{00}),$$

$$\frac{\partial \mathbf{p}}{\partial v}(0, 0) = 3(\mathbf{p}_{01} - \mathbf{p}_{00}),$$

$$\frac{\partial^2 \mathbf{p}}{\partial u \partial v}(0, 0) = 9(\mathbf{p}_{00} - \mathbf{p}_{01} + \mathbf{p}_{10} - \mathbf{p}_{11}).$$

The first three conditions are clearly extensions of our results for the Bezier curve. The fourth can be seen as a measure of the tendency of the patch to divert from

Figure 10.20 Bezier patch.

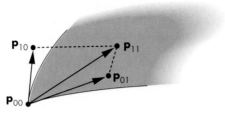

Figure 10.21 Twist at corner of Bezier patch.

being flat, or to **twist**, at the corner. If we consider the quadrilateral defined by these points (Figure 10.21), the points will lie in the same plane only if the twist is zero. Front Plate 3 uses Bezier patches to create a smooth surface from elevation data.

10.7 Cubic B-Splines

In practice, the cubic Bezier curves and surface patches are widely used. They have one fundamental limitation: At the join points (or patch edges, for surfaces), we have only C^0 continuity. If, for example, we were to use these curves to design our model-airplane cross sections as shown in Section 10.2, and then were to attempt to build those cross sections, we might be unhappy with the way that the pieces met at the join points.

It might seem that we have reached the limit of what we can do with cubic parametric polynomials, and that, if we need more flexibility, we have to either go to high-degree polynomials or shorten the interval and use more polynomial segments. Both of these tactics are possibilities—and there is another: We can use the same control-point data but not require the polynomial to interpolate any of these points. If we can come close to the control points and get more smoothness at the join points, we may be content with the result.

10.7.1 The Cubic B-Spline Curve

In this section we illustrate a particular example of a B-spline curve and show how we can obtain C^2 continuity at the join points with a cubic. In Section 10.8 we give a short introduction to a more general approach to splines—an approach that is general enough to include the Bezier curves as a special case. Consider four control points in the middle of a sequence of control points: $\{\mathbf{p}_{i-2}, \mathbf{p}_{i-1}, \mathbf{p}_i, \mathbf{p}_{i+1}\}$. Our previous approach was to use these four points to define a cubic curve such that, as the parameter u varied from 0 to 1, the curve spanned the distance from $\mathbf{p}_{i-2}$ to $\mathbf{p}_{i+1}$, interpolating $\mathbf{p}_{i-2}$ and $\mathbf{p}_{i+1}$. Instead, suppose that as u goes from 0 to 1, we span only the distance between the middle two control points, as shown in Figure 10.22. Likewise, we use $\{\mathbf{p}_{i-3}, \mathbf{p}_{i-2}, \mathbf{p}_{i-1}, \mathbf{p}_i\}$ between $\mathbf{p}_{i-2}$ and $\mathbf{p}_{i-1}$, and $\{\mathbf{p}_{i-1}, \mathbf{p}_i, \mathbf{p}_{i+1}, \mathbf{p}_{i+2}\}$ between $\mathbf{p}_i$ and $\mathbf{p}_{i+1}$. Suppose that $\mathbf{p}(u)$ is the curve we use between $\mathbf{p}_{i-1}$ and $\mathbf{p}_i$, and $\mathbf{q}(u)$ is the curve to its left, used between $\mathbf{p}_{i-2}$ and $\mathbf{p}_{i-1}$. We can match conditions at $\mathbf{p}(0)$ with conditions at $\mathbf{q}(1)$. Using our standard formulation, we are looking for a matrix $\mathbf{M}$, such that the desired cubic polynomial is

$$\mathbf{p}(u) = \mathbf{u}^T \mathbf{M} \mathbf{p},$$

where $\mathbf{p}$ is the matrix of control points

$$\mathbf{p} = \begin{bmatrix} \mathbf{p}_{i-2} \\ \mathbf{p}_{i-1} \\ \mathbf{p}_i \\ \mathbf{p}_{i+1} \end{bmatrix}.$$

We can use the same matrix to write $\mathbf{q}(u)$ as

$$\mathbf{q}(u) = \mathbf{u}^T \mathbf{M} \mathbf{q},$$

where

$$\mathbf{q} = \begin{bmatrix} \mathbf{p}_{i-3} \\ \mathbf{p}_{i-2} \\ \mathbf{p}_{i-1} \\ \mathbf{p}_i \end{bmatrix}.$$

In principle, we could write down a set of conditions on $\mathbf{p}(0)$ that would match conditions for $\mathbf{q}(1)$, and we could write equivalent conditions matching various derivatives of $\mathbf{p}(1)$ with conditions for another polynomial that starts there. For example, the condition

$$\mathbf{p}(0) = \mathbf{q}(1)$$

requires continuity at the join point, without requiring interpolation of any data. Enforcing this condition gives one equation for the coefficients of $\mathbf{M}$. There are clearly many sets of conditions that we can use; each set can define a different matrix.

We can take a shortcut to deriving the most popular matrix, by noting that we must use symmetric approximations at the join point. Hence, any evaluation of conditions on $\mathbf{q}(1)$ cannot use $\mathbf{p}_{i-3}$, because this control point does not appear in the equation for $\mathbf{p}(u)$. Likewise, we cannot use $\mathbf{p}_{i+1}$ in any condition on $\mathbf{p}(0)$. Two conditions that satisfy this symmetry condition are

$$\mathbf{p}(0) = \mathbf{q}(1) = \frac{1}{6}(\mathbf{p}_{i-2} + 4\mathbf{p}_{i-1} + \mathbf{p}_i),$$

$$\mathbf{p}'(0) = \mathbf{q}'(1) = \frac{1}{2}(\mathbf{p}_i - \mathbf{p}_{i-2}).$$

Figure 10.22 Four points that define a curve between the middle two points.

If we write $\mathbf{p}(u)$ in terms of the coefficient array $\mathbf{c}$,

$$\mathbf{p}(u) = \mathbf{u}^T \mathbf{c},$$

these conditions are

$$\mathbf{c}_0 = \frac{1}{6}(\mathbf{p}_{i-2} + 4\mathbf{p}_{i-1} + \mathbf{p}_i),$$

$$\mathbf{c}_1 = \frac{1}{2}(\mathbf{p}_i - \mathbf{p}_{i-2}).$$

We can apply the symmetric conditions at $\mathbf{p}(1)$:

$$\mathbf{p}(1) = \mathbf{c}_0 + \mathbf{c}_1 + \mathbf{c}_2 + \mathbf{c}_3 = \frac{1}{6}(\mathbf{p}_{i-1} + 4\mathbf{p}_i + \mathbf{p}_{i+1}),$$

$$\mathbf{p}'(1) = \mathbf{c}_1 + 2\mathbf{c}_2 + 3\mathbf{c}_3 = \frac{1}{2}(\mathbf{p}_{i+1} - \mathbf{p}_{i-1}).$$

We now have four equations for the coefficients of $\mathbf{c}$, which we can solve for a matrix $\mathbf{M}_S$, the **B-spline geometry matrix**,

$$\mathbf{M}_S = \frac{1}{6} \begin{bmatrix} 1 & 4 & 1 & 0 \\ -3 & 0 & 3 & 0 \\ 3 & -6 & 3 & 0 \\ -1 & 3 & -3 & 1 \end{bmatrix}.$$

This particular matrix yields a polynomial that has several important properties. We can see these properties by again examining the blending polynomials:

$$\mathbf{b}(u) = \mathbf{M}_S^T \mathbf{u} = \frac{1}{6} \begin{bmatrix} (1-u)^3 \\ 4 - 6u^2 + 3u^3 \\ 1 + 3u + 3u^2 - 3u^3 \\ u^3 \end{bmatrix}.$$

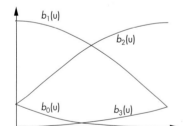

Figure 10.23 Spline-blending functions.

These polynomials are shown in Figure 10.23. We can show, as we did for the Bezier polynomials, that

$$\sum_{i=0}^{3} b_i(u) = 1,$$

and, in the interval $0 \leq u \leq 1$,

$$0 \leq b_i(u) \leq 1.$$

Figure 10.24 Convex hull for spline curve.

Thus, the curve must lie in the convex hull of the control points, as shown in Figure 10.24. Note that the curve is used for only part of the range of the convex hull. We defined the curve to have C^1 continuity; in fact, however, it has C^2 continuity,[7] as we can verify by computing $\mathbf{p}''(u)$ at $u = 0$ and $u = 1$, and seeing that the values are the same for the curves on the right and left. It is for this reason that spline curves are so important. From a physical point of view, metal will bend such that the second derivative is continuous. From a visual perspective, a curve made of cubic segments with C^2 continuity will be seen as smooth, even at the join points.

Although we have used the same control-point data as those we used for the Bezier cubic to derive a smoother cubic curve, we must be aware that we are doing three times the work that we would do for Bezier or interpolating cubics. The reason is that we are using the curve between only control point $i - 1$ and control point i. A Bezier curve using the same data would be used from control point $i - 2$ to control point $i + 1$. Hence, each time we add a control point, a new spline curve must be computed, whereas for Bezier curves, we add the control points three at a time.

10.7.2 B-Splines and Basis

Instead of looking at the curve from the perspective of a single interval, we can gain additional insights by looking at the curve from the perspective of a single control point. Each control point contributes to the spline in four adjacent intervals. This property guarantees the locality of the spline; that is, if we change a single control point, we can affect the resulting curve in only four adjacent intervals. Consider the control point $\mathbf{p}_i$. In the interval between $u = 0$ and $u = 1$, it is multiplied by the blending polynomial $b_2(u)$. It also contributes to the interval on the left through $\mathbf{q}(u)$. In this interval, its contribution is $b_1(u + 1)$—we must shift the value of u by 1 to the left for this interval.

The total contribution of a single control point can be written as $B_i(u)\mathbf{p_i}$, where B_i is the function

$$B_i(u) = \begin{cases} 0 & u < i - 2, \\ b_0(u + 2) & i - 2 \leq u < i - 1, \\ b_1(u + 1) & i - 1 \leq u < i, \\ b_2(u) & i \leq u < i + 1, \\ b_3(u - 1) & i + 1 \leq u < i + 2, \\ 0 & u \geq i + 2. \end{cases}$$

This function is pictured in Figure 10.25. Given a set of control points $\mathbf{p}_0, \ldots, \mathbf{p}_m$, we can write the entire spline with the single expression[8]

$$\mathbf{p}(u) = \sum_{i=1}^{m-1} B_i(u)\mathbf{p}_i.$$

---

7. If we are concerned with only G^2, rather than with C^2, continuity, we can use the extra degrees of freedom to give additional flexibility in the design of the curves; see Barsky [Bar83].
8. We determine the proper conditions for the beginning and end of the spline in Section 10.8.

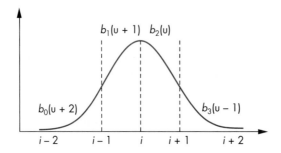

$b_1(u + 1)$ $b_2(u)$

$b_0(u + 2)$

$b_3(u - 1)$

$i - 2$ $i - 1$ i $i + 1$ $i + 2$

Figure 10.25 Spline basis function.

This expression shows that, for the set of functions $B(u - i)$, each member is a shifted version of a single function, and the set forms a basis for all our cubic B-spline curves. Given a set of control points, we form a piecewise polynomial curve $\mathbf{p}(u)$ over the whole interval as a linear combination of basis functions. Figure 10.26 shows the function and the contributions from the individual basis functions. The general theory of splines that we develop in Section 10.8 expands this view by allowing higher-degree polynomials in the intervals and by allowing different polynomials in different intervals.

10.7.3 Spline Surfaces

B-spline surfaces can be defined in a similar way. If we start with the B-spline blending functions, the surface patch is given by

$$\mathbf{p}(u, v) = \sum_{i=0}^{3} \sum_{j=0}^{3} b_i(u) b_j(v) \mathbf{p}_{ij}.$$

This expression is of the same form as are those for our other surface patches, but, as we can see from Figure 10.27, we use the patch over only the central area, and we must do nine times the work that we would do with the Bezier patch. However, because of inheritance of the convex-hull property and the additional continuity at the edges from the B-spline curves, the B-spline patch

$\mathbf{P}_{i-2}$ $\mathbf{P}_{i-1}$ $\mathbf{P}_i$ $\mathbf{P}_{i+1}$ $\mathbf{P}_{i+2}$ $\mathbf{p}(u)$

$i - 2$ $i - 1$ i $i + 1$ $i + 2$ u

Figure 10.26 Approximating function over interval.

$\mathsf{Figure}\ 10.27$ Spline surface patch.

is considerably smoother than a Bezier patch constructed from the same data would be.

10.8 General B-Splines

Suppose that we have a set of control points, $\mathbf{p}_0, \ldots, \mathbf{p}_m$. The general approximation problem is to find a function $\mathbf{p}(u) = [\ x(u) \quad y(u) \quad z(u)\ ]^T$, defined over an interval $u_{min} \le u \le u_{max}$, that is smooth and is close, in some sense, to the control points. Suppose we have a set of values $\{u_k\}$, called **knots**, such that

$$u_{min} = u_0 \le u_1 \le \ldots \le u_n = u_{max}.$$

We call the sequence $u_0, u_1, \ldots, u_n$ the **knot array**.[9] In splines, the function $\mathbf{p}(u)$ is a polynomial of degree d between the knots,

$$\mathbf{p}(u) = \sum_{j=0}^{d} \mathbf{c}_{jk} u^j, \quad u_k < u < u_{k+1}.$$

Thus, to define a spline of degree d, we must define the $n(d+1)$ three-dimensional coefficients $\mathbf{c}_{jk}$. We get the required conditions by applying various continuity requirements at the knots and interpolation requirements at control points.

For example, if $d = 3$, then we have a cubic polynomial in each interval, and, for a given n, we must define $4n$ conditions. There are $n-1$ internal knots. If we want C^2 continuity at the knots, we have $3n-3$ conditions. If, in addition, we want to interpolate the $n+1$ control points, we have a total of $4n-2$ conditions. We can pick the other two conditions in various ways, such as by fixing the slope at the ends of the curve. However, this particular spline is global; we must solve a set of $4n$ equations in $4n$ unknowns, and each coefficient will depend on all the control points. Thus, although such a spline provides a smooth curve that interpolates the control points, it is not well suited to computer graphics and CAD.

---

9. Most researchers call this sequence the *knot vector*, but that terminology violates our decision to use *vector* for only directed line segments.

figure 10.28 First three basis functions.

10.8.1 Recursively Defined B-Splines

The approach taken in B-splines is to define the spline in terms of a set of basis or blending functions, each of which is nonzero over only the regions spanned by a few knots. Thus, we write the function $\mathbf{p}(u)$ as an expansion:

$$\mathbf{p}(u) = \sum_{i=0}^{m} B_{id}(u)\mathbf{p}_i,$$

where each function $B_{id}(u)$ is a polynomial of degree d, except at the knots, and is zero outside the interval $(u_{i_{\min}}, u_{i_{\max}})$. The name *B-splines* comes from the term *basis splines*, in recognition that the set of functions $\{B_{id}(u)\}$ forms a basis for the given knot sequence and degree. Although there are numerous ways to define basis splines, of particular importance is the set of splines defined by the **Cox–deBoor recursion**:[10]

$$B_{k0} = \begin{cases} 1, & u_k \leq u \leq u_{k+1}; \\ 0, & \text{otherwise} \end{cases}$$

$$B_{kd} = \frac{u - u_k}{u_{k+d} - u_k} B_{k,d-1}(u) + \frac{u_{k+d} - u}{u_{k+d+1} - u_{k+1}} B_{k+1,\,d-1}(u).$$

Each of the first set of functions, B_{k0}, is constant over one interval and is zero everywhere else; each of the second, B_{k1}, is linear over each of two intervals, and is zero elsewhere; each of the third, B_{k2}, is quadratic over each of three intervals; and so on (Figure 10.28). In general, B_{kd} is nonzero over the $d+1$ intervals between u_k and u_{k+d+1}, and it is a polynomial of degree d in each of these intervals. At the knots, there is C^{d-1} continuity. The convex-hull property holds because

$$\sum_{i=0}^{m} B_{i,d}(u) = 1, \qquad \text{and} \qquad 0 \leq B_{id}(u) \leq 1.$$

---

10. This formula is also known as the *deCasteljau recursion*.

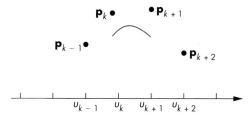

Figure 10.29   Uniform B-spline.

However, because each B_{id} is nonzero in only $d + 1$ intervals, each control point can affect only $d + 1$ intervals, and each point on the resulting curve is within the convex hull defined by these $d + 1$ control points.

Note that careful examination of the Cox–deBoor formula shows that each step of the recursion is a linear interpolation of functions produced on the previous step. Linear interpolation of polynomials of degree k produces polynomials of degree $k + 1$.

A set of spline basis functions is defined by the desired degree and the knot array. Note that we need what appears to be $d - 1$ "extra" knot values to define our spline, because the recursion requires u_0 through u_{n+d} to define splines from u_0 to u_{n+1}. These additional values are determined by conditions at the beginning and end of the whole spline.

Note that we have made no statement about the knot values other than that $u_k \leq u_{k+1}$. If we define any $0/0$ term that arises in evaluating the recursion as equal to 1, then we can have repeated, or multiple, knots. If the knots are equally spaced, we have a **uniform spline**. However, we can achieve more flexibility by allowing not only nonuniform knot spacing, but also repeated ($u_k = u_{k+1}$) knots. Let us examine a few of the possibilities.

10.8.2 Uniform Splines

Consider the uniform knot sequence $\{0, 1, 2, \ldots, n\}$. The cubic B-spline we discussed in Section 10.7 could be derived from the Cox–deBoor formula with equally spaced knots. We use the numbering that we used there (which is shifted from the Cox–deBoor indexing); between knots k and $k + 1$, we use the control points $\mathbf{p}_{k-1}$, $\mathbf{p}_k$, $\mathbf{p}_{k+1}$, and $\mathbf{p}_{k+2}$. Thus, we have a curve defined for only the interval $u = 1$ to $u = n - 1$. For the data shown in Figure 10.29, we define a curve that does not span the knots. In certain situations, such as that depicted in Figure 10.30, we can use the periodic nature of the control-point data to define the spline over the entire knot sequence. These **uniform periodic B-splines** have the property that each spline basis function is a shifted version of a single function.

Figure 10.30   Periodic uniform B-spline.

10.8.3 Nonuniform B-Splines

Repeated knots have the effect of pulling the spline closer to the control point associated with the knot. If a knot at the end has multiplicity $d + 1$, the B-spline of degree d must interpolate the point. Hence, one solution to the problem of the spline not having sufficient data to span the desired interval is to repeat knots at the ends, forcing interpolation at the endpoints, and using uniform knots everywhere else. Such splines are called **open splines**.

The knot sequence $\{0, 0, 0, 0, 1, 2, \ldots, n - 1, n, n, n, n\}$ is often used for cubic B-splines. The sequence $\{0, 0, 0, 0, 1, 1, 1, 1\}$ is of particular interest, because, in this case, the cubic B-spline becomes the cubic Bezier curve. In the general case, we can repeat internal knots, and we can have any desired spacing of knots.

10.8.4 NURBS

In our development of B-splines, we have assumed that $\mathbf{p}(u)$ is the array $[\, x(u) \quad y(u) \quad z(u) \,]^T$. In two dimensions, however, we could have replaced it with simply $[\, x(u) \quad y(u) \,]^T$, and all our equations would be unchanged. Indeed, the equations remain unchanged if we go to four-dimensional B-splines. Consider a control point in three dimensions:

$$\mathbf{p}_i = [x_i \quad y_i \quad z_i].$$

The weighted homogeneous-coordinate representation of this point is

$$\mathbf{q}_i = w_i \begin{bmatrix} x_i \\ y_i \\ z_i \\ 1 \end{bmatrix}.$$

The idea is to use the weights w_i to increase or decrease the importance of a particular control point. We can use these weighted points to form a four-dimensional B-spline. The first three components of the resulting spline are simply the B-spline representation of the weighted points,

$$\mathbf{q}(u) = \begin{bmatrix} x(u) \\ y(u) \\ z(u) \end{bmatrix} = \sum_{i=0}^{n} B_{i,d}(u) w_i \mathbf{p}_i.$$

The w component is the scalar B-spline polynomial derived from the set of weights:

$$w(u) = \sum_{i=0}^{n} B_{i,d}(u) w_i.$$

In homogeneous coordinates, this representation has a w component that may not be equal to 1; thus, we must do a perspective division to derive the three-dimensional points:

$$\mathbf{p}(u) = \frac{1}{w(u)} \mathbf{q}(u) = \frac{\sum_{i=0}^{n} B_{i,d}(u) w_i \mathbf{p}_i}{\sum_{i=0}^{n} B_{i,d}(u) w_i}.$$

Each component of $\mathbf{p}(u)$ is now a rational function in u, and, because we have not restricted the knots in any way, we have derived a **nonuniform rational B-spline (NURBS)** curve.

NURBS curves retain all the properties of our three-dimensional B-splines, such as the convex-hull and continuity properties. They have two other properties that make them of particular interest in computer graphics and CAD.

If we apply an affine transformation to a B-spline curve or surface, we get the same function as the B-spline derived from the transformed control points. Because perspective transformations are not affine, most splines will not be handled correctly in perspective viewing. However, the perspective division embedded in the construction of NURBS curves ensures that NURBS curves are handled correctly in perspective views.

Quadric surfaces are usually defined as algebraic implicit forms. If we are using nonrational splines, we can only approximate these surfaces. However, quadrics can be shown to be a special case of quadratic NURBS curve; thus, we can use a single modeling method, NURBS curves, for the most widely used curves and surfaces; see Exercises 10.14 and 10.15. Color Plate 5 shows the mesh generated by a NURBS modeling of the surfaces that make up the object in Color Plate 1. OpenGL ultimately renders this mesh with polygons. Color Plates 17 and 18 show a NURBS surface used to model moving water in an animated film from Dreamworks Animation Studio. In this example, a particle system (Chapter 11) was used to alter vertices in the mesh.

10.9 Rendering of Curves and Surfaces

Once we have defined a scene with curves and surfaces, we must find a way to render it. There are several approaches. In one, we compute points on the object that are the intersection of rays from the center of projection through pixels with the object. However, except for quadrics (Section 10.11), the intersection calculation requires the solution of nonlinear equations of too high a degree to be practical for real-time computation. A second approach involves evaluating the curve or surface at a sufficient number of points that we can approximate it with our standard flat objects. We focus on this approach for parametric polynomial curves and surfaces.

10.9.1 Polynomial Evaluation Methods

Suppose that we have a representation over our standard interval

$$\mathbf{p}(u) = \sum_{i=0}^{n} \mathbf{c}_i u^i, \quad 0 \le u \le 1.$$

We can evaluate $\mathbf{p}(u)$ at some set of values $\{u_k\}$, and we can use a polyline (or GL_LINE_STRIP) to approximate the curve. Rather than evaluate each term u^k independently, we can group the terms as

$$\mathbf{p}(u) = \mathbf{c}_0 + u(\mathbf{c}_1 + u(\mathbf{c}_2 + u(\dots + \mathbf{c}_n u))).$$

This grouping shows that we need only n multiplications to evaluate each $p(u_k)$; this algorithm is known as **Horner's method**. For our typical cubic $\mathbf{p}(u)$, the grouping becomes

$$\mathbf{p}(u) = \mathbf{c}_0 + u(\mathbf{c}_1 + u(\mathbf{c}_2 + u\mathbf{c}_3)).$$

If the points $\{u_i\}$ are spaced uniformly, we can use the method of **forward differences** to evaluate $\mathbf{p}(u_k)$ using $O(n)$ additions and no multiplications. The forward differences are defined iteratively by the formulas

$$\Delta^{(0)}\mathbf{p}(u_k) = \mathbf{p}(u_k),$$

$$\Delta^{(1)}\mathbf{p}(u_k) = \mathbf{p}(u_{k+1}) - \mathbf{p}(u_k),$$

$$\Delta^{(m+1)}\mathbf{p}(u_k) = \Delta^{(m)}\mathbf{p}(u_{k+1}) - \Delta^{(m)}\mathbf{p}(u_k).$$

If $u_{k+1} - u_k = h$ is constant, then we can show that, if $\mathbf{p}(u)$ is a polynomial of degree n, then $\Delta^{(n)}\mathbf{p}(u_k)$ is constant for all k. This result suggests the strategy illustrated in Figure 10.31 for the scalar cubic polynomial

$$p(u) = 1 + 3u + 2u^2 + u^3.$$

We need the first $n + 1$ values of $p(u_k)$ to find $\Delta^{(n)}p(u_0)$. But, once we have $\Delta^{(n)}p(u_0)$, we can copy this value across the table and work upward, as shown

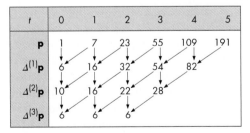

Figure 10.31 Construction of a forward-difference table.

Figure 10.32 Use of a forward-difference table.

in Figure 10.32, to compute successive values of $p(u_k)$, using the rearranged recurrence

$$\Delta^{(m-1)}(p_{k+1}) = \Delta^{(m)}p(u_k) + \Delta^{(m-1)}p(u_k).$$

This method is efficient, but is not without its faults: It applies only to a uniform grid, and it is prone to accumulation of numerical errors.

10.9.2 Recursive Subdivision of Bezier Polynomials

The most widely used rendering method performs recursive subdivision of the Bezier curve. The method is based on the use of the convex hull, and never requires explicit evaluation of the polynomial. Suppose that we have a cubic Bezier polynomial (the method also applies to higher-degree Bezier curves). We know that the curve must lie within the convex hull of the control points. We can break the curve into two separate polynomials, $l(u)$ and $r(u)$, each valid over one-half of the original interval. Because the original polynomial is a cubic, each of these polynomials also is a cubic. Note that, because each is to be used over one-half of the original interval, we must rescale the parameter u for l and r, so that, as u varies over the range $(0, 1)$, $l(u)$ traces the left half of $p(u)$, and $r(u)$ traces the right half of p. Each of our new polynomials has four control points that both define the polynomial and form its convex hull. We denote these two sets of points by $\{l_0, l_1, l_2, l_3\}$ and $\{r_0, r_1, r_2, r_3\}$; the original control points for $p(u)$ are $\{p_0, p_1, p_2, p_3\}$. These points and the two convex hulls are shown in Figure 10.33. Note that the convex hulls for l and r must lie inside the convex hull for p, a result known as the **variation-diminishing property** of the Bezier curve.

Consider the left polynomial. We can test the convex hull for flatness by measuring the deviation of l_1 and l_2 from the line segment connecting l_0 and l_3. If they are close, we can draw the line segment instead of the curve. If they are not close, we can divide l into two halves and test the two new convex hulls for flatness. Thus, we have a recursion that never requires us to evaluate points on a polynomial, but we have yet to discuss how to find $\{l_0, l_1, l_2, l_3\}$ and $\{r_0, r_1, r_2, r_3\}$.

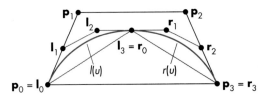

Figure 10.33 Convex hulls and control points.

We shall find the hull for $\mathbf{l}(u)$; the calculation for $\mathbf{r}(u)$ is symmetric. We can start with

$$\mathbf{p}(u) = \mathbf{u}^T \mathbf{M}_B \begin{bmatrix} \mathbf{p}_0 \\ \mathbf{p}_1 \\ \mathbf{p}_2 \\ \mathbf{p}_3 \end{bmatrix},$$

where

$$\mathbf{M}_B = \begin{bmatrix} 1 & 0 & 0 & 0 \\ -3 & 3 & 0 & 0 \\ 3 & -6 & 3 & 0 \\ -1 & 3 & -3 & -1 \end{bmatrix}.$$

The polynomial $\mathbf{l}(u)$ must interpolate $\mathbf{p}(0)$ and $\mathbf{p}\left(\frac{1}{2}\right)$; hence,

$$\mathbf{l}(0) = \mathbf{l}_0 = \mathbf{p}_0,$$
$$\mathbf{l}(1) = \mathbf{l}_3 = \mathbf{p}\left(\frac{1}{2}\right) = \frac{1}{8}(\mathbf{p}_0 + 3\mathbf{p}_1 + 3\mathbf{p}_2 + \mathbf{p}_3).$$

At $u = 0$, the slope of $\mathbf{l}$ must match the slope of $\mathbf{p}$, but, because the parameter for $\mathbf{p}$ covers only the range $\left(0, \frac{1}{2}\right)$ while u varies over $(0, 1)$, implicitly we have made the substitution $\bar{u} = 2u$. Consequently, derivatives for $\mathbf{l}$ and $\mathbf{p}$ are related by $d\bar{u} = 2du$, and

$$\mathbf{l}'(0) = 3(\mathbf{l}_1 - \mathbf{l}_0) = \mathbf{p}'(0) = \frac{3}{2}(\mathbf{p}_1 - \mathbf{p}_0).$$

Likewise, at the midpoint,

$$\mathbf{l}'(1) = (\mathbf{l}_3 - \mathbf{l}_2) = \mathbf{p}'\left(\frac{1}{2}\right) = \frac{3}{8}(-\mathbf{p}_0 - \mathbf{p}_1 + \mathbf{p}_2 + \mathbf{p}_3).$$

These four equations can be solved algebraically. Alternatively, this solution can be expressed geometrically, with the aid of Figure 10.34. Here, we construct

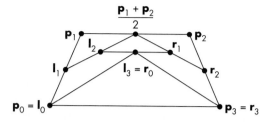

Figure 10.34 Construction of subdivision curves.

both the left and right sets of control points concurrently. First, we note that the interpolation condition requires that

$$l_0 = p_0,$$
$$r_3 = p_3.$$

We can verify by substitution in the four equations that the slopes on the left and right yield

$$l_1 = \frac{1}{2}(p_0 + p_1),$$

$$r_2 = \frac{1}{2}(p_2 + p_3).$$

The interior points are given by

$$l_2 = \frac{1}{2}\left(l_1 + \frac{1}{2}(p_1 + p_2)\right),$$

$$r_1 = \frac{1}{2}\left(r_2 + \frac{1}{2}(p_1 + p_2)\right).$$

Finally, the shared middle point is given by

$$l_3 = r_0 = \frac{1}{2}(l_2 + r_1).$$

The advantage of this formulation is that we can determine both sets of control points using only shifts (for the divisions by 2) and adds. However, one of the advantages of the subdivision approach is that it can be made adaptive, and only one of the sides may require subdivision at some point in the rendering. Also, note that, because the rendering of the curve need not take place until the rasterization stage of the pipeline and can be done in screen or window coordinates, the limited resolution of the display places a limit on how many times the convex hull needs to be subdivided (Exercise 10.18).

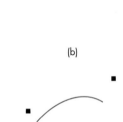

(a)

(b)

(c)

Figure 10.35 Cubic polynomials generated as Bezier curves by conversion of control points. (a) Bezier polynomial. (b) Interpolating polynomial. (c) B-spline polynomial.

10.9.3 Rendering of Other Polynomial Curves by Subdivision

Just as any polynomial is a Bezier polynomial, it is also an interpolating polynomial, a B-spline polynomial, and any other type of polynomial for a properly selected set of control points. The efficiency of the Bezier subdivision algorithm is such that we usually are better off converting another curve form to Bezier form, and then using the subdivision algorithm. A conversion algorithm can be obtained directly from our curve formulations. Consider a cubic Bezier curve. We can write it in terms of the Bezier matrix $\mathbf{M}_B$ as

$$\mathbf{p}(u) = \mathbf{u}^T \mathbf{M}_B \mathbf{p},$$

where $\mathbf{p}$ is the **geometry matrix** of control points. The same polynomial can be written as

$$\mathbf{p}(u) = \mathbf{u}^T \mathbf{M} \mathbf{q},$$

where $\mathbf{M}$ is the matrix for some other type of polynomial and $\mathbf{q}$ is the matrix of control points for this type. We assume that both polynomials are defined over the same interval. The polynomials will be identical if we choose

$$\mathbf{q} = \mathbf{M}^{-1} \mathbf{M}_B \mathbf{p}.$$

For the conversion from interpolation to Bezier, the controlling matrix is

$$\mathbf{M}_B^{-1} \mathbf{M}_I = \begin{bmatrix} 1 & 0 & 0 & 0 \\ -\frac{5}{6} & 3 & -\frac{3}{2} & \frac{1}{3} \\ \frac{1}{3} & -\frac{3}{2} & 3 & -\frac{5}{6} \\ 0 & 0 & 0 & 1 \end{bmatrix}.$$

For the conversion between cubic B-splines and cubic Bezier curves, it is

$$\mathbf{M}_B^{-1} \mathbf{M}_S = \frac{1}{6} \begin{bmatrix} 1 & 4 & 1 & 0 \\ 0 & 4 & 2 & 0 \\ 0 & 2 & 4 & 0 \\ 0 & 1 & 4 & 1 \end{bmatrix}.$$

Figure 10.35 shows four control points and the cubic Bezier, interpolating, and spline polynomials. All three were generated with OpenGL's Bezier evaluators. The interpolating and spline forms were generated as Bezier curves, from the new control points derived from the matrices $\mathbf{M}_B^{-1} \mathbf{M}_I$ and $\mathbf{M}_B^{-1} \mathbf{M}_S$. Note that for the spline case, the resulting curve is generated between only the second and third of the original control points.

10.9.4 Subdivision of Bezier Surfaces

We can extend our subdivision algorithm to Bezier surfaces. Consider the cubic surface in Figure 10.36, with the 16 control points shown. Each four points in a row or column determine a Bezier curve that can be subdivided. However, our

P_{30} P_{33}

P_{00} P_{03}

Figure 10.36 Cubic Bezier surface.

Figure 10.37 First subdivision of surface.

Figure 10.38 Points after second subdivision.

subdivision algorithm should split the patch into four patches, and we have no control points along the center of the patch. We can proceed in two steps.

First, we apply our curve-subdivision technique to the four curves determined by the 16 control points in the v direction. Thus, for each of $u = 0, \frac{1}{3}, \frac{2}{3}, 1$, we create two groups of four control points, with the middle point shared by each group. There are then seven different points along each original curve; these points are indicated in Figure 10.37 by circles. We see that there are three types of points: original control points that are kept after the subdivision (gray), original control points that are discarded after the subdivision (white), and new points created by the subdivision. We now subdivide in the u direction using these points. Consider the rows of constant v, where v is one of $0, \frac{1}{3}, \frac{2}{3}, 1$. There are seven groups of four points. Each group defines a Bezier curve for a constant v. We can subdivide in the u direction, each time creating two groups of four points, again with the middle point shared. These points are indicated in Figure 10.38. If we divide these points in four groups of 16, with points on the edges shared (Figure 10.39), each quadrant contains 16 points that are the control points for a subdivided Bezier surface.

Compared to the calculation for curves, the test for whether the new convex hull is flat enough to stop a subdivision process is more difficult. Many renderers use a fixed number of subdivisions, often letting the user pick the number. If a high-quality rendering is desired, we can let the subdivision continue until the projected size of the convex hull is less than the size of one pixel.

Figure 10.39 Subdivided quadrant.

10.10 The Utah Teapot

We conclude our discussion of parametric surfaces with an example of recursive subdivision of a set of cubic Bezier patches. The object that we show has become known as the **Utah teapot**. The data for the teapot were created at the University of Utah by M. Newell for testing of various rendering algorithms. These data have been used in the graphics community for over 30 years. The teapot data consist of the control points for 32 bicubic Bezier patches. They are given in terms of 306 vertices (numbered from 1 to 306). The first 12 patches define the body of the teapot; the next four define the handle; the next four define the spout; the following eight define the lid; and the final four define the bottom. These data are widely available.

For purposes of illustration, let us assume that we want to subdivide each patch n times and, after these subdivisions, we will render the final vertices using either line segments or polygons passing through the four corners of each patch. Thus, our final drawing can be done with the function (for line segments)

```
void draw_patch(point3 p[4][4])
{
    glBegin(GL_LINE_LOOP);
        glVertex3fv(p[0][0]);
        glVertex3fv(p[3][0]);
        glVertex3fv(p[3][3]);
        glVertex3fv(p[0][3]);
    glEnd();
}
```

We build our patch subdivider from the curve subdivider for a cubic curve c, using our point3 type

```
void divide_curve(point3 c[4], point3 r[4], point3 l[4])
{
int i;
point3 t;
for(i=0;i<3;i++)
    {
    l[0][i]=c[0][i];
    r[3][i]=c[3][i];
    l[1][i]=(c[1][i]+c[0][i])/2;
    r[2][i]=(c[2][i]+c[3][i])/2;
    t[i]=(l[1][i]+r[2][i])/2;
    l[2][i]=(t[i]+l[1][i])/2;
    r[1][i]=(t[i]+r[2][i])/2;
    l[3][i]=r[0][i]=(l[2][i]+r[1][i])/2;
    }
}
```

The patch subdivider is easier to write—but is slightly less efficient—if we assume that we have a matrix-transpose function transpose. This code is then

```
void divide_patch(point3 p[4][4], int n)
{
point3 q[4][4], r[4][4], s[4][4], t[4][4];
point3 a[4][4], b[4][4];
int i,j, k;
if(n==0) draw_patch(p);
else
    {
    for(k=0; k<4; k++) divide_curve(p[k], a[k], b[k]);
    transpose(a);
    transpose(b);
    for(k=0; k<4; k++)
        {
        divide_curve(a[k], q[k], r[k]);
        divide_curve(b[k], s[k], t[k]);
        }
    divide_patch(q, n-1);
    divide_patch(r, n-1);
    divide_patch(s, n-1);
    divide_patch(t, n-1);
    }
}
```

A complete teapot-rendering program using shaded polygons is given in Appendix A. That program contains the teapot data.

The teapot is available as an object in the GLUT library with automatic generation of normals for shading. Here, we are interested in using it to demonstrate our recursive-subdivision algorithm. Figure 10.40 shows the teapot as a wire frame at three levels of subdivision, along with a simple rendering with constant shading. Note that the various patches have different curvatures and sizes; thus, carrying out all subdivisions to the same depth can create many unnecessarily small polygons.

The OpenGL Bezier curve functions that we introduce in Section 10.12 will allow us to render the patches through the API, using only a few function calls. These functions are usually implemented by means of recursive subdivision, but should be more efficient than an implementation in the user program would be.

Figure 10.40 Rendered teapots.

10.11 Algebraic Surfaces

Although quadrics can be generated as a special case of NURBS curves, this class of algebraic objects is of such importance that it merits independent discussion. Quadrics are the most important case of the algebraic surfaces that we introduced in Section 10.1.

10.11.1 Quadrics

Quadric surfaces are described by implicit algebraic equations in which each term is a polynomial of the form $x^i y^j z^k$, with $i + j + k \leq 2$. Any quadric can be written in the form

$$q(x, y, z) = a_{11}x^2 + 2a_{12}xy + a_{22}y^2 + a_{33}z^2 + 2a_{23}yz + 2a_{13}xz$$
$$+ b_1 x + b_2 y + b_3 z + c = 0.$$

This class of surfaces includes ellipsoids, parabaloids, and hyperboloids. We can write the general equation in matrix form in terms of the three-dimensional column matrix $\mathbf{p} = [\, x \quad y \quad z \,]^T$ as the **quadratic form**

$$\mathbf{p}^T \mathbf{A} \mathbf{p} + \mathbf{b}^T \mathbf{p} + c = 0,$$

where

$$\mathbf{A} = \begin{bmatrix} a_{11} & a_{12} & a_{13} \\ a_{12} & a_{22} & a_{23} \\ a_{13} & a_{23} & a_{33} \end{bmatrix}, \qquad \mathbf{b} = \begin{bmatrix} b_1 \\ b_2 \\ b_3 \end{bmatrix}.$$

The 10 independent coefficients in $\mathbf{A}$, $\mathbf{b}$, and c determine a given quadric. However, for the purpose of classification, we can apply a sequence of rotations and translations that reduces a quadric to a standard form without changing the type of surface. In three dimensions, we can write such a transformation as

$$\mathbf{p}' = \mathbf{M}\mathbf{p} + \mathbf{d}.$$

This substitution creates another quadratic form with $\mathbf{A}$ replaced by the matrix $\mathbf{M}^T\mathbf{A}\mathbf{M}$. The matrix $\mathbf{M}$ can always be chosen to be a rotation matrix that such $\mathbf{D} = \mathbf{M}^T\mathbf{A}\mathbf{M}$ is a diagonal matrix. The diagonal elements of $\mathbf{D}$ can be used to determine the type of quadric. If, for example, the equation is that of an ellipsoid, the resulting quadratic form can be put in the form

$$a'_{11}x'^2 + a'_{22}y'^2 + a_{33}z'^2 - c' = 0,$$

where all the coefficients are positive. Note that because we can convert to a standard form by an affine transformation, quadrics are preserved by affine transformations, and thus fit well with our other standard primitives.

10.11.2 Rendering of Surfaces by Ray Casting

Quadrics are easy to render because we can find the intersection of a quadric with a ray by solving a scalar quadratic equation. We represent the ray from $\mathbf{p}_0$ in the direction $\mathbf{d}$ parametrically as

$$\mathbf{p} = \mathbf{p}_0 + \alpha\mathbf{d}.$$

Substituting into the equation for the quadric, we obtain the scalar equation for α:

$$\alpha^2\mathbf{d}^T\mathbf{A}\mathbf{d} + \alpha\mathbf{d}^T(\mathbf{b} + 2\mathbf{A}\mathbf{p}_0) + \mathbf{p}_0^T\mathbf{A}\mathbf{p}_0 + \mathbf{b}^T\mathbf{d} + c = 0.$$

As we may for any quadratic equation, we may find zero, one, or two real solutions. We can use this result to render a quadric into the frame buffer, or as part of a ray-tracing calculation. In addition, we can apply our standard shading model at every point on a quadric because we can compute the normal by taking the derivatives

$$\mathbf{n} = \begin{bmatrix} \frac{\partial q}{\partial x} \\ \frac{\partial q}{\partial y} \\ \frac{\partial q}{\partial z} \end{bmatrix} = 2\mathbf{A}\mathbf{p} - \mathbf{b}.$$

This method of rendering can be extended to any algebraic surface. Suppose that we have an algebraic surface

$$q(\mathbf{p}) = q(x, y, z) = 0.$$

As part of the rendering pipeline, we cast a ray from the center of projection through each pixel. Each of these rays can be written in the parametric form

$$\mathbf{p}(\alpha) = \mathbf{p}_0 + \alpha\mathbf{d}.$$

Substituting this expression into q yields an implicit polynomial equation in α:

$$q(\mathbf{p}(\alpha)) = 0.$$

We can find the points of intersection by numerical methods, or, for quadrics, by the quadratic formula. If we have terms up to $x^i y^j z^k$, we can have $i + j + k$ points of intersection, and the surface may require considerable time to render.

10.11.3 Subdivision Curves and Surfaces

Let us reexamine our subdivision formula from Section 10.9.2 from a slightly different perspective. We start with four points—$\mathbf{p}_0, \mathbf{p}_1, \mathbf{p}_2, \mathbf{p}_3$—and end up with seven points. We can call these new points $\mathbf{s}_0, \ldots, \mathbf{s}_6$. We can view each of these sets of points as defining a piecewise-linear curve, as in Figure 10.41.

(a)

(b)

Figure 10.41 (a) Piecewise-linear curve determined by four points. (b) Piecewise-linear curve after one subdivision step.

We can use our subdivision formulas to relate the two sets of points

$$s_0 = p_0$$

$$s_1 = \tfrac{1}{2}(p_0 + p_1),$$

$$s_2 = \tfrac{1}{4}(p_0 + 2p_1 + p_2),$$

$$s_3 = \tfrac{1}{8}(p_0 + 3p_1 + 3p_2 + p_3),$$

$$s_4 = \tfrac{1}{4}(p_1 + 2p_2 + p_3),$$

$$s_5 = \tfrac{1}{2}(p_2 + p_3),$$

$$s_6 = p_3$$

The second curve is said to be a **refinement** of the first. As we saw in Section 10.9.2, we can continue the process iteratively and in the limit converge to the B-spline. However, in practice, we want to carry out only enough iterations so that the resulting piecewise-linear curve connecting the new points looks smooth. How many iterations we need to carry out depends on the size of the projected convex hull, that can be determined from the camera specifications. Thus, we have a method which allows us to render curves at different levels of detail.

These ideas and their benefits are not limited to B-splines. Over the past few years, a variety of methods for generating these **subdivision curves** have appeared. Some interpolate points—such as p_0 and p_3—while others do not interpolate any of the original points. But in all cases, the refined curves converge to a smooth curve.

The next issue to examine is how can we apply these ideas to surfaces. We saw one method in Section 10.9.2, but of even greater interest is how we might apply these ideas to meshes of polygons. Let us return to the subdivision schemes we used to generate the Sierpinski gasket in Chapter 2 and the sphere approximation in Chapter 6. Consider a triangle before and after a subdivision, as in Figure 10.42.

Regardless of whether we are using midpoint subdivision or working in two or three dimensions, we can observe that the three original vertices are still parts of only a single triangle, while the new vertices are parts of multiple triangles and thus have more than two edges meeting at them. We can also note that as we do more subdivisions, the original vertices and the new vertices retain this difference. Thus, while we have a subdivision scheme that is fairly easy to describe graphically, it is much more difficult to state the algorithm mathematically or analyze it. For example, how do we number the old vertices and write a formula for the new (postsubdivision) vertices. If we consider a general mesh as in Figure 10.43, these problems are even more difficult. For example, we can create gaps in the surface if we are not careful. These problems are not unsolvable. The references at the end of the chapter should help to get you started.

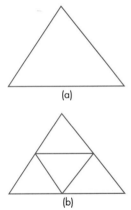

Figure 10.42 (a) Triangle. (b) Triangles after one subdivision.

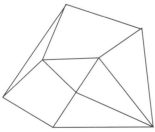

Figure 10.43 General mesh.

A theory of **subdivision surfaces** has emerged that deals with both the theoretical and practical aspects of these ideas. The figures in Color Plate 29 were developed using subdivision surfaces. Figure 10.44 shows a sequence of meshes generated by a subdivision-surface algorithm and the rendered surface from the highest resolution mesh.

Figure 10.44 Successive subdivisions of polygonal mesh and rendered surface. (Images courtesy Caltech Multi-Res Modeling Group).

10.12 Curves and Surfaces in OpenGL

OpenGL supports Bezier curves and surfaces through mechanisms, called **evaluators**, that can be used to compute values for the Bernstein polynomials of any order. Evaluators do not require uniform spacing of control points, and, because we can use Bezier curves and surfaces to generate other types of polynomial curves and surfaces by generating new control points, this mechanism is flexible. We can use evaluators to generate one-, two-, three-, and four-dimensional curves and surfaces. Curves use one-dimensional evaluators, which evaluate the Bernstein polynomials in one variable. We might use one-dimensional evaluators to define color maps or paths in time for animations. The GLU library uses this mechanism in four dimensions to provide NURBS curves. Two-dimensional evaluators evaluate the Bernstein polynomials in two variables and are used primarily to generate surfaces. In addition to defining curves and surfaces, the OpenGL evaluator functions can also provide colors, normals, and texture coordinates.

10.12.1 Bezier Curves

For curves, we define a one-dimensional evaluator through the function

```
glMap1f(type, u_min, u_max, stride, order, point_array)
```

as part of our initialization. The `type` parameter specifies the type of objects that we want to evaluate using Bezier polynomials. Options include three- and four-dimensional points, RGBA colors, normals, indexed colors, and one- through four-dimensional texture coordinates. The control-point data are in the array pointed to by `point_array`. The values `u_min` and `u_max` define the range of the parameter. The value of `stride` is the number of values of the parameter between curve segments. For example, in our cubic B-spline, we stride three points for each curve segment. The `order` parameter is 1 greater than the degree of the polynomial. Thus, for our cubic B-spline defined over $(0, 1)$, we set up an evaluator for a three-dimensional curve by

```
point data[]={...}
glMap1f(GL_MAP_VERTEX_3, 0.0, 1.0, 3, 4, data);
```

We can define multiple evaluators that are active at the same time, and can use them to evaluate, for example, curves and normals at the same time. Each evaluator must be enabled through

```
glEnable(type);
```

Once an evaluator has been set up, whenever we need a value from the active evaluators, we use the function

```
glEvalCoord1f(u);
```

Thus, `glEvalCoord1f` can replace any combination of `glVertex`, `glColor`, and `glNormal`, depending on which evaluators have been enabled. Suppose that we have defined evaluators for the cubic Bezier curve over (0,10) and the array of control points. We can get 100 equally spaced points on the curve by the call

```
glBegin(GL_LINE_STRIP)
    for(i=0; i<100; i++) glEvalCoord1f( (float) i/100.0);
glEnd();
```

OpenGL provides an alternative if the values of u are equally spaced. In this case, we can use the functions

```
glMapGrid1f(100,0.0, 10.0);
glEvalMesh1(GL_LINE, 0, 100);
```

The first function sets up the uniform grid with 100 intervals; the second function generates the desired curve.

10.12.2 Bezier Surfaces

Bezier surfaces are generated in a manner similar to curves. We can use the functions `glMap2` and `glEvalCoord2`, but now there are two parameters, u and v, to specify. For example, a bicubic Bezier surface over the region $(0, 1) \times (0, 1)$ can be set up with the function call

```
glMap2f(GL_MAP_VERTEX_3, 0.0, 1.0, 3, 4, 0.0, 1.0, 12, 4, data);
```

We have to specify the order and stride for both parameters, allowing additional flexibility in defining the surface. Note that the stride for the second variable is 12 because the array `data` stores the information by rows. Hence, we step forward three floats to get the next element on the same row, but must go through 12 floats to get to the element in the next column. The corresponding evaluator calls depend on whether we want to draw a mesh or to create a set of polygons for shading. For the mesh, we have to make sets of calls to the evaluator of the form

```
for(j=0; j<100; j++)
{
    glBegin(GL_LINE_STRIP);
        for(i=0; i<100; i++)
          glEvalCoord2f( (float) i/100.0, (float) j/100.0);
    glEnd();
    glBegin(GL_LINE_STRIP);
        for(i=0; i<100; i++)
          glEvalCoord2f( (float) j/100.0, (float) i/100.0);
    glEnd();
}
```

For quadrilaterals, the calls look like

```
for(j=0; j<99; j++)
{
    glBegin(GL_QUAD_STRIP);
    for(i=0; i<=100; i++)
    {
      glEvalCoord2f( (float) i/100.0, (float) j/100.0);
      glEvalCoord2f( (float) (i+1)/100.0, (float) j/100.0);
    }
    glEnd();
}
```

For uniform meshes, we can use `glMapGrid2` and `glEvalMesh2`. Thus, as part of the initialization, we specify

```
glMapGrid2f(100, 0.0, 1.0, 100, 0.0, 1.0);
```

As part of the display function, we call

```
glEvalMesh2(GL_FILL,0,100,0,100);
```

There is still a problem. Unless we enable lighting, if we display these polygons, we will see a flat filled area. We can enable lighting as in Chapter 6, but the shading calculations require the normals at the vertices. Although we could evaluate these normals ourselves by differentiating the appropriate polynomials, we can also ask OpenGL to generate normals automatically as the evaluators are used. We need only to enable the option

```
glEnable(GL_AUTO_NORMAL);
```

when we enable the lighting options.

10.12.3 Displaying the Teapot

We can display the teapot using OpenGL Bezier functions. Suppose that we first read in the vertex and patch information, and place it in an array

```
GLfloat data[32][4][4];
```

If we want to display the teapot as a wire frame, we can simply initialize the grid:

```
void myinit()
{
  glEnable(GL_MAP2_VERTEX_3);
  glMapGrid2f(20, 0.0, 1.0, 20, 0.0, 1.0);

}
```

Then, in the display callback, we draw the line segments:

```
for(k=0;k<32;k++)
{
  glMap2f(GL_MAP2_VERTEX_3, 0, 1, 3, 4, 0, 1, 12, 4,
                  &data[k][0][0][0]);
  for (j = 0; j <= 8; j++)
  {
    glBegin(GL_LINE_STRIP);
    for (i = 0; i <= 30; i++)
        glEvalCoord2f((GLfloat)i/30.0, (GLfloat)j/8.0);
    glEnd();
    glBegin(GL_LINE_STRIP);
    for (i = 0; i <= 30; i++)
        glEvalCoord2f((GLfloat)j/8.0, (GLfloat)i/30.0);
    glEnd();
  }
}
```

Note the necessity of setting up a map for each of the patches. To display a shaded teapot, we need a more complex initialization that enables lighting and sets the required material properties:

```
void myinit()
{
  glEnable(GL_MAP2_VERTEX_3);
  glEnable(GL_AUTO_NORMAL);
  glMapGrid2f(8, 0.0, 1.0, 8, 0.0, 1.0);
  glEnable(GL_DEPTH_TEST);

  glEnable(GL_LIGHTING);
  glEnable(GL_LIGHT0);

  glLightfv(GL_LIGHT0, GL_AMBIENT, ambient);
  glLightfv(GL_LIGHT0, GL_DIFFUSE, diffuse);
  glLightfv(GL_LIGHT0, GL_POSITION, position);

  glMaterialfv(GL_FRONT, GL_DIFFUSE, mat_diffuse);
  glMaterialfv(GL_FRONT, GL_AMBIENT, mat_ambient);

}
```

We can then render a teapot by two lines in display function:

```
for(k=0;k<32;k++)
{
    glMap2f(GL_MAP2_VERTEX_3, 0, 1, 3, 4, 0, 1, 12, 4,
                  &data[k][0][0][0]);
    glEvalMesh2(GL_FILL,0,8,0,8);
}
```

10.12.4 NURBS Functions

We can use evaluators to generate nonuniform spacing of points and to generate four-dimensional curves and surfaces. If we recall our earlier observation that we can change any of the polynomial forms to a Bezier form by generating a proper set of control points, then we see that we have all the information necessary to define NURBS curves and surfaces. Rather than have the application programmer go through all these steps, the OpenGL Utility library, GLU, provides a set of NURBS functions. These functions also allow the user to specify various additional parameters that enable finer control of the rendering. There are five NURBS functions for surfaces:

```
gluNewNurbsRenderer
gluNurbsProperty
gluBeginNurbsSurface
gluNurbsSurface
gluEndNurbsSurface
```

The first two functions set up a new NURBS object and define how we would like it rendered. The final three are used to generate the surface. For NURBS curves, the final three are replaced by the functions gluBeginNurbsCurve, gluNurbsCurve, and gluEndNurbsCurve.

The GLU library provides an additional useful facility called trimming curves. **Trimming curves** are closed curves that we can use to render a surface from which the areas defined by curves have been removed. Figure 10.45 illustrates a trimmed surface. The user can define a trimming curve either as a NURBS curve using gluNurbsCurve or as a piecewise linear curve, through the gluPwlCurve function. The trimming curves are defined after the call to glNurbsSurface, and their vertices are specified between calls to glBeginTrim and glEndTrim.

10.12.5 Quadrics

OpenGL supports several quadric objects—disks, cylinders, and spheres—through GLU. These objects can be treated like other graphical objects: They can be scaled, translated, rotated, shaded, and texture mapped. The quadric routines allow for automatic generation of normals and texture coordinates. OpenGL im-

Figure 10.45 Trimmed surface.

plements these objects by approximating them with polygons, although we can specify how many polygons are to be used in the approximation.

Suppose that we want to use a cylinder for the base of the robot in Chapter 9 (see Appendix A). The first step is to define a new quadric object by

```
GLUquadricObj *p;
p=gluNewQuadric();
```

We can then define how we would like the quadric to be rendered. For example, if we want a wire frame, using the present drawing color, we use the function call

```
gluQuadricDrawStyle(p, GLU_LINE);
```

We can now create the cylinder, centered at the origin, with its length along the y-axis, by using

```
gluCylinder(p, BASE_RADIUS, BASE_RADIUS, BASE_HEIGHT, 5, 5);
```

The first three parameters specify the top and bottom radii, and the height. The final two parameters specify by how many slices we divide each circle of constant y, and into how many sections we slice the cylinder in the y direction.

10.13 Summary and Notes

Once again, we have only scratched the surface of a deep and important topic. Also once again, our focus has been on what we can do on a graphics system using a standard API such as OpenGL. From this perspective, there are huge advantages to using parametric Bezier curves and surfaces. The parametric form is robust and is easy to use interactively, because the required data are points that can be entered and manipulated interactively. The subdivision algorithm for Bezier curves and surfaces gives us the ability to render the resulting objects to any desired degree of accuracy.

We have seen that, although Bezier surfaces are easy to render, splines can provide additional smoothness and control. The texts in the suggested readings discuss many variants of splines that are used in the CAD community.

Quadric surfaces are used extensively with ray tracers, because solving for the points of intersection between a ray and a quadric requires the solution of only a scalar quadratic equation. Deciding whether the point of intersection between a ray and the plane determined by a flat polygon is inside the polygon can be more difficult than solving the intersection problem for quadric surfaces. Hence, many ray tracers allow only infinite planes, quadrics, and, perhaps, convex polygons.

10.14 References and Notes

The book by Farin [Far88] provides an excellent introduction to curves and surfaces. It also has an interesting preface in which Bezier discusses the almost simultaneous discovery by him and deCasteljau of the surfaces that bear his name. Unfortunately, deCasteljau's work was described in unpublished technical reports, so deCasteljau did not, until recently, receive the credit he deserved for his work. Books such as those by Rogers [Rog90], Foley [Fol90], Bartels [Bar87], and Watt [Wat93] discuss many other forms of splines. See Rogers [Rog00] for an introduction to NURBS.

The book by Faux [Fau80] discusses the coordinate-free approach to curves and surfaces and the Frenet frame.

Although the book edited by Glassner [Gla89] primarily explores ray tracing, the section by Haines has considerable material on working with quadrics and other algebraic surfaces.

There has been much recent activity on subdivision curves and surfaces. For some of the seminal work in the area, see [Che95], [Deb96], [Gor96], [Lev96], [Sei96], and [Tor96].

Exercises

10.1 Consider an algebraic surface $f(x, y, z) = 0$, where each term in f can have terms in x, y, and z of power up to m. How many terms can there be in f?

10.2 Consider the explicit equations $y = f(x)$ and $z = g(x)$. What types of curves do they describe?

10.3 Suppose that you have a polynomial $p(u) = \sum_{k=0}^{n} c_k u^k$. Find a polynomial $q(v) = \sum_{k=0}^{n} d_k v^k$ such that, for each point of p in the interval (a, b), there is a point v in the range $0 \leq v \leq 1$, such that $p(u) = q(v)$.

10.4 Show that, as long as the four control points for the cubic interpolating curve are defined at unique values of the parameter u, the interpolating geometry matrix always exists.

10.5 Show that in the interval $(0, 1)$, the Bernstein polynomials must be less than 1.

10.6 Verify the C^2 continuity of the cubic spline.

10.7 In Section 10.9 we showed that we can write a cubic polynomial as a cubic Bezier polynomial by choosing a proper set of control points, or equivalently, the proper convex hull. Using this fact, show how to render an interpolating curve using the Bezier renderer provided by OpenGL.

10.8 Find a homogeneous-coordinate representation for quadrics.

10.9 Suppose that we render Bezier patches by adaptive subdivision, so that each patch can be subdivided a different number of times. Do we maintain continuity along the edges of the patches? Explain your answer.

10.10 Write an OpenGL program that will take as input a set of control points, and that will produce the interpolating, B-spline, and Bezier curves for these data.

10.11 Suppose that you use a set of spline curves to describe a path in time that an object will take as part of an animation. How might you notice the difference between G^1 and C^1 continuity in this situation?

10.12 Extend the painting program from Chapter 3 to include Bezier curves. The user should be able to manipulate the control points interactively.

10.13 Derive a simple test for the flatness of a Bezier surface patch.

10.14 Derive the open rational quadratic B-spline with the knots $\{0, 0, 0, 0, 1, 1, 1, 1\}$ and the weights $w_0 = w_2 = 1$ and $w_1 = w$.

10.15 Using the result of Exercise 10.14, show that, if $w = \frac{r}{1-r}$, for $0 \le r \le 1$, you get all the conic sections. *Hint*: Consider $r < \frac{1}{2}$ and $r > \frac{1}{2}$.

10.16 Find the zeros of the Hermite blending functions. Why do these zeros imply that the Hermite curve is smooth in the interval $(0, 1)$?

10.17 What is the relationship between the control-point data for a Hermite patch and the derivatives at the corners of the patch?

10.18 For a 1024×1280 display screen, what is the maximum number of subdivisions that are needed to render a cubic polynomial surface?

10.19 Suppose you have three points, P_0, P_1, and P_2. First, connect successive points with parametric line segments where u ranges from 0 to 1 for each. Next, linearly interpolate between successive pairs of line segments by connecting points for the same value of u with a line segment and then using the same value of u to obtain a value along this new line segment. How can you describe the curve created by this process?

10.20 Extend Exercise 10.19 by considering four points. Linearly interpolate, first between the three curves constructed as in that exercise and, second, between the two curves thus created. Describe the final curve determined by the four points.

10.21 What happens in the cubic Bezier curve if the values of the control points P_0 and P_1 are the same?

10.22 Suppose that we divide a Bezier surface patch, first along the u direction, and then in v we only subdivide one of the two patches we have created. Show how this process can create a gap in the resulting surface. Find a simple solution to this difficulty.

Procedural Methods

T hus far, we have assumed that the geometric objects that we wish to create can be described by their surfaces, and that these surfaces can be modeled (or approximated) by convex planar polygons. Our use of polygonal objects was dictated by the ease with which we could describe these objects and our ability to render them on existing systems. The success of computer graphics attests to the importance of such models.

Nevertheless, even as these models were being used in large CAD applications and for flight simulators, both users and developers recognized the limitations of these techniques. Physical objects such as clouds, smoke, and water did not fit this style of modeling. Adding physical constraints and modeling complex behaviors of objects were not part of polygonal modeling. In response to such problems, researchers have developed procedural models, which use algorithmic models to build representations of the underlying phenomena, generating polygons only as needed during the rendering process.

11.1 Reasons for Using Procedural Models

When we review the history of computer graphics, we see that the desire to create increasingly more realistic graphics has always outstripped advances in hardware. Although we can render more than 10 million polygons per second on existing hardware (including on personal computers), applications such as flight simulation, virtual reality, and computer games can demand rendering speeds greater than 100 million polygons per second. Furthermore, as rendering speeds have increased, database sizes also have increased dramatically. A single data set may contain more than 1 billion polygons.

Often, however, applications have such needs because they use existing software and modeling paradigms. Astute researchers and application programmers have suggested that we would not require as many polygons if we could render a model generating only those polygons that both are visible and project to an area at least the size of one pixel. We have seen examples of this idea in previous chapters, for example, when we considered culling polygons before they reached the rendering pipeline. Nevertheless, a more productive approach has been to reexamine the way in which we do our modeling and seek techniques,

known as **procedural methods**, that generate geometrical objects in a different manner from what we have seen thus far. Procedural methods span a wide
range of techniques. What they have in common is that they describe objects in
an algorithmic manner and produce polygons only when needed as part of the
rendering process.

In many ways, procedural models can be understood by an analogy with
methods that we use to represent irrational numbers—such as square roots, sines,
and cosines—in a computer. Consider, for example, three ways of representing
$\sqrt{2}$. We can say that numerically

$$\sqrt{2} = 1.414\ldots,$$

filling in as many digits as we like; or, more abstractly, we can define the $\sqrt{2}$ as
the positive number x such that

$$x^2 = 2.$$

However, within the computer, $\sqrt{2}$ might be the result of executing an algorithm, such as Newton's method

$$x_{k+1} = \frac{x_k}{2} + \frac{1}{x_k},$$

starting with $x_0 = 1$. From this perspective, $\sqrt{2}$ is defined by an algorithm;
equivalently, it is defined through a program. For objects we deal with in
computer graphics, we can take a similar approach. For example, a sphere
centered at the origin can be defined as the mathematical object that satisfies
the equation

$$x^2 + y^2 + z^2 = r^2.$$

It also is the result of the tetrahedron subdivision process that we developed in
Chapter 6 and of our program for doing that subdivision. A potential benefit of
the second view is that when we render spheres, we can render small spheres (in
screen space) with fewer triangles than we would need for large spheres.

A second type of problem with polygonal modeling has been the difficulty
of combining computer graphics with physical laws. Although we can build and
animate polygonal models of real-world objects, it is far more difficult to make
these graphical objects act as solids and not penetrate one another.

We introduce two of many possible approaches to procedural modeling. In
the first, we work with particles that obey Newton's laws. We then design systems
of particles that are capable of complex behaviors that arise from solving sets of
differential equations—a routine numerical task for up to thousands of particles.
The positions of the particles yield the locations at which to place our standard
geometric objects in a world model.

The second approach—algorithmic models—enables us to control complexity
by replacing polygonal models with language-based models, similar to those used
for both natural and computer languages. With these models we can approximate

many natural objects with a few rules that generate the required graphical entities. Combined with fractal geometry, these models allow us to generate images using only the number of polygons required for display.

11.2 Physically Based Models and Particle Systems

One of the great strengths—and weaknesses—of modeling in computer graphics is that we can build models based on any principles we choose. The graphical objects that we create may have no connection with physical reality. This flexibility allows mathematicians to "see" shapes that do not exist in the usual three-dimensional space and allows engineers to construct prototypes of objects that are not limited by our ability to construct them with present materials and equipment. However, when we wish to simulate objects in the real world, and to see the results of this simulation on our CRT, we can get into trouble. Often, it is easy to make a model for a group of objects moving through space, but it is far more difficult to keep track of when two objects collide, and to have the graphics system react in a physically correct manner. Indeed, it is far easier in computer graphics to let a ball go directly through a wall than to model the ball bouncing off the surface, incorporating the correct elastic rebound.

Recently, researchers have become interested in **physically based modeling**, a style of modeling in which the graphical objects obey physical laws. Such modeling can follow either of two related paths. In one, we model the physics of the underlying process and use the physics to drive the graphics. For example, if we want a solid object to appear to tumble in space and to bounce from various surfaces, we can, at least in principle, use our knowledge of dynamics and continuum mechanics to derive the required equations. This approach is beyond the scope of a first course in computer graphics, and we shall not pursue it. The other approach is to use a combination of basic physics and mathematical constraints to control the dynamical behavior of our objects. We follow this approach for a group of particles.

Particle systems are collections of particles, typically point masses, in which the dynamic behavior of the particles can be determined by the solution of sets of coupled differential equations. Particle systems have been used to generate a wide variety of behaviors in a number of fields. In fluid dynamics, people use particle systems to model turbulent behavior. Rather than solving partial differential equations, we can simulate the behavior of the system by following a group of particles that is subject to a variety of forces and constraints. We can also use particles to model solid objects. For example, a deformable solid can be modeled as a three-dimensional array of particles that are held together by springs. When the object is subjected to external forces, the particles move and their positions approximate the shape of the solid object.

In computer graphics, people have used particles to model such diverse phenomena as fireworks, the flocking behavior of birds, and wave action. In these applications, the dynamics of the particle system gives the positions of the particles, but at each location we can place a graphical object, rather than a point.

In all these cases, we work with a group of particles, each member of which we can regard as a point mass. We use physical laws to write equations that we can solve numerically to obtain the state of these particles at each time step. As a final step, we can render each particle as a graphical object—perhaps as a colored point for a fireworks application, or as a cartoon character in an animation.

11.3 Newtonian Particles

We consider a set of particles that is subject to Newton's laws. Although there is no reason that we could not use other physical laws or construct a set of our own (virtual) physical laws, the advantage of starting with Newtonian particles is that we can obtain a wide range of behaviors using simple, well-understood physics. A Newtonian particle must obey Newton's second law, which states that the mass of the particle (m) times that particle's acceleration ($\mathbf{a}$) is equal to the sum of the forces ($\mathbf{f}$) acting on the particle, or, symbolically,

$$m\mathbf{a} = \mathbf{f}.$$

Note that both the acceleration and force are vectors, usually in three dimensions. One consequence of Newton's laws is that, for an ideal point-mass particle— one whose total mass is concentrated at a single point—its state is completely determined by its position and velocity. Thus, in three-dimensional space, an ideal particle has 6 degrees of freedom, and a system of n particles has $6n$ state variables—the positions and velocities of all the particles. Within some reference frame, the state of the ith particle is given by two three-element column matrices,[1] a position matrix

$$\mathbf{p}_i = \begin{bmatrix} x_i \\ y_i \\ z_i \end{bmatrix},$$

and a velocity matrix

$$\mathbf{v}_i = \begin{bmatrix} \dot{x}_i \\ \dot{y}_i \\ \dot{z}_i \end{bmatrix} = \begin{bmatrix} \frac{dx}{dt} \\ \frac{dy}{dt} \\ \frac{dz}{dt} \end{bmatrix}.$$

Knowing that acceleration is the derivative of velocity and that velocity is the derivative of position, we can write Newton's second law for a particle as the six

---

1. We have chosen to use three-dimensional arrays here, rather than homogeneous coordinate representations, both to be consistent with the way these equations are usually written in the physics literature and to simplify the resulting differential equations.

coupled first-order differential equations

$$\dot{\mathbf{p}}_i = \mathbf{v}_i,$$

$$\dot{\mathbf{v}}_i = \frac{1}{m_i}\mathbf{f}_i(t).$$

Hence, the dynamics of a system of n particles is governed by a set of $6n$ coupled ordinary differential equations.

In addition to its state, each particle may have a number of attributes, including its mass (m_i), and a set of properties that can alter what its behavior is and how it is displayed. For example, some attributes govern how we render the particle and determine its color, shape, and surface properties. Note that, although the dynamics of a simple particle system is based on each particle being treated as a point mass, the user can specify how each particle should be rendered. For example, each particle may represent a person in a crowd scene, or a molecule in a chemical-synthesis application, or a portion of a cloth piece in the simulation of a flag blowing in the wind. In each case, the underlying particle system governs the location, and the velocity, of the center of mass of the particle. Once we have the location of a particle, we can place the desired object at this location.

The set of forces on the particles, $\{\mathbf{f}_i\}$, determines the behavior of the system. These forces are based on the state of the particle system and can change with time. We can base these forces on simple physical principles, such as spring forces, or on physical constraints that we wish to impose on the system; or we can base them on external forces, such as gravity, that we wish to apply to the system. By designing the forces carefully, we can obtain the desired system behavior.

The dynamic state of the system is obtained by numerical methods that involve stepping through approximations to the set of differential equations. A typical time step is based on computing the forces that apply to the n particles through a user-defined function, using these forces to update the state through a numerical differential-equation solver, and finally using the new positions of the particles and their attributes to render whatever graphical objects we wish to place at the particles' locations. Thus, in pseudocode, we have a loop of the form

```
float time, delta; float state[6n], force[3n];
state=get_initial_state();
for(time=t0; time<time_final; time+=delta)
 {
 /* compute forces */
    force=force_function(state, time);

 /* apply standard differential equation solver */
    state=ode(force, state, time, delta);

 /* display result */
    render(state, time);
}
```

The main component that we must design in a given application is the function that computes the forces on each particle.

11.3.1 Independent Particles

There are numerous simple ways that particles can interact and determine the forces that act on each particle. If the forces that act on a given particle are independent of other particles, the force on the ith particle can be described by the equation

$$\mathbf{f}_i = \mathbf{f}_i(\mathbf{p}_i, \mathbf{v}_i).$$

A simple case occurs where each particle is subject only to a constant gravitational force

$$\mathbf{f}_i = \mathbf{g}.$$

If this force points down, then

$$\mathbf{g} = \begin{bmatrix} 0 \\ -g \\ 0 \end{bmatrix},$$

where g is positive, and each particle will trace out a parabolic arc. If we add a term proportional to the velocity, we can have the particle subject to frictional forces, such as drag. If some of the attributes, such as color, change with time, and if we give each particle a (random) lifetime, then we can simulate phenomena such as fireworks. More generally, external forces are applied independently to each point. If we allow the particles to drift randomly and render each as a large object, rather than as a point, we can model clouds or flows with independent particles.

Color Plate 13 shows the use of independent particles to model the sparks generated by welding. Each particle is independent of the others, is subject to gravity, and has a random lifetime.

11.3.2 Spring Forces

If, in a system of n particles, all particles are independent, then the force calculation is $O(n)$. In the most general case, the computation of the forces on a given particle may involve contributions due to pairwise interactions with all the other particles, an $O(n^2)$ computation. For large particle systems, an $O(n^2)$ can slow the computation significantly. Often, we can reduce this complexity by having a particle interact with only those particles that are close to it.

Consider the example of using particles to create a surface whose shape varies over time, such as a curtain or a flag blowing in the wind. We can use the location of each particle as a vertex for a rectangular mesh, as shown in Figure 11.1. The shape of the mesh changes over time, as a result both of external forces that act

Figure 11.1 Mesh of particles.

on each particle, such as gravity or wind, and of forces between particles that give the mesh the appearance of being a solid surface. We can approximate this second type of force by considering the forces between a particle and the latter's closest neighbors. Thus, if $\mathbf{p}_{ij}$ is the location of the particle at row i, column j of the mesh, the force calculation for $\mathbf{p}_{ij}$ needs to consider only the forces between $\mathbf{p}_{i,j}$ and $\mathbf{p}_{i+1,j}$, $\mathbf{p}_{i-1,j}$, $\mathbf{p}_{i,j+1}$, and $\mathbf{p}_{i,j-1}$—an $O(n)$ calculation.

One method to model the forces among particles is to consider adjacent particles as connected by a spring. Consider two adjacent particles, located at $\mathbf{p}$ and $\mathbf{q}$, connected by a spring, as shown in Figure 11.2. Let $\mathbf{f}$ denote the force acting on $\mathbf{p}$ from $\mathbf{q}$. A force $-\mathbf{f}$ acts on $\mathbf{q}$ from $\mathbf{p}$. The spring has a resting length s, which is the distance between particles if the system is not subject to external forces and is allowed to come to rest. When the spring is stretched, the force acts in the direction $\mathbf{d} = \mathbf{p} - \mathbf{q}$; that is, it acts along the line between the points. This force obeys **Hooke's law**:

Figure 11.2 Particles connected by a spring.

$$\mathbf{f} = -k_s(|\mathbf{d}| - s)\frac{\mathbf{d}}{|\mathbf{d}|},$$

where k_s is the spring constant. This law shows that the farther apart the two particles are stretched, the stronger is the force attracting them back to the resting position. Conversely, when the ends of the spring are pushed together, the force pulls them back such that their positions move to a separation by the resting length. As we have stated Hooke's law, however, there is no damping (or friction) in the system. A system of masses and springs defined in such a manner will oscillate forever when perturbed. We can include a **drag** or **damping term** in Hooke's law. The damping force operates in the same direction as the spring force, but depends on the velocity between the particles. The fraction of the velocity that contributes to damping is proportional to the projection of the velocity vector onto the vector defined by the two points as shown in Figure 11.3. Mathematically, Hooke's law with the damping term is given by

$$\mathbf{f} = -\left(k_s(|\mathbf{d}| - s) + k_d\frac{\dot{\mathbf{d}} \cdot \mathbf{d}}{|\mathbf{d}|}\right)\frac{\mathbf{d}}{|\mathbf{d}|}.$$

Figure 11.3 Computation of the spring damping force.

Here, k_d is the damping constant, and

$$\dot{\mathbf{d}} = \dot{\mathbf{p}} - \dot{\mathbf{q}}.$$

A system of masses and springs with damping that is not subjected to external forces will eventually come to rest.

The four images in Color Plate 31 show a mesh that is generated from the locations of a set of particles. Each interior particle is connected to its four neighbors by springs. The particles are also subject to external forces—the wind. At each time step, once the positions of the particles are determined, we can render the mesh using techniques such as texture mapping (Section 7.5) to create the detailed appearance of the surface.

11.3.3 Attractive and Repulsive Forces

Whereas spring forces are used to keep a group of particles together, repulsive forces push particles away from one another and attractive forces pull particles toward one another. We could use repulsive forces to distribute particles over a surface, or, if the particles represent locations of objects, to keep objects from hitting one another. We could use attractive forces to build a model of the solar system or to create applications that model satellites revolving about the earth. The equations for attraction and repulsion are essentially the same except for a sign.

For a pair of particles, located at $\mathbf{p}$ and $\mathbf{q}$, the repulsive force acts in the direction $\mathbf{d} = \mathbf{p} - \mathbf{q}$ and is inversely proportional to the particles' distance from each other. For example, we could use the expression

$$\mathbf{f} = -k_r \frac{\mathbf{d}}{|\mathbf{d}|^3}$$

for an inverse-square-law term. Changing the minus sign to a positive sign and replacing k_r by $(m_a m_b)/g$ gives us the attractive force between two particles of mass m_a and m_b, where g is the gravitational constant.

In the general case, where each particle is subject to forces from all other particles, the computation of attractive and repulsive forces is $O(n^2)$. Unlike meshes of particles connected by springs, where we attempt to keep the particles in the same topological arrangement, particles subject to attractive and repulsive forces usually change their positions among themselves. Hence, strategies to avoid the $O(n^2)$ force calculation are more complex. One approach is to divide space into three-dimensional cells, each of which can contain multiple particles or even no particles, as shown in Figure 11.4.

For forces that are inversely proportional to distance, we can choose a cell size such that the forces on a particle from particles in other than its own or adjacent cells are negligible. If this partitioning is possible, then the $O(n^2)$ calculation is reduced to $O(n)$. However, there is a cost to partitioning, and particles can

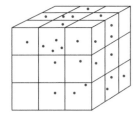

Figure 11.4 Division of space into cells.

move from one cell to another. The difficulty of the first problem depends on the particular application, as we can often obtain an initial particle distribution with little effort, but at other times we might have to do a sort. We can solve the second problem by looking at the particle positions after each time step and redistributing the particles or, perhaps, changing the cells. We can use various data structures to store the particles and cell information.

One other approach that is often used is to replace interactions among particles by interactions between particles and a force field. For example, when we compute the gravitational force on a point mass on the surface of the earth, we use the value of the gravitational field rather than the point-to-point force between the point mass of the particle and a second large point mass at the center of the earth. If we were concerned with only the mass of the earth and our point on the surface, the two approaches would require about the same amount of work. However, if we were to also include the force from the moon, the situation would be more complex. If we used point masses, we would have two point-to-point forces to compute for our mass on the surface, but if we knew the gravitational field, the calculation would be the same as before. Of course, the calculation of the field is more complex when we consider the moon; for particle systems, however, we can often neglect distant particles, so the particle-field method may be more efficient. We can often compute the approximate field on a grid, then use the value at the nearest grid points to give the forces on each particle. After the new state of each particle has been computed, we can update the field. Both of these strategies can often reduce the $O(n^2)$ calculation of forces to $O(n \log n)$.

11.4 Solving Particle Systems

Consider a particle system of n particles. If we restrict ourselves to the simple forces that we just described, the entire particle system can be described by $6n$ ordinary differential equations of the form

$$\dot{\mathbf{u}} = \mathbf{g}(\mathbf{u}, t),$$

where $\mathbf{u}$ is an array of the $6n$ position and velocity components of our n particles, and $\mathbf{g}$ includes any external forces applied to the particles. Thus, if we have two particles $\mathbf{a}$ and $\mathbf{b}$ connected by a spring without damping, we might have

$$\mathbf{u}^T = [\, u_0 \quad u_1 \quad u_2 \quad u_3 \quad u_4 \quad u_5 \quad u_6 \quad u_7 \quad u_8 \quad u_9 \quad u_{10} \quad u_{11} \,]$$
$$= [\, a_x \quad a_y \quad a_z \quad \dot{a}_x \quad \dot{a}_y \quad \dot{a}_z \quad b_x \quad b_y \quad b_z \quad \dot{b}_x \quad \dot{b}_y \quad \dot{b}_z \,].$$

Given the external forces and the state of the particle system $\mathbf{u}$ at any time t, we can evaluate

$$\mathbf{g}^T = \left[\, u_3 \quad u_4 \quad u_5 \quad -kd_x \quad -kd_y \quad -kd_z \quad u_9 \quad u_{10} \quad u_{11} \quad kd_x \quad kd_y \quad kd_z \,\right].$$

Here k is the spring constant and d_x, d_y, and d_z are the components of the normalized vector d between $\mathbf{a}$ and $\mathbf{b}$. Thus, we must first compute

$$\mathbf{d} = \frac{1}{\sqrt{(u_0 - u_5)^2 + (u_1 - u_6)^2 + (u_2 - u_7)^2}} \begin{bmatrix} u_0 - u_6 \\ u_1 - u_7 \\ u_2 - u_8 \end{bmatrix}.$$

Numerical ordinary differential equation solvers rely on our ability to evaluate $\mathbf{g}$ to approximate $\mathbf{u}$ at future times. We can develop a family of differential equation solvers based upon Taylor's theorem. The simplest is known as Euler's method. Suppose that we integrate the expression

$$\dot{\mathbf{u}} = \mathbf{g}(\mathbf{u}, t)$$

over a short time h:

$$\int_t^{t+h} \dot{\mathbf{u}} d\tau = \mathbf{u}(t + h) - \mathbf{u}(t) = \int_t^{t+h} \mathbf{g}(\mathbf{u}, \tau) d\tau.$$

If h is small, we can approximate the value of $\mathbf{g}$ over the interval $[t, t + h]$ by the value of $\mathbf{g}$ at t; thus,

$$\mathbf{u}(t + h) \approx \mathbf{u}(t) + h\mathbf{g}(\mathbf{u}(t), t).$$

This expression shows that we can use the value of the derivative at t to get us to an approximate value of $\mathbf{u}(t + h)$, as shown in Figure 11.5.

This expression matches the first two terms of the Taylor expansion; we can write it as

$$\mathbf{u}(t + h) = \mathbf{u}(t) + h\dot{\mathbf{u}}(t) + O(h^2) = \mathbf{u}(t) + h\mathbf{g}(\mathbf{u}(t), t) + O(h^2),$$

showing that the error we incur in making the approximation is proportional to the square of the step size.

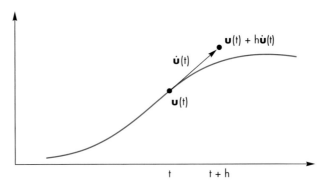

Figure 11.5 Approximation of the solution of a differential equation.

This method is particularly easy to implement. We evaluate the forces (both external and among particles) at time t, compute $\mathbf{g}$, multiply it by h, and add it to the present state. We can apply this method iteratively to compute further values at $t + 2h, t + 3h, \ldots$. The work involved is one calculation of the forces for each time step.

There are two potential problems with Euler's method: accuracy and stability. Both are affected by the step size. The accuracy of Euler's method is proportional to the square of the step size. Consequently, to increase the accuracy we must cut the step size, thus increasing the time it takes to solve the system. A potentially more serious problem concerns stability. As we go from step to step, the per-step errors that we make come from two sources: the approximation error that we made by using the Taylor series approximation and the numerical errors that we make in computing the functions. These errors can either cancel themselves out as we compute further states, or they can accumulate and give us unacceptably large errors that mask the true solution. Such behavior is called **numerical instability**. Fortunately, for the standard types of forces that we have used, if we make the step size small enough, we can guarantee stability. Unfortunately, the required step size for stability may be so small that we cannot solve the equations numerically in a reasonable amount of time. This unstable behavior is most pronounced for spring–mass systems, where the spring constant determines the stiffness of the system and leads to what are called **stiff** sets of differential equations.

There are two general approaches to this problem. One is to seek another type of ordinary differential equation solver, called a stiff equation solver—a topic that is beyond the scope of this book. Another is to find other differential equation solvers similar in philosophy to Euler's method but with a higher per-step accuracy. We derive one such method because it gives us insight into the family of such methods. References to both approaches are given at the end of the chapter.

Suppose that we start as before by integrating the differential equations over a short time interval to obtain

$$\mathbf{u}(t + h) = \mathbf{u}(t) + \int_t^{t+h} \mathbf{g}(\mathbf{u}, \tau)d\tau.$$

This time, we approximate the integral by an average value over the interval $[t, t + h]$

$$\int_t^{t+h} \mathbf{g}(\mathbf{u}, \tau)d\tau \approx \frac{h}{2}(\mathbf{g}(\mathbf{u}(t), t) + \mathbf{g}(\mathbf{u}(t + h), t + h)).$$

The problem now is we do not have $\mathbf{g}(\mathbf{u}(t + h), t + h)$; we have only $\mathbf{g}(\mathbf{u}(t), t)$. We can use Euler's method to approximate $\mathbf{g}(\mathbf{u}(t + h), t + h)$; that is, we can use

$$\mathbf{g}(\mathbf{u}(t + h), t + h) \approx \mathbf{g}(\mathbf{u}(t) + h\mathbf{g}(\mathbf{u}(t), t), t + h).$$

This method is known as the **improved Euler method** or the **Runge–Kutta method of order 2**. Note that to go from t to $t + h$, we must evaluate **g** twice. However, if we were to use Taylor's theorem to evaluate the per-step error, we would find that it is now $O(h^3)$. Thus, even though we are doing more work per step, we can use larger step sizes, and the method is stable for step sizes larger than those for which Euler's method was stable. In general, we can use increasingly more accurate per-step formulas and derive a set of methods called the Runge–Kutta formulas. The most popular is the fourth-order method that has a per-step error of $O(h^4)$ and requires four function evaluations per step. In practice, we can do even better with this number of function evaluations, achieving errors of $O(h^5)$. More important, good solvers adjust their own step size so as to ensure stability.

11.5 Constraints

Simply allowing a group of particles to change state according to a set of differential equations often is insufficient to model real-world behavior such as collisions. Although the impact of an object hitting a wall is subject to Newton's laws, if we were to model the object as a collection of particles, the resulting system would be too complex for most purposes. Instead, we regard conditions such as the one in which two solid objects cannot penetrate each other as constraints that can be stated separately from the laws governing individual particle behavior.

There are two types of constraints that we can impose on particles. **Hard constraints** are those that must be adhered to exactly. For example, a ball must bounce off a wall; it cannot penetrate the wall and emerge from the other side. Nor can we allow the ball just to come close and then to go off in another direction. **Soft constraints** are those that we need only to come close to satisfying. For example, we might want two particles to be separated approximately by a specified distance, as in a particle mesh.

11.5.1 Collisions

Although, in general, hard constraints can be difficult to impose, there are a few situations that can be dealt with directly for ideal point particles. Consider the problem of collisions. We can separate the problem into two parts: detection and reaction. Suppose that we have a collection of particles and other geometric objects and the particles repel one another. Thus, we need to consider only collisions between each particle and the other objects. If there are n particles and m polygons that define the geometric objects, at each time step we can check whether any particle has gone through any of the polygons.

Suppose that one of the particles has penetrated a polygon, as shown in Figure 11.6. We can detect this collision by inserting the position of the particle into the equation of the plane of the polygon. If the time step of our differential

Figure 11.6 Particle penetrating a polygon.

equation solver is small, we can assume that the velocity between time steps is constant, and we can use linear interpolation to find the time at which the particle actually hit the polygon.

What happens to the particle after a collision is similar to what happens when light reflects from a surface. If there is an **inelastic collision**, the particle loses none of its energy, so its speed is unchanged. However, its direction after the collision is in the direction of a perfect reflection. Thus, given the normal at the point of collision P_c and the previous position of the particle P_0, we can compute the direction of a perfect reflection, as we did in Chapter 6, using the vector from the particle to the surface and the normal at the surface, as shown in Figure 11.7:

$$\mathbf{r} = 2(\mathbf{p}_0 - \mathbf{p}_c) \cdot \mathbf{n} \ \mathbf{n} - (\mathbf{P}_0 - \mathbf{P}_c).$$

The particle will be a distance along this reflector equal to the distance it would have penetrated the polygon in the absence of collision detection, as shown in Figure 11.8.

Figure 11.7 Particle reflection.

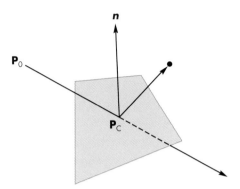

Figure 11.8 Position after collision.

The velocity is changed to be along the direction of reflection, with the same magnitude. Equivalently, the tangential component of the velocity—the part in the plane of the polygon—is unchanged, whereas the direction of the normal component is reversed.

A slightly more complex calculation is required for an **elastic collision** in which the particle loses some of its energy when it collides with another object. The **coefficient of restitution** of a particle is the fraction of the normal velocity retained after the collision. Thus, the angle of reflection is computed as for the inelastic collision, and the normal component of the velocity is reduced by the coefficient of restitution.

The major cost of dealing with collisions is the complexity of detection. In applications such as games, approximate detection often is sufficient. In this case, we can replace complex objects consisting of many polygons by simple objects, such as their bounding rectangles or parallelepipeds, for which collision detection is simpler.

Note that use of particles avoids the complex calculations necessary for objects with finite sizes. In many ways, solving the collision problem is similar to clipping arbitrary objects against each other; the calculation is conceptually simple, but is practically time-consuming and messy. In addition, if we have objects with finite size, we have to consider inertial forces, thus increasing the dimension of the system of equations that we must solve. Consequently, in computer graphics, we are usually willing to accept an approximate solution using ideal point particles, and we obtain an acceptable rendering by placing objects at the location of the particle.

There is another case of hard constraints that arises often and can be handled correctly: contact forces. Suppose that we have a particle that is subject to a force pushing it along a surface, as shown in Figure 11.9. The particle cannot penetrate the surface, and it cannot bounce from the surface because of the force being applied to it. We can argue that the particle is subject to the tangential component

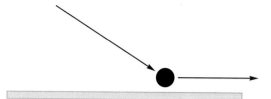

Figure 11.9 Contact force.

of the applied force—that is, the part of the applied force along the surface. We can also apply frictional terms in this direction.

Note that collision detection, as opposed to how we deal with a collision once it has been detected, is often another $O(n^2)$ calculation. Consider, for example, a game, such as pool, in which balls are moving around a table or a simulation of molecules moving within a bounded volume. As any pair of particles can collide, a brute force approach would be to check all pairs of particles at each time step. Faster approaches involve bounding-box methods and hardware support for collision detection.

11.5.2 Particles Inside a Sphere

Before we consider soft constraints, we examine one simple example of hard constraints. We start with a group of particles inside a sphere of radius r centered at the origin. Suppose that these particles are mutually repelling with a force inversely proportional to their distance apart. Particles that collide with the surface of the sphere undergo elastic collisions. Let $\mathbf{p}_i(t)$ and $\mathbf{v}_i(t)$ be the position and velocity of particle i at time t. The distance d_{ij} between particle i and particle j is

$$d_{ij} = \sqrt{(\mathbf{p}_i - \mathbf{p}_j) \cdot (\mathbf{p}_i - \mathbf{p}_j)},$$

and the force on particle i from particle j is along the line between the two particles:

$$\mathbf{f}_{ij} = -k_f \frac{1}{d_{ij}^2} \frac{\mathbf{p}_i - \mathbf{p}_j}{|\mathbf{p}_i - \mathbf{p}_j|} = -k_f \frac{1}{d_{ij}^3} (\mathbf{p}_i - \mathbf{p}_j),$$

where the constant k_f determines the strength of the repelling force. As long as we start with the particles in different positions initially and take small steps in time, and as long as the particles remain inside the sphere, we should have no trouble approximating the solution of the differential equations.

At each time step, we compute a new position and check whether any particle lies outside the sphere. Suppose we have a particle whose position at time t is $\mathbf{p}$ and whose calculated position at time $t + h$ is $\mathbf{q}$. We can denote the corresponding velocities as $\mathbf{v}$ and $\mathbf{u}$. If $\mathbf{q}$ lies inside the sphere, we can accept $\mathbf{q}$ as the next position. If it lies outside the sphere, we proceed as follows. First, we assume that the particle would, if there were no collision, follow a straight line between $\mathbf{p}$ and $\mathbf{q}$. The particle would intersect the sphere at a point $\mathbf{a}$, as shown in Figure 11.10, where

$$\mathbf{a} = (1 - \alpha)\mathbf{p} + \alpha\mathbf{q}.$$

We compute α by finding the distance between $\mathbf{p}$ and the intersection point on the sphere. We want the value of α for which

$$|\mathbf{a}| = r.$$

Figure 11.10 Particle intersecting a sphere.

That yields a simple quadratic equation for α. Once we have this α, the point

$$\mathbf{a} = \mathbf{p} + \alpha(\mathbf{p} - \mathbf{q})$$

is on the sphere, and we can use this point as the point of reflection for the particle. For the sphere, the normal at this point is

$$\mathbf{n} = -\frac{\mathbf{a}}{r}.$$

The direction of reflection (Figure 11.11) is

$$\mathbf{r} = -(\mathbf{p} - \mathbf{a}) + 2\mathbf{n} \cdot (\mathbf{p} - \mathbf{a})\mathbf{n}.$$

Thus, at time $t + h$, the particle will be at $\mathbf{a} + \alpha\mathbf{r}$. We must also change the velocity $\mathbf{v}_q$, because the particle has been redirected by bouncing from the sphere. The component of the velocity along the direction from $\mathbf{p}$ to $\mathbf{q}$ is $(\mathbf{p} - \mathbf{q}) \cdot (\mathbf{v_p} - \mathbf{v_q})$. We can redirect this component along $\mathbf{r}$ and leave the other components of the velocity unchanged. You are asked to create other extensions in the exercises at the end of the chapter.

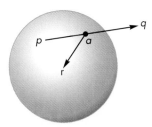

Figure 11.11 Reflections from sphere.

11.5.3 Soft Constraints

Most hard constraints are difficult to enforce. For example, if we want to ensure that a particle's velocity is less than a maximum velocity or that all the particles have a constant amount of energy, then the resulting mathematics is far more difficult than what we have already seen, and such constraints do not always lead to a simple set of ordinary differential equations.

In many situations, we can work with soft constraints: constraints that we need to come only close to satisfying. For example, if we want a particle, whose location is $\mathbf{p}$, to remain near the position $\mathbf{p}_0$, we can consider the **penalty function** $|\mathbf{p} - \mathbf{p}_0|^2$. The smaller this function is, the closer we are to obeying the constraint. This function is one example of an **energy function** whose value represents the amount of some type of energy stored in the system. In physics, such functions can represent quantities, such as the potential or kinetic energy in the system. Physical laws can be written either as differential equations, like those we used for our particles, or in terms of the minimization of expressions involving energy terms. One advantage of the latter form is that we can express constraints or desired behavior of a system directly in terms of potential or energy functions. Conversion of these expressions to force laws is a mechanical process, but its mathematical details are beyond the scope of this book.

Color Plate 27 shows the use of a particle system for scientific visualization. In this example, particles were injected into a three-dimensional data set, and each particle sought to find a surface of constant value—an isosurface. Constraints made the particles seek the desired surfaces, whereas repulsive forces kept the particles separated once they found a surface. The same data can be visualized by other techniques that we introduce in Chapter 12.

11.6 Language-Based Models

Graphs, such as trees and DAGs that we introduced in Chapter 9, offer but one way of representing hierarchical relationships among obejcts. In this section, we look at language-based models for representing relationships. Not only do these methods provide an alternative way of showing relationships, but also they lead to procedural methods for defining objects.

Until now, we have defined geometrical objects in a fixed way: We process a model and generate all the primitives regardless of whether or not they will be visible and, if they are visible, of whether they will make a significant contribution to the scene. Instead, we can define objects by the procedures or algorithms that generate the primitives, rather than by the primitives themselves. We can thus avoid generating the realization of the object—the geometric primitives—until the rendering stage, when we determine which primitives are necessary. These procedural models have the additional advantage that they can be used in conjunction with random-number generators, so that each execution of the procedure generates a different geometric object; each object is similar to the others, but differs in detail. Such methods are particularly useful for generating images of real-world objects such as plants and terrain.

If we look at natural objects, such as plants, we see that, although no two trees are identical, we may have no difficulty telling the difference between two species of trees. Various methods have been proposed that give different realizations each time the program is run, but that have clear rules for defining the structure. We look at the use of tree data structures for generating objects that look like plants.

In computer science, tree data structures are used for describing the parsing of sentences into constituent parts, in both computer and natural languages. For computer programs, doing this parsing is part of compiling the statements in a computer program. For natural languages, we parse sentences to determine whether they are grammatically correct. The tree that results from the parsing of a correct sentence gives the structure or syntax of that sentence. The interpretation of the individual elements in the tree—the words—give the meaning or semantics of the sentence.

If we look at only the syntax of a language, there is a direct correlation between the rules of the language and the form of the trees that represent the sentences.

Figure 11.12 The Koch curve rule.

We can extend this idea to hierarchical objects in graphics, relating a set of rules and a tree-structured model. These systems are known as **tree grammars**. A grammar can be defined by a set of symbols and a set of symbol-replacement rules, or **productions**, that specify how to replace a symbol by one or more symbols. Typical rules are written as

$A \rightarrow BC$,

$B \rightarrow ABA$.

Given a set of productions, we can generate an infinite number of strings. In general, there is more than one rule that we can apply to a given symbol at any time, and, if we select randomly which rule to apply, we can generate a different string each time the program is executed. Programs can be written that not only generate such strings, but also take strings as input and test whether the strings are valid members of the set of strings generated by a given set of rules. Thus, we might have a set of rules for generating a certain type of object, such as a tree or a bush, and a separate program that can identify objects in a scene based on which grammar generates the shape.

The interpretation of the symbols in a string converts the string to a graphical object. There are numerous ways to generate rules and to interpret the resulting strings as graphical objects. One approach starts with the **turtle graphics** (Exercise 2.4) system. In turtle graphics, we have three basic ways of manipulating a graphics cursor, or **turtle**. The turtle can move forward 1 unit, turn right, or turn left. Suppose that the angle by which the turtle can turn is fixed. We can then denote our three operations as F, R, and L. Any string of these operations has a simple graphical interpretation. For example, if the angle is 120 degrees, the string $FRFRFR$ generates an equilateral triangle. We use the special symbols [and] to denote pushing and popping the state of the turtle (its position and orientation) onto a stack (an operation equivalent to using parentheses). Consider the production rule

$F \rightarrow FLFRRFLF$,

with an angle of 60 degrees. The graphical interpretation of this rule is shown in Figure 11.12. If we apply the rule again, in parallel to all instances of F, we get the curve in Figure 11.13(a); if we apply it to a triangle, we get the closed curve in Figure 11.13(b). These curves are known as the **Koch curve** and **Koch snowflake**, respectively. If we scale the geometric interpretation of the curve each time that we execute the algorithm, so as to leave the original vertices in their original locations, we find we are generating a longer curve at each iteration, but

(a)

(b)

Figure 11.13 (a) Koch curve. (b) Koch snowflake.

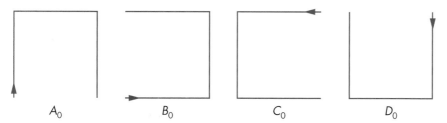

Figure 11.14 The zero-order Hilbert patterns.

this curve always fits inside the same box. In the limit, we have a curve that has infinite length, never crosses itself, but fits in a finite box. It also is continuous but has a discontinuous derivative everywhere.

Another classic example is the **Hilbert curve.** Hilbert curves are formed from 4 simple primitives we can call A_0, B_0, C_0, and D_0, shown in Figure 11.14. Each is a zero-order Hilbert curve. The arrows are there to indicate that we start drawing each in one corner. There are four Hilbert curves of each order N that we can call A_N, B_N, C_N, and D_N. We form each from the order $N-1$ curves by combining the four types according to the following rules:

$$A_N = B_{N-1} \uparrow A_{N-1} \rightarrow A_{N-1} \downarrow C_{N-1}$$
$$B_N = A_{N-1} \rightarrow B_{N-1} \uparrow B_{N-1} \leftarrow D_{N-1}$$
$$C_N = D_{N-1} \leftarrow C_{N-1} \downarrow C_{N-1} \rightarrow A_{N-1}$$
$$D_N = C_{N-1} \downarrow D_{N-1} \leftarrow D_{N-1} \uparrow B_{N-1}$$

The interpretation of theses rules is that the Nth pattern is formed by combining four patterns of order $N-1$ in specified directions. We can see from Figure 11.15, for the first order curve A_1, that **links** corresponding to the arrows in the formulas must be added to connect the patterns. Note also that each pattern starts in a different corner. When the curves are drawn, the arrows are left out, and we obtain curves such as in Figure 11.16.

If we scale the lengths of links as we go to higher order curves, we can verify that, like the Koch curves, the Hilbert curves get longer and longer, never crossing themselves, but always fit in the same box. In the limit the Hilbert curves fill every point in the box and are known as **space-filling curves.**

The push and pop operators allow us to develop side branches. Consider the rule

$$F \rightarrow F[RF]F[LF]F,$$

where the angle is 27 degrees (Figure 11.17). Note that we start at the bottom, and the angle is measured as a deviation from pointing forward.

If we start with a single line segment, the resulting object is that shown in Figure 11.17. We can proceed in a number of ways. One method is to apply the

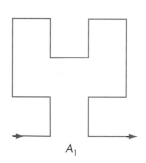

A_1

Figure 11.15 Hilbert rule for type A.

Figure 11.16 Second-order Hilbert curve.

Figure 11.17 The rule $F \rightarrow F[RF]F[LF]F$.

Figure 11.18 Second iteration of the rule in Figure 11.17.

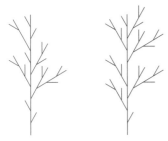

Figure 11.19 Results of random application of the rule from Figure 11.17.

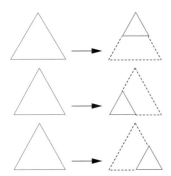

Figure 11.20 Three rules for the Sierpinski gasket.

rule again to each F in the sequence, resulting in the object in Figure 11.18. We can also adjust the length corresponding to a forward movement of the turtle so that branches get smaller on successive iterations. The object resembles a bush and will look more like a bush if we iterate a few more times. However, having only one rule and applying it in parallel results in every bush looking the same.

A more interesting strategy is to apply the rule *randomly* to occurrences of F. If we do so, our single rule can generate both of the objects in Figure 11.19. Adding a few more productions and controlling the probability function that determines which rule is to be applied next allows the user to generate a variety of types of trees. With only slight modifications, we can also draw leaves at the ends of the branches.

One of the attractions of this strategy is that we have defined a class of objects based on only a handful of rules and a few parameters. Suppose that we wish to create a group of trees. The direct approach is to generate as many objects as needed, representing each one as a collection of geometric objects (lines, polygons, curves). In a complex scene, we might then be overwhelmed with the number of primitives generated. Depending on the viewing conditions, most of these primitives might not appear in the image, because they would be clipped out or would be too far from the viewer to be rendered at a visible size. In contrast, using our procedural method, we describe objects by simple algorithms and generate the geometric objects only when we need them and to only the level of detail that we need.

We can also describe a grammar directly in terms of shapes and affine transformations, creating a **shape grammar**. Consider our old friend the Sierpinski gasket. We can define a subdivision step in terms of three affine transformations, each of which scales the original triangle to one-half the size and places the small copy in a different position, as shown in Figure 11.20. We can apply these rules randomly, or we can apply all three in parallel. In either case, in the limit, we derive the gasket.

We now have three related procedural methods that can generate either models of natural objects or models of interesting mathematical objects. The examples of the Koch curve and the Sierpinski gasket introduce a new aspect to the generation process—a method that can be applied recursively and that, each time it is executed, generates detail similar in shape to the original object. Such phenomena can be explored through fractal geometry.

11.7 Recursive Methods and Fractals

The language-based procedural models offer but one approach to generating complex objects with simple programs. Another approach, based on **fractal geometry**, uses the self-similarity of many real-world objects. Fractal geometry was developed by Mandelbrot, who was able to create a branch of mathematics that enables us to work with interesting phenomena with which we cannot deal using the tools of ordinary geometry. Workers in computer graphics have used the ideas of fractal geometry not only to create beautiful and complex objects, but also to model many real-world entities that are not modeled easily by other methods. Graphical objects generated by fractals have been called **graftals.**

11.7.1 Rulers and Length

There are two pillars to fractal geometry: the dependence of geometry on the scale, and self-similarity. We can examine both through the exploration of one of the questions that led to fractal geometry: What is the length of a coastline? Say that we have a map of a coastline. Because the coastline is wavy and irregular, we can take a string, lay it over the image of the coastline, and then measure the length of the string, using the scale of the map to convert distances. However, if we get a second map that shows a closer view of the coastline, we see more detail. The added detail looks much like the view of the first map, but with additional inlets and protrusions visible. If we take our string and measure the length on the second map, taking into account the difference in scale between the two maps, we will measure a greater distance. We can continue this experiment by going to the coast and trying to measure with even greater precision. We find new detail, perhaps even to the level of measuring individual pebbles along the shore. In principle, we could continue this process down to the molecular level, each time seeing a similar picture with more detail and measuring a greater length.

If we want to get any useful information, or at least a measurement on which two people might agree, we must either limit the resolution of the map or, equivalently, pick the minimum unit that we can measure. In computer graphics, if we use perspective views, we have a similar problem, because what detail we see depends on how far we are from the object.

We can approach these problems mathematically by considering our recursion for the Koch snowflake in Section 11.6. Here, each line segment of length 1 was replaced by four line segments of length $1/3$ (Figure 11.21). Hence, each time that we replace a segment, we span the distance between the same two endpoints with a curve four-thirds the length of the original. If we consider the limit as we iterate an infinite number of times, the issue of dimension arises. The curve cannot be an ordinary one-dimensional curve because, in the limit, it has infinite length and its first derivative is discontinuous everywhere. It is not a two-dimensional object, however, because it does not fill a two-dimensional region of the plane. We can resolve this problem by defining a fractional dimension.

figure 11.21 Lengthening of the Koch curve.

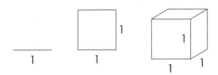

Figure 11.22 Line segment, square, and cube.

11.7.2 Fractal Dimension

Consider a line segment of length 1, a unit square, and a unit cube, as shown in Figure 11.22. Under any reasonable definition of *dimension*, the line segment, square, and cube are one-, two-, and three-dimensional objects, respectively. Suppose that we have a ruler, whose resolution is h, where $h = \frac{1}{n}$ is the smallest unit that we can measure. We assume that n is an integer. We can divide each of these objects into similar units in terms of h, as shown in Figure 11.23. We divide the line segment into $k = n$ identical segments, the square into $k = n^2$ small squares, and the cube into $k = n^3$ small cubes. In each case, we can say that we have created new objects by scaling the original object by a factor of h and replicating it k times. Suppose that d is the dimension of any one of these objects. What has remained constant in the subdivision is that the whole is the sum of the parts. Mathematically, for any of the objects, we have the equality

$$\frac{k}{n^d} = kn^{-d} = 1.$$

Solving for d, we can define the **fractal dimension** as

$$d = \frac{\ln k}{\ln n}.$$

In other words, the fractal dimension of an object is determined by how many similar objects we create by subdivision. Consider the Koch curve. We create four similar objects by the subdivision (scaling) of the original by a factor of 3. The corresponding fractal dimension is

$$d = \frac{\ln 4}{\ln 3} = 1.26186.$$

Figure 11.23 Subdivision of the objects for $h = \frac{1}{3}$.

Now consider the Sierpinski gasket. A scaling step is shown in Figure 11.24. Each time that we subdivide a side by a factor of 2, we keep three of the four triangles created, and

$$d = \frac{\ln 3}{\ln 2} = 1.58496.$$

Figure 11.24
Subdivision of the Sierpinski gasket.

In both examples, we can view the object created by the subdivision as occupying more space than a curve, but less space than a filled area. We can create a solid version of the gasket in a three-dimensional space by starting with a tetrahedron and subdividing each of the faces, as shown in Figure 11.25. We keep the four tetrahedrons at the original vertices, discarding the region in the middle. The object that we create has a fractal dimension of

$$d = \frac{\ln 4}{\ln 2} = 2,$$

Figure 11.25 Solid gasket.

even though it does not lie in the plane. Also note that although the volume is reduced by each subdivision, the surface area is increased. Suppose that we start with a cube and divide it into thirds, as shown in Figure 11.26. Next, we remove the center by pushing out the pieces in the middle of each face and the center, thus leaving 20 of the original 27 subcubes. This object has a fractal dimension of

$$d = \frac{\ln 20}{\ln 3} = 2.72683.$$

Although these constructions are interesting and are easy to generate graphically at any level of recursion, they are by themselves not useful for modeling the world. However, if we add randomness, we get a powerful modeling technique.

Figure 11.26 Subdivision of a cube.

11.7.3 Midpoint Division and Brownian Motion

A fractal curve has dimension $1 \le d < 2$. Curves with lower fractal dimension appear smoother than curves with higher fractal dimension. A similar statement holds for surfaces that have fractal dimension $2 \le d < 3$. In computer graphics, there are many situations where we would like to create a curve or surface that appears random, but that has a measurable amount of roughness. For example, the silhouette of a mountain range forms a curve that is rougher (has higher fractal dimension) than the skyline of the desert. Likewise, a surface model of mountain terrain should have a higher fractal dimension than the surface of farmland. We also often want to generate these objects in a resolution-dependent manner. For example, the detail that we generate for a terrain used in speed-critical application, such as in a flight simulator, should be generated at high resolution for only those areas near the aircraft.

The random movement of particles in fluids is known as **Brownian motion**. Simulating such motion provides an interesting approach to generating natural curves and surfaces. Physicists have modeled Brownian motion by forming

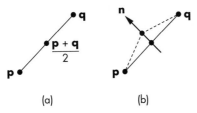

Figure 11.27 Midpoint displacement. (a) Original line segment. (b) Line segment after subdivision.

polylines in which each successive point on the polyline is displaced by a random distance and in a random direction from its predecessor. True Brownian motion is based on a particular random-number distribution that generates paths that match actual particle paths. In computer graphics, we are more concerned with rapid computation and with the ability to generate curves with a controllable amount of roughness; thus, we use the term *Brownian motion* in this broader sense.

Although we could attempt to generate Brownian motion through the direct generation of a polyline, a more efficient method is to use a simple recursive process. Consider the line segment in Figure 11.27(a). We find its midpoint; then, we displace the midpoint in the normal direction, by a random distance, as in Figure 11.27(b). We can repeat this process any number of times to produce curves like those in Figure 11.28. The variance of the random-number generator, or the average displacement, should be scaled by a factor, usually of $\frac{1}{2}$, each time, because the line segments are shortened at each stage. We can also allow the midpoint to be displaced in a random direction, rather than only along the normal. If the random numbers are always positive, we can create skylines. If we use a zero-mean Gaussian random-number generator, with variance proportional to $l^{2(2-d)}$, where l is the length of the segment to be subdivided, then d is the

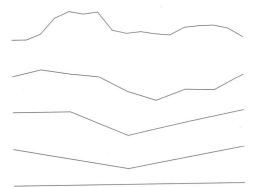

Figure 11.28 Fractal curves with 1, 2, 4, 8, and 16 segments.

Figure 11.29 Midpoint subdivision of a tetrahedron facet.

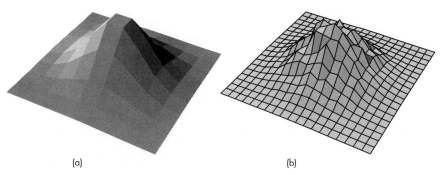

(a)   (b)

Figure 11.30 Fractal terrain. (a) Mesh. (b) Subdivided mesh with displaced vertices.

fractal dimension of the resulting curve. The value $d = 1.5$ corresponds to true Brownian motion.

11.7.4 Fractal Mountains

The best-known uses of fractals in computer graphics have been to generate mountains and terrain. We can generate a mountain with our tetrahedron-subdivision process, by adding in a midpoint displacement. Consider one facet of the tetrahedron, as shown in Figure 11.29. First, we find the midpoints of the sides; then, we displace each midpoint,[2] creating four new triangles. Once more, by controlling the variance of the random-number generator, we can control the roughness of the resulting object. Note that we must take great care in how the random numbers are generated if we are to create objects that are topologically correct and do not fold into themselves; see the suggested readings at the end of this chapter.

This algorithm can be applied equally well to any mesh. We can start with a flat mesh of rectangles in the x, z plane and subdivide each rectangle into four smaller rectangles, displacing all vertices upward (in the y direction). Figure 11.30 shows one example of this process.

---

2. We can also displace the original vertices.

11.8 The Mandelbrot Set

No discussion of fractals, no matter how elementary, would be complete without an introduction to the Mandelbrot set. The Mandelbrot set is easy to generate but shows infinite complexity in the patterns it generates. It also provides a good example of generating images and using color lookup tables. In this discussion, we assume that you have a basic familiarity with complex arithmetic.

We denote a point in the complex plane as

$$\mathbf{z} = x + \mathbf{i}y,$$

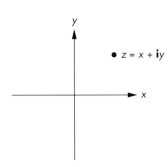

where x is the real part and y is the imaginary part of $\mathbf{z}$ (Figure 11.31). If $\mathbf{z}_1 = x_1 + \mathbf{i}y_1$ and $\mathbf{z}_2 = x_2 + \mathbf{i}y_2$ are two complex numbers, complex addition and multiplication are defined by

$$\mathbf{z}_1 + \mathbf{z}_2 = x_1 + x_1 + \mathbf{i}(y_1 + y_2),$$
$$\mathbf{z}_1\mathbf{z}_2 = x_1x_2 - y_1y_2 + \mathbf{i}(x_1y_2 + x_2y_1).$$

The pure imaginary number $\mathbf{i}$ has the property that $\mathbf{i}^2 = -1$. A complex number $\mathbf{z}$ has magnitude given by

$$|\mathbf{z}|^2 = x^2 + y^2.$$

In the complex plane, a function

$$\mathbf{w} = F(\mathbf{z})$$

maps complex points into complex points. We can use such a function to define a complex recurrence of the form

$$\mathbf{z}_{k+1} = F(\mathbf{z}_k),$$

Figure 11.31   Complex plane.

where $\mathbf{z}_0 = \mathbf{c}$ is a given initial point. If we plot the locations of $\mathbf{z}_k$ for particular starting points, we can see several of the possibilities in Figure 11.32. For a particular function F, some initial values generate sequences that go off to infinity. Others may repeat periodically, and still other sequences converge to points called **attractors**. For example, consider the function

$$\mathbf{z}_{k+1} = \mathbf{z}_k^2,$$

where $\mathbf{z}_0 = \mathbf{c}$. If $\mathbf{c}$ lies outside a unit circle, the sequence $\{\mathbf{z}_k\}$ diverges; if $\mathbf{c}$ is inside the unit circle, $\{\mathbf{z}_k\}$ converges to an attractor at the origin; if $|\mathbf{c}| = 1$, each $\mathbf{z}_k$ is on the unit circle. If we consider the points for which $|\mathbf{c}| = 1$, we can see that, depending on the value of $\mathbf{c}$, we can generate either a finite number of points or all the points on the unit circle.

A more interesting example is the function

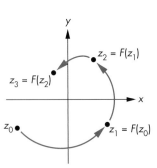

Figure 11.32   Paths from complex recurrence.

$$\mathbf{z}_{k+1} = \mathbf{z}_k^2 + \mathbf{c},$$

with $z_0 = 0 + i0$. The point c is in the **Mandelbrot set** if and only if the points generated by this recurrence remain finite. Thus, we can break the complex plane into two groups of points: those that belong to the Mandelbrot set and those that do not. Graphically, we can take a rectangular region of the plane and color points black if they are in the set and white if they are not (Figure 11.33a). However, it is the regions on the edges of the set that show the most complexity, so we often want to magnify these regions.

The computation of the Mandelbrot set can be time-consuming; there are a few tricks to speed it up. The area centered at $c = -0.5 + i0.0$ is of the most interest, although we probably want to be able to change both the size and the center of our window.

We can usually tell after a few iterations whether a point will go off to infinity. For example, if $|z_k| > 4$, successive values will be larger, and we can stop the iteration. It is more difficult to tell whether a point near the boundary will converge. Consequently, an approximation to the set is usually generated as follows. We fix a maximum number of iterations. If, for a given c, we can determine that the point diverges, we color white the point corresponding to c in our image. If, after the maximum number of iterations, $|z_k|$ is less than some threshold, we decide that it is in the set, and we color it black. For other values of $|z_k|$, we assign a unique color to the point corresponding to c. These colors are usually based on the value of $|z_k|$ after the last iteration.

Appendix A contains a program that generates an approximation to the set. The user can set the size and center of the rectangle, and the number of iterations to be carried out. The magnitudes of the numbers z_k are scaled to be in the range of 0 to 255. We generate an $n \times m$ 1-byte array image by looping over all pixels up to the maximum number of iterations. The display consists of two parts. First,

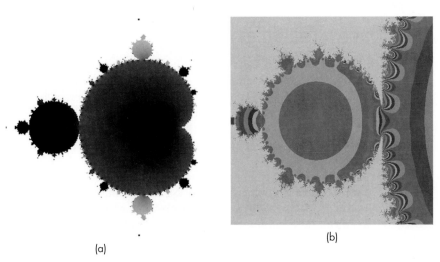

(a)

(b)

Figure 11.33   Mandelbrot set. (a) Black and white coloring. (b) Detail along edges.

we define a color map in the initialization. The map shown uses a floating-point representation of the luminance values over the interval (0.0, 1.0). We define an intensity-to-red map that assigns no red to black (0.0), assigns full red to white (1.0), and linearly interpolates between these values for the other intensities. For blue, we go from full blue for zero intensity to no blue for full intensity. We assign the intensity-to-green values randomly. This green assignment enhances the detail in regions where there are slow changes in intensity (Figure 11.30b). The code is

```
for(i=0;i<256;i++)
{
    redmap[i]=i/255.;
    greenmap[i]=rand()%RAND_MAX; /* a random number between 0.0 and 1.0 */
    bluemap[i]=1.0-i/255.;
}

glPixelMapfv(GL_PIXEL_MAP_I_TO_R, 256, redmap);
glPixelMapfv(GL_PIXEL_MAP_I_TO_G, 256, greenmap);
glPixelMapfv(GL_PIXEL_MAP_I_TO_B, 256, bluemap);
```

You should be able to implement other color maps with no difficulty. The display function requires only clearing of the screen and sending of the pixels to the frame buffer:

```
void display()
{
    glClear(GL_COLOR_BUFFER_BIT);
    glDrawPixels(n,m,GL_COLOR_INDEX, GL_UNSIGNED_BYTE, image);
}
```

11.9 Summary and Notes

We have introduced two more approaches to modeling: systems of particles and language-based methods. Recursion has appeared again; here we use it to generate procedural models that can generate primitives at different levels of detail. A unifying theme is that we can and should work with the basic tools of computer science: data structures, algorithms, graphs, recursion, languages. By interpreting the symbols as graphical objects, we create a toolkit of powerful modeling techniques.

Procedural methods have advantages in that we can control how many primitives we produce and at which point in the process these primitives are generated. Equally important is that procedural graphics provides an object-oriented approach to building models—an approach that should be of increasing importance in the future.

Combining physics with computer graphics provides a set of techniques that has the promise of generating physically correct animations and of providing new modeling techniques. Particle systems are but one example of physically based modeling, but they represent a technique that has wide applicability. One of the most interesting and informative exercises that you can undertake at this point is to build a particle system.

Particle methods are used routinely in commercial animations, both for simulation of physical phenomena, such as fire, clouds, and moving water, and in determining the positions of animated characters.

In this chapter we have introduced the techniques. In Chapter 12, we apply these techniques to data visualization. Several suggested readings include more systematic developments of these areas.

11.10 Suggested Readings

Particle systems were introduced in computer graphics by Reeves [Ree83]. Since then, they have been used for a variety of phenomena, including flocking of birds [Rey87], fluid flow, modeling of grass, and display of surfaces [Wit94a]. Our approach follows Witkin [Wit94b].

There is a wealth of literature on fractals and related methods. The paper by Fournier [Fou82] was the first to show the fractal mountain. For a deeper treatment of fractal mathematics, see the books by Mandelbrot [Man82] and Peitgen [Pei88]. The use of graph grammars has appeared in a number of forms [Pru90, Smi84, Lin68]. Both Hill [Hil90] and Prusinkiewicz [Pru90] present interesting space-filling curves and surfaces. Barnsley's iterated-function systems [Bar93] provide another approach to use of self-similarity; they have application in such areas as image compression.

Exercises

11.1   Find a set of productions to generate the Sierpinski gasket by starting with a single equilateral triangle.

11.2   How could you determine the fractal dimension of a coastline? How would you verify that the shape of a coastline is indeed a fractal?

11.3   Start with the tetrahedron-subdivision program that we used in Chapter 6 to approximate a sphere. Convert this program into one that will generate a fractal mountain.

11.4   We can write a description of a binary tree, such as we might use for search, as a list of nodes with pointers to its children. Write an OpenGL program that will take such a description and display the tree graphically.

11.5   Write a program for a simple particle systems of masses and springs. Render the particle system as a mesh of quadrilaterals. Include a form of interaction that allows a user to put particles in their initial positions.

11.6   Extend Exercise 11.5 by adding external forces to the particle system. Create an image of a flag blowing in the wind.

11.7   Write a program to fractalize a mesh. Try to use real elevation data for the initial positions of the mesh.

11.8   Write a program that, given two polygons with the same number of vertices, will generate a sequence of images that converts one polygon into the other.

11.9   Write a particle system that simulates the sparks that are generated by welding or by fireworks.

11.10   Extend Exercise 11.9 to simulate the explosion of a polyhedron.

11.11   Combine alpha blending (Chapter 7), sphere generation (Chapter 6), and fractals to create clouds.

11.12   Use fractals to generate the surface of a virtual planet. Your output should show continents and oceans.

11.13   In the Lennard-Jones particle system, particles are attracted to each other by a force proportional to the inverse of the distance between them raised to the 12th power but are repelled by another force proportional to the inverse of the same distance raised to the 24th power. Simulate such a system in a box. To make the simulation easier, you can assume that a particle that leaves the box reenters the box from the opposite side.

11.14   Create a particle system in which the region of interest is subdivided into cubes of the same size. A particle can only interact with particles in its own cube and the cubes adjacent to it.

11.15   In animations, particle systems are used to give the positions of the characters. Once the positions are determined, two-dimensional images of the characters can be texture-mapped onto polygons at these positions. Build such a system for characters moving around subject to both external forces that move them in the desired direction and repulsive forces that keep them from colliding. How can you keep the polygons facing the camera?

Visualization

In this chapter, we apply almost everything we have done so far to the problem of visualizing the large data sets that arise in scientific and medical applications. Fortunately, we can bring many tools to bear on these problems. We can create geometric objects. We can color them, animate them, or change their orientation. We can use our buffers for masking, for hidden-surface removal, or for compositing. With all these possibilities, there are multiple ways to visualize a given data set. We explore some of the possibilities in this chapter.

We concentrate on two problems: scalar field visualization, where we have a single value at each spatial point, and flow visualization, where we have a velocity at each spatial point. We shall concentrate on regular data sets so that we can introduce the basic techniques without introducing a great deal of complexity.

12.1 Data + Geometry

Data comprise numbers. They are not geometric objects and thus they cannot be displayed directly by our graphics systems. Only when we combine data with geometry are we able to create a display and to visualize the underlying information. Consider the familiar two-dimensional displays of numerical data, such as graphs and bar charts; we must convert the numbers that we are given to geometry through polylines, rectangles, markers, and other graphical objects. In scientific applications, we obtain data from a variety of sources including mathematical models, simulations, the solution of ordinary and partial differential equations, and measurements. A simple definition of (**scientific**) **visualization** is *the merging of data with the display of geometric objects through computer graphics.*

For the most part, we consider volumetric problems in which we start either with a volume of data obtained at a single time or with multiple volumes that correspond to data obtained at multiple times. Cases where we have only data over a two-dimensional surface often are special cases of our volumetric methods. We consider three types of problems: **scalar visualization**, where we are given a three-dimensional volume of scalars, such as X-ray densities in a medical application; **vector visualization**, where we start with a volume of vector data, such as the velocity at each point in a fluid; and **tensor visualization**, where we have a matrix of data at each point, such as the stresses within a mechanical part.

We must confront several difficulties. One is the large size of the data sets. Many of the most interesting applications involve data that are measured over three spatial dimensions and often also in time. For example, medical data such as from magnetic-resonance imaging can be at a resolution of $512 \times 512 \times 200$ points; the visible-woman data set is a volume of densities that consists of $1734 \times 512 \times 512$ data points. Consequently, we cannot assume that any operation on our data, no matter how conceptually simple it appears, can be carried out easily. Second, these data are only data; they are not geometric objects. Thus, we must translate these data to create and manipulate geometric objects. Third, we may have multidimensional data points. For example, when we measure the flow of a fluid at a point, we are measuring the velocity, a three-dimensional quantity. When we measure the stress or strain on a solid body at some internal point, we collect a 3×3 matrix of data. How we convert these data to geometric objects and select the attributes of those objects determines a variety of visualization strategies.

12.2 Height Fields and Contours

One of the most basic and important tasks in visualization is visualizing the structure in a mathematical function. The problem arises in many forms, the most important ones differing in how we are given the function—implicitly, explicitly, or parametrically—and in how many independent variables define the function. In this section, we consider two problems that lead to similar visualization methods. One is the visualization of an explicit function of the form

$$z = f(x, y),$$

with two dependent variables. This form describes one or more surfaces in three dimensions. Such functions are sometimes called **height fields** because often the dependent variable z represents the height of a point above a plane in which a location is specified by x and y.[1] Topographic data are often described in this form, where x and y are the longitude and latitude of a point on the surface of the earth, and z is the height above sea level. The visualization of f yields a picture of the terrain. This form also arises when we have two-dimensional z, x data that change over time. By replacing y with the time variable t, we can display changes in behavior over time as a surface. If we allow x and y to vary over a region such as a rectangle, the function f describes a surface, as shown in Figure 12.1.

The second form is an implicit function in two variables:

$$g(x, y) = c,$$

Figure 12.1 Surface described by a height field.

---

1. Because we usually draw our coordinate axes with the y direction up, it may seem more natural to use the form $y = f(x, z)$. Equivalently, we can rotate the data as we did for the teapot in Chapter 10.

where c is a constant. This equation describes one or more two-dimensional curves in the x, y plane. There may also be no x, y values that satisfy the equation. As we discussed in Chapter 10, although functions in this form may be known analytically, there is no general method for expressing either of the variables in terms of the other. Familiar examples include quadric curves of the form

$$ax^2 + bxy + cy^2 + dx + ey + d = 0,$$

and the plane

$$ax + by + cz + d = 0.$$

A more complex example is the Ovals of Cassini that are the solutions of the equation

$$g(x, y) = (x^2 + y^2 + a^2)^2 - 4a^2x^2 - b^4.$$

Depending on the values of a and b, this equation describes one or two closed curves. The two problems are related because, for a given value of c, the function g describes a curve that corresponds to a constant z in the equation for f, as shown in Figure 12.2. This curve is called the **contour curve**, corresponding to the **contour value** c.

12.2.1 Meshes

The most common method to display a function $f(x, y)$ is to draw a surface. The surfaces that we discussed in Chapter 10 start with a set of control points. If the function f is known only discretely, then we have a set of samples or measurements of experimental data of the form

Figure 12.2 Surface with contours.

$$z_{ij} = f(x_i, y_j).$$

We assume that these data points are equally spaced such that

$$x_i = x_0 + i\Delta x, \quad i = 0, \dots, N,$$
$$y_j = y_0 + j\Delta y, \quad j = 0, \dots, M,$$

where Δx and Δy are the spacing between the samples in the x and y directions, respectively. If f is known analytically, then we can sample it to obtain a set of discrete data with which to work.

One simple way to generate a surface is through either a triangular or a quadrilateral mesh. We can use the four points z_{ij}, $z_{i+1,j}$, $z_{i+1,j+1}$, and $z_{i,j+1}$ to generate either a quadrilateral or two triangles. Thus, the data define a mesh of either NM quadrilaterals or $2NM$ triangles. The corresponding OpenGL programs are simple. Figure 12.3 shows a rectangular mesh from height data for a part of Honolulu, Hawaii.

There are interesting aspects to and modifications we can make to the OpenGL program. First, if we use all the data, the resulting plot may contain many small

Figure 12.3 Mesh plot of Honolulu data.

polygons. The resulting density of lines in the display may be annoying and can contain moiré patterns. Hence, we might prefer to subsample the data either by using every kth point for some k or by averaging groups of data points to obtain a new set of samples with smaller N and M.

Second, the data in Figure 12.3 were drawn both as black lines and as white filled polygons. The lines are necessary to display the mesh. The polygons are necessary so that data in the front hide the data in the back. Although we can use OpenGL's hidden-surface–removal algorithm to display the polygons correctly, because these data are given in a structured order, we do not need to carry out a standard hidden-surface–removal process. If we display the data by first drawing those in back and then proceeding toward the front, the front polygons automatically hide the polygons farther back. In a system in which hidden-surface removal is done in software, not using a software z buffer and displaying the data in this manner may be faster. Data that are structured in such a manner have been called $2\frac{1}{2}$ **dimensional data sets** because, although the data exist in a three-dimensional world, this special organization leads to efficient rendering algorithms. This structure is not sufficient to represent all three-dimensional surfaces.

There is one additional trick that we used in the display of Figure 12.3. If we draw both a polygon and a line loop with the same data, such as in the code

```
glColor3f(1.0, 1.0, 1.0);
glBegin(GL_QUADS)
  glVertex3i(i,z[i][j],j);
  glVertex3i(i+1,z[i+1][j],j);
  glVertex3i(i+1,z[i+1][j+1],j+1);
  glVertex3i(i,z[i][j+1],j+1);
glEnd();
glColor3f(0.0, 0.0, 0.0);
glBegin(GL_LINE_LOOP)
  glVertex3i(i,z[i][j],j);
```

```
  glVertex3i(i+1,z[i+1][j],j);
  glVertex3i(i+1,z[i+1][j+1],j+1);
  glVertex3i(i,z[i][j+1],j+1);
glEnd();
```

then the polygon and line loop are in the same plane. Even though the line loop is rendered after the polygon, numerical inaccuracies in the renderer often cause parts of a line loop to be blocked by the polygon with the same vertices. Although OpenGL lacks a mode to draw a filled polygon with its edges displayed in a different color, we can enable the **polygon offset mode** and set the offset parameters as in

```
glEnable(GL_POLYGON_OFFSET_FILL);
glPolygonOffset(1.0, 0.5);
```

The first parameter determines the offset; the second is an implementation-dependent scale factor. These functions move the lines slightly toward the viewer relative to the polygon, so all the desired lines are now visible.

The basic mesh plot can be extended in many ways. If we display only the polygons, then we can add lighting to create a realistic image of a surface in mapping applications. The required normals can be computed from the vertices of the triangles or quadrilaterals. Another option is to map a texture to the surface. The texture map might be an image of the terrain from a photograph or other information that might be obtained by digitization of a map. If we combine these techniques, we can generate a display in which, by changing the position of the light source, we can make the image depend on the time of day. It is also possible to obtain smoother surfaces by using the samples in larger groups and defining one of the surface types that we introduced in Chapter 10.

12.2.2 Contour Plots

One of the difficulties with mesh plots is that, although they give a visual impression of the data, it is difficult to make measurements from them. In addition, parts of the surface may be obscured from view if they are behind parts of the surface closer to the viewer. An alternative method of displaying the height data is to display contours—curves that correspond to a fixed value of height.

In the early days of computer graphics, before there were raster displays and good three-dimensional software, users generated curves that corresponded to constant values of z for functions of the form $z = f(x, y)$. The set of contours corresponding to a set of values of z can be displayed in a single plane using only two-dimensional techniques, but can still give much information about the three-dimensional function. We can use this method to construct the topographic (topo) maps used by geologists and hikers. The use of contours is still important, both on its own and as part of other visualization techniques.

If the function f is known analytically, we are looking for curves that satisfy

$$f(x, y) = c,$$

for a particular value of c. Often, we display a set of such curves corresponding to a set of values of c. This problem is an implicit function-display problem, where

$$g(x, y) = f(x, y) - c = 0.$$

For example, if

$$f(x, y) = x^2 + y^2,$$

then, if c is positive, each contour is a circle of radius $\sqrt{c}$. If we start with samples of f, then we have a similar problem, but one of approximating where the contour might lie given only the information in the samples—that is, the height at certain points on our grid. In practice, even if we know f analytically, it is usually easier to find approximate contours by first sampling f to obtain a set of values $\{f_{ij}\}$. We solve the problem for sampled data by a technique called **marching squares**, which is a special case of the marching-cubes method that we introduce in Section 12.4.

12.2.3 Marching Squares

Suppose that we have a function $f(x, y)$ that we sample at evenly spaced points on a rectangular array (or lattice) in x and y, thus creating a set of samples $\{f_{ij} = f(x_i, y_j)\}$ for

$$x_i = x_0 + i\Delta x, \quad i = 0, 1, \ldots, N - 1,$$
$$y_j = y_0 + j\Delta y, \quad j = 0, 1, \ldots, M - 1,$$

where Δx and Δy are the spacing between samples in the x and y directions, respectively. Other than simplifying the development, the equal spacing is not necessary. Equivalently, we might have obtained a set of NM samples by making measurements of some physical quantity on a regular grid, or the samples might have come directly from some device such as a digital camera.

Suppose that we would like to find an approximation to the implicit curve

$$z = f(x, y),$$

for a particular value of z that we denote by c, our contour value. For a given value of c, there may be no contour curve, a single contour curve, or multiple contour curves. If we are working with sampled data, then we only can approximate a contour curve. Our strategy for constructing an approximate contour curve is to construct a curve of connected line segments—a **piecewise linear curve**. We start with the rectangular **cell** determined by the four grid points (x_i, y_j), (x_{i+1}, y_j), (x_{i+1}, y_{j+1}), (x_i, y_{j+1}), as shown in Figure 12.4. Our algorithm finds

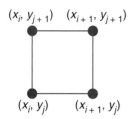

(x_i, y_{j+1}) (x_{i+1}, y_{j+1})

(x_i, y_j) (x_{i+1}, y_j)

Figure 12.4   Rectangular cell.

the line segments on a cell-by-cell basis, using only the values of z at the corners of a cell to determine whether the desired contour passes through the cell.

In general, the sampled values that we have at the corners of the cell are not equal to the contour value. However, the contour curve might still pass through the cell. Consider the simple case where only one of the values at the corners—say, f_{ij}—is greater than c, and the values at the other vertices of the cell are less than c:

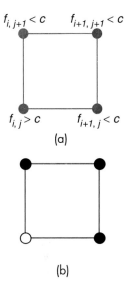

$f_{i,j+1} < c$ $f_{i+1,j+1} < c$

$f_{i,j} > c$ $f_{i+1,j} < c$

(a)

(b)

Figure 12.5 Labeling the vertices of a cube. (a) Thresholding of the vertices. (b) Coloring of the vertices.

$$f_{ij} > c,$$
$$f_{i+1,j} < c,$$
$$f_{i+1,j+1} < c,$$
$$f_{i,j+1} < c.$$

We can show this situation either as in Figure 12.5(a), where we have indicated the values relative to c, or as in Figure 12.5(b), where we have colored black the vertices for which the value is less than c, and have colored white the vertex whose value is greater than c. By looking at this situation, we can see that, if the function f that generated the data is reasonably well behaved, then the contour curve must cross the two edges that have one white vertex and one black vertex. Equivalently, if the function $f(x, y) - c$ is greater than 0 at one vertex and less than 0 at an adjacent vertex, it must be equal to 0 somewhere in between. This situation is shown in Figure 12.6(a).

Figure 12.6(a) shows only one way that the contour might cross the edge. The contour also might cross three times, as shown in Figure 12.6(b), or any odd number of times. Each of these interpretations is consistent with the sampled data. We shall always use the interpretation that a single crossing of an edge by a contour is more likely for smooth functions than are multiple crossings. This choice is an example of the **principle of Occam's razor**, which states that *if there are multiple possible explanations of a phenomenon that are consistent with the data, choose the simplest one*.

Returning to our example cell, if we can estimate where the contour intersects the two edges, then we can join the points of intersection with a line segment. We can even draw this line segment immediately, because the computation for other cells is independent of what we do with this cell. But where do we place the intersections? There are two simple strategies. We could simply place the intersection halfway between the black and the white vertices. However, if a is only slightly greater than c and b is much less than c, then we expect the intersection of the contour with the edge of a cell to be closer to (x_i, y_j) than to (x_{i+1}, y_j). A more sophisticated strategy uses interpolation. Consider two vertices that share an edge of a cell and have values on opposite sides of c—for example,

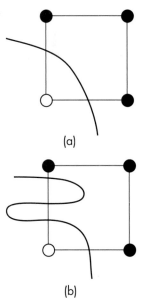

(a)

(b)

Figure 12.6 Contour crossing a cell edge. (a) Once. (b) Multiple times.

$$f(x_i, y_i) = a, \quad a > c,$$
$$f(x_{i+1}, y_j) = b, \quad b < c.$$

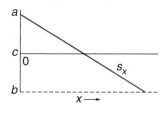

Figure 12.7   Interpolation of the intersection of a cell edge.

If the two vertices are separated by an x spacing Δx, then we can interpolate the point of intersection using a line segment, as shown in Figure 12.7.

This line segment intersects the x-axis at

$$x = x_i + \frac{(a-c)\Delta x}{a-b}.$$

We use this point for one endpoint of our line segment approximation to the contour in this cell, and we do a similar calculation for the intersection on the other edge with a black and a white vertex.

Our discussion thus far has been in terms of a particular cell for which one vertex is colored white and the others are colored black. There are $16\,(=2^4)$ ways that we can color the vertices of a cell using only black and white. All could arise

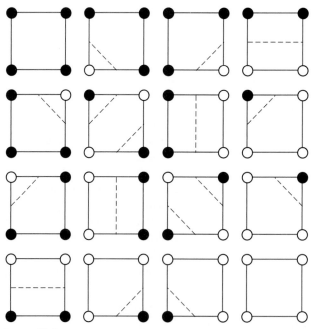

Figure 12.8   Sixteen cases of vertex labelings with contours.

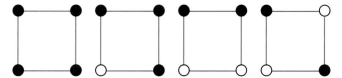

Figure 12.9 Four unique cases of vertex labelings.

in our contour problem. These cases are shown in Figure 12.8, as is a simple way of drawing line segments consistent with the data. If we study these cases, we see that there are two types of symmetry. One is rotational. All cases that can be converted to the same cube by rotation, such as cases 1 and 2, have a single line segment cutting off one of the vertices. There also is symmetry between cases that we can convert to each other by switching all black vertices to white vertices and vice versa, such as cases 0 and 15. Once we take symmetry into account, only four cases are truly unique. These cases are shown in Figure 12.9. Hence, we need code that can draw line segments for only four cases, and we can map all other cases into these four.

The first case is trivial because the simplest interpretation is that the contour does not pass through the cell, and we draw no line segments. The second case is the one that we just discussed; it generates one line segment. The third case is also simple: We can draw a single line segment that goes from one edge to the opposite edge.

The final case is more difficult and more interesting because it contains an ambiguity. We have the two equally simple interpretations shown in Figure 12.10; we must decide which one to use. If we have no other information, we have no reason to prefer one over the other, and we can pick one at random. Alternatively, we could always use only one of the possibilities. But as Figure 12.11 shows, we get different results depending on which interpretation we choose. Another possibility is to subdivide the cell into four smaller cells, as shown in Figure 12.12, generating a new data point in the center. We can obtain the value at this point either from the function, if we know it analytically, or by averaging the values at the corners of the original cell. Hopefully, none of these smaller cells is an ambiguous case. If any is ambiguous, we can further subdivide it.

The code for creating a contour plotter is fairly simple. Suppose that the values at the four vertices are a, b, c, and d. We loop over all cells. If a, b, c, and d are the values at the corner of a cell, then the code to compute which cell type we have is

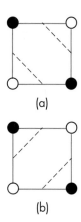

(a)

(b)

Figure 12.10
Ambiguous
interpretation.

```
int cell(double a, double b, double c , double d)
{
/* THRESHOLD = contour value */
    int n=0;
    if(a>THRESHOLD) n+=1;
```

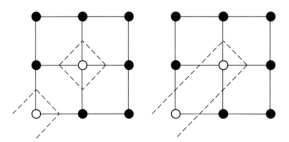

Figure 12.11 Example of different contours with the same labeling.

```
    if(b>THRESHOLD) n+=8;
    if(c>THRESHOLD) n+=4;
    if(d>THRESHOLD) n+=2;
    return n;
}
```

We then can assign the cell to one of the four canonical cases by

```
switch(n)
{
  case 1: case 2: case 4: case 7: case 8:
              case 11: case 13: case 14:
  /* contour cuts off one corner */
  draw_one(num, i,j,a,b,c,d);
  break;
  case 3: case 6: case 9: case 12: /* contour crosses cell */
  draw_adjacent(num,i,j,a,b,c,d);
  break;
  case 5: case 10: /* ambiguous cases */
    draw_opposite(num, i,j,a,b,c,d);
    break;
  case 0: case 15: break; /* no contour in cell */
}
```

Finally, we write the functions that draw the three cases that have line segments in them. For example, the function draw_one deals with the eight cases that draw

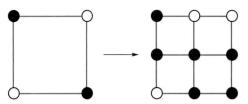

Figure 12.12 Subdivision of a cube.

a line segment from one edge to an adjacent edge of the cell. If the cell has side lengths of s_x and s_y in the *x* and *y* directions, respectively, and the lower-left corner of the cell is at (ox,oy) (Figure 12.13), then the code is, in part,

```
void draw_one(int num, int i, int j, double a, double b,
              double c, double d)
{

/* num = cell type */
/* i, j = coordinates of cell in array */
/* a, b, c, d values at four corners of cell */

/* s_x, s_y = side length of cell */
/* compute the lower left corner of cell here */

  switch(num) /* case type */
  {
   case 1: case 14:
        x1=ox;
        y1=oy+s_y;
        x2=ox+s_x;
        y2=oy;
        break;

/* The other cases go here */
  }
/* draw the line segment */

    glBegin(GL_LINES);
      glVertex2d(x1, y1);
      glVertex2d(x2, y2);
    glEnd();
}
```

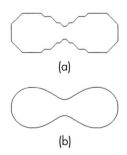

The full code is given in contour.c. Figure 12.14 shows two curves corresponding to a single contour value for the Ovals of Cassini function

$$f(x, y) = (x^2 + y^2 + a^2)^2 - 4a^2x^2 - b^4,$$

with $a = 0.49$ and $b = 0.5$. We constructed the curve on the top always using the midpoint for the point of intersection of the curve with an edge of a cell. We constructed the curve on the bottom using interpolation to obtain the point of intersection. The function was sampled on 50×50 grid. Figure 12.15 shows the Hononlu data-set display with multiple contours at equally spaced contour values.

There are other ways to construct contour curves. One is to start with a cell that is known to have a piece of the contour, and then to follow this contour to adjacent cells as necessary to complete the contour. However, the marching-squares

*(In the margin, top:)*

$(o_x, o_y + s_y)$ $(o_x + s_x, o_y + s_y)$

s_y

s_x

(o_x, o_y) $(o_x + s_x, o_y)$

Figure 12.13 Drawing of the line segment for the adjacent case.

*(In the margin, bottom:)*

(a)

(b)

Figure 12.14 An Oval of Cassini. (a) Using the midpoint. (b) Using interpolation.

Figure 12.15   Contour plot of Honolulu data.

method has the advantage that all cells can be dealt with independently—we march through the data—and the extension to three dimensions for volumetric data is straightforward, as we see in Section 12.4. Several extensions and variations are suggested in the exercises at the end of the chapter.

12.3 Visualizing Surfaces and Scalar Fields

The surface and contour problems of Section 12.2 have three-dimensional extensions. Consider a function f that is defined over some region of three-dimensional space. Thus, at every point within this region, we have a scalar value $f(x, y, z)$ and we say that f defines a **scalar field**. For example, at each point f might be the density inside an object, or the absorption of X rays in the human body as measured by a computed-tomography scan, or the translucency of a slab of glass. Visualization of scalar fields is more difficult than the problems that we have considered thus far for two reasons. First, three-dimensional problems have more data with which we must work. Consequently, operations that are routine for two-dimensional data, such as reading files and performing transformations, present practical difficulties. Second, when we had a problem with two independent variables, we were able to use the third dimension to visualize scalars. When we have three independent variables, we lack the extra dimension to use for display. Nevertheless, if we are careful, we can extend our previously developed methods to visualize three-dimensional scalar fields.

12.3.1 Volumetric Data Sets

Once again, we might have discrete data from a set of measurements or we might obtain data by evaluating (or sampling) the function for a set of points $\{x_i, y_i, z_i\}$, creating a **volumetric data set**.

Assume that our samples are taken at equally spaced points in x, y, and z, as shown in Figure 12.16—a simplifying but not necessary assumption. Thus,

$$x_i = x_0 + i\Delta x,$$
$$y_i = y_0 + j\Delta y,$$
$$z_i = z_0 + k\Delta z,$$

and we can define

$$f_{ijk} = f(x_i, y_j, z_k).$$

Each f_{ijk} can be thought of as the average value of the scalar field within a right parallelepiped of sides Δx, Δy, Δz centered at (x_i, y_j, z_k). We call this parallelepiped a volume element or **voxel**.

The three-dimensional array of voxel values that corresponds to equally spaced samples is called a **structured data set**, because we do not need to store the information about where each sample is located in space. The terms *structured data set* and *set of voxels* often are used synonymously.

Scattered data require us to store this information in addition to the scalar values, and such data sets are called **unstructured**. Visualization of unstructured data sets is more complex but can be done with the same techniques that we use for structured data sets; consequently we shall not pursue this topic.

Even more so than for two-dimensional data, there are multiple ways to display these data sets. However, there are two basic approaches: direct volume rendering and isosurfaces. **Direct volume rendering** makes use of every voxel

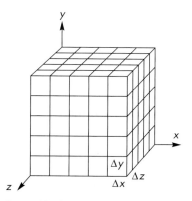

Figure 12.16 A volumetric data set.

in producing an image; isosurface methods use only a subset of the voxels. For a function $f(x, y, z)$ an **isosurface** is the surface defined by the implicit equation

$$f(x, y, z) = c,$$

The value of the constant c is the **isosurface value.** For the discrete problem where we start with a set of voxels, isosurface methods seek to find approximate isosurfaces.

12.3.2 Visualization of Implicit Functions

Isosurface visualization is the natural extension of contours to three dimensions and thus has a connection to visualization of implicit functions. Consider the implicit function in three dimensions

$$g(x, y, z) = 0,$$

where g is known analytically. If any points satisfy this equation, then this function describes one or more surfaces. Simple examples include spheres, planes, more general quadrics, and the torus of radius r and cross section a:

$$(x^2 + y^2 + z^2 - r^2 - a^2)^2 - 4a^2(r^2 - z^2) = 0.$$

As we discussed in Chapter 10, g is a membership function that allows us to test whether a particular point lies on the surface, but there is no general method for finding points on the surface. Thus, given a particular g, we need visualization methods to "see" the surface.

One way to attack this problem involves using a simple form of ray tracing sometimes referred to as **ray casting**. Figure 12.17 shows a function, a viewer, and a projection plane. Any projector can be written in the form of a parametric function:

$$\mathbf{p}(t) = \mathbf{p}_0 + t\mathbf{d}.$$

It also can be written in terms of the individual components:

$$x(t) = x_0 + td_x,$$
$$y(t) = y_0 + td_y,$$
$$z(t) = z_0 + td_z.$$

Substituting into the implicit equation, we obtain the *scalar* equation in t,

$$f(x_0 + td_x, y_0 + td_y, z_0 + td_z) = u(t) = 0.$$

The solutions of this equation correspond to the points where the projector (ray) enters or leaves the isosurface. If f is a simple function, such as a quadric or a torus, then $u(t)$ may be solvable directly. For example, if f is a quadric, then u is a quadratic equation and has at most two real roots that can be found algebraically.

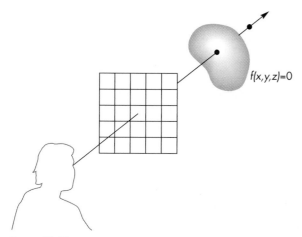

$f(x,y,z)=0$

Figure 12.17 Ray casting of an implicit function.

For higher-order polynomials or more complex forms, such as those involving exponentials and trigonometric functions, we must use numerical methods to obtain the intersections.

Once we have the intersections, we can apply a simple shading model to the surface. The required normal at the surface is given by the partial derivatives at the point of intersection:

$$\mathbf{n} = \begin{bmatrix} \frac{\partial f(x,y,z)}{\partial x} \\ \frac{\partial f(x,y,z)}{\partial y} \\ \frac{\partial f(x,y,z)}{\partial z} \end{bmatrix}.$$

Usually, we do not bother with global lighting considerations and thus do not compute either shadow rays (to determine whether the point of intersection is illuminated) or any reflected and traced rays. For scenes composed of simple objects, such as quadrics, ray casting not only is a display technique, but also performs visible surface determination and often is used with CSG models. For functions more complex than quadrics, the amount of work required by the intersection calculations is prohibitive, and we must consider alternative methods. First, we generalize the problem from one of viewing surfaces to one of viewing volumes.

Suppose that, instead of the surface described by $g(x, y, z) = 0$, we consider a scalar field $f(x, y, z)$, which is defined at every point in some region of three-dimensional space. If we are interested in a single value c of f, then the visualization problem is that of displaying the isosurface:

$$g(x, y, z) = f(x, y, z) - c = 0.$$

Sometimes, displaying a single isosurface for a particular value of c is sufficient. For example, if we are working with computed-tomography data, we might pick c to correspond to the X-ray density of the tissues that we want to visualize. In other situations, we might display multiple isosurfaces.

Finding isosurfaces usually involves working with a discretized version of the problem, replacing the continuous function g by a set of samples taken over some grid. Our prime isosurface visualization method is called marching cubes, the three-dimensional version of marching squares.

12.4 Isosurfaces and Marching Cubes

Assume that we have a data set, $\{f_{ijk}\}$, where each voxel value is a sample of the scalar field $f(x, y, z)$, and, when the samples are taken on a regular grid, the discrete data form a set of voxels. We seek an approximate isosurface using the sampled data to define a polygonal mesh. For any value of c, there may be no surface, one surface, or many surfaces that satisfy the equation. Given how well we can display three-dimensional triangles, we describe a method, called **marching cubes**, that approximates a surface by generating a set of three-dimensional triangles, each of which is an approximation to a piece of the isosurface.

We have assumed that our voxel values $\{f_{ijk}\}$ are on a regular three-dimensional grid that passes through the centers of the voxels. If they are not, we can use an interpolation scheme (see Exercise 12.7) to obtain values on such a grid. Eight adjacent grid points define a three-dimensional cell, as shown in Figure 12.18. Vertex (i, j, k) of the cell is assigned the data value f_{ijk}. We can now look for parts of isosurfaces that pass through each of these cells, based on only the values at the vertices.

For a given isosurface value c, we can color the vertices of each cell black or white, depending on whether the value at the vertex is greater than or less than c. There are $256 = 2^8$ possible vertex colorings, but, once we account for

Figure 12.18 Voxel cell.

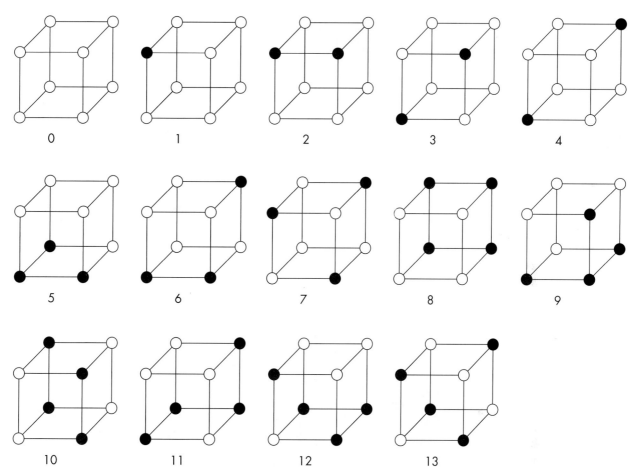

figure 12.19 Vertex colorings.

symmetries, there are only the 14 unique cases shown in Figure 12.19.[2] Using the simplest interpretation of the data, we can generate the points of intersection between the surface and the edges of the cubes by linear interpolation between the values at the vertices. Finally, we can use the triangular polygons to tessellate these intersections, forming pieces of a triangular mesh passing through the cell. These tessellations are shown in Figure 12.20. Note that not all these tessellations are unique.

---

2. The original paper by Lorensen and Cline [Lor87] and many of the subsequent papers refer to 15 cases, but two of those cases are symmetric.

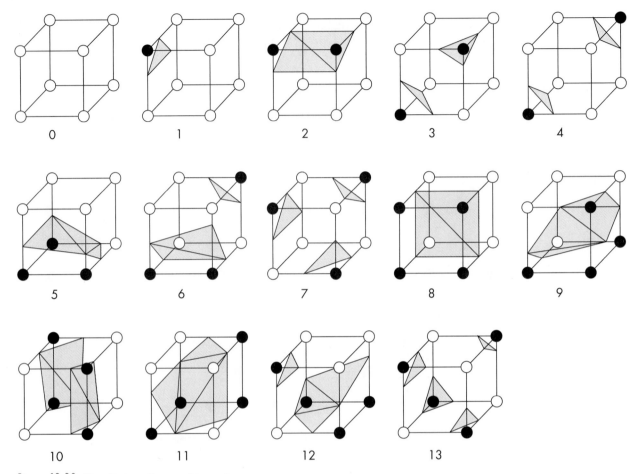

Figure 12.20 Tessellations for marching cubes.

Like the cells from our contour plots, each three-dimensional cell can be processed individually. In terms of the sampled data, each interior voxel value contributes to eight cells. We can go through the data, row by row, then plane by plane. As we do so, the location of the cell that we generate marches through the data set, giving the algorithm its name.

As each cell is processed, any triangles that it generates are sent off to be displayed through our graphics pipeline, where they can be lit, shaded, rotated, texture mapped, and rasterized. Because the algorithm is so easy to parallelize and, like the contour plot, can be table-driven, marching cubes is a popular way of displaying three-dimensional data.

Marching cubes is both a data-reduction algorithm and a modeling algorithm. Both simulations and imaging systems can generate data sets containing from 10^7 to 10^9 voxels. With data sets this large, simple operations (such as reading in the data, rescaling the values, or rotating the data set) are time-consuming, memory-intensive tasks. In many of these applications, however, after executing the algorithm, we might have only 10^3 to 10^4 three-dimensional triangles—a number of geometric objects handled easily by a graphics system. We can rotate, color, and shade the surfaces in real time to interpret the data. In general, few voxels contribute to a particular isosurface; consequently, the information in the unused voxels is not in the image.

We generated Color Plate 26 using the marching-cubes algorithm. Note the differences between this plate and the image in Color Plate 28, which was generated by splatting (Section 12.6). Color Plate 26 shows the effects of rendering three-dimensional objects through the shading of the surfaces—an effect lacking in Color Plate 28.

There is an ambiguity problem in marching cubes, analogous to the problem for contour maps. The problem can arise whenever we have different colors assigned to the diagonally opposite vertices of a side of a cell. Consider the cell coloring in Figure 12.21(a). Figures 12.21(b) and (c) show two ways to assign triangles to these data. If we compare two isosurfaces generated with the two different interpretations, areas where these cases arise will have completely different shapes and topologies. The wrong selection of an interpretation for a particular cell can leave a hole in an otherwise smooth surface. Researchers have attempted to deal with this problem; no approach works all the time. As we saw

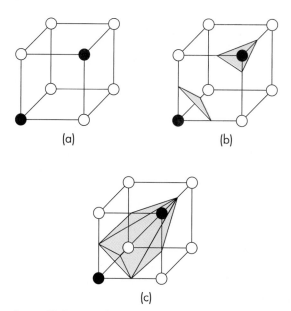

Figure 12.21 Ambiguity problem for marching cubes. (a) Cell. (b) One interpretation of cell. (c) Second interpretation.

with contour plots, an always-correct solution requires more information than is present in the data.

12.5 Mesh Simplification

We have looked at marching cubes as a method of generating small triangular pieces of an isosurface. Equivalently, we can view the output of the algorithm as one or more triangular meshes. These meshes are highly irregular even though they are composed of only triangles. Color Plate 26 shows one such mesh after rendering it using simple shading.

One of the disadvantages of marching cubes is that the algorithm can generate many more triangles than are really needed to display the isosurface. One reason for this phenomenon is that the number of triangles primarily depends on the resolution of the data set, rather than on the smoothness of the isosurface. Thus, we can often create a new mesh with far fewer triangles such that the rendered surfaces are visually indistinguishable. There are multiple approaches to this **mesh simplification** problem.

One popular approach, called **triangle decimation**, seeks to simplify the mesh by removing some edges and vertices. Consider the two simple meshes in Figures 12.22 and 12.23. The mesh in Figure 12.23 was created starting with the mesh in Figure 12.22 and moving vertex A until it coincided with vertex B. Decisions as to which triangles are to be removed can be made using criteria such as the local smoothness or the shape of the triangles. The latter criterion is important because long thin triangles do not render well.

Other approaches are based on resampling the surface generated by the original mesh, thus creating a new set of points that lie on the surface. These points are unstructured, lacking the connectivity in the original mesh. Thus, we are free to connect them in some optimal way. Probably the most popular technique is known as Delauney triangulation. This algorithm creates a triangular mesh in which the circle determined by the vertices of each triangle contains no other vertices. Although this process is fairly complex and beyond the scope of this book, the complexity is $O(n \log n)$ where n is the number of points.

Another approach to resampling is to place points on the original mesh or select a subset of the vertices and then use a particle system to control the final placement of the points (particles). Repulsive forces among the particles cause the particles to move to positions that lead to a good mesh.

Figure 12.22   Original mesh.

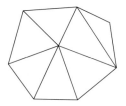

Figure 12.23   Mesh after simplification.

12.6 Direct Volume Rendering

The weakness of isosurface rendering is that not all voxels contribute to the final image. Consequently, we could miss the most important part of the data by selecting the wrong isovalue. **Direct volume rendering** constructs images in which all voxels can make a contribution to the image. Usually these techniques are either extensions of the compositing methods we introduced in Chapter 7 or applications of ray tracing (Chapter 13). Because the voxels typically are located on a rectangular grid, once the location of the viewer is known, there is exists an order in which we can do either front-to-back or back-to-front rendering.

Early methods for direct volume rendering treated each voxel as a small cube that was either completely transparent or completely opaque. If the image was rendered in a front-to-back manner, rays were traced until the first opaque voxel was encountered on each ray; then, the corresponding pixel in the image was colored black. If no opaque voxel was found along the ray, the corresponding pixel in the image was colored white. If the data set was rendered back to front, a painter's algorithm was used to paint only the opaque voxels. Both techniques produced images with serious aliasing artifacts that resulted from treating each voxel as a cube that was projected to the screen. They also failed to display the information in all the voxels. With the use of color and opacity, we can avoid or mitigate these problems.

12.6.1 Assignment of Color and Opacity

We start by assigning a color and transparency to each voxel. For example, if the data are from a computed-tomography scan of a person's head, we might assign colors based on the X-ray density. Soft tissues (low densities) might be red, fatty tissues (medium densities) might be blue, hard tissues (high densities) might be white, and empty space might be black. Often, these color assignments can be based on looking at the distribution of voxel values—the **histogram** of the data. Figure 12.24 shows a histogram with four peaks. We can assign a color to each peak and, if we use indexed color, we can assign red, green, and blue to the color indices through tables determined from curves such as those shown in Figure 12.25. If these data came from a computed-tomography scan, the skull might account for the low peak on the left and be assigned white, whereas empty space might correspond to the rightmost peak in the histogram and be colored black.

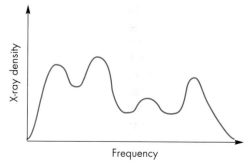

Figure 12.24 Histogram of CT data.

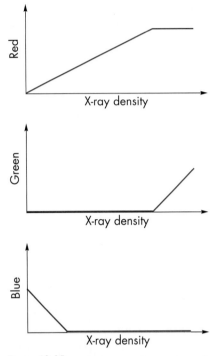

Figure 12.25 Color curves for computed-tomography data.

Opacities are assigned on the basis of which voxels we wish to emphasize in the image. If we want to show the brain but not the skull, we can assign zero opacity to the values corresponding to the skull. The assignment of colors and opacities is a pattern-recognition problem that we shall not pursue. Often, a user interface allows the user to control these values interactively. Here, we are interested in how to construct a two-dimensional image after these assignments have been made.

12.6.2 Splatting

Once colors and opacities are assigned, we can assign a geometric shape to each voxel and apply the compositing techniques from Chapter 7. One method is to apply back-to-front painting. Consider the group of voxels in Figure 12.26. Here, the term *front* is defined relative to the viewer. For three-dimensional data sets, once we have positioned the viewer relative to the data set, *front* defines the order in which we process the array of voxels. As we saw in Chapter 9, octrees can provide an efficient mechanism for storing voxel data sets. Positioning the viewer determines an order for traversing the octree.

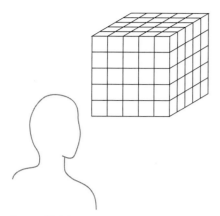

Figure 12.26 Volume of voxels.

One particularly simple way to generate an image is known as **splatting**. Each voxel is assigned a simple shape, and this shape is projected onto the image plane. Figure 12.27 shows a spherical voxel and the associated splat, or **footprint**. Note that if we are using a parallel projection and each voxel is assigned the same shape, the splats differ in only color and opacity. Thus, we do not need to carry out a projection for each voxel, but rather we can save the footprint as a bitmap that can be bitblt into the frame buffer.

The shape to assign each voxel is a sampling issue of the type we considered in Chapter 7. If the process that generated the data were ideal, each splat would be the projection of a three-dimensional sinc function. The use of hexagonal or elliptical splats is based on approximating a voxel with a parallelepiped or ellipsoid rather than using the reconstruction part of the sampling theorem. A better approximation is to use a Gaussian splat, which is the projection of a three-dimensional Gaussian approximation to the sinc function.

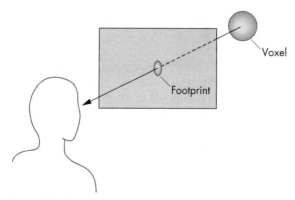

Figure 12.27 Splat, or footprint, of a voxel.

Color Plate 28 is a splatted image of a lobster that we created using the same data set as that we used for Color Plates 26 and 27. Although the image in Color Plate 28 lacks the three-dimensional character of Color Plates 26 and 27 (it looks like a color X-ray image), all voxels contributed to the image.

The key issue in creating a splatted image is how each splat is composited into the image. The data, being on a grid, are already sorted with respect to their distance from the viewer or the projection plane. We go through the data back to front, adding the contributions of each voxel through its splat. We start with a background image and blend in successive splats. We modify slightly our usual way of blending colors and opacities. Consider the formulas for combining source and destination pixels:

$$\mathbf{C}_{d'} = (1 - \alpha_s)\mathbf{C}_d + \alpha_s\mathbf{C}_s,$$

$$\alpha_{d'} = (1 - \alpha_s)\alpha_d + \alpha_s.$$

If we are compositing back to front, and if the source is opaque ($\alpha_s = 1$), then so is $\alpha_{d'}$, and the new destination color is the same as the source color. If the source is transparent, then we retain the original destination color and opacity. We can use OpenGL's blending functions if we first replace the color $\mathbf{C}$ of each voxel by $\alpha\mathbf{C}$, and use source and destination blending factors of 1 and $1 - \alpha_s$, respectively. The major advantage of this back-to-front compositing is that we can process the data in terms of slices of the volume data that correspond to viewing the voxel data as a stacked set of two-dimensional images. Not only are the data often generated in such a manner, but also we do not need to keep the entire data set in memory to do the rendering. However, our approach does not allow us to take advantage of data dependencies that potentially can speed up the processing. For example, if the front of the volume is opaque, a back-to-front renderer nevertheless processes all voxels, even though we see only the front voxels in the final image.

12.6.3 Volume Ray Tracing

An alternative direct volume-rendering technique is front-to-back rendering by ray tracing (Figure 12.28). Using the same compositing formulas that we used for splatting along a ray, we determine when an opaque voxel is reached, and we stop tracing this ray immediately. The difficulty with this approach is that a given ray passes through many slices of the data, and thus we need to keep all the data available. We shall discuss the ray tracing process in greater detail in Chapter 13.

It should be clear that the issues that govern the choice between a back-to-front and a front-to-back renderer are similar to the issues that arise when we choose between an image-oriented renderer and an object-oriented renderer. We have merely added opacity to the process. Consequently, a volume ray tracer can produce images that have a three-dimensional appearance and can make use of all the data. However, the ray-traced image must be recomputed from scratch each time that the viewing conditions change or that we make a transformation

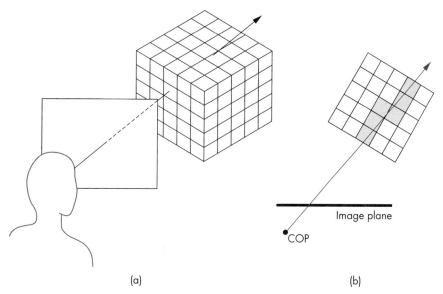

Figure 12.28 Volume ray casting. (a) Three-dimensional view. (b) Top view.

on the data, so the process is not suitable for interactive volume visualization, especially on pipeline architectures.

12.6.4 Texture Mapping of Volumes

The importance of texture mapping in animation has led to the inclusion of large amounts of texture memory in recent graphics systems. Once texture mapping is supported by the hardware, we can render scenes with texture mapping at almost the same rate as we can scenes without texture. From the software perspective, OpenGL 1.2 supports three-dimensional texture mapping. These capabilities suggest a new approach to direct volume rendering.

Suppose that we have sufficient texture memory to hold our entire data set. We can now define a set of planes facing the viewer. We can map texture coordinates to world coordinates such that these planes cut through the texture memory, forming a set of parallel polygons, as shown in Figure 12.29. We now texture map the voxels to these polygons for display. Because we need only a few hundred polygons to be compatible with the number of data points that we have in most problems, we place little burden on our rendering hardware. Unlike all the other volume-rendering methods, this one is fast enough that we can move the viewer in real time and do interactive visualization. There is, however, an aliasing problem with this technique that depends on the angle the polygons make with the texture array.

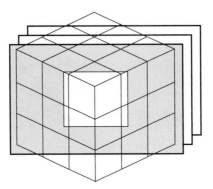

Figure 12.29 Slicing of three-dimensional texture memory with polygons.

12.7 Vector-Field Visualization

Our first visualization task considered a scalar field $f(x, y, z)$ defined over a volume of space. Now suppose that at each spatial point, we measure not a single value but rather a vector of n values. Thus, in three dimensions, we have a volume of values $\mathbf{f}(x, y, z)$, where $\mathbf{f}$ is an n-dimensional vector. The most important examples in which there are three spatial dimensions involve the measurement of three values at each spatial location. For example, in a fluid-flow problem, we might measure the velocity at each point.

In two dimensions, we can consider a surface of values $\mathbf{f}(x, y)$. One application is earth-orbiting satellites that measure properties of the earth from space. The Landsat Multispectral Sensor, for example, makes measurements in 13 different bands of the spectrum. Here, $\mathbf{f}$ is a function of two variables that give the position on the surface of the earth. Such data usually are displayed as two-dimensional color images. The data are mapped to colors that the scientist can identify with information in the measurements. Because this problem has only two spatial dimensions, we shall not pursue it further. In Section 12.7.4 we look at color-mapping techniques that can be applied to this problem.

Our visualization techniques for three-dimensional vector fields employ two primary tools: color and geometric objects. As with visualization of scalar fields, there are multiple techniques for viewing a given data set.

12.7.1 Hedgehogs

We start with a structured data set defined over a right parallelepiped—an assumption made only to simplify our discussion. At each point in this volume, we have a three-dimensional data vector.

Probably the most direct technique is to assume that the vector of data can be displayed as a three-dimensional directed line segment whose orientation and magnitude are determined by the data. Such a line segment is called a **hedgehog**. Displaying hedgehogs is simple, as long as we pay attention to a few problems.

First, because the hedgehogs are projected onto a two-dimensional view surface, the length of the line segment that the viewer sees has been foreshortened and thus its length depends on both the data and the position of the viewer. We can ameliorate this problem by coloring the line segments. For example, we could associate the RGB color cube with the x-, y-, z-axes and color the line segments accordingly. We could also make sure that the viewer can move her position so that she can see the hedgehogs from different locations.

Second, generating a hedgehog at every data point can lead to a cluttered display. We can get around this problem by either subsampling the data by taking every kth data point or by using a subset of the data determined by only those data whose magnitudes exceed some threshold.

Finally, there is a scaling problem: The data must be scaled such that the lengths of the displayed line segments are neither too short nor too long. If there is enough memory to hold the entire data set, this requirement does not pose a serious problem, but it can be a difficulty in real-time visualization when the entire data set is not available.

Figure 12.30 shows a visualization of blood flow in the human carotid artery. The data were collected over a volume. Consequently, the magnitudes of the flow measurements at most points are low, because most points are not in any vein or artery. We avoided cluttering the display with short line segments by thresholding the magnitude of the data vectors. We further reduced the number of line segments by generating a hedgehog for every fifth vector of those remaining after thresholding the magnitude.

12.7.2 Glyphs

Rather than using line segments, we can place other geometric objects, called **glyphs**, at points in space. We usually select glyphs that can be oriented and scaled so that we can show both magnitude and direction. For example, we can use cones, as shown in Figure 12.31.

We can place the base of the cone at the location of the data and can point the axis of the cone in the direction of the vector datum. We can let the size of the cone depend on the magnitude of the datum. Other possible glyphs include various types of arrows.

12.7.3 Color

We can use color either alone or to reinforce other methods of displaying data. The basic idea is that we can assign distinct colors to our hedgehogs or glyphs. Usually, the colors are dependent on the magnitude of data, although more generally we could assign colors to show other information, such as a particular component of the data. We could also try something like mapping three components of the data to each of the three primaries. Although such

Figure 12.30   Blood-flow visualization of the human carotid artery using hedgehogs.

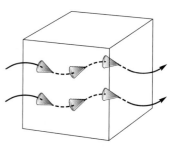

Figure 12.31   Use of oriented glyphs for flow visualization.

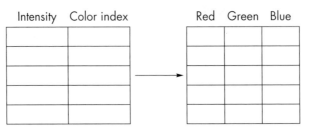

Figure 12.32 Assignment of the color-table entries.

mappings are easy to accomplish within the program, it is less clear that the viewer will be able to interpret an arbitrary color assignment as we wish.

If we are using indexed color, then we carry out color assignment by defining a color table. Thus, we can map the range of magnitudes to the color indices and then assign the colors to the rows of the tables, as shown in Figure 12.32. For RGB color, color assignment is a bit more difficult, since we must define three functions that map magnitude to each of the red, green, and blue primaries.

The more difficult and interesting problem is how we select the colors. As we saw in Chapter 2, there is a huge number of possible color maps for indexed color. For 256-color tables and 8-bit RGB resolution, there are $(2^{24})^{256}$ possible color tables. For RGB color, we have even more possibilities, although it is questionable whether a viewer can make such distinctions visually.

The most common way to assign colors to scalars is to use a thermal scale. Viewers tend to associate the cool colors—blues and greens—with unimportant data and to associate the hot colors—reds, yellows, and white—with important data. Thus, if higher magnitudes of the vectors are more important, we can look for a table or functions that start with blue for the lowest values and go through cyan to green and then to red, yellow, and perhaps white. We can describe such a function through the color cube. We keep the colors on the surface of the cube so as to have the colors as saturated as possible. Such a map is shown on the color cube in Figure 12.33 and as functions that map from magnitude to RGB in Figure 12.34.

We can also try to use color to get a better idea of orientation by adding shading to the glyphs.

12.7.4 Particle Traces and Streamlines

One of the most important applications of vector visualization is flow visualization. Application areas include computational fluid dynamics (CFD), where we solve partial differential equations for the desired physical quantities; medical applications such as Doppler ultrasound, where we measure blood flow; and simulations of wind tunnels, where we track airflow over prototypes of aircraft. What all these applications have in common is that the vector data at each point

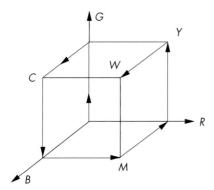

Figure 12.33 Mapping on a color cube.

in space can be thought of as representing the velocity of a fluid at that point. We can have either a single volume of data that form a set of velocities at a particular time, or we can have multiple volumes of data that give us velocities at many times. Rather than look at the velocity vector at many points, we look at how

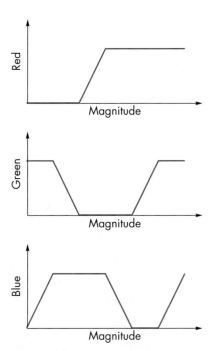

Figure 12.34 Color functions.

particles might flow through the fluid. There are two related types of displays we can create.

A **particle trace** is the path a particle would take in the fluid. Thus, for visualization, we can place a particle in a virtual volume and use the data to trace its trajectory as it flows through the volume. In general, this technique requires data at multiple time steps. If we have steady-state flow, we can use the data at a single time to compute a particle trace by assuming that the forces on a particle do not change with time.

A **streamline** is the curve we obtain by starting at a point and integrating the instantaneous velocity to form a path. In steady-state flow, a particle flows along a streamline. The techniques to display streamlines and particle traces are similar, differing primarily in whether we take the data from a single time or from multiple times.

Suppose that we start with a volume of velocity data at some time t. We can select a point at random within the volume. Thus, we have a position

$$\mathbf{p}(t) = \begin{bmatrix} x(t) \\ y(t) \\ z(t) \end{bmatrix},$$

and a velocity

$$\mathbf{v}(t) = \begin{bmatrix} v_x(t) \\ v_y(t) \\ v_z(t) \end{bmatrix},$$

from the data. If we place a particle at this point, its position a small time later at time $t + h$ is given approximately by

$$\mathbf{p}(t + h) = \mathbf{p}(t) + h\mathbf{v}(t),$$

Figure 12.35 Computation of the points on a streamline.

as shown in Figure 12.35. This position is the next position on the particle trace. If the flow is steady, this position is also on the streamline through $\mathbf{p}(t)$.

If the flow is steady such that particle traces and streamlines are the same, then we can continue the computation with our single volume of data. The new point lies in one of the cells determined by the structured data. We can compute another new position by repeating the calculation starting at the new point. Although the initial point can be chosen to be a point on the structured grid, the new point almost certainly does not lie at a grid point. We can use either the velocity from the closest grid point or that calculated using bilinear interpolation from the data at the four closest grid points. If the flow is not steady and we have data at multiple times, we can let h be equal to the time between data sets, or we can use the data at multiple times to interpolate the data at time $t + h$.

Streamlines can be displayed in other ways. For example, we can take a set of streamlines that start in the same region and bundle them together to form geometric objects called **stream tubes**. Back Plate 4 shows stream tubes for flows in the Caribbean Sea.

Figure 12.36   LIC image.

A small set of streamlines may have a visually appealing look but because of the limited number of streamlines displayed, significant information in the data may not be displayed. However, if we were to display all possible streamlines, the visualization would be very cluttered. An alternative that has been proposed is **line integral convolution** (LIC). In this technique, every possible streamline is computed, but as each streamline is formed, it is convolved as in Chapter 7 with a fixed convolution mask whose entries are random numbers. The effect is to provide a different correlation along adjacent streamlines so that when they are colored for display, they appear different, even though the values along this adjacent pair of streamlines can be almost identical. Figure 12.36 shows an LIC image of surface flows in the Caribbean Sea. Land is shown as a solid color.

12.8 Tensor Visualization

We use tensor visualization when we have data that are themselves related spatially. For example, we might measure stress or strain at every point within a solid material that is subjected to external forces. The stress at a point (x, y, z) in the material can be described by a 3×3 matrix (a rank 2 tensor) of the form

$$\mathbf{M} = \begin{bmatrix} \sigma_x & \tau_{xy} & \tau_{xz} \\ \tau_{yx} & \sigma_y & \tau_{yz} \\ \tau_{zx} & \tau_{zy} & \sigma_z \end{bmatrix}.$$

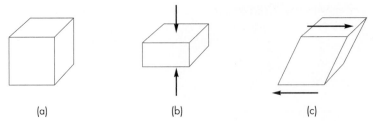

Figure 12.37 Stresses on a small cube. (a) Cube. (b) Normal stress. (c) Shear stress.

Here the diagonal terms are the normal stresses (forces per unit area) that represent the force components that either compress or pull apart the material in directions normal to a small cube located at each point. The off-diagonal terms represent the forces that tend to shear the cube into a parallelepiped, as shown in Figure 12.37.

Replacing the 3×3 matrix by a 1×9 matrix (a rank 1 tensor) would lose much of the structure contained in the 3×3 array; consequently, we cannot apply vector-visualization methods. One method of visualization is to display small cubes, each of which has been distorted by the local stress matrix. Another method is to display properties of the matrix. For example, if the matrix is symmetric—which it will be for most problems—then we can decompose it into its eigenvalues and eigenvectors. That is, we write $\mathbf{M}$ in the form

$$\mathbf{M} = \mathbf{V}^T \Lambda \mathbf{V},$$

where the matrix Λ is diagonal and $\mathbf{V}$ is a rotation matrix, so that $\mathbf{V}^T = \mathbf{V}^{-1}$. The three diagonal elements of Λ, λ_1, λ_2, and λ_3, are the **eigenvalues** of $\mathbf{M}$, and the columns of $\mathbf{V}$ are the **eigenvectors**. The eigenvalues are the most important characteristic of a square matrix (Appendix C).

We can associate an ellipsoid with the three eigenvalues. The isosurfaces of the quadratic form $\mathbf{x}^T \mathbf{M} \mathbf{x}$ are quadrics because

$$\mathbf{x}^T \mathbf{M} \mathbf{x} = \sum_{i=0}^{3} \sum_{j=1}^{3} m_{ij} x_i x_j.$$

If we replace $\mathbf{x}$ by $\mathbf{y} = \mathbf{V}\mathbf{x}$, the quadric form becomes

$$\mathbf{x}^T \mathbf{M} \mathbf{x} = \mathbf{y}^T \mathbf{V}^T \mathbf{M} \mathbf{V} \mathbf{y} = \mathbf{y}^T \Lambda \mathbf{y} = \sum_{i=0}^{3} \lambda_i y_i^2.$$

If the three eigenvalues are positive, the quadric is an ellipsoid, and $\mathbf{V}$ rotates the original frame into one aligned with this ellipse. The eigenvalues determine the length of the three axes of the ellipse. Because this ellipse is tied so closely to the matrix, displaying the ellipse as a glyph gives much of the information in the matrix. The eigenvectors determine the orientation of the ellipse.

12.9 Summary and Notes

Although visualization encompasses everything we do in computer graphics, recent work in visualization has focused on the large data sets that arise in medical applications and from scientific simulations. These data sets are so large that not only can they burden the best of hardware, but also conceptually simple operations, such as reading the data or repositioning the data relative to a viewer, can be difficult. Nevertheless, there is a variety of techniques that can be applied to these problems.

Contours and meshes can be generated easily and fit well with the facilities provided by APIs such as OpenGL.

For volumetric data sets of scalars, we have introduced two general approaches: isosurfaces and volume rendering. In the first, we look for surfaces of a constant value in the data and construct a polygonal mesh that approximates this surface. These techniques are fast and construct geometric objects that can be manipulated interactively with standard graphics hardware. Their weakness is they do not make use of all the data. Direct volume-rendering methods make use of all the data to construct an image, but they can be slow and require a new computation to move the viewer.

Vector-visualization techniques are most important in flow visualization, where we have a volume of velocity data. Here, we have sought to show patterns of flow through a variety of techniques including hedgehogs, glyphs, streamlines, and particle traces.

For problems in which we have data of more than three dimensions at each point, including tensor visualization, it is less clear how we should visualize the information. The difficulties are twofold. First, our graphics systems can display only three-dimensional primitives. Second, although we can use other variables, such as color, to increase the "dimension" of the display, human observers may have difficulty interpreting such displays.

12.10 Suggested Readings

The marching-squares method is a special case of the marching-cubes method popularized by Lorenson and Kline [Lor87]. The method has been rediscovered many times. The ambiguity problem is discussed in [Van94]. Early attempts to visualize volumes were reported by Herman [Her79] and by Fuchs [Fuc77]. Ray-tracing volumes was introduced by Levoy [Lev88]. Splatting is due to Westover [Wes90]. Particles can also be used for visualization [Wit94a, Cro97]. Many other visualization strategies are discussed in [Gal95, Nie97]. One approach to building visualization applications is to use an object-oriented toolkit [Schr98]. The *IEEE Transactions on Visualization and Computer Graphics* contain many examples of recent work in scientific visualization.

Exercises

12.1   Write a program that will display a set of values $\{f_{ij}\}$ as

   a. a set of colored rectangles
   b. a rectangular mesh
   c. a contour plot

12.2   Change the mesh program so that you can display the surface as a lit and shaded surface.

12.3   Change the mesh program so that you can texture map an image to the surface.

12.4   Change the mesh program to use the third-order polynomial surfaces that we introduced in Chapter 10.

12.5   Generate a table that maps the 16 vertex colorings of a rectangular cell to the four ways that a contour curve can pass through the cell.

12.6   There are 256 ways to color the vertices of a cube with two colors; when we eliminate symmetries, however, there are only 14 unique cases. How many of the 256 colorings are included in each of these cases?

12.7   Implement the marching-cubes algorithm. Ignore the ambiguous case; you may use one of the possible interpretations.

12.8   You can display three-dimensional data by displaying local normals for each cell or for some collection of cells. Write a program that will display, for a given contour value, the approximate normal for the portion of the surface that passes through the cell.

12.9   Assume that you have values of a function at the eight vertices of a right parallelepiped. Develop a method of trilinear interpolation, similar to bilinear interpolation, to obtain interior values.

12.10   Develop an isosurface method similar to marching cubes based on tetrahedrons.

12.11   Implement a flow visualization program that will display streamlines or particle traces as tubes that can be colored and shaded.

12.12   Implement a program that decomposes three eigenvalues and eigenvectors and then displays these values as ellipsoids.

12.13 Implement a program that displays a volume of data displaying only points. The density of points in a region should be proportional to the value of the scalar field in the region.

12.14 A simple way to display scalar fields is to form an image from the voxels that lie in a plane. Write a program that will display three such images from three orthogonal planes aligned with the coordinate axes. Allow the user to move these planes interactively.

12.15 How would you alter the basic strategy in marching cubes to use tetrahedra rather than triangles?

Advanced Rendering

In this final chapter, we consider a variety of alternative approaches to the pipeline rendering strategy supported by most hardware and software for interactive applications. We have multiple motivations for introducing these other approaches. We want to be able to incorporate effects, such as global lighting, that are not possible to render in real-time environments. We also want to produce high-quality high-resolution images that go beyond what is needed for standard computer displays.

First, we explore ray tracers. We then look at the rendering equation that provides a physical basis for global rendering. Although we cannot solve the rendering equation in general, we shall look at a special solution for a particular shading model that yields the radiosity approach to rendering.

We consider techniques for displaying large amounts of geometric data using parallel-rendering on clusters of computers. These techniques will also allow us to create images with resolution greater than that of standard display devices.

We also introduce image-based rendering. Here we start with two-dimensional images and go backward to obtain three-dimensional information that can be used to create new images. These techniques combine elements of computer graphics, computer vision, and image processing.

13.1 Going Beyond Pipeline Rendering

Almost everything done so far has led us to believe that, given a scene description containing geometric objects, cameras, light sources, and attributes, we could render it in close to real time using available hardware and software. This view dictated that we would use a pipeline renderer of the type described by the OpenGL architecture and supported by graphics hardware. Although we have developed a reasonably large bag of tricks that enable us to handle most applications and get around the local shading model supported by such renderers, there are still limitations on what we can do. There are many global lighting situations that we cannot approximate well with a pipeline renderer. We would also like to generate images with higher resolution than on a standard workstation and that contain fewer aliasing artifacts. In many situations, we are willing either to render at slower speeds or use multiple computers to achieve these goals. In this chapter, we shall introduce a variety of techniques, all of which are of current interest both to researchers and practitioners.

First, we examine other rendering strategies that are based on the physics of image formation. Our original discussion of image formation was based on following rays of light. That approach is based on a very simple physical model and led to the ray tracing paradigm for rendering. We start by exploring this model in greater detail than in previous chapters and show how to get started writing your own ray tracer.

We can also take approaches to rendering, other than ray tracing, that are also based on physics. We shall examine an approach based on energy conservation and consider an integral equation, the **rendering equation**, that describes a closed environment with light sources and reflective surfaces. Although this equation is not solvable in general, we can develop a rendering approach called **radiosity** that satisfies the rendering equation when all surfaces are perfectly diffuse reflectors.

We shall also look at two approaches that are somewhere between physically correct and real-time renderers. One is the approach taken in RenderMan. The other is an approach to rendering that starts with images. Although these methods are different from each other, both have become important in the animation industry.

Finally, we turn to the problems of working with large data sets and high-resolution displays. These problems are related because large data sets contain detail that requires displays with a resolution beyond what we can get with standard CRTs and LCD panels. We shall consider solutions that use parallelism making use of commodity components, both processors and graphics cards.

13.2 Ray Tracing

In many ways, ray tracing is a logical extension to rendering with a local lighting model. It is based on our previous observation that, of the light rays leaving a source, the only ones that contribute to our image are those that enter the lens of our synthetic camera and pass through the center of projection. Figure 13.1 shows several of the possible interactions with a single point source and perfectly specular surfaces. Rays can enter the lens of the camera directly from the source, from interactions with a surface visible to the camera, after multiple reflections from surfaces, or after transmission through one or more surfaces.

Most of the rays that leave a source do not enter the lens and do not contribute to our image. Hence, attempting to follow all rays from a light source is a time-wasting endeavor. However, if we reverse the direction of the rays, and consider only those rays that start at the center of projection, we know that these **cast rays** must contribute to the image. Consequently, we start our ray tracer as shown in Figure 13.2. Here we have included the image plane, and we have ruled it into pixel-sized areas. Knowing that we must assign a color to every pixel, we must cast at least one ray through each pixel. Each cast ray either intersects a surface or a light source, or goes off to infinity without striking anything. Pixels

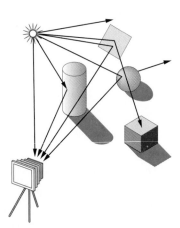

Figure 13.1 Rays leaving source.

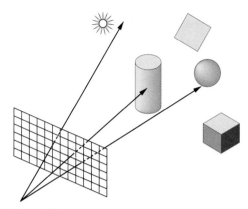

Figure 13.2 Ray-casting model.

corresponding to this latter case can be assigned a background color. Rays that strike surfaces—for now, we can assume that all surfaces are opaque—require us to calculate a shade for the point of intersection. If we were simply to compute the shade at the point of intersection, using the Phong model, we would produce the same image as would our local renderer. However, we can do much more.

Note that the process that we have described thus far requires all the same steps as we use in our pipeline renderer: object modeling, projection, and visible-surface determination. However, as we saw in Chapter 8, the order in which the calculations are carried out is different. The pipeline renderer works on a vertex-by-vertex basis; the ray tracer works on a pixel-by-pixel basis.

In ray tracing, rather than immediately applying our reflection model, we first check whether the point of intersection between the cast ray and the surface is illuminated. We compute **shadow** or **feeler rays** (Figure 13.3) from the point

Figure 13.3 Shadow rays.

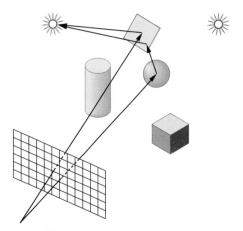

Figure 13.4   Ray tracing with a mirror.

on the surface to each source. If a shadow ray intersects a surface before it meets the source, the light is blocked from reaching the point under consideration, and this point is in shadow, at least from this source. No lighting calculation needs to be done for sources that are blocked from a point on the surface. If all surfaces are opaque and we do not consider light scattered from surface to surface, we have an image that has shadows added to what we have already done without ray tracing. The price we pay is the cost of doing a type of hidden-surface calculation for each point of intersection between a cast ray and a surface.

Suppose that some of our surfaces are highly reflective, like those shown in Figure 13.4. We can follow the shadow ray as it bounces from surface to surface, until it either goes off to infinity or intersects a source. Such calculations are usually done recursively and take into account any absorption of light at surfaces.

Ray tracing is particularly good at handling surfaces that are both reflecting and transmitting. Using our basic paradigm, we follow a cast ray to a surface (Figure 13.5) with the property that, if a ray from a source strikes a point, then the light from the source is partially absorbed, and some of this light contributes to the diffuse reflection term. The rest of the incoming light is divided between a transmitted ray and a reflected ray. From the perspective of the cast ray, if a light source is visible at the intersection point, then we need to do three tasks. First, we must compute the contribution from the light source at the point, using our standard reflection model. Second, we must cast a ray in the direction of a perfect reflection. Third, we must cast a ray in the direction of the transmitted ray. These two rays are treated just like the original cast ray; that is, they are intersected (if possible) with other surfaces, end at a source, or go off to infinity. At each surface that these rays intersect, additional rays may be generated by reflection and transmission of light. Figure 13.6 shows a single cast ray and the path it can follow through a simple environment. Figure 13.7 shows the **ray tree** generated.

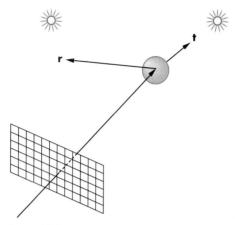

Figure 13.5 Ray tracing with reflection and transmission.

This tree shows which rays must be traced; it is constructed dynamically by the ray-tracing process.

Color Plate 20 was created by ray casting of a three-dimensional data set. Here, shadow rays were not followed. By making the skin transparent and the muscle opaque, however, the ray-tracing paradigm was able to create an image of only the latter. This image was created on a parallel processor, making use of the fact that cast rays can be traced independently of one another.

Although our ray tracer uses the Phong model to include a diffuse term at the point of intersection between a ray and a surface, the light that is scattered diffusely at this point is ignored. If we were to attempt to follow such light, we would have so many rays to deal with that the ray tracer might never complete execution. Thus, ray tracers are best suited for highly reflective environments. Color Plate 23 was rendered with a public-domain ray tracer. Although the scene contains only a few objects, the reflective and transparent surfaces could not have been rendered correctly without the ray tracer. Also, note the complexity of the shadows in the scene, another effect created automatically by ray tracing.

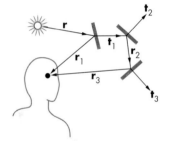

Figure 13.6 Simple ray-traced environments.

13.3 Building a Simple Ray Tracer

The easiest way to describe a ray tracer is recursively, through a single function that traces a ray and calls itself for the reflected and transmitted rays. Most of the work in ray tracing goes into the calculation of intersections between rays and surfaces. One reason that it is difficult to implement a ray tracer that can handle a variety of objects is that, as we add more complex objects, computing intersections becomes problematic. Consequently, most basic ray tracers support only flat and quadric surfaces.

Figure 13.7 Ray tree corresponding to Figure 13.6.

We have seen the basic considerations that determine the ray-tracing process. Building a simple recursive ray tracer that can handle simple objects—quadrics and polyhedra—is quite easy. In this section, we shall examine the basic structure and the functions that are required. Details can be found in the references at the end of the chapter.

We need two basic functions. The recursive function raytrace follows a ray, specified by a point and a direction, and returns the shade of the first surface that it intersects. It will use the function intersect to find the location of the closest surface that the specified ray intersects.

13.3.1 Recursive Ray Tracing

Let us consider the procedure raytrace in pseudocode. We give it a starting point p and a direction d, and it returns a color c. In order to stop the ray tracer from recursing forever, we can specify a maximum number of steps max that it can take. We shall assume, for simplicity, that we have only a single light source whose properties, as well as the description of the objects and their surface properties, are all available globally. If there are additional light sources, we can add in their contributions in manner similar to the way in which we deal with the single source.

```
color c = trace(point p, vector d, int step)
{

    color local, reflected, transmitted;
    point q;
    normal n;

    if(step > max) return(background_color);

    q = intersect(p, d, status);

    if(status == light_source) return(light_source_color);
    if(status == no_intersection) return(background_color);

    n = normal(q);
    r = reflect(q, n);
    t = transmit(q, n);

    local = phong(q, n, r);
    reflected = trace(q, r, step+1);
    transmitted = trace(q, t, step+1);

    return(local + reflected + transmitted);
}
```

If we have exceeded the maximum number of steps, we return a defined background color. Otherwise, we use `intersect` to find the intersection of the given ray with the closest object. This function must have the entire database of objects available to it, and it must be able to find the intersections of rays with all types of objects supported. Consequently, most of the time spent in the ray tracer and the complexity of the code is hidden in this function. We examine some of the intersection issues in Section 13.3.2.

If the ray does not intersect any object, we can return a status variable from `intersect` and return the background color from `trace`. Likewise, if the ray intersects the light source, we return the color of the source. If an intersection is returned, there are three components to the color at this point: a local color that can be computed using the Phong (or any other) model, a reflected color, and, if the surface is translucent, a transmitted color. Before computing these colors, we must compute the normal at the point of intersection, as well as the direction of reflected and transmitted rays, as in Chapter 6. The complexity of computing the normal depends on the class of objects supported by the ray tracer, and this calculation can be part of the function `raytrace`.

The computation of the local color requires a check to see if the light source is visible from the point of closest intersection. Thus, we cast a feeler or shadow ray from this point toward the light source and check whether it intersects any objects. We can note that this process can also be recursive because the shadow ray might hit a reflective surface, such as a mirror, or translucent surface, such as a piece of glass. In addition, if the shadow ray hits a surface that itself is illuminated, some of this light should contribute to the color at q. Generally, we ignore these possible contributions because they will slow the calculation significantly. Practical ray tracing requires that we make some compromises and is never quite physically correct.

Next, we have two recursive steps that compute the contributions from the reflected and transmitted rays starting at q using `raytrace`. It is these recursions that make this code a ray tracer rather than a simple ray-casting rendering such as we saw in Chapter 12. Finally, we add the three colors to obtain the color at p.

13.3.2 Calculating Intersections

Most of the time spent in a typical ray tracer is in the calculation of intersections in the function `intersect`. Hence, we must be very careful in limiting the objects to those for which we can find intersections easily. The general intersection problem can be expressed cleanly if we use an implicit representation of our objects. Thus, if an object is defined by the surface(s)

$$f(x, y, z) = f(\mathbf{p}) = 0,$$

and a ray from a point $\mathbf{p}_0$ in the direction $\mathbf{d}$ is represented by the parametric form

$$\mathbf{p}(t) = \mathbf{p}_0 + t\mathbf{d},$$

then the intersections are given for the values of t such that

$$f(\mathbf{p}_0 + t\mathbf{d}) = 0,$$

which is a scalar equation in t. If f is an algebraic surface, then f is a sum of polynomial terms of the form $x^i y^j z^k$. Finding the intersections reduces to finding all the roots of a polynomial. Unfortunately, there are only a few cases that do not require numerical methods.

One is quadrics. In Chapter 10, we saw that all quadrics could be written as the quadratic form

$$\mathbf{p} = \mathbf{p}^T \mathbf{A} \mathbf{p} + \mathbf{b}^T \mathbf{p} + c = 0$$

Substituting in the equation for a ray leaves us with a scalar quadratic equation to solve for the values of t that yield no, one, or two intersections. Because the solution of the quadratic equation requires only the taking of a single square root, ray tracers can handle quadrics without difficulty. In addition, we can eliminate those rays that miss a quadric object and those that are tangent to it before taking the square root, further simplifying the calculation.

Consider, for example, a sphere centered at $\mathbf{p}_c$ with radius r, which can be written as

$$(\mathbf{p} - \mathbf{p}_c) \cdot (\mathbf{p} - \mathbf{p}_c) - r^2 = 0.$$

Substituting in the equation of the ray

$$\mathbf{f}\mathbf{p} = \mathbf{p}_0 + t\mathbf{d},$$

we get the quadratic equation

$$\mathbf{p}_0 \cdot \mathbf{p}_0 + 2\mathbf{p}_0 \cdot (\mathbf{d} - \mathbf{p}_c)t + (\mathbf{d} - \mathbf{p}_0) \cdot (\mathbf{d} - \mathbf{p}_0) - r^2 = 0.$$

Planes are also simple. We can take the equation for the ray and substitute it into the equation of a plane

$$\mathbf{p} \cdot \mathbf{n} + c = 0,$$

which yields a scalar equation that requires only a single division to solve. Thus, for the ray

$$\mathbf{p} = \mathbf{p}_0 + t\mathbf{d},$$

we find

$$t = -\frac{\mathbf{p}_0 \cdot \mathbf{n} + c}{\mathbf{n} \cdot \mathbf{d}}.$$

However, planes by themselves have limited applicability in modeling scenes. We are usually interested either in the intersection of multiple planes that form convex objects (polyhedra) or a piece of a plane that defines a flat polygon. For polygons, we must decide whether the point of intersection lies inside or outside the polygon. The difficulty of such a test depends on whether the polygon is convex and, if not convex, whether it is simple. These issues are similar to the rendering issues that we discussed for polygons in Chapter 8. For convex polygons there are very simple tests that are similar to the tests for ray intersections with polyhedra that we consider next.

Although we can define polyhedra by their faces, we can also define them as the convex objects that are formed by the intersection of planes. Thus, a parallelepiped is defined by six planes and a tetrahedron by four. For ray tracing, the advantage of this definition is that we can use the simple ray-plane intersection equation to derive a ray-polyhedron intersection test.

We develop the test as follows. Let us assume that all the planes defining our polyhedron have normals that are outwardly facing. Consider the ray in Figure 13.8 that intersects the polyhedron. It can enter and leave the polygon only once. It must enter through a plane that is facing the ray and leave through a plane that faces in the direction of the ray. However, this ray must also intersect all the planes that form the polyhedron (except those parallel to the ray).

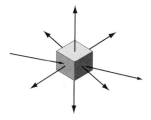

Figure 13.8 Ray intersecting a polyhedron with outward-facing normals shown.

Consider the intersections of the ray with all the front-facing planes—that is those whose normals point toward the starting point of the ray. The entry point must be the intersection farthest along the ray. Likewise, the exit point is the nearest intersection point of all the planes facing away from the start of the ray, and the entry point must be closer to the initial point than the exit point. If we consider a ray that misses the same polyhedron, as in Figure 13.9, we see that that the farthest intersection with a front-facing plane is closer to the initial point than the closest intersection with a back-facing plane. Hence, our test is to find these possible entry and exit points by computing the ray-plane intersection points, in any order, and updating the possible entry and exit points as we find the intersections. The test can be halted if we ever find a possible exit point closer than the present entry point or a possible entry point farther than the present exit point.

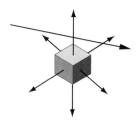

Figure 13.9 Ray missing a polyhedron with outward-facing normals shown.

Consider the two-dimensional example in Figure 13.10 that tests for a ray–convex polygon intersection in a plane. Here lines replace planes, but the logic is the same. Suppose that we do the intersections with the lines in the order 1, 2, 3, 4. Starting with line 1, we find that this line faces the initial point by looking at the sign of the dot product of the normal with the direction of the ray. The intersection with line 1 then yields a possible entry point. Line 2 faces away

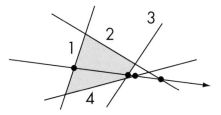

Figure 13.10 Ray intersecting a convex polygon.

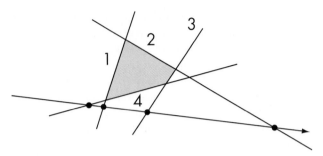

Figure 13.11 Ray missing a convex polygon.

from the initial point and yields a possible exit point that is farther away than our present estimate of the entry point. Line 3 yields an even closer exit point but still one that is farther than the entry point. Line 4 yields a farther exit point that can be discarded. At this point, we have tested all the lines and conclude the ray passes through the polygon.

Figure 13.11 has the same lines and the same convex polygon but shows a ray that misses the polygon. The intersection with line 1 still yields a possible entry point. The intersections with lines 2 and 3 still yield possible exit points that are farther than the entry point. But the intersection with line 4 yields an exit point closer than the entry point, which indicates that the ray must miss the polygon.

13.3.3 Ray-Tracing Variations

Most ray tracers employ multiple methods for determining when to stop the recursive process. One method that is fairly simple to implement is to neglect all rays that go past some distance, assuming that such rays go off to infinity. We can implement this test by assuming that all objects lie inside a large sphere centered at the origin. Thus, if we treat this sphere as an object colored with a specified background color, whenever the intersection calculation determines that this sphere is the closest object, we terminate the recursion for the ray and return the background color.

Another simple termination strategy is to look at the fraction of energy remaining in a ray. When a ray passes through a translucent material or reflects from a shiny surface, we can estimate the fraction of the incoming energy that is in these outgoing rays and how much has been absorbed at the surface. If we add an energy parameter to the ray tracer

```
trace(point p, vector d, int steps, float energy)
```

then we need only to add a line of code to check if there is sufficient energy remaining to continue tracing a ray.

There are many improvements we can make to speed up a ray tracer or make it more accurate. For example, it is fairly simple to replace the recursion in the ray tracer with iteration. Often much of the work in finding intersections can be avoided by the use of bounding boxes or bounding spheres, because the intersection with these objects can be done very quickly. Often, bounding volumes can be used to group objects effectively.

Because ray tracing is a sampling method, it is subject to aliasing errors. As we saw in Chapter 8, aliasing errors occur when we do not have enough samples. However, in our basic ray tracer, the amount of work is proportional to the number of rays. Many ray tracers use a stochastic sampling method in which the decision as to where to cast the next ray is based upon the results of rays cast thus far. Thus, if rays do not intersect any objects in a particular region, few additional rays will be cast toward it, while the opposite holds for rays that are cast in a direction where they intersect many objects. This strategy is also used in RenderMan (Section 13.6). Although we could argue that stochastic sampling only works in a probabilistic sense—as there may well be small objects in areas that are not well sampled—it has the advantage that images produced by stochastic sampling tend not to show the moiré patterns characteristic of images produced using uniform sampling.

Ray tracing is an inherently parallel process, as every ray can be cast independently of every other ray. However, the difficulty is that every ray can potentially intersect any object. Hence, every tracing of a ray needs access to all objects. In addition, when we follow reflected and transmitted rays, we tend to lose any locality that might have helped us avoid a lot of data movement. Consequently, parallel ray tracers are best suited for shared-memory parallel architectures.

13.4 The Rendering Equation

Most of the laws of physics can be expressed as conservation laws, such as the conservation of momentum and the conservation of energy. As light is a form of energy, an energy-based approach can provide an alternative to ray tracing. Consider the closed-environment picture in Figure 13.12. We see some surfaces that define the closed environment, some objects, and a light source inside. Physically all these surfaces are the same. Although each one may have different parameters, each obeys the same physical laws. Any surface can absorb some light and reflect some light. Any surface can be an emitter of light. From the ray-tracing perspective, we can say that that the shades that we see are the result of an infinite number of rays bouncing around the environment, starting with sources and not ending until all the energy has been absorbed. However, when we look at the scene, we see the steady state; that is, we see surfaces each having its own shades. We do not see how the rays have bounced around; we see only the end result. The energy approach allows us to solve for this steady state directly, thus avoiding tracing many rays through many reflections.

Figure 13.12 Closed environment with four objects and a light source.

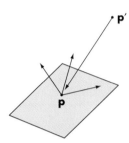

Figure 13.13 A simple surface.

Figure 13.14 Light from p′ arriving at p.

Let us consider just one surface, as in Figure 13.13. We see rays of light entering from many directions and other rays emerging, also possibly in all directions. The light leaving the surface can have two components. If the surface is a light source, then some fraction of the light leaving the surface is from emission. The rest of the light is the reflection of incoming light from other surfaces. Hence, the incoming light also consists of emissions and reflections from other surfaces.

We can simplify the analysis by considering two arbitrary points **p** and **p′**, as in Figure 13.14. If we look at the light arriving at and leaving **p**, the energy must balance. Thus, the emission of energy, if there is a source at **p**, and the reflected light energy must equal the incoming light energy from all possible points **p′**. Let $i(\mathbf{p}, \mathbf{p}')$ be the intensity of light leaving the point **p′** and arriving at the point **p**.[1] The rendering equation

$$i(\mathbf{p}, \mathbf{p}') = v(\mathbf{p}, \mathbf{p}')(\epsilon(\mathbf{p}, \mathbf{p}') + \int \rho(\mathbf{p}, \mathbf{p}', \mathbf{p}'')i(\mathbf{p}', \mathbf{p}'')d\mathbf{p}'')$$

expresses this balance. The intensity leaving **p′** consists of two parts. If **p′** is an emitter of light (a source), there is a term $\epsilon(\mathbf{p}, \mathbf{p}')$ in the direction of **p**. The second term is the contribution from reflections from every possible point (**p″**) that are reflected at **p′** in the direction of **p**. The reflection function $\rho(\mathbf{p}, \mathbf{p}', \mathbf{p}'')$ characterizes the material properties at **p′**. The term $v(\mathbf{p}, \mathbf{p}')$ has two possible values. If there is an opaque surface between **p** and **p′**, then the surface occludes **p′** from **p** and no light from **p′** reaches **p**. In this case, $v(\mathbf{p}, \mathbf{p}') = 0$. Otherwise, we must account for the effect of the distance between **p** and **p′** and

$$v(\mathbf{p}, \mathbf{p}') = \frac{1}{r^2},$$

where r is the distance between the two points.

Although the form of this equation is wonderfully simple, solving it is not an easy task. The main difficulty is the dimensionality. Because **p** and **p′** are points in three-dimensional space, $i(\mathbf{p}, \mathbf{p}')$ has six variables and ρ has nine. In addition, we have not included an additional variable for the wavelength of light, which would be necessary to work with color.

However, we can look at special circumstances that simplify the equation. For example, for perfectly specular surfaces, the reflection function is nonzero only when the angle of incidence equals the angle of reflection and the vectors lie in the same plane. Under these circumstances, ray tracing becomes a special method for solving the rendering equation.

---

1. We are being careful to avoid introducing the units and terminology of radiometry. We see the intensity of light. Energy is the integral of intensity over time, but, if the light sources are unchanging, we are in the steady state, and this distinction does not matter. Most references work with the energy or intensity per unit area (the **energy flux**) rather than energy or intensity.

The other special case that leads to a viable rendering method occurs when all surfaces are perfectly diffuse. In this case, the amount of light reflected is the same in all directions. Thus, the intensity function depends only on **p**. We examine this case in the next section.

13.5 Radiosity

One way to simplify the rendering equation is to consider an environment in which all the surfaces are perfectly diffuse reflectors. Because a perfectly diffuse reflector looks the same to all viewers, the corresponding reflection function is far simpler than the general cases considered by the rendering equation.

Note, however, that although a perfectly diffuse surface reflects light equally in all directions, even if the surface is flat, it can show variations in shading that are not shown when we render using the Phong lighting model. Suppose that we have a simple scene, such as that shown in Figure 13.15, in which all the surfaces are perfectly diffuse. If we render this scene with a distant light source, each polygon surface is rendered as a constant color. If this were a real scene, however, some of the diffuse reflections from the red wall would fall on the white wall, causing red light to be added to the white light reflected from those parts of the white wall that are near the red wall. Diffuse light reflected from the white wall would have a similar effect on the red wall. Our simple shading model has not considered these **diffuse–diffuse interactions**.

An ideal global renderer would capture these interactions. The radiosity method can approximate them very well using an energy approach that was originally used for solving problems in heat transfer.

The basic radiosity method breaks up the scene into small flat polygons, or **patches**, each of which can be assumed to be perfectly diffuse and renders in a constant shade. What we must do first is to find these shades. Once we have found them, we have effectively assigned a color to each patch that is independent of the viewer. Effectively, we have assigned colors to a set of polygon patches in a three-dimensional environment. We can now place the viewer wherever we wish and render the scene in a conventional manner, using a pipeline renderer.

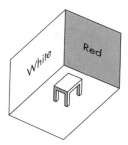

Figure 13.15 Simple scene with diffuse surfaces.

13.5.1 The Radiosity Equation

Let us assume our scene consists of n patches numbered from 1 to n. The radiosity of patch i, b_i, is the light intensity (energy/unit time) per unit area leaving the patch. Typically, the radiosity would be measured in units such as $watts/meter^2$. As we are measuring intensity at a fixed wavelength, we can think of a radiosity function $b_i(\lambda)$ that determines the color of patch i. Suppose that patch i has area a_i. Because we have assumed that each patch is a perfectly diffuse surface, the total intensity leaving patch i is $b_i a_i$. Following reasoning similar to that which we used to derive the rendering equation, the emitted intensity consists of an emissive component, also assumed to be constant across the patch, and a reflective component due to the intensities of all other patches whose light strikes patch i,

$$b_i a_i = e_i a_i + \rho_i \sum_{j=0}^{n} f_{ji} b_j a_j.$$

The term f_{ij} is called the **form factor** between patch i and patch j. It represents the fraction of the energy leaving patch j that reaches patch i. This term depends on how the patches are oriented relative to each other, how far they are from each other , and whether any other patches occlude the light from patch j and prevent it from reaching patch i. We shall discuss the calculation of these factors in the next subsection. The reflectivity of patch i is ρ_i.

Because the form factors depend on the geometric relationship between pairs of patches, there is a simple relationship between the factors f_{ij} and f_{ji} known as the **reciprocity equation**

$$f_{ij} a_i = f_{ji} a_j.$$

Substituting into the equation for the equation for the patch intensities, we find

$$b_i a_i = e_i a_i + \rho_i \sum_{j=0}^{n} f_{ij} b_j a_i.$$

We can now divide by a_i, obtaining an equation for the patch radiosity

$$b_i = e_i + \rho_i \sum_{j=0}^{n} f_{ij} b_j.$$

This result is called the **radiosity equation**.

Assuming that we have computed the form factors, we have a set of n linear equations in the n unknown radiosities. Comparing this equation to the rendering equation, we can see that if the patches were made smaller and smaller, in the limit we would have an infinite number of patches. The sum would become an integral, and the resulting radiosity equation would be a special case of the rendering equation in which all surfaces are perfectly diffuse reflectors.

We can put these equations in matrix form by defining the column matrix of radiosities

$$\mathbf{b} = [b_i],$$

a column matrix of the patch emissions

$$\mathbf{e} = [e_i],$$

a diagonal matrix from the reflection coefficients

$$\mathbf{R} = [\, r_{ij} \,], \qquad a_{ij} = \begin{cases} \rho_i & \text{if } i = j; \\ 0 & \text{otherwise,} \end{cases}$$

and a matrix of the form factors

$$\mathbf{F} = [f_{ij}].$$

Now the set of equations for the radiosities becomes

$$\mathbf{b} = \mathbf{e} - \mathbf{RFb}.$$

We can write the formal solution as

$$\mathbf{b} = [\mathbf{I} - \mathbf{RF}]^{-1}\mathbf{e}.$$

13.5.2 Solving the Radiosity Equation

Although it can be shown that the radiosity equation must have a solution, the real difficulties are practical. A typical scene will have thousands of patches, so that solving the equations by a direct method, such as Gaussian elimination, usually is not possible. Most methods rely on the fact that the matrix $\mathbf{F}$ is sparse. Most of its elements are zero because most patches are sufficiently far from each other so that almost none of the light that they emit or reflect reaches most other patches.

Solution of sets of equations involving sparse matrices are based on iterative methods that require the multiplication of these sparse matrices, an efficient operation. Suppose that we use the equation for the patches to create the iterative equation

$$\mathbf{b}^{k+1} = \mathbf{e} - \mathbf{RFb}^k.$$

Each iteration of this equation requires the matrix multiplication $\mathbf{RFb}^k$, which, assuming $\mathbf{F}$ is sparse, requires $O(n)$ operations, rather than the $O(n^2)$ operations for the general case. In terms of the individual radiosities, we have

$$b_i^{k+1} = e_i - \sum_{j=1}^{n} \rho_i f_{ij} b_j^k.$$

This method, which is known as Jacobi's method, will converge for this problem regardless of the initial starting point $\mathbf{b}^0$.

In general, patches are not self-reflecting so that $f_{ij} = 0$. If we apply updates as soon as they are available, we obtain the Gauss–Seidel method

$$b_i^{k+1} = e_i - \sum_{j=1}^{i-1} \rho_i f_{ij} b_j^{k+1} - \sum_{j=i+1}^{n} \rho_i f_{ij} b_j^k.$$

There is another possible iteration that provides additional physical insight. Consider the scalar formula

$$\frac{1}{1-x} = \sum_{i=0}^{\infty} x^i,$$

which holds if $|x| < 1$. The matrix form of this equation for $\mathbf{RF}$ is[2]

$$[\mathbf{I} - \mathbf{RF}]^{-1} = \sum_{i=0}^{\infty} (\mathbf{RF})^i.$$

Thus, we can write $\mathbf{b}$ as

$$\mathbf{b} = \sum_{i=0}^{\infty} (\mathbf{RF})^i \mathbf{e}$$

$$= \mathbf{e} + (\mathbf{RF})\mathbf{e} + (\mathbf{RF})^2 \mathbf{e} + (\mathbf{RF})^3 \mathbf{e} + \dots$$

We can use this expression, terminating it at some point, to approximate $\mathbf{b}$. Each term has an interesting physical interpretation. The first term, $\mathbf{e}$, is the direct light emitted from each patch so that an approximate solution with just this term will show only the sources. The second term, $(\mathbf{RF})\mathbf{e}$, adds in the light that is the result of exactly one reflection of the sources onto other patches. The next term adds on the contribution from double reflections, and so on for the other terms.

13.5.3 Computing Form Factors

At this point, we have ways of solving for the patch radiosities that are reasonably efficient, but we have yet to discuss the calculation of the form factors. We start with a general derivation of an equation for the form factor between two patches, and then we shall look at how we might find approximate form factors using the tools that we have available.

Consider two perfectly diffuse flat patches, P_i and P_j, as in Figure 13.16, which we have drawn without any other patches that might cause occlusion. Each patch has a normal that gives its orientation. Although each patch emits light equally in all directions, the amount of light leaving two different points on P_j that reaches any point on P_i is different because of the different distances between two points on P_j and a point on P_i. Thus, to collect all the light from P_j that falls on P_i, we must integrate over all points on P_j. The same reasoning applies to two points on P_i that receive light from a point on P_j; they will receive a different amount of light, and thus to determine the light falling on P_i, we must also integrate over all points on P_i.

We can derive the required integral based on our understanding of diffuse shading from Chapter 6. Consider a small area on each patch, da_i and da_j. Each can be considered to be an ideal diffuse reflector (Figure 13.17). They are a distance r apart, where r is the distance between two points, $\mathbf{p}_i$ and $\mathbf{p}_j$, at the center of the two small areas. The light leaving da_j goes in the direction

Figure 13.16   Two patches.

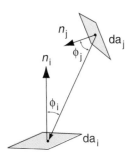

Figure 13.17   Foreshortening between two small patches.

2. The formula converges if the magnitudes of all the eigenvalues of $\mathbf{BF}$ are less than unity, a condition that must be true for the radiosity equation.

$\mathbf{d} = \mathbf{p}_i - \mathbf{p}_j$. However, the intensity of this light is reduced or foreshortened by $\cos \phi_j$, where ϕ_j is the angle between the normal for patch j and the vector $\mathbf{d}$. Likewise, the light arriving at da_i is foreshortened by $\cos \phi_i$, where ϕ_i is the angle between the normal for patch i and the vector $\mathbf{d}$. To obtain the desired form factor, f_{ij}, we must also account for the distance between the patches and the possibility of occlusion. We can do both by defining the term

$$o_{ij} = \begin{cases} 1 & \text{if } \mathbf{p}_j \text{ is visible from } \mathbf{p}_i; \\ 0 & \text{otherwise,} \end{cases}$$

Finally, by averaging over the total area of the patch, we obtain the form-factor equation

$$f_{ij} = \frac{1}{a_i} \int_{a_i} \int_{a_j} o_{ij} \frac{\cos \phi_i \cos \phi_j}{\pi r^2} \, da_i \, da_j.$$

Although the form of this integral is simple, there are only a few special cases for which it can be solved analytically. For real scenes, we need numerical methods. Because we there are n^2 form factors, most methods are a compromise between accuracy and time.

We shall sketch two approaches. The first method starts with the notion of two-step mappings that we used in our discussion of texture mapping in Chapter 7. Consider two patches again, this time with a hemisphere separating them as in Figure 13.18. Suppose that we want to compute the light from P_i that reaches P_j at a point $\mathbf{p}_i$. We center the hemisphere at this point and orient the patch so that the normal is pointing up. We can now project P_j onto the hemisphere and observe that we can use the projected patch for our computation of the form factor rather than the original patch. If we convert to polar coordinates, the form factor equation becomes simpler for the projected patch. However, for each small area of P_i we have to move the hemisphere and add the contribution from each area.

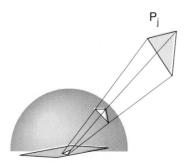

Figure 13.18 Projecting patch on a hemisphere.

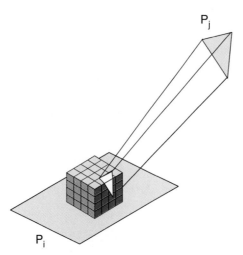

P_j

P_i

Figure 13.19 Projecting patch on a hemicube and onto another patch.

A simpler approach for most graphics applications is to use a hemicube rather than a hemisphere, as shown in Figure 13.19. The hemicube is centered like the hemisphere but its surface is divided into small squares called pixels. The light that strikes patch i is independent of the type of intermediate surface that we use. The advantage of the hemicube is that its surfaces are either parallel to or orthogonal to P_i. Consequently, it is straightforward to project P_j onto the hemicube and to compute the contribution of each pixel on the hemicube to the light that reaches point $\mathbf{p}_i$. Thus, if the surface of the hemicube is divided into m pixels, numbered 1 to m, then we can compute the contribution of those pixels which are projections of P_j and are visible from $\mathbf{p}_i$ and add them to form the **delta form factor** Δf_{ij}, which is the contribution of P_j to the small area da_i at the center of the hemicube. We then get the desired form factor by adding the contributions of all the delta form factors. The contributions from each pixel can be computed analytically once we know whether P_j projects on it, a calculation that is similar to the ray-tracing calculation required to determine whether an object is visible from a light source. The details are included in the references at the end of the chapter.

Another approach to computing form factors exploits our ability to use a graphics system to compute simple renderings very rapidly. Suppose that we want to compute f_{ij}. If we illuminate P_i with a known amount of light only from P_j, we will have an experimental measurement of the desired form factor. We can approximate this measurement by placing point light sources on P_j and then rendering the scene with whatever renderer we have available. Because of the possibility that another patch obscures P_i from P_j, we must use a renderer that can handle shadows.

13.5.4 Carrying Out Radiosity

In practice, radiosity rendering has three major steps. First, we divide the scene into a mesh of patches, as in Figure 13.20. This step requires some skill as more patches require the calculation of more form factors. However, it is the division of surfaces into patches that allows radiosity to yield images with subtle diffuse–diffuse interactions. Often the creation of the initial mesh can be done interactively, allowing the placement of more patches in regions such as corners between surfaces where we expect to see diffuse–diffuse interactions. Another approach is based on the observation that the radiosity of a large surface is equal to the area-weighted sum of the radiosities of any subdivision of it. Hence, we can start with a fairly rough mesh and refine it later (**progressive radiosity**). Once we have a mesh, we can compute the form factors, the most computationally intense part of the process.

Once we have mesh and the form factors, we can solve the radiosity equation. We form the emission array **e** using the values for the light sources in the scene and assign colors to the surfaces, forming **R**. Now we can solve the radiosity equation to determine **b**.

The components of **b** act as the new colors of the patches. We can now place the viewer in the scene and render with a conventional renderer.

figure 13.20 Division of surfaces into patches. (Courtesy of A. Van Pernis, K. Rasche, and R. Geist, Clemson University.)

The image in Color Plate 24 was rendered using radiosity. It started with the initial mesh in Figure 13.20, which was then altered with a particle system to achieve a better set of patches. It shows the strength of radiosity for rendering interiors that are composed of diffuse reflectors.

13.6 RenderMan

There are other approaches to rendering that have arisen from the needs of the animation industry. Although interaction is required in the design of an animation, real-time rendering is not required when the final images are produced. Of greater importance is producing images free of rendering artifacts such as the jaggedness and moiré patterns that arise from aliasing. However, rendering the large number of frames required for a feature-length film cannot be done with ray tracers or radiosity renderers, even though animations are produced using large numbers of computers—**rendering farms**—whose sole task is to render scenes at the required resolution. In addition, neither ray tracers nor radiosity renderers alone produce images that have the desired artistic qualities.

The RenderMan interface is based on the use of the modeling-rendering paradigm that we introduced in Chapter 1. The design of a scene is done interactively, using simple renderers of the type that we discussed in Chapter 6. When the design is complete, the objects, lights, material properties, cameras, motion descriptions, and textures can be described in a file that can be sent to a high-quality renderer or to a rendering farm.

In principle, this off-line renderer could be any type of renderer. However, given the special needs of the animation industry, Pixar developed both the interface (RenderMan) and a renderer called Reyes that was designed to produce the types of images needed for commercial motion pictures. Like a ray tracer, Reyes was designed to work a pixel at time. Unlike a ray tracer, it was not designed to incorporate global lighting effects. By working a pixel at a time, Reyes collects all the light from all objects at a resolution that avoids aliasing problems. Reyes divides (**dices**) objects—both polygonal and curved—into **micropolygons**, which are small quadrilaterals that project to a size of about half of a pixel. Because each micropolygon projects to such a small area, it can be flat shaded, thereby simplifying its rendering. The smooth shading of surfaces is accomplished by coloring the micropolygons carefully during the dicing process.

Reyes incorporates many other interesting techniques. It uses random or stochastic sampling rather than point sampling to reduce visible aliasing effects. Generally, it works on small regions of the frame at one time to allow efficient use of textures. Note that even with its careful design, a single scene with many objects and complex lighting effects can take hours to render.

There are many renderers of this type available, some either public domain or shareware. Some renderers are capable of incorporating different rendering styles within one product. Thus, we might use ray tracing on a subset of the objects that have shiny surfaces. Likewise, we might want to use radiosity on some other subset of the surfaces. In general, these renderers support a large variety of effects and allow the user to balance rendering time against sophistication and image quality.

13.7 Large-Scale Rendering

In many applications, particularly in scientific visualization of large geometric data bases, we create images from data sets that might contain more than 500 million data points and generate more than 100 million polygons. This situation presents two immediate challenges. First, if we are to display this many polygons, how can we do so when typical CRT displays contain only about one million pixels. Second, if we have multiple frames to display, either from new data or because of transformations of the original data set, we need to be able to render this large amount of geometry faster than can be achieved even with high-end systems.

A popular solution to the display-resolution problem is to build a **power wall**, a large projection surface that is illuminated by an array of projectors (Figure 13.21), each with the resolution of a CRT (usually 1024 × 1280 or 1024 × 768). Generally the light output from the projectors is tapered at the edges, and the displays are overlapped slightly to created a seamless image. We can also create high-resolution displays from arrays of standard size LCD panels,

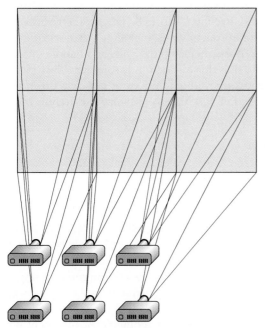

Figure 13.21 Power wall using six projectors.

although at the cost of seeing small separations between panels, which can give the appearance of a window with multiple panes.

Our approach to both these problems is to use clusters of standard computers connected with a high-speed network. Each computer might have a commodity graphics card. Note that such configurations are one aspect of a major revolution in high-performance computing. Formerly, supercomputers were composed of expensive fast processors that usually incorporated a high degree of parallelism in their designs. These processors were custom designed and required special interfaces, peripheral systems, and environments that made them extremely expensive and thus affordable only by a few government laboratories and large corporations. Over the last few years, commodity processors have become extremely fast and inexpensive. The same technology has led to a variety of add-on graphics cards whose performance can be measured in millions of polygons per second and hundreds of millions of pixels per second. Computers assembled from such components can be connected by standard networks that run at gigabit-per-second rates. Thus, we can put together a cluster of these machines for a cost in the range of $1,000–$3,000 per node.

However, there are multiple ways we can distribute the work that must be done to render a scene among the processors. We shall examine three possibilities. In this taxonomy, the key difference is where in the rendering process we assign primitives to the correct areas of the display. Where we place this step leads to the designations **sort first**, **sort last**, and **sort middle**.

Suppose that we start with a large number of processors of two types: geometry processors and raster processors. This distinction corresponds to the two phases of the rendering pipeline that we discussed in Chapter 8. The geometry processors can handle front-end floating-point calculations, including transformations, clipping, and shading. The raster processors manipulate bits and handle operations such as scan conversion. Note that this distinction is somewhat historical, as the present general-purpose processors and graphics cards can each do either of these tasks. However, this distinction will help us organize the architectural possibilities.

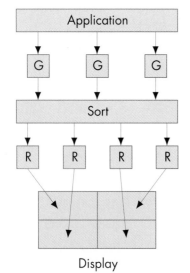

Figure 13.22 Sort-middle rendering.

13.7.1 Sort-Middle Rendering

Consider a group of geometry processors (each labeled with a G) and raster processors (each labeled with an R) connected as in Figure 13.22. Suppose that we have an application that generates a large number of geometric primitives. It can use multiple geometry processors in two obvious ways. It can run on a single processor and send different parts of the geometry generated by the application to different processors. Alternatively, we can run the application on multiple processors, each of which generates only part of the geometry. At this point we need not worry about how the geometry gets to the geometry processors—as the best way is often application dependent—but on how to best employ the geometry processors that are available.

Assume that we can send any primitive to any of the geometry processors, each of which acts independently. When we use multiple processors in parallel, a major concern is **load balancing**, that is, having each of the processors do about the same amount of work, so that none are sitting idle for a significant amount of time, thus wasting resources. One obvious approach would be to divide the world-coordinate space equally among the processors. Unfortunately, this approach often leads to poor load balancing because in many applications the geometry is not uniformly distributed in the problem space. An alternative approach is to distribute the geometry uniformly among the processors as it is generated, independently of where the geometric objects are located. Thus, with n processors, we might send the first geometric entity to the first processor, the second to the second processor, the nth to the nth processor, the $n + 1$-st to the first processor, and so on. Now consider the raster processors. We can assign each of these to a different region of the frame buffer or, equivalently, assign each to a different region of the screen. Thus, each one renders a fixed part of the display.

Now the problem is how to assign the outputs of the geometry processors to the raster processors. Note that each geometry processor can process objects that could go anywhere on the display. Thus, we must sort their outputs and assign primitives that emerge from the geometry processors to the correct raster processors. Consequently, some sorting must be done before the raster stage. We refer to this architecture as *sort middle*.

This configuration was popular with high-end graphics workstations a few years ago, when special hardware was available for each task and there were fast internal buses to convey information through the sorting step. With commodity computers connected by a standard network, the sorting step can be a bottleneck, and two other approaches have proven simpler.

13.7.2 Sort-Last Rendering

With sort-middle rendering, the number of geometry processors and the number of raster processors could be different. Now suppose that each geometry processor is connected to its own raster processor, as in Figure 13.23. This configuration would be what we would have with a collection of standard PCs, each with its own graphics card. Once again, let us not worry about how each processor gets the application data and instead focus on how this configuration can process the geometry generated by the application.

Just as with sort middle, we can load-balance the geometry processors by sending primitives to them in an order that ignores where on the display they might lie once they are rasterized. However, precisely because of this way of assigning geometry and lacking a sort in the middle, each raster processor must have a frame buffer that is the full size of the display. Because each

Figure 13.23 Sort-last rendering.

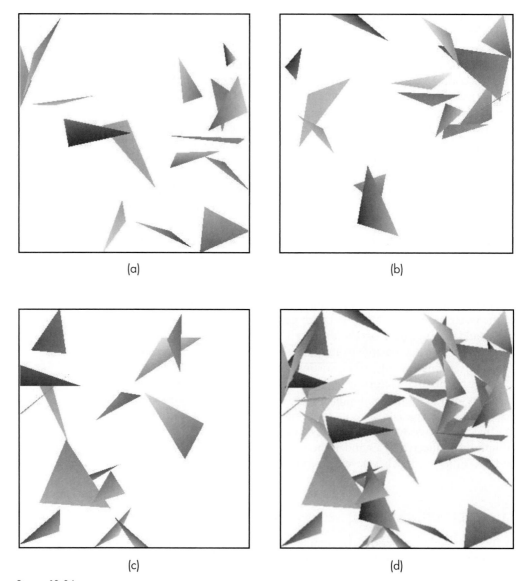

(a)

(b)

(c)

(d)

Figure 13.24 Example of sort-last rendering. (a), (b), (c) Partial renderings. (d) Composited image. (Courtesy of Ge Li, University of New Mexico.)

geometry/raster pair contains a full pipeline, each pair produces a correct hidden-surface–removed image *for part of the geometry*. Figure 13.24 shows three images that are each correct, while the fourth shows how they must be combined to form a correct image containing all the geometry.

We can combine the partial images with a compositing step, as in Figure 13.23. For the compositing calculations, we need not only the images in the color

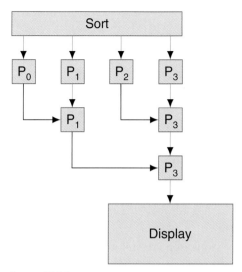

Figure 13.25 Binary-tree compositing.

buffers of the geometry processors but also the depth information, because we must know for each pixel which of the raster processors contains the pixel corresponding to the closest point to the viewer.[3] Fortunately, if we are using our standard OpenGL pipeline, the necessary information is in the z buffer. For each pixel, we need only compare the depths in each of the z buffers and write the color in the frame buffer of the processor with the closest depth. The difficulty is determining how to do this comparison efficiently when the information is stored on many processors.

Conceptually, the simplest approach, sometimes called **binary-tree compositing**, is to have pairs of processors combine their information. Consider the example in Figure 13.25, where we have four geometry/raster pipelines, numbered 0–3. Processors 0 and 1 can combine their information to form a correct image for the geometry they have seen, while processors 2 and 3 do they same thing concurrently with their information. Let us assume that we form these new images on processors 1 and 3. Thus, processors 0 and 2 have to send *both* their color buffers *and* their z buffers to their neighbors (processors 1 and 3, respectively). We then repeat the process between processors 1 and 3, with the final image being formed in the frame buffer of processor 3. Note that the code is very simple. The geometry/raster pairs each do an ordinary rendering. The compositing step requires only the use of glReadPixels and some simple comparisons. However, in each successive step of the compositing process, only half

---

3. For simplicity, we are assuming that all the geometric objects are opaque.

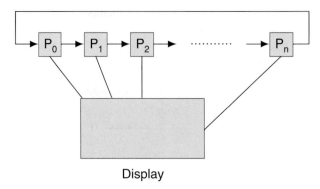

Figure 13.26 Binary-swap compositing.

the processors that were used in the previous step are still needed. In the end, the final image is prepared on a single processor.

There is another approach to the compositing step know as **binary-swap compositing** that avoids the idle processor problem. In this technique, each processor is responsible for one part of the final image. Hence, for compositing to be correct, each processor must see all the data. If we have n processors involved in the compositing, we can arrange them in a round-robin fashion as in Figure 13.26. The compositing takes n steps (rather than the $\log n$ steps required by tree compositing). On the first step, processor 0 sends portion 0 of its frame buffer to processor 1 and receives portion n from processor n. The other processors do a similar send and receive of the portion of the color and depth buffers of their neighbors. At this point, each processor can update one area of the display that will be correct for the data from a pair of processors. For processor 0 this will be region n. On the second round, processor 0 will receive from processor n the data from region $n - 1$, which is correct for the data from processors n and $n - 1$. Processor 0 will also send the data from region n, as will the other processors for part of their frame buffers. All the processors will now have a region that is correct for the data from three processors. Inductively, it should be clear that after $n - 1$ steps, each processor has $1/n$ of the final image. Although we have taken more steps, far less data has been transferred than with tree compositing, and we have used all processors in each step.

13.7.3 Sort-First Rendering

One of the most appealing features of sort-last rendering was that we could pair geometric and raster processors and use standard computers with standard graphics cards. Suppose that we could decide first where each primitive lies on the final display. Then we could assign a separate portion of the display to each geometry/raster pair and avoid the necessity of a compositing network. The configuration might look as in Figure 13.27. Here we have included a processor at the front end to make the assignment as to which primitives go to which processors.

This front-end sort is the key to making this scheme work. In one sense, it might seem impossible, since we are implying that we know the solution—where primitives appear in the display—before we have solved the problem for which we need the geometric pipeline. But things are not hopeless. Many problems are structured so that we may know this information in advance. We also can get the information back from the pipeline using glGetFloatv to find the mapping from world coordinates to screen coordinates. In addition, we need not always be correct. A primitive can be sent to multiple geometry processors if it straddles more than one region of the display. Even if we send a primitive to the wrong processor, that processor may be able to send it on to the correct processor. Because each geometry processor performs a clipping step, we are assured that the resulting image will be correct.

Sort-first rendering does not address the load-balancing issue, because, if there are regions of the screen with very few primitives, the corresponding processors may not be very heavily loaded. However, sort-first rendering has one important advantage over sort-last rendering: it is ideally suited for generating high-resolution displays. Suppose that we want to display our output at a resolution much greater than we get with typical CRT or LCD displays that have a resolution in the range of 1–2 million pixels. Such displays are needed when we wish to examine high-resolution data that might contain more than 100 million geometric primitives.

One approach to this problem is to build a tiled display or power wall consisting of an array of standard displays (or tiles). The tiles can be CRTs, LCD panels, or the output of projectors. From the rendering perspective, we want to render an image whose resolution is the array of the entire display, which can exceed 4000×4000 pixels. Generally, these displays are driven by a cluster of PCs with commodity graphics cards. Hence, the candidate rendering strategies are sort first and sort last.

However, sort-last rendering cannot work in this setting because each geometry/rasterizer processor must have a frame buffer the size of the final image, and, for the compositing step, extremely large amounts of data must be exchanged between processors. Sort-first renderers do not have this problem. Each geometry/processor pair need only be responsible for a small part of the final image, typically an image the size of a standard frame buffer.

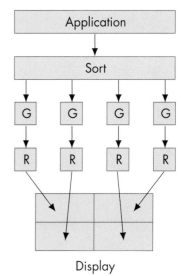

Figure 13.27 Sort-first rendering.

13.8 Image-Based Rendering

Recently there has been a great deal of interest in starting with a set of two-dimensional images and either extracting three-dimensional information or forming new images from them. This problem has appeared in many forms over the years. Some of the most important examples in the past have included the following:

- Using aerial photographs to obtain terrain information
- Using a sequence of two-dimensional X rays to obtain a three-dimensional image in computerized axial tomography (CT)
- Obtaining geometric models from cameras in robotics
- Warping one image into another (morphing)

Newer applications have focused on creating new images from a sequence of stored images that have been carefully collected. For example, suppose that we take a sequence of photographs of an object—a person, a building, or a CAD model—and want to see the object from a different viewpoint. If we had a three-dimensional model, we would simply move the viewer or the object and construct the new image. But what can we do if we have only two-dimensional information? These problems all fit under the broad heading **image-based rendering**. Techniques involve elements of computer graphics, image processing, and computer vision.

13.8.1 A Simple Example

We can get some idea of the issues involved by considering the problem shown on Figure 13.28. On the left is a perspective camera located at a point $\mathbf{p}_1$, and on the right is a second located at $\mathbf{p}_2$. Consider a point $\mathbf{q}$ that is imaged by both cameras. Assuming that we know everything about these cameras—their locations, orientations, fields of view—can we determine $\mathbf{q}$ from the two images produced by the cameras? Figure 13.29 has a top view of a simplified version of the problem with the two cameras both located on the x-axis and with their image planes parallel at $z = d$. Using our standard equations for projections, we have the two relationships

$$\frac{x_1 - x_{p1}}{d} = \frac{x - x_1}{z},$$

$$\frac{x_2 - x_{p2}}{d} = \frac{x - x_2}{z}.$$

These are two linear equations in the unknowns x and z that we can solve, yielding

$$z = \frac{d\,\Delta x}{\Delta x_p - \Delta x},$$

$$x = \frac{x_{p1}\Delta x - x_1 \Delta x_p}{\Delta x_p - \Delta x},$$

where $\Delta x = x_2 - x_1$ and $\Delta x_p = x_{p2} - x_{p1}$.

q

P_1 P_2

Figure 13.28 Two cameras imaging the same point.

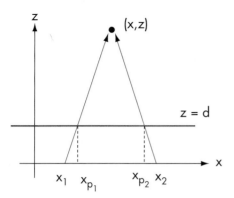

Figure 13.29 Top view of the two cameras.

Thus, we have determined **q** from the two images. This result does not depend on where the cameras are located; moving them only makes the equations a little more complex. Once we have **q** we can obtain an image from any viewpoint.

On closer examination, we can see some practical problems. First, there are numerical problems. Any small errors in the measurement of the camera position can cause large errors in the estimate of **q**. Such numerical issues have plagued many of the traditional applications, such as terrain measurement. One way around such problems is to use more than two measurements and then to determine a best estimate of the desired position.

There are other serious problems. For example, how do we obtain the points **p**$_1$ and **p**$_2$? Given the images from the two cameras, we need a method of identifying corresponding points. This problem is one of the fundamental problems in computer vision and one for which there are no perfect solutions. Note that if there is occlusion, the same point may not even be present in the two images, as in Figure 13.30.

Many early techniques were purely image based, using statistical methods to find corresponding points. Other techniques were interactive, requiring the user to identify corresponding points. Recently, within the computer graphics community, there have been some novel approaches to the problem. We shall mention a few noteworthy approaches. The details of each are in the suggested readings at the end of the chapter.

One way around the difficulties in pure image-based approaches has been to use geometric models rather than points for the registration. For example, in a real environment, we might know that there are many objects that are composed of right parallelepipeds. This extra information can be used to derive very accurate position information.

One use of image-based techniques has been to generate new images for a single viewer from a sequence of images. Variations of this general problem have

Figure 13.30 Imaging with occlusion.

been used in the movie industry, in providing new images in a virtual reality applications, such as Apple's QuickTime VR, and for viewing objects remotely.

Another use of image-based techniques has been to reduce the number of times a scene has to be rendered. One often-exploited observation is that for small movements of the viewer, instead of reprojecting the objects, we can simply shear their images slightly. This technique has been used in Microsoft's Talisman architecture.

Others have looked at the mathematical relationship between two-dimensional images and the light distribution in a three-dimensional environment. Each two-dimensional image is a sample of a four-dimensional light field. In a manner akin to how three-dimensional images are constructed from two-dimensional projections in computerized axial tomography, two-dimensional projections from multiple cameras can be used to reconstruct the three-dimensional world. Two of these techniques are known as the **lumigraph** and **light-field rendering**.

13.9 Summary and Notes

This chapter has illustrated that there are many approaches to rendering. The physical basis for rendering with global lighting is contained in the rendering equation. Unfortunately, it contains too many variables to be solvable, even by numerical methods, for the general case. Radiosity and ray tracing can handle some global effects, although they make opposite assumptions on the types of surfaces that are in the scene.

Although the speed and cost of computers make it possible to ray-trace scenes and do radiosity calculations that were not possible a few years ago, it appears that these techniques alone have limited utility in the real world. If we look at what has been happening in the film, television, and game industries, it appears that we can create photorealistic imagery using a wealth of modeling methods and a variety of commercial and shareware renderers. However, there is a growing acceptance of the view that photorealism is not the ultimate goal. Hence, we see increasing interest in such areas as combining realistic rendering and computer modeling with traditional hand animation. The wide range of image-based methods fit in well with many of these applications.

Most of what we see on the consumer end of graphics is driven by computer games. It appears that no matter how fast and cheap processors are, the demands of consumers for more sophisticated computer games will continue to force developers to come up with faster processors with new capabilities. Most likely as high-definition television (HDTV) becomes more accepted, we will see a greater variety of high-resolution displays available at a reasonable prices.

On the scientific side, the replacement of traditional supercomputers by clusters of commodity computers will continue to have a large effect on scientific visualization. The enormous data sets generated by applications run on these clusters will drive application development on the graphics side. Not only will these applications need imagery generated for high-resolution displays, but also the difficulties of storing these data sets will drive efforts to visualize these data as fast as they can be generated.

13.10 Suggested Readings

Ray tracing was introduced by Appel [App68] and popularized by Whitted [Whi80]. Many of the early papers on ray tracing are included in a volume by Joy and colleagues [Joy88]. The book by Glassner [Gla89] is particularly helpful if you plan to write your own ray tracer. Many of the tests for intersections are described in Haines's chapter in [Gla89] and in the Graphics Gems series [Gra90, Gra91, Gra92, Gra94, Gra95].

The Rendering Equation is due to Kajiya [Kaj86]. Radiosity is based on a method first used in heat transfer [Sie81]. It was first applied in computer graphics by Goral and colleagues [Gor84]. Since its introduction, researchers have done a great deal of work on increasing its efficiency [Coh85, Coh88, Coh93] and incorporating specular terms [Sil89]. The method of using point light sources to find form factors appeared in [Kel97].

The RenderMan Interface is described in [Ups89]. The Reyes rendering architecture was first presented in [Coo87]. Maya [Wat02] allows multiple types of renderers.

The sorting classification of parallel rendering was suggested by Molnar and colleagues [Mol94]. The advantages of sort-middle architectures were used in SGI's high-end workstations such as the InfiniteReality Graphics [Mon97]. The sort-last architecture was developed as part of the Pixel Flow architecture [Mol92]. Binary-swap compositing was suggested by [Ma94]. Software for sort-last renderings using clusters of commodity computers is discussed in [Hum01]. Power walls are described in [Her00, Che00].

Image-based rendering by warping frames was part of Micorsoft's Talisman hardware [Tor96]. Apple's Quicktime VR [Che95] was based on creating new views from a single viewpoint from a 360-degree panorama. Debevec and colleagues [Deb96] showed that by using a model-based approach, new images from multiple viewpoints could be constructed from a small number of images. Other warping methods were proposed in [Sei96]. Work on the Lumigraph [Gor96] and light fields [Lev96] established the mathematical foundations for image-based techniques.

Exercises

13.1 Devise a test for whether a point is inside a convex polygon based on the idea that the polygon can be described by a set of intersecting lines in a single plane.

13.2 Extend your algorithm from Exercise 13.1 to polyhedra that are formed by the intersection of planes.

13.3 Derive an implicit equation for a torus whose center is at the origin. You can derive the equation by noting that a plane that cuts through the torus reveals two circles of the same radius.

13.4 Using the result from Exercise 13.3, show that you can ray trace a torus using the quadratic equation to find the required intersections.

13.5 Consider a ray passing through a sphere. Find the point on this ray closest to the center of the sphere. Hint: consider a line from the center of the sphere that is normal to the ray. How can you use this result for intersection testing?

13.6 We can get increased accuracy from a ray tracer by using more rays. Suppose for each pixel, we cast a ray through the center of the pixel and through its four corners. How much more work does this approach require as compared to the one-ray-per-pixel ray tracer.

13.7 In the sort-middle approach to parallel rendering, what type of information must be conveyed between the geometry processors and raster processors?

13.8 What changes would you have to make to our parallel rendering strategies if we were to allow translucent objects?

13.9 One way to classify parallel computers is by whether their memory is shared among the processors or distributed so that each processer has its own memory that is not accessible to other processors. How does this distinction affect the various rendering strategies that we have discussed?

13.10 Generalize the simple example of imaging the same point from two viewers to the general case in which the two viewers can be located at arbitrary locations in three dimensions.

13.11 Build a simple ray tracer that can handle only planes and spheres. There are many interesting data sets available on the Internet with which to test your code.

13.12 Suppose that you have an algebraic function in which the highest term is $x^i y^j z^k$. What is the degree of the polynomial that we need to solve for the intersection of a ray with the surface defined by this function?

13.13 Consider again an algebraic function in which the highest term is $x^i y^j z^k$. If $i = j = k$, how many terms are in the polynomial that is created when we intersect the surface with a parametric ray.

13.14 For one or more OpenGL implementations, find how many triangles per second can be rendered. Determine what part of the rendering time is spent in hidden-surface removal, shading, texture mapping, and rasterization. If you are using a commodity graphics card, how does the performance that you measure compare with the specifications for the card?

13.15 Determine the pixel performance of your graphics card. Determine how many pixels per second can be read or written. Do the reading and writing of pixels occur at different rates? Is there a difference in writing texture maps?

13.16 Build a sort-last renderer using OpenGL for the rendering on each processor. You can do performance tests using applications that generate triangles or triangular meshes.

13.17 Explain why, as we add more processors, the performance of sort-first rendering will eventually get worse.

Sample Programs

This appendix contains the source code for many of the example programs that we developed in the text. These programs and others that are referred to in the text are also available by means of anonymous ftp from `ftp.cs.unm.edu` under the directory /pub/angel/BOOK. See `http://www.cs.unm.edu/~angel` for updates. A makefile that should work on most UNIX implementations is also available there, as are additional sample programs. Other examples, including those in the *OpenGL Programmer's Guide* and GLUT, can be obtained starting from SGI's OpenGL home page (`http://www.sgi.com/software/opengl/`) or from the OpenGL organization (`http://www.opengl.org`).

OpenGL is provided with all Silicon Graphics workstations and with Microsoft Windows. Sources of OpenGL for other systems are referenced on the OpenGL home page. There are versions available for most UNIX workstations, Windows, and the Macintosh—either through the manufacturers or through third-party suppliers. There is a free OpenGL API called MESA available over the Internet (`http://www.mesa3D.org`). It runs on most systems including LINUX.

The programs that follow use the GLUT library for interfacing with the window system. GLUT is available over the Internet. See the OpenGL home pages. The naming of the functions follows the *OpenGL Programmer's Guide* and the *GLUT Users Guide*. These programs share much of the same code. You should find functions, such as the reshape callback, the initialization function, and the `main` function, almost identical across the programs. Consequently, only the first instance of each function contains extensive comments.

In all these programs, illustration of graphical principles, other than efficiency, was the most important design criterion. You should find numerous ways both to extend these programs and to make them run more efficiently. In some instances, the same visual results can be generated in a completely different manner, using OpenGL capabilities other than the ones we used in the sample program. These programs, additional programs, and other information are contained in the CD that comes with this book.

The programs that follow include

1. A program that generates 5,000 points on the Sierpinski gasket (Chapter 2)
2. A version of the gasket program using recursion (Chapter 2)
3. A three-dimensional point version of the gasket program (Chapter 2)
4. A three-dimensional recursive version of the gasket program (Chapter 2)

A.1 Sierpinski Gasket Program

```
/* Two-Dimensional Sierpinski Gasket          */
/* Generated Using Randomly Selected Vertices */
/* And Bisection                              */

#include <GL/glut.h>

/* You may have to change the include to <glut.h> or
elsewhere depending on where it is stored on your system */

/* glut.h includes gl.h and glu.h */

void myinit()
{

/* attributes */

     glClearColor(1.0, 1.0, 1.0, 1.0); /* white background */
     glColor3f(1.0, 0.0, 0.0); /* draw in red */

/* set up viewing */
/* 500 x 500 window with origin lower left */

     glMatrixMode(GL_PROJECTION);
     glLoadIdentity();
     gluOrtho2D(0.0, 500.0, 0.0, 500.0);
     glMatrixMode(GL_MODELVIEW);
}
```

```
void display()
{

/* define a point data type */

    typedef GLfloat point2[2];

    point2 vertices[3]={{0.0,0.0},{250.0,500.0},{500.0,0.0}}; /* A triangle
*/

    int i, j, k;
    int rand();        /* standard random number generator */
    point2 p ={75.0,50.0};  /* An arbitrary initial point inside triangle */

    glClear(GL_COLOR_BUFFER_BIT);  /*clear the window */


/* compute and plot 5000 new points */

    for( k=0; k<5000; k++)
    {
        j=rand()%3; /* pick a vertex at random */


    /* Compute point halfway between selected vertex and old point */

        p[0] = (p[0]+vertices[j][0])/2.0;
        p[1] = (p[1]+vertices[j][1])/2.0;

    /* plot new point */

        glBegin(GL_POINTS);
            glVertex2fv(p);
        glEnd();
    }
    glFlush(); /* clear buffers */
 }

void main(int argc, char** argv)
{

/* Standard GLUT initialization */

    glutInit(&argc,argv);
    glutInitDisplayMode (GLUT_SINGLE | GLUT_RGB); /* default, not needed */
    glutInitWindowSize(500,500); /* 500 x 500 pixel window */
    glutInitWindowPosition(0,0); /* place window top left on display */
    glutCreateWindow("Sierpinski Gasket"); /* window title */
    glutDisplayFunc(display);
```

```
                                  /* display callback invoked when window opened */

        myinit(); /* set attributes */

        glutMainLoop(); /* enter event loop */
}
```

A.2 Recursive Generation of Sierpinski Gasket

```
/* Recursive subdivision of triangle to form Sierpinski gasket */
/* Number of recursive steps given on command line */

#include <GL/glut.h>

typedef float point2[2];

/* initial triangle */

point2 v[]={{-1.0, -0.58}, {1.0, -0.58}, {0.0, 1.15}};

int n;

void triangle( point2 a, point2 b, point2 c)

/* display one triangle   */
{
    glBegin(GL_TRIANGLES);
        glVertex2fv(a);
        glVertex2fv(b);
        glVertex2fv(c);
    glEnd();
}

void divide_triangle(point2 a, point2 b, point2 c, int m)
{

/* triangle subdivision using vertex numbers */

    point2 v0, v1, v2;
    int j;
    if(m>0)
    {
        for(j=0; j<2; j++) v0[j]=(a[j]+b[j])/2;
        for(j=0; j<2; j++) v1[j]=(a[j]+c[j])/2;
        for(j=0; j<2; j++) v2[j]=(b[j]+c[j])/2;
        divide_triangle(a, v0, v1, m-1);
        divide_triangle(c, v1, v2, m-1);
```

```
            divide_triangle(b, v2, v0, m-1);
    }
    else triangle(a,b,c); /* draw triangle at end of recursion */
}


void display()
{


    glClear(GL_COLOR_BUFFER_BIT);
    divide_triangle(v[0], v[1], v[2], n);
    glFlush();
}

void myinit()
{

    glMatrixMode(GL_PROJECTION);
    glLoadIdentity();
    gluOrtho2D(-2.0, 2.0, -2.0, 2.0);
    glMatrixMode(GL_MODELVIEW);
    glClearColor (1.0, 1.0, 1.0, 1.0);
    glColor3f(0.0,0.0,0.0);
}

void
main(int argc, char **argv)
{
    n=atoi(argv[1]);
    glutInit(&argc, argv);
    glutInitDisplayMode(GLUT_SINGLE | GLUT_RGB);
    glutInitWindowSize(500, 500);
    glutCreateWindow("Sierpinski Gasket");
    glutDisplayFunc(display);
    myinit();
    glutMainLoop();
}
```

A.3 Three-Dimensional Sierpinski Gasket

```
/* 3D Sierpinski Gasket GL program */

#include <GL/gl.h>
#include <GL/glu.h>
#include <GL/glx.h>
#include <GL/glut.h>
```

```
/* define a point data type */

typedef struct {float x,y,z;} point3;

point3 vertices[4]={{0,0,0},{250,500,100},
   {500,250,250},{250,100,250}}; /* A tetrahedron */

int j;
point3 new, old={250,100,250};

void clear()
{
 glClear(GL_COLOR_BUFFER_BIT);
}

void display()

/* compute and plot a single new point */

{
long rand();

int i;
j=rand()%4; /* pick a vertex at random */


/* Compute point halfway between vertex and old point */

new.x = (old.x+vertices[j].x)/2;
new.y = (old.y+vertices[j].y)/2;
new.z = (old.z+vertices[j].z)/2;

/* plot point */

glBegin(GL_POINTS);
glColor3f(1.0-new.z/250.,new.z/250.,0.);
glVertex3f(new.x, new.y,new.z);
glEnd();


/* replace old point by new */

 old.x=new.x;
 old.y=new.y;
 old.z=new.z;


 glFlush();
}
```

```
void mouse(int btn, int state, int x, int y)
{
  if(btn==GLUT_LEFT_BUTTON&state==GLUT_DOWN)  glutIdleFunc(display);
  if(btn==GLUT_MIDDLE_BUTTON&state==GLUT_DOWN)  glutIdleFunc(NULL);
  if(btn==GLUT_RIGHT_BUTTON&state==GLUT_DOWN)   exit();
}

int main(int argc, char** argv)
{


  glutInit(&argc,argv);
  glutInitDisplayMode (GLUT_SINGLE | GLUT_RGB);
  glutInitWindowSize(500,500);
  glutInitWindowPosition(0,0);
  glutCreateWindow("Sierpinski Gasket");
  glutIdleFunc (display);
  glutMouseFunc (mouse);
  glClearColor(1.0, 1.0, 1.0, 0.0); /* white background */
  glColor3f(1.0, 0.0, 0.0);
  glMatrixMode(GL_PROJECTION);
  glLoadIdentity();
  glOrtho(0.0, 500.0, 0.0, 500.0, -500.0, 500.0);
  glMatrixMode(GL_MODELVIEW);
  glutDisplayFunc(clear);


 glutMainLoop();

}
```

A.4 Recursive Three-Dimensional Sierpinski Gasket

```
/* Recursive subdivision of tetrahedron to form 3D Sierpinski gasket */
/* Number of recursive steps given on command line */

#include <stdlib.h>
#include <GL/glut.h>

typedef float point3[3];

/* initial tetrahedron */

point3 v[]={{0.0, 0.0, 1.0}, {0.0, 0.942809, -0.33333},
      {-0.816497, -0.471405, -0.333333}, {0.816497, -0.471405, -0.333333}};

static GLfloat theta[] = {0.0,0.0,0.0};
```

```
int n;

void triangle( point3 a, point3 b, point3 c)

/* display one triangle using a line loop for wire frame, a single
normal for constant shading, or three normals for interpolative shading */
{
    glBegin(GL_POLYGON);
        glNormal3fv(a);
        glVertex3fv(a);
        glVertex3fv(b);
        glVertex3fv(c);
    glEnd();
}

void divide_triangle(point3 a, point3 b, point3 c, int m)
{

/* triangle subdivision using vertex numbers
right-hand rule applied to create outward-pointing faces */

    point3 v1, v2, v3;
    int j;
    if(m>0)
    {
        for(j=0; j<3; j++) v1[j]=(a[j]+b[j])/2;
        for(j=0; j<3; j++) v2[j]=(a[j]+c[j])/2;
        for(j=0; j<3; j++) v3[j]=(b[j]+c[j])/2;
        divide_triangle(a, v1, v2, m-1);
        divide_triangle(c, v2, v3, m-1);
        divide_triangle(b, v3, v1, m-1);
    }
    else triangle(a,b,c); /* draw triangle at end of recursion */
}

void tetrahedron( int m)
{

/* Apply triangle subdivision to faces of tetrahedron */

 glColor3f(1.0,0.0,0.0);
    divide_triangle(v[0], v[1], v[2], m);
 glColor3f(0.0,1.0,0.0);
    divide_triangle(v[3], v[2], v[1], m);
 glColor3f(0.0,0.0,1.0);
    divide_triangle(v[0], v[3], v[1], m);
 glColor3f(0.0,0.0,0.0);
    divide_triangle(v[0], v[2], v[3], m);
}
```

```
void display()
{


    glClear(GL_COLOR_BUFFER_BIT | GL_DEPTH_BUFFER_BIT);
    glLoadIdentity();
    tetrahedron(n);
    glFlush();
}


void myReshape(int w, int h)
{
    glViewport(0, 0, w, h);
    glMatrixMode(GL_PROJECTION);
    glLoadIdentity();
    if (w <= h)
        glOrtho(-2.0, 2.0, -2.0 * (GLfloat) h / (GLfloat) w,
            2.0 * (GLfloat) h / (GLfloat) w, -10.0, 10.0);
    else
        glOrtho(-2.0 * (GLfloat) w / (GLfloat) h,
            2.0 * (GLfloat) w / (GLfloat) h, -2.0, 2.0, -10.0, 10.0);
    glMatrixMode(GL_MODELVIEW);
    glutPostRedisplay();
}


void
main(int argc, char **argv)
{
    n=atoi(argv[1]);
    glutInit(&argc, argv);
    glutInitDisplayMode(GLUT_SINGLE | GLUT_RGB | GLUT_DEPTH);
    glutInitWindowSize(500, 500);
    glutCreateWindow("3D Gasket");
    glutReshapeFunc(myReshape);
    glutDisplayFunc(display);
    glEnable(GL_DEPTH_TEST);
    glClearColor (1.0, 1.0, 1.0, 1.0);
    glutMainLoop();
}
```

A.5 Square Drawing Program

```
/* This program illustrates the use of the GLUT library for
interfacing with a window system */
```

```
/* The program opens a window, clears it to black,
then draws a box at the location of the mouse each time the
left button is clicked. The right button exits the program.
The program also reacts correctly when the window is
moved or resized by clearing the new window to black*/

#include <GL/glut.h>

/* globals */

GLsizei wh = 500, ww = 500; /* initial window size */
GLfloat size = 3.0;   /* half side length of square */


void drawSquare(int x, int y)
{

   y=wh-y;
   glColor3ub( (char) rand()%256, (char) rand()%256, (char) rand()%256);
   glBegin(GL_POLYGON);
      glVertex2f(x+size, y+size);
      glVertex2f(x-size, y+size);
      glVertex2f(x-size, y-size);
      glVertex2f(x+size, y-size);
   glEnd();
   glFlush();
}


/* reshaping routine called whenever window is resized
or moved */

void myReshape(GLsizei w, GLsizei h)
{

/* adjust clipping box */

   glMatrixMode(GL_PROJECTION);
   glLoadIdentity();
   glOrtho(0.0, (GLdouble)w, 0.0, (GLdouble)h, -1.0, 1.0);
   glMatrixMode(GL_MODELVIEW);
   glLoadIdentity();

/* adjust viewport and clear */

   glViewport(0,0,w,h);
   glClearColor (0.0, 0.0, 0.0, 1.0);
   glClear(GL_COLOR_BUFFER_BIT);
   glFlush();
```

```
/* set global size for use by drawing routine */

    ww = w;
    wh = h;
}

void myinit()
{

    glViewport(0,0,ww,wh);

/* Pick 2D clipping window to match size of screen window
This choice avoids having to scale object coordinates
each time window is resized */

    glMatrixMode(GL_PROJECTION);
    glLoadIdentity();
    glOrtho(0.0, (GLdouble) ww , 0.0, (GLdouble) wh , -1.0, 1.0);

/* set clear color to black and clear window */

    glClearColor (0.0, 0.0, 0.0, 1.0);
    glClear(GL_COLOR_BUFFER_BIT);
    glFlush();



/* callback routine for reshape event */

    glutReshapeFunc(myReshape);

}

void mouse(int btn, int state, int x, int y)
{
    if(btn==GLUT_RIGHT_BUTTON && state==GLUT_DOWN)    exit();
}

/* display callback required by GLUT 3.0 */

void display()
{}

int main(int argc, char** argv)
{

    glutInit(&argc,argv);
    glutInitDisplayMode (GLUT_SINGLE | GLUT_RGB);
    glutCreateWindow("square");
```

```
    myinit ();
    glutReshapeFunc (myReshape);
    glutMouseFunc (mouse);
    glutMotionFunc(drawSquare);
    glutDisplayFunc(display);

    glutMainLoop();

}
```

A.6 Paint Program

```
/* A simple painting program with text, lines, triangles,
rectangles, and points */


#define NULL 0
#define LINE 1
#define RECTANGLE 2
#define TRIANGLE  3
#define POINTS 4
#define TEXT 5

#include <GL/glut.h>

void mouse(int, int, int, int);
void key(unsigned char, int, int);
void display();
void drawSquare(int, int);
void myReshape(GLsizei, GLsizei);

void myinit();

void screen_box(int, int, int);
void right_menu(int);
void middle_menu(int);
void color_menu(int);
void pixel_menu(int);
void fill_menu(int);
int pick(int, int);

/* globals */

GLsizei wh = 500, ww = 500; /* initial window size */
GLfloat size = 3.0;   /* half side length of square */
int draw_mode = 0; /* drawing mode */
int rx, ry; /*raster position*/
```

```
GLfloat r = 1.0, g = 1.0, b = 1.0; /* drawing color */
int fill = 0; /* fill flag */

void drawSquare(int x, int y)
{

        y=wh-y;
        glColor3ub( (char) rand()%256, (char) rand()%256, (char) rand()%256);
        glBegin(GL_POLYGON);
                glVertex2f(x+size, y+size);
                glVertex2f(x-size, y+size);
                glVertex2f(x-size, y-size);
                glVertex2f(x+size, y-size);
        glEnd();
}


/* reshaping routine called whenever window is resized
or moved */

void myReshape(GLsizei w, GLsizei h)
{

/* adjust clipping box */

        glMatrixMode(GL_PROJECTION);
        glLoadIdentity();
        glOrtho(0.0, (GLdouble)w, 0.0, (GLdouble)h, -1.0, 1.0);
        glMatrixMode(GL_MODELVIEW);
        glLoadIdentity();

/* adjust viewport and  clear */

        glViewport(0,0,w,h);
        glClearColor (0.8, 0.8, 0.8, 1.0);
        glClear(GL_COLOR_BUFFER_BIT);
        display();
        glFlush();

/* set global size for use by drawing routine */

        ww = w;
        wh = h;
}

void myinit()
{

 glViewport(0,0,ww,wh);
```

```
/* Pick 2D clipping window to match size of X window
This choice avoids having to scale object coordinates
each time window is resized */

        glMatrixMode(GL_PROJECTION);
        glLoadIdentity();
        glOrtho(0.0, (GLdouble) ww , 0.0, (GLdouble) wh , -1.0, 1.0);

/* set clear color to black and clear window */

        glClearColor (0.8, 0.8, 0.8, 1.0);
        glClear(GL_COLOR_BUFFER_BIT);
        glFlush();
}

void mouse(int btn, int state, int x, int y)
{
    static int count;
    int where;
    static int xp[2],yp[2];
    if(btn==GLUT_LEFT_BUTTON && state==GLUT_DOWN)
    {
       glPushAttrib(GL_ALL_ATTRIB_BITS);
       where = pick(x,y);
       glColor3f(r, g, b);
       if(where != 0)
       {
          count = 0;
          draw_mode = where;
       }
       else switch(draw_mode)
       {
         case(LINE):
          if(count==0)
          {
             count++;
             xp[0] = x;
             yp[0] = y;
          }
          else
          {
             glBegin(GL_LINES);
                glVertex2i(x,wh-y);
                glVertex2i(xp[0],wh-yp[0]);
             glEnd();
             draw_mode=0;
             count=0;
          }
          break;
```

```
case(RECTANGLE):
  if(count == 0)
  {
      count++;
      xp[0] = x;
      yp[0] = y;
  }
  else
  {
      if(fill) glBegin(GL_POLYGON);
      else glBegin(GL_LINE_LOOP);
          glVertex2i(x,wh-y);
          glVertex2i(x,wh-yp[0]);
          glVertex2i(xp[0],wh-yp[0]);
          glVertex2i(xp[0],wh-y);
      glEnd();
      draw_mode=0;
      count=0;
  }
  break;
case (TRIANGLE):
  switch(count)
  {
    case(0):
      count++;
      xp[0] = x;
      yp[0] = y;
      break;
    case(1):
      count++;
      xp[1] = x;
      yp[1] = y;
      break;
    case(2):
      if(fill) glBegin(GL_POLYGON);
      else glBegin(GL_LINE_LOOP);
          glVertex2i(xp[0],wh-yp[0]);
          glVertex2i(xp[1],wh-yp[1]);
          glVertex2i(x,wh-y);
      glEnd();
      draw_mode=0;
      count=0;
  }
  break;
case(POINTS):
  {
      drawSquare(x,y);
      count++;
  }
```

```
              break;
          case(TEXT):
            {
            rx=x;
            ry=wh-y;
            glRasterPos2i(rx,ry);
            count=0;
            }
              }

              glPopAttrib();
              glFlush();
            }
}

int pick(int x, int y)
{
    y = wh - y;
    if(y < wh-ww/10) return 0;
    else if(x < ww/10) return LINE;
    else if(x < ww/5) return RECTANGLE;
    else if(x < 3*ww/10) return TRIANGLE;
    else if(x < 2*ww/5) return POINTS;
 else if(x < ww/2) return TEXT;
    else return 0;
}

void screen_box(int x, int y, int s )
{
    glBegin(GL_QUADS);
      glVertex2i(x, y);
      glVertex2i(x+s, y);
      glVertex2i(x+s, y+s);
      glVertex2i(x, y+s);
    glEnd();
}

void right_menu(int id)
{
   if(id == 1) exit();
   else display();
}

void middle_menu(int id)
{

}

void color_menu(int id)
```

```
{
   if(id == 1) {r = 1.0; g = 0.0; b = 0.0;}
   else if(id == 2) {r = 0.0; g = 1.0; b = 0.0;}
   else if(id == 3) {r = 0.0; g = 0.0; b = 1.0;}
   else if(id == 4) {r = 0.0; g = 1.0; b = 1.0;}
   else if(id == 5) {r = 1.0; g = 0.0; b = 1.0;}
   else if(id == 6) {r = 1.0; g = 1.0; b = 0.0;}
   else if(id == 7) {r = 1.0; g = 1.0; b = 1.0;}
   else if(id == 8) {r = 0.0; g = 0.0; b = 0.0;}
}

void pixel_menu(int id)
{
   if (id == 1) size = 2 * size;
   else if (size > 1) size = size/2;
}

void fill_menu(int id)
{
   if (id == 1) fill = 1;
   else fill = 0;
}

void key(unsigned char k, int xx, int yy)
{
   if(draw_mode!=TEXT) return;
 glColor3f(0.0,0.0,0.0);
   glRasterPos2i(rx,ry);
   glutBitmapCharacter(GLUT_BITMAP_9_BY_15, k);
 /*glutStrokeCharacter(GLUT_STROKE_ROMAN,i); */
   rx+=glutBitmapWidth(GLUT_BITMAP_9_BY_15,k);

}

void display()
{
 int shift=0;
   glPushAttrib(GL_ALL_ATTRIB_BITS);
   glClearColor (0.8, 0.8, 0.8, 1.0);
   glClear(GL_COLOR_BUFFER_BIT);
   glColor3f(1.0, 1.0, 1.0);
   screen_box(0,wh-ww/10,ww/10);
   glColor3f(1.0, 0.0, 0.0);
   screen_box(ww/10,wh-ww/10,ww/10);
   glColor3f(0.0, 1.0, 0.0);
   screen_box(ww/5,wh-ww/10,ww/10);
   glColor3f(0.0, 0.0, 1.0);
   screen_box(3*ww/10,wh-ww/10,ww/10);
   glColor3f(1.0, 1.0, 0.0);
```

```
        screen_box(2*ww/5,wh-ww/10,ww/10);
        glColor3f(0.0, 0.0, 0.0);
        glBegin(GL_LINES);
            glVertex2i(wh/40,wh-ww/20);
            glVertex2i(wh/40+ww/20,wh-ww/20);
        glEnd();

        glBegin(GL_TRIANGLES);
            glVertex2i(ww/5+ww/40,wh-ww/10+ww/40);
            glVertex2i(ww/5+ww/20,wh-ww/40);
            glVertex2i(ww/5+3*ww/40,wh-ww/10+ww/40);
        glEnd();
        glPointSize(3.0);
        glBegin(GL_POINTS);
            glVertex2i(3*ww/10+ww/20, wh-ww/20);
        glEnd();
        glRasterPos2i(2*ww/5,wh-ww/20);
        glutBitmapCharacter(GLUT_BITMAP_9_BY_15, 'A');
        shift=glutBitmapWidth(GLUT_BITMAP_9_BY_15, 'A');
        glRasterPos2i(2*ww/5+shift,wh-ww/20);
        glutBitmapCharacter(GLUT_BITMAP_9_BY_15, 'B');
        shift+=glutBitmapWidth(GLUT_BITMAP_9_BY_15, 'B');
        glRasterPos2i(2*ww/5+shift,wh-ww/20);
        glutBitmapCharacter(GLUT_BITMAP_9_BY_15, 'C');
        glFlush();
        glPopAttrib();
}


int main(int argc, char** argv)
{
    int c_menu, p_menu, f_menu;

    glutInit(&argc,argv);
    glutInitDisplayMode (GLUT_SINGLE | GLUT_RGB);
    glutCreateWindow("square");
    glutDisplayFunc(display);
    c_menu = glutCreateMenu(color_menu);
    glutAddMenuEntry("Red",1);
    glutAddMenuEntry("Green",2);
    glutAddMenuEntry("Blue",3);
    glutAddMenuEntry("Cyan",4);
    glutAddMenuEntry("Magenta",5);
    glutAddMenuEntry("Yellow",6);
    glutAddMenuEntry("White",7);
    glutAddMenuEntry("Black",8);
    p_menu = glutCreateMenu(pixel_menu);
    glutAddMenuEntry("increase pixel size", 1);
    glutAddMenuEntry("decrease pixel size", 2);
```

```
    f_menu = glutCreateMenu(fill_menu);
    glutAddMenuEntry("fill on", 1);
    glutAddMenuEntry("fill off", 2);
    glutCreateMenu(right_menu);
    glutAddMenuEntry("quit",1);
    glutAddMenuEntry("clear",2);
    glutAttachMenu(GLUT_RIGHT_BUTTON);
    glutCreateMenu(middle_menu);
    glutAddSubMenu("Colors", c_menu);
    glutAddSubMenu("Pixel Size", p_menu);
    glutAddSubMenu("Fill", f_menu);
    glutAttachMenu(GLUT_MIDDLE_BUTTON);
    myinit ();
    glutReshapeFunc (myReshape);
    glutKeyboardFunc(key);
    glutMouseFunc (mouse);
    glutMainLoop();

}
```

A.7 Double-Buffering Example

```
/*
 *  single_double.c
 *  This program demonstrates single and double buffering for
 *  flicker-free animation.  The left and middle mouse
 *  buttons start and stop the spinning motion of the square
 */
#include <GL/glut.h>
#include <stdlib.h>

static GLfloat spin = 0.0;
    int singleb, doubleb;

void displayd()
{
    glClear (GL_COLOR_BUFFER_BIT);
    glRectf (-25.0, -25.0, 25.0, 25.0);
    glutSwapBuffers ();
}

void displays()
{
    glClear (GL_COLOR_BUFFER_BIT);
    glRectf (-25.0, -25.0, 25.0, 25.0);
    glFlush();
}
```

```
void spinDisplay ()
{
    spin = spin + 2.0;
    if (spin > 360.0) spin = spin - 360.0;
    glutSetWindow(singleb);
    glLoadIdentity();
    glRotatef (spin, 0.0, 0.0, 1.0);
    glutPostRedisplay();
    glutSetWindow(doubleb);
    glLoadIdentity();
    glRotatef (spin, 0.0, 0.0, 1.0);
    glutPostRedisplay();
}

void myinit ()
{
    glClearColor (0.0, 0.0, 0.0, 1.0);
    glColor3f (1.0, 1.0, 1.0);
    glShadeModel (GL_FLAT);
}

void mouse(int btn, int state, int x, int y)
{
if(btn==GLUT_LEFT_BUTTON && state==GLUT_DOWN)   glutIdleFunc(spinDisplay);
if(btn==GLUT_MIDDLE_BUTTON && state==GLUT_DOWN)  glutIdleFunc(NULL);
}

void myReshape(int w, int h)
{
    glViewport(0, 0, w, h);
    glMatrixMode(GL_PROJECTION);
    glLoadIdentity();
    if (w <= h)
    glOrtho (-50.0, 50.0, -50.0*(GLfloat)h/(GLfloat)w,
        50.0*(GLfloat)h/(GLfloat)w, -1.0, 1.0);
    else
    glOrtho (-50.0*(GLfloat)w/(GLfloat)h,
        50.0*(GLfloat)w/(GLfloat)h, -50.0, 50.0, -1.0, 1.0);

    glMatrixMode(GL_MODELVIEW);
    glLoadIdentity ();
}

/*  Main Loop
 *  Open window with initial window size, title bar,
 *  RGBA display mode, and handle input events
 */
int main(int argc, char** argv)
{
```

```
    glutInit(&argc,argv);
    glutInitDisplayMode (GLUT_SINGLE | GLUT_RGB);
    singleb=glutCreateWindow("single buffered");
    myinit ();
    glutDisplayFunc(displays);
    glutReshapeFunc (myReshape);
    glutIdleFunc (spinDisplay);
    glutMouseFunc (mouse);
    glutInitDisplayMode (GLUT_DOUBLE | GLUT_RGB);
    doubleb=glutCreateWindow("double buffered");
    myinit ();
    glutDisplayFunc(displayd);
    glutReshapeFunc (myReshape);
    glutIdleFunc (spinDisplay);
    glutMouseFunc (mouse);

    glutMainLoop();

}
```

A.8 Selection-Mode Picking Program

```
#include <stdlib.h>
#include <stdio.h>
#include <GL/glut.h>


void init()
{
   glClearColor (0.0, 0.0, 0.0, 0.0);
}

void drawObjects(GLenum mode)
{
    if(mode == GL_SELECT) glLoadName(1);
    glColor3f(1.0, 0.0, 0.0);
    glRectf(-0.5, -0.5, 1.0, 1.0);
    if(mode == GL_SELECT) glLoadName(2);
    glColor3f(0.0, 0.0, 1.0);
    glRectf(-1.0, -1.0, 0.5, 0.5);
}

void display()
{
    glClear(GL_COLOR_BUFFER_BIT);
    drawObjects(GL_RENDER);
```

```
      glFlush();
}

/*  processHits prints out the contents of the
 *  selection array
 */
void processHits (GLint hits, GLuint buffer[])
{
   unsigned int i, j;
   GLuint ii, jj, names, *ptr;

   printf ("hits = %d\n", hits);
   ptr = (GLuint *) buffer;
   for (i = 0; i < hits; i++)
   { /*  for each hit   */
      names = *ptr;
      ptr+=3;
      for (j = 0; j < names; j++)
      { /*  for each name */
         if(*ptr==1) printf ("red rectangle\n");
         else printf ("blue rectangle\n");
         ptr++;
      }
      printf ("\n");
   }
}

#define SIZE 512

void mouse(int button, int state, int x, int y)
{
   GLuint selectBuf[SIZE];
   GLint hits;
   GLint viewport[4];

   if (button == GLUT_LEFT_BUTTON && state == GLUT_DOWN)
   {
   glGetIntegerv (GL_VIEWPORT, viewport);

   glSelectBuffer (SIZE, selectBuf);
   glRenderMode(GL_SELECT);

   glInitNames();
   glPushName(0);

   glMatrixMode (GL_PROJECTION);
   glPushMatrix ();
   glLoadIdentity ();
/*  Create 5x5 pixel picking region near cursor location     */
```

```
   gluPickMatrix ((GLdouble) x, (GLdouble) (viewport[3] - y),
                  5.0, 5.0, viewport);
   gluOrtho2D (-2.0, 2.0, -2.0, 2.0);
   drawObjects(GL_SELECT);


   glMatrixMode (GL_PROJECTION);
   glPopMatrix ();
   glFlush ();

   hits = glRenderMode (GL_RENDER);
   processHits (hits, selectBuf);

   glutPostRedisplay();
   }
}


void reshape(int w, int h)
{
   glViewport(0, 0, w, h);
   glMatrixMode(GL_PROJECTION);
   glLoadIdentity();
   gluOrtho2D (-2.0, 2.0, -2.0, 2.0);
   glMatrixMode(GL_MODELVIEW);
   glLoadIdentity();
}

void keyboard(unsigned char key, int x, int y)
{
   switch (key)
   {
      case 27:
         exit(0);
         break;
   }
}

/* Main Loop */
int main(int argc, char** argv)
{
   glutInit(&argc, argv);
   glutInitDisplayMode (GLUT_SINGLE | GLUT_RGB);
   glutInitWindowSize (500, 500);
   glutInitWindowPosition (100, 100);
   glutCreateWindow (argv[0]);
   init ();
   glutReshapeFunc (reshape);
   glutDisplayFunc(display);
```

```
            glutMouseFunc (mouse);
            glutKeyboardFunc (keyboard);
            glutMainLoop();
            return 0;
        }
```

A.9 Rotating-Cube Program

```
/* Rotating cube with color interpolation */

/* Demonstration of use of homogeneous coordinate
transformations and simple data structure for representing
cube from Chapter 4 */

/*Colors are assigned to the vertices */
/*Cube is centered at origin */

#include <stdlib.h>
#include <GL/glut.h>


 GLfloat vertices[][3] = {{-1.0,-1.0,-1.0},{1.0,-1.0,-1.0},
 {1.0,1.0,-1.0}, {-1.0,1.0,-1.0}, {-1.0,-1.0,1.0},
 {1.0,-1.0,1.0}, {1.0,1.0,1.0}, {-1.0,1.0,1.0}};

 GLfloat colors[][3] = {{0.0,0.0,0.0},{1.0,0.0,0.0},
 {1.0,1.0,0.0}, {0.0,1.0,0.0}, {0.0,0.0,1.0},
 {1.0,0.0,1.0}, {1.0,1.0,1.0}, {0.0,1.0,1.0}};

void polygon(int a, int b, int c, int d)
{

/* draw a polygon via list of vertices */

 glBegin(GL_POLYGON);
 glColor3fv(colors[a]);
 glVertex3fv(vertices[a]);
 glColor3fv(colors[b]);
 glVertex3fv(vertices[b]);
 glColor3fv(colors[c]);
 glVertex3fv(vertices[c]);
 glColor3fv(colors[d]);
```

```
 glVertex3fv(vertices[d]);
 glEnd();
}

void colorcube()
{

/* map vertices to faces */

polygon(0,3,2,1);
polygon(2,3,7,6);
polygon(0,4,7,3);
polygon(1,2,6,5);
polygon(4,5,6,7);
polygon(0,1,5,4);
}

static GLfloat theta[] = {0.0,0.0,0.0};
static GLint axis = 2;

void display()
{

/* Display callback, clear frame buffer and z buffer,
   rotate cube and draw, swap buffers */

 glClear(GL_COLOR_BUFFER_BIT | GL_DEPTH_BUFFER_BIT);
 glLoadIdentity();
 glRotatef(theta[0], 1.0, 0.0, 0.0);
 glRotatef(theta[1], 0.0, 1.0, 0.0);
 glRotatef(theta[2], 0.0, 0.0, 1.0);

 colorcube();

 glFlush();
 glutSwapBuffers();
}

void spinCube()
{

/* Idle callback, spin cube 2 degrees about selected axis */

 theta[axis] += 2.0;
 if( theta[axis] > 360.0 ) theta[axis] -= 360.0;
```

```
/* display(); */
glutPostRedisplay();
}

void mouse(int btn, int state, int x, int y)
{

/* Mouse callback, selects an axis about which to rotate */

if(btn==GLUT_LEFT_BUTTON && state == GLUT_DOWN) axis = 0;
if(btn==GLUT_MIDDLE_BUTTON && state == GLUT_DOWN) axis = 1;
if(btn==GLUT_RIGHT_BUTTON && state == GLUT_DOWN) axis = 2;
}

void myReshape(int w, int h)
{
    glViewport(0, 0, w, h);
    glMatrixMode(GL_PROJECTION);
    glLoadIdentity();
    if (w <= h)
        glOrtho(-2.0, 2.0, -2.0 * (GLfloat) h / (GLfloat) w,
            2.0 * (GLfloat) h / (GLfloat) w, -10.0, 10.0);
    else
        glOrtho(-2.0 * (GLfloat) w / (GLfloat) h,
            2.0 * (GLfloat) w / (GLfloat) h, -2.0, 2.0, -10.0, 10.0);
    glMatrixMode(GL_MODELVIEW);
}

void
main(int argc, char **argv)
{
    glutInit(&argc, argv);

/* Need both double buffering and z buffer */

    glutInitDisplayMode(GLUT_DOUBLE | GLUT_RGB | GLUT_DEPTH);
    glutInitWindowSize(500, 500);
    glutCreateWindow("colorcube");
    glutReshapeFunc(myReshape);
    glutDisplayFunc(display);
    glutIdleFunc(spinCube);
    glutMouseFunc(mouse);
    glEnable(GL_DEPTH_TEST); /* Enable hidden-surface removal */
    glutMainLoop();
}
```

A.10 Rotating Cube Using Vertex Arrays

```
/* Rotating cube with color interpolation */

/* Demonstration of use of homogeneous coordinate
transformations and simple data structure for representing
cube from Chapter 4 */
/*Colors are assigned to the vertices */
/*Cube is centered at origin */

#include <stdlib.h>
#include <GL/glut.h>


GLfloat vertices[] = {-1.0,-1.0,-1.0,1.0,-1.0,-1.0,
1.0,1.0,-1.0, -1.0,1.0,-1.0, -1.0,-1.0,1.0,
1.0,-1.0,1.0, 1.0,1.0,1.0, -1.0,1.0,1.0};

GLfloat colors[] = {0.0,0.0,0.0,1.0,0.0,0.0,
1.0,1.0,0.0, 0.0,1.0,0.0, 0.0,0.0,1.0,
1.0,0.0,1.0, 1.0,1.0,1.0, 0.0,1.0,1.0};

GLubyte cubeIndices[]={0,3,2,1,2,3,7,6,0,4,7,3,1,2,6,5,4,5,6,7,0,1,5,4};


static GLfloat theta[] = {0.0,0.0,0.0};
static GLint axis = 2;

void display()
{
/* Display callback, clear frame buffer and z buffer,
   rotate cube and draw, swap buffers */

glClear(GL_COLOR_BUFFER_BIT | GL_DEPTH_BUFFER_BIT);
glLoadIdentity();
glRotatef(theta[0], 1.0, 0.0, 0.0);
glRotatef(theta[1], 0.0, 1.0, 0.0);
glRotatef(theta[2], 0.0, 0.0, 1.0);

glDrawElements(GL_QUADS, 24, GL_UNSIGNED_BYTE, cubeIndices);

glBegin(GL_LINES);
  glVertex3f(0.0,0.0,0.0);
  glVertex3f(1.0,1.0,1.0);
glEnd();
```

```
      glFlush();
      glutSwapBuffers();
}

void spinCube()
{

/* Idle callback, spin cube 2 degrees about selected axis */

   theta[axis] += 2.0;
   if( theta[axis] > 360.0 ) theta[axis] -= 360.0;
   glutPostRedisplay();
}

void mouse(int btn, int state, int x, int y)
{

/* mouse callback, selects an axis about which to rotate */

   if(btn==GLUT_LEFT_BUTTON && state == GLUT_DOWN) axis = 0;
   if(btn==GLUT_MIDDLE_BUTTON && state == GLUT_DOWN) axis = 1;
   if(btn==GLUT_RIGHT_BUTTON && state == GLUT_DOWN) axis = 2;
}

void myReshape(int w, int h)
{
    glViewport(0, 0, w, h);
    glMatrixMode(GL_PROJECTION);
    glLoadIdentity();
    if (w <= h)
        glOrtho(-2.0, 2.0, -2.0 * (GLfloat) h / (GLfloat) w,
            2.0 * (GLfloat) h / (GLfloat) w, -10.0, 10.0);
    else
        glOrtho(-2.0 * (GLfloat) w / (GLfloat) h,
            2.0 * (GLfloat) w / (GLfloat) h, -2.0, 2.0, -10.0, 10.0);
    glMatrixMode(GL_MODELVIEW);
}

void
main(int argc, char **argv)
{

/* need both double buffering and z buffer */

   glutInit(&argc, argv);
   glutInitDisplayMode(GLUT_DOUBLE | GLUT_RGB | GLUT_DEPTH);
   glutInitWindowSize(500, 500);
   glutCreateWindow("colorcube");
   glutReshapeFunc(myReshape);
```

```
    glutDisplayFunc(display);
    glutIdleFunc(spinCube);
    glutMouseFunc(mouse);
    glEnable(GL_DEPTH_TEST); /* Enable hidden--surface--removal */
    glEnableClientState(GL_COLOR_ARRAY);
    glEnableClientState(GL_NORMAL_ARRAY);
    glEnableClientState(GL_VERTEX_ARRAY);
    glVertexPointer(3, GL_FLOAT, 0, vertices);
    glColorPointer(3,GL_FLOAT, 0, colors);
    glColor3f(1.0,1.0,1.0);
    glutMainLoop();
}
```

A.11 Rotating Cube with a Virtual Trackball

```
/* Rotating cube demo with trackball*/

#include <math.h>
#include <GL/glut.h>

#define bool int
#define false 0
#define true 1


int  winWidth, winHeight;

float  angle = 0.0, axis[3], trans[3];
bool   trackingMouse = false;
bool   redrawContinue = false;
bool    trackballMove = false;

/*
** Draw the cube.
*/
GLfloat vertices[][3] = {
    {-1.0,-1.0,-1.0}, {1.0,-1.0,-1.0}, {1.0,1.0,-1.0}, {-1.0,1.0,-1.0},
    {-1.0,-1.0,1.0}, {1.0,-1.0,1.0}, {1.0,1.0,1.0}, {-1.0,1.0,1.0}
};

GLfloat colors[][3] = {
    {0.0,0.0,0.0},{1.0,0.0,0.0}, {1.0,1.0,0.0}, {0.0,1.0,0.0},
    {0.0,0.0,1.0}, {1.0,0.0,1.0}, {1.0,1.0,1.0}, {0.0,1.0,1.0}
};
```

```c
void polygon(int a, int b, int c , int d, int face)
{

    /* draw a polygon via list of vertices */

    glBegin(GL_POLYGON);
    glColor3fv(colors[a]);
    glVertex3fv(vertices[a]);
    glColor3fv(colors[b]);
    glVertex3fv(vertices[b]);
    glColor3fv(colors[c]);
    glVertex3fv(vertices[c]);
    glColor3fv(colors[d]);
    glVertex3fv(vertices[d]);
     glEnd();
}

void colorcube()
{

    /* Map vertices to faces */

    polygon(1,0,3,2,0);
    polygon(3,7,6,2,1);
    polygon(7,3,0,4,2);
    polygon(2,6,5,1,3);
    polygon(4,5,6,7,4);
    polygon(5,4,0,1,5);
}

/*
** These functions implement a simple trackball-like motion control.
*/

float lastPos[3] = {0.0F, 0.0F, 0.0F};
int curx, cury;
int startX, startY;

void
trackball_ptov(int x, int y, int width, int height, float v[3])
{
    float d, a;

    /* Project x,y onto a hemisphere centered within width, height */
    v[0] = (2.0F*x - width) / width;
    v[1] = (height - 2.0F*y) / height;
    d = (float) sqrt(v[0]*v[0] + v[1]*v[1]);
```

```
    v[2] = (float) cos((M_PI/2.0F) * ((d < 1.0F) ? d : 1.0F));
    a = 1.0F / (float) sqrt(v[0]*v[0] + v[1]*v[1] + v[2]*v[2]);
    v[0] *= a;
    v[1] *= a;
    v[2] *= a;
}


void
mouseMotion(int x, int y)
{
    float curPos[3], dx, dy, dz;

    trackball_ptov(x, y, winWidth, winHeight, curPos);
if(trackingMouse)
{
    dx = curPos[0] - lastPos[0];
    dy = curPos[1] - lastPos[1];
    dz = curPos[2] - lastPos[2];

    if (dx || dy || dz) {
    angle = 90.0F * sqrt(dx*dx + dy*dy + dz*dz);

    axis[0] = lastPos[1]*curPos[2] - lastPos[2]*curPos[1];
    axis[1] = lastPos[2]*curPos[0] - lastPos[0]*curPos[2];
    axis[2] = lastPos[0]*curPos[1] - lastPos[1]*curPos[0];

    lastPos[0] = curPos[0];
    lastPos[1] = curPos[1];
    lastPos[2] = curPos[2];
        }
}

    glutPostRedisplay();
}

void
startMotion(int x, int y)
{

    trackingMouse = true;
    redrawContinue = false;
    startX = x; startY = y;
    curx = x; cury = y;
    trackball_ptov(x, y, winWidth, winHeight, lastPos);
    trackballMove=true;
}
```

```
                    void
                    stopMotion(int x, int y)
                    {

                        trackingMouse = false;

                        if (startX != x || startY != y) {
                        redrawContinue = true;
                           } else {
                        angle = 0.0F;
                        redrawContinue = false;
                        trackballMove = false;
                           }
                    }

                    void display()
                    {
                        glClear(GL_COLOR_BUFFER_BIT|GL_DEPTH_BUFFER_BIT);

                        /* View transform */

                        if (trackballMove) {
                         glRotatef(angle, axis[0], axis[1], axis[2]);

                        }
                     colorcube();
                        glutSwapBuffers();
                    }


                    void mouseButton(int button, int state, int x, int y)
                    {
                     if(button==GLUT_RIGHT_BUTTON) exit();
                     if(button==GLUT_LEFT_BUTTON) switch(state)
                     {
                        case GLUT_DOWN:
                        y=winHeight-y;
                        startMotion( x,y);
                        break;
                        case GLUT_UP:
                        stopMotion( x,y);
                        break;
                            }
                    }

                    void myReshape(int w, int h)
                    {
                        glViewport(0, 0, w, h);
                        winWidth = w;
```

```
        winHeight = h;
}

void spinCube()
{
        if (redrawContinue) glutPostRedisplay();
}



void
main(int argc, char **argv)
{
        glutInit(&argc, argv);
        glutInitDisplayMode(GLUT_DOUBLE | GLUT_RGB | GLUT_DEPTH);
        glutInitWindowSize(500, 500);
        glutCreateWindow("colorcube");
        glutReshapeFunc(myReshape);
        glutDisplayFunc(display);
        glutIdleFunc(spinCube);
        glutMouseFunc(mouseButton);
        glutMotionFunc(mouseMotion);
        glEnable(GL_DEPTH_TEST);
        glMatrixMode(GL_PROJECTION);
        glLoadIdentity();
        glOrtho(-2.0, 2.0, -2.0, 2.0, -2.0, 2.0);
        glMatrixMode(GL_MODELVIEW);
        glutMainLoop();
}
```

A.12 Moving Viewer

```
/* Rotating cube with viewer movement from Chapter 5 */
/* Cube definition and display similar to rotating-cube
program */

/* We use the Lookat function in the display callback to point
the viewer, whose position can be altered by the x, X, y, Y, z,
and Z keys.
The perspective view is set in the reshape callback */

#include <stdlib.h>
#include <GL/glut.h>


 GLfloat vertices[][3] = {{-1.0,-1.0,-1.0},{1.0,-1.0,-1.0},
  {1.0,1.0,-1.0}, {-1.0,1.0,-1.0}, {-1.0,-1.0,1.0},
```

```
        {1.0,-1.0,1.0}, {1.0,1.0,1.0}, {-1.0,1.0,1.0}};

        GLfloat normals[][3] = {{-1.0,-1.0,-1.0},{1.0,-1.0,-1.0},
        {1.0,1.0,-1.0}, {-1.0,1.0,-1.0}, {-1.0,-1.0,1.0},
        {1.0,-1.0,1.0}, {1.0,1.0,1.0}, {-1.0,1.0,1.0}};

        GLfloat colors[][3] = {{0.0,0.0,0.0},{1.0,0.0,0.0},
        {1.0,1.0,0.0}, {0.0,1.0,0.0}, {0.0,0.0,1.0},
        {1.0,0.0,1.0}, {1.0,1.0,1.0}, {0.0,1.0,1.0}};

        void polygon(int a, int b, int c , int d)
        {
         glBegin(GL_POLYGON);
          glColor3fv(colors[a]);
          glNormal3fv(normals[a]);
          glVertex3fv(vertices[a]);
          glColor3fv(colors[b]);
          glNormal3fv(normals[b]);
          glVertex3fv(vertices[b]);
          glColor3fv(colors[c]);
          glNormal3fv(normals[c]);
          glVertex3fv(vertices[c]);
          glColor3fv(colors[d]);
          glNormal3fv(normals[d]);
          glVertex3fv(vertices[d]);
         glEnd();
        }

        void colorcube()
        {
         polygon(0,3,2,1);
         polygon(2,3,7,6);
         polygon(0,4,7,3);
         polygon(1,2,6,5);
         polygon(4,5,6,7);
         polygon(0,1,5,4);
        }

        static GLfloat theta[] = {0.0,0.0,0.0};
        static GLint axis = 2;
        static GLdouble viewer[]= {0.0, 0.0, 5.0}; /* initial viewer
                                                       location */

        void display()
        {

         glClear(GL_COLOR_BUFFER_BIT | GL_DEPTH_BUFFER_BIT);

        /* Update viewer position in model-view matrix */
```

```
 glLoadIdentity();
 gluLookAt(viewer[0],viewer[1],viewer[2], 0.0, 0.0, 0.0,
                                    0.0, 1.0, 0.0);

/* rotate cube */

 glRotatef(theta[0], 1.0, 0.0, 0.0);
 glRotatef(theta[1], 0.0, 1.0, 0.0);
 glRotatef(theta[2], 0.0, 0.0, 1.0);
 colorcube();

 glFlush();
 glutSwapBuffers();
}

void mouse(int btn, int state, int x, int y)
{
 if(btn==GLUT_LEFT_BUTTON && state == GLUT_DOWN) axis = 0;
 if(btn==GLUT_MIDDLE_BUTTON && state == GLUT_DOWN) axis = 1;
 if(btn==GLUT_RIGHT_BUTTON && state == GLUT_DOWN) axis = 2;
 theta[axis] += 2.0;
 if( theta[axis] > 360.0 ) theta[axis] -= 360.0;
 display();
}

void keys(unsigned char key, int x, int y)
{

/* Use x, X, y, Y, z, and Z keys to move viewer */

   if(key == 'x') viewer[0]-= 1.0;
   if(key == 'X') viewer[0]+= 1.0;
   if(key == 'y') viewer[1]-= 1.0;
   if(key == 'Y') viewer[1]+= 1.0;
   if(key == 'z') viewer[2]-= 1.0;
   if(key == 'Z') viewer[2]+= 1.0;
   display();
}

void myReshape(int w, int h)
{
 glViewport(0, 0, w, h);

/* Use a perspective view */

 glMatrixMode(GL_PROJECTION);
 glLoadIdentity();
 if(w<=h) glFrustum(-2.0, 2.0, -2.0 * (GLfloat) h/ (GLfloat) w,
      2.0* (GLfloat) h / (GLfloat) w, 2.0, 20.0);
```

```
        else glFrustum(-2.0, 2.0, -2.0 * (GLfloat) w/ (GLfloat) h,
            2.0* (GLfloat) w / (GLfloat) h, 2.0, 20.0);

    /* Or we can use gluPerspective */
     /* gluPerspective(45.0, w/h, 1.0, 10.0); */

    glMatrixMode(GL_MODELVIEW);
    }


    void
    main(int argc, char **argv)
    {
     glutInit(&argc, argv);
     glutInitDisplayMode(GLUT_DOUBLE | GLUT_RGB | GLUT_DEPTH);
     glutInitWindowSize(500, 500);
     glutCreateWindow("colorcube");
     glutReshapeFunc(myReshape);
     glutDisplayFunc(display);
     glutMouseFunc(mouse);
     glutKeyboardFunc(keys);
     glEnable(GL_DEPTH_TEST);
     glutMainLoop();
    }
```

A.13 Sphere Program

```
/* Recursive subdivision of cube (Chapter 6). Three display
modes: wire frame, constant, and interpolative shading */

/*Program also illustrates defining materials and light sources
in init() */

/* mode 0 = wire frame, mode 1 = constant shading,
mode 3 = interpolative shading */

#include <stdlib.h>
#include <GL/glut.h>


typedef float point[4];

/* initial tetrahedron */

point3 v[]={{0.0, 0.0, 1.0}, {0.0, 0.942809, -0.33333},
        {-0.816497, -0.471405, -0.333333}, {0.816497, -0.471405, -0.333333}};
```

```
static GLfloat theta[] = {0.0,0.0,0.0};

int n;
int mode;


void triangle( point3 a, point3 b, point3 c)

/* Display one triangle using a line loop for wire frame, a single
normal for constant shading, or three normals for interpolative shading */
{
    if (mode==0) glBegin(GL_LINE_LOOP);
    else glBegin(GL_POLYGON);
        if(mode==1) glNormal3fv(a);
        if(mode==2) glNormal3fv(a);
        glVertex3fv(a);
        if(mode==2) glNormal3fv(b);
        glVertex3fv(b);
        if(mode==2) glNormal3fv(c);
        glVertex3fv(c);
    glEnd();
}

void normal(point3 p)
{

/* Normalize a vector */

    double sqrt();
    float d =0.0;
    int i;
    for(i=0; i<3; i++) d+=p[i]*p[i];
    d=sqrt(d);
    if(d>0.0) for(i=0; i<3; i++) p[i]/=d;
}

void divide_triangle(point3 a, point3 b, point3 c, int m)
{

/* Triangle subdivision using vertex numbers.
right-hand rule applied to create outward-pointing faces */

    point3 v1, v2, v3;
    int j;
    if(m>0)
    {
        for(j=0; j<3; j++) v1[j]=a[j]+b[j];
        normal(v1);
        for(j=0; j<3; j++) v2[j]=a[j]+c[j];
```

```
            normal(v2);
            for(j=0; j<3; j++) v3[j]=b[j]+c[j];
             normal(v3);
            divide_triangle(a, v1, v2, m-1);
            divide_triangle(c, v2, v3, m-1);
            divide_triangle(b, v3, v1, m-1);
            divide_triangle(v1, v3, v2, m-1);
        }
        else triangle(a,b,c); /* draw triangle at end of recursion */
}

void tetrahedron( int m)
{

/* Apply triangle subdivision to faces of tetrahedron */

    divide_triangle(v[0], v[1], v[2], m);
    divide_triangle(v[3], v[2], v[1], m);
    divide_triangle(v[0], v[3], v[1], m);
    divide_triangle(v[0], v[2], v[3], m);
}

void display()
{

/* Displays all three modes, side by side */

    glClear(GL_COLOR_BUFFER_BIT | GL_DEPTH_BUFFER_BIT);
    glLoadIdentity();
    mode=0;
    tetrahedron(n);
    mode=1;
    glTranslatef(-2.0, 0.0,0.0);
    tetrahedron(n);
    mode=2;
    glTranslatef( 4.0, 0.0,0.0);
    tetrahedron(n);


    glFlush();
}

void myReshape(int w, int h)
{
    glViewport(0, 0, w, h);
    glMatrixMode(GL_PROJECTION);
    glLoadIdentity();
    if (w <= h)
        glOrtho(-4.0, 4.0, -4.0 * (GLfloat) h / (GLfloat) w,
```

```
            4.0 * (GLfloat) h / (GLfloat) w, -10.0, 10.0);
    else
        glOrtho(-4.0 * (GLfloat) w / (GLfloat) h,
            4.0 * (GLfloat) w / (GLfloat) h, -4.0, 4.0, -10.0, 10.0);
    glMatrixMode(GL_MODELVIEW);
    display();
}


void myinit()
{
    GLfloat mat_specular[]={1.0, 1.0, 1.0, 1.0};
    GLfloat mat_diffuse[]={1.0, 1.0, 1.0, 1.0};
    GLfloat mat_ambient[]={1.0, 1.0, 1.0, 1.0};
    GLfloat mat_shininess={100.0};
    GLfloat light_ambient[]={0.0, 0.0, 0.0, 1.0};
    GLfloat light_diffuse[]={1.0, 1.0, 1.0, 1.0};
    GLfloat light_specular[]={1.0, 1.0, 1.0, 1.0};

/* Set up ambient, diffuse, and specular components for light 0 */

    glLightfv(GL_LIGHT0, GL_AMBIENT, light_ambient);
    glLightfv(GL_LIGHT0, GL_DIFFUSE, light_diffuse);
    glLightfv(GL_LIGHT0, GL_SPECULAR, light_specular);

/* Define material properties for front face of all polygons */

    glMaterialfv(GL_FRONT, GL_SPECULAR, mat_specular);
    glMaterialfv(GL_FRONT, GL_AMBIENT, mat_ambient);
    glMaterialfv(GL_FRONT, GL_DIFFUSE, mat_diffuse);
    glMaterialf(GL_FRONT, GL_SHININESS, mat_shininess);

    glShadeModel(GL_SMOOTH); /* enable smooth shading */
    glEnable(GL_LIGHTING); /* enable lighting */
    glEnable(GL_LIGHT0);   /* enable light 0 */
    glEnable(GL_DEPTH_TEST); /* enable z buffer */
    glClearColor (1.0, 1.0, 1.0, 1.0);
    glColor3f (0.0, 0.0, 0.0);
}


void
main(int argc, char **argv)
{
    n=atoi(argv[1]);
    glutInit(&argc, argv);
    glutInitDisplayMode(GLUT_SINGLE | GLUT_RGB | GLUT_DEPTH);
    glutInitWindowSize(500, 500);
    glutCreateWindow("sphere");
```

```
        myinit();
        glutReshapeFunc(myReshape);
        glutDisplayFunc(display);
        glutMainLoop();
}
```

A.14 Pixel-Reading Program

```
#include <stdlib.h>
#include <stdio.h>
#include <GL/glut.h>

int n=300;
int m=300;


void display()
{
    glClear(GL_COLOR_BUFFER_BIT);
    glColor3ub(255, 255, 127);
    glRecti(0,0,n,m);
    glFlush();
}


void myReshape(int w, int h)
{
    glViewport(0, 0, w, h);
    glMatrixMode(GL_PROJECTION);
    glLoadIdentity();
    gluOrtho2D(0.0, (GLfloat) w, 0.0, (GLfloat) h);
    glMatrixMode(GL_MODELVIEW);
}

void mouse(int state, int button, int x, int y)
{
    int i,j;
    GLubyte pixels[3];
    glutPostRedisplay();
    glReadPixels(x,m-y,1,1,GL_RGB,GL_UNSIGNED_BYTE, pixels);
    for(i=0;i<2;i++) for(j=0;j<2;j++)
    {
        printf("%d %d %d\n", pixels[0], pixels[1], pixels[2]);
    }
}
```

```
void myinit()
{
    glClearColor (0.0, 0.5, 1.0, 1.0);
    gluOrtho2D(0.0, 0.0, (GLfloat) n, (GLfloat) m);
    glReadBuffer(GL_BACK);
    glPixelStorei(GL_PACK_ALIGNMENT, 1);
    /* glDisable(GL_DITHER); */

}

main(int argc, char *argv[])
{
    glutInit(&argc, argv);
    glutInitDisplayMode(GLUT_SINGLE | GLUT_RGB);
    glutInitWindowSize(500, 500);
    glutCreateWindow("image");
    myinit();
    glutReshapeFunc(myReshape);
    glutMouseFunc(mouse);
    glutDisplayFunc(display);
    glutMainLoop();
}
```

A.15 Rotating Cube with Texture

```
#include <stdlib.h>
#include <GL/glut.h>
GLfloat planes[]= {-1.0, 0.0, 1.0, 0.0};
GLfloat planet[]= {0.0, -1.0,  0.0, 1.0};
GLfloat vertices[][3] = {{-1.0,-1.0,-1.0},{1.0,-1.0,-1.0},
    {1.0,1.0,-1.0}, {-1.0,1.0,-1.0}, {-1.0,-1.0,1.0},
    {1.0,-1.0,1.0}, {1.0,1.0,1.0}, {-1.0,1.0,1.0}};
GLfloat colors[][4] = {{0.0,0.0,0.0,0.5},{1.0,0.0,0.0,0.5},
    {1.0,1.0,0.0,0.5}, {0.0,1.0,0.0,0.5}, {0.0,0.0,1.0,0.5},
    {1.0,0.0,1.0,0.5}, {1.0,1.0,1.0,0.5}, {0.0,1.0,1.0,0.5}};

void polygon(int a, int b, int c, int d)
{
    glBegin(GL_POLYGON);
    glColor4fv(colors[a]);
    glTexCoord2f(0.0,0.0);
    glVertex3fv(vertices[a]);
    glColor4fv(colors[b]);
    glTexCoord2f(0.0,1.0);
    glVertex3fv(vertices[b]);
    glColor4fv(colors[c]);
```

```
        glTexCoord2f(1.0,1.0);
        glVertex3fv(vertices[c]);
        glColor4fv(colors[d]);
        glTexCoord2f(1.0,0.0);
        glVertex3fv(vertices[d]);
        glEnd();
}

void colorcube(void)
{

/* Map vertices to faces */

    polygon(0,3,2,1);
    polygon(2,3,7,6);
    polygon(0,4,7,3);
    polygon(1,2,6,5);
    polygon(4,5,6,7);
    polygon(0,1,5,4);
}

static GLfloat theta[] = {0.0,0.0,0.0};
static GLint axis = 2;

void display(void)
{
    glClear(GL_COLOR_BUFFER_BIT | GL_DEPTH_BUFFER_BIT);
    glLoadIdentity();
    glRotatef(theta[0], 1.0, 0.0, 0.0);
    glRotatef(theta[1], 0.0, 1.0, 0.0);
    glRotatef(theta[2], 0.0, 0.0, 1.0);
    colorcube();
    glutSwapBuffers();
}

void spinCube()
{
    theta[axis] += 2.0;
    if( theta[axis] > 360.0 ) theta[axis] -= 360.0;
    glutPostRedisplay();
}

void mouse(int btn, int state, int x, int y)
{
    if(btn==GLUT_LEFT_BUTTON && state == GLUT_DOWN) axis = 0;
    if(btn==GLUT_MIDDLE_BUTTON && state == GLUT_DOWN) axis = 1;
    if(btn==GLUT_RIGHT_BUTTON && state == GLUT_DOWN) axis = 2;
}
```

```
void myReshape(int w, int h)
{
    glViewport(0, 0, w, h);
    glMatrixMode(GL_PROJECTION);
    glLoadIdentity();
    if (w <= h)
        glOrtho(-2.0, 2.0, -2.0 * (GLfloat) h / (GLfloat) w,
            2.0 * (GLfloat) h / (GLfloat) w, -10.0, 10.0);
    else
        glOrtho(-2.0 * (GLfloat) w / (GLfloat) h,
            2.0 * (GLfloat) w / (GLfloat) h, -2.0, 2.0, -10.0, 10.0);
    glMatrixMode(GL_MODELVIEW);
}

void key(unsigned char k, int x, int y)
{
    if(k == '1') glutIdleFunc(spinCube);
    if(k == '2') glutIdleFunc(NULL);
    if(k == 'q') exit(0);
}

void
main(int argc, char **argv)
{
    GLubyte image[64][64][3];
    int i, j, r, c;
    for(i=0;i<64;i++)
    {
      for(j=0;j<64;j++)
      {
        c = ((((i&0x8)==0)^((j&0x8))==0))*255;
        image[i][j][0]= (GLubyte) c;
        image[i][j][1]= (GLubyte) c;
        image[i][j][2]= (GLubyte) c;
      }
    }
     glutInit(&argc, argv);
     glutInitDisplayMode(GLUT_DOUBLE | GLUT_RGB | GLUT_DEPTH);
     glutInitWindowSize(500, 500);
     glutCreateWindow("colorcube");
     glutReshapeFunc(myReshape);
     glutDisplayFunc(display);
     glutIdleFunc(spinCube);
     glutMouseFunc(mouse);
     glEnable(GL_DEPTH_TEST);
     glEnable(GL_TEXTURE_2D);
     glTexImage2D(GL_TEXTURE_2D,0,3,64,64,0,GL_RGB,GL_UNSIGNED_BYTE, image);
     glTexParameterf(GL_TEXTURE_2D,GL_TEXTURE_WRAP_S,GL_REPEAT);
     glTexParameterf(GL_TEXTURE_2D,GL_TEXTURE_WRAP_T,GL_REPEAT);
```

```
    glTexParameterf(GL_TEXTURE_2D,GL_TEXTURE_MAG_FILTER,GL_NEAREST);
    glTexParameterf(GL_TEXTURE_2D,GL_TEXTURE_MIN_FILTER,GL_NEAREST);
    glutKeyboardFunc(key);
    glClearColor(1.0,1.0,1.0,1.0);
    glutMainLoop();
}
```

A.16 Scene-Graph Example

```
//Scene.cc

#include "Scene.h"

#define BaseRadius 0.2
#define Radius 0.08
#define BaseLen 1
#define UpLen 0.6
#define LowLen 0.6
#define EyeRadius 0.04
#define ChairLegLen 0.55

int
main(int argc, char **argv)
{

  float v[][3]={{-0.3,-0.2,0.0},{0.3, -0.2, 0.0},
      {0.3, 0.2, 0.0},{-0.3, 0.2, 0.0} };

  //Light nodes
  Light *Light1=new Light;
  Light *Light2=new Light;
  TurnOff *Off1=new TurnOff(Light1);
  TurnOff *Off2=new TurnOff(Light2);

  //Setting Light Values :
  Light1->SetValue(POSITION, -2, -3, 1.5, 1);
  Light1->SetValue(SPOT_DIRECTION, 2, 3, -1.5);
  Light1->SetValue(CUTOFFANGLE, 40.0);
  Light1->TurnOn();

  Light2->SetValue(POSITION, 5, 5, 5, 0);
  Light2->SetValue(SPECULAR, 1.0, 1.0, 1.0, 1.0);
  Light2->SetValue(DIFFUSE, 1.0, 1.0, 1.0, 1.0);
  Light2->TurnOn();
```

```
//Nodes for Camera:
Camera *Camera1=new Camera(PERSPECTIVE);

Camera1->SetValue(POSITION, 2.2, 0.9, 3);
Camera1->SetValue(AIMAT, 0, 0, 0);
Camera1->SetValue(UPDIRECTION, 0, 1, 0);
Camera1->SetValue(ASPECT, 1);
Camera1->SetValue(NEAR, 1);
Camera1->SetValue(FAR, 20);
Camera1->SetValue(YANGLE, 50);

//Nodes for Robot:
Material *RobotMat=new Material;
Material *EyeMat=new Material;

Cylinder *Base=new Cylinder;
Sphere *Head=new Sphere;
Sphere *EyeL=new Sphere;
Sphere *EyeR=new Sphere;
Cylinder *UpperArmL=new Cylinder;
Cylinder *UpperArmR=new Cylinder;
Cylinder *LowerArmL=new Cylinder;
Cylinder *LowerArmR=new Cylinder;
Cylinder *UpperLegL=new Cylinder;
Cylinder *UpperLegR=new Cylinder;
Cylinder *LowerLegL=new Cylinder;
Cylinder *LowerLegR=new Cylinder;
Polygon *Paper=new Polygon;

Transformation *EyeLTrans=new Transformation;
Transformation *EyeRTrans=new Transformation;
Transformation *HeadTrans=new Transformation;
Transformation *UpArmLTrans=new Transformation;
Transformation *UpArmRTrans=new Transformation;
Transformation *LowArmTrans=new Transformation;
Transformation *UpLegLTrans=new Transformation;
Transformation *UpLegRTrans=new Transformation;
Transformation *LowLegTrans=new Transformation;
Transformation *BaseTrans=new Transformation;

//Robot Value:
RobotMat->SetValue(DIFFUSE, 0.0, 0.0, 1.0, 1.0);
RobotMat->SetValue(AMBIENT, 0.0, 0.0, 1.0, 1.0);
RobotMat->SetValue(SPECULAR, 1.0, 1.0, 1.0, 1.0);
RobotMat->SetValue(SHININESS, 100.0);

EyeMat->SetValue(DIFFUSE, 1.0, 1.0, 1.0, 1.0);
```

```
EyeMat->SetValue(AMBIENT, 1.0, 1.0, 1.0, 1.0);
EyeMat->SetValue(SPECULAR, 1.0, 1.0, 1.0, 1.0);
EyeMat->SetValue(SHININESS, 100.0);

Base->SetValue(HEIGHT, BaseLen);
Base->SetValue(RADIUS, BaseRadius);
Head->SetValue(RADIUS, BaseRadius);
EyeL->SetValue(RADIUS, EyeRadius);
EyeR->SetValue(RADIUS, EyeRadius);
UpperArmL->SetValue(HEIGHT, UpLen);
UpperArmL->SetValue(RADIUS, Radius);
LowerArmL->SetValue(HEIGHT, LowLen);
LowerArmL->SetValue(RADIUS, Radius);
UpperArmR->SetValue(HEIGHT, UpLen);
UpperArmR->SetValue(RADIUS, Radius);
LowerArmR->SetValue(HEIGHT, LowLen);
LowerArmR->SetValue(RADIUS, Radius);
UpperLegL->SetValue(HEIGHT, UpLen);
UpperLegL->SetValue(RADIUS, Radius);
LowerLegL->SetValue(HEIGHT, LowLen);
LowerLegL->SetValue(RADIUS, Radius);
UpperLegR->SetValue(HEIGHT, UpLen);
UpperLegR->SetValue(RADIUS, Radius);
LowerLegR->SetValue(HEIGHT, LowLen);
LowerLegR->SetValue(RADIUS, Radius);

Paper->SetVerticesv(v, 4);
Paper->SetMaterial(EyeMat);

EyeLTrans->SetValue(TRANSLATION, BaseRadius-EyeRadius/2, 0, 0, 0);
EyeLTrans->SetValue(ROTATION, 30, 0, 0, 1, 1);
EyeRTrans->SetValue(TRANSLATION, BaseRadius-EyeRadius/2, 0, 0, 0);
EyeRTrans->SetValue(ROTATION, -30, 0, 0, 1, 1);
HeadTrans->SetValue(TRANSLATION, 0, 0, BaseLen+BaseRadius+BaseRadius/3, 0);
UpArmLTrans->SetValue(TRANSLATION, 0, 0, -UpLen, 0);
UpArmLTrans->SetValue(ROTATION, -45, 0, 1, 0, 1);
UpArmLTrans->SetValue(TRANSLATION, 0, BaseRadius+Radius, BaseLen, 2);
UpArmRTrans->SetValue(TRANSLATION, 0, 0, -UpLen, 0);
UpArmRTrans->SetValue(ROTATION, -45, 0, 1, 0, 1);
UpArmRTrans->SetValue(TRANSLATION, 0, -(BaseRadius+Radius), BaseLen, 2);
LowArmTrans->SetValue(TRANSLATION, 0, 0, -UpLen, 0);
LowArmTrans->SetValue(ROTATION, -45, 0, 1, 0, 1);
UpLegLTrans->SetValue(TRANSLATION, 0, 0, -UpLen, 0);
UpLegLTrans->SetValue(ROTATION, -90, 0, 1, 0, 1);
UpLegLTrans->SetValue(TRANSLATION, 0, BaseRadius+Radius, 0, 2);
UpLegRTrans->SetValue(TRANSLATION, 0, 0, -UpLen, 0);
UpLegRTrans->SetValue(ROTATION, -100, 0, 1, 0, 1);
```

```
UpLegRTrans->SetValue(TRANSLATION, 0, -(BaseRadius+Radius), 0, 2);
LowLegTrans->SetValue(TRANSLATION, 0, 0, -UpLen, 0);
LowLegTrans->SetValue(ROTATION, 95, 0, 1, 0, 1);
BaseTrans->SetValue(ROTATION, -90, 1, 0, 0, 0);
BaseTrans->SetValue(ROTATION, -10, 0, 0, 1, 1);

Head->SetTransform(HeadTrans);
EyeL->SetTransform(EyeLTrans);
EyeR->SetTransform(EyeRTrans);
EyeR->SetMaterial(EyeMat);
EyeL->SetMaterial(EyeMat);
UpperArmL->SetTransform(UpArmLTrans);
LowerArmL->SetTransform(LowArmTrans);
UpperArmR->SetTransform(UpArmRTrans);
LowerArmR->SetTransform(LowArmTrans);
UpperLegL->SetTransform(UpLegLTrans);
LowerLegL->SetTransform(LowLegTrans);
UpperLegR->SetTransform(UpLegRTrans);
LowerLegR->SetTransform(LowLegTrans);
Base->SetTransform(BaseTrans);

Paper->SetTransform(ROTATION, 20, 0, 1, 0, 0);
Paper->SetTransform(TRANSLATION, 0.05, -0.15, -0.2, 1);

//Set Relationship in Robot:
RobotMat->AddChild(Light1);
Light1->AddChild(Base);

Base->AddChild(Off1);
Off1->AddChild(Light2);
Light2->AddChild(Head);
Head->AddChild(Off2);
Head->AddChild(EyeL);
Head->AddChild(EyeR);

Base->AddChild(UpperArmL);
UpperArmL->AddChild(LowerArmL);
Base->AddChild(UpperArmR);
UpperArmR->AddChild(LowerArmR);
Base->AddChild(UpperLegL);
UpperLegL->AddChild(LowerLegL);
Base->AddChild(UpperLegR);
UpperLegR->AddChild(LowerLegR);
LowerArmR->AddChild(Paper);

//Nodes for Chair:
Cube *Seat=new Cube(0.7, 0.06, 0.7);
```

```
Line *Leg1=new Line;
Line *Leg2=new Line;
Line *Leg3=new Line;
Line *Leg4=new Line;
DrawStyle *LegStyle=new DrawStyle;
Color *ChairColor=new Color;

//Chair Value:
float v1[][3]={{-0.3, 0, 0.3},{-0.35, -1*ChairLegLen, 0.3}};
float v2[][3]={{0.3, 0, 0.3},{0.35, -1*ChairLegLen, 0.3}};
float v3[][3]={{0.3, 0, -0.3},{0.35, -1*ChairLegLen, -0.3}};
float v4[][3]={{-0.3, 0, -0.3},{-0.35, -1*ChairLegLen, -0.3}};

ChairColor->SetValue(RED);
Seat->SetTransform(TRANSLATION, 0, -0.15, 0, 0);
LegStyle->SetValue(LINEWIDTH, 7);
Leg1->SetStyle(LegStyle);
Leg1->SetVerticesv(v1);
Leg2->SetStyle(LegStyle);
Leg2->SetVerticesv(v2);
Leg3->SetStyle(LegStyle);
Leg3->SetVerticesv(v3);
Leg4->SetStyle(LegStyle);
Leg4->SetVerticesv(v4);
Seat->AddChild(Leg1);
Seat->AddChild(Leg2);
Seat->AddChild(Leg3);
Seat->AddChild(Leg4);
ChairColor->AddChild(Seat);

//Transformation Nodes for both Robot and Chair:
Transformation *Trans1=new Transformation;

Trans1->SetValue(TRANSLATION, -0.5, 0, 0, 2);

Trans1->AddChild(ChairColor);
Trans1->AddChild(RobotMat);

//Root Node:
Node *Root=new Node;

Root->AddChild(Trans1);
Root->AddChild(Camera1);

//Viewer:
GLViewer *MyViewer=new GLViewer;

MyViewer->Init(argc, argv);
MyViewer->SetValue(BACKCOLOR, GRAY);
```

```
  MyViewer->SetValue(BUFFER, DOUBLE);
  MyViewer->CreateWin("Working Hard", 500, 500);

  GLViewer *MyViewer2=new GLViewer;

  MyViewer2->Init(argc, argv);
  MyViewer2->SetValue(BACKCOLOR, MAGENTA);
  MyViewer2->CreateWin("Working Hard2", 200, 200);
  MyViewer2->SetValue(BUFFER, DOUBLE);

  MyViewer->Show(Root);
  MyViewer2->Show(Root);
  return 0;
}
```

A.17 Program for Drawing Bezier Curves

```
/*
**   curves.c
**
**   Bezier curve drawing program.
**
**
**      q - Quit the program
**      c - Clear the screen
**      e - Erase the curves
**      b - Draw Bezier curves
**
*/

#include <GL/glut.h>

void keyboard(unsigned char key, int x, int y);

#define MAX_CPTS  25    /* Fixed maximum number of control points */

GLfloat cpts[MAX_CPTS][3];
int ncpts = 0;
static int width = 500, height = 500;   /* Window width and height */


void drawCurves()
{
    int i;
    for(i=0; i<ncpts-3; i +=3)
```

```
        {
            /* Draw the curve using OpenGL evaluators */

            glMap1f(GL_MAP1_VERTEX_3, 0.0, 1.0, 3, 4, cpts[i]);
            glMapGrid1f(30, 0.0, 1.0);
            glEvalMesh1(GL_LINE, 0, 30);
        }
        glFlush();
}

/* This routine displays the control points */
static void display(void)
{
    int i;
    glClear(GL_COLOR_BUFFER_BIT);


    glBegin(GL_POINTS);
    for (i = 0; i < ncpts; i++)
        glVertex3fv(cpts[i]);
    glEnd();

    glFlush();
}


/* This routine inputs new control points */
static void mouse(int button, int state, int x, int y)
{
    float wx, wy;

    /* We are only interested in left clicks */
    if (button != GLUT_LEFT_BUTTON || state != GLUT_DOWN)
        return;

    /* Translate back to our coordinate system */
    wx = (2.0 * x) / (float)(width - 1) - 1.0;
    wy = (2.0 * (height - 1 - y)) / (float)(height - 1) - 1.0;


    /* See if we have room for any more control points */
    if (ncpts == MAX_CPTS)
        return;

    /* Save the point */
    cpts[ncpts][0] = wx;
    cpts[ncpts][1] = wy;
    cpts[ncpts][2] = 0.0;
    ncpts++;
```

```
    /* Draw the point */
    glColor3f(0.0, 0.0, 0.0);
    glPointSize(5.0);
    glBegin(GL_POINTS);
    glVertex3f(wx, wy, 0.0);
    glEnd();

    glFlush();
}



/* This routine handles keystroke commands */
void keyboard(unsigned char key, int x, int y)
{
    switch (key)
    {
        case 'q': case 'Q':
            exit();
            break;
        case 'c': case 'C':
            ncpts = 0;
            glutPostRedisplay();
            break;
        case 'e': case 'E':
            glutPostRedisplay();
            break;
        case 'b': case 'B':
            drawCurves();
            break;
    }
}



/* This routine handles window resizes */
void reshape(int w, int h)
{
    width = w;
    height = h;

    /* Set the transformations */
    glMatrixMode(GL_PROJECTION);
    glLoadIdentity();
    glOrtho(-1.0, 1.0, -1.0, 1.0, -1.0, 1.0);
    glMatrixMode(GL_MODELVIEW);
    glViewport(0, 0, w, h);
}
```

```
int main(int argc, char **argv)
{
    glutInit(&argc, argv);
    glutInitDisplayMode(GLUT_RGB);
    glutInitWindowSize(width, height);
    glutCreateWindow("curves");
    glutDisplayFunc(display);
    glutMouseFunc(mouse);
    glutKeyboardFunc(keyboard);
    glutReshapeFunc(reshape);
    glClearColor(1.0, 1.0, 1.0, 1.0);
    glColor3f(0.0, 0.0, 0.0);
    glPointSize(5.0);
    glEnable(GL_MAP1_VERTEX_3);
    glutMainLoop();
}
```

Spaces

Computer graphics is concerned with the representation and manipulation of sets of geometric elements, such as points and line segments. The necessary mathematics is found in the study of various types of abstract spaces. In this appendix we review the rules governing three such spaces: the (linear) vector space, the affine space, and the Euclidean space. The **(linear) vector space** contains only two types of objects: scalars, such as real numbers, and vectors. The **affine space** adds a third element: the point. **Euclidean spaces** add the concept of distance.

The vectors of interest in computer graphics are directed line segments and the n-tuples of numbers that are used to represent them. In Appendix C we discuss matrix algebra as a tool for manipulating n-tuples. In this appendix we are concerned with the underlying concepts and rules. It is probably helpful to think of these entities (scalars, vectors, points) as abstract data types, and the axioms as defining the valid operations on them.

B.1 Scalars

Ordinary real numbers and the operations on them are one example of a **scalar field**. Let S denote a set of elements called **scalars**, $\alpha, \beta, \ldots$. Scalars have two fundamental operations defined between pairs. These operations are often called addition and multiplication, and are symbolized by the operators $+$ and $\cdot$,[1] respectively. Hence, for $\forall \alpha, \beta \in S, \alpha + \beta \in S, \alpha \cdot \beta \in S$. These operations are associative, commutative, and distributive, $\forall \alpha, \beta, \gamma \in S$:

$$\alpha + \beta = \beta + \alpha,$$

$$\alpha \cdot \beta = \beta \cdot \alpha,$$

$$\alpha + (\beta + \gamma) = (\alpha + \beta) + \gamma,$$

$$\alpha \cdot (\beta \cdot \gamma) = (\alpha \cdot \beta) \cdot \gamma,$$

$$\alpha \cdot (\beta + \gamma) = (\alpha \cdot \beta) + (\alpha \cdot \gamma).$$

---

1. Often, if there is no ambiguity, we can write $\alpha\beta$ instead of $\alpha \cdot \beta$.

There are two special scalars—the additive inverse (0) and the multiplicative inverse (1)—such that $\forall \alpha \in S$:

$$\alpha + 0 = 0 + \alpha = \alpha,$$

$$\alpha \cdot 1 = 1 \cdot \alpha = \alpha.$$

Each element α has an additive inverse, denoted $-\alpha$, and a multiplicative inverse, denoted $\alpha^{-1} \in S$, such that

$$\alpha + (-\alpha) = 0,$$

$$\alpha \cdot \alpha^{-1} = 1.$$

The real numbers using ordinary addition and multiplication form a scalar field, as do the complex numbers (under complex addition and multiplication) and rational functions (ratios of two polynomials).

B.2 Vector Spaces

A vector space, in addition to scalars, contains a second type of entity: **vectors**. Vectors have two operations defined: vector–vector addition and scalar–vector multiplication. Let u, v, w denote vectors in a vector space V. Vector addition is defined to be closed ($u + v \in V, \forall u, v \in V$), commutative ($u + v = v + u$), and associative ($u + (v + w) = (u + v) + w$). There is a special vector (the **zero vector**) $\mathbf{0}$ defined such that $\forall u \in V$:

$$u + \mathbf{0} = u.$$

Every vector u has an additive inverse denoted by $-u$ such that

$$u + (-u) = \mathbf{0}.$$

Scalar–vector multiplication is defined such that, for any scalar α and any vector u, αu is a vector in V. The scalar–vector operation is distributive. Hence,

$$\alpha(u + v) = \alpha u + \alpha v,$$

$$(\alpha + \beta)u = \alpha u + \beta u.$$

The two examples of vector spaces that we use are geometric vectors (directed line segments) and the n-tuples of real numbers. Consider a set of directed line segments that we can picture as shown in Figure B.1. If our scalars are real numbers, then scalar–vector multiplication changes the length of a vector, but not that vector's direction (Figure B.2).

Vector–vector addition can be defined by the **head-to-tail axiom**, which we can visualize easily for the example of directed line segments. We form the vector $u + v$ by connecting the head of u to the tail of v, as shown in Figure B.3. You should be able to verify that all the rules of a vector field are satisfied.

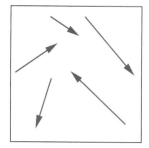

Figure B.1 Directed line segments.

Figure B.2 Scalar–vector multiplication.

Figure B.3 Head-to-tail axiom for vectors.

The second example of a vector space is n-tuples of scalars—usually, real or complex numbers. Hence, a vector can be written as

$$v = (v_1, v_2, \ldots, v_n).$$

Scalar–vector multiplication and vector–vector addition are given by

$$u + v = (u_1, u_2, \ldots, u_n) + (v_1, v_2, \ldots, v_n)$$
$$= (u_1 + v_1, u_2 + v_2, \ldots, u_n + v_n),$$
$$\alpha v = (\alpha v_1, \alpha v_2, \ldots, \alpha v_n).$$

This space is denoted $\mathbf{R}^n$ and is the vector space in which we can manipulate vectors using matrix algebra (Appendix C).

In a vector space, the concepts of linear independence and basis are crucial. A **linear combination** of n vectors $u_1, u_2, \ldots, u_n$ is a vector of the form

$$u = \alpha_1 u_1 + \alpha_2 u_2 + \ldots + \alpha_n u_n.$$

If the only set of scalars such that

$$\alpha_1 u_1 + \alpha_2 u_2 \ldots + \alpha_n u_n = 0$$

is

$$\alpha_1 = \alpha_2 = \ldots = \alpha_n = 0,$$

then the vectors are said to be **linearly independent**. The greatest number of linearly independent vectors that we can find in a space gives the **dimension** of the space. If a vector space has dimension n, any set of n linearly independent vectors form a **basis**. If $v_1, v_2, \ldots, v_n$ is a basis for V, any vector v can be expressed uniquely in terms of the basis vectors as

$$v = \beta_1 v_1 + \beta_2 v_2 + \ldots + \beta_n v_n.$$

The scalars $\{\beta_i\}$ give the **representation** of v with respect to the basis $v_1, v_2, \ldots, v_n$. If $v_1', v_2', \ldots, v_n'$ is some other basis (the number of vectors in a basis is constant), there is a representation of v with respect to this basis; that is,

$$v = \beta_1' v_1' + \beta_2' v_2' + \ldots + \beta_n' v_n'.$$

There exists an $n \times n$ matrix $\mathbf{M}$ such that

$$\begin{bmatrix} \beta_1' \\ \beta_2' \\ \vdots \\ \beta_N' \end{bmatrix} = \mathbf{M} \begin{bmatrix} \beta_1 \\ \beta_2 \\ \vdots \\ \beta_N \end{bmatrix}.$$

We derive $\mathbf{M}$ in Appendix C. This matrix gives a way of changing representations through a simple linear transformation involving only scalar operations for carrying out matrix multiplication. More generally, once we have a basis for a vector space, we can work only with representations. If the scalars are real numbers, then we can work with n-tuples of reals and use matrix algebra, instead of doing operations in the original abstract vector space

B.3 Affine Spaces

A vector space lacks any geometric concepts, such as location and distance. If we use the example of directed line segments as the natural vector space for our geometric problems, we get into difficulties because these vectors, just like the physicist's vectors, have magnitude and direction, but have no position. The vectors in Figure B.4 are identical.

If we think of this problem in terms of coordinate systems, we can express a vector in terms of a set of basis vectors that define a **coordinate system**. Figure B.5(a) shows three basis vectors emerging from a particular reference point, the **origin**. The location of the vectors in Figure B.5(b) is equally valid, however, because vectors have no position. In addition, we have no way to express this special point, because our vector space has only vectors and scalars as its members.

We can resolve this difficulty by introducing an affine space that adds a third type of entity—points—to a vector space. The points $(P, Q, R, \ldots)$ form a set. There is a single new operation, **point–point subtraction**, that yields a vector. Hence, if P and Q are any two points, the subtraction

$$v = P - Q$$

always yields a vector in V. Conversely, for every v and every P, we can find a Q such that the preceding relation holds. We can thus write

$$Q = v + P,$$

Figure B.4 Identical vectors.

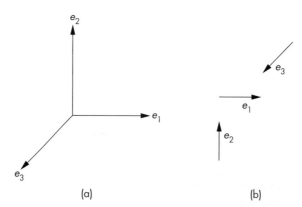

(a)   (b)

Figure B.5 Coordinate system. (a) Basis vectors located at the origin. (b) Arbitrary placement of basis vectors.

defining a vector–point addition. A consequence of the head-to-tail axiom is that for any three points P, Q, R,

$$(P - Q) + (Q - R) = (P - R).$$

If we visualize the vector $P - Q$ as the line segment from the point Q to the point P, using an arrow to denote direction, the head-to-tail axiom can be drawn as shown in Figure B.6.

Various properties follow from affine geometry. Perhaps the most important is that if we use a frame, rather than a coordinate system, we can specify both points and vectors in an affine space. A **frame** consists of a point P_0, and a set of vectors $v_1, v_2, \ldots, v_n$ that defines a basis for the vector space. Given a frame, an arbitrary vector can be written uniquely as

$$v = \alpha_1 v_1 + \alpha_2 v_2 + \ldots + \alpha_n v_n,$$

and an arbitrary point can be written uniquely as

$$P = P_0 + \beta_1 v_1 + \beta_2 v_2 + \ldots + \beta_n v_n.$$

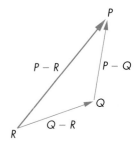

Figure B.6 Head-to-tail axiom for points.

The two sets of scalars, $\{\alpha_1, \ldots, \alpha_n\}$ and $\{\beta_1, \ldots, \beta_n\}$, give the representations of the vector and point, respectively, each representation consisting of n scalars. We can regard the point P_0 as the origin of the frame; all points are defined from this reference point.

If the origin never changes, we can worry about only those changes of frames corresponding to changes in coordinate systems. In computer graphics, however, we usually have to deal with making changes in frames and with representing objects in different frames. For example, we usually define our objects within a physical frame. The viewer, or camera, can be expressed in terms of this frame, but, as part of the image-creation process, it is to our advantage to express object positions with respect to the camera frame—a frame whose origin usually is located at the center of projection.

B.4 Euclidean Spaces

Although affine spaces contain the necessary elements for building geometric models, there is no concept of how far apart two points are, or of what the length of a vector is. Euclidean spaces have such a concept. Strictly speaking, a Euclidean space needs to contain only vectors and scalars.

Suppose that E is a Euclidean space. It is a vector space containing scalars $(\alpha, \beta, \gamma, \ldots)$ and vectors $(u, v, w, \ldots)$. We assume that the scalars are the ordinary real numbers. We add a new operation—the **inner (dot) product**—that combines two vectors to form a real. The inner product must satisfy the properties that, for any three vectors u, v, w and scalars α, β,

$$u \cdot v = v \cdot u,$$

$$(\alpha u + \beta v) \cdot w = \alpha u \cdot w + \beta v \cdot w,$$

$$v \cdot v > 0 \text{ if } v \neq 0,$$

$$0 \cdot 0 = 0.$$

If

$$u \cdot v = 0,$$

then u and v are **orthogonal**. The magnitude (length) of a vector is usually measured as

$$|v| = \sqrt{v \cdot v}.$$

Once we add affine concepts, such as points, to the Euclidean space, we naturally get a measure of distance between points, because, for any two points P and Q, $P - Q$ is a vector, and hence

$$|P - Q| = \sqrt{(P - Q) \cdot (P - Q)}.$$

We can use the inner product to define a measure of the angle between two vectors:

$$u \cdot v = |u||v| \cos \theta.$$

It is easy to show that $\cos \theta$ as defined by this formula is 0 when the vectors are orthogonal, and lies between -1 and $+1$, and has magnitude 1 if the vectors are parallel ($u = \alpha v$).

B.5 Projections

We can derive several of the important geometric concepts from the use of orthogonality. The concept of **projection** arises from the problem of finding the shortest distance from a point to a line or plane. It is equivalent to the following problem. Given two vectors, we can take one of them and divide it into two parts, one parallel and one orthogonal to the other vector, as shown in Figure B.7 for directed line segments. Suppose that v is the first vector and w is the second. Then, w can be written as

$$w = \alpha v + u.$$

The parallel part is αv, but, for u to be orthogonal to v, we must have

$$u \cdot v = 0.$$

Because u and v are defined to be orthogonal,

$$w \cdot v = \alpha v \cdot v + u \cdot v = \alpha v \cdot v,$$

allowing us to find

$$\alpha = \frac{w \cdot v}{v \cdot v}.$$

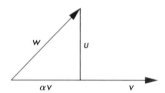

Figure B.7 Projection of one vector onto another.

The vector αv is the projection of w onto v, and

$$u = w - \frac{w \cdot v}{v \cdot v} v.$$

We can extend this result to construct a set of orthogonal vectors from an arbitrary set of linearly independent vectors.

B.6 Gram-Schmidt Orthogonalization

Given a set of basis vectors, $a_1, a_2, \ldots, a_n$, in a space of dimension n, it is relatively straightforward to create another basis $b_1, b_2, \ldots, b_n$ that is **orthonormal**, that is, a basis in which each vector has unit length and is orthogonal to each other vector in the basis, or mathematically:

$$b_i \cdot b_j = \begin{cases} 1 & \text{if } i = j, \\ 0 & \text{otherwise.} \end{cases}$$

Hence, there is no real loss of generality in using orthogonal (Cartesian) coordinate systems.

We proceed iteratively. We look for a vector of the form

$$b_2 = a_2 + \alpha b_1,$$

which we can make orthogonal to b_1 by choosing α properly. Taking the dot product, we must have

$$b_2 \cdot b_1 = 0 = a_2 \cdot b_1 + \alpha b_1 \cdot b_1.$$

Solving, we have

$$\alpha = -\frac{a_2 \cdot b_1}{b_1 \cdot b_1}$$

and

$$b_2 = a_2 - \frac{a_2 \cdot b_1}{b_1 \cdot b_1} b_1.$$

We have constructed the orthogonal vector by removing the part parallel to b_1—that is, the projection of a_2 onto b_1.

The general iterative step is to find a

$$b_k = a_k + \sum_{i=1}^{k-1} \alpha_i b_i$$

that is orthogonal to $b_1, \ldots, b_{k-1}$. There are $k - 1$ orthogonality conditions that allow us to find

$$\alpha_i = -\frac{a_k \cdot b_i}{b_i \cdot b_i}.$$

We can normalize each vector, either at the end of the process, by replacing b_i by $b_i/|b_i|$, or, more efficiently, by normalizing each b_i as soon as possible.

B.7 Suggested Readings

There are many excellent books on linear algebra and vector spaces. For practitioners of computer graphics, the preferred approach is to start with vector-space ideas and to see linear algebra as a tool for working with general vector spaces. Unfortunately, most of the linear-algebra textbooks are concerned with only the Euclidean spaces of n-tuples, $\mathbf{R}^n$. See Bowyer and Woodwark [Bow83] and Banchoff and Werner [Ban83].

Affine spaces can be approached in number of ways. See Foley [Fol90] for a more geometric development.

Exercises

B.1   Prove that the complex numbers form a scalar field. What are the additive and multiplicative identity elements?

B.2   Prove that the rational functions form a scalar field.

B.3   Prove that the rational functions with real coefficients form a vector space.

B.4   Prove that the number of elements in a basis is unique.

B.5   Consider a set of n real functions $\{f_i(x)\}$, $i = 1, \ldots, n$. Show how to form a vector space of functions with these elements. Define *basis* and *dimension* for this space.

B.6   Show that the set of polynomials of degree up to n form an n-dimensional vector space.

B.7   The most important Euclidean space is the space of n-tuples, $a_1, \ldots, a_n$: $\mathbf{R}^n$. Define the operations of vector addition and scalar-vector multiplication in this space. What is the dot product in $\mathbf{R}^n$?

B.8   Suppose that you are given three vectors in $\mathbf{R}^3$. How can you find whether they form a basis?

B.9   Consider the three vectors in $\mathbf{R}^3$: $(1,0,0)$, $(1,1,0)$, and $(1,1,1)$. Show that they are linearly independent. Derive an orthonormal basis from these vectors, starting with $(1,0,0)$.

Matrices

In computer graphics, the major use of matrices is in the representation of changes in coordinate systems and frames. In the studies of vector analysis and linear algebra, the use of the term *vector* is somewhat different. Unfortunately, computer graphics relies on both these fields, and the interpretation of *vector* has caused confusion. To remedy this situation, we use the terms *row matrix* and *column matrix*, rather than the linear-algebra terms of *row vector* and *column vector*. We reserve the *vector* to denote directed line segments, and occasionally, as in Appendix B, to denote the abstract-data-type vector that is an element of a vector space.

This appendix reviews the major results that you will need to manipulate matrices in computer graphics. We almost always use matrices that are 4 × 4. Hence, the parts of linear algebra that deal with manipulations of general matrices, such as the inversion of an arbitrary square matrix, are of limited interest. Most implementations, instead, implement inversion of 4 × 4 matrices directly in the hardware or software.

C.1 Definitions

A **matrix** is an $n \times m$ array of scalars, arranged conceptually as n rows and m columns. Often, n and m are referred to as the row and column **dimensions** of the matrix, and, if $m = n$, we say that the matrix is a **square matrix** of dimension n. We use real numbers for scalars, almost exclusively, although most results hold for complex numbers as well. The elements of a matrix $\mathbf{A}$ are the members of the set of scalars, $\{a_{ij}\}$, $i = 1, \ldots, n$, $j = 1, \ldots, m$. We write $\mathbf{A}$ in terms of its elements as

$$\mathbf{A} = [\, a_{ij} \,].$$

The **transpose** of an $n \times m$ matrix $\mathbf{A}$ is the $m \times n$ matrix that we obtain by interchanging the rows and columns of $\mathbf{A}$. We denote this matrix as $\mathbf{A}^T$, and it is given as

$$\mathbf{A}^T = [\, a_{ji} \,].$$

The special cases of matrices with one column ($n \times 1$ matrix) and one row ($1 \times m$ matrix) are called **column matrices** and **row matrices**. We denote column matrices with lowercase letters:

$$\mathbf{b} = [\, b_i \,].$$

The transpose of a row matrix is a column matrix; we write it as $\mathbf{b}^T$.

C.2 Matrix Operations

There are three basic matrix operations: scalar–matrix multiplication, matrix–matrix addition, and matrix–matrix multiplication. You can assume that the scalars are real numbers, although all these operations are defined in the same way when the elements of the matrices and the scalar multipliers are of the same type.

Scalar–matrix multiplication is defined for any size matrix $\mathbf{A}$; it is simply the element-by-element multiplication of the elements of the matrix by a scalar α. The operation is written as

$$\alpha\mathbf{A} = [\, \alpha a_{ij} \,].$$

We define **matrix–matrix addition**, the sum of two matrices, by adding the corresponding elements of the two matrices. The sum makes sense only if the two matrices have the same dimensions. The sum of two matrices of the same dimensions is given by the matrix

$$\mathbf{C} = \mathbf{A} + \mathbf{B} = [\, a_{ij} + b_{ij} \,].$$

For **matrix–matrix multiplication**, the product of an $n \times l$ matrix $\mathbf{A}$ by an $l \times m$ matrix $\mathbf{B}$ is the $n \times m$ matrix

$$\mathbf{C} = \mathbf{AB} = [\, c_{ij} \,],$$

where

$$c_{ij} = \sum_{k=1}^{l} a_{ik} b_{kj}.$$

The matrix–matrix product is thus defined only if the number of columns of $\mathbf{A}$ is the same as the number of rows of $\mathbf{B}$. We say that $\mathbf{A}$ premultiplies $\mathbf{B}$, or $\mathbf{B}$ postmultiplies $\mathbf{A}$.

Scalar–matrix multiplication obeys a number of simple rules that hold for any matrix $\mathbf{A}$, and for scalars α and β, such as

$$\alpha(\beta\mathbf{A}) = (\alpha\beta)\mathbf{A},$$

$$\alpha\beta\mathbf{A} = \beta\alpha\mathbf{A},$$

all of which follow from the fact that our matrix operations reduce to scalar multiplications on the scalar elements of a matrix. For matrix–matrix addition, we have the **commutative** property. For any $n \times m$ matrices $\mathbf{A}$ and $\mathbf{B}$:

$$\mathbf{A} + \mathbf{B} = \mathbf{B} + \mathbf{A}.$$

We also have the **associative** property, which states that for any three $n \times m$ matrices $\mathbf{A}$, $\mathbf{B}$, and $\mathbf{C}$:

$$\mathbf{A} + (\mathbf{B} + \mathbf{C}) = (\mathbf{A} + \mathbf{B}) + \mathbf{C}.$$

Matrix–matrix multiplication, although associative,

$$\mathbf{A}(\mathbf{BC}) = (\mathbf{AB})\mathbf{C},$$

is almost never commutative. So not only is it almost always the case that $\mathbf{AB} \neq \mathbf{BA}$, but also one product may not even be defined when the other is. In graphics applications, where matrices represent transformations such as translation and rotation, these results express that the order in which you carry out a sequence of transformations is important. A rotation followed by a translation is not the same as a translation followed by a rotation. However, if we do a rotation followed by a translation followed by a scaling, we get the same result if we first combine the scaling and translation, preserving the order, and apply the rotation to the combined transformation.

The identity matrix $\mathbf{I}$ is a square matrix with 1s on the diagonal and 0s elsewhere:

$$\mathbf{I} = [\, a_{ij} \,], \qquad a_{ij} = \begin{cases} 1 & \text{if } i = j; \\ 0 & \text{otherwise.} \end{cases}$$

Assuming that the dimensions make sense,

$$\mathbf{AI} = \mathbf{A},$$

$$\mathbf{IB} = \mathbf{B}.$$

C.3 Row and Column Matrices

The $1 \times n$ and $n \times 1$ row and column matrices are of particular interest to us. We can represent either a vector or a point in three-dimensional space,[1] with respect to some frame, as the column matrix

$$\mathbf{p} = \begin{bmatrix} x \\ y \\ z \end{bmatrix}.$$

----

1. The homogeneous-coordinate representation introduced in Chapter 4 distinguishes between the representation of a point and the representation of a vector.

We use lowercase letters for column matrices. The transpose of $\mathbf{p}$ is the row matrix

$$\mathbf{p}^T = [\,x\quad y\quad z\,].$$

Because the product of an $n \times l$ and a $l \times m$ matrix is an $n \times m$ matrix, the product of a square matrix of dimension n and a column matrix of dimension n is a new column matrix of dimension n. Our standard mode of representing transformations of points is to use a column matrix of two, three, or four dimensions to represent a point (or vector), and a square matrix to represent a transformation of the point (or vector). Thus, the expression

$$\mathbf{p}' = \mathbf{A}\mathbf{p}$$

yields the representation of a transformed point (or vector), and expressions such as

$$\mathbf{p}' = \mathbf{A}\mathbf{B}\mathbf{C}\mathbf{p}$$

describe sequences, or **concatenations**, of transformations. Note that because the matrix–matrix product is associative, we do not need parentheses in this expression.

Many graphics books prefer to use row matrices to represent points. If we do so, using the fact that the transpose of a product can be written as

$$(\mathbf{A}\mathbf{B})^T = \mathbf{B}^T\mathbf{A}^T,$$

then the concatenation of the three transformations can be written in row form as

$$\mathbf{p}'^T = \mathbf{p}^T\mathbf{C}^T\mathbf{B}^T\mathbf{A}^T.$$

The professed advantage of this form is that, in English, we read the transformations in the order in which they are performed; first $\mathbf{C}$, then $\mathbf{B}$, then $\mathbf{A}$. Almost all the scientific, mathematics, and engineering literature, however, uses column matrices rather than row matrices. Consequently, we prefer the column form. Although the choice is conceptually simple, in practice you have to be careful regarding which one your API is using, as not only is the order of transformations reversed, but also the transformation matrices themselves must be transposed.

C.4 Rank

In computer graphics, the primary use of matrices is as representations of points and of transformations. If a square matrix represents the transformation of a point or vector, we are often interested in whether or not the transformation is reversible or **invertible**. Thus, if

$$\mathbf{q} = \mathbf{A}\mathbf{p},$$

we want to know whether we can find a square matrix $\mathbf{B}$ such that

$\mathbf{p} = \mathbf{Bq}$.

Substituting for $\mathbf{q}$,

$\mathbf{p} = \mathbf{Bq} = \mathbf{BAp} = \mathbf{Ip} = \mathbf{p}$

and

$\mathbf{BA} = \mathbf{I}$.

If such a $\mathbf{B}$ exists, it is the **inverse** of $\mathbf{A}$, and $\mathbf{A}$ is said to be **nonsingular**. A noninvertible matrix is **singular**. The inverse of $\mathbf{A}$ is written as $\mathbf{A}^{-1}$.

The fundamental result about inverses is as follows: *The inverse of a square matrix exists if and only if the determinant of the matrix is nonzero.* Although the determinant of $\mathbf{A}$ is a scalar, denoted by $|\mathbf{A}|$, its computation, for anything but low-dimensional matrices, requires almost as much work as does computation of the inverse. These calculations are $O(n^3)$ for an n-dimensional matrix. For the two-, three-, and four-dimensional matrices of interest in computer graphics, we can compute determinants by Cramer's rule and inverses using determinants, or we can use geometric reasoning. For example, the inverse of a translation is a translation back, and thus the inverse of a translation matrix must be a translation matrix. We pursue this course in Chapter 4.

For general nonsquare matrices, the concept of rank is important. We can regard a square matrix as a row matrix whose elements are column matrices or, equivalently, as a column matrix whose elements are row matrices. In terms of the vector-space concepts of Appendix B, the rows of an $n \times m$ matrix are elements of the Euclidean space $\mathbf{R}^m$, whereas the columns are elements of $\mathbf{R}^n$. We can determine how many rows (or columns) are **linearly independent**. The row (column) **rank** is the maximum number of linearly independent rows (columns), and thus *for an $n \times n$ matrix, the row rank and the column rank are the same and the matrix is nonsingular if and only if the rank is n.* Thus, a matrix is invertible if and only if its rows (and columns) are linearly independent.

C.5 Change of Representation

We can use matrices to represent changes in bases for any set of vectors satisfying the rules of Appendix B. Suppose that we have a vector space of dimension n. Let $\{u_1, u_2, \ldots, u_n\}$ and $\{v_1, v_2, \ldots, v_n\}$ be two bases for the vector space. Hence, a given vector v can be expressed as either

$v = \alpha_1 u_1 + \alpha_2 u_2 + \ldots + \alpha_n u_n$

or

$v = \beta_1 v_1 + \beta_2 v_2 + \ldots + \beta_n v_n.$

Thus, $(\alpha_1, \alpha_2, \ldots, \alpha_n)$ and $(\beta_1, \beta_2, \ldots, \beta_n)$ are two different representations of v, and each can be expressed, equivalently, as a vector in the Euclidean space $\mathbf{R}^n$ or as a column matrix of dimension n. When we are working with representations, rather than with the vectors, we have to be careful to make sure that our notation reflects the difference. We write the representations of v as either

$$\mathbf{v} = \begin{bmatrix} \alpha_1 & \alpha_2 & \cdots & \alpha_n \end{bmatrix}^T$$

or

$$\mathbf{v}' = \begin{bmatrix} \beta_1 & \beta_2 & \cdots & \beta_n \end{bmatrix}^T,$$

depending on which basis we use.

We can now address the problem of how we convert from the representation $\mathbf{v}$ to the representation $\mathbf{v}'$. The basis vectors $\{v_1, v_2, \ldots, v_n\}$ can be expressed as vectors in the basis $\{u_1, u_2, \ldots, u_n\}$. Thus, there exists a set of scalars γ_{ij} such that

$$u_i = \gamma_{i1} v_1 + \gamma_{i2} v_2 + \ldots + \gamma_{in} v_n, \quad i = 1, \ldots, n.$$

We can write the expression in matrix form for all u_i as

$$\begin{bmatrix} u_1 \\ u_2 \\ \vdots \\ u_n \end{bmatrix} = \mathbf{A} \begin{bmatrix} v_1 \\ v_2 \\ \vdots \\ v_n \end{bmatrix},$$

where $\mathbf{A}$ is the $n \times n$ matrix:

$$\mathbf{A} = \begin{bmatrix} \gamma_{ij} \end{bmatrix}.$$

We can use column matrices to express both $\mathbf{v}$ and $\mathbf{v}'$ in terms of the vectors' representations as

$$\mathbf{v} = \mathbf{a}^T \begin{bmatrix} u_1 \\ u_2 \\ \vdots \\ u_n \end{bmatrix},$$

where

$$\mathbf{a} = \begin{bmatrix} \alpha_i \end{bmatrix}.$$

We can define $\mathbf{b}$ as

$$\mathbf{b} = \begin{bmatrix} \beta_i \end{bmatrix},$$

and we can write $\mathbf{v}'$ as

$$\mathbf{v}' = \mathbf{b}^T \begin{bmatrix} v_1 \\ v_2 \\ \vdots \\ v_n \end{bmatrix}.$$

The matrix $\mathbf{A}$ relates the two bases, so we find by direct substitution that

$$\mathbf{b}^T = \mathbf{a}^T \mathbf{A}.$$

The matrix $\mathbf{A}$ is the **matrix representation** of the change between the two bases. It allows us to convert directly between the two representations. Equivalently, we can work with matrices of scalars rather than with abstract vectors. For geometric problems, although our vectors may be directed line segments, we can represent them by sets of scalars, and we can represent changes of bases or transformations by direct manipulation of these scalars.

C.6 The Cross Product

Given two nonparallel vectors, u and v, in a three-dimensional space, the cross product gives a third vector, w, that is orthogonal to both. Regardless of the representation, we must have

$$w \cdot u = w \cdot v = 0.$$

We can assign one component of w arbitrarily, because it is the direction of w, rather than the length, that is of importance, leaving us with three conditions for the three components of w. Within a particular coordinate system, if u has components $\alpha_1, \alpha_2, \alpha_3$, and v has components $\beta_1, \beta_2, \beta_3$, then, in this system, the **cross product** is defined as

$$\mathbf{w} = \mathbf{u} \times \mathbf{v} = \begin{bmatrix} \alpha_2 \beta_3 - \alpha_3 \beta_2 \\ \alpha_3 \beta_1 - \alpha_1 \beta_3 \\ \alpha_1 \beta_2 - \alpha_2 \beta_1 \end{bmatrix}.$$

Note that vector w is defined by u and v; we use their representation only when we wish to compute w in a particular coordinate system. The cross product gives a consistent orientation for $u \times v$. For example, consider the x-, y-, and z-axes as three vectors that determine the three coordinate directions of a right-handed coordinate system.[2] If we use the usual x- and y-axes, the cross product $x \times y$ points in the direction of the positive z-axis.

---

2. A right-handed coordinate system has positive directions determined by the thumb, index finger, and middle finger of the right hand used for the x-, y-, and z-axes, respectively. Equivalently, on a piece of paper, if positive x points left to right and positive y points bottom to top, then positive z points out of the page.

C.7 Eigenvalues and Eigenvectors

Square matrices are operators that transform column matrices into other column matrices of the same dimension. Because column matrices can represent points and vectors, we are interested in questions such as, When does a transformation leave a point or vector unchanged? For example, every rotation matrix leaves a particular point—the fixed point—unchanged. Let us consider a slightly more general problem. When does the matrix equation

$$\mathbf{Mu} = \lambda \mathbf{u}$$

have a nontrivial solution for some scalar λ, that is, a solution with $\mathbf{u}$ not being a matrix of zeros? If such a solution exists, then $\mathbf{M}$ transforms certain vectors $\mathbf{u}$—its **eigenvectors**—into scalar multiples of themselves. The values of λ for which this relationship holds are called the **eigenvalues** of the matrix. Eigenvalues and eigenvectors are also called **characteristic values** and **characteristic vectors**, respectively. These values characterize many properties of the matrix that are invariant under such operations as changes in representation.

We can find the eigenvalues by solving the equivalent matrix equation

$$\mathbf{Mu} - \lambda \mathbf{u} = \mathbf{Mu} - \lambda \mathbf{Iu} = (\mathbf{M} - \lambda \mathbf{I})\mathbf{u} = \mathbf{0}.$$

This equation can have a nontrivial solution if and only if the determinant[3]

$$|\mathbf{M} - \lambda \mathbf{I}| = 0.$$

If $\mathbf{M}$ is $n \times n$, then the determinant yields a polynomial of degree n in λ. Thus, there are n roots, some of which may be repeated or complex. For each distinct eigenvalue, we can then find a corresponding eigenvector. Note that every multiple of an eigenvector is itself an eigenvector, so that we can choose an eigenvector with unit magnitude. Eigenvectors corresponding to distinct eigenvalues are linearly independent. Thus, if all the eigenvalues are distinct, then any set of eigenvectors corresponding to the distinct eigenvalues form a basis for an n-dimensional vector space.

If there are repeated eigenvalues, the situation can be more complex. However, we need not worry about these cases for the matrices we shall use in graphics. Thus, if $\mathbf{R}$ is a 3×3 rotation matrix and $\mathbf{p} = [\begin{array}{ccc} x & y & z \end{array}]^T$ is the fixed point, then

$$\mathbf{Rp} = \mathbf{p}.$$

---

3. The general statement, known as the Fredholm alternative, states that the the the n linear equations in n unknowns $\mathbf{Ax} = \mathbf{b}$ have a unique solution if and only if $|\mathbf{A}| \neq 0$. If $|\mathbf{A}| = 0$, there are multiple nontrivial solutions.

Thus, every rotation matrix must have an eigenvalue of 1. This result is the same whether we work in three dimensions or use the four-dimensional homogenous coordinate representation in Chapter 4.

Suppose that $\mathbf{T}$ is a nonsingular matrix. Consider the matrix

$$\mathbf{Q} = \mathbf{T}^{-1}\mathbf{M}\mathbf{T}.$$

Its eigenvalues and eigenvectors are solutions of the equation

$$\mathbf{Q}\mathbf{v} = \mathbf{T}^{-1}\mathbf{M}\mathbf{T}\mathbf{v} = \lambda\mathbf{v}.$$

But if we multiply by $\mathbf{T}$, this equations becomes

$$\mathbf{M}\mathbf{T}\mathbf{v} = \lambda\mathbf{T}\mathbf{v}.$$

Thus, the eigenvalues of $\mathbf{Q}$ are the same as those of $\mathbf{M}$, and the eigenvectors are the transformations of the eigenvectors of $\mathbf{M}$. The matrices $\mathbf{M}$ and $\mathbf{Q}$ are said to be **similar**. Many of the transformations that arise in computer graphics involve similar matrices. One interpretation of this result is that changes of coordinate systems leave fundamental properties, such as the eigenvalues, unchanged. If we can find a similarity transformation that converts $\mathbf{M}$ to a diagonal matrix $\mathbf{Q}$, then the diagonal elements of $\mathbf{Q}$ are the eigenvalues of both matrices.

Eigenvalues and eigenvectors have a geometric interpretation. Consider an ellipsoid, centered at the origin, with its axes aligned with the coordinate axes. It can be written as

$$\lambda_1 x^2 + \lambda_2 y^2 + \lambda_3 z^2 = 1$$

for positive values of λ_1, λ_2, and λ_3, or in matrix form

$$[x \quad y \quad z] \begin{bmatrix} \lambda_1 & 0 & 0 \\ 0 & \lambda_2 & 0 \\ 0 & 0 & \lambda_3 \end{bmatrix} \begin{bmatrix} x \\ y \\ z \end{bmatrix} = 1.$$

Thus, λ_1, λ_2, and λ_3 are both the eigenvalues of the diagonal matrix and the inverses of the lengths of the major and minor axes of the ellipsoid. If we apply a change of coordinate system through a rotation matrix, we create a new ellipsoid that is no longer aligned with the coordinate axes. However, we have not changed the length of axes of the ellipse, a property that is invariant under coordinate system changes.

C.8 Suggested Readings

Some of the standard references on linear algebra and matrices include Strang [Str93] and Banchoff and Werner [Ban83]. See also Rogers and Adams [Rog90] and the *Graphics Gems* series [Gra90, Gra91, Gra92, Gra94, Gra95].

The issue of row versus column matrices is an old one. Early graphics books [New73] used row matrices. The trend now is to use column matrices [Fol90], although a few books still use row representations [Wat00]. Within the API, it may not be clear which is being used, because the elements of a square matrix can be represented as a simple array of n^2 elements. Certain APIs, such as OpenGL, allow only postmultiplication of an internal matrix by a user-defined matrix; others, such as PHIGS, support both pre- and postmultiplication.

Exercises

C.1   In $\mathbf{R}^3$, consider the two bases $\{(1, 0, 0), (1, 1, 0), (1, 1, 1)\}$ and $\{(1, 0, 0), (0, 1, 0), (0, 0, 1)\}$. Find the two matrices that convert representations between the two bases. Show that they are inverses of each other.

C.2   Consider the vector space of polynomials of degree up to 2. Show that the sets of polynomials $\{1, x, x^2\}$ and $\{1, 1 + x, 1 + x + x^2\}$ are bases. Give the representation of the polynomial $1 + 2x + 3x^2$ in each basis. Find the matrix that converts between representations in the two bases.

C.3   Suppose that $\mathbf{i}$, $\mathbf{j}$, and $\mathbf{k}$ represent the unit vectors in the x, y, and z directions, respectively, in $\mathbf{R}^3$. Show that the cross product $u \times v$ is given by the matrix

$$u \times v = \begin{vmatrix} \mathbf{i} & \mathbf{j} & \mathbf{k} \\ u_1 & u_2 & u_3 \\ v_1 & v_2 & v_3 \end{vmatrix}.$$

C.4   Show that, in $\mathbf{R}^3$,

$$|u \times v| = |u||v|| \sin \theta|,$$

where θ is the angle between u and v.

C.5   Find the eigenvalues and eigenvectors of the two-dimensional rotation matrix

$$\mathbf{R} = \begin{bmatrix} \cos \theta & -\sin \theta \\ \sin \theta & \cos \theta \end{bmatrix}.$$

C.6   Find the eigenvalues and eigenvectors of the three-dimensional rotation matrix

$$\mathbf{R} = \begin{bmatrix} \cos \theta & -\sin \theta & 0 \\ \sin \theta & \cos \theta & 0 \\ 0 & 0 & 1 \end{bmatrix}.$$

References

Ado85   Adobe Systems Incorporated, *PostScript Language Reference Manual*, Addison-Wesley, Reading, MA, 1985.

Ake88   Akeley, K., and T. Jermoluk, "High Performance Polygon Rendering," *Computer Graphics*, 22(4), 239–246, 1988.

Ake93   Akeley, K., "Reality Engine Graphics," *Computer Graphics*, 109–116, 1993.

Ang90   Angel, E., *Computer Graphics*, Addison-Wesley, Reading, MA, 1990.

Ang02   Angel, E., *OpenGL, A Primer*, Addison-Wesley, Reading, MA, 2002.

ANSI85 American National Standards Institute (ANSI), *American National Standard for Information Processing Systems—Computer Graphics—Graphical Kernel System (GKS) Functional Description*, ANSI, X3.124-1985, ANSI, New York, 1985.

ANSI88 American National Standards Institute (ANSI), *American National Standard for Information Processing Systems—Programmer's Hierarchical Interactive Graphics System (PHIGS)*, ANSI, X3.144-1988, ANSI, New York, 1988.

App68   Appel, A., "Some Techniques for Shading Machine Renderings of Solids," *Spring Joint Computer Conference*, 37–45, 1968.

Arn96   Arnold, K., and J. Gosling, *The Java Programming Language*, Addison-Wesley, Reading, MA, 1996.

Ban83   Banchoff, T., and J. Werner, *Linear Algebra Through Geometry*, Springer-Verlag, New York, 1983.

Bar93   Barnsley, M., *Fractals Everywhere*, Second Edition, Academic Press, San Diego, CA, 1993.

Bar83   Barsky, B.A., and C. Beatty, "Local Control of Bias and Tension in Beta-Splines," *ACM Transactions on Graphics*, 2(2), 109–134, 1983.

Bar87   Bartels, R.H., C. Beatty, and B.A. Barsky, *An Introduction to Splines for Use in Computer Graphics and Geometric Modeling*, Morgan-Kaufmann, Los Altos, CA, 1987.

Bli76   Blinn, J.F., and M.E. Newell, "Texture and Reflection in Computer Generated Images," *CACM*, 19(10), 542–547, 1976.

Bli77   Blinn, J.F., "Models of Light Reflection for Computer-Synthesized Pictures," *Computer Graphics*, 11(2), 192–198, 1977.

Bow83   Bowyer, A., and J. Woodwark, *A Programmer's Geometry*, Butterworth, London, 1983.

Bre63   Bresenham, J.E., "Algorithm for Computer Control of a Digital Plotter," *IBM Systems Journal*, January, 25–30, 1965.

Bre87   Bresenham, J.E., "Ambiguities in Incremental Line Rastering," *IEEE Computer Graphics and Applications*, May, 31–43, 1987.

Car78   Carlbom, I., and J. Paciorek, "Planar Geometric Projection and Viewing Transformations," *Computing Surveys*, 10(4), 465–502, 1978.

Cas96   Castleman, K.C., *Digital Image Processing*, Prentice-Hall, Englewood Cliffs, NJ, 1996.

Cat75   Catmull, E., "A Hidden-Surface Algorithm with Antialiasing," *Computer Graphics*, 12(3), 6–11, 1975.

Cha98   Chan, P., and R. Lee, *The Java Class Libraries: Java.Applet, Java.Awt, Java.Beans* (Vol. 2), Addison-Wesley, Reading, MA, 1998.

Che95   Chen, S.E., "Quicktime VR: An Image-Based Approach to Virtual Environment Navigation," *Computer Graphics*, 29–38, 1995.

Che00   Chen, K.L. et al., "Building and Using a Scalable Display Wall System," *IEEE Computer Graphics and Applications*, 20(4), 29–37, 2000.

Cla82   Clark, J.E., "The Geometry Engine: A VLSI Geometry System for Graphics," *Computer Graphics*, 16, 127–133, 1982.

Coh85   Cohen, M.F., and D.P. Greenberg, "The Hemi-Cube: A Radiosity Solution for Complex Environments," *Computer Graphics*, 19(3), 31–40, 1985.

Coh88   Cohen, M.F., S.E. Chen, J.R. Wallace, and D.P. Greenberg, "A Progressive Refinement Approach to Fast Radiosity Image Generation," *Computer Graphics*, 22(4), 75–84, 1988.

Coh93   Cohen, M.F., and J.R. Wallace, *Radiosity and Realistic Image Synthesis*, Academic Press Professional, Boston, MA, 1993.

Coo82   Cook, R.L., and K.E. Torrance, "A Reflectance Model for Computer Graphics," *ACM Transactions on Graphics*, 1(1), 7–24, 1982.

Coo87   Cook, R.L., L. Carpenter, and E. Catmull, "The Reyes Image Rendering Architecture," *Computer Graphics*, 21(4), 95–102, July 1987.

Cro81   Crow, F.C., "A Comparison of Antialiasing Techniques," *IEEE Computer Graphics and Applications*, 1(1), 40–48, 1981.

Cro97   Crossno, P.J., and E. Angel, "Isosurface Extraction Using Particle Systems," *IEEE Visualization*, 1997.

Deb96   Debevec, P.E., C.J. Taylor, and J. Malik, "Modeling and Rendering Architecture from Photographs: A Hybrid Geometry- and Image-Based Approach," *Computer Graphics*, 11–20, 1996.

DeR88   DeRose, T.D., "A Coordinate Free Approach to Geometric Programming," SIGGRAPH Course Notes, *SIGGRAPH*, 1988.

DeR89   DeRose, T.D., "A Coordinate Free Approach to Geometric Programming," *Theory and Practice of Geometric Modeling*, W. Strasser and H.P. Seidel (Eds.), Springer-Verlag, Berlin, 1989.

Dre88   Drebin, R.A., L. Carpenter, and P. Hanrahan, "Volume Rendering," *Computer Graphics*, 22(4), 65–74, 1988.

Ebe01   Eberly, D.H., *3D Game Engine Design*, Morgan Kaufmann, San Francisco, CA, 2001.

Ebe98   Ebert, D. (Ed), *Texturing and Modeling*, Academic Press, New York, 1998.

End84   Enderle, G., K. Kansy, and G. Pfaff, *Computer Graphics Programming: GKS—The Graphics Standard*, Springer-Verlag, Berlin, 1984.

Eng68   Engelbart, D.C., and W.K. English, "A Research Center for Augmenting Human Intellect," *Fall Joint Computer Conference*, Thompson Books, Washington, DC, 1968.

Far88   Farin, G., *Curves and Surfaces for Computer Aided Geometric Design*, Academic Press, New York, 1988.

Fau80   Faux, I.D., and M.J. Pratt, *Computational Geometry for Design and Manufacturing*, Halsted, Chichester, England, 1980.

Fol90   Foley, J.D., A. van Dam, S.K. Feiner, and J.F. Hughes, *Computer Graphics*, Second Edition, Addison-Wesley, Reading, MA, 1990 (C Version 1996).

Fol94   Foley, J.D., A. van Dam, S.K. Feiner, J. F. Hughes, and R. Phillips, *Introduction to Computer Graphics*, Addison-Wesley, Reading, MA, 1994.

Fos96   Fosner, R., *OpenGL Programming for Windows 95 and Windows NT*, Addison-Wesley, Reading, MA, 1996.

Fou82   Fournier, A., D. Fussell, and L. Carpenter, "Computer Rendering of Stochastic Models," *CACM*, 25(6), 371–384, 1982.

Fuc77   Fuchs, H., J. Duran, and B. Johnson, "A System for Automatic Acquisition of Three-Dimensional Data," *Proceedings of the 1977 NCC*, AFIPS Press, 49–53, Montvale, NJ, 1977.

Fuc80   Fuchs, H., Z.M. Kedem, and B.F. Naylor, "On Visible Surface Generation by A Priori Tree Structures," *SIGGRAPH 80*, 124–133, 1980.

Gal95   Gallagar, R.S., *Computer Visualization: Graphics Techniques for Scientific and Engineering Analysis*, CRC Press, Boca Raton, FL, 1995.

Gla89   Glassner, A.S. (Ed.), *An Introduction to Ray Tracing*, Academic Press, New York, 1989.

Gla95   Glassner, A.S., *Principles of Digital Image Synthesis*, Morgan-Kaufmann, New York, 1995.

Gol83   Goldberg, A., and D. Robson, *Smalltalk–80: The Language and Its Implementation*, Addison-Wesley, Reading, MA, 1983.

Gon87   Gonzalez, R., and P. Wintz, *Digital Image Processing*, Second Edition, Addison-Wesley, Reading, MA, 1987.

Gor84   Goral, C.M., K.E. Torrance, D.P. Greenberg, and B. Battaile, "Modeling the Interaction of Light Between Diffuse Surfaces," *Computer Graphics (SIGGRAPH 84)*, 18(3), 213–222, 1984.

Gor96   Gortler, S.J., R. Grzeszczuk, R. Szeliski, and M.F. Cohen, "The Lumigraph," *Computer Graphics*, 43–54, 1996.

Gou71   Gouraud, H., "Computer Display of Curved Surfaces," *IEEE Trans. Computers*, C-20, 623–628, 1971.

Gra90   *Graphics Gems I*, Glassner, A.S. (Ed.), Academic Press, San Diego, CA, 1990.

Gra91   *Graphics Gems II*, Arvo, J. (Ed.), Academic Press, San Diego, CA, 1991.

Gra92   *Graphics Gems III*, Kirk, D. (Ed.), Academic Press, San Diego, CA, 1992.

Gra94   *Graphics Gems IV*, Heckbert, P. (Ed.), Academic Press, San Diego, CA, 1994.

Gra95   *Graphics Gems V*, Paeth, A. (Ed.), Academic Press, San Diego, CA, 1995.

Hal89   Hall, R., *Illumination and Color in Computer Generated Imagery,* Springer-Verlag, New York, 1989.

Har96   Hartman, J., and J. Wernecke, *The VRML 2.0 Handbook*, Addison-Wesley, Reading, MA, 1996.

Hea94   Hearn, D., and M.P. Baker, *Computer Graphics*, Second Edition, Prentice-Hall, Englewood Cliffs, NJ, 1994.

Hec84   Heckbert, P.S., and P. Hanrahan, "Beam Tracing Polygonal Objects," *Computer Graphics*, 18(3), 119–127, 1984.

Hec86   Heckbert, P.S., "Survey of Texture Mapping," *IEEE Computer Graphics and Applications,* 6(11), 56–67, 1986.

Her79   Herman, G.T., and H.K. Liu, "Three-Dimensional Display of Human Organs from Computed Tomograms," *Computer Graphics and Image Processing,* 9, 1–21, 1979.

Her00   Hereld, M., I.R. Judson, and R.L. Stevens, "Tutorial: Introduction to Building Projection-Based Tiled Display Systems," *IEEE Computer Graphics and Applications,* 20(4), 22–26, 2000.

Hil01   Hill, F.S., Jr., *Computer Graphics*, Second Edition, Prentice Hall, Upper Saddle River, NJ, 2001.

Hop83   Hopgood, F.R.A., D.A. Duce, J.A. Gallop, and D.C. Sutcliffe, *Introduction to the Graphical Kernel System: GKS*, Academic Press, London, 1983.

Hop91   Hopgood, F.R.A., and D.A. Duce, *A Primer for PHIGS,* John Wiley & Sons, Chichester, England, 1991.

Hum01   Humphreys, G., M. Elridge, I. Buck, G. Stoll, M. Everett, and P. Hanrahan, "WireGL: A Scalable Graphics System for Clusters," *SIGGRAPH 2001.*

ISO88   International Standards Organization, *International Standard Information Processing Systems—Computer Graphics—Graphical Kernel System for Three Dimensions (GKS-3D),* ISO Document Number 8805:1988(E), American National Standards Institute, New York, 1988.

Jar76   Jarvis, J.F., C.N. Judice, and W.H. Ninke, "A Survey of Techniques for the Image Display of Continuous Tone Pictures on Bilevel Displays," *Computer Graphics and Image Processing,* 5(1), 13–40, 1976.

Joy88   Joy, K.I., C.W. Grant, N.L. Max, and L. Hatfield, *Computer Graphics: Image Synthesis*, Computer Society Press, Washington, DC, 1988.

Kaj86   Kajiya, J.T., "The Rendering Equation," *Computer Graphics,* 20(4), 143–150, 1986.

Kel97   Keller, H., "Instant Randiosity," *Computer Graphics*, 49–56, 1997.

Kil94a   Kilgard, M.J., "OpenGL and X, Part 3: Integrated OpenGL with Motif," *The X Journal,* SIGS Publications, July/August 1994.

Kil94b   Kilgard, M.J., "An OpenGL Toolkit," *The X Journal,* SIGS Publications, November/December 1994.

Kil96   Kilgard, M.J., *OpenGL Programming for the X Windows System,* Addison-Wesley, Reading, MA, 1996.

Knu87   Knuth, D.E., "Digital Halftones by Dot Diffusion," *ACM Transactions on Graphics,* 6(40), 245–273, 1987.

Kov97   Kovatch, P.J., *The Awesome Power of Direct3D/DirectX,* Manning Publications Company, Greenwich, CT, 1997.

Kui99   Kuipers, J.B., *Quaternions and Rotation Sequences,* Princeton University Press, Princeton, NJ, 1999.

Las87   Lasseter, J., "Principles of Traditional Animation Applied to 3D Computer Animation," *Computer Graphics*, 21(4), 33–44, 1987.

Lev88   Levoy, M., "Display of Surface from Volume Data," *IEEE Computer Graphics and Applications,* 8(3), 29–37, 1988.

Lev96   Levoy, M., and P. Hanrahan, "Light Field Rendering," *Computer Graphics*, 31–42, 1996.

Lia84   Liang, Y., and B. Barsky, "A New Concept and Method for Line Clipping," *ACM Transactions on Graphics*, 3(1), 1–22, 1984.

Lin68   Lindenmayer, A., "Mathematical Models for Cellular Interactions in Biology" *Journal of Theoretical Biology,* 18, 280–315, 1968.

Lin01   Linholm, E., M.J. Kilgard, and H. Morelton, "A User-Programmable Vertex Engine," *SIGGRAPH,* 2001.

Lor87   Lorensen, W.E., and H.E. Cline, "Marching Cubes: A High Resolution 3D Surface Construction Algorithm," *Computer Graphics,* 21(4), 163–169, 1987.

Ma94   Ma, K.L., J. Painter, C. Hansen, and M. Krogh, "Parallel Volume Rendering Using Binary-Swap Compositing," *IEEE Computer Graphics and Applications,* 14(4), 59–68, 1994.

Mag85   Magnenat-Thalmann, N., and D. Thalmann, *Computer Animation: Theory and Practice,* Springer-Verlag, Tokyo, 1985.

Man82   Mandelbrot, B., *The Fractal Geometry of Nature,* Freeman Press, New York, 1982.

Mat95   The MathWorks, *Student Edition of MatLab Version 4 Users Guide,* Prentice-Hall, Englewood Cliffs, NJ, 1995.

Max51   Maxwell, E.A., *General Homogeneous Coordinates in Space of Three Dimensions*, Cambridge University Press, Cambridge, England, 1951.

Mcc01   McCuskey, M., and A. LaMothe (Editors), *Special Effects Game Programming with DirectX 8.0,* Premier Press, Portland, OR, 2001.

Mia99   Miamo, J., *Compressed Image File Formats*, ACM Press, New York, 1999.

Mol99   Möller, T., and E. Haines, *Real-Time Rendering*, AK Peters, Natick, MA, 1999.

Mol92   Molnar, S., J. Eyles, and J. Poulton, "PixelFlow: High-Speed Rendering Using Image Composition," *Computer Graphics*, 26(2), 231–240, 1992.

Mol94   Molnar, S., M. Cox, D. Ellsworth, and H. Fuchs, "A Sorting Classification of Parallel Rendering," *IEEE Computer Graphics and Applications*, 26(2), 231–240, 1994.

Mon97   Montrym, J., D. Baum, D. Dignam, and C. Migdal, "InfiniteReality: A Real-Time Graphics System," *Computer Graphics*, 293–392, 1997.

Mur94   Murray, J.D., and W. Van Ryper, *Encyclopedia of Graphics File Formats,* O'Reilly and Associates, Sebastopol, CA, 1994.

New73   Newman, W.M., and R.F. Sproull, *Principles of Interactive Computer Graphics*, McGraw-Hill, New York, 1973.

Nie94   Nielson, J., *Usability Engineering*, Academic Press, New York, 1994.

Nie97   Nielson, G.M., H. Hagen, and H. Muller, *Scientific Visualization: Overviews, Methodologies, and Techniques*, IEEE Computer Society, Piscataway, NJ, 1997.

Ope01a   OpenGL Architecture Review Board, *OpenGL Programming Guide*, Third Edition, Addison-Wesley, Reading, MA, 2001.

Ope01b   OpenGL Architecture Review Board, *OpenGL Reference Manual*, Third Edition, Addison-Wesley, Reading, MA, 2001.

OSF89   Open Software Foundation, *OSF/Motif Style Guide,* Prentice-Hall, Englewood Cliffs, NJ, 1989.

Ost94   Osterhaut, J., *Tcl and the Tk Toolkit,* Addison-Wesley, Reading, MA, 1994.

Pap81   Papert, S., *LOGO: A Language for Learning*, Creative Computer Press, Middletown, NJ, 1981.

Pav95   Pavlidis, T., *Interactive Computer Graphics in X*, PWS Publishing, Boston, MA, 1995.

Per89   Perlin, K., and E. Hoffert, "Hypertexture," *Computer Graphics,* 23(3), 253–262, 1989.

PHI89   PHIGS+ Committee, "PHIGS+ Functional Description, Revision 3.0," *Computer Graphics,* 22(3), 125–218, July 1998.

Pho75   Phong, B.T., "Illumination for Computer Generated Scenes," *Communications of the ACM*, 18(6), 311–317, 1975.

Pei88   Peitgen, H.O., and S. Saupe (Ed.), *The Science of Fractal Images,* Springer-Verlag, New York, 1988.

Pik84   Pike, R., L. Guibas, and D. Ingalls, "Bitmap Graphics," *Computer Graphics*, 18(3), 135–160, 1984.

Por84   Porter, T., and T. Duff, "Compositing Digital Images," *Computer Graphics,* 18(3), 253–259, 1984.

Pra78   Pratt, W.K., *Digital Image Processing*, Wiley, New York, 1978.

Pru90   Prusinkiewicz, P., and A. Lindenmayer, *The Algorithmic Beauty of Plants,* Springer-Verlag, Berlin, 1990.

Ree83   Reeves, W.T., "Particle Systems—A Technique for Modeling a Class of Fuzzy Obejcts," *Computer Graphics*, 17(3), 359–376, 1983.

Rey87   Reynolds, C.W., "Flocks, Herds, and Schools: A Distributed Behavioral Model," *Computer Graphics*, 21(4), 25–34, 1987.

Rie81   Riesenfeld, R.F., "Homogeneous Coordinates and Projective Planes in Computer Graphics," *IEEE Computer Graphics and Applications*, 1(1), 50–56, 1981.

Rog85   Rogers, D.F., *Procedural Elements for Computer Graphics,* Second Edition, McGraw-Hill, New York, 1998.

Rog90   Rogers, D.F., and J.A. Adams, *Mathematical Elements for Computer Graphics,* McGraw-Hill, New York, 1990.

Rog00   Rogers, D.F., *An Introduction to NURBS: With Historical Perspective,* Morgan-Kaufmann, San Francisco, CA, 2000.

Sch88   Schiefler, R.W., J. Gettys, and R. Newman, *X Window System*, Digital Press, Woburn, MA, 1988.

Sch97   Schneiderman, B., *Designing the User Interface: Strategies for Effective Human–Computer Interaction*, Third Edition, Addison-Wesley, Reading, MA, 1997.

Sho95   Shoemaker, K., "Animating Rotation with Quaternion Curves," *Computer Graphics*, 19(3), 245–254, 1985.

Schr98   Schroeder, W., K. Martin, and B. Lorensen, *The Visualization Toolkit*, Prentice-Hall, Upper Saddle River, NJ, 1998.

Sei96   Seitz, S.M., and C.R. Dyer, "View Morphing," *Computer Graphics*, 21–30, 1996.

Seg92   Segal, M., and K. Akeley, *The OpenGL Graphics System: A Specification*, Version 1.0, Silicon Graphics, Mountain View, CA, 1992.

Sie81   Siegel, R., and J. Howell, *Thermal Radiation Heat Transfer*, Hemisphere, Washington, DC, 1981.

Sil89   Sillion, F.X., and C. Puech, "A General Two-Pass Method Integrating Specular and Diffuse Reflection," *Computer Graphics*, 22(3), 335–344, 1989.

Smi84   Smith, A.R., "Plants, Fractals and Formal Languages," *Computer Graphics*, 18(3), 1–10, 1984.

Str93   Strang, G., *Introduction to Linear Algebra*, Wellesley-Cambridge Press, Wellesley, MA, 1993.

Sut63   Sutherland, I.E., *Sketchpad, A Man–Machine Graphical Communication System, SJCC*, 329, Spartan Books, Baltimore, MD, 1963.

Sut74a   Sutherland, I.E., and G.W. Hodgeman, "Reentrant Polygon Clipping," *Communications of the ACM*, 17, 32–42, 1974.

Sut74b   Sutherland, I.E., R.F. Sproull, and R.A. Schumacker, "A Characterization of Ten Hidden-Surface Algorithms," *Computer Surveys*, 6(1), 1–55, 1974.

Swo00   Swoizral, H., K. Rushforth, and M. Deering, *The Java 3D API Specification*, Second Edition, Addison-Wesley, Reading, MA, 2000.

Tor96   Torborg, J., and J.T. Kajiya, "Talisman: Commodity Realtime 3D Graphics for the PC," *Computer Graphics*, 353–363, 1996.

Tor67   Torrance, K.E., and E.M. Sparrow, "Theory for Off–Specular Reflection from Roughened Surfaces," *Journal of the Optical Society of America*, 57(9), 1105–1114, 1967.

Tuf83   Tufte, E.R., *The Visual Display of Quantitative Information*, Graphics Press, Cheshire, CT, 1983.

Tuf90   Tufte, E.R., *Envisioning Information*, Graphics Press, Cheshire, CT, 1990.

Tuf97   Tufte, E.R., *Visual Explanations*, Graphics Press, Cheshire, CT, 1997.

Ups89   Upstill, S., *The RenderMan Companion: A Programmer's Guide to Realistic Computer Graphics*, Addison-Wesley, Reading, MA, 1989.

Van94   Van Gelder, A., and J. Wilhelms, "Topological Considerations in Isosurface Generation," *ACM Transactions on Graphics*, 13(4), 337–375, 1994.

Wat92   Watt, A., and M. Watt, *Advanced Animation and Rendering Techniques*, Addison-Wesley, Wokingham, England, 1992.

Wat98   Watt, A., and F. Policarpo, *The Computer Image*, Addison-Wesley, Woking-ham, England, 1998.

Wat00   Watt, A., *3D Computer Graphics*, Third Edition, Addison-Wesley, Woking-ham, England, 2000.

Wat02   Watkins, A., *The Maya 4 Handbook*, Charles River Media, Hingham, MA, 2002.

Wer94   Wernecke, J., *The Inventor Mentor*, Addison-Wesley, Reading, MA, 1994.

Wes90   Westover, L., "Footprint Evaluation for Volume Rendering," *Computer Graphics*, 24(4), 367–376, 1990.

Whi80   Whitted, T., "An Improved Illumination Model for Shaded Display," *Communications of ACM*, 23(6), 343–348, 1980.

Wit94a   Witkin, A.P., and P.S. Heckbert, "Using Particles to Sample and Control Implicit Surfaces," *Computer Graphics,* 28(3), 269–277, 1994.

Wit94b   Witkein, A. (Editor), *An Introduction to Physically Based Modeling,* Course Notes, *SIGGRAPH 94,* 1994.

Wol91   Wolfram, S., *Mathematica*, Addison-Wesley, Reading, MA, 1991.

Wri97   Wright, R.S., Jr., and M. Sweet, *OpenGL Superbible*, Wite Group Press, Corte Madera, CA, 1997.

Wys82   Wyszecki, G., and W.S. Stiles, *Color Science*, Wiley, New York, 1982.

Function Index

This index includes only the first appearance of those functions that are used in the text. The complete list of OpenGL functions is contained in the *OpenGL Reference Manual* and the GLUT documentation. The functions are grouped according to their inclusion in the GL, GLU, or GLUT libraries. Functions with multiple forms, such as glVertex, are listed once.

GL Functions

glAccum, 351
glBegin, 40
glBitMap, 316
glBlendFunc, 345
glCallList, 101
glCallLists, 102
glClear, 62
glClearColor, 62
glColor, 62
glColorMaterial, 297
glColorPointer, 178
glCopyPixels, 318
glDepthFunc, 392
glDepthMask, 346
glDrawBuffer, 131
glDrawElements, 176
glDrawPixels, 318
glEnable, 81
glEnableClientState, 177
glEnd, 40
glEndList, 100
glEvalCoord, 520
glEvalMesh, 521
glFlush, 42
glFog, 349
glFrustum, 241
glGenLists, 102
glGetFloat, 432
glHint, 336
glIndex, 63
glInitNames, 116
glLight, 294
glLightModel, 295
glListBase, 105
glLoadIdentity, 68

glLoadMatrix, 198
glLoadName, 116
glMap, 520
glMapGrid, 521
glMaterial, 296
glMatrixMode, 68
glMultMatirx, 201
glNewList, 100
glNormal, 253
glOrtho, 67
glPixelMap, 319
g;PixelStore, 317
glPointSize, 65
glPolygonOffset, 563
glPopAttrib, 102
glPopMatrix, 102
glPopName, 116
glPushAttrib, 102
glPushMatrix, 102
glPushName, 116
glRasterPos, 55
glReadBuffer, 315
glReadPixels, 318
glRotate, 198
glScale, 198
glSelectBuffer, 116
glShadeModel, 288
glTexCoord, 331
glTexEnv, 336
glTexGen, 336
glTexImage, 330
glTexParameter, 333
glTranslate, 104
glVertex, 39
glVertexPointer, 178
glViewport, 71

Subject Index

Back Plate 1 Rendering of hierarchical robot figure. (Courtesy of University of New Mexico.)

Back Plate 2 Sphere computer by recursive subdivision of tetrahedron. Triangle colors assigned randomly. (Courtesy of University of New Mexico.)

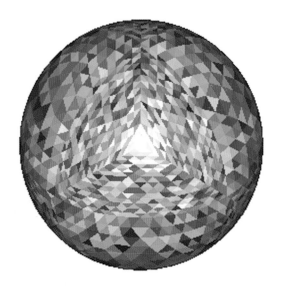